Waqf in Zaydī Yemen

Studies in Islamic Law and Society

VOLUME 46

The titles published in this series are listed at *brill.com/sils*

Waqf in Zaydī Yemen

Legal Theory, Codification, and Local Practice

By

Eirik Hovden

BRILL

LEIDEN | BOSTON

Library of Congress Cataloging-in-Publication Data

Names: Hovden, Eirik, author.
Title: Waqf in Zaydi Yemen : legal theory, codification, and local practice / by Eirik Hovden.
Description: Leiden ; Boston : Brill, 2019. | Series: Studies in Islamic law and society ; volume 46
Identifiers: LCCN 2018030396 (print) | LCCN 2018033239 (ebook) | ISBN 9789004377844 (ebook) | ISBN 9789004377721 (hardback : alk. paper)
Subjects: LCSH: Waqf—Yemen (Republic) | Islamic law—Yemen (Republic)
Classification: LCC KMX1271.35 (ebook) | LCC KMX1271.35 .H68 2018 (print) | DDC 349.533—dc23
LC record available at https://lccn.loc.gov/2018030396

Typeface for the Latin, Greek, and Cyrillic scripts: "Brill". See and download: brill.com/brill-typeface.

ISSN 1384-1130
ISBN 978-90-04-37772-1 (hardback)
ISBN 978-90-04-37784-4 (e-book)

This book is printed on acid-free paper and produced in a sustainable manner.

If Ṣan'ā' was destroyed, the waqf *could rebuild it,*
but if the waqf *was destroyed, Ṣan'ā' could not revive it*[1]

∴

1 Idhā kharibat Ṣan'ā' aqāmahā al-waqf wa-idhā khariba al-waqf lam tuqimhu Ṣan'ā'. Jamāl al-Dīn 'Alī b. 'Abdallāh b. al-Qāsim al-Shihārī, Waṣf Ṣan'ā': Mustall min kitāb al-manshūrāt al-jalīya, ed. 'Abdallāh b. Muḥammad al-Ḥibshī (Sanaa: al-Markaz al-Faransī li-l-Dirāsāt al-Yamaniyya, 1993), 71. See also Tim Macintosh-Smith, City of Divine and Earthly Joys: The Description of San'a (American Institute for Yemeni Studies and The Middle East Studies Association of North America, 2001), 19–20.

Contents

Acknowledgements

I owe my foremost thanks to all those in Yemen who cannot be mentioned by name. Many have helped with information, opinions, practicalities and enthusiasm. The generosity of the Yemenis has been amazing. I would like to thank the two supervisors of my PhD thesis on which this book is based, Professor Knut S. Vikør and Professor Anne K. Bang at the Department of Archaeology, History, Cultural Studies and Religion (AHKR), University of Bergen, Norway. For financial support, I thank the Faculty of Humanities, University of Bergen for providing me with a three-year PhD scholarship and support for the production of this book and the Meltzer foundation for providing additional support for the fieldwork.

At the University of Bergen I owe many thanks to colleagues who have provided a social and intellectual environment during the years of the PhD project, many of who have also commented upon early parts of the draft: John-Erik Sætren, Katja J. Fredriksen, Kjersti G. Berg, Liv Tønnesen, Marianne Bøe, Hilde G. Kjøstvedt, Frode Løvlie, Renate Lunde, Kjetil Fosshagen, Richard J. Natvig, Pernille Myrvold, Ludmila Torlakova.

For commenting upon the draft of the PhD thesis, or parts of it, and encouragement I also wish to thank Andre Gingrich, Daniel Varisco, Laila al-Zwaini, Anna Würth and David Powers. For reworking the draft into a book I received invaluable comments from the two external examiners or the thesis, Brinkley Messick and Randi Deguilhem. During my post doc in Vienna I received useful comments and support from my colleagues at the Institute for Social Anthropology (ISA), Austrian Academy of Sciences (AAS), Andre Gingrich, Magdalena Moorthy-Kloss, Odile Kommer, Daniel Mahoney, Marieke Brandt and especially Johann Heiss, and Paolo Sartori at the Institute of Iranian Studies. I also want to thank the anonymous reviewers and the staff at Brill, and Valerie Joy Turner who copy edited the manuscript and AHKR who provided funds for that.

In Yemen my foremost gratitude is to the learned Mohamed Abdulsalam Mansour who taught me *waqf* law. His enthusiasm for knowledge will always inspire. I am grateful for the research permit provided by the Yemeni Centre for Studies and Research (YCSR) and its director ʿAbd al-Aziz al-Maqāliḥ, and its staff, among them, Khaled al-Surayhi. The French Research Centre in Sanaa (Centre Français d'Archéologie et de Sciences Sociales—CEFAS) and its staff and researchers and the Yemen College for Middle Eastern Studies (YCMES) were most helpful for providing practical help and support. In the Ministry of Awqāf, I wish to thank the former minister, al-Qadi Hamoud al-Hittar, and especially the Director of investments, ʿAlī Muḥammad al-Farrān, for sharing with me a copy of the manuscript of his book on *waqf* in Yemen. Several local public *waqf* administrators in Sanaa and elsewhere provided me with information and showed me helpfully around in their areas. I am grateful to the Imam Zayd bin Ali Cultural Foundation (IZBACF) and their staff for providing me with access to their archives and their digital material in a most professional way. I promised them to translate the *fiqh* texts correctly and I hope that I managed to do that as far as possible. I also appreciate the Ministry of Culture and its former Deputy Minister Sam Yahya al-Ahmar for providing access to the Dār al-Makhṭūṭāt, and The National Centre for Archives in Sanaa and its director al-Qadi Ali Abu l-Rijal and staff. The former director for the project "Conservation of the Historic Cities" Omar al-Hallaj in the GTZ invited me to Hadramawt, where I also was supported by Sālim and 'Alawī BinSumayt in Shibam. In the Ministry of Justice, I wish to thank the supreme court judge Zayd Jaḥḥāf and several other employees, especially Muḥammad al-'Umaysī whose hospitality and knowledge of Yemeni bureaucracy was indispensable. I am very grateful for being given the chance to take part in the annual yearly Canadian Archaeological Mission to Zabid in 2010, directed by Ingrid Hehmeyer, together with employees from The General Authority of Antiquities and Museums (GOAM), among them, Aḥmad al-Mas'abī. In Rayma, the local Director of Antiquities, Mahdī al-Quṭwī, and several others contributed in many ways. I am also grateful to Gerhard Lichtenthäler and Frédéric Pelat who provided advice and support during the fieldwork. While acknowledging the aid and contributions, all shortcomings are mine.

Finally, I wish thank my parents for all the encouragement and support, Astrid Langehaug Hovden and Øystein Hovden.

Figures

Transliteration

The transliteration of Arabic words follows the Brill *EI*³ system. Place names have been Anglicized according to their commonly used forms (e.g., "Sanaa" instead of the Arabic "Ṣanʿāʾ").

Personal Names and Imamic Titles

Incoherent usage of the names of the Zaydī imams can in certain circumstances lead to confusion. In general, the names consist of two parts, the imamic title and the given name. The imamic title is usually a compound of two or more words such as "al-Manṣūr bi-Llāh." A common convention used by some Yemeni and western historians is referring to only the first part of the title, which is then followed by the given name, thus "al-Manṣūr al-Qāsim" and "al-Mahdī al-ʿAbbās." Such a convention is mostly sufficient in discussions of the imams of the Qāsimī dynasty, however, when looking farther back in time, there are several imams with the same name. In *fiqh* texts, short abbreviations occur and there are combinations of names that reoccur inconsistently in different sources; for instance "al-Mahdī li-Dīn Allāh Aḥmad b. al-Murtaḍā" is referred to by any of those names in many of the texts. In such cases I use the most commonly used version of the name; "Ibn al-Murtaḍā," or "al-Manṣūr" for "al-Manṣūr bi-Llāh ʿAbdallah b. Ḥamza," and a sufficient number of names in the beginning of a new section.

The phrase "ʿ*alayhi al-salām*," which translates as "peace be upon him," is often stated after mentioning important imams in *fiqh* texts. This and similar honorary phrases are usually excluded from translations, except when it is interesting to see how a certain imam or scholar is honoured.

Dates

Dates have been converted to the Gregorian/Julian calendar by using the online converter at the homepage of the Asien-Orient Institut, University of Zurich (http://www.oriold.uzh.ch/static/hegira.html). Dates are given in AH/CE wherever possible. If the month is not known and two Gregorian years are possible, they are given as 1775 or 76. The ethnographic present is 2010.

CHAPTER 1

Introduction

Standing in the mountains of western Yemen at the edge of a large rainwater harvesting cistern[1] that I wanted to photograph, and breathing heavily from the climb, my host and informant said: "This cistern is not like the others we saw today, this one is *waqf*." Then he was quiet for a moment, clearly thinking to himself, trying to figure something out. He finally said, "Actually, they are all *waqf*—they are made for the benefit of all Muslims."[2]

In my MA thesis,[3] I describe the use of rainwater harvesting cisterns and their role in local water management and the related system of ownership structure, but I never fully grasped the concept of *waqf*. At that time I had few informants educated in Islamic law who could explain the legal framework of *waqf* and I did not have the language skills to understand the texts of Islamic law. On several occasions, before I was able to investigate the topic of *waqf* in greater depth, I thought, what does it mean that that specific cistern was *waqf*? Or that they all were *waqf*? And what are the implications of that fact in the local society? Would that cistern be taken better care of compared to other cisterns because of its religious status as *waqf*? These basic questions are one of the foundations of this book.

The institution of *waqf* (pl. *awqāf*) in Islamic law is in many ways similar to trusts, endowments or foundations in present day, western law. In premodern Muslim societies, infrastructure—and especially urban infrastructure—was to a large extent established and managed as public foundations, that is, *waqf*. This was not only the case for mosques, which are nowadays the main remnant of official, formal *awqāf*, but also for schools and scholarships for education, services for the poor and sick, the public water supply, community houses for

1 In many areas in Yemen, the population lives on mountaintops and ridges where there is no groundwater. Here, large water tanks (*birka, mājil*) are used to collect and store rainwater for domestic use and for animals. The technology is centuries old and a well-integrated part of society.

2 In the context of his statement, where Muslims are the majority—he was essentially saying that the *waqf*s are for the benefit of people in general (as he did not think in terms of religious minorities).

3 Eirik Hovden, "Rainwater Harvesting Cisterns and Local Water Management: A Qualitative Geographical / Socio-Anthropological Case Study and Ethnographic Description from the Districts of Hajja, Mabyan and Shiris" (MA thesis, University of Bergen, online: bora.uib.no/handle/1956/2001, 2006).

 | DOI:10.1163/9789004377844_002

the reception of officials and travellers, and halls for holding local celebrations and religious festivals.

As a thematic focus, this book concentrates on "non-mosque" public foundations in Yemen and most of the examples are related to the public water supply. Water supply serves as a typical example of the non-mosque related services that the institution of *waqf* was a vehicle for. Water supply is also a type of service, or public infrastructure central to both Yemeni and western development discourses and thus it is a shared, common focus that transcends the secular/religious divide or the divide between Islamic studies, history, and development studies. This book provides a legally oriented ethnographic description of a truly local mode of management of public resources—a local mode that should not be overlooked in the ongoing quest to find locally accepted legal and political vehicles for managing public, common good.

1 *Waqf* as Public Infrastructure and Welfare in Muslim Societies

In the study of Yemen, anthropologists and social historians have been reluctant to look into how local economic and legal institutions were integrated into and related to broader and regional structures of Islamic law. The importance of *waqf* or public foundations in local economic and legal life in Yemen is one such field that has been relatively under-represented, with a few exceptions;[4] this is largely because *waqf* as a phenomenon is situated between the usual foci of historical-ethnographic and Islamic disciplines. I discuss this further in chapter 2.

The institution of foundations (*waqf, awqāf*) in Islamic law has been central to everyday life in the Middle East for centuries, especially in the cities. It is easy to forget how important infrastructure is for a society: What would one do without public wells, schools, scholarships, and stipends for the poor, etc.? And what does it mean that these services are public? What role does "the public" have in taking care of the weak and those in need? What types of discourses of "public affairs" existed? Was there a notion of "welfare society"? Did this overlap with religious values only? Premodern concepts from the Middle East seem to centre around different combinations of customary, local and tribal law, and of course, Islamic law (*sharīʿa*). Islamic law was undoubtedly the most "universal" and formal of those mentioned. It was also more situated in writing and written texts than customary or local law.

4 An example of such an exception is the work of Brinkley Messick, who I refer to in several places in this book.

1.1 *A Non-State Yet Public Legal Institution*

In premodern Islamic law there were mainly two categories for public management and the redistribution of resources: public or charitable foundations (*awqāf ʿāmma, khayriyya*) and the common property of Muslims (*bayt al-māl*). The latter, *bayt al-māl*, was usually managed by the ruler (in Zaydī Yemen; the imam) and held as state property. One could say that state property was a type of public sphere in which there was a good deal of money in circulation, but most of this served to support the state itself. Clearly, *zakāt* and the *bayt al-māl* were important political tools for the state rulers.

The public foundations, in contrast to the public treasury (*bayt al-māl*), were only partly controlled by the state. The state often ascribed to itself the responsibility of inspectorship (*naẓāra*) and legal guardianship (*wilāya*) over *waqf* that had no private guardian (*mutawallī*). However, according to most interpretations of Islamic law, foundations could be made and managed completely without interference from the state. From this perspective, public foundations are "non-governmental." At the same time, Islamic law provides the state, or the supreme Islamic legitimate authority, with the right to interfere in the management of the public foundations if they are misused or in need of protection from usurpers. Thus *waqf* is not entirely non-governmental.

Waqf could be made for both private (*waqf ahlī, dhurrī*) and public (*ʿāmm, khayrī*) purposes; this book focuses mainly on the latter. It must be noted, however, that the distinction between the two categories is often deliberately blurred, as I demonstrate in detail here.

From a legal perspective, *waqf* consists of a transfer of a property or a right from a private owner to a beneficiary, such that God theoretically becomes the new owner and the beneficiary has the right to its use or benefit (usufruct, *manfaʿa*). In the case of a public building, a school, a water stand or a house for the poor, the right of use would be to gain access to these services and physical structures. Those holding the right of use were called "beneficiaries" (*al-mawqūf ʿalayhim, maṣrif*) and in a public *waqf* this right was open to anyone and not restricted, sold or inherited. In a private *waqf* these rights could be transferred to new generations according to specific rules, but not through inheritance proper or sale.[5] This type of *waqf* is usually called "family *waqf*" (*waqf dhurrī,—ahlī,* or—*khāṣṣ*).

From a religious and theological perspective, *waqf* was seen as an excellent form of charity, a so-called "continuous charity" (*ṣadaqa jāriya*): The one who gives something as a foundation (the founder) has performed an act that

5 There are complicated jurisprudential rules related to the prohibition of inheriting or selling a *waqf*; to a great extent these can be circumvented, as I demonstrate in chapters 6 and 7.

produces continuous merit from God (*ajr, thawāb*), even in the future, in the period after the death of the founder and before the day of judgement. According to a well established *ḥadīth* (a saying or an act of the Prophet), which can be found in several different versions, man can only obtain such a continuous merit from God by leaving something good behind him in the world, something that falls under one of the following three categories: Continuous charity, useful knowledge or a good descendant remembering and praying for him.[6] All other types of good deeds stop at the time of death. In Islamic legal theory (*fiqh*), in debates concerning *waqf*, it is stated that *waqf* is such a continuous charity, just mentioned by another term. The term *waqf* as referring to charitable foundation is not found in the Qurʾān and rarely appears in the *ḥadīth*. Other types of charity, such as charity (*ṣadaqa*) intended to help a poor person, only earn the giver reward one time. These two aspects, continuity (*taʾbīd*) and a good and pious purpose or intention (*qurba, taqarrub*) have long been at the very core of Islamic *waqf* theory;[7] at the same time they have proved problematic, since they are difficult to define in practical terms that are legally effective and useful in daily life. In practice, *waqf*s were often made to circumvent inheritance rules, and to keep large estates of land under control of the head of the family or the clan. If not held as *waqf*, land must be divided over the generations according to the Islamic rules of inheritance. Thus without endogamous marriages, a family can lose their land if daughters marry outside the family, as their offspring belong to another patrilineal clan (as demonstrated in chapter 5).

Public foundations could also be drained of resources by actors like the founder's descendants, the administrators or guardians, or the tenants of the assets, any of whom might use grey areas, or ambiquity in the law. Grey areas and ambiguities in the jurisprudence (*fiqh*) meant that it was possible to circumvent the law by legal ruses (*ḥīla, ḥiyal*). Such circumventions often became the new rule if they were allowed to continue; they became recognized at the legal level in courts, though not entirely in an ideal juristic sense and according to the ideal definitions of a *waqf*.

Doctrinal theory and contextualized legal practice can at times be so far apart that the historian and the anthropologist become lost in juristic details that may never have been practiced in reality outside the academic circles of the law schools. In practice, the two aforementioned conditions—"continuity" and "a good, pious purpose" (*qurba*)—were subject to compromises in daily

6 This is a well-known *ḥadīth* that appears in books of *fiqh*; it was also quoted by several informants.

7 Again, with some differences among the schools of law, as I elaborate on later.

interactions with the mundane, social, real world. These compromises were reincorporated into the legal theory under the legal maxims of "custom" (*ʿurf*) and "(public) interest" (*maṣlaḥa*).[8] Judges also had a limited power to enforce pure theory and had to follow established court practice and to a certain degree the wishes of local elites. In reality, the power of the patriarchal, extended family and clans affected the formation of the institution and law of public *waqf*. In that respect, *waqf* law is very much situated in a language of private contractual law, where *waqf* was seen as a private legal personality[9] in a community among other private owners, and much less under "public law," yet the public law component should not be underestimated, and we return to it below.

1.2 *The Transition to the Modern World*

In the twentieth century the old public foundations in the Islamicate world were overtaken by swift economic development as new colonial and later national infrastructures were built. This new infrastructure was owned and managed by the states themselves, not as independent or local foundations. The individual *waqfs*, and the institution of *waqfs* as such, were often perceived by the secular-oriented elite as something premodern and old-fashioned, and as something belonging to the religious sphere rather than the civil, public sphere. The old public foundations were often administered by religious scholars (*ʿulamāʾ*) and conservative actors who were not educated in modern sciences and administration. The old hospitals, orphanages, water stands, wells, Qurʾānic and *sharīʿa* schools were seen by many as remnants of the past that were not terribly useful. Here, it should be noted that the process

8 The main chapters in this book provide an in-depth study of such an incorporation of "interest" and "custom" into the corpus of legal rules.

9 There is a general argument that refers to Schacht, who states that "Islamic law does not recognize the juristic persons." J. Schacht, *An Introduction to Islamic Law* (Oxford: Oxford University Press, 1964), 125. This is re-stated in the *EI*² article on *waqf*. R. Peters, D. S. Powers, Aharon Layish, Ann K. S. Lambton, Randi Deguilhem, R. D. McChesney, M. B. Hooker, and J. O. Hunwick, "Waḳf," in *Encyclopedia of Islam*, second edition, ed. P. J. Bearman, Th. Biancuis, C. E. Bosworth, E. van Donzel, and W. P. Heinrichs (Leiden: Brill Online, 1960–2004), 11:59–99. Doris Behrens-Abouseif argues that this is a matter of definition and that there are arguments in favour of defining *waqf* as a legal personality. Doris Behrens-Abouseif, "The *Waqf*: A Legal Personality?" in *Islamische Stiftungen zwischen juristischer Norm on sozialer Praxis*, ed. Astrid Meier, Johannes Pahlitzsch, and Lucian Reinfandt (Berlin: Akademie-Verlag, 2009). The Yemeni *waqf* decree no. 63 of 1977, article 4, explicitly states that the ministry of *awqāf* is to be considered a legal personality (*shakhṣiyya iʿtibāriyya*). ʿAbd al-Mālik Manṣūr, *al-Awqāf wa-l-irshād fī mawkib al-thawra* (Sanaa: Wizārat al-Awqāf wa-l-Irshād, 1987), 292 [henceforth referred to as *al-Mawkib*].

of modernization took quite different directions in different countries of the region.[10] Areas with little state influence, as in large parts of Yemen, saw less radical change. Much of the land and the assets that belonged to these foundations were often covertly taken over by private individuals, rich landowners, bureaucrats in the *waqf* administration, or overtly by the state itself. Below, we see how the advent of modernity has affected the *waqf*s (pl. *awqāf*) in Yemen (especially in the former Yemen Arab Republic or Northern Yemen).

The mosques did remain as *waqf* after the onset of modernity, and their numbers multiplied. Mosques had been managed as *waqf*, such that each mosque had its own sources of *waqf* income. When the post-colonial nation states were founded, most of them created a separate ministry for foundations (also called endowments, or religious endowments), typically called the "ministry of *awqāf*," often with the addition of the words "religious guidance" (*irshād*). These ministries were responsible for all the public foundation properties and thus the finances of the mosques, and for the regulation of the ideological activities related to them. What in the mediaeval period was a fledging system of supervising various types of public foundations now became a "ministry of religious affairs." This ministry often took on a strong ideological function and came to be used by the state to integrate religious activities into frameworks that the state could control.

The fact that there were once, not so long ago, public foundations that aimed at providing services to people and the society, and that these were also to a large extent private and not state controlled, now tends to be forgotten, both by religious scholars and ordinary people. Occasional attempts are made to revive the institution of *waqf*, but it is difficult to point out clear trends toward this. Some reforms have been made in some Gulf states and interesting legal revivals can be found in Malaysia and Indonesia. In Turkey, foundations, although heavily reformed, remain an important part of civil society.[11]

Because *waqf* is often seen as a part of a religious field, many secular actors are reluctant to engage in a "religious" Islamic discourse over which they feel they have little control. On the other hand, some of the most conservative religious forces, the so-called Salafīs, are reluctant to recognize the institution at all, since most of the *waqf* rules are not mentioned, at least not literally, in the

10 For an overview, see Franz Kogelmann, "Die Entwiklung des islamischen Stiftungswesens im postkolonialen Staat. Prozesse in Ägypten, Algerien und Marokko," in *Islamische Stiftungen zwischen juristischer Norm on sozialer Praxis*, ed. Astrid Meier, Johannes Pahlitzsch, and Lucian Reinfandt (Berlin: Akademie-Verlag, 2009).

11 See, for instance, chapter 2: "Waqf and Islamic Finance: Two Resources for Charity," in *The Charitable Crescent: Politics of Aid in the Muslim World*, ed. Jonathan Benthall and Jerome Bellion-Jourdan (London: I.B. Tauris, 2009).

Qur'ān and only to a limited extent in the Sunna. For Islamists, transactional law such as *waqf* is not given priority of interest over more politically potent and popular parts of the law, such as ritual law (i.e., law that relates to matters of worship). *Waqf* legal theory is necessarily rather academic in nature and must somehow be related to *fiqh* (Islamic legal theory)[12] as formulated in the classical law schools, therefore making it difficult to popularize, especially given the large gap between the ideals and realities of law in the specific legal field of *waqf*.

Generally, when foundations are created, the founders (*wāqif, wāqifūn*) also make a written document (*waqf* document, *waqfiyya*) that is made public and/or entered into public court registers. These documents contain detailed information about who established the foundation, from what assets, and how it should be administered in the future. Even today these documents can be very troublesome, particularly when they reappear after decades and lead to conflicts over who actually owns what. These documents include a standard formulae stating that the individual *waqf*s are the property of God, and "that they cannot be sold, cannot be given away, cannot be inherited, until God inherits the earth and those upon it."

2 Field, Scope, and Focus

2.1 *Yemen, Local Law, and* Waqf

Yemen is a mountainous, in large part tribally organized (although mainly sedentary), poor country located at the southwestern corner of the Arabian Peninsula. For most of the Islamic period, the agriculturally marginal northern highlands have been beyond direct government control and have been governed by local sedentary tribes, while the south, the coastal areas, and the western mountains have been more feudal and politically stable. Although egalitarianism is portrayed as a crucial tribal value, especially in the north and northeastern areas where tribalism is strong, local shaykhs and elites tend to own more land than others and they represent the government locally. They thus connect the local communities with the state through ties of patronage. In the highlands, prior to 1962 the central state was headed by the (Zaydī) imam and often ruled from Sanaa with the military aid of the northern tribes, who extracted taxes from the more politically docile, but agriculturally fertile south and west. Tribal leaders and local elites received percentages of the collected taxes and

12 *Fiqh* means "legal theory," the academic science of Islamic law. I elaborate on this in the next chapter.

FIGURE 1 Map of the northern (western) part of the Republic of Yemen.
COPYRIGHT ERIK GOOSMANN.

filled important positions in the state. In the past the education system and thus the basis for the legal system was geographically fragmented, mainly outside government control,[13] and to a large extent funded by local *waqf* and run by local *'ulamā'*, scholars of Islamic law. From the tenth century CE, Zaydism gradually became the most influential form of Islamic doctrine in the highlands, and was more or less prevalent around and north of Sanaa after

13 The contrast to Egypt and al-Azhar is striking.

1324.[14] The basic tenets of Zaydī state theory are largely oppositional,[15] and together with hundreds of small rural centres of Islamic learning (*hijra, hijar*) each with their own tribal patronage, a semi-autonomous legal system emerged, one that was difficult for the elites in Sanaa to control. It produced a perception of law as something greater, more lasting, and more legitimate than the government or the state itself and at times when the state was weak or even absent, significant aspects of the legal system were still applied locally and effectuated in accordance with local needs. Islamic law, tribal law, local customary law, and state law merged and were codified in ways that differed slightly from area to area and period to period. While the contemporary *waqf* law was constructed by modern state institutions, it still contains strong elements of the aforementioned legal ideologies, especially Islamic legal theory (*fiqh*); we return to this point in more detail, especially in chapters 5, 6, and 7.

Over the centuries, *waqfs* have been used by actors in local communities and notaries and judges have served the local societies' needs for regulating and sanctioning local ownership structures. This was and still is mainly done through the language of Islamic contractual law; each contract or ownership document represents a public confirmation or transfer of a set rights from one legal person to another, and conveys the legal strength, time period, and legal validity that the users request. Not all dispositions were equally important. A transaction that was very important, the validity of which had to be strong, would require prominent, perhaps even nationally renowned witnesses. An example here is the inheritance division of the land of a shaykh in Rayma; the document, which was shown to me, had been signed in the 1950s by the judges of the Supreme Court in far away Taʿizz. Important *waqf* documents similarily involve a large number of witnesses, more than the two required in Islamic contractual law. At the opposite end of the scale we find very simple *waqf* documents, the type that can be drawn up by any person in the village able to write and thus act as a notary. Such a simple *waqf* document would be much cheaper to set up, while the elaborate *waqfs* involved paying for access to the right judges and inviting the right witnesses. Sometimes the founder of a *waqf* did not want it made more "formal" than necessary; if the *waqf* was made simply as a strategy for other means, he or his children might more easily

14 For the early spread of Zaydism, see David Thomas Gochenour, "The Penetration of Zaydi Islam into Early Medieval Yemen" (PhD thesis, Harvard University, 1984).

15 This refers to the well-developed doctrines of polity in Zaydism. The doctrine of *khurūj* is particularly important, as it states that it is a duty to overthrow a ruler that is "unjust." Throughout Yemeni history this doctrine has often been used to legitimize imam pretenders aiming to establish a polity. However, once in power, they must fight off other pretenders both in scholarly matters and militarily.

revoke it and privatize it later. Revocation such as this was only possible if, originally, it was only "sufficiently" strong and, for example, not entered into public registries.

Minor contracts could be oral, yet most of those involving permanent transfers of assets were made in writing and the notaries' or judges' handwriting acted as a proof of authenticity, in addition to the two required witnesses. In this way, the contracts were valid even after the original parties passed away, or valid in a larger geographical area, as the contracts did not depend on local face-to-face knowledge of the villagers. Yemen's thousands of agricultural terraces all have individual names and are defined in such written contracts sanctioned by the local legal system, which is more or less respected by the local community and the local elite.

In this book I am concerned with access to agricultural lands that produce a significant surplus every year, though other forms of assets such as real estate and urban building plots are also important. In *waqf*, these assets were donated to beneficiaries, either private or public or a mix of the two.

2.2 *Understanding* Waqf *in Its Social Context*

The general aim of this book is to deepen our understanding of the role of the institution of public foundations (*waqf*) in Yemeni society, both in the past and the present. In the Yemeni context, there has not been much research undertaken on this topic. Because of Yemen's particular history, landscape, and legal traditions, an extrapolation of academic knowledge of *waqf* studies from, for example, the Ottoman context, must be made with caution. Often academic texts that do treat this topic digress into the problematic relationship between the doctrines and theories of Islamic law on the one hand, and the established, practiced law on the other.

The difference between these two is arguably not only an issue of "theory" versus "practice," but rather, as I argue in the book, more a landscape of different debates and contestations of legitimacy and validities that only partially overlap. As I elaborate below, all these debates have their own "theory" and also "practice." For instance, the scholarly debates in Islamic law are situated in texts and contexts that span centuries and continents, while the everyday *waqf* practices in small rural villages are mostly undertaken by actors who have no insight into the details of theoretical law, and who may even be illiterate. They have their own perception and version of the law in both norms and practices, and these also deserve academic representation. These two "fields of *waqf*," legal theory and local perceptions and practices of *waqf*, are analytically separate study objects, yet are strongly interrelated. This book focuses on and conxtualizes this interrelationship between Islamic scholarly jurisprudence (*fiqh*) and local forms of law.

2.3 *Defining the Geographical, Historical, and Social Field*

The area under scrutiny in this study cannot be defined absolutely in geographical space and historical time. Sometimes the relevant field is a specific village, at other times it is the wider intellectual Islamic tradition of Islamic law. I usually use the term "Yemen," though Yemen is a large and diverse area. Most of the legal texts and cases are from Northern, Upper, Zaydī Yemen and most are less than 500 years old. Most *waqf* and other legal documents[16] are less than 200 years old and come from the wider Sanaa area. Narratives and recorded memoirs span the lifetime of living informants, the majority from Sanaa, but I also made several trips to other cities and regions in Yemen, such as Zabid, Rayma, and Hadramawt. *Waqf* in Yemen is not necessarily best understood when separated into "Zaydī" and "Shāfiʿī" law, or divided into "Qāsimī" or "Republican" *waqf* practices. The resemblances are many and sectarian and historical divisions are not always analytically fruitful. As I demonstrate in this book, some of the main, reoccurring legal problems that relate to human agency are the same in Zaydī and Shāfiʿī areas and are found from the Qāsimī imamate (from 1636), or even before, and until today. Such "legal problems" or "grey areas" are great opportunities for us to see what is actually going on in the field, much more so than analysing rules or cases dealing with "the ideal *waqf*."

2.4 Waqf *and the Development Sector: Engaging in Islamic Law*

The need for more knowledge about the role of *waqf* in Yemen is not purely academic. The development sector is continually looking for ways to anchor the legitimacy of its infrastructure projects in the social and cultural web of local communities, especially in a weak state society like Yemen. They are looking for ways to set up, administer, and create types of project ownership that increase the locals' perception of the legitimacy of development projects. The question of whether the public *waqf* is a suitable institution for the use of the development sector cannot be fully treated in this book; however, certain key issues are clarified. Arguably, the questions that can be raised on the basis of this book are fundamental to those who wish to establish such answers and to use the concept of *waqf* actively in their development projects. As a part

16 At my request the ministry of *awqāf* provided fifty documents, not all of which were *waqf* documents. I have also collected and read a similar number of published and unpublished *waqf* documents, although several of them were shown to me on the condition of anonymity.

of Islamic law or *sharīʿa*, the term *waqf* is readily associated with the many negative connotations of "Islamic law" often found in non-academic, western discourses. At the same time, as a means of managing the public good, the institution of the *waqf* incorporates fundamentally universal aspects that are not endemic to Islamic law or Islamic societies; *waqf* is not a concept that has been fixed once and for all, but rather a set of ideas and practices situated in specific historical and social contexts. Claiming that *waqf* is suitable, or not, for use in the development sector is simply impossible without also engaging in a wide range of local and contemporary debates concerning what *waqf* should be. Perhaps, hypothetically, only certain parts of the local understanding of *waqf* will be found to be compatible with the standards of the development sector; that is, some aspects of the concept can be used and other parts must be rejected. In any case, it is necessary to engage in the debate, even if the arguments must take the form of "*sharīʿa*-language." Choosing to reject such a dialogue and instead introducing a new, imposed sets of morals and "concepts of public good" risks total failure if the locals do not adopt the discourse and see the compatibility. Not only will development aid always carry a political dimension, but it will also carry a legal and institutional aspect. This book provides new background information that may facilitate further research and debate on these topics.

2.5 *Thematic and Methodological Focuses*

The book has the following methodological focuses, both of which are related to the construction of legitimacy, authority, and validity in *waqf* law and practices: One is a focus on the knowledge[17] in use in *waqf* practices and the second is a focus on certain problematic "gray areas" in the legal theory (*waqf fiqh*).

The focus on knowledge makes it possible to see a *waqf* as a legal institution that is used to redistribute certain goods in society, and it allows an anthropological perspective that can be combined with that of the analysis of legal/normative texts. By looking at how legal knowledge is constructed, transmitted, sanctioned, and put into legal use, it becomes possible to focus on how human agency shapes the *waqf* institution and creates local social observable effects, and it also becomes possible to see how "facts on the ground" affect legal theoretical discourses. I elaborate on this below.

A more specific methodological delimitation in this study involves looking at the borders of the legal phenomenon of *waqf*, rather than at its ideal type. In this book the term "validity" is used in a general way. In a narrow legal sense, it refers to the binary distinction so often used in the formulation of legal rules

17 That is, knowledge of law, the law itself, and the local, daily knowledge of *waqf*.

and in legal theory (*fiqh*); "legal" (e.g., *jāʾiz, ṣaḥīḥ*) and "illegal" (e.g., *bāṭil, ghayr ṣaḥīḥ*), or valid and invalid. In more general usage, the term validity is used in a broad sense to include the notion of "right" and "wrong" as expressed by informants, and in this sense the term is not more accurate than other terms such as "authority" or "legitimacy." In any case, it refers to the emic claims of "correctness" and as we see, this is not always clear and univocal, even in legal theory,[18] especially when actually observed practices are far removed from the claimed ideal standard.

By maintaining a methodological focus at the very edge of validity, authority, and legitimacy related to the phenomenon of *waqf*, the definition of what *waqf* is becomes significantly more useful, and it becomes possible to see and analyse forms of *waqf* that do not follow the ideal type, but that are present to a great extent in Yemeni history and society. The core definition of *waqf*, as it is given in introductory books of Islamic law, is well known and fits well as an overview. Yet the historical and social reality is much more complex and this reality is also reflected in Islamic legal theory. The border areas of the *waqf* phenomenon are the most interesting parts of *waqf fiqh* because the dynamics between Islamic law and society can be seen here more readily, as for example, the ways "custom" (*ʿurf*) and "public interest" (*maṣlaḥa*) as legal maxims are drawn upon to validate legal rules otherwise not found in the Qurʾān or the Sunna. This perspective also highlights the ways that human agents continually utilize the frames and language of *fiqh* to create new legal constructions in acts of entrepreneurship. If I had opted to focus on the ideal *waqf*, the relationship between legal theory and local practices would remain difficult to trace beyond assumptions and tautologies.

Borders or "border areas" of validity thus refer to certain debates in the legal theory of *waqf* in which the very foundations of the *waqf* institution are threatened or endangered because of the discrepancy between ideal doctrine and observed practice and thus also refer to an area where doctrine and local practices interact over time. These topics in *waqf*, such as the balance between *waqf* and inheritance law, lease law and other forms of "semi-*waqf*" give us an opportunity to analyse in depth how doctrine is also affected by the presence, or lack of, political systems and enforceability. I argue that the binary distinction of "theory versus practice" is not a fruitful one as legal theory is also situated and located in certain practises, such as the academic *madrasa*s (Islamic schools), and local practises also involve theories in the form of knowledge

18 I use the term "validity" because it is a single term that can be used in all four "fields" of knowledge, and by using one term, commonalities and interconnections between the four fields are more easily seen. I present the four fields below.

about operative *waqf* law, the history of individual *waqfs* and morality in behaviour related to *waqf*. Each of the main chapters in the book (chapters 5 to 7) is centred on one such "topic," where the construction of legal validity is the common focus.

3 Types of Data

At the start of the research, I planned to focus on specific *waqf* cases of public water supply and the administration of public water infrastructure and to use three types of empirical data for each case: (1) observations of physical structures together with (2) informants' narratives, and (3) related texts (*waqf* documents, legal documents). Methodologically, it was difficult to find these three types of data for each specific case simultaneously. Often one or two types of data were missing, creating a patchwork of data that was quite broad, yet weak in the sense that it was too dispersed. The thematic focus on water structures and on public water supply remained, however, since many of the problematic issues for water supply *waqfs* are the same as for other types of *waqf*. Early on I shifted the research focus towards topics in *waqf* legal theory, also relevant for other types of *waqfs*. Thus a fourth type of empirical data became the most important, namely the legal debates. This shifted the research into a more text-oriented study than originally planned.

At times all four types of data are connected in the analysis; this is a costly, but rewarding undertaking. The cost is a lack of statistical certainty because of the low number of cases, while the benefits pertain to understanding the complex two-way relationship between legal theories in texts and practices on the ground, which are investigated in an explorative (as opposed to fixed) and qualitative (as opposed to quantitative) manner.

3.1 *Discourses of God and Good: Laws to Promote the Public Good*

Legitimacy or validity in *waqf*, or "public infrastructure management," is defined according to the texts used in this study and, according to the informants, it is defined as ultimately stemming from either (1) "God" as mediated through certain texts or (2) from what is "the best for society," or (3) as a complex mix of these two. This is a rather philosophical distinction that is partly analogous to the concepts of "ethics of duty" and "ethics of consequence" on the one hand and a division between a "religious" belief system and a "humanitarian" system on the other hand. There is not necessarily a conflict between them, yet for some informants, and for some questions there is a conflict. Theological issues such as whether or not man can, by himself, understand right or wrong outside the text of the revelation is something that is a highly relevant topic in Zaydī theology, but arguably not relevant when looking at legal theory or the "branches of the law" (*fiqh, furūʿ*), such as *waqf* law. The informants' own epistemological reflections over such ultimate sources of validity are incoherent, inconsistent, and unsystematic, yet, some more or less clear patterns can be found. So far, there is nothing necessarily "Islamic" about this; it is more of a question of how to translate the words "God" and the "common good." Identifying the exact nature of the "Islamic component" of *waqf* is not the primary focus of this study, rather the focus is on how the term "Islamic" and hence "Islamic law" and *waqf* are contingent parts of central perceptions of what is "public" and "public interest," and consequently also codified into and acted out as constructions of "law" in a social setting. Terms such as "public infrastructure" and "public interest" are mostly secular terms in western discourses and are situated in certain social and historical contexts and therefore, ultimately, the translations of these terms remain dependent on the knowledge and even the ideology of the reader.

This being said, the frame of reference for the legal theory behind the institution of *waqf* is strongly anchored in the wider tradition of the Islamic sciences and especially the vast body of Islamic legal theory and law. By contrast, *waqf*, or the arguments used in *waqf* discourse, cannot possibly be understood without also seeing them as parts of the vast knowledge tradition of Islamic law in general and Zaydī law specifically. While a single *waqf* is a phenomenon unique to that specific village, situated in face-to-face structures, ownership, village history and memory—the legal institution of *waqf* exists in a knowledge tradition shared over continents and centuries.

3.2 *Separate Fields of* Waqf *Knowledge*

The levels between the "local" and "the Islamic," or the "little and great traditions"[19] cannot be seen only as orderly layers of doctrinal truths—the reality is far more complex than that. In this book I use a model of four such "discourses," or here "fields of knowledge" as an aid to understand approximately where the text, narrative or observation under scrutiny belongs. These "fields" are thus both methodological models of what to look for, and to a certain degree also a model of how to understand the patterns emerging in the analysis. I see the practices and norms related to *waqf* in this book through Fredrik

19 This term, taken from Robert Redfield, is often now seen as an oversimplified dichotomy. Robert Redfield, "The Social Organisation of Tradition," *Far Eastern Quarterly* 15, no. 1 (1955): 13–21.

Barth's knowledge perspective[20] and I use four different "fields" of *waqf* knowledge in the analysis:

1. *Fiqh*, Islamic legal theory;
2. Codifications of *waqf* law;
3. Individual legal and administrative cases and documents; and
4. Local knowledge of daily *waqf* users.

I elaborate on these fields in the next chapter, and reflect on the place of this book in the tradition of studying Islamic law in Yemen.

3.3 *On the Tradition of Western Ethnographic Research in Yemen*

Modern ethnographic fieldwork in Northern Yemen was made possible when the civil war ended around 1968. During the 1970s and 1980s a large number of ethnographic studies were undertaken. Several of these are of excellent quality and have been published as theses, academic monographs or articles. Many of those who undertook ethnographic fieldwork in this period later changed their focus into more text-oriented studies as their language skills and thus abilities to study Islamic and local texts improved. Well-known examples are Daniel Varisco, Paul Dresch, Brinkley Messick, Martha Mundy, and Shelagh Weir. These scholars—originally anthropologists—later wrote historical works and edited historical or legal texts. Most of them did their fieldwork in villages and towns of the highlands. During the 1990s fewer anthropologists made the typical broad spectrum, ethnographic descriptions based on local, rural fieldwork. This was not only due to a change in theoretical focus and fashion in the discipline of social anthropology, but was also related to the feasibility of undertaking long-term, rural fieldwork in Yemen in a hardened political climate. The present study follows this new trend of more narrow thematic focuses. Numerous geopolitical incidents after 2001 have changed the attitude of Yemenis towards foreigners and affected the possibility of undertaking long-term ethnographic fieldwork.

4 Fieldwork

Fieldwork in Yemen presents some very clear challenges and limitations.[21] The logistical challenges of fieldwork to a large extent shape the process of col-

20 I elaborate on this in the following chapter. Fredrik Barth, "An Anthropology of Knowledge," *Current Anthropology* 43, no. 1 (2002): 1–18.

21 A fuller and more elaborate verision of this chapter can be found in Eirik Hovden, "Flowers in *Fiqh* and Constructions of Validity: Practices and Norms in Yemeni Foundations of Forever Flowing Charity" (PhD thesis, University of Bergen, 2012).

lecting data. I used both textual analysis and ethnographic methods and read, consulted, or discussed the texts in this study with various informants. This method of combining textual analysis and ethnographic methods was at the core of the research process and laid the foundation for later review of those same texts, and other similar texts, "alone" after departing from the field. Both methods have been mainly qualitative and explorative, though I have also tried to obtain a degree of representativeness by checking that the category or concepts do appear in the data with some degree of statistical evidence. Below I elaborate on the nature of the fieldwork and the methods and some of their main strength and weaknesses.

The fieldwork was not one of classical ethnography that might involve staying in a single local community/social network for a long time. The object of study dictated a multi-site approach.[22] Because *waqf* is only a limited part of local life in a certain village or town, the larger patterns of *waqf* administration and legal systems could not have been followed if I had stayed only in one location. *Waqf* is practiced and "known" by legal and administrative actors and elites in regional networks and institutions of different scales. Thus I directed my time and effort towards these specialists and prioritized them over "normal" informants. Practical and logistical challenges in rural Yemen also affected my ability to choose a single site and undertake long-term, ethnographic fieldwork. As a westerner at this time, in the 2000s, it was difficult to undertake such fieldwork because the Yemeni government increasingly restricted foreigners from staying in the countryside.

I undertook the ethnographic fieldwork for the present study over a total period of eleven months, spread over three separate periods between January 2008 and January 2010. The main bulk of time was spent in Sanaa, with some day trips to villages inside the larger Sanaa area. In addition, I took longer trips to Zabid, Rayma, and Hadramawt. I obtained research permission and a residence permit from the Yemeni Centre for Studies and Research; I originally requested this from the French research centre in Sanaa, CEFAS.

For the most part I met with informants who were formally educated and many of them held bureaucratic positions in the ministry of justice and in the ministry of *awqāf*. In the wider *awqāf* system there was a general scepticism about documenting the many discrepancies between ideals and practices. Thus the most useful informants were those who knew well what *waqf* is all

22 Gerorge E. Marcus, "Ethnography in/of the World System: The Emergence of Multi-Sited Ethnography," *Annual Review of Anthropology* 24 (1995): 95–117. Thus the "plot" (p. 109) followed in this study is the institution of *waqf*. For a deeper discussion of multi-sited fieldwork, see also Mark-Anthony Falzon, *Multi-Sited Ethnography: Theory, Praxis and Locality in Contemporary Research* (Farnham, UK: Ashgate, 2009).

about and had information they wanted to share yet did not have official positions related to *waqf* administration. For example, in Yemen, a fair number of taxi drivers and people one meets in daily life in markets and restaurants in fact have a higher education, but are unemployed. Many of these people provided important information and perspectives; their usefulness was especially related to the fact that they came from all over Yemen and from different parts of society.

Most scholars who have done ethnographic work in Yemen describe the importance of the afternoon *qāt* chews[23] as an important arena where new informants could be met. There, I could explain my project and what I was doing to a wider group and observe reactions, hear stories, and gather information. At best, these were effective semi-structured group interviews or focus groups. However, the setting was difficult, if not impossible to plan and being a guest also limited my ability to insert my research interest upon the group and their discussions. Many of my personal friends and key informants belonged to the *sayyid*[24] and *qāḍī*[25] houses and several were grandchildren of well-known Zaydī scholars and high-ranking administrators, civil servants, and lawyers in the recent past. This younger generation typically tended to have tried traditional, higher studies of Islamic law and some were at the time studying at the faculty of *sharīʿa* and law (Kulliyyat al-Sharīʿa wa-l-Qānūn) and at the university in general. Some had also worked as lawyers, judges, other bureaucrats in the beginning of their careers.

Many of the middle class and the new rich do not value education in the humanities or the traditional religious sciences and have little knowledge about a topic like *waqf*. I met many people, even some with doctoral degrees, who had little knowledge of what *waqf* was, other than "mosques, cheap flats, and cheap urban building plots." Such perceptions are also important for the study, but in terms of the time I spent with different groups and networks of informants, my main focus was on those who did have a relationship with and knowledge about *waqf*. The same applies to interviewing daily users of *waqf* water stands

---

23 *Qāt* is a stimulant, which is consumed daily after lunch, often in groups. For a detailed description of the public nature of these afternoon *qāt* chews, see Lisa Wedeen, *Peripheral Visions: Publics, Power and Performance in Yemen* (Chicago and London: University of Chicago Press, 2008).

24 A *sayyid* (pl. *sāda*) is a person who claims descent from the Prophet. In the Zaydī areas of Yemen they form a distinct part of society, have a special religious status, and seldom marry "down" into the tribes.

25 A *qāḍī* (pl. *quḍāh*) is a member of an educated family that specializes in Islamic law, but is not a *sayyid*. The *sāda* and *quḍāh* had and still have important administrative positions in the state.

or other *waqf* services and structures. Information related to these issues usually came along with the daily routine of life in the city, and events such as being unexpectedly invited to the homes of friends of friends; therefore such meetings were often not planned. When I visited villages I would go with someone with a relation to the field area, either a relative or a professional official of some sort. I developed a rough interview guide, although most of the time the conversations flowed freely. Usually, the visit took place during the daily after lunch *qāt* session, but often, it was hard to reject invitations for lunch as well. Quite a few of the informants enthusiastically welcomed me and took me around to visit their friends and relatives without informing me in advance of the plans. Thus a large part of the flow of information was obtained during occasions that were quite unplanned and unexpected. The hospitality of the many informants that gave their time and took me around cannot be overstated and on such occasions it was often difficult to reject their friendship simply because they did not know enough about *waqf*. Fieldwork merged with the role of being a guest and a friend. Many of the documents I asked for were difficult to find and even more difficult to copy. Thus in some cases I was able to see *waqf* documents and even registers (*miswaddāt*), but was not allowed to copy them. In a few cases I was allowed to copy them, but not to publish them.

It took much time and effort to approach the ministry of *awqāf* and its archives and engage in learning *waqf* legal theory and understand the reasons, according to the informants, that this knowledge is important. The fieldwork was facilitated by following certain focuses or common tasks that could be shared with informants based on their interests. One of these tasks was obtaining historical material in the form of *waqf* documents, the other was engaging in the world of Zaydī *waqf fiqh*.[26] I paid for an assistant and a teacher to create a certain daily continuity in at least some areas of the fieldwork. By seeking private instruction in *fiqh*, I could focus on the topics important to me, rather than following the normal career of a *sharīʿa* student and beginning with the basics; this would have meant a totally different course of study. The knowledge I acquired by studying *fiqh* was a crucial door opener and conversational "ice-breaker" and my entry point to important intellectual engagements with informants.

From the perspective of most informants, *waqf* was merely a part of the larger concept of Islamic law (*sharīʿa*) and "Islam." In the eyes of my well-educated informants these are not absolute agreed upon categories and often

---

26 The original thesis included two parts: first, how to read with informants and study *waqf fiqh* with a teacher, and the second concerns dealing with the ministry of *awqāf*. Hovden, "Flowers in *Fiqh*," 30–41.

the discussions that took place were well beyond my ability to understand them. Nonetheless, I became part of such discussions. In Yemen, individuals interested in history and society are not only found in academic circles connected to the university. Social history and public memory is politicised, even in the local village context. Often it was easier to discuss the broad trends than to discuss local history in a village where the actors in the room were partly involved in that history.

The practice of reading texts with informants was less systematically applied. In most cases I simply presented them with some fragments of the material in order to see what was intelligible and to whom. The most interesting cases were the instances in which informants interpreted documents from their own family, as these documents held a social meaning or some degree of legal power for them personally. Unfortunately, the political nature of such documents (locally) made this a rare event. Many informants told me that they would be happy to show me their documents, provided their families gave permission. Usually this ended without result. I read a wide range of texts with a number of informants, and covered broad geographical and historical periods; this resulted in a useful explorative approach, but one that could not be systematized. What held the endeavour together, analytically, was the focus on *waqf* as a general legal and social institution and the focus on specific cases of *waqf* as a collection of the most common responses to and comments on this textual material.

Most of my informants were, by far, male. As a male researcher I had limited access to women's arenas and most public positions are held and represented by males. However, women are often seen as independent legal actors who are able to set up *waqf*s, as can be seen in several cases mentioned in this book. The special position of women, which varies greatly by social setting, could not be made into a main topic in this study.

5 Archival Material

The ministry of *awqāf* was only one of several public archives in which to search for sources related to *waqf*, however, it is the most important institutional actor in the field of *waqf* and was therefore given the most attention. It turned out that there were few, if any, *waqf* documents available from them. In general, in archives in Yemen, only parts of the content have been catalogued and in several of the public archives and collections, the catalogues provide little more than the title. Between the various archives there is a great difference in the level of professionalism of those managing the facilities. I received help from Yemeni historians who clarified what I could obtain from which archives.[27]

The issue of "*qāt* money" or money to facilitate the acquisition of archives arose at several places. Sometimes, a small sum is mandatory if the service requested involves the time and effort of the archivist or official, though some officials increased their price when dealing with foreigners. There are many good reasons for not engaging in this type of interaction and it must be pointed out that maintaining a strict position with regard to these questions contributed to my lack of success in some of the archives/offices. Various Yemenis also seek to obtain *waqf* documents or entries from the registers (*miswaddāt*), in order to "erase" issues from the past. Thus my quest for *waqf* documents was somehow parallel to theirs, though for a different purpose. Originally, these documents were public information and theoretically they still are, but today they exist in an opaque space between private and public. Perhaps it is wise and indeed correct for the archivists and their families to keep these documents beyond the public domain for the time being. The presence of doubt in terms of the degree of "publicness" is itself an argument for anonymization. Those documents obtained with the approval of the minister of *awqāf* are not anonymized in this study, since they were officially given to me by the ministry, yet even here I exercised caution.

Textual material from courts is quite useful as legal-historical sources. Court cases between private or state actors and the ministry of *awqāf* not only contain the text of the judgment itself, but often also copies of related documents, including copies of original *waqf* documents. Visiting courts was possible, but not very rewarding, as Yemenis did not welcome foreigners who wanted to observe cases over time and record what takes place. The work done by Anna Würth,[28] who sat in court and observed what was taking place, seems impractical in today's political climate. Also, court cases, especially those involving large and valuable areas of land, as is often the case in *waqf* disputes, tend to go on for years. Ultimately I was given access to, and copies of, six full court cases with all related documents from the Sanaa and Jawf Court of Appeal (Maḥkamat al-isti'nāf Ṣan'ā' wa-l-Jawf) dealing with conflicts between the ministry of *awqāf* and private or public actors. This material is very rich and

27 Among the most useful archives in terms of service was the Dār al-Makhṭūṭāt, which belongs to the ministry of culture. I am very grateful for the assistance of the undersecretary, Sām b. Yaḥyā al-Aḥmar, in swiftly providing a permit.

28 Anna Würth, *Ash-sharī'a fī Bāb al-Yaman; Recht, Richter und Rechtspraxis an der familienrechtlichen Kammer des Gerischts Süd-Sanaa (Republik Jemen) 1983–1995* (Berlin: Dunker & Humblot, 2000).

consists of several hundred pages, but several of the actors involved in the cases did not want to share their views and did not want the cases to receive any attention, and in the end I decided not to follow up on that further.

Several times I visited a young "private" neighbourhood judge (*muḥakkam*), who came from a family of traditional *sayyids* in one of the districts in the far northwest of Yemen. He mainly dealt with cases in which the degree of the dispute was low, such as marriage contracts, sales, leases, and simple inheritance divisions. I visited him and sat in his reception room several afternoons. My relationship to him is representative of my relations with many informants; after a certain period there comes a phase in which it is impractical for me to remain; the relationship cannot be developed further and stagnates. The role of a guest is highly respected and well defined, and visiting someone's work place regularly necessitates a specific and good reason for being there. Only a handful of such relationships could be maintained over a long time.

Comparatively few contemporary or present-day legal cases involve *waqf*, and if they do, there is a tendency to keep them as private as possible since theoretically the state has rights in such *waqfs*. An example to illustrate this was a case I saw (but did not copy) between a famous *sayyid* family and the ministry of *awqāf*; it concerned a large tract of land that is now owned by one of the major embassies in Sanaa. The *sayyid* family had sold the land to the embassy, claiming that they could do so since it was a family *waqf*, while the ministry claimed that the land was, in part, a public *waqf* and that they should receive compensation. The case had been suspended for several years. The *sayyid* family preferred that the case be forgotten. Thus the historical material I obtained is not only fragmented and heterogeneous, but large parts of it are also not entirely public according to some of the actors or informants involved. As a rule I have used caution with this material; much of the material is simply referred to without the names of persons and places and it has not been reprinted in its entirety.

I should note that there were just as many informants with the opposite viewpoint: they took a more ideological stand and claimed that "information relating to *waqf* is public," and "should certainly not be hidden from the public sphere," especially not from researchers with the necessary permissions. In practice the whole question of who owns what is rather opaque and not entirely public, especially in cities and urban areas where a great deal of land has changed hands during recent years. The challenges involved with gaining access to information in the original *waqf* registers (*miswaddāt*) is an excellent way to study how ownership in an opaque political setting falls between the categories of public and private information.

The issue of *waqf* documents and registers, and especially those located in Sanaa appeared to be and never ceased to be, a matter of mystery. As I mention in chapter 3, since the 1930s in particular, the state has increasingly registered some types of *waqfs* by force. Some informants in Zabid pointed out that during the period when Ḥusayn b. Aḥmad al-Sayāghī was minister of *awqāf* in the 1960s the original registers were confiscated, and other cities and villages were left with copies only. If this is really what happened, then the archive in Sanaa must be very rich indeed. The first post-revolution decree organizing the ministry of *awqāf* and its responsibilities (Republican decree no. 26 of 1968, article 10) states:

> All old *waqf* documents (*wathā'iq al-waqf al-qadīma*) are to be registered (*tuḥaṣṣar*) and taken (*tuḍbaṭ*) from every province (*qaḍā'*) and district (*nāḥīya*) and a copy is to be made, separately, whereupon the originals that require special care are to be kept at the archives of the ministry of *awqāf* in the special storage that is made for this purpose **in the dome (*qubba*) in the middle of the courtyard of the Great Mosque,**[29] and a caretaker is to be appointed to receive and catalogue these documents.[30]

Which documents were actually transferred, or were originally present from before is not known. There are rumours of a major armed robbery of the archive of the Great Mosque during the 1990s, but no one would provide any details about this. The minister of *awqāf*, al-Qāḍī Ḥamūd al-Hitār,[31] mentioned the episode and the lack of information about it as an example of the delicacy of the issue of these *waqf* registers and *miswaddāt*. He further ensured that most of the *miswaddāt* were mysteriously replaced by the thieves shortly after the break-in. The same mystery surrounds the project of scanning these important documents, a process that is supposed to be taking place. For historical purposes, and for those wishing to secure the *awqāf* in Sanaa and Yemen, such a project is naturally extremely important. Yet, there are many interests working against such a program. Previous *waqf* administrators and present-day private and public landowners have acquired *waqf* land at less than the market prices or simply by seizure. The modern present-day registers are partly electronic and are the result of several previous "reforms" of re-registration, as

29 These words appear in a bolder font in the original text.

30 Translated from Manṣūr, *al-Mawkib*, 280.

31 The ethnographic present refers to 2010. In March 2011 Ḥamūd al-Hitār was dismissed or resigned and his predecessor, Ḥamūd 'Ubād took over.

I explain in chapter 3. The common story is that for each such re-registration, less land and fewer assets were registered as *waqf*. One person who worked in the latest ongoing registration project (*al-ḥaṣr*) told me quite clearly that "it is prohibited to see the old registers." In theory no one has the power to prohibit this; yet in practice the discrepancy between information in the old registers and the new ones is potentially controversial. A full-fledged legal document written and witnessed by known figures could still win in a court case today, that is, if the court is not corrupt. Many informants pointed this out. The documents are still valid, and even if they are not valid today (in practice), they could be valid again, under a new regime in the future.

One informant explained that he had gone to the ministry to "liberate" (*taḥrīr*) two pieces of his land. *Taḥrīr* is a concept in which *waqf* land is "sold" by the ministry to the tenant, usually for half the free market value of the land.[32] The ministry takes the money and in theory buys an asset and creates another *waqf* somewhere else, thus making an *istibdāl*, or *waqf* asset exchange.[33] The reason for doing this, he said, was to ensure his family's good name: while he himself gladly paid the yearly rent to the *waqf* and he respected the *waqf*, he was not sure his son would continue to do this after he inherits[34] the tenancy of the land. If his son failed to respect the *waqf* and pay the rent, this would bring shame and God's wrath on the family. Therefore, being rid of the *waqf* would mean getting rid of a heavy responsibility. He claimed (and this is why I mention the episode here), that many were not as pious as he was in these matters and that many "obtained" the original documents to ensure that the *waqf* was forgotten and that no legal memory existed.[35] This is especially true of *waqf*s that have some sort of public character or component. Note that the *waqf* of the so-called *waṣāyā* type (treated in chapter 3, 5, and 7) is of a more private character than the "absolute" mosque *waqf*s and thus privatizing them is not very controversial, even in the *fiqh*. And if the *waqf*s have been non-operative for several decades and were not registered in the latest re-registration reforms, then the only "memory" might exist in a local register made by a diligent *waqf*

32 This was presented by several informants as "custom" (*ʿurf*) and one informant called it a *fatwā*. It is also mentioned in Serjeant, *Ṣanʿāʾ*, 152, thus it has been practiced at least since the mid 1980s. Ḥusayn al-ʿAmrī and R. B. Serjeant, "Administrative Organisation," in *Ṣanʿāʾ: An Arabian Islamic City*, ed. R. B. Serjeant and R. Lewcock (London: World of Islam Festival Trust, 1983), 152.

33 In Zaydī *fiqh* this is allowed. Indeed it can even be compulsory if it is in the interest of the *waqf*.

34 In the ideal *waqf fiqh*, tenancy cannot be inherited, yet legally, it can be in several forms. See chapter 6.

35 Public knowledge of the status of *waqf* ownership is called *shuhra* and this is, in theory, equal to written *waqf* documents in terms of legal validity.

inspector in the past. An in-depth study of *waqf* assets in a particular village or area would be useful to have and having access to registers from different periods would be important data for a historical study. Yet in the context of the present study of this book, this was not possible.

•••

In this chapter I elaborate on the background for the present study. There were clear limitations in the fieldwork, as I have pointed out. These limitations were faced in constructive ways, but as a result of the challenges, the focus of the study shifted into more legally-oriented issues centring on certain topics where the validity and legitimacy of *waqf* is at stake.

The research questions focus on what "validity" means in the various fields of knowledge; what is validity in *waqf* law or in *fiqh* and what is it in a local village? How are these connected through codified law and decrees, and in court cases and administrative documents? How does local village life affect *fiqh* and vice versa? How is the validity of the *sharīʿa* constructed or portrayed in the various fields of *waqf* knowledge?

In order to look at constructions of validity I have chosen the approach of looking not at the ideal type of *waqf*, but rather at forms of *waqf* that exist around the edges of the definition of the ideal *waqf*. On these edges or borders dynamic constructions of validity are more visible than in the centre of the ideal type of *waqf*. Examples include *waqf*s used to circumvent inheritance rules, *waqf*s that combine private and public beneficiaries as strategies for various purposes, and the strong rights of the tenant ascribed by custom, and the issues of the inheritance of tenancy. I analyse all of these topics in detail in the coming chapters. Chapter 2 also provides additional reflection on how knowledge and validity (in *waqf*) must be seen as consisting of a more or less shared and agreed upon corpus of ideas, as consisting of mediums and modes of communications and the transmission of knowledge, and finally also as consisting of the social setting and arena where it is used and played out.

6 The Structure of the Book

In chapter 1 I present the background for the research and elaborate on the different layers of research questions. In chapter 2 I discuss and clarify central terms related to the academic study of "Islamic law" and *waqf* and address some of the challenges of such an interdisciplinary study. Finally, I present a model of four different fields in which knowledge about *waqf* is used.

Chapter 3 is a general introduction to *waqf* in Yemen and in it I briefly review previous ethnographic, historical, and jurisprudential literature on *waqf* in Yemen. I present the history of the centralized public *waqf* administration, mainly as a synthesis of already published material. In chapter 4 I situate the texts and sources that I use in the following chapters in a historical and political context with a focus on Zaydī *fiqh* and codified law.

In chapters 5 to 7 I address specific topics situated on the border of what is a valid *waqf*. These chapters share a common methodological approach, in that each focuses on a specific topic relevant in the legal history of *waqf* in Yemen rather than dealing with an ideal *waqf*. They focus on all four spheres of knowledge (*fiqh*, codification, legal cases, and daily knowledge of *waqf*) in order to show that in crucial aspects the practices on the ground affect the upper level doctrines as well as the other way around. The topics that each constitute a separate chapter are issues like circumvention of the inheritance rules, combined public and private *waqf*, and the problem of the strong tenant. Some chapters are more *fiqh*-oriented and some are more practice-oriented. Still, all focus on the ties and interconnections between the various fields of knowledge. In chapter 8, I take up a meta-perspective on the topic of the sources of validity in *waqf* law and draw some conclusions.

CHAPTER 2

Representing Validity in Islamic Law

> I think that in pursuing our studies in the peasant communities that lie within the great civilizations the contextual studies of anthropologists will go forward to meet the textual studies made by historians and humanists of the great traditions of that same civilization. In doing this we shall expand our own contexts and extend our concepts.
>
> ROBERT REDFIELD[1]

∵

Which glasses we put on when looking at the world, or which lenses we choose to use affects what we can see, whether we are studying centuries-old normative Islamic texts or the ethnography of present-day local, legal practices. The study underlying this book uses an interdisciplinary approach to study *waqf* by combining sources, methods, and theories from Islamic studies, history, and anthropology.[2] In this chapter I present the "lenses" I use in the study and the ways in which they are best combined.

In the western academic study of Islamic law there are two main clusters of perspectives; the first involves textually-oriented studies mainly in the disciplines and studies of the Arabic language, Orientalism, Islamic studies, the history of Islamic law, and the general, wider focus on the Islamic intellectual tradition. The second cluster of perspectives, which is also somewhat newer, consists of ethnography/anthropology and social and legal history. The first cluster is oriented towards the normative texts, which are often quite old, and the second, newer cluster is oriented towards describing, understanding, and explaining local behaviour, that is, the social perception of the normative texts, but often without focusing on the content of the texts or the "tradition" that these texts build upon. The field that bridges the two perspectives is still young

1 Redfield, "Social Organisation," 17.

2 Several other disciplines could be mentioned as many of them partially overlap and share a historical development. My undergraduate background is in geography, anthropology, and Arabic.

 | DOI:10.1163/9789004377844_003

and actively being developed, and thus many scholars and sub-disciplines remain in one of the two perspectives noted above.

In this chapter I argue that it is necessary to bridge the two perspectives, while at the same time remain critical when importing analytical concepts, theories, and models into the new combined perspective. Uncritically importing representations of "disconnected" and de-contextualized legal norms into a study of local law risks inventing a "law" that is/was simply not there in the first place. In order to bridge the two perspectives in this book in a sound way, I use Fredrik Barth's theoretical concept of "knowledge," and more specifically, I present an apparatus of analysis that ultimately centres on constructions of "validity" and the criteria for validity in various forms of legal knowledge. As we see in the rest of the book, "validity" in *waqf* is very different among different groups of actors and in different contexts, even though the actual legal institution referred to by these actors (*waqf*) and the frames around it (Islamic law) are the same.

A norm can be "real" and "exist" and thus be represented in at least two ways: As a re-statement of a normative text/statement or as an observation or representation of an observation of an invocation of a norm and the subsequent action that follows the norm (or does not). For a modern jurist, "law" is a norm, and the relationship of law to its context and application in modern society is fairly well known. The letter of the law and the practices of the law are closely related. One can assume that there is an existing apparatus of legal training, enforcement by the police, punishment executed by a state; it is the exceptions that interest the jurists—the case in which, for some reason, the law is not followed, or cannot be followed. Thus the letter of the law for the modern jurist is fairly "real" and not just any narrative statement. However, in "Islamic law," or more specifically in the representation of Islamic law, this relationship between norm and actual application is much more problematic for several reasons; I deal with these reasons in this chapter. A certain ideal, norm, or legal doctrine related to *waqf* cannot be assumed to "exist" because a law book from the fifteenth century (presumably) claims that this is the law. A law or a legal institution can "exist" in a book, or in normative or ideological representations, but may not necessarily exist in a sociological/historical sense. On the other hand, a regular practice or pattern of behaviour alone cannot confirm the ultimate existence of an underlying norm and it certainly cannot confirm the existence of a "law." Which of them is the "real" law? Perhaps the exact nature of the relationship between norms and actions should be left to the philosophers.[3] Yet both need representation; the more relevant question in this chapter is how to represent them in a way that scrutinizes the interplay

3 For a sceptical view of a empiricist perspective and an argument in favor of looking at the norms the way locals categorize them, see Paul Dresch, "Legalism, Anthropology, and History:

between them and does not simply assume this interplay in one or the other way. Much of the Islamic academic jurisprudential debates (*fiqh*) are indeed very concerned with this relationship and elaborate upon it in great detail, as we shall see.

In this chapter I begin by presenting a typical legal definition of *waqf* and further demonstrate and argue why this very normal legal definition *waqf* is problematic in the descriptive sciences like anthropology and history. In relation to this, I review some of the important cross-disciplinary debates on how to represent Islamic law (in general, not only related to *waqf*). I conclude by investigating and elaborating upon theories of how norms constitute a form of "knowledge" that must constantly be reproduced and transmitted in a certain social setting; thus norms cannot be seen as merely statements, they are in their very nature also acts. At the same time there are different arenas or "fields" where such knowledge is situated: *Fiqh* schools, the judge's court, the local village. These fields have their own parameters that affect what law "is." These "fields of knowledge" have their own criteria of validity that can be seen in texts and in behaviour. The fields and parameters presented in this chapter form a foundation for analysis in the later chapters of this book.

1 Normative and Descriptive Models of *Waqf*

1.1 *The Basic* Waqf *Model*

The "basic *waqf* model" or the "ideal *waqf* model" is a fundamental starting point to define *waqf*:[4]

	God	
The founder (*al-wāqif*)	The asset (*al-mawqūf, al-ʿayn, al-raqaba*)	The beneficiary (*al-mawqūf ʿalayhi, al-maṣrif*)
	The administrator/guardian (*al-mutawallī*)	

FIGURE 2 The basic ideal legal *waqf* model.

A View from Part of Anthropology," in *Legalism: Anthropology and History*, ed. Paul Dresch and Hanna Skoda (Oxford: Oxford University Press, 2012), 1–37.

4 The model is inspired by a version found in Randi Deguilhem, "The Waqf in the City," in *The City in the Islamic World*, ed. Salma K. Jayyusi, Renata Holod, Attilio Petruccioli, and André Raymond (Leiden: Brill, 2008), 938. See also Peters, et al., "Waḳf."

The model is abstract, easily translatable from Islamic legal theory and easy to re-present. In English the term *waqf* can mean both the act of setting up a *waqf*, and the actual outcome that lasts beyond its foundation. In this ideal setting, the institution of *waqf* and the individual *waqf* are one and the same.[5] The model presents four "actors" and one "thing." The first actor is the founder (*al-wāqif*). He "owns" the "thing" before the act of making it into a *waqf*. The thing or asset is the object of *waqf*; what is given or donated or made into a *waqf*. The beneficiary is the recipient of the *waqf*. A very crucial, yet rather theoretical, aspect in setting up a *waqf* is a concept that is situated in the wider realm of ownership law; the ownership over the thing (*milk*)[6] and the right to use it (usufruct, *manfaʿa*) are separated. That is, God takes over the ownership, while the beneficiary (*al-mawqūf ʿalayhi*) takes over the right of use.[7] Another more abstract and impersonal concept referring to the beneficiary is the "place of expenditure" (*al-maṣrif*).

"God" comes into the picture in many ways; not only is He the formal recipient and owner of the actual *waqf* and hence all *waqf*s, He is also, according to many Muslims, the source of the laws (*al-sharīʿa*) regulating the institution of *waqf* itself. According to many Muslims God is also fundamental in many moral and legal aspects concerning the institution at large. God will "refund" the founder of the *waqf* with merit (*ajr, thawāb*); this of course can be a strong motivation for setting up a *waqf*.

The final actor in the model is the administrator (guardian, *nāẓir, walī, mutawallī*, sometimes trustee). The founder may decide to retain this role for himself, but since the *waqf* is made to last perpetually,[8] an administrator or chain of administrators must be appointed for the *waqf* for the future. This can be a member of the founder's family and thus "inherited," or it can be someone from the "formal public," such as a judge or a government representative. Just as the asset is split into one aspect (usufruct) for the beneficiary and one aspect (ownership) for God, the *mutawallī* also, although less explicitly, receives an important right, namely the main financial and managerial control over

5 In Arabic, form I, II, and form IV of the verb are used to describe the act of establishing a *waqf*; the *maṣdar* is "*waqf*."

6 Not *mulk*, which is "kingship" or God's rule. *Milk* is usually pronounced *mulk*, and in Yemeni usage often means "private lands," with or without sharecropping agreements. The terms *milk* and *māl* are used fairly interchangeably.

7 All these details are subject to variation in the different law schools. In Zaydism, God is the new owner, while the beneficiaries "own" the right of use and it can even be "inherited." The difference between to "own" and to "possess," or for that matter other similar terms, relates to legal theory that I elaborate on later. Here, the model is given for the sake of overview only.

8 At least in mainstream Zaydī *waqf fiqh*.

the asset. As I demonstrate in chapter 7, this is no small right, both in terms of power and in terms of economic gain.

There are two doctrinal concepts that are fundamental in (Zaydī) *waqf*, but that are difficult to represent in the model above: perpetuity and piety. Most doctrinal views hold that *waqf* must be perpetual (*mu'abbad, ta'bīd*), or almost so.[9] The asset to be made into a *waqf* must be of a "lasting character" (*baqā' 'aynihi*) in addition to being "useful" (*al-intifā' bihi*).[10] Most *waqf*s referred to in this study are agricultural fields that produce a yearly harvest for the beneficiary. The revenue or income is called *al-ghalla*. If the thing is of direct use, such as a book or a house, the value given to the beneficiaries is not the house, but the right to use it, the usufruct (*al-manfa'a*, pl. *manāfi'*). The founder is free to stipulate how his *waqf* should function and to whom the benefit should go. In more ethnographic terms, and if we ignore for a moment the religious dimension, *waqf* as presented here is merely a type of ownership law, in which individuals come together in societies and agree on rules on how to regulate access to resources.

In addition to the doctrine of perpetuity (*ta'bīd*) there is also a doctrine of "piety" (*qurba, taqarrub*). This last doctrine separates *waqf* from most other transactions; a *waqf* cannot be made for selfish means, it must serve a purpose that pleases God (at least in Zaydism). Both these doctrines are important in the doctrinal discourse, but in practical legal fields compromises must be made. In this book I demonstrate these compromises in detail and discuss how the jurists themselves perceive these compromises. Therefore, saying that *waqf* "must" be perpetual or pious is a normative statement referring to the doctrine, not to law as practiced in courts.[11] Thus, it is difficult to decide whether or not *waqf*s are similar to different types of western (charitable?) trusts, as this depends on which level of doctrine is referred to and in which context the comparison is made. The same applies to its religious basis: to what extent can

---

9 For instance, a book that is made into *waqf* cannot be expected to last for centuries if it is in daily use, so this criterium is not absolute.

10 Ibn Miftāḥ, *al-Muntazi' al-mukhtār min al-ghayth al-midrār al-ma'rūf bi-Sharḥ al-azhār* (Sanaa: Wizārat al-'Adl / Maktabat al-Turāth al-Islāmī, 2003), 8:175 [henceforth *Sharḥ al-azhār*].

11 Even the status of the doctrines themselves is explicitly questioned in some of the law schools. A Shāfi'ī *waqf* does not need to be pious, and a Mālikī *waqf*, and partly also the Zaydī, may revert back to the founder's family, and therefore, in practical terms, it is not perpetual. Further, a wide range of legal ruses to circumvent these doctrines are considered legally valid and discussed in minute details in the *fiqh*. This is an example of the problem of which "law" to represent, the ideal, or one that is more "real." In any case, the ideal component is important as a framework for the legal discourses and for religious and moral inspiration.

(the "Islamic") God be compared to ("western, secular") Good.[12] Such reflections do not arise in this study unless the topic appears in the texts and the narratives of informants. The focus of this book lies in a much narrower definition of "law," which is also much more contextualized. The doctrines do play an important role in *waqf* in Yemen, but mainly as ideals of inspiration and as frames for much more mundane and practically oriented legal discourses related to certain controversial rules of Zaydī *waqf* law.

In conclusion, the basic *waqf* model above serves as an illustration of key concepts, key actors, and the relations between these. However, the model is abstract, de-contextualized, and can only serve as a starting point for understanding how the institution of *waqf* is acted out in a specific context. Below are some important elaborations on the legal aspects of this model. These elaborations are not to be understood as representations of theoretical findings from this study, they are rather to be seen as tools to better understand the complexity of *waqf* as a legal phenomenon, before we come to the more empirical chapters.

1.2 *The Direct and Indirect Usufruct* Waqf

A *waqf* can be an object that is used directly. An example is a book given as *waqf*, or a house where the beneficiaries live. The "indirect usufruct *waqf*" becomes important if that house is not given to be lived in, but to be rented out and the rent to be given to the beneficiaries designated by the founder. In this case the asset of the *waqf*, and the place where the beneficiaries can enjoy the *waqf*, are physically separated. Such a *waqf* has a side that produces income and a side where the income is spent. In such cases where the usufruct of the *waqf* is indirect, the economic management of the asset becomes crucial. The people who live in a *waqf* house or till a *waqf* agricultural field literally live and work in and on the *waqf* asset, but they are not beneficiaries, they are only tenants (*musta'jirūn, shurakā'*). If the administrator is a good businessman in the service of the *waqf*, the tenants will be required to pay something like full market rent.

In simple, direct usufruct *waqf*, there is little need for a *mutawallī*; a book that is made a *waqf* can follow a certain family for generations and the beneficiaries (the same family) can take care of it. But in an indirect usufruct *waqf*, the *mutawallī* is a significant actor. And the tenants, who were not even

---

12 For an up to date debate on these issues, see Armando Salvatore and Mark LeVine (eds.), *Religion, Social Practice, and Contested Hegemonies: Reconstructing the Public Sphere in Muslim Majority Societies* (New York: Palgrave, 2005); Armando Salvatore and Dale Eickelman (eds.), *Public Islam and the Common Good* (Leiden: Brill, 2006).

mentioned in the basic *waqf* model above, are also important actors both legally and practically. In the strict ideal model, they have no other rights than other tenants on the free market would have.

1.3 Waqf *for* Waqf

As noted, many *waqf*s are indirect usufruct *waqf*s, where the value of the *waqf* is converted into some type of currency so that the beneficiary can make use of it efficiently. For example, an agricultural field is made a *waqf* for the sake of a local mosque. The agricultural field is then part of the income producing side of the *waqf*, while the mosque is the beneficiary. If the mosque is also a *waqf* (as they often are) then we have a situation with a *waqf* for a *waqf* (an indirect usufruct *waqf* for a direct usufruct *waqf*).

Strictly speaking, the mosque, as a *waqf*, is a beneficiary of another, different *waqf*, unless the same founder made the two at the same time. In practice, the lines of distinction between them become blurred. The agricultural field has a special status in that it is preferred over the mosque because the income of the asset must first be used for the maintenance of the asset itself.[13] If we call them primary and secondary *waqf*s, the primary *waqf* can be seen as a separate legal unit and like any other indirect usufruct *waqf*s, the *mutawallī* is obliged to take care of and maintain it before he can give away any surplus to the beneficiary/secondary[14] *waqf*. This is anchored in the doctrine of continuity. The mosque and the agricultural field are two different *waqf*s and can have two different *mutawallī*s. In practice, the mosque is often administered together with the assets that belong to it (its income producing primary *waqf*s) as one administrative unit, and often under one *mutawallī*. If so, the borders between the two *waqf*s (the primary and the secondary) become diluted and unclear over time.

1.4 *Multiple Asset* Waqf

In all the examples above, one and the same *waqf* can also contain several different assets. For example, five agricultural fields can be made by the same founder, simultaneously, for the benefit of one mosque. They are different assets, but under the same legal unit as one *waqf*. What makes them different

---

13 See article 55 in the *waqf* law: Wizārat al-Shu'ūn al-Qānūniyya, Qānūn al-waqf al-sharʿī (qānūn raqm 23 1992) wa lā'iḥat tanẓīm ijrā'āt al-ta'jīr wa-l-intifāʿ bi-amwāl wa-ʿaqārāt al-awqāf wa-istithmārihā (qarār jumhūrī raqm 99 1996), 2nd ed. (Sanaa: Wizārat al-Shu'ūn al-Qānūniyya, 2007).

14 Here the "receiving" *waqf* is called "secondary." However, the primary *waqf* would often be more recent than the secondary one, thus if we look at the chronology of their establishment, the terms could have been used in reverse order. It is by looking at the flow of revenue that the terms "primary" and "secondary" fit with the usage above.

assets are their physical character as five fields in perhaps five different locations, but they are ruled by the same contract (*waqf* document) and law as one unit. The *waqf* must be delimited and defined, but need not necessarily be one "thing."

1.5 Waqf *Clusters*

If a mosque has several primary *waqf*s attached to it in order to provide it with income, these are often administered under the *mutawallī* of the mosque. His role is one that is more or less "public," to the extent that the mosque is public, at least to the users of the mosque. The other possible alternative is that the founders of the primary *waqf*s insist on retaining the right to administer their *waqf*s for themselves.[15]

If, for various reasons, the primary *waqf*s are administered together, one may see this as a de facto merging of *waqf*s. This often depends on practical circumstances: Over time, the original founders may be forgotten, the *waqf* documents lost, and what is left is a public memory (*shuhra*) that those particular agricultural fields or houses are *waqf* and belong to the local mosque (or any other beneficiary). Typically, the administrator then produces new documentation in the form of inventory lists or *waqf* registers (*miswaddāt*) that define which properties in the village are *waqf*. He may bring important witnesses such as scholars, judges, and wealthy landowners to witness the validity of the inventory list.

Typically, if under the jurisdiction of a strong state, the state will claim to be a sort of "meta-*mutawallī*." If so, all the public *waqf*s, such as mosques, may be included in one large state affiliated administration. In areas such as Yemen that are unstable and politically fragmented for long periods of time, every city has its own *waqf* administration, often influenced by the local scholars and the wealthy. Indeed, in Yemen one of the meanings of the term *al-waqf* (with the definite article), in addition to the legal institution as such, is the name of the regional, public *waqf* administration that administered or supervised the major mosques and other public *waqf* services in their city and nearby countryside. *Waqf*s that were privately managed, or managed by certain families could still exist, but these would be separate "clusters."[16]

15 This is an important field of *waqf fiqh* that is treated several places in this book, but mainly in chapter 7.

16 See chapter 3.

1.6 *Mixed Beneficiary* Waqf

A *waqf* can be made for a public beneficiary, which theoretically means that the benefits of the *waqf* are open to anyone (*waqf khayrī, ʿāmm*). It can also be made for the benefit of a specific family, in which case it is called a private *waqf* or a family *waqf* (*waqf khāṣṣ, ahlī*). But a *waqf* can also be a combination of private and public elements.

Many of the smaller public *waqfs*, or *waqf* clusters, are administered by members of a certain family and the role of *mutawallī* can be, in practice, semi-hereditary. Often, the founder of a public *waqf* may wish to include and reserve a special place for his family and descendants. For example one agricultural field could be given as a *waqf* for both a village water cistern and for the family and descendants of the founder. The division between the two beneficiaries is according to the stipulations of the founder. Alternatively, some of the "benefit" could be taken from the *waqf* by giving the *mutawallī* the surplus of the *waqf* after maintaining a specific public service,[17] or by letting the descendants of the founder rent the *waqf* asset for a rent that is below market rates.[18]

Now we see that the ideal, basic legal model of the *waqf* fades into something much more legally complicated and yet more pragmatic. Obviously, such a model is more empirically oriented (sociologically or historically) and is partly based on patterns of behaviour and actual cases and not only on simplified ideal legal norms.

1.7 *The Biographical* Waqf *Model*

If we continue in the direction of models of sociological or historical validity, other aspects arise in the material. One such "lens" or "model" involves examining the biographies, or lives, of individual *waqfs*. The biographical *waqf* model is rather different from those above. The intention behind the model is to remind the reader that a *waqf* continues after the act of founding and the death of the founder, and continues with new actors, many of whom inherited the roles or statuses. Generations come and go and have to share the benefit of the *waqf* according to certain rules. The term *waqf* sounds very abstract and as a legal term it is abstract; in practice, we are mainly talking about concrete physical things, like a certain agricultural field, a certain water cistern, and a certain mosque. New generations of administrators, tenants, and beneficiaries come and go. Their internal division of power and access to the revenues and resources may change over time, which is why the *waqf* itself is also under pressure from actors and groups of actors who may each want to maximize

17 See chapter 7.

18 See chapter 6 and 7.

their share. Typically, the heirs of the founder will try to have the *waqf* rendered invalid by a *sharīʿa* judge in order to regain the *waqf* from the beneficiaries. Similarly, the modern state tries to increase its control. Threats can also come from natural disasters or changes in the economy or technology.

Over a long duree we can imagine a local landscape of *waqfs* that are initiated, exist in more or less stable conditions, then eventually change, split, or merge, and disappear, if they are not revived. The history of one specific *waqf* and its biography can perhaps tell us about periods of calm and periods of conflict. Once the many small *waqfs* are established, the critical moments in their biography arise when one actor takes the place of the other; for example when a new administrator takes over from the old one. The *waqf* can only exist when a certain number of people respect it and keep it "alive" and new actors bring with them new ideas and knowledge of what is a good, proper, and valid *waqf*.

The individual *waqfs* can also reveal the history of a local public infrastructure, such as a mosque or a public well, even though theoretically and legally the *waqf* and the physical thing are not the same.

In most *waqf* laws it is valid for someone to sell a *waqf* asset and buy a new one if it is in the interest of the *waqf* to do so (*istibdāl, ibdāl*). In any case few *waqfs* are constant over time, in terms of the spirit of the *waqf* in the original idea of the founder, or in terms of the physical asset. The aspect of conflict and change is also highly "legal," but one that cannot be predicted by the ideal legal *waqf* model. In reality most *waqfs* have a history, a biography.

1.8 *The Operational* Waqf *Model*

The operational *waqf* model is a reminder that many *waqfs* are not apparent to researchers unless there are clear conflicts or significant changes in the *waqf* because the picture we see is one of normality.[19] The tenant of the land or the house or the shop pays the administrator the rent and the administrator takes care of the *waqf*, be it a water cistern or a mosque. It is simply part of local economic life and it is only recently that social historians have attempted to see this important institution actively operating in local society, and not just as a legal construct appearing with conflict.

19 There are other reasons that *waqfs* are not easily "seen" in the field. During fieldwork many informants felt free to talk about *waqf* in the village in general, but significantly fewer were willing to point out exactly which assets and structures were *waqfs*. Even fewer showed me the legal documents related to *waqfs*. This seems to relate to the semi-private nature of *waqf* tenancy and management; many of the rights attached to a *waqf* are customary and not fully legally defined and if the law were full applied this would often mean a loss to tenants and local administrators.

In practical terms the operational *waqf* has no founder, and is not necessarily part of any state apparatus. It is an ongoing activity or income and involves the maintenance of both asset and beneficiaries, and payments to those hired to perform various jobs related to the *waqf*. The economic activity mainly centres on the issues of lease and the daily use of the *waqf* by users or beneficiaries. An example is an agricultural field that has been made *waqf* for a mosque and a water cistern. This model allows us to see the tenant tilling the land on a daily basis, and the one who prays in the mosque, and the one who daily fetches water from the village *waqf* cistern. These actors are parts of the *waqf*, legally, socially, and culturally. *Waqf* as seen as a legal document, or contract, here fades into daily practices, knowledges, memories, and perceptions of those practices and physical structures. The *waqf* may thus exist as various forms of "perceptions" that are more or less present and "known." This is not necessarily so, as a legal construct cannot be defined once and for all, and wrapped in logical, formal language that has a beginning and an end; rather it is an ongoing knowledge, often tacit and taken for granted. Methodologically and practically, the *waqf* must be "known" and seen by the researcher. When we as researchers look at a snapshot in history, or at a legal document recorded on paper, what we see is, of course, a tiny fraction of a much larger phenomenon both in time and space.

1.9 *Actors Involved in* Waqf

When looking at the above models, each one highlights a specific set of actors. When we look at all the potential actors involved in a *waqf* as a list, we see that there are many types of actors that are easily overlooked in the basic *waqf* model. Such a list or model of potential actors involved in a *waqf* is useful as a "check-list" when studying a specific *waqf* case.

A: Actors that are part of the basic *waqf* model.

1 God
2 The founder (*al-wāqif*)
3 The piece of property donated (*al-ʿayn, al-raqaba, al-mawqūf*) that is, the "object" made into *waqf* is also an actor in case a slave is made *waqf*
4 The beneficiary (*al-mawqūf ʿalayhi, al-maṣrif*)
5 The *waqf* administrator (*mutawallī*)

B: Actors in addition to those found in the basic *waqf* model.

6 The tenant (*al-mustaʾjir*)
7 The unlawful possessor (*al-mughtaṣib*) of a *waqf* asset or usufruct (often a tenant)
8 The local judge/notary involved in making *waqf* documents/contracts

9 Witnesses to *waqf* documents/contracts
10 The judge
11 The public *waqf* inspector/minister
12 The local representative of the public *waqf* administration (in Yemen; *ʿāmil al-waqf, mudīr al-waqf*)
13 Islamic scholars; *ʿulamāʾ*. Actors and structures involved in forming traditional and modern *waqf* laws.
14 Any potential beneficiary, or *waqf* "user" (if emically perceived as one, self ascribed or by the community)—the unlawful/unintended user of a *waqf* service; a "free rider".

C: Actors who are descendants of those above.
The model allows us to realize and expect a higher number of conflicting interests and a more complicated struggle of power than in the simpler models. We can also expect *waqf fiqh* and law to regulate the balance of power between all these actors mentioned in the model. This model also leads us to a highly important aspect: That of knowledge distribution. *Waqf* related activity is highly dependent on specialized knowledge(s) such as knowledge about the law and the legal system. And the legal knowledge might be quite distinct and specialized compared to knowledge of best possible agricultural practice. Knowledge of what is a "good" and valid *waqf*, and proper *waqf* behaviour, is often unevenly distributed in the society. When attempting to describe the knowledge in use and its distribution, we must also situate this in groups of actors and social settings.

The models above start with a basic legal, ideal, and simplified definition of *waqf*. To what extent this legal definition is one of how *waqf* should be (normative, prescriptive), or one of what *waqf* is (descriptive), is a question that we cannot address at this stage of the argument in this chapter, but most would claim that both are necessary. Below, I review a number of theoretical debates related to how to approach this problem in the academic representation of Islamic law; is it fundamentally a "norm," or "practice," or if both, how can they be approached and represented in a sound manner? The review begins with a historical overview of the academic study of Islamic law, of which *waqf* law is an integral part.

2 Academic Debates on Islamic Law

Waqf law is an integral part of Islamic law (*sharīʿa, fiqh*) and indeed a separate chapter in most Islamic legal works. Islamic law as a whole has been under scrutiny by western academic scholars for around two centuries. This has led to an academic tradition that forms the basis for our academic understanding of Islamic law today; this tradition has produced important debates and insights into both the texts and the social processes of Islamic law. In recent decades, other academic disciplines have also taken up the study of Islamic law, each from their own perspective. The categorization of the academic study of Islamic law into historical or disciplinary paradigms must be undertaken cautiously in order not to invent polemical debates and straw men.

Knut Vikør presents four main types of "schools" or perspectives of scholarship on Islamic law; below I partly adopt his typology,[20] but append my own views.

2.1 *Early Orientalists (Before About 1880)*

The first school Vikør presents is that of western scholars before about 1880. For the sake of clarity, I refer to them as the "early orientalists." According to Vikør, these scholars portrayed Islamic law in very much the same way Muslim scholars did, as something that grew out of the Prophet's own actions and sayings (*ḥadīth*), which was later consolidated into the four (or more) schools of law. They tended to accept the contents of these sources as a historical reality, that is, that Islamic history and the idea that the narratives (*ḥadīth*s) of the sayings and actions of the Prophet were historically correct and thereby provided a "true" normative basis for the *sharīʿa*.[21]

It was only toward the end of the 1800s that historical knowledge and methods of textual criticism enabled the formation of a critical view of Islamic history and Islamic law.[22] Scholars of this period contributed little to the descriptive sciences, which were at the time somewhat ideological; rather the focus of this generation of scholars was on the normative texts. The scholars of this period translated and edited many important Islamic theological and jurisprudential works. Their works on grammar, dictionaries, editions, and translations are still used by historians and social scientists today and the philological tradition of this generation continues into today's field of Islamic studies.

20 Knut Vikør, *Between God and the Sultan: A History of Islamic Law* (Oxford University Press, 2005), 12–19.

21 Ibid., 12.

22 Already in 1848 Gustav Weil suggested "that a substantial bulk of the *ḥadīth* should be regarded as spurious." Wael B. Hallāq, "The Authenticity of Prophetic Ḥadīth: A Pseudo-Problem," *Studia Islamica* 89 (1999), 1. More significant is the fact that certain schools and sects of Muslim scholars have themselves always been critical of the authority of parts of the *ḥadīth* material.

2.2 *The Revisionists*

Vikør uses Joseph Schacht (d. 1969) as the core example of a revisionist. Schacht's *Introduction to Islamic Law*[23] is unavoidable for most scholars of the field even today. The revisionists criticized the authenticity of the *ḥadīth*s by using textual criticism to show that many *ḥadīth*s were fabricated and circulated one or two centuries after the time of the Prophet. Schacht also developed other theories significant for the study of Islamic law: He argued that Islamic law was mainly an academic, intellectual tradition that was used by the judiciary to a limited extent[24] and further, that in legal practice a system of "ad hoc rules" were used. He claimed that there were no significant developments in Islamic law since the end of the formative period and thereby he approved of the theoretical dogma many western and Muslim scholars claimed throughout history, that "the door of *ijtihād*" (new formulation of law on the basis of original sources) had been closed.[25] A third theory was that the role of the eponymous founders of the four law schools were largely an invention of later scholars who sought to construct coherent law schools and systematic genealogies of legitimacy.

The revisionists began to question the nature of the *sharīʿa* as "true" and introduced the perspective of social constructivism and the linguistic turn to

23 Schacht, *Introduction to Islamic Law*.

24 Vikør here states that Schacht followed Weber in his theory of *Kadijustiz*, which meant that the judges did not follow an external coherent body of rules.

25 This theory is dependent on the definition of the term *sharīʿa*; if Schacht meant the didactic works of legal rules (*mukhtaṣarāt*), then yes, little development has taken place since the classical period. But if the court decisions, *fatwās*, *fiqh*-margins and commentaries, sultanic and imamic decrees, legal ruses, the "flexible elements" (*istiṣlāḥ, isitḥsān*, etc.), and the practice-oriented *fiqh* in general are included in the definition of *sharīʿa*, then there has been a continuous development of the *sharīʿa*. There is a question of what empirical data was available at Schacht's time, but we must also consider his definition of *sharīʿa* as "jurisprudence" rather than actual, local, practised legal systems. Schacht was more aware of this than what he has later been criticized for. For instance, Schacht explicitly points out that the concept of legal ruses (*ḥiyal*) is an important topic for further studies. He uses the term "legal ruses" in a wide sense and explicitly states that Muslim jurists incorporated the legal needs of the society into the law, for example with custom. Another field in which flexibility and development could take place was in the way legal documents were written. Schacht addressed this in his comments on the topic of *shurūṭ*. He also pointed out that the *fatwā* genre represents a window to the more flexible uses of the law. To say that Schacht denied the post-classical development of Islamic law or flexibility in the law is to miss the point and is a typical example of paradigmatic polemical debate. See Jörn Thielmann, "A Critical Survey of Western Law Studies on Arab-Muslim Countries," in *Legal Pluralism in the Arab World*, ed. Dupret Baudouin, Berger Maurits, and Laila al-Zwaini (The Hague, London, and Boston: Kluwer Law International, 1999), 44. Schacht, *Introduction to Islamic Law*, 73–75, 80–85, 210–211.

understand how social forces shaped the body of the law. The law was seen as having been shaped by social agency in a political context. This inclusion of social theories as dynamic forces constantly acting upon a corpus of normative material represented the first step away from the text itself as an isolated object of study. It also opened up a way to see the *sharīʿa* as a theoretical concept or an emic ideal that has been implemented to a limited extent and suggests that there existed something in historical reality, a reality that diverged, sometimes significantly, from this normative corpus. The relationship between the normative texts and practices on the ground remained rather unresolved and was not theorized by the revisionists, mainly because they lacked historical and anthropological studies of Islamic law in actual use. At this point (ca. 1960) there was only limited empirical knowledge of local legal practices.

2.3 *The Post-Schacht Generation*

The post-Schacht generation is less homogeneous as a group; first, some were anti-revisionists. Some of these are apologists for "reformed Islam," and argued against the claims of lack of historicity of the texts of revelation and thus against the potential critique of authenticity of Islamic law, while others simply argued that the revisionists went too far in emphasizing the inventions. Vikør then mentions "the historians of practice"; from this point on, when much richer empirical material became available, they criticized Schacht's theory that Islamic law had not changed.

Some of these debates took a polemical turn and the terms for "law," "Islamic," "change," *ijtihād* (new production of law), and *taqlīd* (following established law), were often used in confusing and polemical ways. As noted, the debate of whether or not Islamic law had changed ("the closure of the door of *ijtihād*")[26] is irrelevant to this study unless the hypothesis is much more specific and contextualized. These historians[27] seem to use the term "Islamic law" or *sharīʿa* as

---

26 See the footnote above. See also Hallaq's article on the continued open door of *ijtihād* and the role of *muftīs* and *fatwās*. Wael B. Hallāq, "From Fatwās to Furūʿ; Growth and Change in Substantive Islamic Law," *Islamic Law and Society* 1, no. 1 (1994): 29–65.

27 Again, it is problematic to make very firm claims and categorise scholars in this paradigm. Wael Hallaq is an example of someone who sees the "*sharīʿa*" as the totality of the Islamic tradition. Rudolph Peters is an example of a "historian of practise." He treats Islamic criminal law in admirable detail by first elaborating on "classical doctrine," and then proceeding to the "historical" part. He states: "… [I] will refrain from paying attention to the historical development of the doctrine, although I am well aware that the doctrine was not static and immutable. However, this is only recently recognized and there are still many gaps in our knowledge." Rudolph Peters, *Crime and Punishment in Islamic Law: Theory and Practice from the Sixteenth to the Twenty-First Century* (Cambridge: Cambridge University Press, 2006), 60.

a concept that refers to Islamic law in a wider sense, while Schacht used the term in a much narrower sense, that is, as the corpus of the most agreed upon established rules from the four Sunnī law schools, as presented in medieval student textbooks or judges' manuals (*mukhtaṣarāt*). The claim of the post-Schacht generation, that the *sharīʿa* was indeed in use both as an ideal theory and a legal practice, is an example of how the term *sharīʿa* is used to mean something that exists as a jurisprudential corpus and a social practice at the same time, but without sufficiently theorizing and defining the relationship between the two.

2.4 *The Interdisciplinary Focus*

Vikør mentions how social scientists now started to focus on how actors use the *sharīʿa*.[28] This current is rather diverse in its approaches. It is a question of where Islamic legal studies or the history of Islamic law ends, and where an interdisciplinary study of Islamic law starts. And the sheer numbers of researchers and scholarly works produced in recent decades is not comparable with that of earlier generations of scholars of Islamic law.

After World War II, much more attention and resources were given to the study of the Middle East, partly due to the new geopolitical constellations. In the United States especially, significant public funding was diverted to create centres for Middle Eastern studies in the interdisciplinary genre of "area studies." This trend came somewhat later to Europe, but when it came, it usually adopted and incorporated the academic orientalists who now became specialists on Islam or the Middle East instead. (After 1978 and the publication of Edward Said's *Orientalism*, they usually did not want to be called "Orientalists," or later, even less "Islamicists"). In the United States, government funding was first and foremost designed to provide the state bureaucracy with resources related to languages and the culture of the Middle East. The staff in these centres belonged to all types of political directions and academic interests. Much hope was given to the interdisciplinary method itself.[29] Vikør states that this new interdisciplinary current of scholarship produced a valuable correction in terms of "anti-essentialism."[30]

The rest of this part of the chapter will depart from the historical roots of the study of Islamic law and elaborate upon two important epistemological

28 Vikør, *Between God and the Sultan*, 16–17.

29 Aaron W. Hughes, *Situating Islam: The Past and Future of an Academic Discipline* (London and Oakville, CT: Equinox, 2008).

30 Vikør, *Between God and the Sultan*, 17–18.

debates: How to conceptualize "Islam" as an object of study and how to conceptualize "(Islamic) law."

2.5 *Anthropology of Islam(s)*

Anthropology (or sociology) of Islam and legal anthropology are two subdisciplines which arose rather separately from the discipline of Islamic legal history, but in the post-Schacht generations they have intertwined and merged together with the earlier textually-oriented study of Islamic law. Today the borders between the disciplines are blurred and the theoretical debates fade into each other.

Until recently anthropologists had not made significant advances in the study of Islamic law. They did and partly still do relatively little in the field of Islamic legal studies, or the study of textual Islam in general, even when producing ethnographic studies from the Middle East. Daniel Varisco discusses the reasons behind this and concludes that it may be related to pragmatic reasons, such as the lack of proficiency in formal, classical Arabic. Thus a "division of labour" arose between anthropologists on the one hand and Islamicists and Arabists on the other. The former dealt with local life and the latter with texts. This divide has only recently started to be bridged; the present study situates itself in the new tradition that bridges the two.

In the past, Islamic law was seen as textual Islam, not the Islam that could be studied by observation of local practices or listening to what "normal" people say. From that perspective, *sharīʿa*, or Islamic law, was considered a part or a sub-category of Islam, if not the most essential part of textual, "high," Islam.[31] In his book *Islam Obscured*, Daniel Varisco criticizes previous anthropological representations of Islam. The term "Islam," as an analytical category and as a starting point for the analysis has itself been subject to much criticism. Varisco quotes Michael Gilsenan's 1983 introduction: "… it is almost an obligatory starting point in scholarly treatment to acknowledge that 'There is no monolithic Islam'"[32] The discussion of whether or not to use the term "Islam" with a capital "I," indicating its "existence," or even in plural, "islams," or even to use it at all, quickly descends into polemical disagreement. Abdul Hamid El-Zein is often quoted as one of the first scholars to reject the idea that there "is" something called "Islam."[33] However, when El-Zein is used to illustrate this

31 D. M. Varisco, *Islam Obscured: The Rhetoric of Anthropological Representation* (New York: Palgrave Macmillan, 2005), 15–18.

32 Michael Gilsenan, *Recognizing Islam: An Anthropologist's Introduction* (London: Croom Helm, 1983); Varisco, *Islam Obscured*, 149.

33 Abdul Hamid el-Zein, "Beyond Ideology and Theology: The Search for the Anthropology of Islam," *Annual Review of Anthropology* 6 (1977): 227–254.

seemingly extreme post-modernist position, his more detailed arguments are overlooked; El-Zein argues that any analysis must start with the categories of the informant, even if they contradict one or the other types of "correct" doctrines of Islam. It is in this objective, analytical level that correct "Islam" is not relevant:

> … the utility of the concept "Islam" as a predefined religion with its supreme "truth" is extremely limited in anthropological analysis.… This logic of relations implies that neither Islam nor the notion of religion exists as a fixed and autonomous form referring to positive content which can be reduced to universal and unchanging characteristics. Religion becomes an arbitrary category which as a unified and bounded form has no necessary existence. "Islam" as an analytical category dissolves as well.[34]

El-Zein argues for the study of contextualized, localized, and situated Islam, and claims that there is no Islam that is not contextualized, at least not as an anthropological object of study. I would extend this important point more specifically to Islamic law and hereunder *waqf* law; a mere presentation of a norm or ideology is not evidence of its "existence" and certainly not if "Islam" and "Islamic law" are represented in a highly generalized way. From this it follows that there is also no Islamic law and no *waqf* law that are not contextualized, at least not that are relevant to anthropological or historical analysis.[35]

Talal Asad, in responding to El-Zein, disagreed that it is a constructive solution to completely drop "Islam" as a theoretical category.[36] Perhaps misinterpreting El-Zein,[37] many others also rejected what they saw as an attempt to say "there is no Islam" and hence, "there is no anthropology of Islam." For those calling themselves "anthropologists of Islam" this must have been a sensitive situation. Asad does provide a constructive way forward in his article from 1986; in it he argues that Islam should be seen as a discursive tradition, or traditions in plural, situated in social contexts and that the social context

34 Ibid., 252.

35 This point is important. As I elaborate later in this chapter, *fiqh* debates and even the most philosophical Islamic debates have a social setting of use and transmission, and a certain medium through which it is expressed. When text-oriented scholars analyse a text, they see the text, but overlook the influences of the context at the time in which the text was created or debated. This study uses Fredrik Barth's knowledge theory in these questions.

36 Talal Asad, "The Idea of an Anthropology of Islam," in *Occasional Paper Series* (Washington, DC: Center for Contemporary Arab Studies, 1986), 4.

37 El-Zein used Levi Strauss' theories of structuralism; in the 1980s this was quite dated and easy to criticise, or simply dismiss altogether.

is what is formative: "... it should be the anthropologist's first task to describe and analyse the kinds of reasoning and the reasons for arguing, that underlie Islamic traditional practices."[38] In this, Asad is not opposing El-Zein, on the contrary, and the previous disagreement is perhaps only of a polemical character, which is also the impression of Varisco.[39] Asad further states: "An anthropology of Islam will therefore seek to understand the historical conditions that enable the production and maintenance of specific discursive traditions, or their transformation—and the efforts of practitioners to achieve coherence."[40] The last words in this quote are especially important in this study. Coherence is a central quality of law. This book will follow El-Zein and Talal Asad's view, but with the further elaboration of Fredrik Barth's theory of knowledge.[41] Barth's theory does not deal specifically with Islam, but with "traditions of knowledge" in general. The above discussion of how to analyse "Islam" is directly relevant to the question of how to analyse Islamic law. The focus on *waqf* as a legal institution in this study takes us back to the more legal dimensions of "Islam" and *sharīʿa* and here it is necessary to review another debate that is fundamental to conceptualizing Islamic law.

2.6 *From Legal Pluralism Towards Codification*

The attempts to study Islamic law or *sharīʿa* in a comparative academic perspective using universal social science theories mainly arose in the academic disciplines of sociology and the anthropology of law, new fields that are still being developed, especially in Islamic contexts.[42] The sociology or anthropology of law originated with attempts to understand the system of law in "primitive" cultures and the dynamics between official state law and sub-fields of local and customary laws.[43] One of the most significant debates in recent decades have been over the concept of "legal pluralism."

It is critical for any academic discussion of the analytical potential of the term "Islamic law" (or the term, *sharīʿa*) that we take a stand towards the use of

38 Asad, "The Idea of an Anthropology of Islam," 16.

39 Varisco, *Islam Obscured*, 147–148. For a useful review of this debate of anthropology of "Islams" versus the "one Islam-position" see Gabriele Marranci, *The Anthropology of Islam* (Oxford and New York: Berg, 2008), chapter 3, "From Studying Islam to Studying Muslims," 31–51; and Jens Kreinath (ed.), *The Anthropology of Islam Reader* (London: Routledge, 2012).

40 Asad, "The Idea of an Anthropology of Islam," 17.

41 Barth, "An Anthropology of Knowledge."

42 For a more thorough review, see Thielmann, "A Critical Survey."

43 A central contribution but one that is not discussed here is the concept of the "semi-autonomous field": Sally F. Moore, "Law and Social Change: The Semi-Autonomous Social Field as an Appropriate Subject of Study," *Law & Society Review* 7, no. 4 (1973): 719–746.

the term "law" as an analytical category. This is especially important in a field in which there is relatively little primary data available, and where a great deal of knowledge circulates as quotations of previous research, using the term "Islamic law," "Islamic law says." Often the division between the researcher's concept of law and that of the informants' or the texts' is not well distinguished and developed. The danger is that the researcher may be producing knowledge only related to his own idea of "law" by a priori creating a body of laws to look for in his study, while excluding others. Many scholars of Islamic law have been tempted by the term "legal pluralism" (or its related term "interlegality") because it seems, at first sight, to resolve the theoretical problem of there being, simultaneously, different "bodies" of law in the field of study, such as "classical Islamic law," "Muslim state law" or different versions of "customary law," "case law" or "tribal law."

Leon Buskens has attempted to solve or clarify this problem by using the concept of the "Islamic triangle";[44] in this configuration, state law, *sharīʿa*, and customary law are so intertwined that they cannot be analysed separately. Most scholars would agree that there is legal pluralism in the Muslim world, while at the same time admitting that there are some fields where the application of law, in a narrow legal sense, is usually limited to a hybrid, yet rather defined[45] range of legal rules. It is rare for the actors to simply be able to choose between different equal, parallel existing bodies of laws.

Baudouin Dupret offers a detailed treatise of the debates on legal pluralism as an analytical concept in the anthropology and sociology of law.[46] Interestingly, his argument is similar to those who criticize an essentialist use of the term *sharīʿa*. He calls his solution "praxiology": "Instead of elevating law to the rank of an analytical instrument, I would suggest going back to the observation of social practices and considering, in the broad field of the many normativities, that law is what people refer to as law."[47] He continues:

> In other words, whereas Tamanaha rightly criticizes legal pluralism for its overinclusiveness, i.e. its inclusion of phenomena that most people

---

44 Leon Buskens, "An Islamic Triangle: Changing Relationships between Sharīʿa, State Law and Local Customs," *ISIM Review* (2000), 8.

45 These rules are "defined" in the sense that they are more or less known by the actors in court, while the same rules in the *fiqh* may remain open. Conflicting parties of course will not know in advance their case or the judge's opinion, yet they can consult other experts about court practice on such questions.

46 Baudouin Dupret, "What is Plural in the Law? A Praxiological Answer," Égypte/Monde arabe, Troisième série, 1 (2005), online: http://journals.openedition.org/ema/1869; doi: 10.4000/ema.1869.

47 Ibid.

> would not consider to be law, and its under-inclusiveness, i.e. its exclusion of phenomena that many would consider to be law, he queers the pitch by underestimating people's practical and context-sensitive understanding of the word "law" or its equivalents.... In other words, the question of legal pluralism does not arise from scholars looking at the social world from outside, but it becomes a topic in its own right when it emerges out of people's practices that they orient to a situation of co-existing, conflating and/or conflicting multiple laws.[48]

Dupret insists that "legal pluralism" cannot be an a priori analytical category or a theoretical starting point. It is only fruitful if the local practitioners of law identify it in relation to their own definitions and practices of law, and state that what they have is multiple parallel legal systems, and thereby legal pluralism.[49] Dupret suggests studying how practices and norms are related to each other instead of trying to identify the norms and systematize them in advance of the observation (of norms in contextualized use). This does not lead to the problem that "everything can be law," according to Dupret, who argues for an approach to the study of law that is methodologically "praxiological":

> ... since activities in legal settings are characterized, as are human activities in general, by the general orientation to the production of intelligibility, coordination and order, it would be rather surprising to observe such an anarchical proliferation of laws *without observable attempts to reduce it*. This last question addresses the authority which is granted by conventionalism to social actors to initiate new kinds of law. The realistic answer stresses that law as a social institution is necessarily produced by social actors, and that recognizing these actors' authority only threatens the authority of social and legal theorists. This holds true in a praxiological perspective. Moreover, it should be said that it is not up to legal sociologists and anthropologists to determine whether or not to grant social actors the authority to initiate new laws. All that social sciences can do

48 Ibid.

49 For support of this view and a thorough discussion see Gordon R. Woodman, "The Idea of Legal Pluralism," in *Legal Pluralism in the Arab World*, ed. Dupret Bauduion, Berger Maurits, and Laila al-Zwaini (The Hague, London, and Boston: Kluwer Law International, 1999). See also Maarten Bavenick and Gordon R. Woodman, "Can There be Maps of Law?" in *Spatializing Law: An Anthropological Geography of Law in Society*, ed. Frans von Benda-Beckmann, Keebet von Benda-Beckmann, and Anne Griffiths (Burlington, VT: Ashgate, 2009). See also Thielmann, "A Critical Survey."

> is to observe and describe how real people in real settings orient to the production of a phenomenon which they call law.[50]

In this last statement he touches upon what I would call the very opposite of legal pluralism, namely "legal monism"; how laws are constantly debated with the purpose of narrowing down the scope of possible legally valid outcomes.[51] This is a twist in the debate that leads us away from the circular philosophic arguments and back to a social arena; the rational purpose of law (of law in a narrow sense that is), is to regulate social behaviour. This is not to deny that there are "grey areas" in the law which remain vague, "flexible elements" or areas "outside" one or the other body of law. Most lawyers can attest that such grey areas exist even in western law, which is partly the reason lawyers are needed in the first place. But this is not an argument for not trying to see the regularities, together with our informants, before identifying the exceptions. It is important not to begin with a top-down normative analysis that builds on ideal normative definitions, but rather to look at what happens in practice and build models based on this, in dialogue with our informants, whether the object is court cases or legal debates. In chapters 5, 6, and 7 of this book, I demonstrate how major questions of "Islamic" *waqf* law cannot be understood without examining its dependence on local custom (*ʿurf*) and ideas of utility and public interest (*maṣlaḥa*). In *fiqh* debates concerning the "meeting" between Islamic law and local custom, we observe a present awareness of the degrees of compatibility between Islamic law and local custom.

The debates over which rules to choose as the "more correct and valid rules" to be used by the judges either takes place among specialists of law, in which case we can refer to it as academic legal theory, jurisprudence (*fiqh*), or it can take place among various groups of "commoners" in which case it could be called "public legal debates," whether in the modern mass media or in a traditional, everyday afternoon village gathering. Only after some type of political debate and process of delimiting the scope of rules has taken place can some

---

50 Dupret, "What is Plural in the Law?." Emphasis mine.

51 Woodman uses "conflict," "integration," "separation," "unification" and "recognition" of "one law by another" here, again, the definition of law is crucial, and such a typology of relationships between different "laws" requires some degree of comparability. In any case, the actors themselves must to a certain extent share the perception of legal pluralism with the researcher. Woodman, "The Idea of Legal Pluralism." See Bälz on definitions of legal pluralism based on parallel systems of binary codes. Kilian Bälz, "Sharīʿa and Qānun in Egyptian Law: A Systems Theory Approach to Legal Pluralism," *Yearbook of Islamic and Middle Eastern Law* 2 (1995), 41.

rules be chosen,[52] agreed upon, and enforced. What takes place in a legal debate is not a process by which the actors agree that all potential rules are equal, on the contrary, the actors conclude that some rules are better, more valid, and more just than others. If the debate is carried out in order to produce new, coherent law that can be implemented in courts, then this is the act of codification, something we come back to below.

In a theoretically pure common law system, the decision of the judge becomes future law. Hence the term "law" in English covers both the process around the law in court and the normative statements regulating the social action. The English word "ruling" is indicative: it covers both a court decision and a legal rule.[53] In an absolute model of civil law, the judge, ideally, does not look at previous cases and simply applies the letter of the law or the "code." Arguably, Islamic law can take the form of either ideal types, common and civil law, but it is usually a mix of the two. More importantly, both ideal types involve some components of legal precedence and some degree of regulation or code-giving from an external political-legislative body situated above or outside the court and the judge.[54] This body external to the court can be a democratically elected assembly, a privy council, an Islamic state council or a consensus of aristocrats, landowners or elders in the village.

52 In this perspective, if one insists that "*sharīʿa*" was used, then it must also have been codified. One could argue that the *mukhtaṣar* genre is a step in the direction of codification, as argued by Fadel: "The *mukhtaṣar* functioned as the authoritative collection of a legal school's doctrine, and, for that reason, I argue that Islamic law in the age of *mukhtaṣars* is best understood as a codified Common Law" (abstract) Mohammed Fadel, "The Social Logic of *taqlīd* and the Rise of the *mukhtaṣar*," *Islamic Law and Society* 3, no. 2 (1996): 193–233. In chapter 4 I argue that *fiqh* is caught between the duality of the academic ideal of plurality of knowledge and polyvocality on the one hand, and the struggle to provide subjects with clear, univocal law on the other. Whether this or that is "inside" or "outside" "the *sharīʿa*" is hardly relevant unless the actors themselves make a point of it.

53 In other European law systems which are built on civil law, the term "law" usually consists of two terms that tend to separate the process of the law and the letter of the law, or in other words, the normative corpus and the social system around it (Norwegian: Lov og rett, or German: Gesetz and Recht).

54 Some argue that Islamic law is a special type of its own. At times such arguments overlook the necessity that a law be accepted, endorsed, and sanctioned at the political level. If Islamic law is purely "religious" or apolitical or independent, this may be so for certain genres of literature, but it is a mistake to claim that this can be the case for all Islamic law. Again, this is a problem of definition that arises only if keeping a rather essentialist view of Islamic law. A related argument is that Islamic law is a third and unique type—or "jurist's law," that is, the law of the *muftī* or the scholar. See Vikør, *Between God and the Sultan*, 6–11. Again, the issue of when and where the *ʿulamāʾ* could operate freely and when they were tightly tied to a specific political polity is open for debate.

If the researcher observes the action in the court, then he can understand and examine both the freedom and the constraints of the judge. The "letter of the law," or legal theory in general, is obviously only a part of what takes place in court.[55] In other words, "legal theory" (jurisprudence, *fiqh*) and "observed law" must be two different analytical concepts or levels. A concept such as "codification" can include the use of consistency, coherence, logic, legibility, predictability, applicability, and sanctionability, all important parts in the efficacy and perception of the law. Legal theory, debates, codification, legislation, and the judge's decision are all important parts of what takes place in the courtroom. "Codification" can thus be an analytical category or tool that ties together the ideology and theories of Islamic law (*fiqh*) with the observable law found in the courts and in the legal documents. Layish argues that modern codification is something "outside" the "classical *sharīʿa*,"[56] while Fadel argues that strong aspects of codification arose in the *mukhtaṣar* genre in the late classical era and that therefore codification is not something new and not "outside" the *sharīʿa*.[57]

Above I indicate that we are in need of analytical categories, such as "codification," despite the fact that some Muslim jurists would claim that such a thing does not "exist" in the *sharīʿa*, or that it can never be fully "Islamic". If local Muslim jurists and legal experts are given too much definitional power of what the *sharīʿa* is and how it is internally built up, we end up simply reproducing their version of God's law, rather than studying law as situated in social and political contexts. Dupret's praxiology is therefore an important theoretical tool of guidance, away from "legal pluralism" and towards the study of how validity is constructed in Islamic law, and an important correction to previous norm-based theories of what Islamic law is.

2.7 *Reviewing the Inductive Turn*

In order to move forward towards a constructive theoretical perspective it is helpful to first look back at what we are leaving behind. The following is a generalized model of an epistemology with "Islam" as its starting point and other concepts subordinated, and arranged systematically in sub-branches. I call it the "Islam, *sharīʿa*, *fiqh*, *waqf* model":

---

55 Lawrence Rosen focuses on the importance of the local notables in a rural setting in Morocco and their power over the processes of law. Lawrence Rosen, *The Justice of Islam: Comparative Perspectives on Islamic Law and Society* (Oxford: Oxford University Press, 2000).

56 Aharon Layish, "The Transformation of the Sharīʿa from Jurists' Law to Statutory Law in the Contemporary Muslim World," *Die Welt des Islams* 44, no. 1 (2004): 85–113.

57 Fadel, "Social Logic of *taqlīd*."

Culture? System of norms			
Islam ("religion"?)	**Islamic law (*sharīʿa*)** (morals, system of norms, law?)	legal theory, jurisprudence (***fiqh***)	***waqf*** (a legal institution)
observable practice?			

FIGURE 3 The Islam, *sharīʿa, fiqh, waqf* model.

This is a model that is often expressed by informants, but also appears in some branches of academic study, and in western public debate. The model refers to the general idea that *waqf* is a part of *fiqh, fiqh* is a part of the *sharīʿa* and *sharīʿa* is a part of Islam, and finally, Islam is a religion (though for some it is even a political ideology with a "content" that dictates sub-categories from the top down). The model is built upon the fundament that there is "something" more or less coherent which is called "Islam." For most Muslim believers this also includes a hierarchy of authority and truth. Often its systematic aspects are claimed, and when the foundations of the claim cannot be defined, informants reply that only very educated individuals are able to produce theories specifying exactly what the *sharīʿa* entails. The *ʿulamāʾ* know. Usually, "normal" informants would say "because it is in the Qurʾān," even if this is objectively incorrect (for example, there are few if any references to *waqf* in the Qurʾān). More educated informants, and indeed specialists in *fiqh*, can and do produce longer and more elaborate chains of references, all going back to some idea of God, heaven and hell, and to the very reason for having a law. It is not the place to discuss these emic models of Islamic epistemology here.

The problem arises when there are traces of such thinking in academic disciplines and especially so in disciplines and texts that are necessary to relate to as fundaments for our present day academic knowledge. It is not a problem if the goal is to give a simplified version of the works and views of a certain medieval scholar. The problem arises when the idea of *sharīʿa* is given strength as a factor in explanations of social behaviour, i.e., in the assumption that "norms" lead to actions and that the norms are a priori defined and systematized in a fixed system called *sharīʿa*.[58]

As noted, the problems do not originate in the orientalists' and Islamic scholars' study and reproduction of normative texts. Their effort and results were admirable. The problem arises when a corpus of law and norms are taken

58 In the original thesis I elaborate on five problems that must be addressed. Hovden, "Flowers in *Fiqh*," 85–90.

out of their context, simplified, and projected onto a frame of social and historical reality where it did not exist originally. That is, it is problematic to import, uncritically, the orientalists' or believers' models into other academic disciplines, by unreflexive interdisciplinarity and to thereby ascribe an ontological reality that it never claimed in the first place. This study rejects the "deductive" use of any essential "Islam" and rather bases itself on an "inductive"[59] perspective where empirical reality must be a corrective priority. Dupret and Ferrie further argue against theorizing over abstract generalities and instead advocate further contextualization. They argue that when norms are invoked by actors, this does not mean that the norm "exists" in advance (be it "Islam" or a specific rule).[60] Thus the praxiological perspective we see develop from Dupret rather focuses on how the norms are put forward and claimed.[61] Although the actors clearly cannot choose freely what to claim in any moment, or freely invent new categories, we should not create abstract, systematic hierarchies of norms on their behalf. The "structure" (Islamic law) framing the "agency" cannot be assumed to be exactly the same way Muslim scholars portray it (or the way it is portrayed in other idealized versions).[62] As this book demonstrates, the systematicity between the ideal doctrinal norms of *waqf* and the more applicable *waqf* law is not at all clear; this is something the Zaydī jurists point out themselves. The researcher can overlook important and interesting doubt,

59 Here, the terms "deductive" and "inductive" are used only to conceptualize which end of the hierarchy of norms the researcher gives methodological priority to, that is, in a legally oriented research. The argument follows the argumentation of Dupret, quoted several times below, who argues for a methodological reorientation toward the usage of the norms, rather than an examination of the upper level, doctrinal, decontextualized norms only.

60 Baudouin Dupret and Jean-Noël Ferrie, "Constructing the Private/Public Distinction in Muslim Majority Societies: A Praxiological Approach," in *Religion, Social Practice, and Contested Hegemonies: Reconstructing the Public Sphere in Muslim Majority Societies*, ed. Armando Salvatore and Mark LeVine (New York: Palgrave Macmillan, 2005).

61 This is also, in part, what Paul Dresch argues for. For him, "legalism" is how people think in legal categories and "how such classifications of the world are accepted, contested, or manipulated." However, he seems to be critical of an empiricist perspective. Dresch, "Legalism, Anthropology, and History."

62 The conclusion of the same book argues in favour of not seeing "Islam" in a universalistic frame, and suggests that the concept of "casuistry" adds contextual aspects in the analysis of moral reasoning. Cecelia Lynch, "Public Spheres Transnationalized: Comparisons Within and Beyond Muslim Majority Societies," in *Religion, Social Practice, and Contested Hegemonies: Reconstructing the Public Sphere in Muslim Majority Societies*, ed. Armando Salvatore and Mark LeVine (New York: Palgrave Macmillan, 2005). Perhaps we could even talk of "analytical casuistry."

"grey areas," tensions, and inconsistencies if he insists on representing the law of the "ideal *waqf*" only.

We shall now move away from the general focus on Islam and Islamic law and focus more specifically on *waqf* and academic *waqf* studies. There are now a number of studies on *waqf* that have elaborated our understanding of *waqf* as a historical and social phenomenon much in line with the reflections above.[63] Most of these do treat the problem of defining the study object, and the problem of finding theories of Islamic law that incorporate power and agency into the social use of legal concepts and normative texts. Below, I use two theoreticians to demonstrate how *waqf* can be conceptualized as "norms in use." One of these is van Leeuwen, who is an excellent example of a historian of practice.

> It will be argued below that in the course of time, the concept of *waqf* was "institutionalized," in the sense developed by Bourdieu, and that gradually a field was formed in which various parties "invested" their material and symbolic capital in order to derive profit and symbolic power from it. The concept of the field, moreover, seems to allow for a representation of the *waqf* institution both in its "essential" and its historical manifestations, since it is the dialectic between these two that determines the dynamic force of history, and the reproduction of structures within the framework of the field.[64]

This is a good example of how the ideal legal definition of *waqf* is exchanged for one of a social "field" that is subject to social forces and for which there is a dialectical relationship over time between something more essential and doctrinal and on the other side practices situated in history. Few would disagree with

63 Many could be mentioned here, perhaps the most important are Haim Gerber, *Islamic Law and Culture 1600–1840* (Leiden: Brill, 1999), although *waqf* is not the main focus; Miriam Hoexter, *Endowments, Rulers, and Community: Waqf al-Haramayn in Ottoman Algiers* (Leiden: Brill, 1998); Amy Singer, *Constructing Ottoman Beneficence: An Imperial Soup Kitchen in Jerusalem* (New York: State University of New York Press, 2002); Alejandro García Sanjuán, *Till God Inherits the Earth: Islamic Pious Endowments in al-Andalus (9–15th centuries)* (Leiden: Brill, 2007). In addition, there are a number of published articles and conference papers by scholars like Gabriel Baer, Randi Deguilhem, Aharon Layish, David Powers, and Paolo Sartori. As for *waqf* in Yemen, Messick's study of the local economy in the town of Ibb is an example of an economic entry point into the study of *waqf*. Brinkley Messick, "Transactions in Ibb: Economy and Society in a Yemeni Highland Town" (PhD thesis, Princeton University, 1978).

64 Richard van Leeuwen, *Waqfs and Urban Structures: The Case of Ottoman Damascus* (Leiden: Brill, 1999), 27–28.

the necessity of such a twofold model.[65] *Waqf* is no longer explained primarily as a sub-category of Islam or as something that is primarily Islamic. Rather, it is a social field or part of a social field, an institution that can be observed as patterns of social behaviour. To be more explicit, when analysing, I suggest that we set aside "Islam" and "*sharīʿa*" in the "Islam, *sharīʿa, fiqh, waqf*" model mentioned above, and we are left with *fiqh* and *waqf*. I argue against using Islam or *sharīʿa* as analytical categories because these terms are so ambiguously used, by researchers and informants, as well as by the public in popular debate.

On the other hand, *fiqh* is an inherently Islamic academic field of legal knowledge and the term "legal theory" is very appropriate.[66] It is a tradition in the Asadian meaning that is essentially "Islamic" and incomparable with other traditions of legal theory in the sense that it is a corpus which to a very high degree refers, in an intertextual way, to itself, yet the term legal theory could be used to highlight more universal aspects of *fiqh* like formality, logic, specialist knowledge, rootedness in texts, transmission in an academic and school-like setting, etc.

This specific study, however, looks into Zaydī *waqf* law and how it has developed in parallel with certain problems or challenges. Instead of reviewing *waqf* studies in general, I focus on the unique Zaydī and Yemeni situation and the relationship between the religious authority and legal judgements.

2.8 *Levels of Norms*

The model of only one level of law, or structure, and another level of practice or agency needs to be elaborated. More levels and more accurate levels are needed in our analysis. I use an article by Brinkley Messick as the starting point.[67] Messick describes a court ruling from 1947 in which the judge annulled a *waqf* due to a new decree from Imam Yaḥyā (the religious, judiciary, and state leader of

65 As for the model with one core doctrinal debate interplaying with the local use of these doctrines, Dupret remains sceptical and argues that this duality should not be the main theory, just because it fits certain contexts. Dupret and Ferrie, "Constructing the Private/ Public Distinction," 150.

66 To translate *fiqh* as "legal theory" is not an established use of the term. Some would reserve the word "theory" for the more theoretical sides of *fiqh* such as *uṣūl al-fiqh*. I would argue that the distinction between *uṣūl* and *furūʿ* is not that clear, although they are usually recognized as two separate "genres."

67 Brinkley Messick, "Textual Properties: Writing and Wealth in a Shari'a Case," *Anthropological Quarterly* 68, no. 3 (1995): 157–170. In general, Brinkley Messick's work is important theoretically; it is also highly relevant for this study because most of his empirical material is from Yemen.

the time) restricting the use and validity of family *waqfs*.[68] In the conclusion of the article Messick calls the decree from the imam an "intermediary doctrine" among "levels" of normative texts. Although he does not state these explicitly, we can see clearly at least three "levels" in Messick's article; the initial and lowest one is the legal document or verdict made by the judge, the second one is the decree from the Imam, and the highest one, situated above the imamic decree is a level of scholarly, academic *fiqh*: "… to illustrate the importance of working backward from a local text such as a judgment to intermediate ones, here imamic opinions. To work still further back, to higher or prior doctrine, would require an equivalent sort of close reading of the ikhtiyarat."[69] Messick suggests starting at the level of the ethnographic and historical information and then working "backward." We may only reach "Islam" in the end, at such a distance that it does not need to be clearly defined. The study object is much closer. Messick uses the terms "levels" and "genres of doctrines," but leaves us to conceptualize exactly how these levels are connected and relate to each other. Should they be seen as ever larger circles around the written judgement or as levels on top of each other, hierarchically? What sort of determinacy does one level impose on the subordinated ones? The exact way of imagining the landscape of these levels is not important here, rather the importance here lies in the willingness and attempt to systematize and to make models of what most others simply refer to as *sharīʿa, fiqh* or the "normative texts" or even "textual authority." The normative texts are situated in complex landscapes, genres, or even discourses that we must make maps of, or models of, in order to relate to them, and in order to understand how our informants related to them and used them in actual social interaction. Only then do we have something that other scholars can relate to and constructively criticize. As for Messick's mentioning of "levels of doctrines," I use the model immediately below to separate distinct discourses, traditions, or fields of *waqf* knowledge and hereafter refer to these as "fields". Thus I imply that *waqf* is not one field only, but several interconnected fields of legal knowledge. Their interconnections mean that they affect each other and that actors borrow, mix, and reconstruct knowledge, symbols, legitimacy and validity in acts of entrepreneurship, though they remain separated by fundamental contextual constraints.

---

68 That is, limiting the possibility of circumventing the inheritance rules. It was common to do this by establishing a *waqf* in which the children of exogamously married women are granted fewer rights than they would have in a normal inheritance division; I elaborate on this in chapter 7.

69 Messick, "Textual Properties," 167.

1 Legal theory (*fiqh*)
2 Codification (decrees, state legislation)
3 Judge's law (legal and administrative documents, court verdicts)
4 Everyday *waqf* related knowledge and practices

With regard to the definition of "law" and "legal" in a more narrow sense, it is now possible to distinguish between legal theory that first and foremost takes place in *madrasa* academic school settings and law in a more narrow sense as the established practice of the judge, and possibly also the imamic/state decrees. The judge's "law" is therefore more sociologically oriented; it is something that can be seen in enforced judgements. Moreover, all fields in the model contain some type of text (corpus) and context. It is not that the *fiqh* is "text" while "practice" is what is found "on the ground." Too often we hear about ideals as "theory" and the local as "practice." "Texts" and "theories" are present and used in all four fields in the model above, at least if we include oral narratives and common knowledge as texts. Each field of *waqf* law has its own dynamic of "text and context" and we must take great care when comparing a text from one field with a context from another. The claims of validity of a specific argument in one field do not automatically follow the criteria for validity in the other fields, even if the wording of the argument seems similar from a distance.

2.9 *Connecting Practice and Norm in Fredrik Barth's Knowledge Theory*

Legal knowledge, whether inside or outside a narrow definition of "law" must be "known" by "knowers." Without those who "know" the orientalists and philologists would only have texts to study—without social context, agency, and effects as sociological objects of study. The "knowers" of *waqf* must constantly use their knowledge and transmit it to others, and this must be done through a certain medium in a specific social setting. These are the concepts that Fredrik Barth suggests we look at when studying the knowledge that our informants use as they engage in their daily lives. The following elaboration is based on his article "An Anthropology of Knowledge."[70]

Barth starts the article with no small proposition; he claims that anthropologists should exchange the concept of "culture" for one of "knowledge." His definition of knowledge is wide: "What a person employs to interpret and act upon the world. Under this caption I wish to include feelings (attitudes) as well as information, embodied skills as well as verbal taxonomies and concepts: all the ways of understanding that we use to make up our experienced, grasped

70 Barth, "An Anthropology of Knowledge."

reality."[71] When Geertz asked him, what then, is the difference between "culture" and "knowledge," Barth replied that the term "culture" is so laden with misconceptions in the history of anthropology that a new term may be more useful and thus provide a blank page to fill:

> Knowledge provides people with materials for reflection and premises for action, whereas "culture" too readily comes to embrace also those reflections and those actions. Furthermore, actions become knowledge to others only after that fact. The concept of "knowledge" situates its items in a particular and unequivocal way relative to events, actions and social relationships.
>
> Knowledge is distributed in a population, while culture makes us think in terms of diffuse sharing. Our scrutiny is directed to the distributions of knowledge—its presence or absence in particular persons—and the processes affecting these distributions can become objects of study.
>
> Differences in knowledge provide much of the momentum for our social interaction, from gossip to the division of labour. We must share some knowledge to be able to communicate and usually must differ in some knowledge to give focus to our interaction.[72]

The fact that knowledge is unevenly distributed in the population is particularly true in terms of legal knowledge and consciousness of law and legal practices. Quoting the philosopher Russell, Barth goes on to state that knowledge can be based on "inference." The processes of inference create chains of references, or chains of validity. This is something that I demonstrate in the analytical chapters of this book. Rarely is absolute certainty invoked and indeed most such links in chains of references are based on degrees of trust and the use of trust in validating true knowledge. On this Barth remarks:

> By our acceptance of valid inference, we all extend the reach and scope of our knowledge immensely, relying on judgements based on whatever criteria of validity we embrace—above all, what others whom we trust tell us they believe.

---

71 Ibid., 1. For other uses of Barth's article in relation to theorizing Islam, see Ahmet Yukleyen, "Production of Mystical Islam in Europe: Religious Authorization in the Süleymanlı Sufi Community," *Contemporary Islam* 4, no. 3 (2010), 272. For a more general perspective on Islamic knowledge, see, for instance, Martiin van Bruinessen and Stefano Allievi, *Producing Islamic Knowledge: Transmission and Dissemination in Western Europe* (London and New York: Routledge, 2011).

72 Barth, "An Anthropology of Knowledge," 1–2.

> As a consequence, much of our knowledge we have accumulated by learning from others—including, indeed, the criteria for judging validity that we have learned to use. This makes a great deal of every person's knowledge conventional, constructed within the traditions of knowledge of which each of us partakes.[73]

The criteria of validity are thus very much founded upon consensus. Chains of references (explicitly to and in Islamic texts) do not necessarily have to be crystal clear, logical, and reach all the way back to a source. Often vital links in the chain are simply "known" to be true, or "known" to be telescoped long enough back to a certain something. The very stop in the chain of reference, or lack of reference at all, is just as relevant to analyse and represent as trying to "help" the informant by linking his idea to the "actual" fundament in the texts of revelation (Qur'ān and Sunna). The extent of the elaboration of such chains of trust, or chains of references or validity is what is interesting. That is, how deep must arguments in different fields of *waqf* be, in order for the informants to "accept" the knowledge as true or valid? Law is a special field of knowledge; one may disagree with the judge, but it is the judge who holds power. In *fiqh* however, extremely elaborate chains of "truth" can be found in an enormous variety.

Barth claims that we should break with the "cultural perspective" and proceed to the "analytical operation of dividing the shapes, instruments and encasements from each other, to better analyse the internal processes of differently constituted traditions of knowledge."[74] As for the framework of analysis, he suggests that we look at three distinct aspects of knowledge. These three aspects are interconnected and mutually influence each other. He states that it is not at all his intention to divide the concept of knowledge into separate subcategories, but rather to say that knowledge cannot be understood without looking at all three simultaneously: (1) corpus, (2) medium, and (3) social setting of transmission and use. This perspective allows agency into the analysis and it becomes easier to understand the construction of the criteria of validity that govern knowledge in any particular tradition. It is a very important theoretical contribution that "corpus" ("norms") and "social setting of transmission and use" ("practices") are seen as two sides of the same coin. Norms and practices, text and context cannot be separated and analysed in isolation. We may then be able to ask for, and identify, the circumstances that produced what we see, be it in history or the present.

73 Ibid., 2.

74 Ibid.

> We may then be able to analyse the *trajectory* of a changing corpus of knowledge by identifying the potentials and constraints that these criteria of validity and feasibility provide for the production and transmission of knowledge in concrete traditions. This conjunction of factors will have the effect of pointing native thinkers and actors in particular directions of effort, creativity, and representation.[75]

With the above mentioned concepts we are given a wide range of new analytical concepts and tools. In this way we can further identify the degrees of coherence or systematicity that are found in various fields[76] of knowledge. After that, Barth introduces what he calls "exogene factors" which are always important, but for the sake of clarity are presented "outside" his main arguments above. The exogene factors refer to: (1) Material circumstances, which determine the pragmatics under which local human life unfolds, and (2) relations of power that arise outside the local social setting.[77] Neither of these are minor "omissions" and it is not the intention here to make them less important.

As for the first, the material circumstances, we must recall that the *waqf* referred to in this study mainly consists of agricultural terraces in a premodern peasant grain economy, while the second factor refers to higher and external levels of the political arena. The Zaydīs have their geographical and political setting, while a judge serves a specific constituency or jurisdiction and a certain landowning elite may hold power in a certain area. All such arenas or fields of knowledge that we identify as the object of study are more or less situated in wider circles of power. (The judge must somehow answer to the imam in Sanaa, etc.). But the inclusion of these relations of power that exist outside our object of study must only be done when necessary, otherwise there would be no defined object of study.

Barth makes two additional important remarks: First, methodological relativism must be used in the analysis. This often goes without saying, but the relativism he refers to is the same one referred to earlier in this chapter; namely, that it is not up to the researcher to decide what is "correct *waqf* law" or "correct Islam" to use as a starting point for the analysis. Second, he emphasizes that we must assume that there is a systematic relation between knowledge and the uses to which it is put. This means that we should expect the *waqf fiqh*

75 Ibid., 3.

76 Barth uses the term "traditions"; following Asad, "knowledge tradition" is a term suitable to *fiqh*. The term "field," which I use, better fits better the way *waqf* as an institution "exists" and is perceived by local, non-scholarly informants.

77 Barth, "An Anthropology of Knowledge," 3–4.

to address problems that arise in *waqf* management, be these administrative, agricultural or political, not only "Islamic" in character.[78]

3 Arriving at an Analytical Framework

If we "pair" the four levels of *waqf* knowledge (*fiqh*, codification, judge's law, etc.) with those new "aspects" of knowledge provided by Barth, a table of three columns by four rows emerges. One can add a fourth column of the "criteria of validity":

	Corpus of knowledge	**Medium**	**Social setting of transmission and use**	**Criteria of validity**
Fiqh				
Codification and law				
Judge's decisions and legal documents				
Everyday *waqf* related knowledge				

FIGURE 4 Table of main analytical concepts of *waqf* knowledge.

Below I elaborate on each level of the table:

3.1 Fiqh

Fiqh, or Islamic legal theory, is a highly specialised body of knowledge that requires years of education to master. The trajectory of this body of knowledge has been relatively stable over time and space; its vocabulary and conventions have remained consistent for centuries and stretches over continents. It is an "academic" type of knowledge that is mainly acquired in settings of higher education with actors such as students (*ṭālib*, pl. *ṭullāb*) and teachers (*ʿālim, faqīh, shaykh ʿilm*). *Fiqh* fits very well with the term "tradition" used by Talal Asad and Fredrik Barth.

78 Ibid., 10.

3.2 *The* Fiqh *Corpus*

The corpus of *fiqh* is varied, but the core consists of textbooks in legal theory; these are typically condensed abridgements (*mukhtaṣar, -āt*) (*matn, mutūn*) from the classical period. Prominent examples are the book *al-Hidāya* for the Ḥanafīs, *Minhāj al-ṭālibīn* for the Shāfiʿīs, and the *Kitāb al-Azhār* for the Zaydīs. These books are quite short and intended to be learned by heart, at least for each lecture. These "law manuals" are simply a long string of legal rules, a condensed version of the most agreed-upon rules from the law school (*madhhab*), covering the whole spectrum of the law.[79] In the basic Zaydī law manual, *Kitāb al-Azhār*, there is a "Chapter of Waqf" (*Kitāb al-Waqf*) of 80 to 100 individual rules, grouped in nine sections. In the narrow sense, these rules are the corpus of Zaydī *waqf fiqh*. In addition to these basic texts, there is the genre of commentaries and explanations (*sharḥ, shurūḥ*). For the Zaydīs, one of the most famous commentaries is the *Sharḥ al-azhār*. These commentaries must be studied by the intermediate student; advanced students must be able to thoroughly understand the discussions related to each of the rules. In addition to such works there are a wide range of other sub-genres or Islamic subjects, such as Arabic grammar (*naḥw wa-ṣarf*) and morphology (*iʿrāb*), logic (*manṭiq*), theology (*uṣūl al-dīn, kalām*), Qur'ānic exegesis (*tafsīr*), *ḥadīth* compilations or commentaries (*muṣannafāt*), and principles of law (*uṣūl al-fiqh*). These other subjects are fundamental to the study of *fiqh*, but not part of *fiqh* in a narrow sense. In Yemen, the more practical of these subjects, such as language and logic, were called the "instruments" (*ālāt*). The corpus of *fiqh*, although depending on the level of the *fiqh*, consists of a string of rules in addition to the literature of explanation and discussion surrounding those rules.

The typical actor in *fiqh*, in terms of number, is the student, not unlike other systems of learning. As the student advances, more and more leave their studies and ultimately only a few scholars are left from their age group. Thus the largest number of actors are those that leave early; these students become imams of local mosques, a secretary or *waqf* administrator. The most rare actors are those experts that write authoritative works and treatises later used by other scholars and students.

3.3 Fiqh *Medium*

Until the late nineteenth century, the medium of these texts was handwritten manuscripts; in Yemen this was true well into the twentieth century. These were immensely expensive and learning took the form of memorizing highly

79 See Fadel, "Social Logic of *taqlīd*."

compressed texts (*matn, mutūn*) along with selected commentaries. This made it possible to study without possessing, or even having access to, such a physical book at least for the early stages of the study. In the late nineteenth century, printed books started to be used Yemen and in the early twentieth century the important *fiqh* work, *Sharḥ al-azhār* slowly became available in print form; thus it became much more possible to consult the physical texts directly. Today, the use of PDF files, USB sticks, handheld mobile devices, and a wide range of electronic formats, along with access to the Internet means that the possibilities and constraints of the medium are fundamentally different than they were a hundred years ago.

The most important medium was and still is the human memory. Vast amounts of knowledge must be accumulated before any sort of independent reasoning can be made. This knowledge is shared through written texts, but it can hardly make sense without participation in a traditional study circle. From this we can also see that studying *fiqh* is also a study of power, discipline, and respect, perhaps we can even use the word indoctrination in its original sense.

The most dedicated students and teachers travelled around Yemen and the Muslim world and brought with them new knowledge and texts. Most students only travelled to the closest city, but those who visited the major scholars of their law schools or indeed other law schools could participate in very advanced debates that questioned the very fundaments of knowledge and religion.

3.4 Fiqh *Social Setting of Transmission and Use*

The mere attempt to separate and isolate the two previous parameters ("*fiqh* corpus" and "*fiqh* medium") was not successful in the sense that both seem inseparable and intertwined with the knowledge field called "social setting of transmission and use." This illustrates how intimately these parameters are interwoven into each other. The stability or instability of these parameters are important: For example, once printed books became available, *fiqh* did not necessarily have to be studied in a *madrasa*; young educated men[80] could approach the corpus themselves.[81] Perhaps this changes the meaning and how the texts

80 Of course the same is true of women; the phenomenon of contemporary women *fiqh* students could not be investigated in this study, but is obviously important.

81 See Messick's chapter on the new lawyers' association and their periodical "*al-Qistas*": Brinkley Messick, "Cover Stories: A Genealogy of the Legal Public Sphere in Yemen," in *Religion, Social Practice, and Contested Hegemonies: Reconstructing the Public Sphere in Muslim Majority Societies*, ed. Armando Salvatore and Mark LeVine (New York: Palgrave Macmillan, 2005).

are interpreted. A traditional setting of *fiqh* teaching is also framed in ritual gestures and special clothing that add levels of meaning to the knowledge.[82]

3.5 Fiqh *Criteria of Validity*

As for the criteria of validity, this is a topic that is central to chapters 5 to 8; I only mention it briefly here. The student only needs to know the validity required for his goals and his level of study. Above him, or behind him, is a community and a hierarchy of scholars fading out into chains of famous imams and *ʿulamāʾ* of the past. When attempting to produce a map of sources of validity and "certain" knowledge, many western scholars use the emic scheme of (1) the Qurʾān, (2) Sunna, (3 or 4) analogy (*qiyās*) or consensus (*ijmāʿ*), and some add *ijtihād* (the production of new law) or various forms of "flexible elements". However, such a classification is idealized and quickly becomes self-contradictory as the actual strings of validity behind the rules in the *fiqh* often do not go all the way "back" to the texts of revelation. The chains of reference, "inference" and "trust" usually stop long before the Qurʾān. For the literalists and traditionists such ultimate anchors of certainty are more often invoked in comparison to more intellectual rationalists who claim that there is hardly any certain knowledge in the *sharīʿa* and that all rules must be understood and interpreted by fallible human minds.[83] There is a tendency for Zaydīs to rely on references to the statements of earlier Zaydī imams, which are based upon doctrines that emphasize the role of the 'house of the Prophet' (*ahl al-bayt*); similarly Shāfiʿīs focus on the rules of interpretation laid out by al-Shāfiʿī and other major scholars, which focus on the thousands of narratives (*ḥadīth*) of the Sunna of what the Prophet said and did. Neo-traditionists like al-Shawkānī and present day Salafīs place even more emphasis on the perfection of the revelation and the importance of skipping over the classical tradition and directly look at the *ḥadīth* material. But this perspective is highly textual in the sense that it builds, to a large extent, on how Muslim historians and jurists themselves have presented legitimacy, how validity is situated and reasoned differently in different sects and law schools. If one studies a *fiqh* book together with a student of *sharīʿa*, one is left with a rather different picture, one where chains of trust and genealogies of references are rather short and accepted even though they do not extend far back. The study of texts through ethnography and praxiology

82 See for instance Michael Lambek, "Certain Knowledge, Contestable Authority: Power and Practice on the Islamic Periphery," *American Ethnologist* 17, no. 1 (1990): 23–40.

83 For an inter-law school debate over *sharīʿa* epistemology, certainty, and doubt, see Robert Gleave, *Inevitable Doubt: Two Theories of Shīʿī Jurisprudence* (Leiden: Brill, 2000).

allow us to study the act of reference to norms, ideals, and validity, instead of the internal (in)consistency of the system of norms.

Just as the chains of references in the Zaydī *waqf* chapter go relatively deep in some works (like the *Sharḥ al-azhār*), other works intended more for practical application by administrators and judges (like *al-Tāj al-mudhhab*) have few references if any at all. And for a professor at the faculty of *sharīʿa* and law at the University of Sanaa, the reference (claim) that something is a *qiyās* ("analogy") may not be the same as *qiyās* was for al-Shāfiʿī himself. Whether a chain of reference to its source of validity is long and elaborate, or whether it is short or even absent depends on the very local context and the "need" for validity there and then in that specific setting. To be effective in a certain legal setting, it is not always necessary, perhaps not even fruitful, to produce the full chains of validity. Such chains are, after all, also vulnerable and once fleshed out they may be subject to critique and attack. Another strategy may be *not* giving the chain of validity or the argument behind a rule, rather simply letting it end on an authoritative name, which consensus and convention has already validated. Perhaps the chains of references are also in this way partly circular; the law school validates the rule, and the way the rule is respected together with other rules validate the concept of the law school. Much of the *fiqh* is intended for one's own pre-defined audience who have already accepted certain frames of conventions. Although genres like *uṣūl al-fiqh* (principles or methodology of law) exist in all law schools, such high-level exercise is not what the average *fiqh* actor engages in. The average *fiqh* actor learns law in order to become a local teacher, scribe, notary or a judge, not in order to question the fundaments. A personal religious quest for a modern educated individual is again something quite different and *waqf fiqh* would not be a main focus for such a student.

Most actors of *fiqh* begin as students who are not permitted to question the knowledge they learn. The very few that do advance are allowed, and later indeed expected, to question and discuss and deconstruct legal rules and be able to state the sources of the authority of individual rules. The higher the level one reaches, the more important is the debate itself and the search for true knowledge of what God intended with the revelation or the true purpose of the law. The validity thus also comes from one's level of study: For the beginner, the knowledge is valid because the teacher says it is, for the expert, it is valid because he is able to access rare and new and authoritative sources and use multiple methods. And ultimately it comes down to degrees of doubt and certainty. The expert knows that no knowledge is absolutely certain. *Waqf* is arguably not mentioned in the Qur'ān. Everything in between is related to chains of trust, trust in persons, and trust in other's knowledge.[84]

Fiqh usually refers to the premodern debates and if too many modern words and concepts are used, the image of "proper" *fiqh* is lost and the debate changes into a debate that the traditional *faqīh* simply refuses to take an interest in. Today, many Islamic scholars carefully avoid politics and instead deal mostly with theories of correct prayer positions and what types of music are good and bad; in short they address moral issues rather than "legal" issues such as *waqf* law.

This is not to say that the premodern theories of transactional law (*muʿāmalāt*) are not still alive in traditional study circles today. They are, but these are not very "interesting" for the public, or for religious movements that claim attention in the mass media or vie for the attention of the public and Muslims at the Friday prayer. Today, many students of *fiqh* do not come from learned families, and Salafī-oriented actors hardly focus on *waqf* at all. As Zaydīs also operate in a doctrinal "war" against such forms of neo-traditionism, even more focus is taken away from "dry and boring" transactional law. The transactional law now used by the courts is similar to premodern law, with only minor changes; for the most part these changes are the addition of modern words and terms related to procedure. Thus there is a tendency to see "original" *fiqh* as "religious" and thus a personal moral quest and the present-day applied law as something related to a profession. If we are to focus on the more legal *fiqh* and not on the religious one, we see that *waqf fiqh* fades into modern law during the twentieth century, yet the validity of the modern *waqf* law is far from strong, purely descriptively speaking, in terms of the extent to which it is actually followed. The modern, present-day *waqf* law is caught between *sharʿī* validity and a modern discourse of law, as traditional, Muslim jurists (*fuqahā'*) are not the only actors with education and authority anymore.[85] Law gradually takes other forms in other forums, yet in a country like Yemen, the tradition remains strong; this can be seen in the ways legal documents are written, in ways that scholars (*ʿulamā'*) manifest their authority (through dress and behaviour) and in the way they refer to old *fiqh* works when court decisions are written.

84 A literalist or traditionist would of course claim that the Qur'ān and the canonical collection of *ḥadīths* is certain knowledge and that these texts can be used without applying humanly fallible reason. This emic claim is discussed in several places elsewhere in this book.

85 See Messick, "Cover Stories."

The mention of court leads us into a more narrow understanding of law and to the field of codification.

3.6 *Codification*

The term "codification" in this study mainly refers to the creation of imamic decrees, the creating of the present-day *waqf* law, and the historical processes behind this creation. In a narrow sense, the present-day codification is the *waqf* laws of Yemen as published by the ministry of justice and the ministry of legal affairs. Since the 1970s laws have been drafted by the "codification committee" (*lajnat al-taqnīn*). In 1976 most of the present *waqf* law was drafted and issued. Before the Republican revolution in 1962, codification was a task of the Zaydī imam, indeed it was also a duty, in matters where the *fiqh* was too broad and needed to be narrowed in scope in the face of diverging, alternative, possible rules. In theory the imams had sole monopoly in issuing valid law, and the judges of the country, also appointed by the imam, were obliged to follow these laws. When an imam died, a new imam took over and issued his own codification.

The field of codification, even today, is caught between, and interacts with both *fiqh* and the local notaries and judges, as we discuss in chapters 4, 5, 6, and 7. In this book, I intend to examine premodern codification (as the imamic decrees arguably were), and consider codification in a wider perspective. Codification is the ideal, the process of narrowing down the scope of possible rules, and it is also the product of that process—the set of coherent, enforceable rules. "Codification" is more specific than "law." It specifically centres on the need for coherence, applicability, and enforceability. It must also be "known."

3.7 *Codification Corpus*

The "corpus" of codification is law in decree form that states in clear, coherent language what is "legal" and the binary opposite, what is "illegal." Since *waqf* is a contractual law regulating the transfer of property or rights from one legal person to another, a main focus is what constitutes a valid contract. There is a need to limit the destructive scope of contradictory alternative rules found in the *fiqh* literature. "Destructive" because as a debate, most suggestions for rules in *fiqh* have a potential counter-suggestion. Thus we should not forget that attempts at codification are found already at the *fiqh* level. A large part of *fiqh* and several special works are dedicated to giving the judge or the introductory student or reader a clear and defined corpus of rules to follow. Some rules are better than others, more valid, according to the *madhhab*, as elaborated upon in chapter 4.[86] Codification seeks to limit the law to one choice only, so that all judges and legal actors make the same rulings in similar cases, at least at the local level.[87] Systematicity is an underlying fundament. Codification uses specialist legal language that judges can apply, yet it also draws on the language and validity of *fiqh*. When codification is not intended to be applied, but is rather meant as a political or doctrinal statement, it is perhaps better to characterise it as such. In the modern Yemeni *waqf* law we find some ideal but impractical elements—these we outline in chapter 6, in order to highlight the relationship between *waqf* law and *fiqh* and *sharīʿa*. The codification is not entirely cut off from *fiqh*, but draws on it, this is something that makes codification and *fiqh* at times hard to distinguish if one does not also look at the setting of its transmission and use.

3.8 *Codification Medium*

The ideal type of imamic codification was decrees in the form of letters to the judges or public *fatwā*s they were obliged to follow. At the city or village level, local market laws,[88] tribal laws,[89] and village water irrigation laws could also be formulated as a public, collective contract on which prominent witnesses and judges attested, and also in written form. Yet these laws are only partly *sharʿī*, and the *waqf* laws were usually not a part of these local codifications. As we see in chapter 4, much of the premodern Yemeni *waqf* codification was built into *fiqh* works like the *Sharḥ al-azhār* and *al-Tāj al-mudhhab*, the former being a work that also involves legal debate, while the latter is much more univocal and coherent, with fewer alternative rules.

---

86 See, for example, Fadel, "The Social Logic of *taqlīd*."

87 It is common to hear that "the *sharīʿa* cannot be codified." Some argue that there is no Saudi codification and that judges consult *fiqh* directly and thus arrive at rules independently. This may be an ideal in some states and perhaps partly a practice, but one must assume that both judges and those who use the court system communicate with each other and further, that some rules are known to be more valid than others. There may be an implicit standard that judges must follow. This does not mean that coherence and systematization and therefore codification in the ideal form described in this chapter *must* exist at all time and in all places.

88 See R. B. Serjeant and Ismāʿīl al-Akwaʿ, "The Statute of Ṣanʿāʾ (*Qānūn Ṣanʿāʾ*)," in *Ṣanʿāʾ: An Arabian Islamic City*, ed. R. B. Serjeant and R. Lewcock (London: World of Islam Festival Trust, 1983).

89 A prominent example is the work Paul Dresch, *The Rules of Barat: Tribal Documents from Yemen* (Sanaa: Le Centre Français d'Archéologie et de Sciences Sociales, 2006).

3.9 *Codification Setting of Transmission and Use*

Codification was drafted by individuals who understood the politics of balance between various interests: those of the ruler, the *ʿulamāʾ*, and the landowning elite. Politics are balanced against *fiqh* discourse and solutions must be successful and acceptable for a wide range of actors, not only the *ʿulamāʾ*. A rule can be ideal, but ill-suited to local context for various reasons. Codification is an ongoing process that involves listening to the thoughts of the local actors and, at the same time, being a tool of the ruling interests. Usually, codification is formulated by a few state-appointed, well-educated experts who, in effect, resemble state employees, or bureaucrats, though they vigorously insist on their impartiality and loyalty to doctrinal principles and religion. Power is, however, a necessary component, whether the codification is meant to be enforced by a state or by members of a tribe or community. In modern Yemeni *waqf* codification, the author presents himself as an Islamic scholar and the party issuing the law is the state. Previously the Zaydī imam held both roles. The actors involved in the process of codification are educated in legal theory and debate; this legal debate and other preparations of the code take place before (and perhaps after) the process of codification. In a narrow sense, it is only the moment of issuing and subsequent implementation, upholding, and defending the law code that constitutes its "use" and "transmission." Prior to that point, and perhaps parallel to it, it is a debate, or legal theory. As we see later in this book, *waqf* law is not only formulated in a top-down model, from the centre of power and imposed on the peripheries; rather local customs and local elites, *waqf* actors, and *waqf* administrators were also important to the process and must have discussed and made local adaptations to the *waqf* law.

3.10 *Codification Criteria of Validity*

The imamic codification was highly saturated in *fiqh* language. The *fatwās* or the decrees (*ikhtiyārāt*) issued by the imams balanced between raw political power and the need to build the law on the validity of *fiqh*. This book, especially chapter 5, focuses on the history of the codification of *waqf* law. The act of codification could also be "reflexive," as noted by Bernard Haykel.[90] By codifying the laws, the imams could publicly confirm their roles as imams, lawgivers, *mujtahid* scholars, and guardians of society and of Islam. The ability to issue law legitimizes the state.

90 Bernard Haykel, *Revival and Reform in Islam: The Legacy of Muhammad al-Shawkānī* (Cambridge: Cambridge University Press, 2003), 202.

Codification requires some degree of institutionalized power in order to be enforceable, a system of courts and administrators and some type of police or military that can enforce the decisions of administrators and judges. In some geographical areas or during periods when the state is weak, one may rightly ask where this enforcement comes from. The level of codification can also be resisted or circumvented by local judges and users of law; they can go directly to the jurists and make their own codifications. Here it is important to bear in mind that the *waqf fiqh* serves a need in the society and most enforcement of *waqf* law can indeed be done on a local, non-state level as long as there is a certain degree of local political stability. The judges only need witnesses from the village and a general consensus in the village that everyone should respect everyone's contracts and ownership documents.

The validity of codification partly lies in the raw force of the government and the local political power, be it elites in a village, members of a tribe or a state that can implement a set of coherent rules. If asked, most actors are unable to elaborate upon the exact relation between *sharīʿa* and codification and to what extent the *sharīʿa* can be codified at all without destroying its legitimacy. Only rather well educated actors would openly admit that the *sharīʿa* is self-contradictory, and because they are well educated, they know very well when to put forward such a statement and when not to. Public political debates cannot escape the hierarchy of validity in the *fiqh*,[91] but that does not mean that arguments from *fiqh* debates can be simply taken out of the *fiqh* context and enter into the public debate over what the law (code) should be. The actors involved in modern codification debates are not necessarily versed in the same details as the traditional actors of *fiqh*, thus arguments can be formulated slightly differently. The same words may be used, but the new context and actual usage gives a new range of meaning and a new range of validity.

The public debate that takes place in a modern society, with multiple means of communication, and the debate that takes place in a traditional, premodern society are very different. Even in one and the same society, a variety of debates can take place in different fields and levels of the society. Methodologically

91 I am referring to the basis on which people accept that laws are legitimate. For example, when asked in public, Muslims would likely claim that the Qur'ān, God, and the Prophet are the source of all laws, these are followed by the *ahl al-bayt* (for Zaydīs), and imams and scholars from the classical period who formulated *fiqh*, then the practical rules that were added later, along with custom. For a jurist (*faqīh*) there is a hierarchy of sources, but for a layman who wants to make an argument in a court case or in a public debate, he may skip some of this "ideal" hierarchy and refer directly to a rule that originally came from custom but can now be found in a *fiqh* book. For him the fact that it is in the *fiqh* book renders it sufficiently valid.

and analytically, the field of codification is more difficult to define than that of *fiqh*; the discrepancy between the normative reality and the sociological reality is even more pressing, especially when parts of the Yemeni *waqf* law is not used and arguably not intended for use, as illustrated in chapter 6. Codification is supposed to serve local life and actual legal problems, therefore describing in detail a law that is only partially used appears to be even more problematic. Many scholars, both western academic and Muslim, also tend to see the level of codification as less interesting since it is not as real, "pure," or authentic as (their view of) the *sharīʿa*. Whether or not the codification is authentic is irrelevant here, what is relevant is why it is formulated as it is, and to what extent it is enforced as law and how people (judges, lawyers, and lay people) think about it and relate to it. This latter form of knowledge takes us to the next social field where knowledge about *waqf* and legal validity is used.

3.11 *The Judge's* Waqf

This is the field of the local notary or the judge and the production of legal documents. It also partly overlaps with administrative knowledge and practice such as *waqf* bookkeeping and the use of *waqf* inventory registers by public *waqf* administrators. We can call this field the "judge's *waqf*" or the "public administrator's *waqf*" and say that it deals with individual *waqf* cases and their validity. It is not necessary to strictly limit this to the judge or the court, it can be extended to all forms of local, formal, usually written *waqf* practices.

3.12 *The Judge's* Waqf *Corpus*

The corpus in the narrow sense is easy to point out; it consists of a written document representing the legal validity of the *waqf*. Thus that piece of paper contains the essence of the *waqf*, there, where it is recorded. A *waqf* can also legally exist solely in the form of public knowledge (*shuhra*); it is not a legal requirement that it be written down, however *waqf* documents are commonly written down in Yemen. In a wider sense, the judge needs more knowledge that what is written in the *waqf* document; he needs knowledge of *fiqh*, and the codified, agreed upon *fiqh*, and state codification. He needs to know the precedence of previous cases and what the local political forces expect from him. And most importantly, he needs to know how to write a valid legal document. Thus the corpus of knowledge is not as clearly defined as the two previous fields, it is more divided into explicit and implicit aspects.

A legal document as a corpus is a rather short text, written, or sometimes oral, that ties the ownership, or right, to a specific person or group. As an aggregate, it is the patterns of such documents; we find a high degree of consistency in how they are formulated.

3.13 *The Judge's Medium*

As indicated immediately above, it is difficult to separate the content or corpus of a *waqf* document from its medium. This becomes clearer if we imagine changes in the medium; changes in ways people keep records and make the content public. In a narrow sense we can simply point to the pen and paper as the medium. In a wider sense we must also look at how such papers are stored in private homes, how they are known, and the crucial importance of a general understanding and respect for such legal documents in the local community.

3.14 *The Judge's Social Setting, Transmission, and the Use of Legal Knowledge*

In a narrow sense, the social setting is the very act of inscribing validity into the *waqf* document. The context is the reception room of the notary (*al-amīn*) or the judge, traditionally, this was often the judge's house. In modern, urban legal cases it would be the courtroom. We must also separate the act of setting up a *waqf* from all other forms of legal action related to *waqf* in general. If we look at the social setting, transmission, and the use of legal knowledge in a wider sense, the judge or public administrator must have some legal education. He must be in contact with colleagues. He must gradually rise in rank from being a secretary in a father's or an uncle's court and learning how to behave and act like a proper notary or a judge.[92]

3.15 *The Judge's Criteria of Validity*

When a property changes hands, or when a *waqf* is initiated or changed, a document is written in legally binding terminology taken from *fiqh* and from previous cases. The document reproduces "facts" like the nature and descriptions of the object, the persons involved and the changes in legal status of the object addressed in the document. Legal documents are heavily dependent on connections to their local context, to witnesses, names of agricultural fields that are known to everyone in the village and they are dependent on a certain degree of publication. Today most such documents are copied into public registers. In the past, if the judge were locally respected, his handwriting in itself would be an autographic guarantee of the authenticity of the legal instrument.[93]

---

92 For more elaboration on the role of judges, see Brinkley Messick, *The Calligraphic State: Textual Domination and History in a Muslim Society* (Berkeley and Los Angeles: University of California Press, 1993), in general and specifically 167–171, 186, 192–200; "Provincial Judges: The *Sharīʿa* Judiciary of Mid-Twentieth-Century Yemen," in *Law, Custom and Statute in the Muslim World*, ed. Ron Shaham (Leiden: Brill, 2006).

93 See for instance Messick, *Calligraphic State*, 215.

In *waqf*, some actors gain and other lose when a *waqf* is set up, and the judge's or the notary's job is to create a legal document as an instrument that is just as strong and enduring as the founder of the *waqf* wishes. The validity of such an instrument exists in a local political order, in mutual agreement among the landowning elites or patriarchically structured clans. In cities, more elaborate political orders exist, including police and other forces that can effectuate judges' decisions. In a context like Yemen, however, one should not take the western concept of the rule of law for granted. Many conflicts are open to negotiation and if the judge makes a ruling according to valid *fiqh* knowing that this ruling cannot be effectuated, he would undermine his own position. Since the judge replicates and produces rulings that are fairly coherent over time, he is also part of a codification project in a common law sense. Still, if asked, judges usually claim that what they do is simply to implement *sharīʿa* by following the old and well-known authoritative *fiqh* books.

3.16 *Local Daily* Waqf *Knowledge*

Locally, at the village level, everyone has a relationship to a *waqf* as a *waqf* user. The local mosque, water basins, and inns for travellers were mostly *waqf*. These structures had houses, shops, and agricultural fields donated as *waqf* for the benefit of the local population. These were rented out and the income was used to take care of the *waqf*s.

Every day, these structures are used, even by persons who cannot read or write or who do not know anything about *waqf* as a legal institution defined in *fiqh*. Counted in number of persons, these are the vast majority of actors related to *waqf*. They grow up with the physical structures around them and learn which house and which agricultural field is *waqf* and what this means in terms of their rights and responsibilities or those of others. The actors often live in face-to-face relationships. Perhaps they even enter into a conflict with other *waqf* actors and come before the judge. Certainly, they will have heard about such conflicts. Daily knowledge of *waqf*s is something that is learned and discussed, but it differs from the other fields of knowledge described above, because it is not dependent on logic, formality or sanctionability, the way, for example, codification or *fiqh* is. It may just as well be built on emotions, memories, and narratives of local good and bad deeds according to local moral standards. Some common narratives are ideal: "How the forefathers used to respect *waqf*, by even washing the plough so that earth from a *waqf* field would not be taken to a private field." Others believe that *waqf* fields and *waqf* assets are a way to allow poor people access to cheap rental flats and building plots. "Its *waqf*, why should they not get cheap rent?"

The field of daily *waqf* knowledge is not easily broken down into separate analytical categories. This is because this field is much more heterogeneous than the other three. The social setting is the local village, the city quarter, the daily interaction like *qāt* gatherings and discussions after the Friday prayer. And the medium is mainly oral narratives. The physical *waqf* structures are also a sort of medium that ideas and memories are attached to. The criteria of validity depends largely on the type of daily knowledge; if we narrow down the scope of knowledge to norms and social control, then this blends with local perceptions of what is moral, and religion is only a part of this.

3.17 *Methodological Aspects in the Different Knowledge Fields*

The division into four fields of *waqf* knowledge also highlights some methodological aspects: The three first levels are usually defined as corpuses in writing and as literary genres although most of the knowledge "around" the writing is situated in knowledge, conventions, and practices. In a society with a high rate of illiteracy, the fact that these kinds of knowledge involve skills of literacy is a very important distinction to bear in mind since being able to read and write was, and still is, limited to parts of the population. It is a skill that requires a high investment in training and resources. This certainly also applies to the researcher who would have to learn handwriting, language, and the conventions as well. In the fields dominated by textual material, there is always a problem of how to access the "original" meaning. Be it the meaning of the one who wrote it, of the ones who read it later, and of present informant-readers. On the positive side, legal texts are by their very nature and purpose relatively clear and free of ambiguities. This does not mean that reading *fiqh* cannot also have ritual aspects or, that large parts of *fiqh* are mainly an internally oriented discourse—this is certainly the case. But when focusing on the parts that deal with mundane legal problems, the *faqīh* author, the reader, and the researcher can to a large extent share a frame of reference and common concepts, despite hundreds of years of separation between the researcher and the text and the users of the text. The field of everyday *waqf* knowledge is a field seldom available to historians because of lack of data. Historians must extrapolate from legal documents or the other textual sources or archaeological sources in order to reconstruct "what actually happened" or "what people were thinking."

If we change the focus of the parameters of the fields of knowledge in order to highlight the key actor in each field, the three upper ones still stand out as more defined than the last field, which remains rather all-encompassing:

The *faqīh, ʿālim* (and his colleagues and his students)
The imam, the state-sponsored scholar, local elites
The judge, the notary and the public *waqf* administrator
"Everyone" who has a relationship to a *waqf*

The fact that the fourth field is so open reduces the value of this field as an analytical tool; this is an argument for specifying it further, especially in a purely ethnographic or anthropological study. This has not been given priority in this study and we shall leave it at that here.

The four fields of *waqf* knowledge are separate from each other for the sake of clarity as a typology of ideal types, yet they are obviously interconnected in ways I discuss below. They are useful as theoretical ideal types both in the process of identifying what to look for and in the process of understanding the complexity of the empirical material. But they should not be claimed to "exist" as a conclusion.

There is a strong "intertextuality" between the ideal types or fields. The actors borrow narratives, concepts, and metaphors from the other fields. Although I give the fields in this chapter as a list, I do not intend to present the fields in an absolutely hierarchical way, nor do I mean that level 2 cannot be directly related to level 4 without the intermediary of level 3 and so on. I present it this way here because most informants do present the "topography of legal norms" in a similar hierarchy.

Of the four fields of *waqf* knowledge it is the field of *fiqh* that stands out most clearly, and fits the ideal type of a "knowledge tradition" or a "field of knowledge." When we attempt to define and relate the other fields to each other we produce more friction. This friction is fruitful. By showing in exactly what ways *fiqh* is not just a closed field, but indeed interconnected with the other fields we can read the very rich *fiqh* material in a new light, and situate it more clearly in historical and social practices.

• • •

How a norm "exists" is very different from one academic discipline to another. At one extreme, Arabists simply translated and edited some of the abridged law manuals like the *Minhāj al-ṭālibīn* and the *Hidāya* and thus re-produced normative knowledge. At the other extreme, a "law" does not "exist" prior to action and power and only reoccurring patterns of behaviour can indicate a social regularity, though one can never be fully "proven" to exist. In intermediary positions there has been a tendency to over-generalize what Islamic law is and to focus on the ironic[94] discrepancy between ideal "theory" and "local practice" even when the actual available sources are fairly contextualised.

94 See Dupret Baudouin, *Practices of Truth: An Ethnomethodological Inquiry into Arab Contexts* (Amsterdam and Philadelphia: John Benjamins Publishing Company, 2011), especially 59–68.

This chapter seeks a level of refinement in these matters. Further, I shift away from a separation of "norms" and "practice" towards using Fredrik Barth's theory of knowledge, which maintains that all knowledge also consists of social contexts, practices, and media. Thus "*sharīʿa*" is not to be seen as the "theory" or, the "doctrine" that affects the local historical and ethnographic practices. This twofold model must be elaborated upon by also looking for legal ideals and pragmatic legal approaches taken by actors in their own context. Only then can we see that *fiqh* has its field, the judge's law has its field and so on, even though discourses and arguments of validity may be inspired from other levels and borrow legitimacy from them. When looking for constructions of validity in *waqf*, this is crucial; the criteria for validity are different in the (here four) different fields.

CHAPTER 3

Central *Waqf* Administration

Wa-kam siqāyatin wa-madrasa
qad aṣbaḥat awqāfuhā munṭamisa[1]

How many a *sabīl* and school
have lost their *waqfs* [or have no proof]
AL-QĀḌĪ ʿALĪ B. ṢĀLIḤ B. ABĪ L-RIJĀL (d. 1135/1722 or 23)

In this chapter I provide background information about the central *waqf* administration in Yemen. The chapter consists of two parts: The first and shorter part elaborates on what has been published about *waqf* in Yemen and how this literature has struggled with defining what "public" *waqf* is. The second and longer part is a historical presentation of what is known about the development of central, public *waqf* administration in Yemen from the time of the first Ottoman occupation (ca. 957/1550) until today. The bulk of this historical presentation focuses on the period from Imam al-Mahdī l-ʿAbbās (r. 1161–89/1748–75) until today. Throughout this period there was a striking degree of continuity in the forms of administration and also in terms of how the central government cooperated with local elites without giving away the potential benefit that can arise from administration of *waqf*. In periods with a strong

1 This is verse number 35 in a *qaṣīda* of 67 verses concerning the mismanagement of *waqf* in Sanaa, written by al-Qāḍī ʿAlī b. Ṣāliḥ Abī l-Rijāl (d. 1135/1722 or 23) for the ruler of Sanaa, Imam al-Muʾayyad Muḥammad b. Ismāʿīl (r. 1092–97/1681–86). Muḥammad b. Muḥammad b. Yaḥyā Zabāra, *Nashr al-ʿarf li-nubalāʾ al-yaman baʿda al-alf* (Beirut: Markaz al-Dirāsāt wa-Buḥūth al-Yamanī, Dār al-Ādāb, 1985), 2:198—the *qaṣīda* is on 2:214–216. (The word "*wa-kam*" is repeated twice, which is a print mistake; the Arabic could read something like *wa-kam siqāya wa-kam madrasa*, which would add a syllable and ease the reading). Serjeant has translated verse 22 and 23 of the same *qaṣīda*: "Don't leave our *waqfs* to an inspector / Who will spend on the furnishings of (his own) belvedere / And, with concrete, his house will be / Well appointed, despite any *qāḍī*" R. B. Serjeant, "The Mosques of Ṣanʿāʾ: The Yemeni Islamic Setting," in *Ṣanʿāʾ: An Arabian Islamic City*, ed. R. B. Serjeant and R. Lewcock (London: World of Islam Festival Trust, 1983), 315.

 | DOI:10.1163/9789004377844_004

central government, parts of the *waqf* administration were further centralized and, for example, under Imam Yaḥyā (r. 1911–1948) "unused" public *waqfs* were re-grouped to form the basis of income for the newly founded ministry of education. This chapter mainly focuses on the centralized public *waqf* administration. Much *waqf* was managed locally or even by the family of the founder, a fact that is difficult to quantify with the available sources, but one that is problematized throughout the chapter.

1 Types of *Waqf* in Yemen

A description of which types of *waqf* existed, or exist, in Yemen depends on the criteria of the "types." Three such criteria are commonly used to classify *waqfs*:

1. According to type of expenditure/beneficiary (mosques, water supply, etc.)
2. According to types of administration (degrees and types of private and public administration)
3. According to type of income-producing asset (agricultural land, shops, etc.)

I do not address the third type here. Suffice it to say that by far the most important type of object made into *waqf* is agricultural land. In the cities there are also a significant number of houses and shops for rent, and *waqf* rental building plots.[2]

It is common to divide the *waqf* beneficiary into two types: private (*ahlī, khāṣṣ, dhurrī*) and public (or charitable *khayrī, ʿāmm*). However, this distinction is not as clear-cut as it may seem. The rest of this chapter shows that the distinction between private and public beneficiaries does not correspond to the distinction of private and public administration, although this simple fact is often overlooked in academic representations of "types" of *waqf* in Yemen. As I argue in several places in this book, the distinction between private and public *waqf* is an ideal and problematic distinction. In practice, it is just as important to distinguish between the state administered *waqfs* and the privately administered *waqfs*. First, I briefly review established typologies of *waqf* beneficiaries

2 For *waqf* shops for rent in the market area of Sanaa, see Walter Dostal, *Der Markt von Ṣanʿāʾ* (Vienna: Verlag der Österreichischen Akademie der Wissenschaften, 1979), 15–18. Mermier also addresses this, partly based on Dostal, see Franck Mermier, "Les Souks de Sanaa et la Societe Citadine" (PhD thesis, Ecole des Hautes Etudes en Sciences Sociales (EHESS), Paris, 1988), 317–323.

in Yemen; this is followed by a similar review of types of *waqf* administration. In modern western and Yemeni academic works there are several such typologies; I present them chronologically, according to when they were published:

1.1 *Types of Beneficiaries of* Waqf *in Yemen: Types of* Waqf *Services*

Serjeant's typology from 1983 seems to be based on a quotation of Ḥusayn al-ʿAmrī, who in turn quotes the minister of *awqāf* at the time, al-Qāḍī Muḥammad b. Luṭf al-Ṣabāḥī.[3] In short it gives these beneficiaries as:

1 Mosques
2 *ʿUlamāʾ* and religious education
3 The sick
4 One's descendants [i.e., family *waqf*]
5 Water supply and shelter for travellers
6 Public baths
7 Animals

In 1987 the ministry and ʿAbd al-Mālik Manṣūr published an official book about the ministry of *awqāf; al-Awqāf wa-l-irshād fī mawkib al-thawra.*[4] At the time, he was the deputy minister. In his book (hereafter called *al-Mawkib*), the list is increased to eight types.[5] The types are presented without a specific historical context.

1 Mosques
2 Education
3 Descendants
4 Disabled persons (*dawū l-ʿāhāt*)
5 Feeding the poor
6 Expenses of the poor related to marriage[6]
7 Village reception halls [for hospitality towards guests]
8 Sick animals

In his book on *waqf* in Yemen Ḥasan ʿAlī Mijallī presents a typology that he claims was given to him by the ministry.[7] This typology is much more elaborate

---

3 Ḥusayn al-ʿAmrī and R. B. Serjeant, "Administrative Organisation," in *Ṣanʿāʾ: An Arabian Islamic City*, ed. R. B. Serjeant and R. Lewcock (London: World of Islam Festival Trust, 1983), 152.

4 ʿAbd al-Mālik Manṣūr, *al-Mawkib.*

5 Ibid., 148–152.

6 See Serjeant's treatment of this topic. al-ʿAmrī and Serjeant, "Administrative Organisation," 152.

7 Ḥasan ʿAlī Mijallī, *al-Awqāf fī l-Yaman: al-Itār al-sharʿī wa-l-qānūnī li-l-waqf wa-maqāṣidihi al-ʿāmma wa-tārīkh al-waqf wa-dawrihi al-iqtiṣādī wa-l-ijtimāʿī* (Sanaa: Maktabat Khālid b.

than the previous ones and consists of the main types with a further division into sub-types:

Main types

A. Mosques
B. Education, *ʿulamāʾ* and the learned (*al-mutaʿallimūn*)
C. Health; support for the sick
D. Graveyards in general and graves of saints and dignitaries
E. Religious festivals of different types
F. Water services
G. Housing, roads, and travellers
H. "Social"; the poor, orphans, and food support
I. Animals
J. Public *waqf*s where the beneficiary has become unknown.

For example, "type F, water services" includes the following sub-types:[8]

F.	**Water services**	
1.	*Waqf al-ghuyūl*	For the repair and maintenance of the springs of the *ghuyūl*[a] [*qanāt*], cleaning, and repair of the conduits and canals.
2.	*Waqf* for wells	For digging wells for drinking water, and for ongoing maintenance and repairs.
3.	*Waqf al-sabīl*	For the building of drinking water *sabīl*s for anyone who passes by, their maintenance, and distribution of water for anyone in need.
4.	*Waqf* for cisterns (*birak, mawājil*)	For the building of cisterns that collect rainwater, which are used by the local inhabitants, and for their maintenance and upkeep.
5.	*Waqf* for water basins (*aḥwāḍ*)	For the construction of water basins, for drinking water for livestock, and for the ongoing repair and maintenance and the distribution of water from them.
6.	*Waqf* for dams (*sudūd wa-ḥawājiz*)	For the construction of dams to collect water after flash floods and rainwater and their maintenance.

al-Walīd, 2002), 17–22. His source in the ministry may be ʿAlī Muḥammad al-Farrān, who has presented a very similar typology, see below.

8 Mijallī, *al-Awqāf fī l-Yaman*, 20.

(*cont.*)

F.	**Water services**	
7.	*Waqf* for well equipment (*sabala*)	For the repair and purchase of ropes (and buckets, skins, rope-wheels) that are used in hoisting water from the wells.[b]
8.	Others	

a See ʿAbd al-Wahhāb Muḥammad ʿAslān, *Ghuyūl Ṣanʿāʾ: Dirāsa tārīkhiyya āthāriyya wathāʾiqiyya* (Damascus and Beirut: Dar al-Fikr al-Muʿāṣir, 2000).

b I have photocopies of two *waqf* document register entries from Zabid that specify such a beneficiary.

A typology made by ʿAlī Muḥammad al-Farrān in his unpublished manuscript *al-Awqāf wa-l-tanmīya fī l-Yaman*[9] is very similar to the one of Mijallī above and was probably made by the same person(s), or taken from the same sources in the ministry of *awqāf*. Al-Farrān's typology is the most comprehensive one available and he mentions more than a hundred types of beneficiaries.[10] Unfortunately, many of these types are not, historically speaking, "proven" to exist at all. For instance, few, if any, *waqf* documents related to health services have been edited and published until now. Thus the whole field of "health *waqf*" may very well be an important type, but we do not know much about it and how common it actually was. Al-Farrān's typology is also completely ahistorical and sometimes gives the impression that it covers types of *waqf* outside Yemen as well. As for the focus on "Yemen," it is also problematic to mix types of *waqfs* from Hadramawt with types of *waqfs* from Sanaa for example. For instance, *waqfs* for Sufi lodges may be quite widespread in the Shāfiʿī regions, but rare in the Zaydī regions. A "national history of *waqf*" has its own logic, for example, it portrays the institution of *waqf* as a very important part of the national history of Yemen by including as many types of *waqf* as possible. The book of al-Farrān is by far the most detailed to date, and he does provide new historical information about *waqf* administration. Some of the types he mentions are indeed

9 ʿAlī b. Muḥammad al-Farrān, *al-Awqāf wa-l-tanmīya fī l-Yaman* (unpublished manuscript). Al-Farrān kindly provided me with his manuscript in electronic form. A shorter version of the manuscript was published as *Athar al-waqf wa-l-mubarrirāt fī l-takāful and ijtimāʿī* (Taʿizz: Muʾassasat al-Saʿīd li-l-ʿUlūm wa-l-Thaqāfa, 2009).

10 al-Farrān, *Athar al-waqf*, 69–91.

documented by examples of *waqf* documents, not to mention many types of administrative documents related to *waqf*.

One problem in making such typologies of *waqf* is that some of the "services" may, in part, overlap. A mosque can, for instance, be used as a community hall, a village school, it can have a water supply facility attached to it, which in turn is important for the local inhabitants and so forth. In this case, these "extra" services attached to the mosque "disappear" if any actual *waqf* is listed only under the type "mosques."

So far, there is too little information available to create sound typologies of what types of *waqf* services existed and still exist in Yemen. *Waqf* for mosques, religious education, help for the poor and sick, water supply, and village community houses were certainly all important and indeed fundamental to local economic, political, and social life. Yet research has yet to establish how important each type was, in which geographical area, in which social context, and in which historical period.

1.2 *Types of* Waqf *Administration: Public* Waqf *and Private* Waṣāyā

If we look at the present-day Yemeni ministry of *awqāf* and religious guidance, hereafter called the "ministry," we immediately notice a lack of transparency in their organisational structure and mode of operation. We see a ministry that has obviously inherited a structure from the pre-Republican, premodern past, but exact information is difficult to obtain and even controversial. Looking at the official information available and relying on the knowledge of various types of informants, we are quickly confused and must ask; what is the ministry actually in charge of? What is actually taking place in the ministry? And what other *waqf* structures and practices are there in addition to those managed by the ministry? What happened to all the individual *waqfs*, since what appears to remain today only relates to medium-sized and important mosques? To define *waqf* from the present *waqf* law and the present state public *waqf* administration as they present themselves in governmental decrees produces an opaque and even contradictory picture.

On the other hand, by looking at the historical background of today's public *waqf* administration, we can see fairly stable modes of administration, which can further help us to understand what to look for in the field and why exact information can be controversial. It is important to point out that a *waqf* for a public purpose does not have to be publicly managed, according to local customs and Zaydī *fiqh* rules. Yet, what we do see over time is a clear attempt by state actors to try to draw the administration of ever more types of *waqf* into state structures and state controlled forms. But contrary to these state forces, we also see in *waqf* documents that the founder very often stipulates that he himself will have the right of administration or guardianship (*naẓar, wilāya*), and subsequently, that this right passes to the "best among his descendants," which practically means the leading member of his family and clan. Thus many *waqf*s have been formed with the explicit intention that the *waqf* not be passed on to the government to control. In this, we can therefore see forces working the opposite way, trying to keep *waqf*s out of reach of the government and even outside of full public/state knowledge, in order to ensure that the *waqf*, in practical terms, continues to be available and useful to the descendants of the founder.

We must also remember that the construction of the state was and is highly porous. Traditionally, the state leader, the imam, delegated administrative responsibility and thereby rights and positions to local, powerful actors and families; this also often included the right to administer "clusters" or "portfolios" of public *waqf*s. These individuals represented both the imam and the state, but also themselves and their family and clan. Furthermore, we see that these individuals often privatized the very administration by keeping administrative knowledge and even the accounts, registers, and documents to themselves. Some families and clans have administered public *waqf*s for centuries while states and dynasties have come and gone.[11]

A typology of forms of *waqf* administration is a very different issue from that of a typology of beneficiaries. The main divide is between what is controlled and administered by the central government through a more or less coherent structure and those *waqf*s that are not controlled by the government, but are privately managed. There are also several grey areas between these two. These in-between types that exist in the grey areas are mentioned and discussed below and also in chapter 7. The most well-known published historical representation of public *waqf* administration is part of a chapter found in Serjeant and Lewcock's edited book *Ṣanʿāʾ: An Arabian Islamic City*[12] called "Administrative Organisation".[13]

1.3 Waqf *in the Chapter "Administrative Organisation"*

After a short introductory passage, this section presents five types of *waqf* based on the work of al-Ṭayyib Zayn al-ʿĀbidīn (al-Tayib Zein al-Abdin).[14] The

11 Examples will be given in the historical presentation in this chapter.

12 R. B. Serjeant and Ronald Lewcock, *Ṣanʿāʾ: An Arabian Islamic City* (London: World of Islam Festival Trust, 1983).

13 Ḥusayn al-ʿAmrī and R. B. Serjeant, "Administrative Organisation," 151–152.

14 Al-Tayib Zein al-Abdin, "The Role of Islam in the State, Yemen Arab Republic (1940–72)" (PhD thesis, University of Cambridge, 1975), 218–219.

typology presents five types of *waqf*, or rather, separate types of *waqf* that each has its own separate public administration office:

1 *al-waqf al-dākhilī* (the internal *waqf*) and *waqf al-ṣawāfī*[15]
2 *al-waqf al-khārijī* (the external *waqf*)[16]
3 *waqf al-waṣīyy* (the trustee's *waqf*)[17]
4 *al-waqf al-muthallath* (the three-[tenths] *waqf*)
5 *muthallath al-Ḥaramayn* (the three-[tenths] of the holy cities)

Some clarification is necessary. First, the last two types of *waqf* can easily be omitted, since they do not seem to have been very important in Sanaa or Yemen. We know that there was a *nāẓir al-Ḥaramayn* supervising the Ḥaramayn *waqf*s, and he sent funds and grain to various recipients in Mecca and Medina.[18] A common narrative told by informants today is that Yemen used to send *waqf* grain to Mecca and Medina and also specifically to the pigeons of Mecca. Yet little if any information exists concerning the quantity of this type of *waqf*.

---

15 As for the term *ṣāfīya, ṣawāfī*: Historically, this seems to have been estate land belonging to castles or lords. See Wilferd Madelung, *Religious and Ethnic Movements in Medieval Islam* (Aldershot, UK: Variorum, 1992), ch. 11: "Land Ownership and Land Tax in Northern Yemen and Najrān: 3rd–4th/9th–10th Century," 196. In the Qāsimī period, *ṣawāfī* seems to be close to the concept of state land; we know that the state held *ṣawāfī* land and there was a minister (*wazīr*) of *ṣawāfī*. Haykel, *Revival and Reform*, 71. Non-state *ṣawāfī* from the same time is mentioned in Ḥusayn 'Abdallāh al-'Amrī, *The Yemen in the 18th and 19th Centuries: A Political and Intellectual History* (London: Ithaca Press, 1985), 76. The verb *istaṣfā* seems mean "to confiscate" in Ibn 'Abd al-Majīd, *Bahjat al-zaman fī tārīkh al-Yaman*, ed. 'Abdallāh Muḥammad al-Ḥibshī and Muḥammad Aḥmad al-Sanabānī (Sanaa: Dār al-Ḥikma al-Yamāniyya, 1988), 97. For a description of the *waqf al-dākhilī*, Serjeant quotes al-'Ābidīn: "The entire income of this category of *waqf* is devoted to maintaining existing mosques or building new ones, and forms the bulk of the revenue of the present day Ministry of *Awqāf*." al-'Amrī and Serjeant, "Administrative Organisation," 151–152.

16 al-'Amrī and Serjeant, "Administrative Organisation," 151–152. "This is controlled by a member of the donor's family, the Ministry nowadays supervising to ensure that the beneficiaries receive their rightful shares. The Ministry receives five per cent and the remainder is distributed among the donor's relatives in accordance with the distribution laid down by the *sharī'ah* for inheritance."

17 Ibid.: "No part is given to the *Awqāf* but the donor specifies a particular pious activity, usually a mosque, to be maintained. The rest of the income is distributed among the relatives according to the law of inheritance. The Ministry hardly interferes in this *waqf*; it is controlled by a trustee, *waṣiyy*, usually the eldest member of the family, named by the donor. The *Awqāf* appoints a supervisor to keep a registry of the land and to settle cases of dispute, for which he receives two and a half per cent of the income. Through this and the proceeding *waqf* some tribes attempt to exclude women from inheritance by dedicating the *waqf* to their male descendants. Imām Yaḥyā, and the later Ministry of Justice, ruled against the validity of such an arrangement."

18 Gabriele Vom Bruck, *Islam, Memory, and Mortality in Yemen: Ruling Families in Transition* (New York: Palgrave Macmillan, 2005), 118.

Types 1, 2, and 3 are, on the other hand, very important: Serjeant has used the commentaries of al-Abdin, who in turn refers to the so-called "Tesco-report,"[19] a survey of the agricultural potential around Zabid from 1971. There are two problems in this: First, Serjeant quotes al-Abdin stating that the administration of *waqf al-khārijī* is controlled by a member of the founder's family. This is not the essence of the *dākhilī/khārijī* division and was perhaps even misunderstood: As Messick states in his PhD thesis (five years before the book *Ṣanʿāʾ* was published), the *dākhilī* administration was the administration of the *waqf*s related to Sanaa. The *khārijī* administration was also located in Sanaa, but dealt with public *waqf*s elsewhere in Yemen. Thus the *khārijī* administration also had sub-offices in other cities in Yemen, for example in Ibb.[20] The *khārijī waqf* administration is thus a parallel to the *dākhilī*, and as we shall see below, it is a fairly new term introduced around 1890. The *khārijī* refers to "what goes on out there," from the perspective of Sanaa. Both the *dākhilī* and the *khārijī* administrations dealt with the same type of *waqf*; mainly *waqf*s for maintaining and funding mosques and mosque-related expenses and activities.

A second problem relates to the type "*waqf al-waṣiyy*" (hereafter called the *waṣāyā*). In terms of beneficiaries, this type can be both fully private, as in a family *waqf*, or partly or even fully public. The essence, however, is that they are administered by a descendant of the founder. Some of them were and are registered by the state and inspected by the *nāẓir al-waṣāyā*, and thus they probably pay a certain percentage of the income to him. However, many such *waṣāyā* are not registered by the state at all and simply remain under private administration. This typology found in the aforementioned section of Serjeant's book (151–152) has later been quoted uncritically by Mermier[21] and Ḥusayn al-ʿAmrī.[22]

In addition to Sanaa, each of the major villages and cities had its own *al-waqf* in definite form, or sometimes called *al-waqf al-kabīr*. It could also be called *al-awqāf al-Ṣanʿānīyya, al-awqāf al-Dhamāriyya, Thulāʾiyya, Sharafiyya*, and so on. Both the *dākhilī* and the *khārijī waqf* were of the same type in that they were controlled and administrated by local *ʿulamāʾ* and/or government

---

19 al-Abdin, "Role of Islam in the State," 218. This report, published by the UNDP/FAO is well known in Yemeni studies and is called the "Tesco-report": Tesco-Viziterv-Vituki, "Survey of the Agricultural Potential of Wādī Zabīd" (Rome and Budapest: UNDP/FAO, 1971).

20 Messick, "Transactions in Ibb," 250.

21 Mermier, "Les Souks de Sanaa," 343.

22 Ḥusayn ʿAbdallāh al-ʿAmrī, *Yamaniyyāt fi l-tārīkh wa-l-thaqāfa wa-l-siyāsa II* (Damascus: Dār al-Fikr al-Muʿāṣir, 2000), 85–98. This publication is a direct translation of chapter 11 of Serjeant and Lewcock, *Ṣanʿāʾ*, into Arabic.

appointed administrators (*ʿāmil*, pl. *ʿāmilūn*, or *ʿummāl*[23]). The difference between this type and that of the third type above (the *waṣāyā*), is that the third type is administered by a private individual from the family of the founder, regardless of whether the beneficiary is private or public.

1.4 *The Four-Field Model of* Waqf *Administration*

Even though the distinction between private and public beneficiaries and between private and public management is unclear, some tendencies can be seen better in a four-field model. *Waqf* administration is then, theoretically, broken down into four ideal types, A, B, C, and D:

		Type of Administration	
		Public	**Private**
Type of Beneficiary	Public	A *waqf, awqāf* (non-mosque types A: *waṣāyā*)	B *waṣāyā*
	Private	C *waṣāyā*	B/D *waṣāyā* D *waṣāyā*

FIGURE 5 Types of *waqf* according to type of administration and type of beneficiary.

Type A would be a typical public *waqf* and today these *waqf*s are the bulk of those administered by the ministry. The type belonging to the ministry is usually called, colloquially, *waqf* or *awqāf*. Most of this type is agricultural land which was originally made *waqf* for specific mosques, but that today (should) enter into a common, national, central *waqf* budget.

Type B is a type of public *waqf* that is managed by a private individual, often a descendant of the founder. In Yemen both this type and type D (family *waqf*) are usually referred to as *waṣāyā*,[24] not *waqf* (although no one with knowledge

23 The plural, *ʿummāl*, is not used as often; it refers to the position or the salary of the *ʿāmil*; *ʿumāl*, *ʿummāl*, *ʿamāla*.

24 When talking about the type as such, or even the institution, the term *waṣāyā* is usually given in plural. Rarely does one see "*waṣīya*" in singular, unless speaking of a specific *waṣīya*. This stands in contrast to *waqf*, which often appears in the singular, especially in its definite form, when it means "*waqf* in general." This is probably because *waṣāyā* are indeed several individual cases, while *waqf* are, in practice, often merged together and administered as a whole and so can be referred to more easily in the singular. Although it is not entirely satisfactory, I use the English plural *waqf*s, since most of the discussions

of *fiqh* would deny its close relation to *waqf* in a legal sense). Types B and D can also be combined, as is the case when there are two simultaneous beneficiaries, one private and one public. A pure family *waqf* (D)—privately administered and with a private beneficiary—is also called, colloquially, a *waṣīya*, pl. *waṣāyā*. The term *waqf dhurrī* is a more formal and academic term. Chapters 5 and 7 clarify how and why the term *waṣīya* came into use, and why the right to private administration and guardianship is highly important.

Type C is a theoretical oddity in the table above, but in reality it exists. In the early twentieth century, some family *waqf*s were brought under a public inspector called *nāẓir al-waṣāyā*. Such *waqf*s could be, at least theoretically, placed in this type, and they are also called *waṣāyā*.[25]

In all of the types above, the state has always sought to maximise its control. The *waqf* (type A) was always under the direct control of the imam or the state, through local *waqf* representatives and administrators (*ʿāmil*); at various stages the *waṣāyā* types were also registered and "inspected." These reforms of registration and inspection (to the extent that we can call them reforms) were not very successful, and there are still some legal grey areas between types A and B, particularly regarding the exact role of the state and the role of the private administrator. Both types B and D were, and still are inspected by the *nāẓir al-waṣāyā*, though his exact role is not very clear. In the theoretical usage of the table above, we should therefore make the line between private and public administration less clear, and include between the private and public a zone with varying degrees of government control. The terms "private" and "public" are problematic since they carry connotations of western modernity; here "public" simply means that the service of the *waqf* was open to all (Muslims, in the case of mosques).

We must also distinguish between what ministry officials claim they control, what the state law allows them to control, what the *fiqh* allows them to control, and what they actually control. Not all mosques are controlled by the ministry, even in Sanaa or the larger cities. We must also realize that certain families had the right to the positions as public administrators and kept these positions for centuries, and sometimes occupied small "fiefs" of the administration. Thus a certain family may have administered a certain mosque for generations, and still does so within the structure of the ministry of *awqāf*. A very important

concern individual hypothetical legal cases; *waqf*s, not *awqāf* as in a general category of land, as in the minstry of *awqāf*.

25 This position seems to have existed at least since the late second Ottoman period, around 1890. It could also be older.

methodological point here is that only type A would be counted as "*waqf*" in public *waqf* registers. The rest would often (but not always) in official surveys[26] be considered "private" land. The legal status of the types B and C is not considered as strong as a "pure, absolute" *waqf* (A). As I demonstrate in several places in the book, the *waqf* status of these *waṣāyā* is often unclear and open for interpretation, something the ideal (normative) *waqf* model and definitions cannot fully capture. In other words they are not "full" (absolute, *muṭlaq*) *waqf*s, even if this is somewhat controversial in Zaydī *fiqh*, as we see below.

Furthermore, a *waqf* may have more than one administrator (*mutawallī*). The *mutawallī* of type A tends to be the Zaydī imam and his appointed deputies, or today, the ministry of *awqāf*. Yet attempts to control the *waṣāyā* saw the insertion of a second level of guardianship, the "inspector" (*nāẓir*)[27] above the *mutawallī*s. Ideally, the imam,[28] or the judiciary was the ultimate guardian of all *waqf*. The ministry today claims such a role, though in reality its legitimacy and powers are much more limited. The *fiqh* only regulates the "old" constellation of authority and naturally does not mention the republican state. The *fiqh* clearly states that the founder is free to appoint a member of his family as an administrator and that this position can remain in his family, also in the case of "public" *waqf*s. The judiciary and the imam can only take over his position if the administrator does something illegal and leaves no descendants or appointed deputy. Or, if for some reason, the private administrator disappears.

Creating a *waqf* does not necessitate a state approval or registration according to Zaydī *fiqh*, thus, the ministry and the lawmakers of today face challenges when trying to limit these private rights, by using *fiqh* arguments. The terms *wilāya* and *naẓāra* cover terms such as "guardianship," "administration," "authority," while the meaning depends on the context. The term *mutawallī* tends to be used for the administrator of private individual *waqf*s, while the term *nāẓir*[29] refers to the level of the minister. *Naẓar*, however, is often used synonymously with *wilāya* as is found in many *waqf* documents: *ishtaraṭa al-naẓar ilā awlādihi….* ("he stipulated the authority to his sons …"). In this book, I use the terms "administration" and *mutawallī* wherever possible.

---

26 Most land surveys seem to totally overlook this point. When estimating the amount of *waqf*, would the *waṣāyā* count as well? It was likely under-reported, since many preferred to keep their *waṣāyā* un-registered.

27 Even though the public *waqf mutawallī*, or "minister" of the past was called *nāẓir al-waqf* by some.

28 In this work, by "imam" I generally refer to the Zaydī religious leader and not to the leader of the prayers in a mosque. The role of the Zaydī imam is discussed in chapter 4.

29 The verbal noun related to this usage is *naẓāra*.

In practice however, many public *waqfs*, including mosques that are outside the control of the ministry still exist. As the state and the ministry are seen as inefficient, partly corrupt and partly illegitimate, few *waqfs* are now "given away" voluntarily to state administration. The *waqfs* that were completely taken over by the state (type A) were those in which the original founder and administrator and the related documents were lost or forgotten and thus in need of public administration. Some founders also donated *waqfs* to the public *waqf* (A) by giving away the right to their administration (*wilāya*).

Because of the religious status of the institution of *waqf* and because of the pious character of the activities it funds, such as mosques, schools, and salaries for scholars and students, it is natural that the scholars, the *ʿulamāʾ* had a central role. The *ʿulamāʾ* tended to emphasize their independent role as neutral, apolitical guardians of society and religion, and as self-made, intellectual men. In reality, many were part of the political elite and wealthy families or supported by wealthy patrons. This adds to the grey area between public and private as the state appointed *waqf* administrators often came from certain privileged families (*bayt, buyūt*) of the *sayyid* and *qāḍī* classes.

Over time, we can expect that *waqf* types B, C, and D gravitate towards A as they may "lose" connection with their original administrators and beneficiaries. In this sense, type A is, theoretically, cumulative over time. An important aspect that works counter to this accumulation is the ever-present problem of mismanagement and corruption.

We can expect an equally strong gravitation out of the table; many *waqfs* of types B and D revert to private property. Indeed Zaydī *waqf* doctrine, contrary to Ḥanafī *waqf* doctrine for example, states that *waqf* can revert to the founder's descendants if the designated goal of the *waqf* ceases to exist. In Ḥanafī *waqf*, the ultimate goal for any *waqf* must be type A. While in Zaydī *waqf*, it can revert to type D.[30] Type D is often considered a private matter and not as "holy" as the other forms of *waqf*. Since this type was partly abolished by Imam Yaḥyā in the 1920s, many *waqfs* "disappeared" and were dissolved and privatized.[31] Martha Mundy also states that many such smaller *waqfs* only lasted for a generation or two.[32]

Before focusing on the empirical historical presentation of central *waqf* administration, a summary of the above reflections gives us a hypothesis to look for in the empirical presentation: The crux of validity and legality lies in the

30 Of course arguably, and mainly, types that are close to B and B/D to begin with.

31 Imam Yaḥyā's decrees concerning this are treated in chapter 5.

32 Martha Mundy, *Domestic Government: Kinship, Community and Polity in North Yemen* (London: Tauris, 1995), 232 n61.

actual process of registration. If a *waqf* is not registered in a public register, it can more easily be reverted to private property. It should also be noted that while types B, C, and D tend to be called *waṣāyā*, type A is also at times called *waṣāyā*,[33] although today this is rare. Type A is most commonly called *waqf* or *awqāf*. In this book the terms *waqf* or *awqāf* are used wherever possible and the term *waṣāyā* is only used when necessary. In a legal sense, they are all *waqf* and they are usually called *waqf* in the *fiqh*.

Over time we see that the public *waqf* (A) is fairly stable in terms of modes of administration. Each city or major village or *hijra*[34] had its so-called *al-waqf al-kabīr*: the "main *waqf*" or "*the waqf*" (*al-waqf*). Thus while administered as a unit, each mosque could have its own assets registered and there could be great differences in income from mosque to mosque. Often, the "main *waqf*" was conceptually attached to the main mosque, the Friday mosque or congregational mosque (*al-jāmiʿ*), of which there was usually only one.

We see a development over time, where funds are taken from rich mosques and given to poorer mosques, but first only within the city's own main *waqf*. The funds were not shared with other cities. It is only the Qāsimī imams, and certainly later under Imam Yaḥyā, that we have clear evidence that the surplus of the main *waqf* was seen as a potential income for the *waqf*s of other cities, and this legal and administrative innovation also made it possible to control the economic surplus of the mosques. Not all mosques, and *waqf*s in favour of mosques, were forced equally into the main *waqf*; some important mosque *waqf*s remained fairly independent and were administered by certain families.

The main expenditure of the *waqf* (A) was the upkeep of the city mosques, and payments to imams, caretakers (*sadana*), scholars, teachers, and even students. The services that the mosques provided were not restricted to religious services only. Often the mosque had a *sabīl* attached to it, in which case the *sabīl* was administered as a part of the mosque. Most services other than mosques and the larger religious schools seem to have belonged to the *waṣāyā* types B or B/D which remained outside state *waqf* administration and supervision at least until the period of Imam Yaḥyā.

---

33 The term "absolute *waṣāyā*" (*waṣāyā muṭlaqa*) refers to mosque *waqf*s that are solely for the mosque, that is, those that do not have any private rights attached, in practice this is type A or B. For an example of this see al-Hādī ʿIzz al-Din b. al-Ḥasan, *Majmūʿ rasāʾil wa fatāwā l-Imām al-Hādī ʿIzz al-Dīn b. al-Ḥasan b. ʿAlī b. al-Muʾayyad: al-Mujallad al-thānī: Jumla min al-fatāwa al-mufīda ʿalā l-masāʾil al-fādiḥa al-farīda*, ed. ʿAbd al-Raḥmān b. Ḥusayn Shāʾim al-Muʾayyadī (Sanaa: Muʾassasat al-Imām Zayd b. ʿAlī l-Thaqāfiyya, forthcoming), 469.

34 A *hijra* is a non-tibal town or village under the protection of surrounding tribes; they are inhabited by *sāda* or *quḍāh* and are sometimes centres of learning.

Before the administration was centralized, any surplus could be spent locally. During periods of centralisation, it was naturally the surplus, the funds left after salaries and maintenance were paid, that the central administration wanted to take. The normal local expenses for maintenance and salaries were allowed to continue, while any surpluses were sent to Sanaa. The exact account of this history is unknown and more historical research is needed to see how much surplus was extracted in different historical periods.

2 Historical Overview of Centralized State *Waqf* Administration

Most of the information in the following part of the chapter, especially for the period before Imam Yaḥyā (r. 1911–48), is taken from the most readily available Yemeni chronicles and biographical dictionaries. These were thoroughly read and quoted by Serjeant in his authoritative work *Ṣanʿāʾ: An Arabian Islamic City*, but topics related to *waqf* are spread out and appear sporadically throughout the book. I have re-read these passages in the chronicles that Serjeant refers to, and found some additional mention of this type of information.[35]

In Shāfiʿī *fiqh*, the role of administration of *waqf* is mainly given to the local judge. In Zaydī Yemen, however, the doctrine of state polity was, at least in theory, more centralized. It was ultimately the imam's responsibility to appoint administrators of *waqfs* in the event that no other person held the right to administration (*wilāya*) (type A). To what extent the imam was actually able to freely appoint and dismiss tax collectors and *waqf* administrators was highly dependent on his power.

2.1 *The Islamic Schools of Lower Yemen and the* Waqfs

This book focuses on the Zaydī areas of Yemen and the Zaydī law school and its relation to society. The Shāfiʿī areas are generally not included in this study before the Zaydī military expansion to Lower Yemen and the Tihama in the mid seventeenth century. Thus the Sunnī sultanates like the Rasūlids and Tahirids are not included, that is, I do not examine *waqfs* in Lower and Coastal Yemen before 1636 when the Ottomans were expelled and when the Zaydī Qāsimī state took over these areas. In general the eastern sultanates and the Hadramawt are

35 Yemeni historians also provide some references to *waqf* in these works, but none can be compared to that of Serjeant. Several contemporary Yemeni historians also quote him, including, ʿAbd al-Mālik Manṣūr, the author of *al-Mawkib*. This would seem to indicate that there has been little new research done on the topic since Serjeant's time.

also not included here.[36] However, a few points regarding these areas must be mentioned. The sultanate and dynasty of the Rasūlids centred mainly around the cities of Zabid and Ta'izz. Concerning the many Islamic schools in the area, the work of Ismā'īl al-Akwa', *al-Madāris al-Islamiyya*[37] stands as an authoritative work. It is an encyclopaedia of the Islamic schools, many of which were founded under this dynasty; several of the entries end with "and this school had plenty of *waqf*s attached to it." For a study of *waqf*s from this period from Ta'izz, see Muḥammad 'Abd al-Raḥīm Jāzim's forthcoming work.[38] Many of these *waqf*s were later regrouped as the schools themselves disappeared or ceased operating. In Zabid, many of the *waqf*s for the schools were included in large clusters, such as the Kawā'in (Zabid), and the *waqf al-kabīr*,[39] where the *waqf* administration of the city of Zabid was allowed to keep a part of the income and the rest was sent to Sanaa. Today these *waqf* clusters are partly privatized. To reconstruct what happened to the individual *waqf*s is an important historical task, but also a problematic one from the point of view of the new owners.

2.2 *The Register of the Forgotten Mosques*

In his introduction to the book *Masājid Ṣan'ā'*[40] from 1942, al-Ḥajarī states that a large re-structuring of the *waqf*s took place in the city of Sanaa after the plague in 933/1526–27. The plague left a large number of properties without inheritors. Imam al-Mutawakkil Sharaf al-Dīn Yaḥyā (d. 965/1558) took these properties and made them into new *waqf*s and distributed them to one mosque in every quarter of the city and made sure that each of the mosques

36 A short book dealing with *awqāf* in Hadramawt is 'Abd al-Raḥmān 'Abdallāh 'Iwaḍ Bakīr, *al-Waqf fī Ḥaḍramawt bayna al-Salaf wa-l-Khalaf* (n.p.: al-Jama'iyya al-Khayriyya li-Ta'līm al-Qur'ān al-Karīm, far' Ḥaḍramawt, Mukallā', Dār Ḥaḍramawt li al-Dirāsāt wa-l-Nashr, 2002).

37 Ismā'īl b. 'Alī l-Akwa', *al-Madāris al-islāmiyya fī-l-Yaman* (Sanaa and Beirut: al-Jīl al-Jadīd, Mu'assasat al-Risāla, 1986).

38 Muḥammad 'Abd al-Raḥim Jāzim, "Un nouveau corpus documentaire d'époque rasūlide: Les actes de waqf de Ta'izz," Chroníques du Manuscrít au Yémen 10 (2010), online: https://cmy.revues.org/1900 (accessed 12 November 2015).

39 For the history of *waqf* in Zabid where such *waqf* clusters are also mentioned, see 'Abdū 'Alī 'Abdallāh Hārūn, *al-Durr al-naḍīd fī taḥdīd ma'ālim wa-āthār madīnat Zabīd* (Sanaa: Wizārat al-Thaqāfa wa-l-Siyāḥa, 2004); 'Abd al-Raḥmān 'Abdallāh al-Ḥaḍramī, *Zabīd: Masājiduhā wa-madārisuhā l-'ilmiyya fī l-tārīkh* (Sanaa: al-Markaz al-Faransī li-Dirāsāt al-Yamaniyya bi-Ṣan'ā', al-Ma'had al-Faransī li-Dirāsāt al-'Arabiyya bi-Dimashq, 2000).

40 Muḥammad b. Aḥmad al-Ḥajarī, *Masājid Ṣan'ā: 'Āmiruhā wa-muwafīhā* (Sanaa: Maktabat al-Irshād, 2007 [1942]). The introduction is translated in the informative article of Tim Macintosh-Smith, "The Secret Gardens of Sana'a," *Saudi Aramco World* 57, no. 1 (2006). Serjeant and Lewcock also comment on its content: *San'ā'*, 321.

were properly equipped and supplied with water, including basins for public domestic water supply (*muttakhidhāt*). The water in the ablution pools (*maṭāhir*) was changed daily by professional water lifters (*sānī, sunāh*) using inclined well-ramps (*mirnāʿ, marāniʿ*), and the wastewater was used to irrigate the mosque gardens[41] (*maqshama, maqāshim*). As the inhabitants now had access to a proper mosque, they stopped using the many small, unfurnished mosques that had no water supply or lighting, and over time these mosques fell into decay, and eventually ruin; many of these disappeared completely and were built over. As for the historicity of this account, there is little evidence available, but this narrative is an example of a way to conceptualize "the beginning" of today's structure of *waqf* administration in Sanaa, that is, it originated from a major re-structuring after a crisis. The "forgotten mosques" are registered in the so-called the "register of forgotten mosques" (*Miswaddat al-masājid al-mansiyya*). This register, or *miswadda*, is quoted numerous times in al-Ḥajarī's book. Together with *al-Miswadda al-sinānịyya*, these are the most quoted sources in his encyclopaedia-like work of the mosques of Sanaa. Al-Ḥajarī is the only historian(!) to ever have had access to these two most important documentary sources.

2.3 *The First Ottoman Occupation (ca. 957–1045/1550–1636)*

The Ottomans undoubtedly brought with them knowledge of centralized *waqf* administration from elsewhere in the Islamicate world, but there are few sources from this period that explicitly mention the organisation of *waqf* management. One of the documentary sources is *al-Miswadda al-sinānịyya* as mentioned above; Serjeant himself was very interested in gaining access to this unique source:

> [that there ...] is one major omission in that, because of its virtual inaccessibility, we were unable to make a direct study of the *Miswaddah* of Sinān Pāshā,[42] preserved in the Chancellery of the Jāmiʿ Mosque. The

41 The gardens are still partly in use. See Macintosh-Smith, "The Secret Gardens."

42 Sinān Bāshā: There are at least two men by that name, both were governors of Yemen during the first Ottoman occupation: The first is Sinān Bāshā Beylerbeyi (1506–96), who was also a governor of Egypt and an Ottoman grand vizier (in 1580). The second is Sinān Bāshā l-Kaykhiyā, who was appointed governor of Yemen in 1604–5. There is some information about him and his period as governor in the *Ghāyat al-amānī* and it was he who ordered the famous *waqf* register to be made and also built the Kaʿba-like building (*al-Qubba*) in the middle of the courtyard of the Great Mosque, where, until today the old *waqf* registers are kept. Sinān is buried in al-Mukhā' next to the famous saint al-Shādhilī. See R. B. Serjeant, "The Post-Medieval and Modern History of Ṣanʿā' and the Yemen,

> authorities had not, as yet, permitted it to be photographed for reference and study at leisure. During our all too brief stays in Ṣanʿāʾ, with many fundamental data to establish, it was out of the question to copy out passages by hand. An edition of the *Miswaddah* with professional identification of places, families, etcetera, is an indispensable preliminary to anything near a comprehensive history of Ṣanʿāʾ.[43]

Al-Miswadda al-sināniyya is the oldest major register of *waqf*s known to exist in Sanaa. The reason for focusing on this type of document in historical studies is clear; such documents give us insight into the ownership structures of the time and if subsequent registers are found and made available, changes over time can be traced. In his chapter "Administrative Organisation," Serjeant states,

> The Jāmiʿ Mosque contains a document of the highest importance for the history of Ṣanʿāʾ, the register, usually called *Miswaddat* Sinān, of the Turkish Pasha of the first Ottoman occupation (1604–07). "He it was," says Yaḥyā b. al-Ḥusayn, "Who compiled a comprehensive roll (*daftar jāmiʿ*) of the *waqf*s of Ṣanʿāʾ, and commanded the *qāḍīs* to rule on its validity—which they did. He appointed a number of the ulema to bear witness to this roll, including the very learned Sayyid Muḥammad b. ʿIzz al-Dīn al-Muʾayyadī and others" [...] In December 1973 I saw the *Miswaddat* Sinān in the Chancellery of the Jāmiʿ, the *Qubbah* which contains only modern furniture and steel cupboards. It is a long, narrow but thick volume nicely bound in probably contemporary plum-coloured leather with embossed design in the middle of the covers. The paper is polished yellow-brown or buff colour and the writing is beautiful and clear to read.[44]

Further, he speculates on the reason he was not allowed to copy it:

> Unfortunately, requests to photocopy this book have, in the past, not met with response, whether it be for some vaguely religious reason, or because so much of Ṣanʿāʾ being *waqf* and parts of this possibly appropriated to private families there is reluctance to publish its contents. This

ca. 953-1382/1515-1962" in *Ṣanʿāʾ: An Arabian Islamic City*, ed. R. B. Serjeant and R. Lewcock (London: World of Islam Festival Trust, 1983), 71–72.

43 Serjeant and Lewcock, *Sanʿāʾ*, 11.

44 al-ʿAmrī and Serjeant, "Administrative Organisation," 153.

> would be a valuable source for the history of the mosques until the beginning of the 11th/17th century.[45]

Until today, no one has copied the register of Sinān Bāshā and Serjeant's frustration is still very much felt by western and Yemeni historians alike. The mention of *al-Miswadda al-sināniyya* marks the beginning of the chronological, historical presentation in this chapter. Throughout the periods and incidents discussed below, and until today, this register has remained in the "Kaʿba-like" structure with a dome, called *al-Qubba*,[46] in the middle of the courtyard of the Great Mosque in Sanaa, built by the same Sinān Bāshā. The *qubba* and the *Miswadda* symbolize the very geographical and physical nexus of *waqf* administration in Yemen. The source Serjeant quotes above is from the chronicle by Yaḥyā b. al-Ḥusayn, *Ghāyat al-amānī*.[47] The same chronicle states that in the year [1016/]1607–08 Sinān Pāshā was exchanged with Bāshā Jaʿfar. At the end of the description of the happenings of that year, the author remarks dryly: "In these days Bāshā Jaʿfar killed Muḥammad b. Aḥmad al-Bawnī, *Nāẓir al-Waqf* in Sanaa, because of the complaints from the inhabitants of the city of his confiscation of their properties and including them into the *waqf*."[48] This passage is the first account, according to the sources available and used in this study, of the position of *nāẓir al-waqf*, a public *waqf* minister or "inspector." In the forthcoming work of Muḥammad Jāzim on *waqf*s in Taʿizz, we know that in 1595 there was an Ottoman *nāẓir al-nuẓẓār* by the name Bahāʾ al-Dīn b. Qāsim; he served under the vizier of Yemen, Ḥasan Bāshā.[49] Thus we may assume that the Ottomans brought with them new ideas of forms of centralized *waqf* administration and supervision, but we do not know much about this from historical sources. They certainly sought to coordinate the *waqf* administration over geographical areas that the Zaydīs had not held before, as it was from this period and onwards that Lower Yemen[50] and the Tihāma were also, in theory,

45 Serjeant, "Mosques of Ṣanʿāʾ," 321.

46 For a photograph of the *qubba* inside the Jāmiʿ, see *Sanʿāʾ*, 205, plate 18.

47 Yaḥyā b. al-Ḥusayn b. al-Qāsim b. Muḥammad, *Ghāyat al-amānī*, ed. Saʿīd ʿAbd al-Fattāḥ ʿĀshūr and Muḥammad Muṣṭafā Ziyāda (Cairo: Dār al-Kātib al-ʿArabī li-l-Ṭibāʿa wa-l-Nashr bi-l-Qāhira, 1968), 2:792–793.

48 See also Serjeant, "The Post Medieval and Modern History of Ṣanʿāʾ and the Yemen, ca. 953–1382/1515–1962," in Serjeant and Lewcock, *Ṣanʿāʾ*, 73.

49 Jāzim, "Un nouveau corpus documentaire."

50 Lower Yemen refers to the areas around Ibb and Taʿizz, and sometimes also includes the Tihāma and the western mountains. Upper Yemen is usually defined as the area from the Sumāra pass above Ibb. Often the distinction between Upper and Lower Yemen is said to be the distinction between the Zaydī and Shāfiʿī areas, but this is not a clear geographical border.

controlled from Sanaa. In practice, in terms of actual control over *waqf* administration, we cannot expect the Ottomans to have achieved much outside the major cities and towns they occupied.

3 *Waqf* Administration Under the Qāsimī Dynasty (1045–1289/1636–1872)

Starting with the Ottoman notion of a state *waqf* inspector, *nāẓir al-waqf*, we see that from this point on in history, the state tried to increase its role in *waqf* administration and even interfered and included individual *waqf*s and types of *waqf* that originally were not related to the state at all. The Zaydī Imam al-Qāsim b. Muḥammad (d. 1029/1620), also called al-Qāsim the Great, led the wars against the Ottomans for several years and his son al-Mu'ayyad Muḥammad (d. 1054/1644) finally evicted them in 1045/1636. The following imams were his descendants (hence the Qāsimī dynasty)[51] and during their reign, the state quickly expanded to include the fertile western mountains and Lower Yemen as well as the coastal plain, Tihāma. For a short while they also held Hadramawt and Aden. The Qāsimī state sustained itself to a large extent on the tax income from the rich agricultural areas south and west of Sanaa. During much of the seventeenth century and into the eighteenth century, they held a monopoly of production of coffee for the world, an income that mainly came from Lower Yemen.

The Qāsimī state mainly ruled over Shāfiʿī areas and especially towards the end of their rule, they were Zaydī imams and rulers in name, but only loosely controlled the tribal and Zaydī areas north of Sanaa. The later Qāsimī imams separated the office of the imam into a political leader called the imam and a religious and legal leader, called the chief *qāḍī* or the *shaykh al-Islam*, of which Muḥammad al-Shawkānī (1760–1834) was the most famous. In doctrinal matters, the state made use of Sunnī-oriented scholars, creating a grey area between Hādawī-Zaydīs and traditionists,[52] or neo-Sunnī doctrines in theology and law.

---

51 For a useful genealogical map of the different Qāsimī rulers, see the beginning of Haykel, *Revival and Reform*.

52 The term traditionist is thoroughly elaborated by Haykel and refers to the view that the *ḥadīth* sciences (and hence the term "tradition") and the *ḥadīth*s in general are authoritative primary sources for law. There are several such famous scholars that opposed or "added" to Zaydism by using the authority of the Sunnī *ḥadīth* collections, of which Muḥammad al-Shawkānī (d. 1834) is the latest and most famous of them. The term "neo-Sunnī" is used similarly, but the term "neo" refers more specifically to the newer tendency

The Qāsimī state did not remain intact until 1872. In the very beginning of the nineteenth century they started losing control over the coastal areas, which were first taken by the Wahhābīs and later by the Egyptians. It is doubtful that they ever directly controlled the tribal areas of the north, and the various regional governors could have quite independent powers, at times even branching off into separate states (*dawlas*). In the mid nineteenth century the Qāsimī state was dissolving and local elites ruled the fertile south and west. The Ottomans gradually took over the coastal areas and subsequently the southern highlands (Lower Yemen) until they took Sanaa permanently in 1872.[53]

During the period of the Qāsimī dynasty we see a development of state-like structures. The Qāsimīs developed a system of ministers and governors.[54] Taxation, especially from the fertile western mountains and lower Yemen, was crucial for the income for the state. The tax system was complicated, and involved several types of taxes. It was often collected from the areas of relative political stability such as the western mountains and Lower Yemen, while the strong tribes in the north paid less tax and their shaykhs were allowed to keep a large part for themselves. A dual system of harvest estimators (*khurrāṣ*) and tax collectors was at times employed,[55] and the tribal system became part of the structure of tax collection, in the sense that the tribes were collectively responsible for the tax burden. The powerful shaykhs of the north were given a portion of the taxes for themselves; this was done to enhance their loyalty and to discourage tribal attacks on the state. The northern tribes were used as auxiliary armies and were commissioned to subdue the population in the fertile Lower Yemen.

Perhaps the most important sources of the history of state *waqf* administration can be found in the many biographical dictionaries, encyclopaedia, and chronicles that exist from this period. Below I review quotations from these sources in order to assess the tools that the state used in their attempt to take control of an increasing number of and types of *waqf*.

As an example of the many small mentions in the biographical dictionaries, we can read that a certain Muḥammad b. Mahdī l-Shabībī l-Dhamārī was in charge of (*tawallā*) the *waqf* of Jibla and the areas of Ibb. He died in 1729 or

---

to reject the law schools altogether, something that al-Shawkānī also did. See Haykel, *Revival and Reform*, 10.

53 For the Qāsimī period in general, see especially Haykel, *Revival and Reform* and Paul Dresch, *Tribes, Government, and History in Yemen* (Oxford: Clarendon Press, 1989), 198–235.

54 Haykel, *Revival and Reform*, 17–18.

55 For taxation, see al-ʿAmrī and Serjeant, "Administrative Organisation," 154–160.

1730.[56] Below we follow the references to several such persons and incidents. By paying attention to their titles, the areas they controlled, and their relationship to the political power, we can learn how the public, central administration of *waqf* developed over time.

3.1 *Aḥmad Qāṭin al-Ṣanʿānī (d. 1199/1785)*[57]

Al-Qāḍī Aḥmad Qāṭin al-Ṣanʿānī was born in Ḥabāba in 1118/1706. He studied in nearby Shibām and Kawkabān. Zabāra quotes al-Shawkānī who states that Qāṭin was administrator of the *awqāf* in Thulāʾ[58] (*walī l-awqāf al-thullāʾiyya*) for a period. Later Imam al-Mahdī l-ʿAbbās (d. 1189/1775) made him administrator of the *awqāf* of Sanaa (*wallāhu al-awqāf al-Ṣanʿāniyya*).

Zabāra quotes different historians' views of Qāṭin's life and biography; these often give slightly diverging stories, for example, in the details of the many disputes he was involved in and the speculations about the reasons he fell from favour with the imam.

Al-Shawkānī states in his *Badr* that Qāṭin was a student of the then chief *qāḍī* in Sanaa, al-Sayyid Aḥmad al-Shāmī. For some reason, and al-Shawkānī states exactly "for some reason" (*ḥāditha kāna bi-sabbabihā ʿuzila ṣāḥib al-tarjama*) Qāṭin was dismissed as a *waqf* administrator: Under Imam al-Mahdī l-ʿAbbās he was also appointed judge of Thulāʾ and built a great house there. He fell out with the scholar Qāsim al-Kibsī. Apparently, Qāṭin managed to convince the imam to give him a third of the *waqf* administrator position and salary (*ʿamāla*) from Thulāʾ.[59] Al-Kibsī went to the imam and claimed that a crime had been committed (*iḥtaṣaba ʿalayhi*) when Qāṭin built his house (illegally) on top of a graveyard. It is not clear if this was the real reason for his imprisonment. This may be the first source mentioning that the imam delegated the position as public *waqf* administrator for an area outside Sanaa and that with this position also came the right to take percentages of the whole income (as will be shown below, usually 10 per cent). Further, al-Shawkānī states: "When he administered the *awqāf*, the income of the *awqāf* increased significantly."[60]

56 Muḥammad b. Muḥammad b. Yaḥyā Zabāra, *Nayl al-waṭar min tarājīm rijāl al-Yaman fī l-qarn al-thālith ʿashar min hijrat sayyid al-bashar ṣ*, ed. ʿAdil ʿAḥmad ʿAbdallāh al-Mawjūd and ʿAlī Muḥammad Muʿawwiḍ, 2 vols. (Beirut: Dar al-Kutub al-ʿIlmiyya, 1998), 3:213.

57 In general, see Zabāra, *Nashr al-ʿarf*, 1:274–285.

58 The towns Thulāʾ, Ḥabāba, Shibām, and Kawkabān are located around 40 km northwest of Sanaa.

59 Zabāra, *Nashr al-ʿarf*, 1:279.

60 Ibid., 1:278; Zabāra quotes al-Shawkānī. See also Muḥammad b. ʿAlī l-Shawkānī, *al-Badr al-ṭāliʿ bi-maḥāsin man baʿda al-qarn al-sābiʿ* (Damascus and Beirut: Dār Ibn Kathīr, 2006), 144.

There was a strong disagreement between Qāṭin and the chief *qāḍī* Yaḥyā l-Saḥūlī. Qāṭin was jailed in the fortress of Sanaa for two years by Imam al-Mahdī l-ʿAbbās because of this quarrel. Positions turned around "in matters too long to discuss here" and he was later pardoned again. Al-Saḥūlī himself was imprisoned in 1758–59 while Qāṭin was given the role as inspector (*al-nāẓir*) over the *awqāf* of "Lower Yemen and Thulā' and other areas" and he was made head of the imamic *dīwān*, or something like prime minister (*wa-jaʿalahu raʾīs al-qaḍāʾ bi-l-dīwān al-imām*). He was then jailed for a second time in 1774–75; Imam al-Mahdī l-ʿAbbās died shortly after and al-Mahdī's son, Imam al-Manṣūr ʿAlī, pardoned Qāṭin.[61] As for the reason he was imprisoned, Qāṭin himself[62] produced a rather lengthy and complicated story around his legal position in the question of the imam's right to take and decide over the *zakāt* of *waqf* lands:[63] "Sīdī l-Mawlā [al-Mahdī l-ʿAbbās] May God grant him mercy, said to me relating to the issue of *zakāt* of the *waqf*; it was indeed to be paid (*tuqbaḍ*).... Al-Faqīh Aḥmad al-Nihmī pressured me because of this and Mawlāna al-Mahdī [al-ʿAbbās] did the same."[64] Qāṭin himself continues and explains:

> In the *waqf* of Sanaa, there are stipends (*muqarrarāt*) for the poor. I showed him, by opening the books,[65] the way the *zakāt* had been used. And I said to them, "this is the usage! And to change this is injustice! (*ẓulm*)." Then al-Mahdī became quiet for some days and observed the

61 Zabāra, *Nashr al-ʿarf*, 1:227.

62 Ibid., 2:143.

63 Should God's property be taxed? The recent historical practices seem to indicate that *waqf* lands are rented out and that the tenant must pay the *zakāt*. However, it is quite easy to see the argument that the *zakāt* of *waqf*, if taken, should go to the *waqf* beneficiaries themselves, as Zaydī *waqf* beneficiaries are pious by definition and worthy recipients and taxation of God's property seems odd. In any case, most of these *waqf* beneficiaries were mosques. Thus one could easily argue that such a taxation is unnecessary in the first place. Or, as Qāṭin himself stated before the imam, this should return to the *waqf* as stipends for the poor and if the *zakāt* was diverted away from the *waqf* (to the *bayt al-māl*) "the poor would suffer." Another reference to the issue of *zakāt* from *waqf* states that in 1817 "the new imam, al-Mahdī ʿAbdallāh decided to follow the practice of his father in the issues of *zakāt* of *waqf* and argued (*istaḥajja*) that it was to go back to the *waqf* ... however it did not show on the upkeep of the mosques." Luṭf Allāh b. Aḥmad Jaḥḥāf, *Ḥawliyyāt al-muʾarrikh jaḥḥāf*, ed. Ḥusayn b. ʿAbdallāh al-ʿAmrī (Beirut: Dār al-Fikr al-Muʿāṣir, 1998), 83. At the time Qāṭin made his argument, al-Shawkānī was supposed to have had a strong influence on legal matters, however, he is not mentioned.

64 Zabāra, *Nashr al-ʿarf*, 2:143.

65 The verb "to show" *aṭlaʿa* is used for bringing forward and opening a book or consulting a book.

> management of the *waqf* and its incomes and left the issue. Instead he decided to take some of the administrator's salary (*ʿamāla*). The imam gave to the *waqf* administrator, shaykh ʿAbdallāh al-ʿArāsī, two thirds only …[66]

Here we gain some insight into the intrigues between "civil servants." We can see that the imam had power, but that he was at the same time dependent on the knowledge and loyalty of his civil servants. As a state *waqf* administrator, Aḥmad Qāṭin had several secretaries; one of them was Muḥammad Aḥmad al-Sharafī (d. ca. 1800). Qāṭin states "he was my secretary the days I worked in the *waqf*" (*kataba maʿī ayyām ʿamālatī fī-l-waqf*).[67] Another secretary was Zayd b. Muḥammad al-Shāmī.[68] The term *ʿamāla* is important here: It seems to mean both the position as a *waqf* inspector and the salary itself. Aḥmad Qāṭin died in 1785.[69]

3.2 *Al-Qāḍī l-ʿArāsī (d. 1187/1773)*

Al-Qāḍī ʿAbdallāh Muḥyī l-Dīn al-ʿArāsī was appointed to be public *waqf* administrator when Aḥmad Qāṭin was dismissed, as mentioned above. Zabāra quotes al-Sayyid Ibrāhīm b. Muḥammad al-Amīr who states about al-ʿArāsī that: "… he was the *walī* of the *awqāf* of Sanaa and later for all of Yemen. He improved the income and gave to the poor. He took control (*ḍabaṭa*) of all *awqāf* in Yemen by setting up *waqf* registers (*miswaddāt*) and this had never been done by anyone before him."[70] Qātin states: "Al-ʿArāsī was *walī l-awqāf* after me. And Imam al-Mahdī l-ʿAbbās gave him only two-thirds of an *ʿushr* whereas my *ʿamāla* used to be a full *ʿushr* [10 per cent], which is the usual *ʿamāla*."[71] Here the size of the salary of the public *waqf* administrator is confirmed. This is no small sum. As we shall see, this tenth seems to be a norm that was kept until today. Al-ʿArāsī died in 1773.[72] Around 1750, al-Mahdī l-ʿAbbās appointed Aḥmad b. Ṣāliḥ b. Abī l-Rijāl to be a secretary of the *awqāf* (*kitābat al-awqāf*). Abī l-Rijāl worked under the *mutawallī l-awqāf*, ʿAbdallāh al-ʿArāsī and "they met every week to discuss the matters related to the interests of the *awqāf*."[73]

66 Zabāra, *Nashr al-ʿarf*, 2:143.
67 Ibid., 2:411.
68 Ibid., 1:278.
69 Ibid., 1:283. al-Shawkānī, *al-Badr al-ṭāliʿ*, 145.
70 Zabāra, *Nashr al-ʿarf*, 2:143.
71 Ibid.
72 Ibid., 2:147. ʿĪd al-fiṭr, 1187 AH.
73 Zabāra, *Nashr al-ʿarf*, 1:139: "al-Qāḍī Aḥmad b. Ṣāliḥ b. Abī l-Rijāl (1727–77) was given the position of secretary of the *awqāf* by al-Maḥdī l-ʿAbbās. He was also made minister or governor of al-Ḥayma, Ḥufāsh, and Wuṣāb.

The role of the secretaryship was kept in the family of (*bayt*) Abī l-Rijāl from about 1750 until 1938–39![74]

3.3 *Al-Sayyid ʿAlī b. Muḥammad ʿĀmir (d. 1196/1782 or 83)*

When al-ʿArāsī died, ʿAlī b. Muḥammad ʿĀmir was appointed by Imam al-Mahdī l-ʿAbbās in 1773 to be *nāẓir al-awqāf*. He and Imam Mahdī quarrelled over his salary; ʿĀmir wanted a full tenth (*ʿushr*), and after some days of negotiations, the imam gave in.[75]

Apparently, ʿĀmir was skilled in *waqf* administration and knew how to extract the most of the potential income. Before the appointment, he had worked for Qāṭin as his assistant (*muʿayyan*). This is a clear example of how the imam was dependent on knowledgeable administrators. It is also an example of how the inspection or administration of public *waqf* was "outsourced" to scholars in a way similar to that of tax fiefs, which were given to local shaykhs.

Zabāra quotes Aḥmad Qāṭin, who says that he was a close friend of al-Sayyid ʿAlī b. Muḥammad ʿĀmir. Qāṭin gives us important information about the *waqf* administration of ʿĀmir:

> ʿĀmir was a *waqf walī* in the areas of Taʿizz for a period. He took back lands that had been illegally taken from the *waqf* and he revived the mosques and there were no complaints. Then later, a delegation of some of those who had taken *waqf* lands went to Sanaa and complained about him, and they continued to do so until al-Badr [Muḥammad b. Ismāʿīl] al-Amīr and Qāḍī ʿAbd al-Jabbār believed them and gave in.[76]

Here Qāṭin explains the essence of the problem:

> In *waqf* there is a something called "*waqf* payment" (*ḍarāʾib*) which is the "mother of problems" (*umm al-ṣawāʾib*). Qāḍī ʿAbd al-Jabbār told me himself that ʿĀmir was the *walī* of the *waqf* of Yemen and that some of the *waqf* tenants (*shurakāʾ al-waqf*) came to him and they agreed to pay a fixed rent for the *waqf* and further, to pay a fixed rent for the *waqf* land every year, whether there was a harvest or not (*sawaʾan kāna hunāka thamara aw lā*). And this situation is now continuing. So even if al-ʿĀmir is removed, another *ʿāmil waqf* would take his place and the same people

74 Ibid., 1:142.
75 Ibid., 2:236.
76 Ibid., 2:235–36.

> will complain to him about the size of the *waqf* rent. Subsequently, and over time, they will pay a rent a little lower than before.[77]

Here Qāṭin criticises the problem inherent in fixed rents, as opposed to a sharecropping agreement. A fixed rent payment is easier to complain about, especially during years of drought when such a payment could be presented as "unfair." What we do not know is whether this was a practice that existed under ʿĀmir only or if it was more common. In *fiqh*, as we see in chapter 6, the sharecropping type of leases seem to be the most prevalent and considered more "safe" for the *waqf*. Fixed leases would, however, be cheaper to administer since it is not necessary to assess the harvest every year in order to estimate the rent, thus the episode described above could be an example of an "administrative shortcut" made by ʿĀmir. The term *ḍarāʾib* in *waqf* leases reappears in al-Shijnī's (d. 1201/1786 or 87) *fatwā* translated in chapter 7, which indicates that the *ḍarāʾib* type of payment was common around the time of the *fatwā*.[78] These lease practices are an important part of *waqf* and more research is needed in order to draw conclusions.

When Imam al-Mahdī l-ʿAbbās died and his son Imam al-Manṣūr ʿAlī took over in 1776, the new imam dismissed (*ʿazalahu*) ʿĀmir and Sayyid Muḥammad al-Ḥaṭaba was appointed (*ʿayyanahu*) to the position as *waqf* administrator. The reason for this, according to Jaḥḥāf,[79] was ʿĀmir's protest when the minister ʿAlī b. Ḥasan al-Akwaʿ built a mosque (Masjid Ḥurqān) and did not establish, simultaneously, any *waqfs* for the mosque. When al-Akwaʿ wanted to register it in the general *waqf* register (*al-miswadda al-ʿāmma*), ʿĀmir refused to do this since it would have provided the mosque with "free" income from the main Sanaa *waqf*. The quarrel resulted in ʿĀmir's dismissal. ʿĀmir died in 1196 or 97/1782 or 83. ʿAlī b. Ḥasan al-Akwaʿ was appointed *nāẓir al-waqf*, though probably not for long; Muḥammad al-Ḥaṭaba took the position after him.[80]

3.4 *Al-Sayyid Muḥammad b. Ḥasan al-Ḥaṭaba (d. 1205/1791)*

Al-Sayyid Muḥammad b. Ḥasan al-Ḥaṭaba took over the position as the public *waqf* inspector (*tawallā naẓārat al-awqāf*). He lowered the wages for some of the employees (*ahl al-waẓaʾif wa-aʿmāl al-waqf*) and sent the resulting surplus

77 Zabāra, Ibid.

78 *Ḍarāʾib waqf* rent is also mentioned in Mijallī, *al-Awqāf fī l-Yaman*, 122–123.

79 As given by Luṭf Allāh Jaḥḥāf in Zabāra, *Nashr al-ʿarf*, 2:236. See also Serjeant and Lewcock, *Ṣanʿāʾ*, 315 n59.

80 Zabāra, *Nashr al-ʿarf*, 2:236–237.

to the public treasury (*bayt al-māl*). He became highly unpopular[81] and died in 1206/1791.[82] As for regional *waqf* administrators in this period, there are, for example, references to a certain Sayyid ʿAlī b. Aḥmad b. ʿAlī (d. 1198/1784) who was *mutawallī waqf Dhamār*.[83] This indicates that other cities had their own "main *waqf*," but we do not know the nature of their relationship to the government in Sanaa; nor do we know to what extent these regional *waqf* administrations were required to send the surplus to the capital.

3.5 *Al-Khafanjī's (d. 1180/1766 or 67) Poem*

Al-Khafanjī's poem, translated in Serjeant's *Ṣanʿāʾ*,[84] is a *qaṣīda*[85] that portrays a comic drama in rhyme. In the poem, the various mosques of Sanaa are each given personalities. The drama is about a poor little mosque, the ʿAddil Mosque, which feels sorry for itself and dreams of becoming something more important and grandiose. The mosque complains about his state and looks to other, richer mosques, and asks them for support. The Jāmiʿ (the Jāmiʿ al-Kabīr) is portrayed as very rich. Several of the other mosques present their case for the Jāmiʿ and the Jāmiʿ replies, after some time, that he unfortunately cannot help them since the *waqf* documents[86] seem to have been lost. The ʿAddil Mosque is poor, has no *waqf* lands of his own, and dreams of becoming a rich mosque with a garden, a *waqf* shop to provide rental income; it dreams of being well-supplied with lamp oil and water, having a paid imam and a *muʾadhdhin*, and

81 Zabāra, *Nayl al-waṭar*, 2:298–301. Dallāl wrote some lines of poetry about him, translated in al-ʿAmrī and Serjeant, "Administrative Organisation," 153.

82 Zabāra, *Nashr al-ʿarf*, 2:147; here it states that he died in 1305 AH (i.e., 1887 or 1888), and Serjeant quotes this al-ʿAmrī and Serjeant, "Administrative Organisation," 153. The correct year is one hundred *hijrī* years earlier, 1205/1791 (that is, the year 1305 in the *Nashr* is a misprint and should be 1205). This is confirmed in Zabāra, *Nayl al-waṭar*, 2:298–301.

83 Al-Sayyid ʿAlī b. Aḥmad b. ʿAlī (d. 1198/1784) was "*mutawallī waqf Dhamār*." He studied under al-Qāḍī Ahmad b. Ṣāliḥ b. Abū l-Rijāl and under al-Qāḍī ʿAlī b. Aḥmad b. Nāṣir al-Shijnī (who issued the *fatwā* in chapter 7) He was in charge of the *awqāf* of Dhamār in the days of Imam al-Manṣūr ʿAlī (son of al-Mahdī l-ʿAbbās). See Zabāra, *Nashr al-ʿarf*, 2:170–171.

84 Serjeant remarks that the poem was also translated by Harald Vocke in 1973 into German and that this translation was based on another source and that his comments are even fuller. Serjeant and Lewcock, *Sanʿāʾ*, 317–321. The poem was recently published in the newest edition of al-Ḥajarī, *Masājid Ṣanʿā*, 79–81.

85 According to Serjeant, epic dramas in which mosques are the main characters are not uncommon; he claims to have seen one from Hadramawt as well. Serjeant and Lewcock, *Sanʿāʾ*, 318. For other such dramas see "The marriage between the Madhhab Mosque and the Murādiyya Mosque," Zabāra, *Nashr al-ʿarf*, 2:204–216.

86 Note that the term *waṣīya* is used.

being a place where the "*Azhār*,[87] the *Bayān*,[88] and the *Mulḥa*"[89] are taught. The poem is full of humour that is difficult to reproduce; one example is the small mosque's dream to perform the call to prayer so loud that the jinn would fart when they heard it. The political and legal problem that this poem raises is the issue of distributing *waqf* income from rich mosques to poorer ones; that is, the inter-beneficiary transfer of funds (called inter-beneficiary because both *waqfs* have the same type of beneficiary, in this case, mosques). There were certainly rich and poor mosques at this time. Opening the legal possibility of transferring income between them leads to the problem of potentially disrespecting the founders' will. But, if this will is no longer present in the form of public memory or documentation, then it is clearly tempting to take a more flexible stand on these questions. As I point out below, the tendency to allow transfers between *waqfs* within the public *waqf* administration has increased over time until today.

3.6 *An Open Letter from Muḥammad b. Ismāʿīl al-Amīr to Imam al-Mahdī l-ʿAbbās (1180/1767)*

In what became an important and well-known incident in the history of the *waqf* in Sanaa, the great scholar al-Badr Muḥammad b. Ismāʿīl al-Amīr (d. 1183/1769)[90] (hereafter called Ibn al-Amīr) wrote a letter in 1181/1767 in which he publicly criticised Imam al-Mahdī l-ʿAbbās's effort to exchange the *waqf* lands of Shuʿūb, outside Sanaa, for those of other areas. The imam would have benefited from this because he had repaired the irrigation system called Ghayl al-Barmakī and Ghayl al-Aswad[91] that conducted water to the Shuʿūb area just north of Sanaa, outside the city walls, and he wanted the *waqf* land

87 That is (Ibn Miftāḥ), *Sharḥ al-azhār*.

88 The *al-Bayān al-shāfī* is discussed in chapter 4.

89 That is *Mulḥat al-iʿrāb*. Together with *al-Ajrūmiyya*, these two are the most commonly used introductory works of Arabic grammar in traditional education. The *Mulḥa* is mentioned several times as an important part of the curriculum in Arabic grammar, see for instance al-Shawkānī's own "ideal-curriculum" in his work *Adab al-ṭalab* as translated by Haykel, *Revival and Reform*, 105 n103. And, for instance Vom Bruck, *Islam, Memory, and Mortality*, 117.

90 For his life, see Zabāra, *Nashr al-ʿarf*, 3:29–69.

91 Al-Mahdī l-ʿAbbās repaired the two famous underground water canals, called Ghāyl al-Aswad and Ghayl al-Barmakī. These water tunnels are often called *qanāt* elsewhere; in Yemeni dialect they are referred to as "*ghuyūl*." They start at several wells some distance to the south of the city, pass under the city with several openings for public access and mosque ablutions, and exit on the lower, northern side of the city, called Shuʿūb. For these two *ghayls* in general see R. B. Serjeant, Paolo Costa, and Ronald Lewcock, "The Ghayls of Ṣanʿāʾ," in *Ṣanʿāʾ*, ed. Serjeant and Lewcock (London: World of Islam Festival Trust, 1983); and ʿAslān, *Ghuyūl Ṣanʿāʾ*.

as his own private property, now more fertile because of the repaired irrigation system. To do this, he needed to "move" the *waqf* lands[92] somewhere else. His attempt was criticized and the episode became an example of how independent, free speaking *ʿulamāʾ* tried to correct what was perceived as corrupt government behaviour in *waqf* management.

Ibn al-Amīr was born in 1688 and was a well-known and respected scholar with neo-traditionist leanings, that is, a Sunnī-oriented Zaydī scholar of Yemen. He studied in several cities in Yemen and several times went to the holy cities (Mecca and Medina) for hajj and to study. He was a judge and a preacher in the Great Mosque (al-Jamīʿ al-Kabīr). In 1748[93] Imam al-Mahdī l-ʿAbbās made him *waqf* administrator of Sanaa (*wallāhu awqāf Ṣanʿāʾ wa-bilādihā*), but shortly after he withdrew from the position. Ibn al-Amīr became unpopular in the eyes of the Zaydī imam and his family, in particular for not mentioning the name of the imam during the Friday sermon (this practice was customary as a way of recognizing the hierarchy of power) in the Great Mosque of Sanaa where he was a preacher. He was imprisoned, but his biographer says he turned the prison into a place of study; scholars came to discuss and learn from him, especially the *ḥadīth* sciences.[94]

In Zaydī *fiqh* exchanging (*istibdāl*)[95] a *waqf* asset is fully legal, in fact there are few arguments against it. The validity hinges upon the interests of the *waqf* in question, and indeed, if it is in the interest of the *waqf* to do so, then changing the asset is required. In practice, however, *waqf* assets are often ascribed a special "holy" status, and changes of *waqf* are often viewed with suspicion.[96]

92 Most probably, not all Shuʿūb land was *waqf*, but there were a high number of *waqf* fields interspersed among private fields. The sales document is edited and analysed in Ḥusayn ʿAbdallāh al-ʿAmrī, *Miʾat ʿām min tārīkh al-Yaman al-ḥadīth* (Damascus: Dār al-Fikr, 1988), 33–43. And similarly in Ḥusayn ʿAbdallāh al-ʿAmrī, "A Document Concerning the Sale of Ghayl al-Barmakī and al-Ghayl al-Aswad by al-Mahdī ʿAbbās, Imam of Yemen, 1131–89/1718–75," in *Arabian and Islamic Studies*, ed. R. L. Bidwell and G. R. Smith (London and New York: Longman, 1983). The sale took place in February 1767.

93 Ramaḍān 1161.

94 Zabāra, *Nashr al-ʿarf*, 3:32.

95 There are several terms in use that all mean "exchange": *ʿiwaḍ, ibdāl,* and *istibdāl*. In Ḥanafī areas, the term *istibdāl* seems to be used more consistently.

96 In some treatises the question of whether or not it is legal to "sell" *waqfs* seems to have reappeared as a legal topic. In order to undertake an *istibdāl* it is also necessary to sell the original *waqf* asset. To sell the *waqf*, without buying a new *waqf* asset, would not be an *istibdāl* and certainly illegal; it looks as if Ibn al-Amīr speculated about this aspect for his argumentation. The question of selling a *waqf*, and how to define "necessity," is addressed in an unpublished treatise found in the Maktabat al-Waqf called "*Taʾkīd al-taʾsīs al-mabnā ʿalā wujūb dawām al-taḥbīs*," Majāmīʿ 23, "Fiqh," folio 28–30. The treatise, from 1654, is signed by al-Ḥusayn b. Nāṣir ʿAbd al-Ḥafīẓ; it is divided into two parts, the second of which

The question here is more complicated, because Imam al-Mahdī l-ʿAbbās wanted to "move" the *waqf* properties out of Shuʿūb to somewhere else, so that he could benefit from the land value, which increased after he repaired the irrigation system. And the argument against such an exchange in the letter from Ibn al-Amīr to Imam al-Mahdī does not address this very particular fact, but rather criticizes the more general idea of "selling and buying *waqf*." Further, it builds on the notion that a *waqf* asset has a more "holy" status than other forms of property. In his argument in favor of this, he mentions several details about which types of *waqf*s existed at the time and important details about the *waqf* type called *waṣāyā* as we see below. The edited letter, dated 1767, is found under the entry of "al-Mahdī l-ʿAbbās" in the biographical encyclopaedia *Nashr al-ʿarf*. The main part is translated below, and divided into sections. After a long and eloquent introduction, Ibn al-Amīr directly criticizes the *waqf* transactions:

> [... A]nd the worst of sins is that of the purchase (*shirāʾ*) of the *awqāf* and its exchange from *waqf* into private property. Our Lord [the imam] did, after all, invalidate the sale undertaken by the former *waqf* administrator (*ʿāmil*), the one who was administrator before al-Shaykh al-ʿArāsī, and took it back according to what is right, and so be it.[97]

Here, Ibn al-Amīr refers to the *waqf* administrator "before al-ʿArāsī," which was Aḥmad Qāṭin, mentioned earlier in this chapter. It seems that Qāṭin also sold some of the *waqf* lands, but that these sales were later invalidated by the Imam and al-ʿArāsī. Ibn al-Amīr gives the Imam Mahdī credit for this corrective action. Then comes a long section in which Ibn al-Amīr claims that privatizing *waqf* is illegal in principle because of its "holy status." It is a peculiar argument since we are presumably talking about an "exchange" (*istibdāl*), which is legal when it is done in the interest of the *waqf*; however, Ibn al-Amīr focuses on the aspect of privatization in isolation, that is, on the fact that the imam wanted to buy the *waqf* lands personally.

> You know the statements of the *ʿulamāʾ* of your time and your judges; that selling *waqf* is *ḥarām*! I have attached a list with their signatures, and my signature is the first one. You surely know that the first *waqf* in Islam was the *waqf* of ʿUmar b. al-Khaṭṭāb, may God be pleased with him, and

is called "*al-Baḥth al-nafīs al-muttaṣil bi-taʾkīd al-taʾsīs al-mabnā ʿalā* ..." A photocopy is in the author's possession.

97 Zabāra, *Nashr al-ʿarf*, 2:21–24.

> according to him, the Prophet, peace be upon him and his descendants, came and he ['Umar] said; Oh Prophet of God, I have acquired land [of quality or quantity] that I have never acquired before, and I want to undertake an act of charity with it, in order to become closer to God (*an ataqarraba bihi ilā Allāh taʿālā*). The Prophet said: "Retain the asset and give away its fruits" (*ḥabbis al-aṣl wa-sabbil al-thamara*). And [according to] the wording of al-Bukhārī, the Prophet said: "Not to be sold, not to be given away, but its fruits are to be enjoyed," and in an account by al-Dhahabī: "Give away its fruits and retain the asset, not to be sold and not to be inherited." And he ['Umar] did so, and therefore the restriction of sale is in the essence of *waqf*. The jurists therefore say that God's property is not to be taken out of the state of *waqf* (*lā yukhraj ʿan al-waqfiyya*) under any circumstances. And Our Lord [al-Mahdī l-ʿAbbās] is the best among living men created by God to execute the orders of his grandfather [the Prophet].[98]

These *ḥadīths* are often quoted in *fiqh* as the foundation of the institution of *waqf*, and they are widely used and known. The wording "not to be sold, not to be given away" is a phrase that is very often found in individual *waqf* documents. Following this is a section that is very important to understanding the difference between *waqf* and *waṣāyā* in Zaydī Yemen (the issue is also further elaborated in chapter 7):

> So, the sale of *waqf* is prohibited as are other types of transactional dispositions of *waqf* (*munāqala bihi*). Yes, it is legal (*ḥalāl*) to sell a *waṣīya* that has been donated [in exchange] for reading the Qur'ān and the *waṣīya* for charities, and also to exchange them (*ibdāluhā*) with something that is better and more useful. These are not *waqf* (*hādhihi laysat awqāfan*)[99] and therefore it is also legal to sell what the administrators (*ʿummāl*) [of this type of *waqf*] have acquired from the surplus of the *waqf* since it is not *waqf* [in the first place]. Property cannot be owned by [something] inanimate (*al-jamād*) and the acquired [object obtained by the] surplus is not the property of the administrator, because he has not paid anything for it from his own pocket, but with income from the *waqf*; thus this surplus [and the land or objects bought from this surplus] is not the property of anyone and if there is a preponderant interest, then it can

98 Ibid., 2:23.

99 He must mean that *waqf*s of the *waṣīya* type do not carry the same legal implications as "absolute *waqf*." In this case *waṣīya* clearly refers to a type of *waqf*.

> be legally sold, but it is not a true purchase (*bayʿ ḥaqīqī*), but more of a bilateral transaction (*muʿāwaḍa*), because it is not the property of the administrator. Few have proper knowledge about these issues.[100]

He is quite explicit in stating that *waṣāyā* is not *awqāf* and that the restrictions on the sale of *waqf* do not concern *waṣāyā*. He ascribes the right of *istibdāl* to the *waṣāyā* type and thereby he implicitly[101] claims that it might not be legal in *awqāf*. He seems to bolster the notion of restricting the sale of *waqf* and upgrading it to be considered *ḥarām*. Again, to the vast majority of jurists, a sale is indeed valid if it is part of an *istibdāl* (a *waqf* asset exchange), so making the sale absolutely invalid, as Ibn al-Amīr does, is a peculiar argument. He seems rather to construct a new difference between *awqāf* and *waṣāyā: awqāf* cannot be sold, while *waṣāyā* can.

The second half of the paragraph above refers to another topic in *waqf fiqh*; whether or not a thing bought from the surplus of the *waqf* automatically becomes *waqf*, or if it remains private property (*milk*), and thereby "free," and "saleable." This is a matter discussed in detail in the *waqf* chapter of the *Sharḥ al-azhār* and the *madhhab* favours[102] the view that such objects do not acquire *waqf* status.[103] So again, Ibn al-Amīr argues in an unconventional way, though he was probably using arguments that were more or less known among his intended readers. We should not see the section above as mainly a jurisprudential argument with the aim of affirming law or *fiqh*, but rather as an argument against contemporary "human" political interference in the specific *awqāf* cases of Sanaa. It is thus more a political critique, or one framed in populist terms, and this is probably the reason his arguments are more polemical than logical extracts of Zaydī *fiqh* debate. He continues:

> Note Our Lord, that the best [agricultural] properties in Sanaa are those at Shuʿūb since they are so close to the city. They are useful for the mosques in terms of herbs (*qaḍb*), tamarisk trees (*athl*), [they] supply grain continuously, and [because of] their proximity, therefore, there is nothing that can replace these lands. It is hoped and indeed also expected that with

100 Zabāra, *Nashr al-ʿarf*, 2:23.

101 Note that in the letter, he never explicitly states that *istibdāl* in *waqf* should be illegal.

102 The *madhhab* "favours" this by indicating *ijmāʿ* with the use of validation signs; *taqrīr* and *tadhhīb*. These indications, which are vital to understanding the *Sharḥ al-azhār*, are explained in chapter 4.

103 ʿAbdallāh Abū l-Ḥasan Ibn Miftāḥ, *al-Muntaziʿ al-mukhtār min al-ghayth al-midrār al-maʿrūf bi-Sharḥ al-azhār* (Sanaa: Wizārat al-ʿAdl / Maktabat al-Turāth al-Islāmī, 2003), 8:239.

> your good intention, which God will hopefully reward, the water tunnel that was buried for so long will be re-excavated to irrigate the *waqf* lands at Shuʿūb in order to provide grain for those on the pay lists of the *waqf* (*ahl al-waẓāʾif*).[104] Indeed, every year since the first *waqf* administrator they have been deprived of four months of salary.[105] By God, look to your grandfather, al-Mahdī Aḥmad b. al-Ḥasan,[106] may God show him mercy, how he excavated his water tunnel in al-Rawḍa[107] and made it available for the people, and [he] made the grapes for the people,[108] without taking any of the surplus, so God blessed him. And the grapes that he irrigated became the best grapes in al-Rawḍa and are sold for a high price because of his pious intention and deed. This *ghayl* (water channel) belongs to the public treasury (*buyūt amwāl*) and was constructed by dirhams from the public treasury and therefore it was not for him to take the surplus privately, and because of his pious intention, God passed on his rule (*khilāfa*) to his descendants for more than eighty years.[109]

In this section of the letter, Ibn al-Amīr describes the importance of the *waqf* lands at Shuʿūb for the mosques and for those on the pay lists (*ahl al-waẓāʾif*), be they mosque caretakers, preachers, teachers, students or worthy poor. He points out that he expects the imam to proceed with the restoration of the water supply system, but that he should do it for the *awqāf* like his (great-) grandfather did, not for himself.

In the last paragraph of the letter, not included in the translation above, Ibn al-Amīr points out to al-Mahdī that he has become one of the richest imams in the history of Yemen, and receives private income even from distant southern areas such as Qaṭaʿba and Radāʿ, and he reminds him that he should show gratitude towards God for this wealth.

Zabāra states in the end (presumably still quoting Qāṭin) that this advice from Ibn al-Amīr made an impression on the imam, and the imam left the *waqf* lands at Shuʿūb as they had been in the past.

---

104 Probably it can mean both employees and people receiving stipends like students and the worthy poor.

105 Here he may be referring to Qāṭin, as he has referred to him above as "the one before al-ʿArāsī"?

106 He reigned from 1676 to 1681; he was a grandson of al-Qāsim and the great great grandfather of al-Mahdī l-ʿAbbās.

107 It is called Ghayl al-Mahdī, see Serjeant, Costa, and Lewcock, "Ghayls of Ṣanʿāʾ," 30.

108 The wording is not entirely clear. The *ghayl* is well known. Al-Rawḍa, which is near Sanaa, to the north, is still known for its grapes.

109 Zabāra, *Nashr al-ʿarf*, 2:23–24. This text is partly treated by Serjeant, "The Post Medieval and Modern History of Ṣanʿāʾ," in Serjeant and Lewcock (eds.), *Ṣanʿāʾ*, 85–86.

3.7 *Other* Waqf *Administrators*

Ibn al-Amīr's son, Ibrāhīm b. Muḥammad b. Ismāʿīl al-Amīr (d. 1213/1799) was also a *waqf* administrator: "His father helped him in the *naẓārat al-waqf*."[110] In 1802 we know that Sayyid Ismāʿīl b. al-Ḥasan al-Shāmī was *ʿāmil al-awqāf*[111] (1741 or 1742–1819). He was a deputy of al-Sayyid ʿAlī b. Muḥammad ʿĀmir (*kāna yanūbu ʿanhu fī kathīr min al-aʿmāl*[112]) and later worked for the *waqf* of the city of Thulāʾ. After that, he took over the *waqf* of Sanaa and settled into that position (*istaqarra fī wilāyat waqf* Ṣanʿāʾ).[113] Some time after this, the position was given to Sālim Muḥammad al-Ṭashshī. In 1816 the chief *qāḍī* al-Shawkānī advised Imam al-Mahdī ʿAbdallāh to replace the *ʿāmil al-awqāf* al-Ṭashshī with the aforementioned Ismāʿīl b. Ḥasan al-Shāmī[114] When al-Shawkānī was writing the *Badr*, al-Shāmī was still in charge of the *awqāf* of Sanaa.[115]

A few months later, in the beginning of 1817, Imam al-Mahdī ʿAbdallāh again changed ministers and Ismāʿīl al-Shāmī's position was given to Yaḥyā b. Muḥammad Ḥaṭaba,[116] who was probably the son of Muḥammad b. Ḥasan al-Ḥaṭaba (d. 1205/1791) mentioned above, who took over after ʿĀmir. From 1795 until his death in 1834, Muḥammad b. ʿAlī l-Shawkānī was the chief *qāḍī* and a central political figure. Al-Shawkānī was also an administrator of local *waqf* clusters in areas outside Sanaa; he was granted "charities" (*ṣadaqāt*) and *waṣāyā* by the imam (*aqṭaʿahu al-imām*). This mention of the "granting of fiefs" together with *waqf*-like "charities" and *waṣāyā* indicates that being given the right to administer *waqf* was lucrative, and comparable to being given tax fiefs.[117]

---

110 Zabāra, *Nayl al-waṭar*, 1:93.

111 al-ʿAmrī, *Yemen in the 18th and 19th Centuries*, 117.

112 The terms *ʿamāla* and *aʿmāl* seem to be used in relation to the granting of rights to public *waqf* admninistration. See also Muḥammad Abū Zahra, *Muḥāḍarāt fī l-waqf* (Cairo: Dar al-Fikr al-ʿArabī), 340.

113 al-Shawkānī, *al-Badr al-ṭāliʿ*, 178.

114 al-ʿAmrī, *Yemen in the 18th and 19th Centuries*, 77; Luṭf Allāh, *Ḥawliyyāt al-muʾarrikh Jaḥḥāf*, 29.

115 al-Shawkānī, *al-Badr al-ṭāliʿ*, 178.

116 Luṭf Allāh, *Ḥawliyyāt al-muʾarrikh Jaḥḥāf*, 87.

117 This is mentioned by Haykel, who quotes the *Ḥawliyyāt Yamāniyya* and the *Nayl al-waṭar*. Haykel writes that it was never clear to him what these *waṣāyā* were. Most probably, they were once local *waqf*s or clusters of *waqf*s: Either large landholdings carrying the names of *waṣāyā*, which indicate that they could just as well have been family controlled *waqf*s, which were confiscated by the state for some reason. Or, it could be the right to supervise local, "normal" public *waqf*s in these specific local areas. In either case, al-Shawkānī would probably have the right to take ten percent of the total income in return for administering the leases and taking care of the local mosques (or other beneficiaries). The actual administrative work could in turn be delegated to someone else, while al-Shawkānī could still obtain a sizeable surplus. For instance, from al-Ḥayma alone he received one hundred

And as we know from Qāṭin, the common salary of a *waqf* administrator of a specific area was 10 per cent of the income. While we cannot discuss taxation policies and the tax collection system here, we can note that the similarity between it and the *waqf* administration system is striking; tax collectors took percentages and it was thus a potentially very lucrative position.[118] After the death of al-Shawkānī in 1834, the following period was characterized by increasing unrest and state disintegration. Already some years before that, the Qāsimīs had begun to lose some parts of the Tihāma. The following decades are often referred to as the "period of chaos." The power of the elites in Sanaa over Lower Yemen diminished, as did their control over *waqf* in these areas. *Waqf* was probably administered by local elites.

3.8 Waqf *Administration Under the Second Ottoman Occupation (1872–1911)*

The Ottomans arrived in 1849 for what was to be their second period of occupation. It was, however, only in the 1870s that they took more direct control over Sanaa, the Tihāma, the western mountains, and Lower Yemen. We know little about their ideas and actions in *waqf* administration reforms in Yemen. They would have had knowledge about a wide range of types of *waqf* administration from areas they had previously ruled. They would also have been very aware of the pragmatic benefits of leaving existing structures and elites in place, despite

---

silver pieces (*qirsh*) monthly. Al-Shawkānī used one of his students, Muḥammad b. ʿAlī l-ʿAmrānī, to manage his "fiefs" and a conflict between the two led to the imprisonment of his student. Haykel, *Revival and Reform*, 56–57. Zabāra, *Nayl al-waṭar*, 2:346. *Ḥawliyyāt Yamaniyya: al-Yaman fī l-qarn al-tāsiʿ ʿashar al-mīlādī*, ed. ʿAbdallāh b. Muḥammad al-Ḥibshī (Sanaa: Dār al-Ḥikma al-Yamaniyya, 1991), 279.

118 Tax collection and the *waqf* administration were mainly occupied by local elites. We must expect that the tax collection system was more dominated by local, tribal shaykhs than the *waqf* administration, as even tribal areas with little or few *waqf* institutions still paid taxes. Tax collection was an important part of the tribal system, since powerful tribal shaykhs were allowed to keep a large part of the collected tax for themselves. The *waqf* administration was in turn more influenced by the scholarly families; *waqfs* tend to be more concentrated in urban areas and in areas where *sayyids* and *quḍāh* are found. A fundamental difference between the two systems was that in the *waqf* administration, most funds presumably reverted to local beneficiaries and in the Qāsimī period we do not know to what extent *waqf* surplus was sent to Sanaa. There were many types of taxes, but the most important, the *zakāt* (*ʿushr*), was sent, in part, to the central government, although there were many local expenditures as well, which Messick points out, though his focus was on the historical period that follows this. Messick, "Transactions in Ibb," 168–173. Shelag Weir writes about the shaykhs' role in tax practices in Rāziḥ; see Shelagh Weir, *A Tribal Order: Politics and Law in the Mountains of Yemen* (Austin: University of Texas Press, 2007), 251–255.

their aims of reforming and "civilizing" governmental structures.[119] There are only a few references in the biographical dictionaries to *waqf* administration from this period; most are referred to by Serjeant in his book on *Ṣanʿāʾ*. Indeed, the administration of the judiciary and the state in general in this period has not yet been studied in detail, although Ottoman policies have been the subject of some research.[120] In general, despite the Ottoman intervention, most *waqf* administration seems to have continued along the same lines as before and in close cooperation with the same scholarly Yemeni elites.

3.9 *The Division of the* Waqf *Administration into* Dākilī *and* Khārijī

As noted early in this chapter, in this period one new aspect emerges, at least to the extent that we can judge by the few sources available. This is the division of the *waqf* administration into the "internal *waqf*" (*al-awqāf al-dākhiliyya*) and the external *waqf* (*al-awqāf al-khārijiyya*). The internal (*dākhilī*) were the *waqfs* of Sanaa, most likely only the city of Sanaa and "its" *waqfs*.[121] The external (*khārijī*) consisted of all other similar urban *waqf* clusters in other cities, such as Dhamār, Ibb, etc., which all had their own *waqf* cluster(s) for the great mosque and/or separate sub-clusters, like *waqf* for religious education.[122] Both sections had their own *nāẓir*, perhaps best translated as minister, or "inspector."[123]

The fact that the *waqfs* outside Sanaa were to be inspected and overseen by the central government in Sanaa was not new during the Ottoman period. As

119 This point was elaborated by Thomas Kühn in his presentation at the annual meeting of the Middle East Studies Association, Washington, DC (Nov. 2014). He referred to several Ottoman administrative documents and communications that emphasize the conscious pragmatic approach to local elites.

120 For a study of this period see Thomas Kühn, "Shaping Ottoman Rule in Yemen, 1872–1919" (PhD thesis, New York University, 2005); Thomas Kuehn, *Empire, Islam, and Politics of Difference: Ottoman Rule in Yemen, 1849–1919* (Leiden: Brill, 2011). Hümeyra Bostan, "Institutionalizing Justice in a Distant Province: Ottoman Judicial Reform in Yemen (1872–1918)" (MA thesis, Istanbul Sehir University, 2013).

121 Presumably there could still be *waqfs* in other nearby areas in favour of certain mosques in Sanaa. For example, informants in Sanaa said that the Qubbat al-Mahdī had *waqfs* in Ānis, Dhamār. I have also seen administrative documents in Rayma (although from the early reign of Imam Yaḥyā), that there existed *waqfs* in favour of public beneficiaries in Sanaa called *al-maḥāsin al-mutawakkiliyya* ("the Mutawakkili public works and services").

122 Messick writes that in Ibb there was a local *waqf* administration for the *waqfs* that support the religious education in the city (*waqf darasa*). Messick, "Transactions in Ibb," 163.

123 Technically, many of the mosque *waqfs* did not have private *mutawallīs*, therefore it was the imam who was the *mutawallī* for these *waqfs*. The term "inspector" only implies supervision, though in fact the inspector was actually a *mutawallī*, at least the *dākhilī* one.

we saw, the Qāsimīs had appointed *walīs* for the *waqf* of Yemen, but the term *al-awqāf al-khārijiyya* seems to be new from the second Ottoman period onwards. We can expect an attempt of renewal of state control over the peripheries in this period after several decades of disintegration. This was especially so in the densely populated and fertile Lower Yemen.

In 1849, we know that the *nāẓir al-awqāf* was al-Qāḍī ʿAbd al-Raḥmān al-ʿAmrānī.[124] The last *ʿāmil waqf* before the Ottomans took Sanaa was al-Sayyid Ḥusayn Ghumdān al-Kibsī.[125] These titles probably only refer to the *waqfs* of Sanaa. Toward the end of the Qāsimī dynasty and into the "period of unrest" we must expect that *waqfs* (that is, the city mosque *waqf* clusters) were administered locally and that Sanaa lost control to local elites.

We know that there was a "*waqf* office council," (*majlis qamsiyūn al-awqāf*), in Sanaa in 1890, when Aḥsan b. Aḥsan al-Akwaʿ[126] was the *raʾīs*. He died that year.[127] We also know that al-Qāḍī Ḥusayn b. ʿAlī l-ʿAmrī[128] was *nāẓir al-waqf*[129] and that he was "in authority of the *waqf*" (*wilāya*),[130] but in 1894 he was removed (*ʿuzila*) from the position, which then was given to ʿAlī b. Muḥammad al-Muṭāʿ.[131] Judging by al-ʿAmrī's title, this must have been just before the division of the *waqf* administration. The position of al-Muṭāʿ as mentioned by al-Wāsiʿī, was called *naẓārat al-waqf al-dākhilī*. Further, he states:

> The *awqāf* were neglected and the tribes (*al-qabāʾil*) took the harvest because the government did not exercise power. When the new *nāẓir* [al-Muṭāʿ] took over the position with the help from the [Ottoman]

124 Serjeant, "The Post Medieval and Early Modern History of Ṣanʿāʾ," in Serjeant and Lewcock (eds.), *Ṣanʿāʾ*, 90.

125 Anon., *Ḥawliyāt Yamaniyya*, 314.

126 He was also the *muftī* of *al-Ḥanafiyya*.

127 Anon., *Ḥawliyāt Yamaniyya*, 365.

128 b. 1848 or 1849, d. 1942 or 1943.

129 Anon., *Ḥawliyāt Yamaniyya*, 527. He may be the same person mentioned in *Ḥawliyāt Yamaniyya*, 364, if not, Aḥsan al-ʿAmrī was *nāẓir al-awqāf* in the year 1890.

130 al-Ḥajarī, *Masājid Ṣanʿā*, 65.

131 Anon., *Ḥawliyāt Yamaniyya*, 527. Here, the *Hawliyyāt* refers to a version of the *Aʾimma* that I do not have, 1:2:143. As for al-Muṭāʿ being a *nāẓir*, I have seen references in a contemporary court case to a *waqf* property at al-Rawḍa that refers to the "Muṭāʿī *waqf* register," *al-Miswadda al-Muṭāʿiyya* as an authoritative legal source. For his biography see Zabāra, *Nuzhat al-naẓar*, 466. There Zabāra states that he was both the "*naẓārat al-awqāf al-dākhiliyya wa-l-khārijiyya*" and that he was member of the administrative council under the Ottomans. Bāsha Ḥilmī imprisoned him for a long period until Imam Yaḥyā took over and set him free. Later al-Muṭāʿ became governor over the *qaḍāʾ* of Radāʿ.

> governor, they took back the control over the *awqāf* and punished those who had taken the *waqf*s.[132]

Al-Wāsiʿī adds that with the newly acquired funds they revived many mosques. Naturally, one must examine the historicity of such claims critically, but it is interesting to see how a central government is seen as necessary to enforce the correct flow of revenues. Henceforth, the division of the *waqf* administration is reflected in the titles: *nāẓir al-awqāf al-dākhiliyya* and *nāẓir al-awqāf al-khārijiyya*. In 1898–99 the Ottoman governor ordered the aforementioned *nāẓir al-awqāf al-dākhiliyya*, al-Sayyid ʿAlī l-Muṭāʿ al-Ṣanʿānī to step down and the *ʿulamāʾ* to choose another to fill the position.[133] Zayd [b. Aḥmad] al-Kibsī[134] was *nāẓir al-waqf al-khārijī*, but was dismissed by the Ottoman governor Aḥmad Faydī. Al-Kibsī died in 1898–99.[135] ʿAlī Aḥmad al-Mujāhid al-Ṣanʿānī[136] (d. 1910) was a secretary (*kātib*) of *al-waqf al-khārijī*, while the secretaryship of the *dākhilī waqf* was held by the Abū l-Rijāl family for the whole period.[137] Serjeant mentions that the *nāẓir al-awqāf al-khārijiyya* attended the bi-weekly "vilayet-council" held by the Ottoman governor and that this indicates the political importance of that role.[138] What power the *nāẓir al-awqāf al-khārijiyya* actually held, and over which geographical areas, is not known. For instance, could he demand to take the surplus of the mosques and religious schools? Or were these more visions and plans than reality? Perhaps the goal of the Ottomans was to "civilize" and standardize the *waqf* administration rather than to exploit it economically; however, according to the few sources reviewed here, it does not seem as if the Ottomans managed to change the system significantly.

3.10 *The Third* Waqf *Administration:* Nāẓir al-waṣāyā

There is a third type of administration, which is important, yet seldom mentioned during this period. In 1913–14 Muḥammad b. Yaḥyā b. Muḥammad al-Manṣūr died; Zabāra states that he was *nāẓir al-waṣāyā* in Sanaa, and that later he was *nāẓir al-waqf al-dākhilī* in Sanaa, though Zabāra does not

---

132 ʿAbd al-Wāsiʿ b. Yaḥyā l-Wāsiʿī, *Tārīkh al-Yaman al-musammā Farḥat al-humūm wa-l-ḥuzn fī ḥawādith tārīkh al-Yaman* (Sanaa: Maktabat al-Irshād, 2007), 255.

133 al-ʿAmrī and Serjeant, "Administrative Organisation," 153 n11.

134 Also mentioned in Anon., *Ḥawliyāt Yamaniyya*, 314.

135 al-ʿAmrī and Serjeant, "Administrative Organisation," 153 n11.

136 Zabāra states that he was also a judge for the "Turks" in the area of al-Ḥayma. Muḥammad b. Muḥammad b. Yaḥyā Zabāra, *Aʾimmat al-Yaman bi-l-qarn al-rābiʿ ashar li-l-hijra* (Cairo: al-Maṭbaʿa al-Salafiyya wa-Maktabatuhā, n.d.), 2:1:156.

137 Zabāra, *Nashr al-ʿarf*, 1:142.

138 al-ʿAmrī and Serjeant, "Administrative Organisation," 153. *Aʾimma*, 1:2:215. (Serjeant refers to *Aʾimma* 2:2:215.).

state exactly when he held these positions.[139] Sayyid Muṣṭafā Sālim quotes a document from late 1899 with Muḥammad b. Yaḥyā l-Manṣūr's signature as *nāẓir waṣāyā*.[140] In July 1912, shortly after the Daʿʿān treaty, there was a *nāẓir al-waṣāyā* under Imām Yaḥyā by the name Muḥammad b. Yaḥyā l-Yadūmī.[141] The house (*bayt*) of al-Manṣūr is one of the scholarly *sayyid* houses and has held the position of *nāẓir al-waṣāyā* for several subsequent periods and does so until today.

As already discussed, the term *waṣāyā* has many meanings. In the 1930s, as we see below, Imam Yaḥyā further clarified this administrative category and it became equivalent to those *waqf*s that are administered by private administrators. (Thus type B in addition to type D in the four-field model at the beginning of this chapter.) At a certain point the idea arose that all *waqf*s with private *mutawallī*s (B/D) should be publicly supervised so that if the *mutawallī*s did not perform their task satisfactorily, the *nāẓir*, and here it is absolutely correct to use the term "inspector," could discover the mismanagement and take corrective action. We do not know whether or not this supervision actually involved following up and reviewing the accounts or merely the registration of assets. In addition, some of these *waqf*s were also without a beneficiary, or the beneficiary (such as that for a water cistern), disappeared or "ceased to exist." In such cases it is possible to argue that the public component of such *waqf*s could not be taken back by the founder's family. Thus there was a need to administer "lost" public *waqf*s, be it "lost" on the side of the founder, the administrator, or the beneficiary.

Many of the family *waqf*s (D) were very large and the important *sayyid* and *qāḍī* houses of Sanaa usually had extensive family *waqf*s. These were subject to much conflict as the rules for how the *waqf*s are to be shared follow genealogy and descent, which after a few generations of intermarriage become very

139 Zabāra, *Aʾimmat al-Yaman*, 2:1:296; Sayyid Muṣṭafā Sālim, *Wathāʾiq Yamaniyya: Dirāsa wathāʾiqiyya tārīkhiyya* (N.p.: al-Maṭbaʿa al-Fanniyya, 1985), 138–141. With regard to why this office appeared during the Ottoman occupation, one theory relates to the fact that for Ḥanafīs, private *waqf*s have a much more important official role because, according to Ḥanafī law, they are only private while the beneficiaries are alive. If the family line, or any other specific beneficiary die out, the *waqf* becomes an open, public *waqf*. Therefore, in Ḥanafī areas there was a strong incentive to register all private *waqf*s, in order to make sure they did revert to public *waqf*s and were not taken by private individuals. Thus the ideas and the practices of registering private *waqf*s would have been common administrative knowledge among the Ottomans. There is also a possibility that this practice was begun by Imam Yaḥyā, since his *waqf* administrators were appointed in 1911. In this case Muḥammad al-Manṣūr must have occupied these two positions for a very short time.

140 Sālim, *Wathāʾiq Yamaniyya*, 138.

141 Ibid., 228–231.

complicated. Many of the beneficiaries, including the women, were well educated and knew their legal rights and how to use legal arguments in the court system. There was therefore a need for someone in authority to register one's family *waqf* somewhere, and to ensure that everyone received the correct share. Much later, Messick refers to informants who note that Aḥmad al-Sayāghī, the local governor in Ibb in the 1940s, tried to force people to register their family *waqfs* under the supervision of the local branch of the *waṣāyā* administration.[142] Again, it must be pointed out that our estimate of the relative amount of the *waṣāyā* that was "supervised" is speculative; we only know of the existence of the term and the office itself. In fact, in the late Ottoman period, we do not know whether both of these tasks (supervising B or D) were actually ascribed to the *nāẓir al-waṣāyā*, nor do we know if it was first something local to Sanaa only, or if the geographical administrative jurisdiction was larger.

4 The *Waqf* Administration of Imam Yaḥyā and Imam Aḥmad (1911–62)

From the early twentieth century, we have access to more sources than in earlier periods. The following presentation of the *waqf* administration under Imam Yaḥyā's rule is divided chronologically and thematically.

Imam Yaḥyā claimed the imamate in 1904 when his father Imam al-Manṣūr bi-Llāh Muḥammad Ḥamīd al-Dīn died. Al-Manṣūr gathered support from the tribes in the northern areas in order to lead military campaigns against the Ottomans. He used the rhetoric of *jihād* and Zaydism to portray the Ottomans as unlawful occupants. At the time, the Ottomans mainly held Sanaa and the areas south and west of Sanaa. As early as 1906 Imam Yaḥyā suggested a compromise on how to divide the political power between him and the Ottomans.[143] The compromise was rejected, but the wording of one of the clauses in the compromise indicates the importance of the matter of the *awqāf*: Condition five concerns the transfer of the *awqāf*, "to our custody, so as to revive the education in this country."[144] Imam Yaḥyā also demanded the right to remove and appoint judges and the right to take the *zakāt* and to appoint local shaykhs to

142 Messick, "Transactions in Ibb," 252.

143 For a version of this compromise, see Zabāra, *A'immat al-Yaman*, 2:1:74–76. And al-Wāsi'ī, *Tārīkh al-Yaman*, 329.

144 Iḥālat al-awqāf ilā 'uhdatinā li-iḥyā' al-ma'ārif fī hādhihi al-bilād. The suggested compromise (*ṣulḥ*) is dated 4 August 1906. Zabāra, *A'immat al-Yaman*, 2:1:75.

collect it. These conditions were also meant to include Lower Yemen. The Ottomans refused. The next compromise, in 1911, was agreed upon and called the Treaty of Daʿʿān after the village in which it was signed. Article nine[145] states: "The matters of *awqāf* and *waṣāyā* are to be under the authority of the imam."[146] Both versions of the conditions indicate the political importance of the public *waqf* administration. In the following year, Imam Yaḥyā ordered the establishment of an appeal court (*maḥkamat al-istiʾnāf*) to be headed by Ḥusayn b. ʿAlī l-ʿAmrī. For the administration of the *awqāf*, Imam Yaḥyā appointed al-Sayyid Qāsim b. Ḥusayn al-ʿIzzī Abū Ṭālib[147] as *nāẓir li-awqāf Ṣanʿāʾ al-dākhiliyya*, al-Qāḍī ʿAbdallāh b. Qāsim al-Ghisālī l-Ṣanʿānī as *wakīl li-naẓārat al-awqāf al-khārijiyya*,[148] and al-Qāḍī Muḥammad b. Yaḥyā b. ʿAlī l-Yamānī as a *nāẓir al-waṣāyā bi-Ṣanʿāʾ*.[149] From the period of the late Qāsimī dynasty through the second Ottoman period, and well into the reign of Imam Yaḥyā until 1938–39, the secretaryship of the *waqf dākhilī* was kept in the Abī l-Rijāl family.[150]

As seen above, the court apparatus and the *waqf* administration began before the Ottomans pulled out in 1918, and it was only after their withdrawal that Imam Yaḥyā himself settled fully in Sanaa. In the course of the next decade, Imam Yaḥyā gained political control over Yemen in a way the Ottomans never did. He initiated reforms of the *waqf* administration in an effort to take control of poorly managed *waqfs* or those that had been taken over by private individuals. He also sought to control the surplus of several types of *waqf* and redirect these funds to other *waqfs* and indirectly, to other parts of the state budget. But in order to do this, he had to make new laws, and these were, in part, contrary to the Zaydī *madhhab*. The major changes did not come until the late 1920s and 1930s. Around this time, he ordered a much tighter grip on *waqf* administration, and demanded that *waqfs* be registered and accounted for; indeed, the surplus of entire types of *waqfs* was to be diverted to the state budget in Sanaa, more specifically so they could be "redirected" into other *waqfs* for education.

---

145 Article 10 as found in *Aʾimmat al-Yaman*, 2:1:205. In other works it seems to be article 9. The wording is the same.

146 "10—Takūnu masāʾil al-awqāf wa-l-waṣāyā manūṭatan bi-l-imām." *Aʾimmat al-Yaman*, 2:1:205. Interestingly, this time the *waṣāyā* are explicitly pointed out in addition to *waqf*.

147 See also Serjeant and Lewcock, *Ṣanʿāʾ*, 428. Thereby we know that he held that position at least until 1918.

148 The title indicates that he was not the *nāẓir*, but only a deputy of the *nāẓir*, or that the position was not officially called *nāẓir*, but the somewhat more modern *wakīl*. Undoubtedly, the Sanaa administration was much older and perhaps even more traditional than the newer *khārijī* administration.

149 The title indicates that this position had jurisdiction over Sanaa only. Zabāra, *Aʾimmat al-Yaman*, 2:1:232.

150 Zabāra, *Nashr al-ʿarf*, 1:139–142. This reference is also mentioned by Haykel, *Revival and Reform*, 70.

He founded al-Madrasa al-ʿIlmiyya, an Azhar-inspired and Ottoman-inspired state *sharīʿa* college that employed *ʿulamāʾ* as teachers, and produced judges, jurists, and administrators in a formalized school setting. In the following sections, we return to these questions in more detail.

4.1 *Taking Control Over Usurped, Unused, and "Lost" Public* Waqfs

Below is an entry (*maktab*) from a public *waqf* register (*miswadda*) that describes the legal process of "taking back" a *sabīl waqf.* The text describes a legal incident in which it was discovered that two private individuals, a man and a woman, had used *waqf* land without taking care of the *sabīl*, a duty entailed by that specific agricultural field. The governmental representatives gave them the choice between continuing to till the land and pay the full *waqf* rent, or taking the harvest themselves, but promising to maintain the *sabīl.* The fact that they were given this choice indicates that this practice was not considered a major crime, rather it was something that required a change in behaviour.

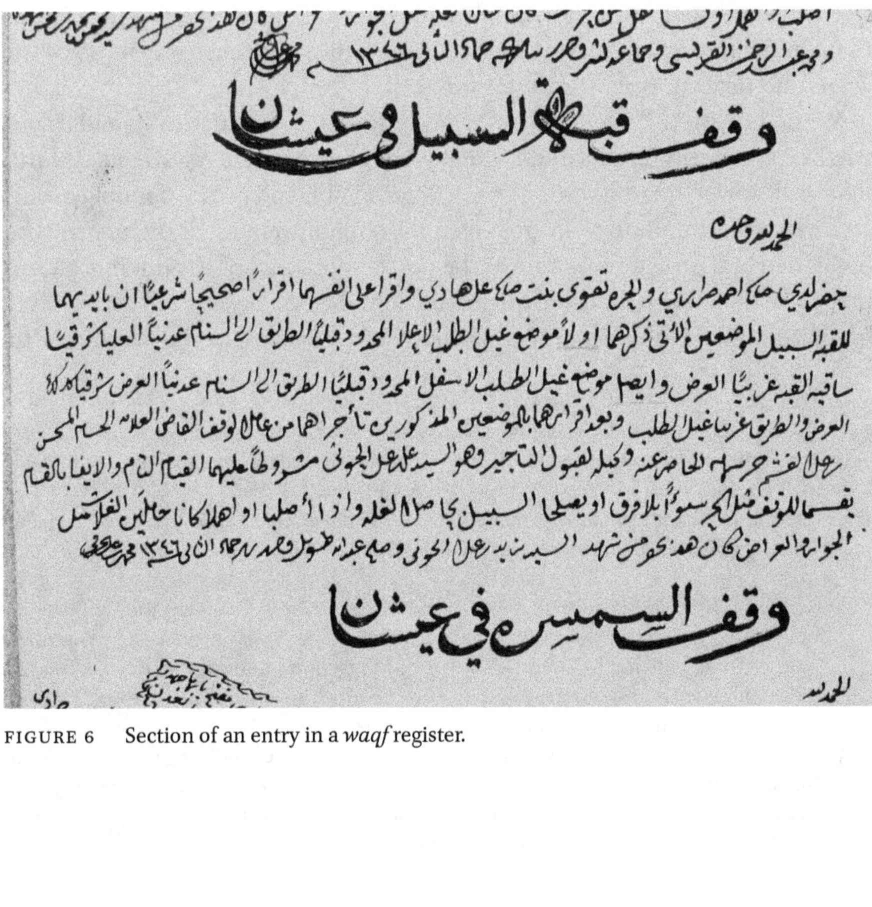
وقف قبلة السبيل في عيشان

الحمد لله وحده

وقف السمسرة في عيشان

FIGURE 6 Section of an entry in a *waqf* register.

Waqf for the Sabīl of the Qubba in ʿAyshān[151]

Thanks be to God, Him alone,

[line 1] The two came to me: Ṣāliḥ Aḥmad Ṣirārī and the free woman Taqwā, daughter of Ṣāliḥ ʿAlī Hādī, and they acknowledged (*aqarrā*) by themselves, a true, *sharʿī* acknowledgement (*iqrār*), that they are in possession of, [2] belonging to the *sabīl* of the *qubba*,[152] two pieces of land [4 ...] Then, after their acknowledgement of [possessing] the two aforementioned pieces of land, they rented them from the local public *waqf* administrator (*ʿāmil al-waqf*) al-Qāḍī l-ʿAllāma al-Ḥusām[153] al-Muḥsin [5] b. ʿAlī l-Ghāshm, [...] It is conditioned upon them [the tenants] that they either provide the full payment of the share[154] (*qisām*) of the harvest [... 6 ...] or, they can choose to take care of the *sabīl* with the provided income. [... 7 ...] This was witnessed by al-Sayyid Zayd b. ʿAlī l-Ḥūthī and Ṣāliḥ ʿAbdallāh Ṭawīl and was written in November/December 1927.[155]

The entry is only one of a list. By re-documenting such *waqf*s, or *waṣāyā*, the state ensured that local individuals could not take over *waqf*s and privatize them in the future. By creating these registers, the state had a way to "seize" the *waqf*s and take control of (*dabaṭa*) them.

We do not know if such reforms were carried out systematically, and if so, to what extent, in which areas, and which types of *waqf*s were registered. Unfortunately these documentary sources are not available today. The opening of such archives would undoubtedly give us a more comprehensive picture of what happened and provide a picture of the power dynamics of the imamic government and its strategy in these questions. In the case above, a key point would be that the *waqf* in question was perhaps not a *waṣīya*, in the sense that the

151 Most probably the village ʿAyshān, 10 km west of the city of Dhamār.

152 The word *qubba* means "dome"; often *sabīls* have a small dome as a roof and are therefore called *qubba*.

153 Here al-Ḥusām is a poetic title that is used before the name Muḥsin, just as al-ʿIzzī before Muḥammad, al-Ṣafiyy before Aḥmad and so on, cf. Serjeant and Lewcock, *Ṣanʿāʾ*, 428 n262.

154 Judging by the *fatwā* translated at the end of chapter 7, demanding the "full" share is quite strict unless this *waqf* was originally an "absolute" *waqf* in which the descendants of the founder did not hold any rights. The two persons mentioned above could also have been unrelated to the founder, i.e., they were tenants who had usurped the *waqf*. Since no *mutawallī* is mentioned, the latter is less probable.

155 The full translation is give in Hovden, "Flowers in *Fiqh*," appendix 2, 528–532. A copy of the document was given to the author by Aḥmad al-Siyānī (the keeper of the *waqf* registers, *ḥāfiz al-miswaddāt* in the ministry of *awqāf*. It was given as a photocopy on a sheet of A4 paper—the original format is not known.

tenants may not have had a right to the position as the *mutawallī* did, or they may not have had rights to parts of the rent.[156] In any case it is truly an act of "inspection" and systematic public correction of local *waqf* (mis)management.

Serjeant refers to another example of how Imam Yaḥyā sought to increase the income for the *waqf* in Sanaa. In 1918 the lease agreement between the *waqf* and the Jews for plots in the Jewish quarter, Qāʿ al-Yahūd, was re-negotiated. The old registers were taken out to confirm previous rental agreements, since these had not been kept up recently. In the process, the *waqf* administrators used legal arguments based on Zaydī *fiqh* to claim that since many of the assets in the form of plots of urban land were not properly delimited, and the distinction between *waqf* and private property had become blurred, the whole area should become public property (*al-maṣāliḥ*). This decision was enforced, whereupon the Imam sold back to the Jews the right to use the properties in the Jewish quarter.[157]

4.2 *Legal Changes*

Around the same time, legal changes started to take place: by invoking the Zaydī institution of *ikhtiyārāt* (lit., "choices") Zaydī doctrine allows and indeed expects the imam to produce laws in areas where *fiqh* remains open, and where the Zaydī Hādawī *madhhab* does not provide a strong consensus or where no "clear textual proof" (*nāṣṣ, ṣarīḥ, qaṭʿī*) exists in the revealed texts. The legal changes he made can be categorised into two related fields: one restricts the use of family *waqf* to prevent families from circumventing the inheritance rules, and a second empowers the state to re-group *waqf* beneficiaries[158] according to "public interest." The first was regarded as a part of his official *ikhtiyārāt* and the courts were ordered to follow them.[159] The second was not related to the judiciary in the same way, but were simply given as orders to the *waqf* administration. Imam Yaḥyā's legal innovations in this field have not

156 This is elaborated further in chapter 7.

157 Serjeant and Lewcock, *Ṣanʿāʾ*, 427–431.

158 This is a complicated topic that may be summarized: The principle is that the will of the founder must be respected, thus if this will is known and can be executed, then there is no doubt that this must be done, unless the *waqf* is invalid for some other reason. However, a multitude of potential problems can arise: for example, if the actual beneficiary ceases to exist, the question arises as to whether or not the family of the founder can take the *waqf* back, or, if the *waqf* should go to a similar beneficiary, or even to another type of beneficiary in another location. The basic view expressed in the *Sharḥ al-azhār* allows for the descendants of the founder to take the *waqf* back (as *waqf*, not as private property). Thus Imam Yaḥyā's legal view was clearly a way to limit this more local and flexible way of managing *waqf* in favour of the state overtaking "lost" *waqfs*.

159 This is elaborated upon in chapter 5.

been categorized as *ikhtiyārāt* as such,[160] yet they do appear as footnotes in *al-Tāj al-mudhhab*, the same way the *ikhtiyārāt* do.[161] Another related legal view condemned, on moral grounds, most overt aspects of saint worship; this served to support the legal decision whereby income from *waqfs* to maintain saints' graves and pay for festivals for saints could be taken by the state.

4.3 *The Creation of the Fourth* Waqf *Administration:* Awqāf al-Turab

Once Imam Yaḥyā had given himself the power to reorganize and take control of *waqfs* he also established a fourth *waqf* administration (*dā'ira*) parallel to the other three, namely the *turab*. *Turab* literally means "soil" and usually it refers to cemeteries and graveyards, but in Yemeni *waqf* administration the term refers to *turab al-awliyā'*, tomb complexes for saints and holy men. The cult of saints is mostly found in Shāfi'ī areas; it is common for a village to have one or more whitewashed domes in which a saint is buried and where local festivals and rituals are performed. Some of these are regionally famous, like that of Aḥmad b. 'Alwān near Ta'izz. Imam Yaḥyā made a decision that because worship of saints is religiously immoral, most of the *waqfs* for the maintenance of such tombs of saints should be registered by the state and the funds from these *waqfs* should be taken and diverted to other public purposes. The practice of saint worship generally occurs in Shāfi'ī areas and various other religious movements have opposed and condemned this as idolatry. The idea that *waqfs* for saints' graves were invalid was not new at Imam Yaḥyā's time, but it is the first time we know that administrative reform was implemented.[162] Thus a

160 For instance, they were not included in the list and commented upon by al-Shamāḥī: 'Abdallāh b. 'Abd al-Wahhāb al-Mujāhid al-Shamāḥī, *Ṣirāṭ al-'ārifīn ilā idrāk ikhtiyārāt amīr al-mu'minīn* (Sanaa: Maṭba'at al-Ma'ārif, 1937).

161 Aḥmad b. Qāsim al-Yamānī l-San'ānī l-'Ansī, *al-Tāj al-mudhhab li-aḥkām al-madhhab* (Sanaa: Maktabat al-Yaman al-Kubrā), 309–312. Here, al-Qāḍī Ḥusayn b. Aḥmad al-Sayāghī (d. 1806) is quoted by al-'Ansī. It is a short treatise that refers to *ḥadīths* and "public interest" in *fiqh* language; in sum, it validates the concept of "transfer" or "change" of the beneficiary of *waqfs* (*taḥwīl*). Al-'Ansī states that this legal view "is chosen" by the Imam (*yakhtāru al-jawāz*). The main argument is that this is a legal question for which no "clear text" exists and for which all *mujtahids* are correct, and therefore the question is open to interpretation by the imam.

162 Al-Shawkānī had strong opinions on the issue of the moral status of respecting various forms of graves and practices related to these. Doctrinally, he had to restrict his criticism because the Wahhābīs, his enemies, were also against grave visitation and in Lower Yemen the custom of grave visitation was a widespread aspect of local religious life. For this and more information concerning this topic in general, see Haykel, *Revival and Reform*, 127–138. Imam Yaḥyā and his close political allies may have been inspired by al-Shawkānī in this matter; the latter stated: "And similarly what exists of *awqāf* for graves: Verily they are devilish *waqf* (*ḥubs*) and misleading customs. It is has never been allowed (*lam yaḥill*) to

fourth parallel *waqf* administration was formed: *naẓārat awqāf al-turab*. Most of this seems to have been done in the name of "education," as the funds were mainly spent on the Madrasa al-ʿIlmiyya. As for the *turab* administration itself, there is fairly little information. Most of its funds came from Lower Yemen and it is unclear to what extent there was an *ʿāmil al-turab* in every district (*nāḥiya* at the time), or if the administrators of the *turab* were only present in certain areas. The job of *ʿāmil al-turab* was likely done simultaneously by whoever held the job of *ʿāmil al-waqf*.

4.4 *Al-Madrasa al-ʿIlmiyya,* Waqf *Education in Transition to Modernity*

In 1926, Imam Yaḥyā opened al-Madrasa al-ʿIlmiyya and a school for ophans in Sanaa. Al-Madrasa al-ʿIlmiyya was used to train bureaucrats and judges.[163] This school was to be the main beneficiary of the diverted *turab waqf* funds. Ever since, the ministry of education and the *turab waqf* have been connected. The ministry of education, the *turab waqf*, and the institutionalization of the *ʿulamāʾ* through al-Madrasa al-ʿIlmiyya hereafter formed a new "triangle" of power that merged *waqf* management with state finances and the reproduction of judicial knowledge. Imam Yaḥyā and his son Imam Aḥmad also built schools elsewhere in Yemen, for example in Taʿizz and Zabid, but their exact administrative relationship with al-Madrasa al-ʿIlmiyya is not known, though they probably also received their funding from the ministry of education. Al-Madrasa al-ʿIlmiyya was considered to be the highest state academy.

Ismāʿīl al-Akwaʿ states that the annual income for al-Madrasa al-ʿIlmiyya was about 50,000 *riyāls* (Maria Theresa silver thalers). The school paid the salaries of the teachers and many of the students (there were approximately 550 students) were given food and lodging.[164] Still, there was a considerable surplus and this was used to buy new agricultural land in the areas around Sanaa, which thereafter belonged to the *turab waqf*.[165] In addition, al-Madrasa al-ʿIlmiyya also possessed a good bit of land confiscated from the Ismaʿīlīs in the Ḥarāz Mountains west of Sanaa,[166] probably also organized through the

---

validate anything related to such *waqfs*, nor to keep quiet about them, indeed, the diverting of these to the public good for the Muslims (*maṣāliḥ al-muslimīn*) is one of the most important and necessary issues. If such a protest and invalidation is not done, then this is among the greatest sins … leading to a form of *shirk*." Muḥammad b. ʿAlī l-Shawkānī, *Adab al-ṭalab wa-muntahā l-arab*, ed. ʿAbdallāh b. Yaḥyā l-Surayḥī (Sanaa: Maktabat al-Irshād, Dār Ibn Ḥazm, 1998), 246.

163 See Messick, *Calligraphic State*, 108–109.

164 See also Messick, *Calligraphic State*, 107–114.

165 Here al-Akwaʿ mentions "Bānī Bahlūl, Bilād al-Rūs, Ṣanḥān and other areas."

166 He uses the term "Makārima" for the Ismāʿīlīs. Other terms commonly used are "al-Baṭiniyya." Al-Akwaʿ, *al-Madāris*, 402–403. The issue of land confiscation and converting

turab waqf. The first director of the al-Madrasa al-ʿIlmiyya was Luṭf b. Ghālib al-ʿAmrī who later became *mudīr* (director) of *awqāf* Dhamār and later also of *awqāf* Taʿizz.[167]

The systematization and centralisation of religious and judicial education had consequences; Vom Bruck quotes ʿAbdallāh al-Iryānī who states that the *waqf*[168] in their village, Hijrat al-Iryān (between Yarīm and Ibb), was originally controlled by a member of his family. Then, Imam Yaḥyā took over the *waqf* administration whereby the local mosque, which previously had teachers and students, was now left without a budget for these services and the local *sharīʿa* students had to go to Sanaa, to the al-Madrasa al-ʿIlmiyya. Further, he indicates that this was the case for other *hijras*[169] as well and that *ʿulamāʾ* in many *hijras* complained that they had to abandon their teaching. The flight of students was not only because of the lack of funds left in the *hijras*, but also because of the reputation and the high quality of al-Madrasa al-ʿIlmiyya.[170]

Not much is known about the actual local consequences of the centralisation of *waqf* funds and how this differed in other areas of Yemen. Most schools in the *hijras* and the mosques in the rural areas were very small and informal; often the mosque itself was used as a school (*miʿlama*), or a simple room adjacent to it served the purpose. The teaching positions were rarely full-time or even formalized. It is simply not known to what extent these registration and centralisation reforms were actually carried out and in what geographical areas. In addition, we do not know who may have been able to resist the reforms.[171] By quoting travel accounts from the mid 1900s, Würth suggests that literacy had been much higher in the past, but that after the centralisation of the *waqf* it dropped to a minimum because the many local schools had to close.[172] This is probably an overstatement of the effect of the *waqf* reforms. We simply do not know if these reforms were applied consistently in all geographical

it to *waqf* is also mentioned briefly by Mijallī, who states that the Zaydī state has several times confiscated property "of the Baṭiniyya in Ḥarāz." Mijallī, *al-Awqāf fī l-Yaman*, 25.

167 al-Akwaʿ, *al-Madāris*, 414.

168 Note the use of the term "the" *waqf*. This is an example of a local "public" *waqf* cluster similar to that of Sanaa or Dhamār, but smaller, probably native to the *hijra*.

169 *Hijra, hijar: sayyid* villages/towns where scholarly activities took place, usually enclaves in otherwise tribal territory.

170 Vom Bruck, *Islam, Memory, and Mortality*, 285 n25; Vom Bruck, "Disputing Descent-Based Authority in the Idiom of Religion: The Case of the Republic of Yemen," *Social Anthropology* 4, no. 2 (1998), 165.

171 In this context vom Bruck states that Imam Yaḥyā "strengthened some favoured Zaydī enclaves, notably Sa'da, Huth, Dhamar, Thula, and Shahara," but she does not give references. Vom Bruck, "Disputing Descent-Based Authority," 167 n38.

172 Würth, *Ash-sharīʿa fī bāb al-Yaman*, 60–62.

areas or to what extent they were applied. Further, she argues that the change in state control over the production of judicial knowledge (as in the Madrasa al-ʿIlmiyya) did not mark a fundamental break with the past in terms of knowledge; clearly, when examining the curriculums, we see that the content remained quite similar to what was taught in *sharīʿa* schools before the Madrasa al-ʿIlmiyya was founded.[173] We can reasonably conclude that along with the transfer of *waqf* funds to Sanaa, *some* power over education, both primary and advanced legal education, was transferred along with it. But the transfer was certainly not enough to extinguish private *sharīʿa* schools and non-state practices of transferring and reproducing judicial knowledge. Far more research is needed in order to say anything more accurate. Other societal changes during the period of Imam Yaḥyā, including the growth in population and historical change in the rural economy, make it difficult to construct a contra-factual history of what might have happened if Imam Yaḥyā's reforms had not been enacted. Additional studies are needed to understand the importance of these local education *waqfs*, what role they played in general literacy rates, for advanced education, in intellectual life, and how they were actually affected by the *waqf* reforms. More general but related questions could be raised about the role of the *hijras* and local Islamic schools and what role the *waqf* still has in the management of these, especially in the core Zaydī areas.

4.5 *A Decree Organising the* Awqāf *Administration, 1937*

The Madrasa al-ʿIlmiyya opened in 1926 and was, presumably, in immediate need of financial income. Exactly when the first *turab waqf* reforms were initiated is not known. The first "ministries" were created in 1937 and first minister of education was Imam Yaḥyā's son, prince[174] (*Sayf al-Islām*) ʿAbdallāh. In a decree[175] dated 1937 addressed to the inspectors of the *khārijī*, the *turab*, and the *waṣāyā* administrations, the three inspectors were requested to identify certain types of *waqf*, to register them, to initiate plans to supervise them, and

173 This is a general statement, but still fairly easy to verify by looking at traditional curriculums as portrayed in the biographical dictionaries and comparing them with the curriculum in al-Madrasa al-ʿIlmiyya.

174 Over the years Imam Yaḥyā changed the rhetoric from one of a Zaydī imamate more in direction of a kingdom (*mamlaka*), officially known as the Mutawakkilite Kingdom. The crown prince was called *walī l-ʿahd*. Haykel, *Revival and Reform*, 210–212. With regard to the princes being called *Sayf al-Islām*, this seems to be an older tradition going back to the Qāsimīs.

175 An electronic copy of the letter was kindly provided by a high-ranking official in the ministry of *awqāf*; ʿAlī Muḥammad al-Farrān; it will be published in the appendix of his forthcoming book. Al-Farrān, *al-Awqāf wa-l-tanmīya fī l-Yaman*. The decree is edited and translated in Hovden, "Flowers in *Fiqh*," appendix 3, 532–540.

also to present all accountancies for the imam's review, or literally, "the noble gaze" or "scrutiny" (*al-naẓar al-sharīf*). The decree orders the registration of all *waqf*s, regardless of type. It mentions three categories of inspectors, with their own separate administrations and accounting, but with some revenue shared among them. The *dākhilī* administration is not mentioned, probably because it was already fairly organised and not in need of reform. The three other separate, parallel administrations mentioned in the decree are *khārijī waqf*s, *turab waqf*s, and the *waṣāyā waqf*s.

4.6 *The* Khārijī Waqfs

This refers to the *waqf*s of individual mosques or larger clusters of mosques in areas outside Sanaa. The decree states that the surplus from such *waqf*s is to be taken by the *khārijī* administration after the needs of the mosque are taken care of. What we know from other sources is that from this time and until today, the local caretaker of the mosque must present requests to the *waqf* administration in order to cover his expenses.[176] It is important to remember that in practice, mosques could also have local private *mutawallī*s (contrary to the decree), and many smaller village mosques tend to be of this type.[177] It is not known to what degree these smaller and more private mosque *waqf*s were brought under imamic supervision, either before or after this reform. There may have been geographical differences in this as well. Even when mosques were registered and included under the *khārijī* administration, local elites administering them could still have under-reported the surpluses or over-reported the actual expenditures. The power to define the "needs" of a certain mosque was, to a large extent, dependent on the local political context.

4.7 *The* Turab Waqfs

The *turab waqf*s were a new category created by Imam Yaḥyā; they still exist under a separate administration today. According to the decree, the *turab* consists of the following types: (1) *khāliṣa*, or "absolute": This refers to tomb complexes with tombs only. In these, all the income of the *waqf*s is to be taken. (2) *Mukhtalaṭa* refers to mixed tomb/mosque complexes: in these, the mosque is

176 According to informants, this is clearly the case today. I have seen mosque employees coming to the ministry to complain that the local *mudīr waqf* had to sign the requests to buy daily necessities for the mosque. The situation in Imam Yaḥyā's time is indicated in Manṣūr, *al-Mawkib*, 159.

177 Even if some of the *waqf* fields for such a smaller village mosque were registered and entered into the *khārijī* administration, this does not mean that the mosque did not have funding from other, privately managed *waqf*s, or other sources like gifts. The smaller village mosques, without imams and *mu'adhdhins*, did not require much regular income.

to be maintained according to local tradition (but not more than half of the income of the *waqf*), and the rest is to go to the *turab* administration budget. Expenses for the mosques are to be clarified by the *khārijī waqf* accountancy, and also clarified by the *turab waqf* accountancy.[178] (3) *Waqf mundaris, munqaṭiʿ al-maṣrif*[179] refers to all types of unused *waqfs* with a public purpose, or unused *waqfs* for which no one makes a legal claim. The income of these *waqfs* was redirected to the "public good" (*al-maṣāliḥ*). It would not be valid to take funds out of the *waqf* realm and enter them into the treasury (*bayt al-māl*). Imam Yaḥyā therefore established the ministry of education as the main recipient of the *turab waqfs* generally, and al-Madrasa al-ʿIlmiyya in particular, since public education could be defined as a new beneficiary. Thus he redirected the *waqf* income while the *waqf* assets remained *waqfs* (as before), separate from other state revenue sources.[180]

4.8 *The* Waṣāyā Waqfs

The concept of the *waṣāyā* was very clearly defined in the decree of 1937. These consist of *waqfs* with private *mutawallīs* and can be of two main types: Public non-mosque beneficiaries such as *sabīls*, village reception rooms (*dawāwīn*), food for the poor, etc. (type B). Or, they could be private, such as family *waqfs* (type D). Both were allowed to remain in effect if they were made for a specific beneficiary and with a valid legal purpose, but they were all required to be registered "whenever they became known" to the *waṣāyā* administration, and they were to be inspected by the *nāẓir al-waṣāyā*. Actually, the word *mutawallī* is not mentioned in the decree at all, and the decree leaves the reader with the sense that private guardianship is simply irrelevant. In practice, however, the *waṣāyā* meant any *waqf* in which there could exist a private *mutawallī*.

178 It is not known whether these mosques are then paid by the general *khārijī* budget and managed by the *khārijī* administration, but this seems logical.

179 *Mundaris* means "disappeared." *Munqaṭiʿ al-maṣrif* means that the *waqf*, for some reason or another, is "cut off" from its beneficiary, e.g., the beneficiary has "disappeared." According to the Zaydī *madhhab*, *waqfs* that no longer have beneficiaries revert to the descendants of the founder, but only as *waqf*, not as property. There is much disagreement around this question and the famous al-Mu'ayyad Aḥmad b. al-Ḥusayn (d. 411/1020) states that they should go to the public good "*al-maṣāliḥ*." Here, Imam Yaḥyā takes the Zaydī stand by allowing descendants of the founder to take the *waqf* back, and by confirming that the rule above only refers to *waqfs* (or rather *waṣāyā*) where no such claims exist. In these cases the "someone" who has taken the *waqf* is usually the tenant and his descendants. This requires that the existence of the *waqfs* be "proven" either by old registers of by public memory (*shuhra*).

180 These three types of *turab waqfs* are also mentioned in Messick, "Transactions in Ibb," 254.

If no *mutawallī* existed, the *waqf* belonged to the *turab* in cases of "confiscated" *waqfs*. Other non-mosque *waqfs* that were still allowed to operate were to be under the *waṣāyā* administration. Thus all types of *waqf* would belong to one of the aforementioned categories, and be supervised by the imam and his appointed inspectors according to the decree.

If the decree is interpreted correctly, the latter of the two types of *waṣāyā* mentioned, the family *waqfs*, or perhaps even all the *waṣāyā* are to surrender one-third of their income to the *waṣāyā* administration. Perhaps the ministry of education was in need of more income than it could get from the *turab*. The appropriation of this third from the *waṣāyā* is not mentioned anywhere else and we do not know if this part of the decree was ever executed. It is even harder to believe that this third referred to all types of *waṣāyā*.[181] It is unlikely that this would have been accepted; rather the third that was to be taken likely became much smaller.[182] Even the registration reform of the *waṣāyā* does not seem to have taken place completely. More investigation is necessary in order to reveal this, and access to the *waṣāyā* archives is required. Many of the powerful families refused to register their *waqfs* altogether and until today continue to administer them themselves.[183] The legal restrictions on family *waqfs* made by Imam Yaḥyā also led to the invalidation and privatization of a large part of such *waqfs*.[184] Thus the number of such *waqfs* greatly declined from the late 1930s.

According to this decree the office of the *waṣāyā* administration is different from the others (the *khārijī* and the *turab* administration), in that it had few or small *waqfs* of its own,[185] it inspected the management and revenue flows

181 Usually, a family *waqf* cannot have a surplus because if the harvest increases in a certain year, the beneficiaries simply receive more that year. As stated in the decree, the *nāẓir al-waṣāyā* also controlled local charity and food *waqfs*, and these could potentially have a surplus after local needs were covered. The third to be taken could be from such a surplus, or this third could be the sharecropping fraction of the harvest that was to be submitted to the *nāẓir*, while the tenants (who are often the descendants of the founder) are allowed to keep the rest. The term used, *al-rājiʿ*, was also the term noted by Dresch as the part a shaykh could keep from the taxes he collected. Dresch, *Tribes*, 228.

182 It could be the 2.5 per cent that al-Abdin refers to that was taken by the inspector. Al-Abdin, "The Role of Islam," 219.

183 This is also supported by findings from Ibb, as presented by Messick, "Transactions in Ibb," 165–166. There is no doubt that such family *waqfs* still exist, but we simply do not know how widespread the phenomenon was, and in which areas it was practiced.

184 This issue is treated in chapter 5.

185 We do not know to what extent there existed "non-mosque type A" in which no private individual claimed the right to administer it and so it was fully taken over by the *nāẓir al-waṣāyā*. However, one should not rule out the possibility that this could be the case in some geographical areas or in some specific cases. In yearly rent registers of recent years

of non-mosque *waqfs*. Again, it is important to point out that little is known about the actual implementation of this decree.

4.9 *Administration in Practice*

During the reign of Imam Yaḥyā, we see a definite change in policy, as exemplified by the decree, which clearly illustrates the states' aspirations to take more direct control over *waqf* by taking potential surplus, redirecting certain *waqf* funds, and confiscating unused *waqfs* or those being used for activities considered unorthodox. All this was undertaken by the administrative instruments of registers (*miswaddāt, dafātir*) and by the creation of new administrations parallel to the existing one(s). All *waqfs* had to be inspected and presented for the "imamic gaze" *al-naẓar al-sharīf*. An all-inclusive register of several volumes was made, called the comprehensive register (*al-miswadda al-shāmila*).[186]

Each *nāẓir* had local representatives, usually at the district level (*nāḥiya*) called *ʿāmil* (pl. *ʿāmilūn* or *ʿummāl*), who in turn sent their accounts to their respective *nāẓirs* in Sanaa every year.[187] In rich agricultural areas there were sometimes several *ʿāmils*, and they in turn may have had several assistants and secretaries or even agents (*wakīl, wukalāʾ*) under them.[188] This system does not seem to have been fully and consistently applied, but rather was applied in those areas where there were many *waqfs* that were productive, and where opposition to the government did not destroy the larger project of collecting taxes and *waqf* funds—mainly Lower Yemen (areas around the cities of Ibb and Taʿizz), the western mountains, the Tihāma, and the highland plains

---

(similar to appendix 8 in Hovden, "Flowers of *Fiqh*") I have seen the category "*waṣāyā and turab*." This could indicate that some *waqfs* do belong to the *waṣāyā*. Perhaps they were once confiscated. Here it is important to note that many of the non-mosque "public" *waqfs* were, in practice, combined *waqfs* in which the family of the founder had significant rights, as elaborated upon in chapter 7. For instance the family of the founder could have the right to the surplus after the mosque has been taken care of.

186 I could not obtain access to this, I was only told about its existence. So I cannot know how "inclusive" it was; it could also be a patchwork of previous registers, but it is fair to expect that the reforms initiated by Imam Yaḥyā necessitated new, updated inventory registers. Needless to say, such registers are fundamental information for historians, and hopefully one day they will be available.

187 Manṣūr, *al-Mawkib*, 159. I have seen such books, and have some copies of letters summing up the end of each year, written from the local *ʿāmil* to the *nāẓir* in Sanaa, stating something like "I hereby send—amount of the income of the *waqfs* from such and such agricultural fields." The answer and approval by Sanaa is written on the same page.

188 An example is that of al-Jabīn, Rayma, where there is still one *ʿāmil al-waqf* and one *ʿāmil al-waṣāyā*. Or, as they are officially called today, *mudīr*. Yet, it should be noted that several informants there told me of privately administered *waqfs* that have no relationship to the state.

around Sanaa and south of Sanaa. The populations in areas north and east of Sanaa were more rebellious and we do not have much information about the *waqf* administration there. Local *hijras* (*sayyid* enclaves) probably had their own local *waqf* administration in these areas. The city of Sa'da is known to have many *waqfs*, but it is unlikely that the state in Sanaa was able to interfere in these the way it did in the areas further south. In some areas, the *ʿāmils* systematically sent out crop assessors (*khurrāṣ, qubbāl, ṭuwwāf*) to estimate (*kharṣ, ṭiyāfa*) the size of the crop before the harvest. This was similar to what was done in the *zakāt* collection system, which was in many ways parallel to the *waqf* revenue. The *zakāt* collection system also consisted of local *ʿāmils* (not *ʿāmil waqf*, but *ʿāmil zakāt*) who also typically received one-tenth of the income, much like the *waqf ʿāmils*.[189] These positions were assigned or taken away by the imam and his closest ministers, although often the local elites were in the best position to extract the full potential from both the *waqf* and from the *zakāt*.

In the early years of Imam Yaḥyā's reign it seems that each mosque in Sanaa still had a specified amount of income. In al-Ḥajarī's book about the mosques of Sanaa, he mentions that the well-known mosque called Qubbat Ṭalḥa was one of the best-equipped mosques in Sanaa, with beautiful carpets and furnishing, and plenty of running water.[190] This was written about a time before the more systematic and centrally controlled administration began to take control of the *waqfs*. We know that around 1930 Crown Prince Aḥmad (later imam) finished the *waqf* reforms in Zabid and took control over the "Ayyūbī and Rasūlī" *waqfs* and ordered them to be spent on schools and mosques.[191] In 1933 Imam Yaḥyā finished the restoration of the important public water supply basin (*siqāya ʿāmma*) outside the Abhar Mosque in Sanaa and attached *waqfs* to the water basin for its maintenance.[192] He also established the *waqf* library in Sanaa, collected manuscripts and books, made the *waqf* for various mosques, and placed them in a new storey above the south wing of the Jāmiʿ al-Kabīr, which then became a public library.[193]

189 Even today *waqf ʿāmils* receive a similar amount and even far higher if they also administer the upkeep of their local mosques.

190 al-Ḥajarī, *Masājid Ṣanʿā*, 76.

191 Zabāra, *A'immat al-Yaman*, 2:2:332.

192 Ibid. This was a very large *sabīl* that supplied water for much of the southern part of the city. For a description of the construction of the *sabīl* at Abhar see al-Ḥajarī, *Masājid Ṣanʿā*, 9–10.

193 For more information about the library, see Messick, *Calligraphic State*, 119–123.

4.10 *The* Waqf *Administration Under Imam Aḥmad (1948–62)*

The creation of the first ministry of *awqāf* was initiated in 1948 when Imam Aḥmad took over after his father, Imam Yaḥyā, was assassinated. Shelagh Weir refers to an interesting document described as a "pledge of allegiance," dated 1948 from Jabal Rāziḥ in the very northwest of Yemen. It was written by the local shaykhs and notables and included a list of conditions that the local shaykhs optimistically hoped the new imam would accept. For instance, they suggest that the shaykhs keep one-fifth of the *zakāt* revenue themselves (twice as much as before), and more importantly, that "heirs should control the proceeds of family *waqf*s."[194] The mere mention of this topic implies that state control over family *waqf*s had been an issue under Imam Yaḥyā, even in areas as distant as Rāziḥ. We do not know whether or not this was accepted for Jabal Rāziḥ, but Messick states that in Ibb, in the period under Imam Aḥmad the governor Aḥmad al-Sayāghī forcibly registered family *waqf*s under the *waṣāyā* administration.[195] Such measures were probably easier to carry out in the areas under the strongest direct state control, such as in the major cites and Lower Yemen.

The first minister of *awqāf* after the ministry was established in 1948 was al-Sayyid ʿAbd al-Qādir b. ʿAbdallāh b. ʿAbd al-Qādir (1908–2004). ʿAbd al-Qādir was first *nāẓir al-awqāf al-ḥaramayn* during Imam Yaḥyā's time and held this position until 1962.[196] However, immediately after 1948, he was given the position as a minister of *awqāf*.[197]

In general the period of Imam Aḥmad saw a continuation of the policy of his father. Imam Aḥmad moved the capital to Taʿizz and Lower Yemen became the focus of new, minor *waqf* reforms. Aḥmad al-Sayāghī,[198] the governor of Ibb, initiated local administrative reforms and opened "offices" (*maktabāt al-awqāf*) in Ibb, Taʿizz, and Zabid to serve as sub-branches of the ministry. The

194 Document D1948: "Al-Naẓīr pledge loyalty to Imām Aḥmad Ḥamīd al-Dīn, with conditions," Weir, *Tribal Order*, 273.

195 Messick, "Transactions in Ibb," 252.

196 In Wādī Zabid there is a particularly sizeable *waqf* for the two holy cities. However, it does not seem to be common elsewhere. Some informants say that all *waqf*s that benefit these cities were included in the general *waqf* budget after the revolution, to be spent inside Yemen, since from this time on Yemen was much poorer than Saudi Arabia, and for some years since 1962 it was also at war with them. It is no surprise that al-Abdin found this type of *waqf* here, since he bases himself on the Tesco report which focuses on Wādī Zabid.

197 Manṣūr, *al-Mawkib*, 185. For a full biography, see Vom Bruck, where he describes his career as a student, *ʿālim*, and state employee. Vom Bruck, *Islam, Memory, and Mortality*.

198 Al-Qāḍī Aḥmad b. Aḥmad, born in Saʿda in 1905–06. He was a governor of Ibb and famous for administering the building of the new road in the Sumāra pass, thus connecting Ibb to Sanaa. He died in Marib fighting during the civil war in 1964. Zabāra, *Nuzhat al-naẓar*, 58.

local *waqf* administration was reorganized into one administration (*dāʾira*) merged under one *mudīr waqf*, and the separate accountancies of the three previously separate administrations were retained. At this time and well into the 1970s, much of the local *waqf* economy was still taken, stored, and paid in sorghum grain.[199]

In Zabid, two informants related to the present-day *waqf* administration claimed that it was in this period and under the orders of Ḥusayn al-Sayāghī that the old *waqf* registers were taken to Sanaa, among them the *miswadda al-Rasūliyya, miswadda al-Manṣūriyya*, and one *miswadda* from the period of al-Mahdī l-ʿAbbās (d. 1189/1775).[200] The *waṣāyā* registers were taken to Sanaa shortly after the revolution in 1962 and only copies were left in Zabid.[201] With regard to the many *waqf*s in Zabid, other informants there also claimed that the city was given the amount of 100,000 *riyāl*s to maintain the mosques and schools and anything in excess of this was sent to Sanaa.[202]

Because this period is closer to the present, it is much more controversial to research and write about because "what actually happened" to specific *waqf* assets and areas of land many not coincide with "what should have happened." Compared to the number of sources that should be available, few sources can be found. Legal documents from this period could still be valid in court. Little has been published about the history of *waqf* from this period, despite the presence of living informants. From this point on, the politics of information of what actually happened is part of contemporary politics, and many actors are reluctant to speak, much less provide documents. Memories and documents from this period are still binding and valid evidence in court.

At this time the *nāẓir al-waṣāyā* was Muḥammad b. Muḥammad al-Manṣūr (d. 2016),[203] a position he has held more or less continuously until today.[204] In 1949 Imam Aḥmad visited Bayt al-Faqīh north of Zabid and "took control over"

199 Messick, "Transactions in Ibb," 162–168, 246–265.

200 I could not confirm this in Sanaa, though several other informants claimed that a certain al-Sayāghī did bring all original *waqf* documents he could find to the capital Taʿizz and subsequently to Sanaa. Ḥusayn al-Sayāghī became minister of *awqāf* after the revolution in 1962 and continued to hold the post during the civil war years, thus the exact timing is unclear and his work with the *waqf* administration and reform stretches over a long time period.

201 I have seen one such handwritten copy of a *miswadda* in Zabid; it contains the wording of individual *waqf* documents, in entries one after the other. I have photocopies of four such entries concerning water supply *waqf*s, mainly *waqf* for the maintenance of public wells.

202 Personal communication with historian ʿAbduh ʿAlī Hārūn, Zabid, 26 December 2009.

203 Born in 1915. He was also a minister of justice and held the position as minister of *awqāf* in 1978.

204 Personal communication with Muḥammad al-Manṣūr, Sanaa, January 2010.

awqāf there (*kharaja, ḍabaṭa*) and built a school.[205] The year after, the *awqāf* in Radāʿ, southeast of Dhamār, were "taken back from the locals" (*ikhrāj*) by its governor al-Sayyid ʿAlī l-Muṭāʿ.[206] These types of statements are typical of the historical narratives often found in the biographical encyclopaedia that describe the pious and just notables as agents acting against corrupt local elites and on behalf of religion and the common good; for these reasons they "took back" the *waqf* properties and "revived" the *waqf*. The counter narratives, namely that such and such person usurped *waqf* land also circulate as common knowledge, but only in more confined, personal settings.

5 The Ministry of *Awqāf* After the Revolution (1962–)

5.1 *The 1962 Revolution and the Following Civil War*

During the 1962 revolution and the years of civil war that followed, the *waqf* administration lost much of its legitimacy and power. The war mainly took place in the northern areas, while the western mountains, Dhamār and Lower Yemen, were not affected as much as the tribal north. When the new governments in the late 1960s and in the beginning of the 1970s sought to resume and reform administration, many documents and registers were lost. Many of the former employees, or rather those with the right to a percentage of *waqf*s, wanted to retain their positions and rights. If we imagine the creation of the new republican ministry as the top of a pyramid, we must bear in mind that only the top part of the pyramid was new. The base of the pyramid, the hundreds of local public *waqf* administrators, continued to a large extent in their positions, although the overall position of the *waqf* institution was weaker and much *waqf* land was usurped. The areas immediately around the cities saw a very fast urban development and agricultural fields were a source for building plots. When the revolution started in 1962 it was much influenced by and based on Egyptian Arab socialism. Many saw the *awqāf*, its practices and administration, as something connected to the oppressive, primitive past.

The previous state *waqf* administration before the revolution had been strongest in areas where the state had a significant control, especially Lower Yemen, and the state had used the *waqf* institution to channel funds from rural areas towards Sanaa. When the new ministry of *awqāf* was established, it had to determine its responsibilities. Would it be right to continue to transfer *waqf* funds from Lower Shāfiʿī Yemen? Some tentative decrees and laws were made,

205 Zabāra, *A'immat al-Yaman*, 2:2:251.

206 Ibid., 2:2:269.

but it took many years after the civil war ended (around 1968) before the ministry grew to become what it is today. The first minster was al-Qāḍī ʿAbd al-Salām Muḥammad Zabāra, who was also a member of the *Majlis qiyādat al-thawra* ("the leadership committee of the revolution"). The ministry was named, first, the ministry of *awqāf* and social affairs (Wizārat al-awqāf wa-l-shu'ūn al-ijtimāʿiyya). Then after a month, the last part was substituted for "tribal affairs" (Shu'ūn al-qabā'il), which was soon removed, leaving only Wizārat al-awqāf. The term *irshād*, "guidance," was not added until 1978: Wizārat al-awqāf wa-l-irshād.

5.2 *The Early Formative Years (1968–78)*

From 1968 onwards several decrees and laws were issued regarding the organisation of the ministry. However, no new *waqf* law (as a contractual law regulating the legal phenomenon as such) was issued until 1976; so until that point the 68 *qarārāt* that the appeal court had issued in 1970 remained in effect.[207]

The first decree organising the new ministry was the republican decree no. 26 of 1968 which was issued to structure the administration in the ministry; it was made at the request of the then minister al-Qāḍī Muḥammad b. Luṭf al-Ṣabāḥī. Article 3 stated that the ministry was to have authority over the charitable *waqf*s that were not managed by the descendants of founders and over *waqf*s in which the beneficiaries were no longer known.[208]

Ministerial decree no. 20 of 1968 concerns the formation of a judiciary committee for the administration of guardianship in questions of *waqf*, presented by the same minister of *awqāf*. The republican decree no. 73 of 1969 gave the ministry an administrative structure, though this was not very detailed: the minister, his deputy (*wakīl*), and the administrations (*idārāt*):

1. a common administration for *awqāf* matters,
2. an administration for *waqf al-waṣāyā* (*subul, wa-l-qirā'a, wa-duwar al-ḍiyāfa*), and
3. an administration for the administration and economy.[209]

Later, additional administrative sections were added, among them, an administration for religious matters and guidance (*irshād*), a general administration for the identification and registration of *waqf* assets (*ḥaṣr*), and a general

207 These mainly concerned the issue of family *waqf* and are treated in chapter 5.

208 Manṣūr, *al-Mawkib*, 186.

209 Ibid., 285.

administration for investments and technical issues. Ministerial decree no. 100 of 1969 further specified some of the responsibilities of the ministry.[210]

The first *waqf* law was the "leading council's decree no. 78 of 1976 concerning *waqf*"; this was almost identical to the one in place today. It is the product of the codification committee and its language and content follow Zaydī *fiqh* quite closely. This was followed by the "leading council's decree no. 63 of 1977 concerning the organisation of the ministry of *awqāf* and definition of its field of responsibility." It was made by Muḥammad Luṭf al-Ṣabāḥī, and it elaborates on the organisational structure and strategies for the future. After these decrees, many years passed without new decrees, until law no. 7 of 1987 concerning the reorganisation of the ministry of *awqāf* and *irshād* and the definition of its responsibilities.[211]

Historically, the judges held the power to decide *waqf* questions, outside those limits that the validated *fiqh*[212] gives to any *mutawallī*. Early on, in 1968 with decree no. 26, a committee was formed. Members included the minister of *awqāf*, the president of the appeal court, and various other ministers.[213] This committee gave the ministry the power that had previously been in the hands of a *sharīʿa* judge (*ḥākim sharʿī*). This committee was to discuss and decide upon matters relating to *waqf* asset exchanges (*badal, istibdāl*), matters related to the definition of worthy beneficiaries, matters of record keeping (*istidāna*), and the approval of leases of *waqf* assets longer than three years. The committee could decide on these matters without relying on a court or a judge.[214] The committee was the theoretical, conceptual bridge between the ministry, the state, and the *sharīʿa*-based judiciary and it also constitutes the political leadership of the ministry. It was given the powers of a *sharīʿa* judge, as it was essentially a *mutawallī* and a judge at the same time. After 1986 it was called *al-majlis al-aʿlā li-l-awqāf wa-l-irshād* and the list of its members expanded.[215]

The decree no. 26 of 1968 article 13b ordered an end to the former *dākhilī* and *khārijī* division.[216] Since then, there have been several decrees regulating

---

210 These include regulating leases and the dissolution of *ḥaqq al-yad* in previous leases. See chapter 6.

211 For the decrees in general see Manṣūr, *al-Mawkib*, 277–309.

212 Validated *fiqh* refers to rules that have been chosen by consensus, or "codified."

213 Ibid., 283.

214 Ibid., 186.

215 Ibid., 298.

216 Ibid., 281. The previous *dākhilī* and *khārijī* administrations were merged under the name *waqf* or *awqāf*.

the administration of the two other types, the *turab* and the *waṣāyā*,[217] but until today, they have remained separate from the *waqf* administration per se. Thus in general, what remained for the ministry were the mosques and their *waqfs*.

Until the 1980s, much of the "currency" in the *waqf* economy was still sorghum grain stored in the traditional way in local grain storage pits (*madāfin*); the first *waqf* decrees after the revolution also refer to grain.[218] After that, grain was sold on the market by the *ʿāmils* and the accountancies later mostly refer to monetary currency. However, even today, the electronic registers and accountancies mention buckets of grain or baskets of grapes, because the yearly payments by the tenants have not been re-negotiated and converted to monetary currency. The old estimates are kept as indications of the value of the rights that are taken as income from the *waqfs*.[219] Much *waqf* land has never been measured in terms of physical area and therefore the only information about the assets is the name of the assets and the value of the estimated or average expected *harvest*, not the size or borders of the asset, even though almost every *waqf* law and decree from 1968 until today has ordered *waqf* assets to be properly registered and defined.

The early years of the ministry were characterised by a high turnover of ministers. In just 13 years, between 1962 and 1975, more than 25 ministers were appointed, many of whom served several times. In some years there were more than three new appointments. The author of *al-Mawkib*, ʿAbd al-Mālik Manṣūr, states that this undoubtedly had a negative effect.[220] He also admits that the actual administrative structure varied a great deal from those planned in the decrees above.[221] This is also the overall picture that is described by most informants.

In the 1970s, al-Qāḍī ʿAlī b. ʿAbdallāh al-ʿAmrī and Yaḥyā b. ʿAbdallāh al-Ḍaḥyānī both held the position of minister several times. Muḥammad b. Muḥammad al-Manṣūr held the position a short while in 1978; there were a

217 In decree no. 73 from 1969, article 1.4 that organises the new ministry defines the *waṣāyā* as "*subul, wa-l-qirāʿa, wa duwar al-ḍayāfa.*" In practice this refers to public, non-mosque *waqfs* with private administrators. Manṣūr, *al-Mawkib*, 285.

218 Such as article 13 in the law from 1968, Manṣūr, *al-Mawkib*, 281. See also Messick, "Transactions in Ibb," 175–181.

219 I have copies of several such lists of *waqf* and *turab-waṣāyā* income from the districts near Sanaa. See appendix 8 in Hovden, "Flowers in *Fiqh*."

220 Manṣūr, *al-Mawkib*, 186.

221 Ibid., 190.

few others between them (among them Muḥammad b. Luṭf al-Ṣabāḥī again). From 1978 until 1990, the position was held by al-Qāḍī ʿAlī b. ʿAlī l-Sammān.

5.3 *The* Turab, Waṣāyā *and* al-Awqāf al-Ṣiḥḥiyya *After the Revolution*

Since its creation the *turab* administration has funded state education. The *dākhilī* and the *khārijī waqf* administrations and account books were merged together, but the *turab* and the *waṣāyā* remained separate administrations, only part of the ministry in name. As mentioned above, some of the income from the *turab waqfs* was also used to acquire new *waqf* land in the areas around Sanaa. After the revolution, the funds from the *turab waqf* were directed to the ministry of education (Wizārat al-tarbīya wa-l-taʿlīm). In 1987, the administration of the *turab waqfs* was in theory given back to the ministry of *awqāf*.[222] In real terms, it was never actually included as part of the ministry of *awqāf* and until today the funds go to the ministry of education via the ministry of finance.[223]

Today the *turab waqf* are special in that they do not fund services in the local areas where the income is taken, rather the income goes to the central budget for state education.[224] On the other hand, the (mosque) *waqf* income is mainly spent for local mosques and local salaries, and only the surplus effectively goes to the ministry in Sanaa. The law of 1977 article 2e states that the ministry is to oversee (*ishrāf*) the *awqāf al-turab wa-l-ṣiḥḥiyya*.[225] Law no. 7 of 1987 (art. 3 sub. 7) states that the ministry is to administer the *turab*, but in special books and registers (*sijillāt khāṣṣa*) and to present the accountancy to the ministry of finance and the funds are to enter the public state treasury (*al-khizāna al-ʿāmma*). The same applies to health *waqf* (*al-awqāf al-ṣiḥḥiyya*).[226] As for the *awqāf al-ṣiḥḥiyya*, even less is known.[227] It is likely that this is a remnant from the hospital set up by Imam Yaḥyā; it was probably given its own *waqfs* like the ministry of education was, and it remained a separate administrative unit

222 As in the above mentioned decree of that year.

223 Mijallī, *al-Awqāf fī l-Yaman*, 26.

224 Some claim that it still funds the state-funded Islamic schools and "institutes," but this has not been investigated in this study.

225 Manṣūr, *al-Mawkib*, 289.

226 Ibid., 297–298.

227 Al-Qirshī states that the ministry of *awqāf* has not been given any details about the health *waqfs*. Ghālib ʿAbd al-Kāfī, *al-Awqāf wa-l-waṣāyā bayna al-sharīʿa wa-l-qānūn al-Yamanī* (Sanaa: Iwān li-l-Khidmāt al-Iʿlāmiyya, 2008), 100.

since then. Until today, the old registers for these *waqf*s are kept at the ministry of health and not handed over to the ministry of *awqāf*.[228]

There is now a section (*qiṭāʿ*) in the ministry especially for *waṣāyā* and *turab*, headed by a ministerial secretary (*wakīl li-shuʾūn al-waṣāyā wa-l-turab*),[229] but in practice his responsibilities do not include the *waṣāyā*, which is still held by the *nāẓir al-waṣāyā*, the famous scholar al-Sayyid Muḥammad al-Manṣūr (b. 1915). The *nāẓārat al-waṣāyā* is located directly under the office of the president, and was affirmed by a presidential decree, thus it bypasses the whole ministry.[230] Al-Qirshī writes (in a footnote) that both he and his predecessor as *waqf* ministers had written requests to the present day *nāẓir al-waṣāyā* to hand over the administration of these *waqf*s, in accordance with the law made in 1987 and to order the *ʿāmil*s under him to come to the ministry for training and resume their work under it, "... but no such thing happened."[231]

In articles 88 and 89 the *waqf* law states that any public *waqf* is to be supervised by the ministry, even if there are private *mutawallī*s. This also includes the *turab*, *ṣiḥḥiyya*, and *waṣāyā*. Article 89 also states that in *waṣāyā* (or any *waqf*) with a public purpose, "the ministry is to receive what the founder stipulated for the *mutawallī*, and if it is not defined, the ministry is to take 5 per cent of the income of the *waqf*."[232] However, this is only the case if there is no other legally valid *mutawallī* present.[233] The right to private guardianship or administration (*wilāya*) is undisputed in the *waqf fiqh*. This relates to the doctrinal concept of respecting the founder's will and the idea that the institution of *waqf* is a private initiative and not a part of the state. In the context of a weak state, people are resistant to the idea that the ministry has supreme power over all *waqf*s and can invalidate private guardianship altogether. Ministerial decree no. 18 of 2001 (*bi-shaʾn ilghāʾ al-naẓarāt al-khāṣṣā*) finally abolished the right to private guardianship. However, the decree caused so much resistance that a new decree was issued (ministerial decree no. 51 of 2002) abolishing the

228 al-Farrān, *Athar al-waqf*, 119 and 189.

229 This was true until spring 2011; Muḥammad b. Yaḥyā b. Luṭf al-Fāṣīl, according to decree no. 284 of 2002.

230 Al-Manṣūr told me that he had a letter of appointment from the president and that this was still in effect. Personal communication with Muḥammad al-Manṣūr, Sanaa, January 2010.

231 al-Qirshī, *al-Awqāf wa-l-waṣāyā*, 101.

232 Ibid., 100.

233 But if there is a *mutawallī*, and the state has registered the *waṣīya* and supervises it, if we read Serjeant/al-Abdin's description of the *khārijī waqf*, we see that the inspector is entitled to 2.5 per cent. This seems reasonable, and the difference would be whether or not a registered *waṣīya waqf* has a legal *mutawallī* present or not. Al-ʿAmrī and Serjeant, "Administrative Organisation," 151; al-Abdin, "Role of Islam," 219.

former decree.[234] Thus private guardianship is again legally valid. Since the law gives the ministry the right to register, "supervise," and review the accountancy of the *waṣāyā* type of *waqf*, the *mutawallī* is reduced to being a paid manager and is no longer the ultimate "guardian." But this is a fairly theoretical discussion and in fact we must expect legal norms and practices to diverge in diverse ways.

5.4 *The Iṣlāḥī Years (1993–97)*

After the unification between North Yemen and the Peoples Democratic Republic of Yemen (previous South Yemen, PDRY), the Islamist Iṣlāḥ party was allowed a more prominent place in politics. In the 1980s, the ministry was fairly traditional, weak, and in a phase of development, struggling to find its role in a modernizing state bureaucracy. The ministry did not have a politically important role. With the Islamization of the late 1980s and the 1990s control over the mosques and what took place in the mosques became much more important. Since that time the *irshād* part of the ministry, which is little mentioned in this book, has grown steadily and is now far more important in terms of state support than the *waqf* part of the ministry.

In 1990 Muḥsin Muḥammad al-ʿUlufī from the GPC (the General People's Congress, the president's ruling party) became minister. In April 1993 Ghālib ʿAbd al-Kāfī l-Qirshī, from the Iṣlāḥ party took the position and held it until May 1997, when the position went to Aḥmad Muḥammad al-Shāmī from the Zaydī l-Ḥaqq party. Al-Shāmī only held the position for a year until 1998 when he resigned because of the chaotic state of the ministry and lack of real power. There was simply not much he could do.[235] The many reforms in the administrative structure and techniques seem hardly to have been effectuated at all, and in many districts it seems as if the *ʿāmil*s managed to retain their positions and ways of administration.

In Upper Yemen, which is Zaydī, these years saw the build up to the open sectarian conflict that resulted in the so-called Ḥūthī rebellions centred on the areas around Sa'da. The power of the Wahhābī and Salafī oriented forces grew. Wahhābī schools, institutes, and mosques were built, and the ministry of *awqāf* became an arena where this power struggle was very much felt. Many of the new mosques and schools were not subjected to the authority of the ministry, but many mosques were still registered under the ministry as *waqf*, and thus had the right to maintenance and salaries from the central *waqf* budget. These

234 al-Farrān, *Athar al-waqf*, 181.

235 Personal communication with al-Shāmī, January 2010. His letter of resignation is well known and he provided me with a copy.

new mosques should have been built with their own *waqf*s attached to them, but they were established and registered in such a way that their maintenance and the salaries associated with them is paid from the ministry.

In addition, traditionally Shāfiʿī areas have resisted government attempts at centralisation, and in the newly incorporated territories in the south and east, such as Hadramawt, people felt that it was better to keep what was left of their *awqāf* hidden, rather than submit them to Sanaa.

5.5 *The Ministry Today*

The Iṣlāḥī leaders in the ministry did not manage to control the *ʿāmil*s in the traditional Zaydī areas who refused to fund Wahhābī or Salafī projects. The ministry was left in a state of chaos that affected the way it was perceived by the population. In addition to this there were other challenges related to internal corruption in the ministry and the openly illegal seizure of *waqf* lands by powerful private individuals and state institutions. Today, many tenants refuse to pay full rent and see themselves as worthy recipients of access to low priced rent of urban land and cheap rental flats and shops. Looking back at these challenges, which to a large extent still exist today, it has been a formidable task simply to keep the ministry functioning. Its very existence today can be attributed to loyal administrators and tenants both inside and outside the official structure. It is the notion of community, tradition, and religious piety that makes it possible for the *waqf* ministry to operate under these circumstances.

In May 2003 the minister Ḥamūd Muḥammad ʿUbād took over. In the years from 2007 until March 2011, al-Qāḍī Ḥamūd Muḥammad al-Hittār was minister. He is known to have prioritized the ever more important *irshād* section and has become famous in the western media for his "rehabilitation programs" of radical Islamists. On 13 March 2011, after the street protests, a presidential decree no. 64 was issued giving Ḥamūd Muḥammad ʿUbād the position of minister of *awqāf* and *irshād*. Al-Hittār stated that he had not been dismissed, but had withdrawn in protest to the violent response of the government towards the demonstrators.

5.6 *The Project of Registration and Mapping of* Waqf *Assets*

Perhaps the most important reform program that is presently under way relates to the registration and mapping of *waqf* assets in electronic databases by using GPS and GIS, and even scanning and digitizing important documents and old *waqf* registers (*mashrūʿ al-ḥaṣr*). It is not yet clear what the outcome of this project may be and there are frequent delays in the project.

Many conflicting interests emerge in the process of transferring information from the old registers into the new ones. An informant working in the registration project told me that with the new electronic *waqf* registers, the old registers are not accessible anymore and people are "prohibited" from consulting them. Obviously, discrepancies between the old registers and the new ones are problematic and every change in *waqf* asset that is not properly documented, witnessed, and attested by the proper authorities will continue to pose a threat to the legitimacy of the ministry.

Many districts (*mudīriyyāt*)[236] have no *ʿāmil*s (*ʿāmilūn*,[237] *ʿummāl*) today,[238] though in some districts there are several. In some areas the local *waqf* office is located directly under the ministry, while in others the local *ʿāmil*s have other regional offices or there are *ʿāmil*s that work between them and the ministry. Sometimes, the titles *nāẓir* or *walī* are also used. The ministry is in a process of creating offices (*maktab, makātib, maktabāt*) in every district (*mudīriyya*), headed by a director (*mudīr al-waqf*) over that district. This reform has still not reached all districts. The administrative map is therefore complicated and there are areas in which several layers of older reforms have not yet been implemented. In practice, the system works almost as it always has; it is very much dependent on local elites. Some areas are able to retain the local *waqf* funds for local needs, while others are under the control of the ministry in such a way that the ministry is able to take the unused surplus, or even most of the income.

To a large extent, the local *ʿāmil*s still inherit their positions, and may take a quite high percentage of the total *waqf* income as salary (i.e., local *ʿāmil*s take their salaries from income from the agents under them). The *ʿāmils* are not state employees, and do not receive benefits in the form of retirement and insurance the way state employees do. Their salary is still made up of percentages of the local income. The percentage varies and depends on the responsibilities included in the job. First, 2.5 per cent is taken for the work of crop estimation (*ṭiyāfa*), which can be done by another person; ideally, the estimate should be approved by the ministry (now the district *waqf* office) before the *ʿāmil* is given an order to collect the estimated amount of the crop. Then, the *ʿāmils*' personal, local representatives (*wakīl, wukalāʾ*) undertake the process of

236 Administratively, Yemen is divided into governorates (*muḥāfaẓat*), districts (*mudīriyyāt*), and sub-districts (*ʿuzla*, pl. *ʿuzal*). There are around 300 districts and 2,000 sub-districts.

237 The plural for *ʿāmil* is also *ʿāmilūn*, not to be confused with "*ʿumāl*" which is the same as the contemporary term for the *ʿamāla*. The term *aʿmāl* refers to a geographical administrative area in several historical periods.

238 al-Farrān, *Athar al-waqf*, 180.

collecting the income or harvest; for this the *ʿāmil* receives an additional 2.5 to 10 per cent. The *ʿāmil* can take 10 per cent of the total income for supervising and accounting and for the process of sending the surplus to the district *waqf* office. The district *waqf* office takes at most 2.5 per cent for accounting for all the *ʿāmils* in their district and reviewing their books. Most of this work is concentrated around harvest time, although some crops are not as regular as the sorghum harvest in the autumn.[239]

In 1995 the ministry of *awqāf* issued decree no. 42 regulating the percentages obtained from *waqf* income. In this decree, the allotted percentages are specified, but vary a great deal according to the type of work and the nature of the assets. If the assets are old, in need of maintenance and are physically distant from each other (therefore entailing time to administer), the percentage granted to the *ʿāmil* can be higher. If the *ʿāmil* is an official employee, thus also receiving a state salary, the percentages are lower. The highest percentage allowed for a non-state employee *ʿāmil* is 25 per cent if he is also doing the crop estimation (*ṭiyāfa*), the crop collection, the accountancies (*kitāba*) and the administration of local mosques and other beneficiaries (*maḥāsin*) that are in his geographical area of responsibility. As for the actual percentages, no reliable studies exist and even the ministry's own accounts are not easily available to critical research.

From its surplus, the ministry has built new mosques in several cities, new market complexes, and housing complexes. The yearly turnover is difficult to estimate, since most of the income reverts to local administrators and local beneficiaries and is also, partly, paid in kind. Many of the key figures in the accountancy, such as the building of new mosques or investment projects, are listed according to "programs" (*khiṭṭa*) that stretch over several years and are therefore difficult to compare. In 2002 the Central Statistical Authority stated that about 30 per cent of agricultural land is *waqf*.[240] Other estimates tend towards 10 per cent.[241] Around the larger cities, this could be significantly

---

239 See Farrān, *Athar al-waqf*, 174–190. Some of the information is based on the unpublished manuscript version of the *Athar al-waqf* called *al-Waqf wa-l-tanmīya fī l-Yaman* and on conversations with al-Farrān.

240 ʿAlī Muḥammad al-Farrān refers to "al-Yaman bi-l-arqām 2002," by al-Jihāz al-Markazī li-l-Iḥṣāʾ.

241 Varisco's unpublished report from 1985, "Land Tenure and Water Rights in the Central Highlands of Yemen" states that this is 10 to 15 per cent as quoted in Aden Aw-Hassan, Mohammed Alsanabani, and Abdul Rahman Bamatraf, "Impact of Land Tenure and other Socioeconomic Factors on Mountain Terrace Maintenance in Yemen," *CAPRi Working paper* 3 (2000), 8. In their 1997 field study they found 20 to 23 per cent *waqf*. Gerholm quotes Dequin (1975:45), who undertook a field survey in Yemen, and claimed that 15 to 20

higher. Since the ministry does not have exact information themselves, and under-reporting in field studies must be expected, and since the understanding and definition of *waqf* is not absolute, any estimate must be taken with great caution.

---

per cent *waqf* was taken. Tomas Gerholm, "Market, Mosque and Mafraj; Social Inequality in a Yemeni Town" (PhD thesis, University of Stockholm, 1977), 60. Serjeant (*Ṣan'ā'*, 154) quotes al-Abidin ("Role of Islam," 218) who quotes al-Akhraṣ, who estimates 15 to 20 per cent *waqf*. Hishām al-Akhraṣ, "A Note on Land Tenure in Yemen," a report for the Central Statistical Planning Organisation, September 1972 (not consulted here).

CHAPTER 4

Main Texts of Zaydī *Waqf Fiqh* and Law

In this chapter I introduce the texts that I analyse in the following chapters in this book. These texts belong to different genres, including various forms of *fiqh* works, *fatwā* collections, and imamic and governmental decrees. The conventions[1] of these texts are an important part of the texts themselves. I present the texts chronologically, preceded by a short introduction to Zaydism. This is followed by a presentation of the most important texts of Zaydī codification, which constitute a fundamental part of Zaydism and the Zaydī law school (*madhhab*). The law school is also a sort of common, general frame of reference for the texts; it is in this arena that "Zaydism" exists as an academic discipline and field of knowledge. The chronological presentation of the texts adds contextual historical information about the text, its author, its readership and patrons, and its importance (or lack of) today. Approaching the modern period, the chapter fades into a history of Yemeni republican codification in general and of *waqf* law specifically.

In addition to a historical, chronological presentation, I also make use of an anthropological perspective in which "Zaydism" and "validity" are constructed also in the present. In conversations in the field with legal experts, students of law, and "ordinary" people, it is possible to see how the validity of *waqf*s specifically, and of Islamic law in general, are rooted in texts. The constructions of validity as narrated to me by informants are in many ways inverted, at least in comparison to a historical presentation of the development in the *fiqh*. The validity extends back from the present, and is rooted in ever more distant texts and statements. The historical timelines that informants construct are not as clear as they are for a historian and certain texts and persons (authors) are given much more attention than others. Thus "the map" of relevance and validity is not just inverted, it is also partly divergent. The informants, when asked the question: "What are the important texts concerning this issue?" often portray a dynamic genealogical map of the important texts, rather than a strict historical presentation about which argument came first. Obviously, this is an inescapable challenge; different informants and groups of informants see truth, relevance, and validity differently and point out different

1 I refer to the "conventions of the texts" in a broad sense: how they are structured, around which elements they are structured, how they are taught and transmitted, what abbreviations are used, and prerequisite knowledge needed by those using the texts.

 | DOI:10.1163/9789004377844_005

textual genealogies of validity. Thus the structure of this chapter is historical and chronological, but the relative anthropological importance of the texts, in constructions of validity today, is something that I point out and discuss alongside the chronological presentation.

In such a long time line, there are many "presents" and contemporary contexts, all of them incorporating older texts. Because many of the *fiqh* texts have a strong dialectical nature it is usually possible to reconstruct, at least academically, how a certain idea has been perceived and interpreted at various points of history. A certain text, say a specific rule (*ḥukm*) or statement (*qawl*), is interpreted by scholar B, which is commented upon by scholar C one hundred years later. Again one hundred years later, all the views of A, B, and up to Y are interpreted and re-constructed in a text by scholar Z. Or, maybe only the arguments of A, G and H "survived" history. Today, one can sit down with informants and ask and observe how they understand the same topic. Very often, only some of these texts "survive" history while most are either forgotten completely or only exist as seldom read manuscripts in a library. It is impossible to construct a single coherent historical structure of Zaydism or Zaydī *fiqh*. The tradition of Zaydism as such, cannot be simply or completely defined and will always remain, in part, an essentialist and emic term. Today, with the advent and possibilities afforded by new technology such as printed books and electronic data formats, new texts from the past "emerge," sometime in new forms. A *sharīʿa* student today has access to a totally different range of texts than what was available one hundred years ago, or even ten years ago. Some of the texts are preferred because of their clear language, usefulness, comprehensiveness, accuracy, etc. The views of informants also differ of course, depending on whether he is well-educated or not, or if he comes from a specific branch of Zaydism. Since the texts in this study have been chosen because of their focus of *waqf*, we must expect that other texts and chains of texts would appear if we had chosen other legal topics. Yet in all this complexity of authors, texts, contexts, and readers, clear patterns emerge and the main pattern(s) is what is presented in this chapter in chronological order. The result is a mix of "objective" history with the commentaries of native historians and legal experts. In the following analysis the cumulative intertextuality that is thoroughly documented in the following chapters binds all these texts firmly together. As for whether or not "author G" was really a skilful scholar, or whether book "K" is truly "authoritative" or "original," these are necessarily subjective views. The texts' relevance is situated and localized, be it in historical, political, geographical, intellectual or legal contexts.

Above, though it may seem that an author always presents his own views and that a text and an author constitute the same single view, this is usually not the case. Many of the texts and genres were created by multiple authors and some books have accumulated layers of comments over centuries. This does not necessarily complicate the analysis; it can also make the "debate" more readily available as a study object. Instead of the researcher collating various views into an "artificial" debate, often the stage has already been set, especially in multi-vocal *fiqh* commentaries, as we shall see.[2]

1 Zaydism

1.1 *Early Zaydism and Caspian Zaydism*

Most portrayals of Zaydism begin with its early roots, debates, sects, and persons.[3] Thus we should start with mentioning Zayd b. ʿAlī (d. 122/740), who revolted against the Umayyad dynasty and became the eponymous "founder" of Zaydism. Zaydism arose in present day Iraq.[4] One of the early authorities, al-Qāsim b. Ibrāhīm al-Rassī (d. 246/860), was from Medina; his branch of Zaydism is referred to as al-Qāsimiyya. His grandson, Yaḥyā b. al-Ḥusayn (d. 298/911) took the title *al-Hādī ilā l-haqq* [the guide to truth] when he brought Zaydism to Yemen, where, in 897, he had come to serve as a mediator between the tribes of Saʿda. Often, his branch of Zaydism is called al-Hādawiyya, or Hādawī-Zaydī to denote the core of traditional Yemeni Zaydism.[5]

Zaydism spread to the Caspian areas of present-day Iran, and mainly the areas of the fertile northern slopes of the Elburz Mountains, called Daylam, Jilan, and Tabaristan. Zaydism existed there and in Yemen (after 284/897) in parallel communities for about four centuries. The Caspian Zaydiyya divided into other branches: Some continued to follow the Qāsimiyya, while many

2 One text stands out as particularly important for present-day Zaydīs, namely Ibn Miftāḥ, *Sharḥ al-azhār* [The commentary on the book of flowers], which I present below.

3 See the authoritative accounts by Madelung, *Religious and Ethnic Movements; Der Imam al-Qāsim ibn Ibrāhīm und die Glaubenslehre der Zaiditen* (Berlin: Walter de Gruyter & Co., 1965); "Zaydiyya," *Encyclopaedia of Islam*, second edition, ed. P. Bearman, Th. Bianquis, C. E. Bosworth, E. van Donzel, and W. P. Heinrichs (Leiden: Brill, 1960–2004). For a more accessible, shorter overview see Eirik Hovden, "Shiʿa: Zaydi (Fiver)," *Encyclopedia of Islam and the Muslim World*, ed. Richard C. Martin (New York: Macmillan, forthcoming). For Zaydī reflections of what it means to be a distinct *madhhab*, see Bernard Haykel and Aron Zysow, "What Makes a Madhhab a Madhhab: Zaydī Debates on the Structure of Legal Authority," *Arabica* 59, nos. 3–4 (2012): 332–371.

4 For a recent study on very early Zaydism, see Najam Haider, *The Origins of the Shīʿa* (New York: Cambridge University Press, 2014).

5 For instance, Anna Würth uses the term "Hādawī" for Zaydī, while Bernard Haykel often uses the term "Zaydī-Hādawī." Würth, *Ash-sharīʿa fī Bāb al-Yaman*; Haykel, *Revival and Reform*.

followed al-Nāṣir al-Ḥasan b. ʿAlī l-Uṭrūsh (d. 304/917), his branch was called "al-Nāṣiriyya." Another Caspian branch or sub-branch was established by the Mu'ayyadiyya: the two brothers al-Mu'ayyad Aḥmad b. al-Ḥusayn (d. 411/1020) and al-Nāṭiq Abū Ṭālib Yaḥyā b. al-Ḥusayn (d. 424/1033).[6] Both are frequently referred to in the later classical Yemeni Zaydī *fiqh* texts.[7]

In Yemeni Zaydism, no such sub-branches are explicitly referred to in the *fiqh*, although the term Hādawī is used to mean, in a narrow sense, those views held by al-Hādī, and in wider sense, the "pure" Zaydism as opposed to that which was later influenced by neo-Sunnism and traditionism as exemplified by al-Shawkānī and his students. "Zaydism" today can thus refer to a quite diverse corpus of ideas. If we make generalizations about this early period, we can see that it is necessary to understand some patterns that serve as foundations for the later classical, Yemeni Zaydism.

1.2 *Doctrinal Foundations and Debates*

First, as a branch of the Shīʿa, the Zaydīs in general do not automatically consider the *ḥadīth*s and *ḥadīth* collections of the Sunnīs authoritative. This important Zaydī stand gradually changed and a parallel line of *ḥadīth*-oriented Zaydīs emerged and culminated in important works of the reformist, neo-Sunnī, traditionist[8] Muḥammad b. ʿAlī l-Shawkānī (d. 1834). However, this tendency was not as strong in the early or classical period. The "proper" Zaydīs (today, the term Hādawiyya is used for this purpose) have their own authoritative *ḥadīth* collection, the *Musnad* of Imam Zayd b. ʿAlī. However, this collection is much smaller than the Sunnī *ḥadīth* collections and in practice, it is not often referred to in later Zaydī *fiqh* as we see.

Second, the Zaydīs held that the descendants of the Prophet (*ahl al-bayt*), through the descendants of ʿAlī and Fāṭima, passed on knowledge over generations, and that this knowledge is authoritative in itself, especially if it is

6 They are also called the "two *Hārūnīs*" from the name of their grandfather Hārūn, or the "two imams." See also Yahyā b. al-Ḥusayn al-Shijarī, *Sīrat al-Imām al-Mu'ayyad bi-Llāh al-Hārūnī*, ed. Ṣāliḥ ʿAbdallāh Aḥmad Qurbān (Sanaa: Mu'assasat al-Imām Zayd b. ʿAlī l-Thaqafiyya, 2003); Madelung, "Zaydiyya."

7 For example in the chapter on *waqf* of the *Kitāb al-Azhār* the views of al-Mu'ayyad are the only ones quoted as alternatives to the Hādawī-Yemeni school in the *matn* of Ibn al-Murtaḍā. I discuss this below. By "classical, Yemeni" Zaydism, I refer to the period starting with al-Hādī's arrival in Yemen in 897 and ending with the first Ottoman invasion in 1550s, though this is not a conventional usage of the term. In terms of *fiqh* we see much increased activity after approximately 1300.

8 The term traditionist refers to the focus on "traditions" (i.e., *ḥadīths*) and is not related to being "traditional." This is a good example of how a term may have a specific meaning in Islamic studies, a meaning that may be quite different in, for example, anthropology.

supported by a relative consensus in the Zaydī community. While this authoritative knowledge itself is not considered inheritable in a strictly genealogical sense and non-*sayyid* scholars are also authoritative and indeed referred to, until today the true descendants of the Prophet have a special "holy" status as carriers of authority, enlightenment, and knowledge. This claim of inherited "holiness" was and still is controversial and the degree to which it is claimed or refuted varies with context.[9] These descendants are now called *sayyid*s (pl. *sāda*) and are a special category of Yemeni society; they marry only within their group.[10] The idea that knowledge (*ʿilm*) has such a mystical, inheritable quality is of course relevant to the construction of borders between those who know and those who do not and in the construction of chains of validity. The neo-Sunnīs like al-Shawkānī strongly emphasized scholarly genealogy through a system of *ijāza* certificates of quality and validity given by teacher to students.[11]

Third, some of the Zaydī epistemological and theological doctrines are different from their Sunnī counterparts. The relevance of mentioning these doctrines in a much more detailed subject like *waqf* law can and should be questioned. The distance, for example, between the doctrines of theology and the corpus of legal rules (*furūʿ*) is vast, and this discrepancy is not a main focus of this study. Yet, we should mention the following: The Zaydīs lean towards the Muʿtazila,[12] and today educated Zaydīs are very well aware of this and often explicitly point this out as a sign that Zaydism is a knowledge tradition based in reason (*ʿaql*), in contrast to their Wahhābī and Salafī counterparts, and further, that Yemeni Zaydīs are "the carriers of the Muʿtazila,"[13] whereas in most other Muslim sects Muʿtazilī doctrines have disappeared; an exception being among Twelver Shīʿīs. In relation to this, Zaydīs view human rationality and reason (*ʿaql*), as an important element in theories of knowledge, including legal knowledge and the process of obtaining theological and legal knowledge with degrees of probability and validity. This results in a tendency to emphasize the

9 For the self perception and construction of this special status of the *sayyids* today, see Vom Bruck, *Islam, Memory, and Mortality*.

10 Their role in traditional and contemporary Yemeni society is well described in most of the historical and ethnographic works referred to in the list of references.

11 Haykel, *Revival and Reform*, 194–195.

12 D. Gimaret, "Muʿtazila," *Encyclopaedia of Islam*, second edition, ed. P. Bearman, Th. Bianquis, C. E. Bosworth, E. van Donzel, and W. P. Heinrichs (Leiden: Brill, 1960–2004). See also the research published on Zaydī theology in recent years by Sabine Schmidtke, Hassan Ansari, and Jan Thiele; their work greatly enhances the visibility, accessibility, and understanding of Zaydī studies.

13 See for example ʿAbd al-ʿAzīz al-Maqāliḥ, *Qirāʾa fī fikr al-zaydiyya wa-l-muʿtazila* (Beirut: Dār al-ʿAwda, 1982). Al-Maqāliḥ is a well known Yemeni intellectual.

role of free will over predestination and insist that the meaning of texts must be interpreted and understood and not simply read. What exact role this fundamental focus on *ʿaql* implies in *waqf fiqh* is problematic; the Zaydī *waqf fiqh* does not appear fundamentally different from Sunnī *waqf fiqh*. While Zaydīs themselves often claim that they were continuously *mujtahid*s, that is, they have continued to research and evaluate their knowledge of the branches of the law (*furūʿ*) against its sources (*uṣūl*), and produce new law, scholars like al-Shawkānī accused them of being *muqallid*s, those who blindly and uncritically follow the views of their imams, while scholars like himself were the true *mujtahids* tracing knowledge back to its true sources.[14] This book uses an inductive and praxiological perspective on the role of *fiqh* in *waqf* practices; thus I do not give priority to establishing the link between high level doctrines and law. Nonetheless, if we look at the broad differences between Sunnism and Zaydism in the construction of validity in *fiqh*, we can say that the main difference lies in the relative weight the Zaydīs give to the views of their imams and scholars, while Sunnīs and especially the newer trends of Zaydism represented by al-Shawkānī, give more weight to the Sunnī canonical *ḥadīth* collections. The former also give more importance to reason, while the latter emphasize the availability and priority of "clear" textual sources.

Fourth, from around the eighth/fourteenth century, Zaydism mainly only existed in the highlands of Yemen. Thus the geographical area of the Zaydīs was fairly confined. This, combined with several specific doctrines endemic to Zaydism regarding the relationship between the imam, the state, and the Muslims, enhanced the legal role of the law school and made the political[15] role of the imam highly important. Ever since Zayd b. ʿAlī's uprising, the doctrine of *khurūj* was important, if not fundamental to Zaydism; to fight an unjust ruler is not only allowed, but indeed a duty (this is contrary to most Sunnī views). The educated elite (*ahl al-ḥall wa-l-ʿaqd*, lit. "those who untie and bind") should agree upon and support a new imam and proclaim their allegiance (*bayʿa*) to him.[16]

14 Note that the term *muqallid* can be derogatory, but it is not always used in this way. The Zaydīs, along with many other sects and schools of law, hold that those who have little knowledge should follow those who have more knowledge and that only the highest degree of *mujtahids* can follow their own understandings of the law. The terms *muqallid* and *mujtahid* are used ambiguously in a broad Muslim context and in academic debates and the meaning of the term must be understood in context.

15 Arguably, the political role of the imam would be different if the population of Zaydīs was spread throughout the Islamic world. Their concentration in Yemen, and the fact that during certain periods the imam did act as the political leader, also affirmed his position as a lawgiver.

16 Doctrinally, recognition is not a condition for the imamate, but in fact the processes of recognition are crucial.

The imam is fallible, but his rules are to be followed as law as long as he lives. When a new imam takes over, new laws may be made by the new imam. In later periods, the laws or rules made by the imam are called *ikhtiyārāt*. For Zaydīs, the rules in the *sharīʿa* that are unquestionable are relatively few. In addition to the clear indisputable rules a larger corpus of rules are supported, in terms of validity, by the consensus of the law school. The remaining open "holes," or rules on which there is strong disagreement, must be clarified and determined by imamic decrees. Thus the role of the imam in the political and legal system is distinct in Zaydism, whereas in Sunnism this is covered by a duality between the ruler (*sulṭān*) and the *ʿulamāʾ*, thus the concept of codification and the implementation of religious law is less clear. In Zaydism, the imam makes the law where it is necessary. The imamate is not hereditary, but should be chosen among the descendants of ʿAlī and Fāṭima.[17] In practice, in certain periods the imamate was indeed hereditary, and a specific few mainly rich and educated *sayyid* families held the position of imam. Henceforth, in this work Zaydism refers to Yemeni Zaydism and more specific sub-branches of Zaydism are only be mentioned if necessary.

1.3 *Classical Yemeni Zaydism: From al-Hādī Until the First Ottoman Occupation*

In this book I use the term "classical" Yemeni Zaydism to refer to the period from 987 until around 1550 (from the introduction of Zaydism to Yemen by Imam al-Hādī Yaḥyā b. al-Ḥusayn until the first Ottoman occupation around 1550),[18] though it is not an established term. In this period, Zaydism was confined to Saʿda and the highlands north of Sanaa. The southern limit was in the areas of Dhamār, but for long periods even Sanaa was occupied by local non-Zaydī dynasties.[19] In Lower Yemen, this period saw several strong dynasties of Sunnī rulers centring on the cities of Zabid and Taʿizz. Other polities, especially in the western mountains, were influenced by the Ismāʿīlīs and Fāṭimids. At times, the Zaydīs were confined to the tribal areas north of Sanaa and existed only in *hijras* (*sayyid*, non-tribal village enclaves) there and in the city of Saʿda. The strength of the Zaydī state varied much and often it disintegrated completely when rival imams opposed each other, while powerful shaykh families ruled locally. During this period, tribes and tribal elites were crucial in Zaydī politics. This was in contrast to later periods, when Zaydī imams and elites also ruled

17 Usually via the two grandsons of the Prophet, al-Ḥasan and al-Ḥusayn.

18 For the introduction of Zaydism to Yemen and the following period, see Gochenour, "Penetration of Zaydi Islam."

19 Smith, "Early and Medieval History."

over the less tribal and more feudal and fertile Lower Yemen.[20] After al-Hādī, his two sons, al-Nāṣir Aḥmad and al-Murtaḍā Muḥammad held the positions as imams. Following this, al-Hādī's descendants held the position occasionally and several other imam claimants came from outside Yemen and established Zaydī family dynasties, many of whom were also descendants of al-Qāsim al-Rassī. Various imams made their capitals in areas between and including Sa'da and Sanaa.[21] From 1324 onward, when the Zaydīs took back Sanaa from the Rasūlids, there was a stronger Zaydī presence in the Sanaa area.

1.4 *Qāsimī Zaydism*

During the first Ottoman occupation (ca. 1550–1636), Zaydism became a unifying ideology of opposition in Upper Yemen and especially north of Sanaa. When the Ottomans were evicted, the Zaydī Qāsimī imams established themselves mainly in Sanaa and Dhamār, and from this point on, ruled most of Lower Yemen. Bernard Haykel describes in detail how the political context at the time influenced Zaydī theological and jurisprudential debates: The period saw the rise of several Sunnī-oriented scholars, who can be termed "neo-Sunnī" as they claimed to focus their criteria of validity directly on Sunnī *ḥadīth*s, in addition to the Qur'ān, thus bypassing the traditional law schools. These scholars were also partly breaking with Zaydī *madhhab* consensus. Prominent examples are Muḥammad b. Ibrāhīm al-Wazīr (d. 840/1436), al-Ḥasan b. Aḥmad al-Jalāl (d. 1084/1673), Ṣāliḥ b. Mahdī l-Maqbalī (d. 1108/1696), and Muḥammad b. Ismā'īl al-Amīr (d. 1182/1769).[22]

As the Zaydī rulers now mainly ruled Shāfi'ī subjects, the borders of Zaydism and Sunnism in *sharī'a* discourse started to blur and the anti-Sunnī antagonism once employed in the anti-Ottoman rhetoric was partly set aside. The office of the imam was divided into two: the imam came to be the political ruler whose position was, in effect, hereditary, and the chief *qāḍī* (or later also *shaykh al-Islām*) was the supreme judge, a role formerly executed by the imam. The most prominent of these were Muḥammad b. 'Alī l-Shawkānī (d. 1834) who held the position as chief *qāḍī* for thirty-five years, under three imams; during this time he produced a number of important works in this new non-*madhhab*, neo-Sunnī, traditionist school. The discourse between the neo-Sunnīs and the

20 For a description of the complex relationship between "state" and tribes in the far north, see, for instance Weir, *A Tribal Order*; Andre Gingrich, "Tribes and Rulers in Northern Yemen," in *Studies in Oriental Culture and History*, ed. Andre Gingrich, Sylvia Haas, Gabriele Paleczek, and Thomas Filliz (Vienna, Frankfurt, and New York: Peter Lang, 1993); Dresch, *Tribes, Government, and History in Yemen*.

21 Ibid., 167–173.

22 Haykel, *Revival and Reform*, 10.

traditional Zaydīs, or Hādawī-Zaydīs, produced important new dimensions that have inspired modern, non-*madhhab*, *ḥadīth*-oriented Islamic thought, which later became very important in the formation of "Yemeni Republican Islam."[23] Legal aspects of these discourses, as exemplified in *waqf fiqh*, are treated in the following chapters.

During the Qāsimī dynasty, Zaydism also expanded southward from Sanaa and many new *hijras* were established in the areas west and south of Dhamār and well into today's Ibb governorate. As can be seen from the names of important scholars and state employees of the time, many came from these "new" Zaydī areas and many of them were more friendly to the state than the "older" Zaydīs in the northern areas. Many of the most influential *sayyid* and *qāḍī* families were cosmopolitan (within the bounds of Zaydī Yemen); they travelled as students and teachers and were posted in various places by the imam as governors, judges, and tax and *waqf* administrators.

1.5 *Zaydism Under Imam Yaḥyā and Imam Aḥmad*

Imam Yaḥyā came to power (1911) by invoking, per traditional Zaydism, the quest for liberation against an unlawful ruler, this time, the second Ottoman occupation. However, he quickly ended up in a position similar to that of the Qāsimī imams: he was a Zaydī imam ruling over Shāfiʿī subjects, and the ruler of a hereditary polity, the Mutawakkilī kingdom (al-Mamlaka al-Mutawakkiliyya). In legal matters, he claimed to be a *mujtahid*-ruler who ruled according to the *sharīʿa* and who issued decrees with *sharʿī* validity. As for Zaydism as a legal tradition, the major Zaydī texts from around the ninth/fifteenth century, like the *Sharḥ al-azhār*, were still authoritative texts, though new details in the *fiqh* had been added in the footnotes.

1.6 *Republican Zaydism (1962–)*

Following the revolution in 1962, the Zaydīs were associated with the *sayyids* and the imamate, and as something oppressive, backwards, and anti-modern. This was despite the fact that several of the important *sayyid* families included both proponents and opponents of the revolution. After the civil war, in which Saudi Arabia and partly Britain backed the imamate and the Egyptian-backed republicans were defeated, it took some time for Zaydīs to develop a new self-image. This new Zaydism of the republican state was portrayed as "normal" and not deviant, "almost" Sunnī. Especially in the judiciary of the new republic, which was almost exclusively held by persons educated in Zaydī *fiqh*, there was a need to create a new, neutral, and technocratic self-image. In several of

23 Ibid., 217–224.

the anthropological works from this period, Zaydism is described as "moderate," perhaps in response to the Iranian Islamic revolution as a backdrop. The difference between the established law schools in Yemen, Zaydī and Shāfiʿī, was downplayed to the extent that it became almost (only) a matter of variations in the positions of prayer.

In this short presentation of Zaydism, it must not be forgotten that "Zaydism" is mainly an intellectual tradition, not a fixed social reality. The majority of "Zaydīs" were, and to a large extent still are, Zaydīs because they were born in a Zaydī area, taught to pray like Zaydīs and because their scholars and judges are Zaydīs. This does not mean that an average Zaydī has knowledge about the doctrine of *khurūj* or about *fiqh*. In the past, the notion of Zaydism was very much related to the ideal of the *sayyids*, their knowledge and their genealogical lines of descent; it was also strongly linked to the imamate. Even though anyone could in theory become an *ʿālim* or *qāḍī*,[24] in practice, it was difficult to access paid positions and employment without belonging to the already established *sayyid* or *qāḍī* houses. Thus after the revolution, Zaydism was to some degree perceived as "aristocratic" and conservative, at least from the viewpoint of the liberal socialists and the emerging popular Islamists. In recent years much research attention has been directed towards the very important phenomena of the emerging Salafī trend and Zaydī revival, a topic that lies outside the scope of this book, but that nonetheless must be mentioned.

1.7 *Salafism and the Zaydī Revival*

In the 1980s, a new form of Islam emerged in Yemen, mainly an apolitical, individualistic, piety-oriented form of Islam.[25] Religious schools were built, often with donors in Saudi Arabia. This trend became very noticeable in the 1990s; it was politicized as a useful counterweight for the state against both Zaydism and socialism. Salafism appealed to many, especially those from the lower classes and from the tribal segment who, in the traditional conservative Zaydī society of rural Yemen, had little social mobility.[26] Salafism often gave simple and clear answers, where Zaydism had an informal, but strong hierarchy

---

24 In Zaydī Yemen, the term *qāḍī* (pl. *quḍāt*, or *quḍāh*) refers not primarily to a judge, but to a scholar, jurist or educated person of non-sayyid *qabīlī* (tribal) origin.

25 See Laurent Bonnefoy, "Varieties of Islamism in Yemen: The Logic of Integration under Pressure," *Middle East Review of International Affairs* 13, no. 1 (2009).

26 In Yemen, there are three main "classes": The lowest class is called the *mazāyina* (sing. *muzayyin*). Together with the old slave class they performed services perceived as polluting; they were considered "weak" and as clients. Above this class is that of the *qabīlīs*, those who are members of a tribe. The "highest" class is that of the *sayyids*. In the past, the classes rarely intermarried.

and advanced books of *fiqh* and philosophy of law and religion. Heated confrontations took place, first noticeable in the areas of Sa'da. Later attacks on the property and symbols of the Zaydī elite became apparent. The 2000s also saw the so-called "six Sa'da wars" in which the Salafī/Zaydī ideological conflict was fuelled by a complex web of various local political actors. One local *sayyid* family in Sa'da, the Ḥūthī family, became especially prominent in organising anti-government campaigns by invoking traditional Zaydism. In all this, Zaydism remained diverse in that the Sanaa scholars rejected the violence and the Zaydī al-Ḥaqq party had long ago refuted the original doctrine of the imamate. Others insisted on a separation between religion and politics. Yet the security apparatus perceived Zaydism as a potential danger and feared that a hidden imam would appear and foment political opposition to the government. During this, the very notion of Zaydism was thoroughly debated. Many from the educated Zaydī families engaged in sophisticated discourse around these issues. The new focus on Zaydism also led to an interest in the old texts and much work has been done by various non-governmental organisations and individuals to collect, edit, and publish central Zaydī textual material.[27] The Zaydī revival has not been a central focus of this study, nor has Salafism. This was partly because the topic is controversial for many types of informants.[28]

A topic like *waqf* also makes the focus on such "isms" less relevant. *Waqf* is a legal topic and mainly educated informants understand what it is, be it landowners, *waqf* administrators, *'ulamā'* or scholars in general. It is not a "religious" topic per se and it does not readily lend itself as a focus for constructing doctrinal or sectarian differences. Most Salafī-oriented informants I met had

27 G. Vom Bruck, "Regimes of Piety Revisited: Zaydī Political Moralities in Republican Yemen," *Die Welt des Islams* 50 (2010): 185–223; Laurent Bonnefoy, "Salafism in Yemen: A 'Saudisation'?" in *Kingdom Without Borders*, ed. Madawi al-Rasheed (London: Hurst and Co., 2008); Bonnefoy, "Varieties of Islamism in Yemen"; Bernard Haykel, "A Zaydi Revival?" *Yemen Update* 36 (1995): 20–21; Shelagh Weir, "A Clash of Fundamentalisms," *Middle East Report* 204, no. 27 (1997); James Robin King, "Zaydī Revival in a Hostile Republic: Competing Identities, Loyalties and Visions of State in Republican Yemen," *Arabica* 59, nos. 3–4 (2012).

28 Such debates were easily observed during fieldwork; they mainly related to defending Zaydism and portraying it as an "open minded" sect under threat from fundamentalist Salafīs. Many uneducated informants were uncomfortable discussing these matters, out of fear of being perceived as Ḥūthī sympathizers. Individuals with higher social positions spoke quite freely, and usually criticized the government's handling of the conflict. A handful of informants had been imprisoned for their views on these matters. The ethnographic present is around 2009 and since then the Ḥūthīs have become significant political actors, although it remains unclear what role Zaydism plays and which form of Zaydism they claim to follow.

few ideas about the difference between religion and law, and had almost no knowledge of *waqf* as a legal topic. As shown in following chapters, the number of *ḥadīths* upon which one could build a Salafī, "non-*madhhab*" *waqf fiqh* are very few, especially if human reason, public interest or custom are not employed as a major sources for law. The whole topic of *waqf* law is simply not of interest to Salafīs, a fact which also seems to project onto the anti-Salafī Zaydīs; they too are preoccupied with the discourse on correct praying positions, whether or not to say "*amīn*" after reciting the *Fātiḥa* etc.,[29] and young Zaydī scholars who study *fiqh* for the sake of personal religious interest often see transactional and contractual *fiqh* as less important.

This overview of what Zaydism *is*, fades into the questions elaborated in chapter 2: Zaydism is a knowledge tradition with political and religious aspects; in this book I scrutinize the legal aspect, a set of frames of judicial knowledge of which *waqf* is a part.

2 Zaydī *Fiqh* Texts and Authors

In this section, we shall review the main authors and texts relevant for this study. This should not be seen as an exhaustive presentation of the history of Zaydī *fiqh*, the aim is to give a rough overview in general and specifically focus on those texts and authors that appear in the chapters on *waqf*.

2.1 *Imam al-Hādī Yaḥyā b. al-Ḥusayn* (*d. 298/911*)

Imam Yaḥyā b. al-Ḥusayn, who took the imamic title *al-Hādī ilā l-ḥaqq* (The guide to the truth, hereafter al-Hādī) was a Zaydī scholar who settled in the northern highlands of Yemen in 284/897. He and his followers came to an area occupied by tribes who were later portrayed as ignorant of religion and in a state of continuous war with each other.[30] Yemeni Zaydī *fiqh* and historiography tend to portray al-Hādī's arrival as "year zero" and somehow analogous to the case of the Prophet, in that al-Hādī brought Islamic law to the area,

29 A similar issue discussed among young scholarly Zaydī informants was whether or not one should utter the *tarḍiya* ("may God be pleased with him") after mention of the names of the Companions of the Prophet who had rejected ʿAlī.

30 For a thorough analysis of this period, see Gochenour, "Penetration of Zaydi Islam." Whether al-Hādī came to Yemen because he was "invited" or because he wanted to insert himself and his state-building project is of course debatable. The city of Sa'da and the area around it were already divided in their views on the Sunnī ʿAbbāsids and the proto-Shīʿī ʿAlids.

whatever the situation had been previously.[31] There were important Zaydī scholars before al-Hādī,[32] but these were not geographically tied to Yemen. Over the centuries and until today al-Hādī has remained a central figure of authority, constantly cited in the later debates. Of his books, perhaps the most important in *fiqh* questions are the *Kitāb al-Muntakhab*[33] and the *Kitāb al-Aḥkām fī l-ḥalāl wa-l-ḥarām.*[34]

2.2 *Imam ʿAbdallāh b. Ḥamza*

Today Imam al-Manṣūr bi-Llāh ʿAbdallāh b. Ḥamza (d. 614/1217) is seen as one of the main figures in classical Yemeni Zaydism, especially in the period between al-Hādī and the many works produced in the 1400s. He is much quoted in later *fiqh* works. He is one of the Yemeni imams who also propagated *daʿwa* for the imamate to the Caspian Daylam, Jilan, and Tabaristan, where the Friday sermon was cited in his name.[35] For this book, I have used his recently edited and published *fiqh* and *fatwā* collection, *al-Majmūʿ al-manṣūrī.*[36]

31 For the biography of al-Hādī, see ʿAlī b. Muḥammad b. ʿUbayd Allāh al-ʿAbbāsī l-ʿAlawī, *Sīrat al-Hādī ilā l-Ḥaqq Yaḥyā b. al-Ḥusayn*, ed. Suhayl Zakkār (Beirut: Dār al-Fikr li-l-Ṭibāʿa wa-l-Nashr wa-l-Tawzīʿ, 1401/1981); Johann Heiss, "Tribale Selbstorganisation und Konfliktreglung Der Norden des Jemen zur Zeit des ersten Imams (10. Jahrhundert)" (PhD thesis, University of Vienna, 1998); A. B. D. R. Eagle, "Ghayat al-Amani and the Life and Times of al-Hadi Yahya b. al-Husayn: An Introduction, Newly Edited Text and Translation with Detailed Annotation" (MA thesis, University of Durham, 1990); ʿAlī Muḥammad Zayd, *Muʿtazilat al-Yaman: Dawlat al-Hādī wa-fikrihi* (Sanaa: Markaz al-Dirāsāt wa-l-Buḥūth al-Yamaniyya, 1985).

32 For Yemeni Zaydīs the most relevant is al-Hādī's grandfather al-Qāsim al-Rassī, see Madelung, "al-Rassī, al-Ḳāsim b. Ibrāhīm b. Ismāʿīl Ibrāhīm b. al-Ḥasan b. al-Ḥasan b. ʿAlī b. Abī Ṭālib," *Encyclopaedia of Islam*, second edition, ed. P. J. Bearman, Th. Biancuis, C. E. Bosworth, E. van Donzel, and W. P. Heinrichs (Leiden: Brill, 1960–2004).

33 In this study, only the *Muntakhab* has been consulted and only in a limited way, from a version downloaded from the Internet.

34 Around 648/1250, al-Amīr al-Ḥusayn b. Badr al-Dīn Muḥammad (d. 662/1263 or 64) commented in a well-known work called *Shifāʾ al-uwām fī aḥādīth al-aḥkām li-l-tamyīz bayna al-ḥalāl wa-l-ḥarām*. See Ibn Miftāḥ, *Sharḥ al-azhār*, 1:48. There are many references to this work in the chapter on *waqf* of the *Sharḥ al-azhār*. Letters and *fatwā*s of al-Hādī were also collected in the work of al-Hādī ilā l-Ḥaqq Yaḥyā b. al-Ḥusayn, *al-Majmūʿa al-fākhira: Majmūʿ kutub wa-rasāʾil al-Imām al-Hādī ilā l-Ḥaqq Yaḥyā b. al-Ḥusayn* (Sanaa: Dār al-Ḥikma al-Yamaniyya li-l-Tijāra wa-l-Tawkīlāt al-ʿĀmma, 2000).

35 E. van Donzel, "al-Manṣūr Biʾllāh ʿAbd Allāh b. Ḥamza b. Sulaymān b. Ḥamza," *Encyclopaedia of Islam*, second edition, ed. P. J. Bearman, Th. Biancuis, C. E. Bosworth, E. van Donzel, and W. P. Heinrichs (Leiden: Brill, 1960–2004), 6:433–434.

36 al-Imām al-Manṣūr bi-Llāh ʿAbdallāh b. Ḥamza, *al-Majmūʿ al-manṣūrī (al-qism al-thānī) Majmūʿ rasāʾil al-Imām al-Manṣūr bi-Llāh ʿAbdallāh b. Ḥamza*, ed. ʿAbd al-Salām b. ʿAbbās al-Wajīh (Sanaa: Dār al-Imām Zayd b. ʿAlī l-Thaqāfiyya li-l-Nashr wa-l-Tawzīʿ, 2001). The work consists of three volumes with slightly different names. Vol 2 and 3 are used in this study.

As we see from al-Manṣūr's texts analysed in chapter 5, he took an independent stand, and disregarded several of the Hādawī rulings. His works have been printed recently, and are examples of works that "re-emerge" after having existed only in manuscript form. Previously, his views were mainly known through quotations from his works in *fiqh* debates, such as the *Sharḥ al-azhār*. Today al-Manṣūr is seen as controversial because he put down the very important popular Zaydī movement at the time called the Muṭarrifiyya and declared it heretical (*takfīr*). This and the vivid theological debates going on at the time makes this a distinct phase in Yemeni Zaydism.[37]

2.3 *Imam Yaḥyā b. Ḥamza and the* Intiṣār

The Imam al-Mu'ayyad bi-Llāh Yaḥyā b. Ḥamza b. ʿAlī l-ʿAlawī (d. 749/1348 or 49) was a prolific scholar and an important imam in Yemeni Zaydism.[38] His famous multi-volume *fiqh* compilation *al-Intiṣār ʿalā ʿulamāʾ al-amṣār*[39] [The victory of the scholars of the cities] has recently been partly edited and published[40] and enjoys much respect. It is an important part of the Zaydī revival. Several informants are of the opinion that this work is second only to the

37 ʿAlī Muḥammad Zayd, *Tayyārāt muʿtazilat al-Yaman fī l-qarn al-sādis al-hijrī* (Sanaa: al-Markaz al-Faransī li-l-Dirāsāt al-Yamaniyya, 1997); ʿAbd al-Ghanī Maḥmūd ʿAbd al-ʿĀṭī, *al-Ṣirāʿ al-fikrī fī l-Yaman bayna al-Zaydiyya wa-l-Muṭarrifiyya: Dirāsa wa-nuṣūṣ* (Cairo: ʿAyn li-l-Dirāsāt wa-l-Buḥūth al-Insāniyya wa-l-Ijtimāʿīyya, 2002); Gregor Schwarb, "Muʿtazilism in the Age of Averroes," in *In the Age of Averroes: Arabic Philosophy in the 6th/12th Century*, ed. Peter Adamson (London: Warburg Institute, 2011), 251–282; Jan Thiele, *Theologie in der jemenitischen Zaydiyya: die naturphilosophischen Überlegungen des al-Ḥasan ar-Raṣṣāṣ* (Leiden: Brill, 2013); Johann Heiss and Eirik Hovden, "Competing Visions of Community in Mediaeval Zaydī Yemen," *Journal of the Economic and Social History of the Orient* 59, no. 53 (2016): 366–407. For al-Manṣūr ʿAbdallāh b. Ḥamza's biography, see Abū Firās Ibn Diʿtham, *al-Sīra al-Manṣūriyya: Sīrat al-Imām ʿAbd Allāh b. Ḥamza 593–614 H*, ed. ʿAbd al-Ghanī Maḥmūd ʿAbd al-ʿĀṭī (Beirut: Dār al-Fikr al-Muʿāṣir, 1993); Abdulla al-Shamahi, "Al-Imām al-Manṣūr ʿAbdulla b. Hamzah b. Sulaymān (d. 614/1217) A Biography by his Disciple Al-Faqīh Ḥumayd b. Ahmad al-Muḥallī (d. 652/1254)," in *Al-Ḥadāʾiq al-Wardiyyah fi Manāqib Aʾimmah al-Zaydiyyah*, v.2 (PhD dissertation, University of Glasgow, 2003).

38 Some use the date 1344 CE for his death. G. J. H. van Gelder, "Yaḥyā b. Ḥamza al- ʿAlawī," *Encyclopaedia of Islam*, second edition, ed. P. Bearman, Th. Bianquis, C. E. Bosworth, E. van Donzel, and W. P. Heinrichs (Leiden: Brill, 1960–2004): 11:246.

39 The full title is *al-Intiṣār ʿalā ʿulamāʾ al-amṣār fī taqrīr al-mukhtār min madhāhib al-aʾimma wa-aqāwīl ʿulamāʾ al-umma fī l-masāʾil al-sharʿiyya wa-l-muḍṭaribāt*. See Aḥmad ʿAbd al-Razzāq al-Ruqayḥī, ʿAbdallāh Muḥammad al-Ḥibshī, and ʿAlī Muḥammad al-Ānisī, *Fihrist makhṭūṭāt Maktabat Jāmiʿ al-Kabīr Ṣanʿāʾ* (Sanaa: Wizārat al-Awqāf wa-l-Irshād, 1984), 2:913.

40 al-Muʿayyad bi-Llāh Yaḥyā b. Ḥamza, *al-Intiṣār ʿalā ʿulamāʾ al-amṣār*, ed. ʿAbd al-Wahhāb b. ʿAlī l-Muʾayyad and ʿAlī b. Aḥmad Mufaḍḍal (Sanaa: Muʾassasat al-Imām Zayd b. ʿAlī l-Thaqāfiyya, 2002).

Sharḥ al-azhār in importance. Thus far the chapter on *waqf* is, unfortunately, considered lost; thus it is not part of the recently printed edition. However, a *mukhtaṣar* (abridgement) of the *Instiṣār*, the *Nūr al-abṣār al-muntaziʿ min kitāb al-Intiṣār*[41] does exist in manuscript form and has been consulted for this study.

2.4 *The* Sharḥ al-azhār *Cluster*

Around the middle of the ninth/fifteenth century several *fiqh* works appeared that are closely related each other; several of them are commentaries on Ibn Murtaḍā's *Kitāb al-Azhār* [The book of flowers], or variations of it.

2.5 *Ibn al-Murtaḍā and His Works*

Ibn al-Murtaḍā—al-Imam al-Mahdī li-Dīn Allāh Aḥmad b. Yaḥyā b. al-Murtaḍā (764–840/1362–1437[42])—is usually known as Ibn al-Murtaḍā.[43] He was a prolific writer and a scholarly imam who was more proficient in the Islamic sciences than in politics and warfare. Ibn al-Murtaḍā was born in Dhamār, was orphaned, then travelled to Thulā', where he studied under relatives living there.[44] He became a scholar of rank and took part in the advanced debates of the central scholars of the day. In his works he quotes many of them, scholars that are now almost unknown, at least when compared to the frequency with which they are cited in the *Sharḥ al-azhār*. He was chosen as imam by an assembly of the *ʿulamā'* in the Jamāl al-Dīn mosque in Sanaa shortly after the death of Imam al-Nāṣir Salāḥ al-Dīn in 793/1391. He was sent to prison in the fortress of Sanaa in the year 794/1392 by his rival to the imamic title; he

41 al-Muʿayyad bi-Llāh Yaḥyā b. Ḥamza, *Nūr al-abṣār al-muntaziʿ min kitāb al-intiṣār* (Electronically photographed manuscript 43 n. 4, mentioned in *Fihrist al-makhṭūṭat al-muṣawwara bi-Mu'assasat Zayd b. ʿAlī*). The text is in black ink with occasional important words in red. Only the sections relevant for chapters 5 and 6 have been consulted.

42 Donaldson refers to the debate over the date of his birth and notes that al-Shawkānī claimed it took place in 1373: William J. Donaldson, *Sharecropping in the Yemen: A Study in Islamic Theory, Custom and Pragmatism* (Leiden: Brill, 2000), 94.

43 He is also often cited in the *fiqh* texts as "al-Mahdī," or in the *Sharḥ al-azhār* simply as *mawlānā* ("Our Lord"). R. Strothmann, "Mahdī li-Dīn Allāh Aḥmad," *Encyclopaedia of Islam*, second edition, ed. P. Bearman, Th. Bianquis, C. E. Bosworth, E. van Donzel, and W. P. Heinrichs (Leiden: Brill, 1960–2004): 5:1240; Ibrāhīm b. al-Qāsim b. al-Mu'ayyad, *Ṭabaqāt al-Zaydiyya al-kubrā: al-Qism al-thālith wa-yusammā: Bulūgh al-murād ilā maʿrifat al-isnād*, ed. ʿAbd al-Salām b. ʿAbbās al-Wajīh (Sanaa: Mu'assasat al-Imām Zayd b. ʿAlī l-Thaqafiyya, 2001), 1:226–233.

44 He also taught his sister *fiqh*. Al-Shawkānī states that *al-Sharīfa* Dahmā' bt. Yaḥyā b. al-Murtaḍā later wrote a four-volume commentary (*sharḥ*) on the *Azḥar*. She also produced other scholarly works and taught students at the city of Thulā'. She died there and is buried in a famous domed grave (*qubba*). Al-Shawkānī, *al-Badr al-ṭāliʿ*, 288.

remained there seven years. During the time in prison he wrote many of his works, among them the *Kitāb al-Azhār*. Ibn al-Murtaḍā was known to have been a very prolific writer,[45] though two works on *fiqh* stand out as his most famous and have been consulted in this study: *al-Baḥr al-zakhkhār* and the *Kitāb al-Azhār*, both of which are discussed further below. Chronologically, between these two he wrote *al-Ghayth al-midrār*,[46] which is not widely used today, but that also deserves some attention. Most probably, judging by the structure of these works, *al-Baḥr al-zakhkhār* was written first. It is a relatively short legal compilation with strong comparative aspects. Together the *Ghayth* and the *Kitāb al-Azhār* are a *sharḥ-matn* complex: that is, the *Kitāb al-Azhār* is a *mukhtaṣar*[47] and the *Ghayth* is its *sharḥ*, a multi-volume explanation, elaboration, and commentary. The text of a *mukhtaṣar* is called *matn* (pl. *mutūn*). While scholars seem to have lost interest in the *Ghayth*, another *sharḥ* took its place, the *Sharḥ al-azhār*. It was written by another scholar, Ibn Miftāḥ, shortly after Ibn al-Murtaḍa wrote his text. It is assumed that most of the content of the *Ghayth* is incorporated into Ibn Miftāḥ's commentary, but more research is necessary to establish the relationship between the two works.

2.6 *The* Baḥr al-zakhkhār

Ibn al-Murtaḍā probably wrote the legal work *al-Baḥr al-zakhkhār* before the famous abridgement (*mukhtaṣar*) *Kitāb al-Azhār*.[48] Its full title is *al-Baḥr al-zakhkhār al-jāmiʿ li-madhāhib ʿulamāʾ al-amṣār* [The book of the mighty ocean:[49] The compilation of the law schools of the scholars of the cities].

45 Donaldson quotes the editor's introduction to *al-Baḥr al-zakhkhār* where he names more than thirty-three works. Donaldson, *Sharecropping in the Yemen*, 95.

46 Translations of poetic titles can never match the original language. The terms *ghayth* and *midrār* are poetic terms found in the Qurʾān; they mean "rain," especially in the positive, life-giving sense. The full title is *al-Ghayth al-midrār al-mufattiḥ li-kamāʾim al-azhār fī fiqh al-aʾimma al-aṭhār* [The blessed rain, the opener to the gardens of the flowers of the jurisprudence of the purest imams]. Nine copies exist in the Wizārat al-Awqāf wa-l-Irshād, see al-Ruqayḥī, al-Ḥibshī, and al-Ānisī (eds.), *Fihrist makhṭūṭāt*, 3:1112–1116.

47 On the *mukhtaṣar* genre, see Fadel, "Social Logic of *taqlīd*."

48 The reason it must be older lies in its structure. Since the *Kitāb al-Azhār* was written, its structure has been widely used. The structure of *al-Baḥr al-zakhkhār* seems to predate the structure of the *Kitāb al-Azhār*, although this has not been investigated in detail here.

49 The term *baḥr* (pl. *biḥār*), means "ocean," but can also mean "groundwater": The term is used this way in Luṭf Allāh b. Aḥmad Jaḥḥāf, *Ḥawliyyāt al-muʾarrikh Jaḥḥāf*, 557. In Serjeant and Lewcock, *Ṣanʿāʾ*, 80, it is stated that "In 1648 the groundwater rose so much that it became easier to irrigate land from wells." Here the term used for groundwater is "*baḥr*." (Serjeant cites this from *al-Tabaq al-Ḥalwāʾ* 22b.) Therefore, an alternative title might be "The abundant groundwater." The book was written in the highlands of Yemen, for scholars of the highlands for whom an abundance of groundwater is a much more apt

Al-Baḥr al-zakhkhār is an organized compilation of individual rules (*furūʿ al-fiqh*).[50] It is relatively short and fairly condensed, and thus includes only the most relevant arguments and the best known rules. It is not a *mukhtaṣar* (an abridgement), as it elaborates upon and quotes different views, but at the same time it is fairly concise. Nor is it a *sharḥ*, as it is not written to explain a specific *matn*. It is considered a useful and practical compilation. Many manuscripts of it exist[51] and the printed edition is widely available. It was first printed in 1948 and republished in 1975,[52] and again recently. The language is condensed. It uses a system of letters before or after statements to indicate who said what.[53] It frequently quotes sources from other law schools and this fact is often pointed out by Zaydī scholars who want to portray themselves as "moderate," and inter-*madhhab*.[54]

---

and understandable metaphor than are references to the sea or ocean. The groundwater metaphor also relates more to the picture of the "watered fruit garden" that the *Azhār* refers to, which al-Shawkānī responded to with *al-Sayl al-jarrār al-mutadaffiq ʿalā ḥadāʾiq al-azhār*, ed. Muḥammad b. Ḥasan Ḥallāq (Damascus and Beirut: Dār Ibn Kathīr, 2005), which was answered by al-Samāwī's *al-Ghaṭamṭam al-zakhkhār* [The vast ocean]. This last title has no clear connection with groundwater, and the term *Ghaṭamṭam* only exists in the poetic realm. Al-Samāwī (d. 1825 or 1826) explains that these titles centre around the idea of symbolic cleansing of "gardens," the removal of the polluting (*najāsa*) elements of al-Shawkānī's ideas, and that he chose a word in the title with even more water than that of a flood, since a large quantity of water is needed to remove ritual pollution. Muḥammad b. Ṣāliḥ b. Hādī l-Samāwī, *al-Ghaṭamṭam al-zakhkhār al-muṭṭahhir li-riyāḍ al-azhār min āthār al-sayl al-jarrār*, ed. Muḥammad b. Yaḥyā b. Sālim ʿIzzān (Amman: Maṭābiʿ Sharikat al-Mawārid al-Ṣināʿiyya al-Urduniyya, 1994), 1:23–24. "Baḥr" is also a metaphoric term for knowledge, as in the expression often found in biographic encyclopaedias: "… *tabaḥḥara fī jamīʿ al-funūn*" ("He travelled in the ocean of knowledge, in all of the disciplines") as, for example, in the biographical entry about Aḥmad ʿAbd al-Raḥmān al-Mujāhid. Zabāra, *Nayl al-waṭar*, 2:215.

50 *Furūʿ* can mean "branches," as on a tree; the roots are its *uṣūl*.

51 At least 30 manuscripts are registered in the catalogue of the Maktabat al-Awqāf, Wizārat al-Awqāf wa-l-Irshād, see al-Ruqayḥī, al-Ḥibshī, and al-Ānisī, *Fihrist makhṭūṭāt*, 2:932–944.

52 The 1975 edition includes a *sharḥ* by Muḥammad b. Yaḥyā Baḥrān al-Ṣaʿdī (d. 957/1549) called *Jawāhir al-akhbār wa-l-āthār al-mustakhraja min lujjat al-baḥr al-zakhkhār*. This "commentary" seems to be mainly a listing of various *ḥadīths*.

53 For further comments on the work and its conventions, see Donaldson, *Sharecropping in the Yemen*, 93–98.

54 Strothman states: "His most valuable work is still his theological and legal encyclopaedia, *Baḥr al-za<u>kh</u>kh<u>ā</u>r* (Berlin MSS 4894–4907) on which he likewise wrote a commentary. Although not the work of an original scholar, it is a rich and well-arranged compilation, which deserves attention, if only for the part of the introduction which compares the various religions, as the distinctions between them are seen from quite a different point of view to that of al-A<u>sh</u>ʿarī or al-<u>Sh</u>ahrastānī." Strothmann, "Mahdī Li-dīn Allāh Aḥmad," 5:1241. It is not clear what this commentary could have been; he is probably referring

2.7 *The* Kitāb al-Azhār *and the Qualities of the* Mukhtaṣar

The *Kitāb al-Azhār* is the most famous *mukhtaṣar* of Zaydī *fiqh*. It is extremely dense, consisting of a long chain of individual rules separated only by the particle *wa* ("and"). In the *waqf* chapter, there are around 80 such rules.[55] Its full title is *Kitāb al-Azhār fī fiqh al-a'imma al-aṭhār*[56] [The book of flowers in the *fiqh* of the purest imams], hereafter called *Kitāb al-Azhār*.

The *Kitāb al-Azhār* is a typical *mukhtaṣar*, meaning that it is a work intended to be short enough to be memorized, at least pieces at a time. Such a text is also called a *matn*, and "learning the *mutūn*" was an important part of education in the *sharīʿa* sciences, not only in *fiqh*.[57] It is a text for the beginner student of *fiqh*, who may not have had a copy of it in written form; every day the student would memorize a certain section, perhaps using his tablet (*lawḥa*) for aid.

The text is not only a coherent system of rules. All examples below are taken from the chapter of *waqf*: For example in certain rules over which there is much disagreement, the author cites an alternative rule; in the *waqf* chapter these alternative rules come from the Caspian Zaydī Imam al-Mu'ayyad. This occurs only twice in the *waqf* chapter. For a comparison, the famous Shāfiʿī *mukhtaṣar* of al-Nawawī, *Minhāj al-ṭālibīn*, often relativizes the rules by adding that the rule in question is "more" or "less" valid,[58] but this rarely happens in the *Kitāb al-Azhār* which simply lists the rules, fairly univocally[59] and without references.

The most basic way to learn the text was to memorize it, along with a separate explanation for each rule.[60] Often the rule mentioned in the *matn* is not the preferred variant of the rule according to the applied law or even according to the law school.[61] In such cases the student used the *matn* as a framework in

---

to the *Ghayth*, which was a commentary or explanation on the *Azhār*, not on *al-Baḥr al-zakhkhār*. How an encyclopaedia can ever be "original" is also not clear.

55 In the *waqf* chapter, there are approximately 70 to 100 rules, depending on how one defines a rule. Some rules mention several conditions or exceptions and sub-rules, etc.

56 al-Imām al-Mahdī li-Dīn Allāh Aḥmad b. Yaḥyā Ibn al-Murtaḍā, *Kitāb al-Azhār fī fiqh al-a'imma al-aṭhār* (Beirut: Dār Maktabat al-Ḥayat, 1973).

57 For example in Arabic grammar; the *Mulḥat al-iʿrāb*, a work that was much used in Yemen, is also a *matn-sharḥ* text (it is written in some 350 rhyming verses (*abyat*)).

58 For example, *fī l-aṣaḥḥ* ("would be the most valid"). See the *waqf* chapter in Shams al-Dīn Muḥammad b. al-Khaṭīb al-Shirbīnī, *Mughnī l-muḥtāj ilā maʿrifat maʿānī alfāẓ al-minhāj* (Beirut: Dār al-Maʿrifa, 2007).

59 In contrast to works that contain a multiplicity of voices and views. The *Kitāb al-Azhār* presents a string of more or less coherent norms, in one voice.

60 For a description of this traditional process of learning, see Messick, *Calligraphic State*, 84–92.

61 For the process of indicating the valid views of the law schools see below.

the learning process, or as a string of text upon which, in order to be correct, he would also have to know the exceptions to the rules stated in the *matn*. Thus studying the *mutūn* involved more than memorization; it also involved the use of a framework, or scaffolding[62] text like the *Kitāb al-Azhār*, in combination with the practical application of the law, as practiced by a judge. In Zaydī Yemen this twofold, slightly ambiguous view of the *sharīʿa* texts is called learning the "*manṭūq* and the *mafhūm*." *Manṭūq* means "spoken; stated," while *mafhūm* means "understood, implicit, meant." This principle enables the student to engage with and use texts that diverge from practical knowledge, or if you will, legal reality. It creates an intellectual tie between an absolute, theoretically valid, norm on the one hand and valid applicable law on the other. This is demonstrated in detail in chapter 6. This does not mean that the "understood" meaning can simply be "understood" in any way and interpreted in any direction, nor that there is a hidden meaning or "defect" in the *matn*: It simply means that what is stated in the *matn* needs to be contextualized in order to make legal sense, and the *manṭūq-mafhūm* principle is the convention that allows for a flexibility in the use of the *matn* as a jurisprudential tool.

Some comments to the rules in the *matn*—be it in the form of explanations, corrections, references to custom or others—are relevant from a doctrinal perspective, while others are relevant from a pragmatic and practical perspective of how to rule a case as a judge. A specific commentary in book form may choose a certain perspective, while the *manṭūq-mafhūm* concept is a much wider awareness that everything must be studied in a context and for a purpose. Therefore, texts like the *Kitāb al-Azhār* are only inspirations that can never be stronger that the individual "proofs" or "evidences" that underpin each individual legal rule. Such reflections are understandably only put forward by very learned scholars in "controlled" settings. The open public emphasis of the uncertainty of Islamic law would undermine the status of both law and jurists. No one would publicly claim that the *Kitāb al-Azhār* "is mainly a structure without legal essence." Questioning a teacher's explanation or commentary of a specific rule, or choosing another diverging commentary in book form, is something the student cannot do in the beginning. Only a rather advanced student can question these flexible elements of text, and often only as part of a wider dissident group, or under political patronage. Students who

62 For the concept of legal scaffolding, see Jackson, Sherman A. "Taqlīd, Legal Scaffolding and the Scope of Legal Injunctions in Post-Formative Theory. Muṭlaq and ʿĀmm in the Jurisprudence of Shihāb al-Dīn al-Qarāfī," *Islamic Law and Society* 3, no. 2 (1996): 165–192. Jackson took the concept mainly from Alan Watson. Here in this study and this chapter the term is used in a more narrow way, related to how the *matn-sharḥ*/commentaries complex is organized in a structure or skeleton that serves a didactic purpose. This structure then also becomes a central spine of the *madhhab*, in matters of *fiqh*.

continue their studies—those that do not quit to become a local notary or an administrator for the state—may specialize in *fiqh* and become a teacher and a scholar. Certain scholars made their own *fiqh* commentaries in book form. Many such commentaries were made on the *Kitāb al-Azhār*, though one in particular became famous shortly after the *Kitāb al-Azhār* and it has remained authoritative, namely the *Sharḥ al-azhār*.

2.8 *Ibn Miftāḥ's (d. 877/1472)* Sharḥ al-azhār

Its full title is *al-Muntazaʿ al-mukhtār min al-ghayth al-midrār al-mufattiḥ li-kamāʾim al-azhār* [The extracted essence from [the book of] the blessed rain, the key to the gardens of the flowers]. It is more commonly known by the title *Sharḥ al-azhār* [The commentary on the [book of] flowers], and will be referred to thus. As mentioned above, Ibn al-Murtaḍā's own commentary on the *Kitāb al-Azhār*, the *Ghayth*, never became popular in the same way as did the commentary by Ibn Miftāḥ.[63] Today Ibn Miftāḥ is only really known for the *Sharḥ al-azhār*. We do not know much about his life. In an entry in his biographical encyclopaedia, the *Badr al-ṭāliʿ*, al-Shawkānī (d. 1834) states that "[Ibn Miftāḥ] is the author of the *sharḥ* that people incline towards," and that the *Sharḥ al-azhār* is a short version of Ibn al-Murtaḍā's *Ghayth*, which he calls *al-Sharḥ al-kabīr* ["the greater commentary"].[64] Al-Shawkānī calls the *Sharḥ al-azhār* "the pillar of the Zaydīs in all of Yemen,"[65] and the *Sharḥ al-azhār* as "the work which students rely on until today."[66] This is a clear description of the prominent position that this work had at the beginning of the nineteenth century. The fact that its position has continued until today is certain from similar comments. Al-Shawkānī also writes that Ibn Miftāḥ was perhaps a student of Ibn al-Murtaḍā, and indicates the link in the chain of knowledge and scholarship between them, but by using the word "perhaps" (*laʿalla*), al-Shawkānī also points to the uncertainty of this link.[67]

The biography of Ibn Miftāḥ in the recent introduction to the *Sharḥ al-azhār* is fuller on this point: Ibn Miftāḥ studied *fiqh* under Faqīh Zayd al-Dhamārī "and read (lit. "heard" *samaʿa*) the *Ghayth al-midrār* under him, and al-Dhamārī was the connecting link (*al-wāsiṭa*) between the two." More such "connections" are given in order to show that Ibn Miftāḥ was indeed strongly

63 His full name is ʿAbdallāh b. Abī l-Qāsim b. Miftāḥ.

64 Given that al-Shawkānī was constantly trying to undermine Zaydī-Hādawī authority, he is not the one to look to for a glorification of the *Sharḥ al-azhār*. However, he added to the quotation above: "despite it not being any more comprehensive than other *shurūḥ*," al-Shawkānī, *al-Badr al-ṭāliʿ*, 434.

65 This he states in the entry describing Ibn al-Murtaḍā, ibid., 157.

66 Ibid., 434.

67 Ibid.

integrated into the mainstream Zaydī *fiqh* of his time. We can also read this as a contemporary attempt to strengthen the Zaydī self image by citing the "chains of knowledge genealogy" of key Zaydī scholars.[68]

The *Sharḥ al-azhār*, as a commentary on a *mukhtaṣar* or a *matn*, is a typical example of a *sharḥ* genre. The genre called *sharḥ* is usually translated into English as "commentary," but the more literal and exact meaning of the word is "explanation." The term "commentary" is not entirely appropriate because, while Ibn Miftāḥ does change the meaning slightly here and there and thus adds his own perspective, he mainly provides the reader of the *Kitāb al-Azhār* with the necessary words to understand the meaning of the text. This is the case for the first of the two stages of the commentary that follow each rule.

First, Ibn Miftāḥ "de-compresses" the *matn*, by adding additional words to it. This stage is certainly better termed an "explanation" than a "commentary." The second stage involves adding quotations and references to provide the evidence and roots of validity for each rule. Again, the term "commentary" is not entirely appropriate because the author does not openly intrude with his own opinions on the text; he simply quotes the opinions of other scholars and compares and contrasts these arguments. If there is much disagreement on a rule, he quotes several scholars and imams, both contemporary and those from the more distant past. Many of the scholars contemporary to him whom he quotes are no longer considered important today and seem to have lost the relevance that Ibn Miftāḥ ascribed them.

An example of the first stage of "de-compressing" a rule, in which the *sharḥ* "wraps" around the *matn* is the rule that will be analysed in detail in chapter 6:

> *Kitāb al-Azhār*: And the sixth [rule] is to rent it out for less than three years.
>
> *Sharḥ al-azhār*: **And the sixth [rule], is** that the *mutawallī* is allowed **to rent it** [the *waqf* asset] **out** for a defined period, however **for less than three years** only.[69]

The *matn* is broken into pieces shorter than the original rule from the *matn* and the *sharḥ* is "wrapped around" these pieces of *matn*. Sometimes even the word *wa* ("and"), or other words are used for another purpose than the author of the *matn* originally intended, however, they always come in the correct sequence. In the manuscripts, the *matn* is usually written in red, and/or in brackets in

68 Ibn Miftāḥ, *Sharḥ al-azhār*, 1:67.

69 "wa-l-sādisa anna li-mutawallī l-waqf **ta'jīruhu** mudda ma'lūma lākin lā yakūnu illā **dūna thalāth sinīn.**" Ibn Miftāḥ, *Sharḥ al-azhār*, 8:271.

printed books. In the new 2003 edition it appears in bold. If the *matn* had not been written in another colour or put in brackets, then the reader would not be able to see the *matn* at all—the reader would have seen one text only. Not all *sharḥ* works are as eloquent as the *Sharḥ al-azhār*. Ibn Miftāḥ is respected for the way he merged the two texts and for his clear and understandable Arabic language. Several informants have explicitly made this latter point.

Then follows the second stage containing the discussion: "al-Faqīh Yaḥyā l-Buḥaybaḥ said:.... Faqīh ʿAlī said:...." Then Ibn Miftāḥ returns to the active voice and says "Yes, and if...." Then he again quotes someone else's view: "Faqīh Yūsuf says: ..."[70] I give a full analysis of this specific rule in chapter 6. All the scholars quoted here quote other Zaydī and Sunnī authorities. The reader only needs a certain depth in the quotations and the references. It often suffices to say that person "A" states that rule Y is valid and the arguments frequently stop here; other scholars, *ḥadīth*s or texts are not quoted. Person "A" gives the validity, full stop. In Ibn Miftāḥ's time, if Faqīh ʿAlī said that al-Hādī said so and so, then this was valid enough, at least for the ideal reader constructed by Ibn Miftāḥ. We can also assume that Ibn Miftāḥ chose the quotations carefully, from a select number of authorities that he believed would be recognized as sufficiently broad for his ideal readers. This way, we can go back in time and analyse what a valid reference was, for whom, what a valid argument was, and how "deep" a reference had to be for it to be accepted. Over the centuries, later versions of the *Sharḥ al-azhār* have seen the addition of multiple layers of glosses that add more references and views.

In the manuscript versions and the first three printed editions of the *Sharḥ al-azhār*, the names of who said what were replaced with a system of abbreviations, in which letters indicate the names. Thus the chains of validity were originally even less clear to the uninitiated reader than in the case demonstrated above. The reader of the *Sharḥ al-azhār* was probably content with a *sharḥ* that made the text understandable as a readable and useful text, rather than it being *the* ultimate *fiqh* work, scrutinizing every possible detail and chain of validity. The readers of this multi-layered text are/were of different types and the vast majority of readers are/were students, not advanced "*ʿulamāʾ* researchers." Later, when the *Sharḥ al-azhār* became the most widely used scaffolding text to deal with Zaydī *fiqh*, more minute details and critical views were added by experts, as comments written on the margins of the manuscript (*ḥāshiya*, pl. *ḥawāshī* or *hāmish*, pl. *hawāmish* or, *taʿlīqāt*). In the first printed editions these glosses were printed as footnotes. Hereafter I use the term "footnotes" or "notes" instead of "glosses," though this term is only meaningful after the

70 Ibn Miftāḥ, *Sharḥ al-azhār*, 8:271–272.

advent of printed editions. The scholars behind these footnotes lived hundreds of years after those quoted by Ibn Miftāḥ. Often, the new scholars, such as the *qāḍī* Ibāhīm al-Saḥūlī (d. 1060/1650) quotes directly from the earlier Zaydī scholars and uses quotations with references to the original authors, such as al-Hādī or al-Manṣūr, thus "bypassing" the scholars of Ibn Miftāḥ's time. But then, the *Sharḥ al-azhār* from the later period, if seen as a book including new footnotes, is a completely different work and different text. The text can be seen to have "evolved" over time as new historical strata were added. We shall return to this below in the chronology.

One of the main doctrinal differences between Zaydism and Sunnism/traditionism relates to the position of *ḥadīth*s as proof for the validity of any given rule. In the *Sharḥ al-azhār* by Ibn Miftāḥ, most of the relevant *waqf ḥadīth*s are given in the introduction to the *waqf* chapter, before the *matn* that contains the rules. But compared to the content of the *matn*, these *ḥadīth*s are not very decisive for the *waqf* chapter as such. They are few, and most *waqf* rules are based on the views of authoritative persons, that is, what someone has stated as the best possible view, with no reference to *ḥadīth*.[71] The consensus of these earlier scholars and their views seems to be sufficient to validate the rules. Ibn Miftāḥ does not need the support of Sunnī *ḥadīth*s. The authoritative view of Sunnī *ḥadīth*s and what they add to the *waqf fiqh* is something that only rare Zaydī scholars concern themselves with, at least until the late Qāsimī dynasty (after 1750s), when Sunnism and *ḥadīth*s were more actively incorporated by *ḥadīth* scholars like al-Shawkānī.[72]

The commentary of Ibn Miftāḥ has gained legitimacy today because he readily quotes a wide range of conflicting sources and this diversity is seen as a sign of quality; thus, it is more of a scholarly debate than univocal commentaries like that of al-Shawkānī, which is much more polemical and favours one result. In other words, Ibn Miftāḥ's commentary is close to what Messick describes as "the open ended texts."[73]

71 That is true in general. Some *ḥadīth*s are referred to, as is the Qur'ān. The point being that while a reference to *ḥadīth* and Qur'ān may appear, it is either taken for granted or too vague to be quoted and instead the reference to, for instance, al-Hādī is sufficient.

72 Sunnī *ḥadīth*s are not necessarily used to criticize Hādawī-Zaydī views only; they were also used to bolster the Hādawī rules. See Haykel, *Revival and Reform*, 9 and the references he gives there. Parts of the Zaydī *fiqh* tradition are so early that certain *ḥadīth*s may not yet have become authoritative, such as the important *ḥadīth* "no testamentation to an heir," which is central in *al-Risāla al-Mahdawiyya* in chapter 5. For the development of this *ḥadīth* specifically, see D. S. Powers, "On the Abrogation of the Bequest Verses," *Arabica* 29, no. 3 (1982): 256–295.

73 See also "Open Texts," in Messick, *Calligraphic State*, 30–36.

None of the versions of the *Sharḥ al-azhār* in manuscript form have been consulted for this study. Therefore, further explanations of conventions in the text are explained in the part dealing with the printed versions of the *Sharḥ al-azhār* below.

2.9 Al-Bayān al-shāfī

Al-Bayān al-shāfī[74] was written by ʿImād al-Dīn Yaḥyā b. Aḥmad al-Muẓaffar (d. 875/1470 or 71). The *Bayān* was another important and much-used *fiqh* work in manuscript form. One indication of its importance is the more than 30 manuscripts of this work in Imam Yaḥyā's *waqf* library.[75] It appeared early in lithographic print, which made it more available, but not easier to read. In 1984 it was edited and printed in four volumes and for a period it was used extensively by the judiciary, alongside with the *Sharḥ al-azhār*. This was partly because at that time the 1980 edition of the *Sharḥ al-azhār* was just a photocopy of the printed 1913–14 version and was difficult to read because of the many handwritten comments. Thus for a period from 1984 until the most recent *Sharḥ al-azhār* edition of 2003, the *Bayān* was perhaps the most useful in terms of the quality of the edition and ease of use. The *Bayān* is much shorter than the *Sharḥ al-azhār*, and because many of the views in the *Bayān* have been entered into the *Sharḥ al-azhār* as footnotes, it has not been used in this study.

2.10 *The* Fatwā *Collection of Imam al-Hādī ʿIzz al-Dīn (d. 900/1445)*

In his biographical dictionary *al-Badr*,[76] al-Shawkānī says about the *fatwā* collection of Imam al-Hādī ʿIzz al-Dīn[77] "… And he has a *fatwā* collection that is enormous (*ḍakhm*) and useful." The *fatwā* collection has recently been edited

74 ʿImād al-Dīn Yaḥyā b. Aḥmad al-Muẓaffar, *Kitāb al-Bayān al-shāfī l-muntaziʿ min al-burhān al-Kāfī* (Sanaa: Maktabat Ghamḍān li-Iḥyāʾ al-Turāth al-Yamanī, 1984). The full title is *al-Bayān al-shāfī l-muntaziʿ min al-burhān al-kāfī fī fiqh al-aʾimma al-aṭhār wa-ittibāʿihim al-akhyār wa-l-fuqahāʾ al-abrār al-jāmiʿ li-masāʾil* *al-sharḥ* *wa-l-Lumaʿ* *wa-fiqh* *al-Baḥr al-zakhkhār* (the three book titles are underlined). The *Sharḥ* referred to in the title could be the *Sharḥ al-azhār*. The *Baḥr* is referred to in the title, as is *al-Lumaʿ* by al-Amīr ʿAlī b. al-Ḥusayn b. Nāṣir (d. 656/1258). The full title is *al-Lumaʿ fī fiqh ahl al-bayt ʿalayhi l-salām*. It is referred to occasionally in the *Sharḥ al-azhār*.

75 al-Ruqayḥī, al-Ḥibshī, and al-Ānisī (eds.), *Fihrist makhṭūṭāt*, 2:953–962. The *Bayān* is also mentioned along with the *Sharḥ al-azhār* and the *Mulḥa* in the mosque drama by Khafanjī mentioned in chapter 3.

76 al-Shawkānī, *al-Badr al-ṭāliʿ*, 455–456.

77 al-Hādī ʿIzz al-Din, *Majmūʿ rasāʾil*. The chapter on *waqf* ("Kitāb al-waqf") is found at 376–481 and the chapter on *waṣāyā* ("Kitāb al-waṣāyā") at 629–660.

by al-Sayyid ʿAbd al-Raḥmān Shāʾim al-Muʾayyadī and is soon to be printed.[78] The collection is not widely known today, but it has been included in this study because of its important legal and historical value. *Fatwās* give a unique insight into the relationship between *fiqh* and applied law.[79] Imam al-Hādī ʿIzz al-Dīn reigned for twenty-one years; his son compiled their collective *fatwās* in one collection, approximately 130 of which are related to *waqf* and *waṣāyā*.

2.11 Taftīḥ al-qulūb

One of the many works from the time just after the *Sharḥ al-azhār* is *Taftīḥ al-qulūb wa-l-abṣār li-htidāʾ ilā kayfiyyat iqtiṭāf athmār al-azhār* by Muḥammad b. Yaḥyā b. Muḥammad b. Bahrān (d. 957/1550).[80] The *Taftīḥ* is a commentary on the *Kitāb al-Azhār*;[81] it is much longer than the *Sharḥ al-azhār* and is a more univocal, concise commentary. Several copies of the manuscript can be found in the catalogue of Imam Yaḥyā's *waqf* library.[82]

2.12 *The* Wābil

Like the *Taftīḥ*, the *Wābil* is a work that relates to the *Kitāb al-Azhār*, and which is later quoted in the footnotes of the *Sharḥ al-azhār*. The full title is *al-Wābil al-maghzār al-maṭʿam li-athmār al-azhār fī fiqh al-aʾimma al-aṭhār* [The abundant shower, the nourishment for the fruits of the flowers]. It was written by Yaḥyā b. Muḥammad b. Ḥasan (d. 990/1582 or 83).[83] Seven copies exist in the catalogue of Maktabat al-Awqāf.[84] Today it is fairly unknown and therefore a

---

78 His son ʿAlī b. ʿAbd al-Raḥmān kindly gave me the pdf files of the edited version.

79 Many scholars have used *fatwās* in the study of *waqf*, including David Powers, Haim Gerber, and García Sanjuán.

80 Muḥammad b. Yaḥyā b. Aḥmad Bahrān al-Ṣaʿdī, *Taftīḥ al-qulūb wa-l-abṣār li-l-ihtidāʾ ilā kayfiyyat iqtiṭāf athmār al-aẓhār* (*sharḥ kitāb al-athmār*) (Sanaa: Maktabat Zayd b. ʿAlī, forthcoming). About Bahrān, see Ibrāhīm b. al-Qāsim, *Ṭabaqāt al-Zaydiyya*, 2:1103–1109, and Ibn Abī l-Rijāl, *Maṭlaʿ al-budūr*, ed. ʿAbd al-Raqīb Muṭahhar Muḥammad Ḥajar (Sanaa: Markaz Ahl al-Bayt li-l-Dirāsāt al-Islāmiyya, 2004), 4:397–405. A Word document of the *waqf* chapter was given to me by the Zayd bin Ali Cultural Foundation in Sanaa as they were preparing an edition of the whole work.

81 It is, more precisely, a commentary on a later version of the *Kitāb al-Azhār* called *al-Athmār* [The fruits] by Imam al-Mutawakkil ʿalā l-Allāh Sharaf al-Dīn Yaḥyā b. Shams al-Dīn (d. 965/1558). Bahrān, who wrote this commentary, was one of his ministers. See al-Wāsiʿī, *Tārīkh al-Yaman*, 194.

82 al-Ruqayḥī, al-Ḥibshī, and al-Ānisī (eds.), *Fihrist makhṭūṭāt*, 2:993–998. There are 13 copies in the Waqf Library.

83 For Yaḥyā b. Muḥammad b. Ḥasan al-Muqrāʾī see Ibn Abī l-Rijāl, *Maṭlaʿ al-budūr*, 4:510–511 and Ibrāhīm b. al-Qāsim, *Ṭabaqāt al-Zaydiyya*, 3:1256–1260. Ibrāhīm b. al-Qāsim gives his death date as 1572 or 1573, thus 980 AH and not 990 AH as Ibn Abī l-Rijāl does.

84 al-Ruqayḥī, al-Ḥibshī, and al-Ānisī (eds.), *Fihrist makhṭūṭāt*, 3:1233–35.

good example of the almost forgotten commentaries on the *Kitāb al-Azhār*, "overtaken" and perhaps even "co-opted" by the *Sharḥ al-azhār*, given that the *Wābil* is now partly incorporated into the footnotes of the *Sharḥ al-azhār*.[85]

2.13 *Muḥammad b. ʿAlī l-Shawkānī and His Works*

Muḥammad b. ʿAlī l-Shawkānī (d. 1834) was a virtuoso scholar of neo-Sunnī/traditionist[86] inclination, who, at the age of 35, in 1795, became a chief *qāḍī* for three imams in the late Qāsimī dynasty.[87] He was close to, if not at the very centre of political power and much of his scholarly work cannot be understood without understanding the context in which he lived, and seeing his need to attack the authority of the previous Zaydī imams and the Zaydī law school as a source of validity and legitimacy outside Qāsimī authority. He became an authority in his own right, by claiming that the very criteria of validity in *fiqh* had to be changed, as we see below. Especially in his later works he appears very independent and self-confident. He was not the first Zaydī who sought to incorporate Sunnī *ḥadīths*; other prominent scholars and authors who leaned in this direction include Muḥammad b. Ibrāhīm al-Wazīr (d. 840/1436), Ṣāliḥ b. Mahdī l-Maqbalī (d. 1108/1696) and Muḥammad b. Ismāʿīl al-Amīr (d. 1182/1769).[88]

Al-Shawkānī wanted to re-build the *sharīʿa* on textual proofs based directly on the "original" sources, which he claimed that the Zaydīs had overlooked. He tried to present the *sharīʿa* as accessible by methodological inference directly from the texts of the Qur'ān and the canonical Sunnī *ḥadīth* collections without having to rely on the other law schools.

Al-Nayl al-awṭār: In 1795, at the age of 35, he completed his *ḥadīth* commentary, *Nayl al-awṭār* [The achievement of the goals].[89] As we see in chapter 5,

85 For instance the view of the *Wābil* on the three-year rule is given under note 10 of the treatment of the rule in the *Sharḥ al-azhār*. See chapter 6 in this book.

86 The term traditionist refers to those who give *ḥadīths* a relatively prominent role as a source of law. Another related term is *ahl al-sunna*, as opposed to the Zaydīs/Hādawīs/Shīʿīs who give preference to the *ahl al-bayt*, that is, they favour the descendants of the Prophet through ʿAlī and the knowledge and authority they carried and continue to carry until today. This doctrinal divide takes many forms and has many layers; Bernard Haykel shows how al-Shawkānī placed himself in a neo-Sunnī tradition that, with regard to some political and doctrinal questions, is outside classical Zaydism. Haykel, *Revival and Reform*.

87 Al-Manṣūr ʿAlī (r. 1775–1809), al-Mutawakkil Aḥmad (r. 1809–1816) and al-Mahdī ʿAbdallāh (r. 1816–1835). See the genealogical map before the introduction in Haykel, *Revival and Reform*.

88 Haykel, *Revival and Reform*, 10.

89 Ibid., 147. The version of the *Nayl* used in this thesis is Muḥammad b. ʿAlī l-Shawkānī, *Nayl al-awṭār: sharḥ muntaqā l-akhbār min aḥādīth sayyid al-akhyār* (Beirut: Dār Iḥyāʾ al-Turāth al-ʿArabī, 2001).

there is a chapter on *waqf* in this work, but it is more oriented towards the scope of available *ḥadīths* than towards applicable contractual (*waqf*) law.

Al-Fatḥ al-rabbānī: Over the years al-Shawkānī wrote an enormous collection of *fatwās* that have recently been edited and printed under the name *al-Fatḥ al-rabbānī*.[90] Here we find numerous practical legal treatises, in which legal questions are central and the *ḥadīths* or "textual proofs" are added in support of the arguments. Many of the *fatwās* in this work are long and very thorough and indeed full-fledged treatises.

Al-Sayl al-jarrār: In 1819 or 1820[91] he completed *al-Sayl al-jarrār al-mutadaffiq ʿalā ḥadāʾiq al-azhār* [The flash flood flowing towards the gardens of the flowers],[92] which is among the latest of his great works. The book is a criticism of the full corpus of Zaydī *fiqh* rules. He agrees with some Zaydī *fiqh* rules, but he validates them based on his own criteria of evidence; others he sweeps aside in eloquent, self-confident polemical language. The *Sayl* follows the structure and the *matn* of the *Kitāb al-Azhār*, and criticises it sentence by sentence, or rule by rule, in the style of "he said; I say."

Al-Darārī l-muḍīya: Among his later works was a work of *fiqh* in the style of a *matn sharḥ* called *al-Darārī l-muḍīya, sharḥ al-durrar al-bahīya*. It is very short; the *matn* of the chapter on *waqf* is only one paragraph and contains only seven rules. It is a work that exemplifies what *fiqh*, or rather, a corpus of "positive law," would look like if al-Shawkānī's methodology were applied on the texts of revelation. Arguably, his *fiqh* is very "thin" and, as in his jurisprudence of *waqf*, for practical purposes it leaves most judicial decisions to *maṣlaḥa* and *ʿurf*, two sources that he originally claimed were not proper sources of certain law.[93]

90 al-Shawkānī, *al-Fatḥ al-rabbānī: Fatāwā l-Imām al-Shawkānī*, ed. Muḥammad b. Ḥasan Ḥallāq (Sanaa: Maktabat al-Jīl al-Jadīd, 2002). Haykel, *Revival and Reform*, 19.

91 Haykel, *Revival and Reform*, 19.

92 A translation of the full title is, 'The raging flood, destroying the gardens of the flowers.' Again, the reference is to the "gardens" of Zaydī *fiqh*. *Mutadaffiq* can mean destroying, or simply "flowing": Zabāra describes the village of Ḥadda and he uses the term "*anhār mutadaffiqa*" for the spring-fed streams there in a way that likely means something like "upwelling" or "flowing." Zabāra, *A'immat al-Yaman*, 2:1:224. Al-Wāsiʿī uses the term in a similar way to describe the *qanāt* (brook) Ghayl Abū Ṭālib. He says that the "Ghayl Abū Ṭālib *yatadaffiqu ilā* al-Rāwḍa," (i.e., "flows" to al-Rāwḍa). Al-Wāsiʿī, *Tārīkh al-Yaman*, 93. In this case, the "flood" is not "raging" or "destroying," but "irrigating"; "giving life to." Similarly the term "*jarrār*" does not necessarily mean something negative, it can also mean "abundant." Here my point is not to argue for one or the other meaning; the ambiguity of meanings is interesting.

93 For his section on *maṣlaḥa* and *istiḥsān* in his own *uṣūl* work, see Muḥammad b. ʿAlī l-Shawkānī, *Irshād al-fuḥūl ilā taḥqīq al-ḥaqq min ʿilm al-uṣūl*, ed. Muḥammad Ṣubḥī b. Ḥasan Ḥallāq (Damascus and Beirut: Dār Ibn Kathīr, 2000), 786–795.

The result is a model that has two layers of law, one that is "pure," built on "certain knowledge" from the holy texts and is, arguably, fairly thin, and another that admits to other types of knowledge and sources for law, such as various levels of *maṣlaḥa* and *ʿurf*. In his critique of the Zaydī law school, he deliberately mixes these two versions of law by explicitly referring to his textually "proven" law when attacking Zaydī law, but only implicitly admitting that the law has a purpose and that the purpose is related to the real world and necessitates knowledge of the real world. Al-Shawkānī claims that his law is based on clear and obvious "extracts" of the holy texts, while Zaydī law is mere opinion.

Related to these issues of legal validity mentioned above are al-Shawkānī's views on who should be allowed to undertake his methodology. In his book *Adab al-ṭalab*,[94] he produces a set of grades of "knowers" and states that only the ultimate expert, a *mujtahid marjaʿ*, should be allowed to produce law from the holy sources. In practice, one is left to wonder if this leaves him and no one else able to produce laws in this way. One can therefore discuss whether his version of the law can be "understood" at all without relying on experts like him as intermediaries, thus everyone else must employ *taqlīd*.[95]

Haykel's biography of al-Shawkānī makes the argument that his works must be understood as part of the political context of the time. Al-Shawkānī's clear language, polemical style, and erudition of the Islamic sciences are exceptional. In his discussion of specific *fiqh* rules, his argumentation is made into an advanced game, though the practical legal implications of his argument are not always that different from the traditional Zaydī view.[96] After all, he was the chief *qāḍī* in a society where traditional Zaydī legal practices had to be accepted to a large extent, and although he gave the impression that he was implementing a new legal order, in practice, we have little historical evidence that the legal practices related to *waqf* actually underwent any significant changes.

2.14 *Printed Versions of the* Sharḥ al-azhār

The *Sharḥ al-azhār* was printed in four volumes early in the twentieth century. In other parts of the Islamicate world, *fiqh* works had been in print for decades. However, in Yemen, this development took place much later and old manuscripts were still copied, read, and memorized. The reason for this late development is not clear, but could be related to the lack of printing facilities. Some works were printed as lithographs, since this did not involve the same editing process. We do not know of any early lithographic prints of the *Sharḥ*

94 al-Shawkānī, *Adab al-ṭalab*, 108–140.
95 Haykel, *Revival and Reform*, 102–108.
96 This is exemplified in chapters 5 and 6.

al-azhār. There are five printed editions of the *Sharḥ al-azhār*: The first edition was printed in 1913–14, the second in 1921–22, the third in 1938, the fourth in 1980, and the fifth in 2003.

2.15 *The 1913–14 Edition*

The first edition was typeset by hand and printed in Cairo in 1913–14, although there is some debate about this date.[97] The first page states that it was printed at the press of Maṭbaʿat Sharikat al-Tamaddun in Cairo with the support of a certain ʿAlī b. Yaḥyā l-Yamānī. Further, it states that the manuscript used for this edition was a manuscript of the *Kitāb al-Azhār* with the *Sharḥ al-azhār* written by al-Shawkānī himself, and the margins were written by al-Shawkānī's student ʿAlī l-Suhayl in 1792 or 1793.[98] Al-Suhayl studied the *Sharḥ al-azhār* under al-Shawkānī and wrote the margins based on his lessons with al-Shawkānī.[99]

The first page in the 1913–14 edition describes how the structure and conventions of the manuscript had to be slightly changed to accommodate the typesetting process:

---

97 There is some disagreement over this: Messick quotes biographical sources that say it was printed at al-Manār Press in 1920–21 and that it was done by the famous intellectual and historian ʿAbd al-Wāsiʿī with the financial support of al-Shaykh ʿAlī b. Yaḥyā l-Hamdānī. He also quotes Serjeant, who states that it was printed in Cairo in 1910. Messick, *Calligraphic State*, 296 n56. This could have been the *Kitāb al-Azhār*, but not the *Sharḥ al-azhār*. Bernard Haykel mentions a different view: He mainly quotes the same sources and also gives the year 1921, however, he also remarks that the first page of the *Sharḥ al-azhār* explicitly states that it was printed at the Maṭbaʿat Sharikat al-Tamaddun in Cairo in 1914 with the support of ʿAlī b. Yaḥyā l-Yamānī. Haykel, *Revival and Reform*, 207 n66. The 1980 edition volume 1 seems to be based on the 1913–14 edition while volume 3, which includes the *waqf* chapter, might be based on the 1921–22 edition. This could mean that in 1913–14 only volume 1 and perhaps volume 2 were printed while volume 3 was printed first in 1921–22. (I was not able to verify this with the material I had available.).

98 Al-Qāḍī l-ʿAllāma ʿAlī b. ʿAbdallāh Suhayl (d. 1835). On his biography, Haykel quotes the *Tiqṣār* (not consulted here) and states that al-Shawkānī made him judge in Sanaa. See Haykel, *Revival and Reform*, 61.

99 Ṭabʿ (or ṭubiʿa) hādha al-kitāb ʿalā nuskha muṣaḥḥaḥa nusikhat bi-ḥawāshīhā ʿālā nuskhat shaykh al-Islām al-qāḍī l-ʿallāma Muḥammad b. ʿAlī l-Shawkānī sanat 1207 wa-quriʾat ʿalayhi wa-dhālika bi-khaṭṭ al-qāḍī ʿAlī b. ʿAbdallāh Suhayl. ʿAbdallāh Abū l-Ḥasan Ibn Miftāḥ, *Kitāb al-Muntaziʿ al-mukhtār min al-ghayth al-midrār al-mufattiḥ li-kamāʾim al-azhār fī fiqh al-aʾimma al-aṭhār* (*Sharḥ al-azhār*) (Cairo: Maṭbaʿat Sharikat al-Tamaddun, 1913–14), vol. 1, first page. It is not entirely clear if al-Shawkānī himself wrote the *sharḥ* and al-Suhayl the glosses (margins, *ḥawāshī*), but the passage quoted above indicates the connection between them and that the manuscript was in al-Suhayl's hand. Two aspects are important: One is the invocation of the authority of al-Shawkānī, and the second is the irony that al-Shawkānī, an opponent of traditional Zaydī *fiqh*, was also central to the production of the most important work of Zaydī *fiqh* today.

[1] The glosses (*ḥawāshī*) on the margins around the *sharḥ* were made into numbered footnotes under the main text (i.e., under the *sharḥ*).
[2] The *tadhhīb* marks or signs (see below), if occurring over the *sharḥ* text or at the beginning of a gloss could not be practically converted into print and were left out altogether.
[3] The small comments interjected between the lines in the main text could not be printed and were given as footnotes.
[4] The *tadhhīb* signs at the end of sentences are given as a *taqrīr*, represented by the letters "q-r-z" that originated from the scholars of the school (*ahl al-madhhab*) who used this sign (consisting of the letter *rāʾ* with a dot above) to indicate the validity (*al-ṣiḥḥa*) of a statement. "It is a sign of statements that they chose ... and this is a statement [of validation] (*taqrīr*) without using words ... represented by the letters q-r-z."[100]

The *taqrīr* and the *tadhhīb* signs are fundamental parts of the text in the manuscript. The *tadhhīb* signs consist of the letters *hāʾ* joined with a *bāʾ* without a dot, inserted over, or after a statement to indicate *madhhab* consensus regarding that statement. The *taqrīr* is used for the same purpose, but at the end of the sentence. Hereafter, I will use the term "validation signs" for both.[101] These are signs that have been used over the centuries to indicate that some views are stronger than others, and that some of them carry the general consensus of the Hādawī-Zaydī school; this is, to an extent, comparable to the Ḥanafī *ẓāhir al-riwāya*.[102]

As stated, the process of converting the *tadhhīb* signs into print did not work for technical reasons, so signs that originally appeared over the lines were simply omitted. Only those at the end of a line could be printed, which in practice meant the *taqrīr* signs (letters q-r-z). However, since manuscripts continued to be used alongside the printed version, these signs were later added to the printed versions during lessons, usually in handwriting with ink. In this way the validation signs "survived" because of the overlap in the usage of two types of texts and because students wanted to continue the tradition of indicating which legal views had been validated. From 1792–93, until the production of the first printed edition, relatively few changes in the validation signs were made. A few differences may be found in some manuscript copies, but overall

100 al-Shawkānī, *Kitāb al-Muntaziʿ al-mukhtār min al-ghayth al-midrār al-mufattiḥ li-kamāʾim al-azhār fī fiqh al-aʾimma al-aṭhār* (*Sharḥ al-azhār*) (Sanaa: Wizārat al-ʿAdl / Dār Iḥyāʾ al-Turāth al-Islāmī, 1980), 1:1.

101 There is also a third *qawīy* ("strong") which is also used at the end of the sentence, or argument; this indicates not a full validation, but a preference. In the *waqf* chapter this rarely occurs.

102 Vikør, *Between God and the Sultan*, 158–159.

they seem to be fairly coherent and consistent.[103] However since the 1792–93 manuscript, quite a few new glosses/comments have appeared. From around 1920 these appear as handwritten on the margins of the new printed text. These were presumably not part of the 1792–93 manuscript since they were left out at the time of editing. Usually, these comments are elaborations on details only.[104] There is also a biographical encyclopaedia at the beginning of the book that provides information about the names that appear in the text. Moreover, there is also a key to abbreviations, a short collection of applicable *fatwās*, and a list of the legal maxims of the *madhhab*.[105]

2.16 *The 1921–22 Edition*

The 1921–22 edition seems to be the same as the previous one, with minor exceptions.[106] The first page states that it was printed in Cairo[107] at Maṭbaʿat al-Maʿārif.

2.17 *The 1938 Edition*

The 1938 edition is slightly different from the previous editions. This edition has not been used in this study. It was printed at the Maṭbaʿat al-Ḥijāzī in Cairo in September/October 1938. The first page states that this is the second edition, that it contains additional footnotes and that it is an "improved edition" funded by some of the "*sāda* of Yemen."[108] This edition is not mentioned by Messick or Haykel, but is referred to by Serjeant.[109]

2.18 *The 1980 Edition*

The 1980 edition is a page by page photocopy of the 1913–14 edition of the same number of volumes. This reprint was funded by the ministry of justice. In the handwritten foreword to the 1980 edition, the minister of justice points out the importance of availability of books for students of law and for the judiciary

103 This could not be investigated in detail, but a general impression indicates little change.

104 A critical comparative study of several copies of both manuscripts and printed editions would give us more information.

105 I do not know which of these components exist in the following editions, except that they are all present in the 1980 edition, which is based on the 1913–14 edition.

106 I have only the first page of the 1921–22 edition, and only the last lines of the first page are different; these lines state where it was printed and from whom the support for this was given.

107 Lit., "Miṣr."

108 The decorative edge of the front page is also slightly different. The title page comes after the biographical dictionary. I have only seen this version; it has not been used in this study and is not quoted in this book.

109 al-ʿAmrī and Serjeant, "Administrative Organisation," 152 n98.

in general. He states that the students at the Maʿhad al-ʿAlī li-l-Qaḍāʾ ("High Institute for Judges") had to study from handwritten copies and circulate them among themselves in a system that was considered primitive. Both the courts and the judiciary in general were in need of a legal reference work. Then he continues with statements that highlight the importance of the *Sharḥ al-azhār* and explain how the 1980 edition came about. Note his mixture of modern law terms with those of the more traditional "*sharīʿa*-language":

> … therefore we have acquired a number of copies of the book *Sharḥ al-azhār* … as it is considered a fundamental reference for the judiciary (*marjaʿ assāsī li-l-qaḍāʾ*) … [and because it] is a reference for codification (*marjaʿ li-l-taqnīn*) of the Islamic *sharīʿa* rules today … [and it is a book that] covers more than other books and contains views from all the different law schools and the evidences behind these rules (*adillatuhā*), especially in what concerns the legal rules (*furūʿ*) in the fields of transactional civil law (*al-muʿāmalāt al-madaniyya*), criminal law (*jināʾiyya*), personal status laws (*al-aḥwāl al-shakhṣiyya*) and rules of judicial procedure (*ijrāʾāt al-qaḍāʾiyya*). The choice fell on this specific manuscript which has been corrected and used for study for several generations, and therefore contains most of the marginal glosses (*ḥawāshī*) that have accumulated over time in manuscripts of the scholars of law (*mashāʾikh al-ʿilm*) who are known from study circles (*ḥalaqāt*) from all the well known religious schools of Yemen (*madāris al-ʿilmiyya al-mashhūra fī l-Yaman*).[110]

On the first page it further says that the work was led by ʿAbdallāh Ismāʿīl Ghumḍān and that the book that was used as a basis for the photocopy print was the personal copy of the prominent scholar Mutahhar b. Yaḥyā b. Ḥasan al-Kuḥlānī (d. 1957). The 1980 edition is an offset print copied from the 1913–14 edition of al-Kuḥlānī's book, containing his personal notes between the lines, commentaries in the margins and also all the *tadhhīb* signs above the chosen rulings. On some pages that were particularly well used, such as the chapter on sales, the margins are full of comments. In the chapter on *waqf* the extent of the comments varies from page to page as well. For example, the section on how to distribute a family *waqf* to the members of the family is full of comments, while other pages are left with fewer or almost no marginal comments.

110 Ibn Miftāḥ, *Kitāb al-muntaziʿ al-mukhtār*, vol. 1, foreword by the minister of justice (1980 edition).

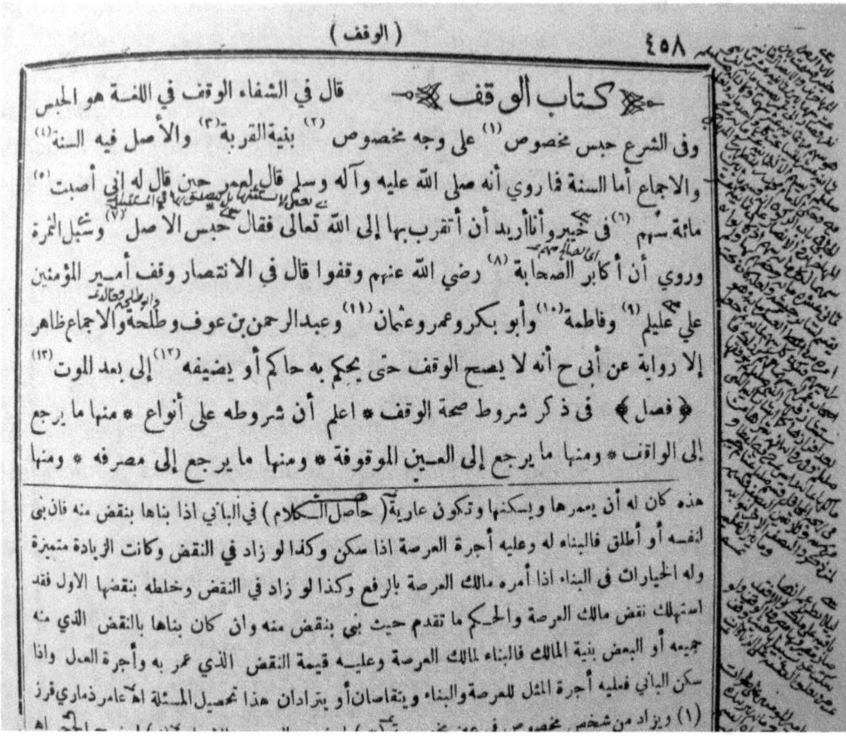
(الوقف) ٤٥٨

كتاب الوقف قال في الشفاء الوقف في اللغة هو الحبس
وفي الشرع حبس مخصوص (١) على وجه مخصوص (٢) بنية القربة (٣) والأصل فيه السنة (٤)
والاجماع أما السنة فما روي أنه صلى الله عليه وآله وسلم قال لعمر حين قال له إني أصبت (٥)
مائة سهم (٦) في خيبر وأنا أريد أن أتقرب بها إلى الله تعالى فقال حبس الاصل (٧) وسبّل الثمرة
وروي أن أكابر الصحابة (٨) رضي الله عنهم وقفوا قال في الانتصار وقف أمير المؤمنين
علي عليه (٩) وفاطمة (١٠) وأبو بكر وعمر وعثمان (١١) وعبدالرحمن بن عوف وطلحة والاجماع ظاهر
إلا رواية عن أبي ح أنه لا يصح الوقف حتى يحكم به حاكم أو يضيفه (١٢) إلى بعد الموت (١٣)
﴿فصل﴾ في ذكر شروط صحة الوقف * اعلم أن شروطه على أنواع * منها ما يرجع
إلى الواقف * ومنها ما يرجع إلى العين الموقوفة * ومنها ما يرجع إلى مصرفه * ومنها

FIGURE 7 Section of the first page of the chapter of *waqf* in the *Sharḥ al-azhār* (1980 edition).

In sum, the 1980 edition has even more layers of texts than previous versions of the *Sharḥ al-azhār*, all of which stem from a specific period. This edition includes:

1. The *matn* of Ibn al-Murtaḍā (d. 840/1437).
2. The *sharḥ* of Ibn Miftāḥ (d. 876/1472).
3. The glosses on the margins, from the time of Ibn Miftāḥ until al-Shawkānī/Suhayl's manuscript in 1792–93.[111]
4. The comments and notes after 1792–93 until (latest al-Kuḥlānī's death, but probably some time earlier) 1957, and the set of validation signs that were omitted in 1913–14, but which stem from the period 1792–93 until (the latest in) 1957. In the 1980 edition, the textual layers 1, 2, and 3 appear

111 That is, minus the validation signs of the type *tadhhīb*, which were not entered in 1913–14 edition.

as printed letters, while textual layer 4[112] still appears in handwriting, as seen in figure 7 above.

In the latest edition from 2003, this final layer was also made into print, as can be seen at the copy of the first page of the *waqf* chapter of the 2003 edition in the very beginning of chapter 8 in this book.

2.19 *The 2003 Edition*

The 2003 edition was much needed. It emerged in a totally different political setting than that of the 1980 edition, in a setting of Zaydī revival, as I discuss below.[113] The reprinting was needed, as the 1980 edition could no longer be found in bookshops and the handwriting of al-Kuḥlānī was difficult to read. Other deficiencies, which also relate to the older versions, were the extensive use of abbreviations for names of scholars, groups of scholars, and books. In all editions except the new 2003 edition, most proper names are not given in full, but only indicated by one or two letters of abbreviation. Where the *Sharḥ al-azhār* 2003 edition reads "al-Faqīh ʿAlī stated," earlier editions often read in passive: "it has been stated by ʿ." In Arabic this appears as "*qīla* ʿ," where the letter *ʿayn* is the abbreviation for ʿAlī as in figure 8 below, the letter *f* for al-Faqīh Yūsuf, etc.[114] This change from "*qīla* + abbreviation" to "*qāla* + full name" was made in the 2003 edition to facilitate the reading of the text by eliminating some of the abbreviations. The inclusion of an explicit subject after the verb in a passive construction is grammatically strange, and also slightly changes the text. By removing the "*qīla*," the meaning is changed, as "*qīla*" meant that the view being quoted is considered weaker than a statement following "*qāla*."[115]

We can see that Ibn Miftāḥ uses *qīla* (evident in the pre-2003 editions) in a subtle way, to include views that are critical and reasonable in their own capacity, but that do not originate from one of the "famous" imams and scholars. Ibn Miftāḥ does this by placing the argument of al-Hādī first and saying "*qāla* al-Hādī," or by using the more grandiose "*qāla Mawlāna ʿalayhi al-salām,*

112 And the *tadhhīb* of text layer 3.

113 For example, in the tense situation in Sanaa during the fieldwork, several bookshops did not sell the *Sharḥ al-azhār* because it was a symbol of Zaydism.

114 For the abbreviation key, see Ibn Miftāḥ, *Kitāb al-muntaziʿ al-mukhtār* (1980 ed.), 1:55–56. Another corresponding key is found in the introduction of *al-Baḥr al-zakhkhār*. Examples of the change from *qīla* to *qāla* are given in chapter 6. Actually, only the letter ʿayn refers to al-Sayyid Abū l-ʿAbbās al-Ḥasanī, but *qīlaʿ* refers to *faqīh* ʿAlī. Thus there is also a distinction here between scholars of the *ahl al-bayt* and those who do not identify as such.

115 Ibn Miftāḥ explicitly points out the intended weakness of Ibn al-Murtaḍā's *matn*, for instance at 8:222 and 8:268, thus Ibn al-Murtaḍā certainly used this convention in the text to indicate the relative strength of the argument. I am not sure that Ibn Miftāḥ's usage is exactly the same.

anna …" (our Lord, peace be upon him, stated that …), where "our Lord" refers to Ibn al-Murtaḍā, the author of the *matn*.

There are various versions of the 2003 edition in a Word file online; these are downloadable in various file formats.[116] The 2003 edition has a distinctly more modern look and a more tidy appearance (see fig. 19). It was printed in 10 volumes in black with a distinct "Islamic" look on the cover and back, with bold, gilded calligraphy that spells out *Sharḥ al-azhār* when all ten volumes are set together on a shelf. Most validation signs and handwritten comments from the 1980 edition are included.[117] The differentiation between the *taqrīr* and the *tadhhīb* validation signs has been maintained. All in all, the text is much easier to read than those of previous editions, especially for someone who is studying the text alone, without a traditional *sharīʿa* education. For the first time the validation signs are printed over the sentence they are supposed to validate, so the printed text matches that of the manuscripts. The *fatwā* collection in the introductory chapter has been omitted, but the biographical encyclopaedia and the list of legal maxims appear.

The new introduction invokes the authority of (the same!) President ʿAlī ʿAbdallāh Ṣāliḥ, the Republic of Yemen and the ministry of justice. There is a foreword by the then minister of justice, Aḥmad ʿAbdallāh al-ʿAqqāb; in many ways this is similar to the foreword of the 1980 edition—it explains the need for a new edition and also emphasizes the unique position of the *Sharḥ al-azhār* in Zaydī and Yemeni *fiqh*.

3 Zaydī Validated *Fiqh*, Imamic Decrees, Yemeni Codification and Laws

3.1 *Making Order in the Validation Marks* (Taqīr, Tadhhīb)

There is a general consensus that most rules relating to *waqf* fall under the category of *masāʾil farʿiyya, ẓanniyya* ("rules built on probable knowledge"), as

116 For example: http://www.yasoob.org/books/htm1/m004/06/n00681.html (accessed April 2015). There are also scanned pdf files and other formats shared on flash disks circulating among young scholars. Some of these files are also organised in online book packages, e.g., "al-Maktaba al-zaydiyya" where the most important Zaydī works are included. A Sunnī counterpart is "al-Maktaba al-shāmila." I did not study these electonic files in detail here; it would be important to include them in future studies.

117 One exception can be found in the treatment of the rule allowing a *waṣīya* for heirs in *Sharḥ al-azhār* (2003 ed.) 10:408, where a validation sign in the *Sharḥ al-azhār* (1980 ed.) is not found in the *Sharḥ al-azhār* (2003 ed.), something that reflects a change in legal opinion, as discussed in chapter 5.

opposed to the category of *masāʾil qaṭʿiyya* ("certain, or absolute knowledge"). It means that most *waqf* rules are open to discussion and cannot be considered certain, or absolute. Most (*sharīʿa* educated) Zaydīs would say that in the case of *waqfs*, validity comes from the good arguments that support the rule, which are often based on some sort of *maṣlaḥa* (interest, utility) and that the important scholars of the past favoured one or the other variant of a rule, while at the same time they respected the debate as such. The consensus of the law school leads to the "best possible view," although the strength of this consensus varied from rule to rule. This is not to be confused with the concept of imamic decrees (*ikhtiyārāt*), in which the imam chooses rules that lack clear validity in the texts of revelation or in the *fiqh*. The scholarly community also have a need to know what is the more correct, valid view when this is not obvious from the discussion about each rule. Thus on an ideal scholarly level, all views are equal (*kulla mujtahid muṣīb*[118]) while on a lower, legal level, for a person without education, every view cannot be equal since contradiction causes confusion and erodes authority. Contradiction in *fiqh* is something that is "academic" and is allowed only at a certain level and certain distance from the applied judiciary and mundane life. This ambiguity is challenging to represent, but one of great importance and our distinction between the knowledge in the field of *fiqh* and the knowledge in the field of codification (as outlined in chapter 2) is useful and necessary. It is necessary to see a distinction in the *fiqh* itself between "open," academic *fiqh* and via the limiting frames of the law school, to the fairly codified applicable *fiqh*, approaching the *fiqh* that the judges find relevant in what they refer to in judgments and what they actually follow in court.

In a work like the *Sharḥ al-azhār*, all these levels can be found at the same time and the textual conventions do distinguish between them. Even in the academic *fiqh* debates, some views or arguments are stronger than others and some views are "validated" over time by generations of scholars. In the *Sharḥ al-azhār* there are two types of this validation, the so-called *taqrīr* (lit., decisions, or validations) and the so-called *tadhhīb* (belonging to the *madhhab*, or school).

The *tadhhīb* is a little sign inserted above the beginning of an argument, in the form of the letters *hāʾ* and *bāʾ*, the *bāʾ* being without a dot. The *taqrīr* occur in the footnotes only, while the *tadhhīb* are also used in the *sharḥ*. As stated above, there were problems in printing the *tadhhīb* signs in the first

118 "Kulla mujtahid fī l-masāʾil al-farʿiyya muṣīb." This is indeed one of the legal maxims listed in the introduction to the *Sharḥ al-azhār*, maxim number 2, Ibn Miftāḥ, *Sharḥ al-azhār* (2003 ed.), 1:14.

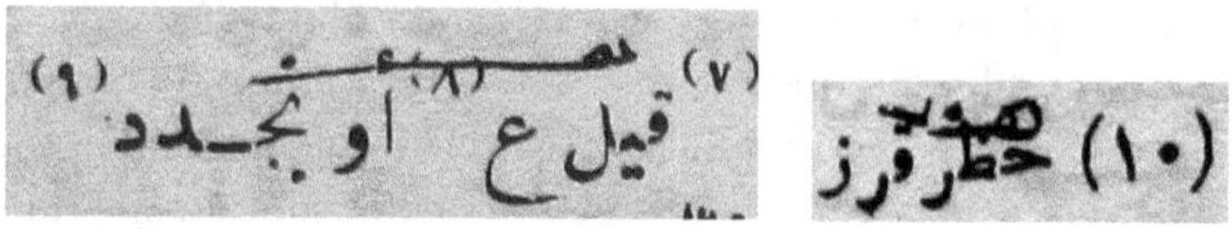

FIGURE 8 *Taqrīr* and *tadhhīb*, "validation marks." *Sharḥ al-azhār* (1980 edition) 3:479 (three-year rule).

printed editions of the *Sharḥ al-azhār* whereas in the 2003 edition they were printed above the rule they validate, as in manuscripts.[119]

It is vital for us to ask, "By what process has this *madhhab* come to such a legal consensus?" And more specifically, "in what political and historical contexts have these consensuses emerged?" Can the law school possibly produce a general consensus over hundreds of years, if the topic in question is politically controversial? The nature of the discussion in Ibn Miftāḥ's *sharḥ* indicates a preference for certain views (as exemplified in chapter 6). The way these views appear is changed by the addition of footnotes, comments, specifications, and validation marks both in the footnotes and in the *sharḥ* itself, all of which are younger than the *sharḥ*. How, since the death of Ibn Miftāḥ in 1472 did this take place?

The history of the validation marks is not known in detail. Most of the information comes from Ḥusayn al-Sayāghī.[120] Al-Sayāghī states that the phenomenon began in the mediaeval period when scholars put small signs above the views they themselves preferred.[121] Al-Sayāghī refers to two important stages in the systematization of the validation marks:

The first stage relates to the scholar Ḥasan b. Aḥmad al-Shabībī (1695 or 1696–1755). Al-Shabībī was born in Ānis, studied in Dhamār, and later in Sanaa and several other towns. He became a teacher and had many students, several of whom later became very well known *ʿulamāʾ*. He specialized in the marginal commentaries (*ḥawāshī*) of the *Sharḥ al-azhār* and those of related works like *al-Bayān al-shāfī*. He became an authority in *tadhhīb* matters and was also later called the "imam of the *madhhab*." It has also been noted that he kept away from government work, perhaps as a way to indicate his scholarly neutrality.[122] Based on this information about al-Shabībī we might believe that he was an

119 For this study, I have only analysed the use of these signs in printed editions, not in manuscripts.

120 Ḥusayn Aḥmad al-Sayāghī, *Uṣūl al-madhhab al-Zaydī l-Yamanī*, unpublished photo copy (1984). This is also pointed out in Würth, *Ash-sharīʿa fī Bāb al-Yaman*, 53–54.

121 Since manuscripts were not consulted with this purpose in mind, I do not address this issue in the present work.

122 Zabāra, *Nashr al-ʿarf*, 1:420–422.

independent, travelling, "academic" *fiqh* specialist, accepted and respected by students, later to be the new generation of scholars. But at the same time, we must be critical, as there are no counter narratives to this account and al-Shabībī himself never taught in the northern areas. Would the Zaydī scholars of Sa'da have validated the same rules he did? This important stage in the long history of Zaydī-Yemeni codification can only be investigated further by comparing the validation marks from different manuscripts from different regions and scholars of the same period, a task that could not be done in this study.

Furthermore, al-Sayāghī elaborates on the second stage of the systematization of the validation marks, and in this account it appears that there were parallel systems of validation marks. At this time, different scholars and regions had their own versions of the validation marks. Imam al-Mahdī ʿAbdallāh (r. 1816–1835) ordered that the validation marks be systematized, since there were diverging views. He ordered the Shaykh al-Islām of the time, Aḥmad b. ʿAbd al-Raḥmān al-Mujāhid to follow the validation marks of the scholar Ḥasan al-Shabībī and this was carried out.[123]

Since we know that few of the validation marks were included in the first printed edition, we must assume that those found in the 1980 edition in al-Kuḥlānī's hand must have "survived" from al-Shabībī and al-Mujāhid. This does not resolve the issue of validation marks by other scholars, including the problem of how the 2003 edition incorporated these (or if it incorporated them), or if the difference is relevant at all. In general, the validation marks in the 1980 edition and 2003 edition seem to overlap.[124]

---

123 This whole process is also referred to by Würth, *Ash-sharīʿa fī Bāb al-Yaman*, 53–54. This account is problematic: if the above were correct then Aḥmad b. ʿAbd al-Raḥmān al-Mujāhid would have been just 26 years old (if he was asked to do this in 1835, the year the Imam died). It seems odd that a man could be *shaykh al-Islām* at this young age. Aḥmad b. ʿAbd al-Raḥmān was not the chief *qāḍī* after al-Shawkānī, as this position went to al-Shawkānī's brother Yaḥyā. Haykel, *Revival and Reform*, 184. His teacher, Aḥmad b. Zayd al-Kibsī, did not die until 1855, when al-Mujāhid became the *ruʾāsat al-tadrīs* (chief teacher)in Sanaa. "And he became the scholar of reference (*marjaʿ*) concerning the systematization of the legal rules of the *madhhab* (*taqrīr ahl al-madhhab*)," Zabāra, *Nayl al-waṭar*, 1:215.

124 The purpose of this study has not been to systematically find discrepancies. However one prominent example is in Ibn Miftāḥ, *Kitāb al-Muntaziʿ al-mukhtār* (1980), 4:516, where we find the rule allowing a *waṣīya* for a heir, and this is given a validation mark, but with a commentary that refers to the well-known controversy about it. In the *Sharḥ al-azhār* (2003 ed.), this specific validation mark is not there and the result is that this rule no longer appears to be valid. *Sharḥ al-azhār*, 10:408. For the discussion about this rule, see chapter 5.

In general, Ibn Miftāḥ, *Sharḥ al-azhār* (2003 ed.), 1:11–24, also contain *fatwās* and discussions of what the *madhhab* actually says in several central practical legal issues, as

3.2 *Codification Under Imam Yaḥyā and Imam Aḥmad (1920s to 1962)*

Codification under Imam Yaḥyā took the form of decrees to the judges, *ikhtiyārāt*, and arguably also imamic support for the publishing of a systematized and univocal *fiqh* work based on the *Sharḥ al-azhār*, the so-called *al-Tāj al-mudhhab*, which we shall come back to.

When Imam Yaḥyā took over from the Ottomans in 1911, Hādawī-Zaydī law had been practiced for centuries and could not be changed or overlooked. It was taught in hundreds of small towns all over the highlands and in the mountains. The imam came to power with the use of religious rhetoric, which was also fundamental to his own legitimacy as a ruler in the following years. He could not simply introduce a new law. He did, however, modify and specify new laws within the framework of Hādawī-Zaydī *fiqh* specifically and within Zaydism and neo-Sunnism in general. When he assumed power from the Ottomans he retained their hierarchical court system and created an appeal court. Earlier, and in classical Zaydism, the judgement of a *sharīʿa* judge could not be changed (as long as the judge stayed within the accepted frames of the law school) and the "system" as such was de-centralized; following the Ottomans, the court system was centralized in a much more systematic way.

Imam Yaḥyā started to issue decrees gradually, but by the 1930s, the list of decrees had accumulated; in 1937 the decrees were printed with comments by ʿAbdallāh b. ʿAbd al-Wahhāb al-Shamāḥī in book form (called *Ṣirāṭ al-ʿārifīn*), in which he gives the legal arguments behind these rules.[125] An example of this is treated in chapter 5, as several of the rules of Imam Yaḥyā's decrees dealt with restrictions on the family *waqf*.

3.3 al-Tāj al-mudhhab

As already stated, the *Sharḥ al-azhār* is a *fiqh* work compiled by several authors, in various stages, and levels. One must be thoroughly trained in order to use this work to search for legal information, as a judge might. Although it contains strong elements of codification, because of its complicated conventions it cannot be considered primarily a handbook for judges.

---

an entity located between ideal *fiqh* and codified rules. In the middle of these discussions the legal maxims of the *madhhab* are presented. All these discussions are extracted from the work *Shudhūr al-dhahab fī taḥqīq al-madhhab* by ʿAbdallāh b. al-Ḥusayn Dallāma (d. 1765), Ibn Miftāḥ, *Sharḥ al-azhār*, 1:11–24. Zabāra states that he was also from Dhamār and was a student of Ḥasan al-Shabībī and several other famous scholars, among them Ibn al-Amīr. Zabāra, *Nashr al-ʿarf*, 2:90–92.

125 al-Shamāḥī, *Ṣirāṭ al-ʿārifīn*. For more about these decrees see Würth, *Ash-sharīʿa fī Bāb al-Yaman*, 40; Haykel, *Revival and Reform*, 204–206, 215–216; Messick, *Calligraphic State*, 4, 38, 48, 211; "Textual Properties." Several of Messick's other works touch upon the topic.

Imam Yaḥyā ordered the publication of a new *fiqh* collection called *al-Tāj al-mudhhab li-aḥkām al-madhhab* [The gilded crown of the rules of the *madhhab*]. It was printed in four volumes in stages from 1938 to 1947[126] and a photocopied reprint was published in the 1970s.[127] It was written by Aḥmad b. Qāsim al-ʿAnsī (d. 1970).[128] It has certainly been used ever since as a reference work, but few would claim that it could ever be considered a substitute for the *Sharḥ al-azhār*; rather it is a useful supplement to it.

Al-Tāj al-mudhhab is in essence an extract of all the validated rules from the *Sharḥ al-azhār*. The *matn* from the *Kitāb al-Azhār* was kept and used in the same way as in the *Sharḥ al-azhār*. Al-ʿAnsī splits up the *Kitāb al-Azhār*, rule by rule, and deals with them individually. Like Ibn Miftāḥ, he also uses the stylistic tool of splitting sentences in the *Kitāb al-Azhār* into words that are given new places in new sentences, thus creating the double layered text, "*Kitāb al-Azhār*/*al-Tāj al-mudhhab*." In this, he invokes the genre and tradition of a traditional *sharḥ*, like Ibn Miftāḥ's *Sharḥ al-azhār*. In contrast to the printed *Sharḥ al-azhār, al-Tāj al-mudhhab* was designed to be read as a printed text. Even so, it is fairly economic with words, but never so condensed that it is difficult for readers to understand. It is a text that can be consulted by an individual alone without the training necessary for the *Sharḥ al-azhār*. The text separates the transactional law (*muʿāmalāt*) from the ritual law (*ʿibādāt*) in two different sections and uses numbered sub-sections (*fuṣūl*) in each chapter. Below this level, the sequence of chapters is kept as in the *Sharḥ al-azhār*. It uses cross-references, very few footnotes and it has punctuation marks. Imam Yaḥyā's decrees are given as footnotes under the respective rule in the text. The voice is univocal, fairly coherent, and not at all polemical. No references to deeper levels of validity are given, nor are there references to who originally made the statements.[129]

While *al-Tāj al-mudhhab* has several characteristics in common with a law code, especially when compared to its origin, the *Sharḥ al-azhār*, it is only an extract of the validated rules of the *Sharḥ al-azhār* and as such it adds nothing new (with the exception of Imam Yaḥyā's *ikhtiyārāt* in the footnotes). And when compared to the modern, republican laws, such as the *waqf* law, it is problematic to define it as an ideal type of codification since it retains so much of the premodern language of *fiqh*. Thus, one can argue that *al-Tāj al-mudhhab*

126 Haykel, *Revival and Reform*, 215.

127 This work was used by scholars like Brinkley Messick and Martha Mundy to access Zaydī *fiqh*.

128 Al-ʿAnsī was also a minister of *awqāf* after the revolution. Manṣūr, *al-Mawkib*, 252.

129 For general information about the context of the *al-Tāj al-mudhhab*, see Haykel, *Revival and Reform*, 215–216.

should be seen as both *fiqh* and codification; the distinction would depend on how it was/is used.

3.4 *Codification Under Imam Aḥmad*

Imam Yaḥyā's son, Imam Aḥmad, reigned from 1948 until the Egyptian supported republican revolution/revolt took place in 1962. Imam Aḥmad's decrees were edited by Haykel in his PhD thesis.[130] Imam Aḥmad also ordered a law compendium, similar to *al-Tāj al-mudhhab*, based on the *Sharḥ al-azhār*. His is much shorter, called *Taysīr al-marām fī masāʾil al-aḥkām li-l-bāḥithīn wa-l-ḥukkām* [Facilitating the quest for the researchers and judges in matters relating to legal rules].[131] The *Taysīr* only deals with transactional law. It was finished in 1951. It is not certain to what extent it has been used.[132] As indicated in chapters 5 and 6, the book is true to the *Kitāb al-Azhār*/*Sharḥ al-azhār*, but is far too short to be useful as law, at least in the field of *waqf* law.

3.5 *Republican* (Waqf) *Codification and Law*

The revolution took place in 1962, however the judiciary and the training of the judiciary was not reformed immediately. Al-Madrasa al-ʿIlmiyya closed, but until recently the judiciary was dominated by a generation of personnel trained in it, or in similar schools. During the first years of the civil war several decrees were issued, but these only related to setting up and organising the public institutions of *waqf* administration, hereunder also the first ministry of *awqāf*. The first law-like decrees came in 1971 when the ministry of justice issued a decree with 68 rulings (*qarārāt*).[133] In general, these are similar to the *ikhtiyārāt* of Imam Yaḥyā and fulfill the same role, in that the fundamentals had already been given in the *Sharḥ al-azhār*; the *qarārāt* were further elaboration on some areas of the law.

The work of codification in a modern, more narrow sense first began under President al-Ḥamdī (r. 1974–77). In 1975 a Codification Committee (Hay'at

130 Haykel, *Revival and Reform*, 213–214; "Order and Righteousness: Muḥammad ʿAlī al-Shawkānī and the Nature of the Islamic State in Yemen" (PhD thesis, Oxford, 1997), 380–382. In this book the decrees related to *waqf* are treated in chapter 5.

131 Qāsim b. Ibrāhīm, ʿAlī b. ʿAbdallāh al-Ānisī, and ʿAbdallāh b. Muḥammad al-Sarḥī, *Kitāb Taysīr al-marām fī masāʾil al-aḥkām li-l-bāḥithīn wa-l-ḥukkām* (Beirut and Sanaa: Manshūrāt al-Madīna, 1986).

132 Haykel, *Revival and Reform*, 216; Würth, *Ash-sharīʿa fī Bāb al-Yaman*, 43; Rashād Muḥammad al-ʿAlīmī, *al-Taqlīdiyya wa-l-ḥadātha fī l-niẓam al-qanūnī l-Yamanī* (Cairo: Maṭābiʿ al-Shurūq, 1986), 129.

133 Muḥammad b. Ismāʿīl al-ʿAmrānī, *Niẓām al-qaḍāʾ fī l-Islām* (Sanaa: Maktabat Dār al-Jīl, 1984), 233–244. The rulings related to *waqf* are given in chapter 5 in this book.

Taqnīn Aḥkam al-Sharīʿa al-Islāmiyya) was set up.[134] One of the earliest laws to be drafted was the *waqf* law of 1976;[135] this has remained almost unchanged until today. As for other important laws, the civil code followed in 1979.

Al-Sayāghī's underlying narrative in the introduction to *al-Bayān al-shāfī*, in which he explains the history of systematization of the validation marks, emphasizes the continuity in the history of codification, so as to imply that the recent republican codification is simply the last stage in a long historical development, rather than a break with the Islamic or *sharʿī* past. By doing so, he projects the validity of the *sharʿī* past onto the new republican codification process, as if to say that codification has always been done through the systemization of the *tadhhīb* signs and through the imamic *ikhtiyārāt*. He states that the codification committee now simply continues the work of finding new valid rules on the basis of the public interest (*maṣlaḥa*) or custom (*ʿurf*), that is, the two important *sharʿī* non-textual sources of law.[136] He goes as far as to say that just as Imam Yaḥyā had his *ikhtiyārāt*, the republic has republican *ikhtiyārāt*.[137] Of course this is not a western "republican" ideology of law based on democracy, but one in which elite Islamic jurists are in power. Such an ideology did not preach a break with the "Islamic" past.

After the revolution the judiciary had to include Shāfiʿī lawyers and judges (this was a new development), from the Shāfiʿī areas previously under Zaydī control, such as Lower Yemen and the Tihāma, and after 1990 also from the newly added areas of former South Yemen. At this time, the Sunnīs gained influence in the judiciary and education of legal personnel; their sole focus was no longer on traditional Shāfiʿī *fiqh*, but rather on newer strains of Sunnism, such as the Muslim Brotherhood, the neo-Sunnīs and even Salafīs. During this period, al-Shawkānī's ideas of a non-*madhhab* law school was often invoked and used as a local, Yemeni way of bridging the law schools, a way that could even be claimed to be Zaydī.[138] The curriculum, at least at the bachelor's level of the faculty of law (Kulliyyat al-Sharīʿa wa-l-Qānūn) was oriented towards a Sunnī and Egyptian law curriculum. However, most informants in Sanaa claim

---

134 Würth, *Ash-sharīʿa fī Bāb al-Yaman*, 44–48. For the wider codification project, see ibid., 36–72.

135 Qarār majlis al-qiyāda bi-l-qānūn raqm 78 li-sanat 1976 bi-sha'n al-waqf; given in full in Manṣūr, al-Mawkib, 313–324.

136 Würth comments on this, *Ash-sharīʿa fī Bāb al-Yaman*, 53–65. That is, to work according to "… ʿalā l-jalab al-maṣāliḥ wa-dafʿ al-mafāsid aw bi-l-ʿurf alladhī lā yuṣādim nāṣṣ," these being two legal maxims on the list of legal rules in the introduction of Ibn Miftāḥ, *Sharḥ al-azhār*.

137 Ḥusayn Aḥmad al-Sayāghī, *Uṣūl al-madhhab al-Zaydī l-Yamanī* (unpublished photocopy, 1984), 16–17.

138 Haykel, *Revival and Reform*, 217–223.

that the master's degree level, i.e., the training of the judges, has retained much its Zaydī character until today.

The present *waqf* law "*qānūn al-waqf al-sharʿī*" is from 1992, and its appendix regulating leases and investments[139] was added in 1996. They are published together in a small booklet.[140] It has a distinct Zaydī character in structure and language, as we shall see in the next three chapters.

Ghālib al-Qirshī,[141] from the Iṣlāḥ party, was the minister of *awqāf* in the 1990s. In the introduction to his student textbook commentary on *waqf* law he states that Yemeni *waqf* law is not biased toward any specific *madhhab*, and that only in rare cases does it contradict the established law schools. In cases of contradictions, proper interpretation (*ijtihād*) has been made by "*ʿulamāʾ* and jurists." Further, he states that his work follows the Egyptian *waqf* law, and that the Egyptian *waqf* law does not contradict the *sharīʿa* in any matters of personal status law (of which *waqf* law could be seen as a part). Finally, he asks the reader to be especially aware of the fact that "the Yemeni Codification Committee (Lajnat Taqnīn al-Sharīʿa al-Islāmiyya) has never deviated from the *sharīʿa*." In al-Qirshī's view al-Azhar (in Cairo) clearly radiates validity and the Yemeni Codification Committee simply built on this. This should be seen as an ideal Sunnī or "Iṣlāḥī" picture. As pointed out by Haykel, from the eighteenth century the state-oriented Zaydīs have not been afraid to search for inspiration and argumentation from the Sunnī law schools. The influence of al-Shawkānī and other neo-Sunnī scholars was strong and gave the rulers an opportunity to dismiss certain Hādawī-Zaydī views. After the revolution of 1962, several other types of Sunnism influenced the judiciary: the Egyptian influence, first as "Azharī quality,"[142] later also Muslim Brotherhood, and Salafīs (i.e., Islamists with non-*madhhab* orientations).

Today, when asked directly, most informants who are not specialized in law believe that *waqf* law comes from "Islam." Yet they rarely have any further explanation as to how Islam and law are connected, as law is, in any case, something that *ʿulamāʾ*, judges, and lawyers deal with. The role of parliament in all this has not been mentioned here, and both doctrinally, and in practice, it seems fairly irrelevant. The validity added to *waqf* law from the modern democratic institution of the state is not something that is often referred to by informants. As a whole, in their eyes the law is for experts. What is often at stake in court

139 Lāʾihat tanẓīm ijrāʾāt al-taʾjīr wa-l-intifāʿ bi-amwāl wa-ʿaqārāt al-awqāf wa-istithmārihā.

140 Wizārat al-Shuʾūn al-Qānūniyya, *Qānūn al-waqf al-sharʿī*.

141 al-Qirshī, *al-Awqāf wa-l-waṣāyā*, 67.

142 On the availability of Egyptian *waqf* law in book form, see Muḥammad Muṣṭafā Shalabī, *Aḥkām al-waṣāyā wa-l-awqāf: al-Maʿmūl bihā fī l-jumhūriyya al-ʿarabiyya al-muttaḥida* (Alexandria: Maṭbaʿat Dār al-Taʾlīf, 1964).

cases related to *waqf* is access to land and wealth, much like ownership law in general. It practice, it centres on the validity of legal documents and witnesses rather than deeper questions of the origins of legal validity. Theoretically, "democratic" elements in *waqf* law enter into *fiqh* and can be seen in the way it has, over the centuries, incorporated both specific rules and flexible tools to formulate new rules and thus serve the local need for *waqf* law. But again, this is a fairly ideological discussion and one can ask how democracy and *sharīʿa* may fit or not. The answers to such questions depend on which groups of informants are asked and the nature of their educational background.

When discussing the final stages of *waqf* law codification, we must bear in mind that many, both laymen and judges, especially in certain geographical areas, are sceptical towards state law and state judges. Codification is necessary in the theoretical sense, in that everything cannot be legal; however, as elaborated upon in this chapter, *fiqh*, as a field of knowledge, has already solved much of this problem. Therefore, the field of codification, that is state codification, in the view of many simply is not "necessary." When asked, even judges often state that what they use is mainly *fiqh*, and that the new laws are mere specifications. An exception to this is the ever-returning problem of family *waqf*, particularly when used to circumvent the effects of the inheritance rules, a topic dealt with in chapter 5. In periods or areas where no collective agreement can be established, the legality of this practice is guaranteed by the absence of a prohibition. A rule stating that something is legal does not have to be enforced, but rules stating that something is illegal require an apparatus of sanction and enforcement. Over various historical periods and in different geographical areas, the state's powers are so limited that speaking of "codification" and "law" is almost meaningless unless it is discussed in terms of what it means at the very local level. As an analytical category "codification" is broader than the modern Yemeni *waqf* law; it is the struggle over which rules should be valid and enforced on the ground in cities and villages. Though the coming chapters may seem to focus, initially at least, on theoretical *fiqh*, they do examine areas of *waqf fiqh* and codified law that interact strongly with local practices in a two-way relationship. This is analysed in a perspective of historical anthropology of Islamic (*waqf*) law (in Yemen).

CHAPTER 5

Family *Waqf* and Inheritance

> Our descendants are the children of our sons, as for our daughters, their children are the descendants of strange men
>
> (Banūnā banū abnā'inā wa-banātunā banūhunna abnā' al-rijāl al-abā'id)

This Yemeni proverb found in the chapter of *waqf* in the *fiqh* work *al-Baḥr al-zakhkhār*[1] (ca. 1400 CE) was quoted by some well-educated informants during discussions as a way to explain the defining features of the patriarchal family system and various options of the intergenerational transfer of wealth in this system, as I elaborate below.

1 Structure and Main Argument of the Chapter

This chapter is structured along the lines of the historical trajectory of the codification of a specific cluster of rules in Zaydī law that regulate the balance between the *waqf*, the testament (*waṣīya*), and the inheritance rules (*al-farā'iḍ, irth, wirātha*). These legal concepts offer different strategies of long-term land ownership control and the allocation of rights of family members to agricultural surplus over time. The chapter focuses on the knowledge field of codification, the second field of the four fields of knowledge defined in chapter 2. Only to a limited extent does it focus on the field of *fiqh* and on individual cases of *waqf* and legal disputes. These "levels" or "fields of knowledge" are ideal types,

1 Ibn al-Murtaḍā, *Kitāb al-Baḥr al-zakhkhār* (Beirut: Mu'assasat al-Risāla, 1975), 155. The same proverb is quoted in the same location in the *waqf* chapter of the *fiqh* work by Yaḥyā b. Ḥamza, *Nūr al-abṣār*. An almost identical proverb is found in 'Abdallāh b. Ḥamza, *al-Majmū' al-manṣūrī*, 2:449.

 DOI:10.1163/9789004377844_006

as treated in chapter 2. Although the structural focus of the chapter is on the ideal type of codification, it becomes clear from the analysis that codification cannot be properly understood without the level of *fiqh* "above it" and without the level of individual cases and legal practice "below" it.

Compared to other legal topics in *waqf*, the matter in question is particularly well-suited to trace a trajectory through the history of Zaydī codification and positive law. No other topic or cluster of topics in *waqf* law has been given so much attention in Zaydī codification (imamic *fatwā*s and decrees)[2] than the role of *waqf* in intergenerational transfer of wealth and its limits. It is a legal topic that reappears in *fatwā* collections and in decrees made by the Zaydī imams to their judges, again and again, throughout classical and Qāsimī Zaydī history. The specific type of *waqf* used to circumvent the inheritance rules is, when seen in a long historical perspective, situated on the very edge of validity, legality, and authority. By tracing the decrees and *fatwā*s we see that roughly half of the imams and scholars favour of the legality of a form of family *waqf* that excludes some of the (otherwise potential) heirs and the other half oppose this form of *waqf*. The types of references and arguments used to legitimize these positions follow certain patterns and are often repeated. By tracing the trajectory of the codified rule, we can see how the field of codification ("law") is affected by the vast tradition of academic, Zaydī and indeed, Islamic *fiqh* (legal theory); at the same time it is also oriented towards more local and contemporary politics of case law, which is constituted by the sum of individual court verdicts and rules wanted by landowning families.

1.1 *Intergenerational Transfer of Wealth in Islamic Legal Theory*

Inheritance as regulated by inheritance laws is only one way of transferring wealth from one generation to the next.[3] The inheritance laws or rules are complex, but the crux is that certain persons inherit certain shares of the property or estate of the diseased. Most importantly, a daughter inherits half the

---

2 It is fairly clear that decrees from the ruler (the imam) to the judges are within the definition of "codification" given in chapter 2. The *fatwā*s are slightly more problematic. Here it must be assumed that the *fatwā*s were of a legally binding character, not simply religious advice and clarifications aimed at moral effect only. The *fatwā*s quoted in this chapter are mainly from ʿAbdallāh b. Ḥamza, al-Hādī ʿIzz al-Dīn, and al-Shawkānī, and were issued in the name of ruling imams or the chief *qāḍī*.

3 See D. S. Powers, "The Islamic Inheritance System: A Socio-Historical Approach," *Arab Law Quarterly* 8, no. 1 (1993): 13–29; "The Islamic Family Endowment," *Vanderbilt Journal of Transactional Law* 32 (1999): 1167–1190.

share of a son. Close relatives like parents and spouses also inherit.[4] In many ways, the inheritance rules are not a very practical model for a patrilineal, tribal, agricultural society to use for the intergenerational transfer of wealth. Giving away parts of the landholdings of the family, or the clan, to "strangers" through inheritance to daughters who marry outside the family may result in an unwanted loss of land.

Theoretically, if a man from family (A) is left with only daughters, and if these daughters marry into another family (i.e., exogamously), the land that they inherit will no longer be under the control of family (A) and will enter into the hands of the other family (B). Since the daughter will later leave most of her inherited land to her children (*awlād al-banāt*), who carry the family name of their father (B), the family (B) will gain control over these lands in the future, and family (A) will lose important sources of income and power. This is an institutional problem in a patrilineal, tribal society if the Islamic inheritance rules are strictly followed. One way of countering this effect is to only marry within the extended family (endogamously). This is a common solution, but among landowning elites, inter-clan marriages are important ways of forging alliances. Another solution is to make sure that over time the two families marry an equal number of women into the family of the other. But the most desirable solution is to be able to prevent the transfer of wealth between the exogamously married woman and her children. The "exclusionary" form of family *waqf* described below is a great tool for this.

Generations come and go and access to land mainly follows the concept of private ownership sanctioned by a local consensus based on respect for ownership documents. Land is not only held by individuals, it is often held in common by an extended family or clan, which are important political entities, in that they provide individuals with food and housing.[5] In such cases, with the notion of communal ownership, even if the land is technically, legally owned by individuals only, there is a significant pressure on individuals from the rest of the extended family to not marry their daughters to outsiders, in order to avoid the subsequent "loss" through inheritance claimed by the children of

4 For an overview of the inheritance rules see Schacht, *Introduction to Islamic Law*, 169–173 and Vikør, *Between God and the Sultan*, 318–321.

5 Many forms of group ownership exist; family *waqf* is one of them. The tribe or clan may also "own" the surrounding grazing land in common, but in Yemen, grazing land is not called property (*māl, amwāl, milk, amlāk*), this mainly refers to agricultural fields and terraces. The land between the agricultural fields and outside them is mainly used for livestock, which is less important than land for growing crops. The system of managing resources for livestock is based much more in tribal and customary practices than in Islamic ownership law.

these women (*awlād al-banāt*). Creating a family *waqf* exclusively in favour of the male descent line (*awlād al-ṣulb*) and excluding the *awlād al-banāt* from the yearly income of the *waqf* is legally possible by setting up a family *waqf* for the descendants of the patrilineal line only. In such a *waqf*, the right to the revenue of the land is given to the living members of the founder's family, while the agricultural fields remain under the status of *waqf*, "not to be bought, not to be sold, and not to be given away as inheritance." The important point here is that such a *waqf* can be made, arguably, with the condition that it excludes (*ikhrāj*) the children of women who married into another family (*awlād al-banāt*), in favour of those children (male and female) who remain in the patrilineal line, the so-called *awlād al-ṣulb*. The latter carry the name of the patrilineal line (*nasab*) of the extended family.[6]

This "exclusion" from the family *waqf*, as we call it hereafter, has been a much used instrument over the centuries in the Islamicate world and also in Zaydī Yemen, where it has been respected by many imams, jurists, local judges, and notaries. At the same time, this norm and practice have been strongly criticized by other imams and scholars, who claim that it is invalid because it is an indirect circumvention of the Islamic inheritance laws. The *awlād al-banāt* are not heirs in the first generation, but from the next generation, they ultimately lose, if the exclusionary *waqf* is chosen instead of the inheritance rules as a model of transferring land from one generation to the next.

In theory, inheritance takes place only after someone's death and a *waqf* is made during the founder's lifetime.[7] As isolated legal concepts in their ideal form they are completely separate. However, in practice, they overlap. Other legal concepts that can be used to transfer wealth from one generation to the next, such as a gift or a testament introduce some complicating factors in this picture and we must make some clarifications:

---

6 See D. S. Powers, "The Maliki Family Endowment: Legal Norms and Social Practices," *International Journal of Middle East Studies* 25, no. 3 (1993): 379–406, especially 394–395: "The wide gap separating these two sets of legal norms—inheritance and endowments—may be illustrated by comparing the group composed of the beneficiaries of a familial endowment with the group composed of the founder's heirs. While most beneficiaries are also heirs, the great majority of heirs do not qualify as beneficiaries. Thus, a man who establishes an endowment for his children and lineal descendants effectively disinherits his spouse, siblings, cousins, uncles, and nephews, to mention just a few."

7 If the *waqf* is made during one's lifetime, but to take effect after death, it is also a testamentary disposition (*waṣīya*), and thus limited to one-third of the estate. It is still a *waqf*.

1.2 *The Relationship Between* Hiba, Waqf, *and* Waṣīya

	Before death[a]	After death
A one-time transfer of property or rights of use (*hiba* and *waṣīya* do not require a pious purpose, but *ṣadaqa* does).	Gift (*hiba, ṣadaqa*)	Testament (*waṣīya*) 1. In all law schools restricted to one-third. 2. In Sunnī law it cannot be given in favour of an heir, in Zaydī (and Shīʿī) law it can be.
A trust-like, perpetual disposition (self-repeating) (it requires a pious purpose in Zaydī and Ḥanafī law, but not in Shāfiʿī law)	*Waqf*	*Waqf-waṣīya*

a More accurately, before the "sickness of [i.e., that leads to] death" (*maraḍ al-mawt*).

FIGURE 9 The relationship between *waqf* and *waṣīya* in schematic form.

A disposition can be made during one's lifetime (inter vivos) for all of one's property, such as, for example, a gift (*hiba*). A gift is not restricted by inheritance rules, nor by the restriction on testaments (*waṣīya*).[8] A testament can only be made for up to one-third of one's property. Theoretically, the individual is free to do what he wants with his property during his life, at least before any sickness that leads to his death (*maraḍ al-mawt*).[9] In practice, however, there is a strong expectation that the individual should hand over land to members of his family, preferably his male children, since land is the very basis of existence, status, identity, honour, and power. Giving away all one's property to a charitable purpose or to a stranger outside one's family can be legally valid

8 In modern Yemeni law, the gift is restricted as well. One might expect that this could be an "outlet," but it seems to have been restricted already by Imam Yaḥyā, as discussed later in the chapter. It is restricted to one-third in all cases and invalid for heirs unless they all approve. This adds to the argument that the four fields merge in practice.

9 See Hiroyuki Yanagihashi, "The Doctrinal Development of 'Maraḍ al-Mawt' in the Formative Period of Islamic Law," *Islamic Law and Society* 5, no. 3 (1998): 326–358.

according to *fiqh*,[10] but morally wrong, highly unusual, and even "un-Islamic" according to most informants.[11]

A student of law reading an introductory *fiqh* textbook about Islamic law studies four distinct, separate concepts. The model above has four separate categories in legal theory (*fiqh*), but in legal practice and in terms of local, non-*fiqh* knowledge, all those fields tend to merge into one; the difference of transactions made before and after death collapses when seen from the long-term intergenerational perspective. The difference between a one-time disposition and a perpetually lasting disposition also collapses, since owning land or having the full right to land is something that largely produces the same effect. The collapse of the borders between the four different legal models causes quite some confusion and inconsistency of terms, both in *fiqh* and in codification. A *waqf* is called a *waṣīya* and vice versa, and the restriction from the *waṣīya* to one-third of one's property becomes imposed onto the *waqf*. This more practical side of the law is then re-integrated back into the more academic *fiqh* in the footnotes of *fiqh* books, as we see below.

Some problems of the "collapse" between the four categories and the resulting confusion also specifically occur in Zaydī *waqf* because of the combination of doctrinal stands that differ from other law schools. Other law schools have different constellations of *waqf* doctrines that lead to other institutionalized dilemmas and inconsistencies than those found in Zaydism. In Shāfiʿī law, for instance, a *waqf* does not necessarily have to be pious. As *waqf* must be pious according to Zaydī doctrine and therefore exploiting the concept of *waqf* to circumvent the inheritance rules produces an even more pressing inconsistency in "the *sharīʿa*." In Sunnī law, a *waṣīya* cannot be given in favour of an heir, and this strengthens the conceptual separation between the two concepts of *waqf*

10 Restriction on charity in the presence of heirs can be claimed through various *ḥadīth*s and different views exist. See below, on ʿAbdallāh b. Ḥamza.

11 The arguments above are rather theoretical, designed to clarify the "problem." Yet, many times I have discussed this question with a wide variety of informants who claim that an individual is not allowed to do what he wants with his property during his lifetime; he is only allowed to give away one-third. This "misunderstanding" is "wrong" according to the ideal *fiqh*, but correct according to local knowledge of morals, law, and "Islam." This ethnographic fact contradicts a "legal" normative fact and perhaps even the understanding of western academic scholars of Islamic law. The chapter shows how the two are combined in the field of codification. One example is Vom Bruck's statement, that "in accordance with Islamic family law, a person may alienate a third of his or her property from the heirs specified in the Qur'an and declare it as a *waqf*." This was told to her by Muḥammad al-Manṣūr. But what Muḥammad al-Manṣūr refers to is not "Islamic law," but Yemeni codification since the time of Imam Yaḥyā. In "Islamic law" no such restriction exists. Vom Bruck, *Islam, Memory, and Mortality*, 73, 290 n29.

and *waṣīya*. However, for Shīʿīs and Zaydīs, a *waṣīya* can indeed be made in favour of an heir. This leads to "picking the best" from both concepts, such as in creating a *waqf* that is "not completely pious," but which is "still legal within the third," and "therefore" can exclude the *awlād al-banāt*. I elaborate on this in this chapter by referring to the way Zaydī scholars see this dilemma and try to solve it.

The topic of circumventing the inheritance rules by using *waqf* is arguably not one of direct relevance to public *waqf*, but it is the single most important—and one of the most controversial debates—in the field of Zaydī *waqf* codification. The topic is thus almost unavoidable when focusing on borders of validity around the concept of *waqf*. As I show in chapter 7, the border between private *waqf*s and public *waqf*s is also often deliberately blurred, making the definition of family *waqf*s even more pressing. By analysing the legal debates behind, and the history and trajectory of codification, several important aspects of public forms of *waqf* also appear. As this chapter shows, the debate clarifies for us, in addition to the legal question itself, other important aspects such as the creative use of *waqf* in economic strategies, the wider history of Zaydī codification, and the very role of Zaydī ownership law in the society.

2 The Arrival of al-Hādī and His *Waqf-Waṣīya* Model

Al-Hādī brought Zaydī *waqf fiqh* and law to Yemen in 897; his family *waqf* model (hereafter called the Hādawī *waqf* model) was a rather special type of family *waqf* that seems to have survived until today. This *waqf* is a family *waqf* that uses a will or testament, a so-called *waṣīya*. Today, this *waqf* is, to a large extent, still called a *waṣīya* instead of its more "correct" legal term, *waqf*.

The Hādawī *waqf* model is based on the premise that one-third of one's property can be given to whomever the founder chooses, including heirs, or some of the heirs. According to the Hādawī *waqf* model, it is permissable to exclude the *awlād al-banāt* from this "free" third. The remaining two-thirds of the property can also be made into a *waqf* excluding the *awlād al-banāt*, but only if all the heirs agree. If they do not, the two-thirds can still become a valid family *waqf*, but the division among the beneficiaries of the remaining two-thirds of the *waqf* must follow the inheritance shares (*waqf ʿalā l-farāʾiḍ*). In other words, the founder is completely free with regard to the first third of his property,[12] and although he is free to make all of his property *waqf* for his heirs,

---

12 The term "his property" is somewhat static in a biographical perspective. I mainly refer to a person in the later stages of life when he is in possession of property. Otherwise, the

for the remaining two-thirds he is restricted in terms of how it must be divided and all the potential heirs must be included.

By calling the family *waqf* a *waṣīya*, one can circumvent the condition of pious intention (*qurba*) and thereby evade the inheritance rules more easily. Of course this *waqf* must be restricted to one-third since it is given in the framework of a *waṣīya* and is executed by the executor or guardian (*waṣīy*). In the Zaydī and Shīʿī *waṣīya*, the testator may give one-third of his property to his heirs and arguably also to a specific group of his heirs. This is why the validity of the Sunnī *ḥadīth* "No testamentation to an heir" (*lā waṣīya li-wārith*) is so controversial in debates about Yemeni family *waqfs*. If the *ḥadīth* is to be held strong or valid, the Hādawī *waqf* model would be invalid. In a *waṣīya* (in contrast to a *waqf*), there is no need for good intention or "piety" (*qurba*)[13] since it is not a charitable disposition in the first place. Circumvention of the inheritance rules by using a *waṣīya* is not as problematic as it would be in a *waqf*. The fact that this combined *waqf-waṣīya* model of al-Hādī is not entirely pious, which is fundamental characteristic of a *waqf*, can be explained by those defending it, who say that this combined model is simply not an "absolute *waqf*" (in contrast to "absolute" *waqfs*—*al-waqf al-muṭlaq*) and therefore this model is not subject to the strict rules of absolute *waqfs* in terms of piety. This implies a breach in the principle of piety and an admission that there are two types of *waqf*; a "real," "pure" or "absolute" *waqf* is one whose purpose is undoubtedly pious, and which can be made during one's lifetime for all of one's property, and also in favour of heirs. But in this case, it should not exclude any heirs. Thus there is a sort of difference in "holiness" between the Hādawī family *waqf* and the "pure" charitable *waqf*, although the distinction between them is often blurred and even denied. Until today, there is a tendency in Yemen to look at family *waqfs* or privately administrated *waqfs* as something close to a private trust, in which both piety and perpetuity are "negotiable." In contrast, publicly administered charitable *waqfs*, for example, for mosques, which are seen as "holy" and "pure," are more liable to the scrutiny of the public.[14]

---

amount of "one-third" would vary greatly in absolute terms, say between a youth who has not yet inherited from his father or gathered wealth, and someone at a late stage of life writing his will.

13 This is fairly agreed upon; a *waṣīya* is simply a transfer similar to a gift, while a *waqf* must, in Zaydī *waqf* doctrine (and Ḥanafī *waqf* doctrine), be pious. The Shāfiʿī *waqf*, on the other hand, simply avoids the whole problem by not specifying that piety (*qurba*) is a requirement for a *waqf*.

14 An example is what is mentioned in the letter from Ibn al-Amīr to al-Mahdī l-ʿAbbās, outlined in chapter 3. An informant from one of the most important *sayyid* houses and a *mutawallī* for all of the family's *waqfs* stated that today many of theirs assets were being sold and that the family *waqf* could, according to the *sharʿī* law, legally be privatized

Al-Hādī left several *fiqh* works, the most well-known among them are the *Muntakhab*[15] and the *Aḥkām*. I do not explain al-Hādī's *waqf* model in more detail here, rather I present it through the eyes of later authoritative observers and commenters, beginning with Imam al-Manṣūr ʿAbdallāh b. Ḥamza (561–614/1166–1217),[16] who looks back at what happened in al-Hādī's days.

3 The *Fatwā*s of Imam al-Manṣūr ʿAbdallāh b. Ḥamza (d. 614/1217)

Imam al-Manṣūr ʿAbdallāh b. Ḥamza was totally opposed to al-Hādī's *waqf* model. In his view, al-Hādī's model produced confusion between *waqf* and *waṣīya*. For al-Manṣūr, a *waqf* is totally different from a *waṣīya*, it is something pious that should not contradict or undermine the rules of inheritance. In his view, excluding the *awlād al-banāt* (children of exogamously married women) could not be valid in a *waqf*, as this could invalidate their right to inheritance. Al-Manṣūr's account is legal, but also "ethnographic." He states that most contemporary *waqf*s were made by use of a *waṣīya*:

> [A] question was asked about a woman who gave by means of testamentation (*awṣat*) a …

(*al-waṣāyā tuḥarrar*), in contrast to *waqf* proper (*waqf, waqf muṭlaq*) which "of course" is something else, and carries another type of sanction. This is in accordance with the legal norms after Imam Yaḥyā and into the present.

15 The *waqf* chapter of the *Muntakhab* is very short and written in *qāla-qultu* style, in which the author, al-Kūfī, "interviews" al-Hādī. Muḥammad b. Sulaymān al-Kūfī, *Kitāb al-Muntakhab* (Sanaa: Dār al-Ḥikma al-Yamaniyya, 1993), 363–365. It is only one-third that is free of exclusion, in the remaining two-thirds the *awlād al-banāt* were included: "And I asked him about a man who made a *waqf* of all his property for his son and the son of his son without the females (*dūna al-ināth*)? He said: That is invalid (*bāṭil*), this must follow God's shares and the *waqf* must be for both males and females according to God's shares (*sihām Allāh*) and the males are to be given a third of the *waqf* without the females (*ināth*)." *Kitāb al-Muntakhab*, 364. In this, the Hādawī *waqf* model is more restrictive than other law schools, which allow for exclusion. Among the Zaydīs this is restricted to one-third anyway, while among the Shāfiʿīs the restriction to one-third in the exclusion does not appear to be there, even though it might be found in other, related rules.

16 One imam between al-Hādī and al-Manṣūr ʿAbdallāh b. Ḥamza was Imam al-Manṣūr al-Qāsim b. ʿAlī l-ʿIyānī (d. 393/1003). He also upheld al-Hādī's *waqf* model. See al-Qāsim al-ʿIyānī, *Majmūʿ kutub wa-rasāʾil al-Imām al-Qāsim al-ʿIyānī*, ed. ʿAbd al-Karīm Aḥmad Jadbān (Sa'da: Maktabat al-Turāth al-Islāmī, 2002), 116–123. However, he seems not to be widely quoted afterward.

> Answer: It is not to be sold because it [this transaction] takes the legal effect of a *waqf* and most *waqf*s in the country are made by the wording of the *waṣīya*.[17]

Al-Manṣūr's *fatwā* collection includes a critical thesis about al-Hādī's *waqf*.[18] He starts by agreeing to the restriction to one-third[19] as given in the *ḥadīth* "A third, and a third is much."[20] This *ḥadīth*, he states, is relevant in some other forms of transactions, but it is not directly related to *waqf*. Then, he proceeds to treat the topic of the legitimacy of the institution of *waqf* in general. He concludes that the only basis for *waqf* is piety, or the intention to do good (*qurba*). He treats several specific sub-questions in which he disagrees with al-Hādī's *waqf* law. The first point is the issue of "*waqf* for some of the heirs excluding others":

> He [al-Hādī] said: If he made all of his property *waqf* for some of the heirs without others, such as in favour of the males without the females among his children and grandchildren; if those who were excluded agree to the *waqf*, then the *waqf* is valid as the founder wishes; if they do not agree, the third is still *waqf* for the males without the females, but the rest is to be *waqf* for all of them, males and females, according to the shares [as outlined] by God the exalted.[21]

This was al-Hādī's *waqf* model. However, al-Manṣūr disagrees and argues:

> The comment on that [is]: What he presented about a *waqf* that has no good intention has no root (*aṣl*) in the *sharīʿa*. And what has no root cannot be validated. It is clear that al-Hādī connected the status of the third to piety[22] in an analogy from the *waṣīya* of a third of one's property

17 ʿAbdallāh b. Ḥamza, *al-Majmūʿ al-manṣūrī*, 2:55.

18 The thesis edited in al-Manṣūr's *fatwā* collection or pages 2:439–463 in *al-Majmūʿ al-manṣūrī*.

19 "The restriction to the third" refers to the restriction in the *waṣīya*, in that one cannot make a *waṣīya* of more than one-third of one's property.

20 According to him it is legal to dispose of all one's property during one's life, although it may be reprehensible to give away so much that one's heirs suffer. This *ḥadīth*, according to him, relates specifically to "*nadhr al-hadāyā ilā bayt Allāh al-ḥarām*" and it does not automatically cover all sorts of dispositions. ʿAbdallāh b. Ḥamza, *al-Majmūʿ al-manṣūrī*, 2:440–441.

21 Ibid., 2:445.

22 As mentioned above, in the *waṣīya* "the third" does not have to be pious. In *waqf*, if this is given by means of a *waṣīya*, is the third dependent on piety or not? Which of the two

(*qiyāsan ʿalā l-waṣīya*), and that the transfer of this third therefore can be done with piety.... However, we think that such a transaction has no piety in it because the females are the weaker part.... And if such a transaction is built upon deficiency (*fasād*), then it becomes deficient in its totality, unlike the sale (*al-bayʿ*) and purchase, and the gift (*al-hiba*) ... There is no fundamental validity [in *waqf*] except good intention ...[23]

The use of the "royal we" recurs in the way the imam calls himself "we." The treatise is long, sometimes repetitive, and some of the cases and examples overlap. Al-Manṣūr states that the "free third" that his predecessors have agreed upon is not entirely free, in that while one can do whatever one wants with it, including non-pious transactions; one cannot contradict the *sharīʿa* with it. It is perfectly fine to give a *waqf* to non-heirs[24] (*ajānib*), but if it is given to heirs in order to circumvent the inheritance rule, then this is not valid, because the first condition of *waqf* is *qurba*. He mentions that females "are the weaker part" in such cases and that it is wrong to leave them without property. Sometimes the terms "females" or "women" are used interchangeably with *awlād al-banāt*. As we see later, the distinction is not crystal clear, and certainly not in the rhetoric of al-Manṣūr; in the Hādawī *waqf* they are all presented as the losing part. Thus it is especially when contrasted to inheritance that the problem of the lack of piety arises:

> As for what is mentioned in the books of al-Qāḍī l-Ḥasan b. ʿAlī b. Muḥammad b. Abī l-Najm as an answer to a question about someone who makes a *waqf* and disinherits his daughters and his brothers, this is invalid, as it is a mere *jāhilī waqf*. [Before Islam] they did not give inheritance to the girls or to their brothers from the same father, and the same [is true] for their younger brothers as well. They gave all the inheritance to the eldest.... And they used to say: Our descendants consist of our sons—the descendants of the women are strangers to us (*abnāʾunā*

concepts (with or without piety) should govern the third if it is both a *waqf* and a *waṣīya*? According to Hādawī-Zaydism, in order to be given to heirs the third must also be pious because this is a condition in *waṣīya* to heirs, according to the chapter of *waṣāyā* in Ibn Miftāḥ, *Sharḥ al-azhār*: "a *waṣīya* is valid, even for heirs, if made in piety" (*wa law li-wārith fī l-qurab*). See "Kitāb al-waṣāyā," *Sharḥ al-azhār* (1980 ed.), 4:516.

23 ʿAbdallāh b. Ḥamza, *al-Majmūʿ al-manṣūrī*, 2:446.

24 He refers to the "two imams" (the two Caspian Hārūnīs, al-Muʾayyad and Abū Ṭālib), who state that it is legal, during one's life, to give to some of one's heirs and even prefer some over others and that this may be pious, according to the intention of the giver, and that there should be an a priori assumption of piety, unless otherwise proven. ʿAbdallāh b. Ḥamza, *al-Majmūʿ al-manṣūrī*, 2:447.

> *banū abnā'inā wa banū l-nisā' abā'id*). Then came the Prophet and he took away their rules and replaced them with God the exalted's rules, and gave the women what God the exalted had ordered ...[25]

Al-Manṣūr makes it appear as if the problem is one of women's rights to inheritance in general and the Hādawī *waqf* model is simply a way to revert to pre-Islamic laws of the intergenerational transfer of wealth. Al-Manṣūr continues:

> ... Then came al-Hādī to Yemen. There were tribes like Hamdān and Khawlān and they used to not give inheritance to their women and [follow] what God the exalted had given them, and the judges followed these rules (*wa-ḥakama bi-dhālika quḍāt al-bilād*). This question was raised to al-Hādī and he abolished this and ordered that one-third could be given to the males (*al-thulth li-l-dhukūr*) [as *waqf*] and the remaining two-thirds was to be divided according to God the exalted's [inheritance] rules, to both males and females. This practice continued in his [al-Hādī's] life and after his death, and is stated as preferred (*rājiḥ*) in the *Muntakhab*.[26]

Al-Manṣūr comments:

> It was said that the Judge 'Alī b. Sulaymān al-Kūfī was al-Hādī's judge and that he judged according [to these rules] and said: The a priori assumption (*al-aṣl*) should be that any *waqf* is valid unless someone makes all his property *waqf*, then it is permissable for a judge to reduce the *waqf* to one-third. The remaining two-thirds, according to him, are to be *waqf* for the heirs, not property (*waqfan, lā milkan*), and according to al-Mu'ayyad bi-Llāh, these two-thirds that are *waqf* can be bought and sold.[27]

Here, al-Manṣūr elaborates on the "confusion" and lack of logic behind the combined *waqf-waṣīya*. The latest scholar to be quoted there, the Caspian Aḥmad b. al-Ḥusayn al-Mu'ayyad bi-Llāh (d. 411/1020), is perhaps the most revered non-Yemeni Zaydī scholar in classical Zaydī law and his views are often quoted. His view that this remaining two-thirds may be bought and sold, sounds, at first, somehow peculiar. This is perhaps a way for al-Manṣūr to strengthen his argument by making the opponent's *waqf* model seem even less pious, since

25 Ibid., 2:449.
26 Ibid., 2:450.
27 Ibid., 2:450.

selling a *waqf* is widely know to be wrong.[28] The remaining two-thirds could be bought and sold, according to al-Mu'ayyad, because it is still private property, not *waqf*.[29] The important point is al-Manṣūr's comment to this: The Hādawī *waqf* model is so wrong that it is indeed "outside religion" (*kharajat bi-dhālika min al-dīn*).[30] Al-Manṣūr adds diplomatically that al-Hādī made this rule as a compromise, given the social context of the time (*jaʿala la-hum al-thulth ṣulḥan*) as al-Hādī probably saw that otherwise the tribes would not change their behaviour, so he made the free one-third into a *sharīʿa*-rule (*fa-sharraʿa la-hum al-thulth*).[31]

Al-Manṣūr also presents his argument as a logical construct, stating that a more specific rule (*farʿ*) cannot be made without a clear fundament (*qāʿida*). In several other statements in the same treatise he repeats this point, that the issue of *qurba* in *waqf* is not simply a matter of interpretation, in which every interpreter is right; there are the fundamental negative implications if the institution of *waqf* is not seen as totally dependant on absolute good purpose (*qurba, qurba maḥḍa*). In the middle of several other questions related to the grey areas between *waqf* and *waṣīya*, he answers repetitively, and one can almost see him losing patience:

> ... I have already made clear to you that the *waṣīya* has its own chapter in the books as the gift has, and there is no connection between these and the chapter of *waqf*, except what they share in their essence. The *waṣīya* has no need for *qurba*, but this is not the case for the *waqf*. A *waqf* without *qurba* is not valid even for one part of a thousand. But this does not apply to the *waṣīya*, which has its own chapter and all its rules are well known.... What was claimed [by al-Hādī and his followers] is only an appearance of a rule (*ṣūratan*), but not real one and it is not constructed

28 This is clarified by al-Manṣūr shortly after this, and also clarified in the *Sharḥ al-azhār*, 8:297 (2003 ed.): al-Mu'ayyad was opposed to al-Hādī's view; he argued that if the *waqf* was opposed during the lifetime of the founder, then indeed the remaining two-thirds are *milk*, not *waqf*. This is probably the reason "it can be bought and sold." Al-Manṣūr states that this is an example of a rule that has been legitimized piece by piece, but that the whole rule as an entity lacks fundamental validity. ʿAbdallāh b. Ḥamza, *al-Majmūʿ al-manṣūrī*, 2:401.

29 The discussion of the status of the remaining two-thirds reveals strong disagreement—this is evident from the footnotes of the *Sharḥ al-azhār*. "ʿĀmir, Muftī, al-Saḥūlī, and Imam Sharaf al-Dīn," all important names in Zaydī *fiqh*, are in favour of the view that the two-thirds remain private property. Ibn Miftāḥ, *Sharḥ al-azhār*, 8:298.

30 ʿAbdallāh b. Ḥamza, *al-Majmūʿ al-manṣūrī*, 2:450.

31 "Wa aqūlu anna al-Hādī, ʿalayhi al-salām, jaʿala la-hum al-thulth ṣulḥan" ʿAbdallāh b. Ḥamza, *al-Majmūʿ al-manṣūrī*, 2:451.

> upon evidence and proofs (*ʿadilla wa-ʿilal*) and the *qiyās* [al-Hādī made] from *waṣīya* [regarding the third] is not valid ... it is only an artificial construction (*ṣūra mawḍūʿa*) that must be corrected back to the truth so that we can have rules that are firmly established (*thābit*).[32]

As a conclusion, we can say that Imam al-Manṣūr ʿAbdallāh b. Ḥamza was crystal clear in his views that *waqf* can only be based on charity and piety and whenever it is so, there is no need for the *qiyās* or "connection" with the *waṣīya*. This does not mean that a *waqf* in favour of heirs or family is not charitable, rather, and more specifically, *waqfs* for some of the heirs may be valid in certain cases, but not as a rule in itself, nor as a rule that allows the exclusion of whole groups in order to circumvent inheritance rules. The *awlād al-banāt* are not heirs in the first generation, but the principle of excluding them as a sub-group of heir-beneficiaries is a misuse of the institution of *waqf*, according to al-Manṣūr. The discussions by ʿAbdallāh b. Ḥamza above can be said to take place in the knowledge field of *fiqh* (legal theory). We know less about the legal decrees (codification) he ordered and we have no individual legal cases from his time. There are, however, two short *fatwā*s by him that state that he did validate the Hādawī *waqf* model for *waqfs* established "before this time," or, if the daughters are given an "equitable" (*mā yaʿdilu*) compensation for being excluded. This view, which is presumably closer to codification, is far less strict than his theoretical rejection.[33]

4 *Instiṣār* and *Nūr al-abṣār*

One of the famous *fiqh* works from the period before the *Sharḥ al-azhār* is the *Intiṣār*[34] by the famous Zaydī Imam al-Muʾayyad bi-Llāh Yaḥyā b. Ḥamza (d. 749 or 50/1348 or 49).[35] The *Kitāb al-Waqf* is no longer extant, and thus it cannot be consulted. An abridgement of the *Intiṣār* called *Nūr al-abṣār al-muntaziʿ min kitāb al-intiṣār* is available as a manuscript and has been consulted.[36]

32 ʿAbdallāh b. Ḥamza, *al-Majmūʿ al-manṣūrī*, 2:458–459.

33 Ibid., 2:277–278 and 3:350–351.

34 Yaḥyā b. Ḥamza, *al-Intiṣār*.

35 Gelder, "Yaḥyā b. Ḥamza al-ʿAlawī."

36 Yaḥyā b. Ḥamza, *Nūr al-abṣār*. This was provided by the Muʾassasat Imām Zayd b. ʿAlī l-Thaqāfiyya, I am most grateful for their assistance. The electronic copy of the manuscript is not paginated.

> … If a *waqf* is made for those who descend from the founder (*ʿalā alladhīna yantasibūna ilayhi*) the *awlād al-banāt* are not included (*lā yadkhulu awlād al-banāt*), because they do not belong to the founder's descent line (*li-annahum lā yantasibūna ilayhi*). Therefore some say: "Our descendants are the children of our sons, as for our daughters, their children are the descendants of stangers."[37]

The *Nūr al-abṣār* is very brief about this specific point. The rule translated here is only one of many that clarifies various legal wordings and definitions of beneficiaries. This rule confirms that the *awlād al-banāt* can be excluded if the wording "*man yantasibūna ilayya*" is used, thus invoking the concept of patrilineage, *nasab*. The controversy identified by al-Manṣūr seems to have been completely forgotten. As we see later, this neutral position is more or less the norm, and by inserting a certain wording in the initiation of the *waqf* (in the *waqf* document),[38] the effect of excluding the *awlād al-banāt* is fairly uncontroversial. However, this could probably only be done within the one-third, as in the Hādawī *waqf* model.

5 The Views of Ibn al-Murtaḍā (d. 840/1437) and Ibn Miftāḥ (d. 877/1472)

Ibn al-Murtaḍā wrote the multivolume legal encyclopaedia called *al-Baḥr al-zakhkhār* [The overflowing ocean] and the *Kitāb al-Azhār* [The book of flowers].[39] Shortly after, this work was commented upon in the typical abridgement and commentary style (*sharḥ*) by Ibn Miftāḥ in a multivolume commentary called the *Sharḥ al-azhār*. This work has since been commented upon and extended throughout the centuries until today, and it represents the mainstream Zaydī *fiqh* discourse. Other commentaries have "branched off" from the

---

37 "Banūnā banū abnāʾinā wa-banātunā banūhunna abnāʾ al-rijāl al-abāʿid." The rules immediately following deal with the word *awlād*, whether or not the term if uttered or written automatically includes the *awlād al-banāt*, and then the term *awlādī* ("my children"). The question of hermaphrodites is also mentioned. After this, the following rule states: "wa law waqqafa hāshimī ʿalā dhālika al-hāshimī dakhala awlād al-banāt in kāna abūhum hāshimī," thus automatically including the *awlād al-banāt* if the beneficiary is a specific *hāshimī* person. Perhaps the *hāshimī*s were somehow considered more pious.

38 A *waqf* establishment does not have to be written, it can be established by words, which produces a legal effect.

39 Ibn al-Murtaḍā, *Kitāb al-Azhār*.

Sharḥ al-azhār and use the *Kitāb al-Azhār* as a structure, such as al-Shawkānī's critique of Zaydī *fiqh* called *al-Sayl al-jarrār*, which is treated below.

Based on its slightly different structure, we assume that Ibn al-Murtaḍā's *al-Baḥr al-zakhkhār* predates the *Kitāb al-Azhār*; almost all *fiqh* work after *Kitāb al-Azhār* follow its structure and division of chapters. *Al-Baḥr al-zakhkhār* is still very popular among Zaydīs today as it strikes a good balance between being concise and it includes most of the recognized diverging views, also some among Sunnī authorities.

To start chronologically, in *al-Baḥr al-zakhkhār* Ibn al-Murtaḍā does not specifically state that a family *waqf* exclusively for males, or excluding the *awlād al-banāt*, is wrong. Rather, the debate concerns which words the founder (*al-wāqif*) should use in establishing the *waqf*, or in the *waqf* document. There is a discussion over which terms include the *awlād al-banāt*[40] and which terms and phrases exclude them. Phrases like "for my children and their children's children" (*'alā awlādī wa-awlād al-awlādī*) include female children (*banāt*) and their children (*awlād al-banāt*), while a simple addition to the previous terms such as "whomever belongs to my descent line" (*man yantasibūna ilayya*) excludes them. Ibn al-Murtaḍā also quotes an anonymous "poet" with the familiar proverb: "our descendants consist of our sons and our daughters, but our daughter's children are strangers to us."[41] The fact that he does not mention more than this points to the general acceptance of the rule by the jurists (*fuqahā'*). Imam al-Manṣūr 'Abdallāh b. Ḥamza is not even quoted.

Further, Ibn al-Murtaḍā allows for *waqf* in favour of heirs from all of the estate if it follows the division of the inheritance rules, and if not, then only one-third can become *waqf*. This is a restatement of the Hādawī model. As for the controversy over the remaining two-thirds, which become *waqf*[42] even if some of the heirs disagree on the *waqf*, he also agrees with al-Hādī, but he quotes three scholars who state that the two-thirds should not take the effect of *waqf*, but should remain private property (*milk*). These three scholars are Imam al-Mu'ayyad Aḥmad (d. 411/1020), Imam Yaḥyā b. Ḥamza, and al-Shāfi'ī.[43]

40 The discussion is further complicated as it not only centres on the *awlād al-banāt*, but sometimes also on females in general. Even the rather hypothetical category of hermaphrodites is treated.

41 Ibn al-Murtaḍā, *al-Baḥr al-zakhkhār*, 5:155.

42 That is, a *waqf* that follows the inheritance rules, that does not contradict them. In this, the *awlād al-banāt* are not directly included, but at least the females are theoretically entitled to a share even if they marry out of the clan. Their children will subsequently "inherit" their share in the *waqf*.

43 Ibn al-Murtaḍā, *al-Baḥr al-zakhkhār*, 5:160–161.

As for the *Kitāb al-Azhār*, we do not see any mention of the rule concerning exclusion. Thus it cannot have been seen as important, and the *awlād al-banāt* could be excluded, but only in a *waqf* made of one-third of one's property.[44]

In the *sharḥ* of Ibn Miftāḥ (*Sharḥ al-azhār*) we find the same trend: The discussion of the exclusion of *awlād al-banāt* mainly occurs in the section concerning the valid wordings for the establishment of the *waqf*. More specifically, these relate to various legal definitions of types of beneficiaries and to which utterances produce which legal effect. There are several footnotes that do treat this topic, but these are much more recent than Ibn Miftāḥ's text. In the footnotes, which are from the period after Ibn Miftāḥ and before al-Shawkānī's time (the printed version of the *Sharḥ al-azhār* is based on a personal manuscript of al-Shawkānī), only a few footnotes refer to the names of their authors. The footnotes diverge and are heterogeneous; they fall under different places in the *waqf* chapter. For instance, the dissent of al-Manṣūr ʿAbdallāh b. Ḥamza is quoted.[45] The legal importance of the footnotes depends on the consensus system of *tadhhīb* and *taqrīr*. The views that are considered authoritative will be analysed from *al-Tāj al-mudhhab*.[46] In conclusion, they allow the exclusion of the *awlād al-banāt* from a *waqf*, either by using specific words, or by claiming that "custom" indicates that the meaning of these words does not include the *awlād al-banāt*.[47]

The conclusion is, as we see below, that the Zaydī *madhhab* has, in general, not prohibited the exclusion of the *awlād al-banāt* in a family *waqf* and it has upheld the Hādawī model, except for several notable, partly neo-Sunnī based opinions. The *ḥadīth*, "no testamentation to an heir" is treated in the "chapter of testaments" (Kitāb al-waṣāyā) and only minimally in the "chapter of *waqf*" (Kitāb al-waqf). The view of the Zaydī *madhhab* is (or at least was) contrary to this *ḥadīth*, namely that a testament can indeed be given in favour of an heir.[48]

A *waqf* made from one-third only would thus automatically be legitimate when excluding the *awlād al-banāt*. Al-Hādī's *waqf* was still the norm, and

44 This again shows that this is mainly an issue when a *waṣīya* is written and that it is meant to take effect after one's death.

45 Ibn Miftāḥ, *Sharḥ al-azhār*, 8:198–199. He is also quoted at 8:203 n3.

46 Some of them belong to the period after Ibn Miftāḥ. For instance, there is a long footnote with a quotation from a *fatwā* by Imam Sharaf al-Dīn (d. 965/1558), ibid., 8:199.

47 In Ibn Miftāḥ, *Sharḥ al-azhār* (2003 ed.), these can be found at 8:199, 201, 203, 205.

48 In Ibn Miftāḥ, *Sharḥ al-azhār* (2003 ed.), 10:408, no validation marks appear. In the *Sharḥ al-azhār* (1980 edition) we find that the rule allowing a *waṣīya* for an heir is allowed, and this is given a validation sign. *Sharḥ al-azhār* (1980 ed.), 4:516.

arguably, his *waqf* model "serves" the need for a family *waqf* that circumvents the inheritance rules.

6 The *Fatwa* Collection of Imam ʿIzz al-Dīn (d. 900/1495)

Imam ʿIzz al-Dīn's *fatwā* collection is important for several reasons. It is perhaps the largest collection of Zaydī/Yemeni *fatwā*s of its time and the *fatwā* genre is important since it is close to codification and applied law. There are around one hundred *fatwā*s in the *waqf* chapter of his *fatwā* collection.[49] Apparently, excluding the children of the daughters was common practice. For example:

> Question: If a man made a *waqf* for his children descending from him (*ʿalā l-awlād, mā tanāsalū*), are the *awlād al-banāt* included in this or not?
>
> The answer: The obvious [thing] is that they are included (*al-ẓāhir dukhūluhum*), because they are also his children and part of his offspring (*al-nasl*). But he did include the words "descending from him" (*mā tanāsalū*), a wording which can only follow local custom (*ʿurf*) in meaning. If the term "children" (*awlād*) does not include *awlād al-banāt*, then this is to be followed. It appears that the commoners (*al-ʿawwām*) think that these are not included in the term "children" and therefore this means that exclusion is in compliance with their intention (*al-ikhrāj muwaffaq li-qaṣdihim*).[50]

Ethnography of "legal consciousness"[51] of commoners and local practice is here used to clarify what was meant in that specific *waqf* wording. Although Imam ʿIzz al-Dīn did not like al-Hādī's form of *waṣīya-waqf* or the exclusion of heirs, he did accept the practice.[52] He also explicitly distanced himself from the views of al-Manṣūr ʿAbdallāh b. Ḥamza: He claims that al-Manṣūr made up a law that is difficult to follow because one cannot prove or disprove the lack

49 al-Hādī ʿIzz al-Din, *Majmūʿ rasāʾil, waqf* 376–481 *waṣāyā* 629–660. The pdf version was kindly given to me by ʿAlī ʿAbd al-Raḥmān Shāʾim.

50 al-Hādī ʿIzz al-Din, *Majmūʿ rasāʾil*, 2:381. For another similarly explicit remark stating that *awlād al-banāt* are usually excluded, see ibid., 2:430. There are many more examples of this in the *fatwā* collection, but these are often only mentioned indirectly in questions referring to something else.

51 This is another theoretical concept that has become important in recent years.

52 See, for instance the *fatwā* on ibid., 2:466–467, which is later re-quoted in the *Risāla al-mahdawiyya* (below in this chapter).

of good intent (*qurba*). If the founder explicitly says "for the sake of God," then what should the judge believe?

> ... as for your claim that he did not intend *qurba*, this needs to be firmly based and established and it must be clear to the judge ... otherwise, the *qurba* is obvious (*wa-illā fa-ẓāhir al-qurba*) since the founder said "for the sake of God" (*fī sabīl Allāh*) and similar [statements]. Or, as you said, that he had excluded the *awlād al-banāt* [and therefore did not intend *qurba*] as according to al-Manṣūr bi-Llāh ... And this is his view only ... and the view of al-Manṣūr is weak, and we do not accept (*lā nusallim lahu*) that excluding some of the heirs (*ikhrāj baʿḍ al-waratha*) contradicts a pious intention (*yunāfī qaṣd al-qurba*). He, al-Hādī, whose *madhhab* preconditioned *qurba*, also excluded the *awlād al-banāt*.... No, this view [of al-Manṣūr] is weak and I do not like to side with it.[53]

Imam ʿIzz al-Dīn's position is clear. We should not forget that ʿIzz al-Dīn was an imam based in Saʿda and was partly a "counter-imam" to various imams in the Sanaa area.

7 *Ikhtiyārāt* of al-Mutawakkil Ismāʿīl (d. 1087/1676)

Imam al-Mutawakkil Ismāʿīl[54] was born in 1610 and ruled from 1644 to 1676 and was the son of the founder of the Qāsimī dynasty, al-Manṣūr al-Qāsim b. Muḥammad[55] who gradually drove out the Ottomans. The Qāsimīs made the imamate hereditary[56] and ruled over a population that consisted more of Shāfiʿīs than Zaydīs; this was a result of state expansion to the south and west. This period also produced several jurists who engaged in the *ḥadīth* sciences and sought to incorporate Sunnī concepts, especially the *ḥadīth* sciences, into Zaydism. Al-Mutawakkil Ismāʿīl was considered a significant scholar and jurist.

53 Ibid., 2:465.

54 Al-Mutawakkil ʿalā Allāh Ismāʿīl b. al-Qāsim b. Muḥammad, r. 1644–1676 (d. 1676).

55 As for his father, he was also a significant scholar and thus his views on the matter in question would be useful to include, however I have not been able to acquire texts on this. One footnote is attributed to him in Ibn Miftāḥ, *Sharḥ al-azhār* (8:199), where he allows for the exclusion of the *awlād al-banāt* in *waqf*.

56 They made the imamate hereditary in practice, yet according to classical Zaydī doctrine, any Ḥasanī or Ḥusaynī can become imam and the position is not hereditary.

He ordered that judges (*ḥukkām*) follow a decree called *al-Masāʾil al-murtaḍāt*.[57] These imamic decrees were later called *ikhtiyārāt*. Imam al-Mutawakkil Ismāʿīl's decree is a four-and-a-half page list; each paragraph begins with "*wa-anna*" in red ink. These apparently align to the chapters and structure of the *Sharḥ al-azhār*. For example: "And, *waqf* that contains an exclusion of an heir or reduces his inheritance is not pious and is therefore invalid."[58] The decree to the judges is very clear: A *waqf* made in favour of some heirs that disadvantages other heirs can be invalidated in court. As such, the rule is against mainstream contemporary Zaydī *fiqh* or Hādawī-Zaydī *fiqh*.

A commentary to the decree, called *Kitāb taftīḥ abṣār al-quḍāt ilā azhār al-masāʾil al-murtaḍāt*,[59] was written to explain the arguments and evidence behind the rules. The catalogue of the Maktabat Jāmiʿ al-Kabīr gives the author as Ṣāliḥ b. Dāwūd al-Ānisī (d. 1062/1651 or 52). Al-Shawkānī mentions that another important scholar and judge of his time, Ismāʿīl b. Yaḥyā l-Ṣadīq (d. 1208/1794), also wrote a commentary (*wa-sharraʿa fī sharḥ al-Masāʾil al-murtaḍāt*) on the decree.[60] Al-Ānisī's commentary, which is used here,[61] is distinctly traditionist in its argumentation in support of Imam al-Mutawakkil's decree. The arguments in favour of the rule are as follows:

First, it refers to Qurʾānic verses, then, to various *ḥadīth*s, often only pieces of the *ḥadīth*s, which were presumably well known to the reader. They are put forward as a long list of arguments supporting the rule, but the direct relationship between the *ḥadīth*s and the rule is not spelled out explicitly. One of them is as follows:

---

57 Ismāʿīl b. al-Qāsim b. Muḥammad al-Mutawakkil, "al-Masāʾil al-murtaḍāt fī mā yaʿtamiduhu al-quḍāt," MS 3013 fols. 104–106 (Dar al-Makhṭūṭāt, Sanaa).

58 Wa-anna al-waqf alladhī fīhi ikhrāj wārith aw naqaṣahu ʿan mīrāthihi lā qurba fīhi fa-lā yaṣiḥhu, ibid., fol. 106.

59 Ṣāliḥ b. Dāwud al-Ānisī [d. 1651 or 1652], "Kitāb Taftīḥ abṣār al-quḍāt ilā azhār al-masāʾil al-murtaḍāt," "Fiqh/ʿilm kalām," MS 693 fols. 8–61 (Dār al-Makhṭūṭāt, Sanaa). The manuscript seems to have been copied in 1950. Bernard Haykel mentions two similar manuscripts, the *Masāʾil* and the *Sharḥ*, from the same library, but with a different manuscript number, and these correspond to the *Masāʾil* and the *Sharḥ* mentioned in this section. Haykel, *Revival and Reform*, 202–203. When I visited the Dār al-Makhṭūṭāt, it seems as if they had recently changed the catalogue system. Al-Shawkānī mentions the *Masāʾil* in the *Badr* under the entry of al-Mutawakkil Ismāʿīl (*Badr al-ṭāliʿ*, 179) and notes that it was commented upon by an important scholar and judge of the time, Ismāʿīl b. Yaḥyā l-Ṣadīq (d. 1794): *wa-sharraʿa fī sharḥ al-Masāʾil al-murtaḍāt*. See al-Shawkānī, *al-Badr al-ṭāliʿ*, 191. Thus, al-Shawkānī was himself aware of this work.

60 al-Ruqayḥī, al-Ḥibshī, and al-Ānisī, *Fihrist makhṭūṭāt*, 2:992.

61 Ṣāliḥ b. Dāwud al-Ānisī, "Kitāb Taftīḥ abṣār al-quḍāt," fols. 49–51.

> From Abī ʿAbbās: There used to be inheritance [only] for the children, and the testament (*waṣīya*) was for the parents and relatives (*al-waṣīya li-l-wālidayn wa-l-aqāribīn* [Q2:180]), then this [verse] was abrogated and God sent the inheritance verses.

The *ḥadīth* "no testamentation to an heir" (*lā waṣīya li-wārith*) is also stated, but the reason this *ḥadīth* is directly relevant for *waqf* is not clarified. Then the argument changes from a listing of texts to a more analytical and argumentative approach concluding: "all these narratives (*akhbār*) tell us about the evil in reducing the inheritance for one's heirs, even with justification, and even in a testament (*waṣīya*), charity (*ṣadaqa*), vow (*nadhr*), or *waqf*, or likewise." Then, a part of a *fatwā* of al-Manṣūr ʿAbdallāh b. Ḥamza is quoted: that a *waqf* that prevents an heir [from taking] his inheritance (*qaṭʿ wārith*) is invalid.[62] The text of the commentary even states "and the son of a daughter is in our view an heir" (*walad al-bint wārith ʿindanā*). As mentioned before, the *awlād al-banāt* are not heirs in the inheritance rules in the first place. More *fatwā*s by al-Manṣūr are then quoted, also the one given above invoking the inheritance practices during the *jāhiliyya*.[63]

The argument quotes the views in favour of the rule only, and one might expect some more "technical" or logical ways of establishing validity, such as explicitly invoking an analogy (*qiyās*) or something similar, in order to "transfer" the authority from the Qur'ān and the *ḥadīth*s to the chosen rule, but this is not done explicitly. It uses an "implicit analogy" to import the validity from a range of quotations from the texts of the Qur'ān and the *ḥadīth*s, as if a "bombardment" of textual proofs might, in sum, appear as a valid argument. This way of argumentation is more often used by the traditionists or those who argue against established views of the Zaydī law school. It would seem that the presumptive reader of such arguments is not a legal specialist. For example, a legal specialist knows that the *ḥadīth* limiting the *waṣīya* to one-third does not, according to established *fiqh*, automatically limit the creation of a *waqf*. The argument ignores counter-arguments or the traditional Hādawī *fiqh* in this field. The same applies to the many *ḥadīth*s arguing for the equal treatment of one's children. These are generally not seen to be specific enough to invalidate a *waqf* that does not follow the inheritance shares. However, these are the only arguments available for those who wish to limit the family *waqf*, as we see in the example of Imam Yaḥyā's decree.

---

62 Ibid., fols. 50–51.

63 Ibid.

The argument of the commentary thus relies on a long list of *ḥadīth*s that are only partially relevant, and on a Zaydī imam, al-Manṣūr, who took a principled stand against the Hādawī *waqf*. The sum of these textual "proofs," however, produces an impressive effect. One wonders if this impressive rhetoric was also meant to be part of a wider anti-Hādawī-Zaydī campaign similar to that undertaken by al-Shawkānī, but this would need more research to establish. Unfortunately we know very little about the actual legal practice and effects produced by this new codification by al-Mutawakkil Ismāʿīl, hopefully in the future historical documentation will show us more.

8 *Al-Risāla al-Mahdawiyya* from 1188/1774

Just one hundred years later a new imamic *ikhtiyārāt*[64] was issued, namely that of Imam al-Mahdī l-ʿAbbās (r. 1161–89/1748–75). It is called *al-Risāla al-Mahdawiyya* and was composed at the very end of 1188/1774 and rewritten at the beginning of 1189/1775, which is also the year al-Mahdī l-ʿAbbās died. By this time, the imams had stopped claiming to be "absolute *mujtahids*"[65] and the role of the imam was split into a legal and religious position that was executed by a chief *qāḍī*, while the imam was the political leader, almost a sultan.[66] Under Imam al-Mahdī l-ʿAbbās the chief *qāḍī* was, for a long time, al-Qāḍī Yaḥyā l-Saḥūlī; he took office around 1153/1740, but was imprisoned in 1173/1759.[67] We do not know who the chief *qāḍī* was around the time the decree was authored in 1188/1774.[68] When the Imam died, his son al-Manṣūr ʿAlī took over and returned al-Saḥūlī to his position where he remained until he died in 1210/1795, the year al-Shawkānī was given the position as chief *qāḍī*.[69]

---

64 There has not been much research on this topic and there may have been *ikhtiyārāt* or codifications issued by imams or chief *qaḍīs* in the meantime. Chief *qāḍī* ʿ Aḥmad b. Abd al-Raḥmān al-Shāmī held his office under the father of al-Mahdī l-ʿAbbās, until Yaḥyā l-Saḥūlī took over the office.

65 In classical Zaydī doctrine there is a long list of conditions for being an imam. One of them is that he must be a *mujtahid*, that is, a scholar so learned that he can rely on his own scholarly authority in all questions of legal interpretation.

66 Haykel, *Revival and Reform*, 43.

67 See ibid., 113–114.

68 Several candidates are possible. One is the influential judge of the time Ismāʿīl b. Yaḥyā l-Ṣadīq (d. 1208/1794), al-Shawkānī, *al-Badr al-ṭāliʿ*, 189. Aḥmad Qāṭin, mentioned earlier, was important in the judiciary and the imamic *dīwān* at this time. Zabāra, *Nashr al-ʿarf*, 2:143.

69 Qāḍī Yaḥyā l-Saḥūlī was one of al-Shawkānī's teachers.

The *Risāla al-Mahdawiyya*[70] only addresses three questions or rules: (1) "no testamentation to an heir," (2) *waqf* for some of the heirs without others, and (3) the validity of legal ruses (*ḥiyal*) in circumventing the right of pre-emption (*shufʿa*). Below I analyse only the two first questions. As an introduction to the decree, we are given the whole genealogy of Imam al-Mahdī l-ʿAbbās up to the founder of the Qāsimī dynasty, al-Manṣūr bi-Llāh al-Qāsim b. Muḥammad; it is also pointed out that he was a descendant of the Prophet:[71]

> [Line 1] Of our Lord al-Mahdī l-ʿAbbās, son of Imam al-Manṣūr Ḥusayn, son of al-Imam al-Mutawakkil Qāsim, son of Ḥusayn, son of al-Mahdī Aḥmad, son of al-Ḥasan, [2] son of al-Ḥasan[72] [3], son of al-Manṣūr al-Qāsim, son of Muḥammad, son of ʿAlī, son of Muḥammad, son of ʿAlī, son[73] of God's Prophet, peace of God be upon him and his descendants.

Then we are presented with more information about the circumstances of the authorship of the decree; that it was sent to all the judges at the very end of 1774:

> [4] [As this is] sent to all judges on 20 Shawwāl 1188 [24 December 1774] and this is what it states: In the Name of God the Compassionate, the Merciful ...[74]

The decree explicitly orders the judges to follow its rulings as these are legal questions that pose severe problems for the judiciary, or "querns of disputes," that continue to grind and revolve around the same problems:

> [6] ... So, because the opinions of the judges in many questions diverge and because this has led to damage and disorder, [7] both specifically and generally ... and [this has caused] the extension of many a [legal] dispute, therefore this decree orders ... all the judges [8] to follow it, in accordance

70 The decree is published as a photocopy in the appendix of the book by Rashād al-ʿAlīmī: al-ʿAlīmī, *al-Taqlīdiyya*, 256. A photo of that page from that book and a transliteration and translation based on the photo is given in Hovden, "Flowers in *Fiqh*," appendix 4.

71 Some of the honorary titles have not been included in the translation.

72 This Ḥasan is not found in the chain on the genealogical chart of the Qāsimīs by Haykel in the beginning of his book, but this could be an inconsistency in the style of the otherwise very elaborate genealogy in the manuscript. Haykel, *Revival and Reform*.

73 It is assumed that this connection is abbreviated or "telescoped."

74 Then follows a long string of eloquent rhyming additions to the *basmala*, not translated here. Even the first passages below end in rhyme; because of the stylistic eloquence I could not translate this section word by word.

> with God's religion and by following the noble law school (*al-madhhab al-sharīf*), and no letter is to be changed ... [9] and [what] follows are some of the most problematic questions around which the quern of dispute revolves:

Then follow the three separate main sections of the decree: (1) that testamentation to heirs is valid, (2) that exclusion of the *awlād al-banāt* in *waqf* is valid, and (3) that circumventions of the rules of pre-emption (*shufʿa*) are valid.[75]

8.1 *The Question of Testamentation to an Heir*

> [9] In the question of testamentation to an heir, the view according to the sound law school (*al-madhhab al-qawīm*) is that it is valid.

The jurisprudential problem concerning the "testamentation to heirs" is not directly relevant for *waqf*, but it is very important indirectly, as *waqf* is often made through a testament in order to take effect after the death of the founder, and this is especially so in cases of family *waqf* in Zaydī Yemen. In the Sunnī law schools testamentation was much more restricted than in Zaydism and in Shīʿī *fiqh*, as mentioned in the beginning of the chapter. This relates to, among other things, a *ḥadīth* that became important quite late in the development of Islamic law; this *ḥadīth* states "no testamentation to heirs." The debate around the status of this specific *ḥadīth* is very well elaborated by David Powers[76] and here I only follow the argumentation as it is presented in the decree, before turning back to the analysis:

> [10] As for how this preference (*tarjīḥ*) came about [towards the validity of this question], we refer to how it was preferred by the great warrior and jurist [11] who this land has benefited so much from, Imam al-Hādī Yaḥyā b. al-Ḥusayn, and in this he was followed by his successor al-Murtaḍā

75 This last third has been left out here, but is given in Hovden, "Flowers in *Fiqh*," appendix 4. *Shufʿa* or pre-emption gives a direct neighbour the right, or first option, to buy a person's property for the same price, if it is put on the market, that is, before any stranger. This ensures that land or houses cannot easily be purchased by people from outside the community. Often legal ruses were used to circumvent a persons right to *shufʿa*.

76 Powers, "On the Abrogation." In this article Powers argues that the *ḥadīth* "no testamentation to an heir" was not put into circulation until the third/ninth century. Both the *isnād* and the *matn* of the *ḥadith* were strengthened at this time. Furthermore, Powers refers to the concept that an *āḥād ḥadīth* cannot abrogate the Qur'ān (see 280). See also Powers, *Studies in Qur'an and Ḥadīth; The Formation of the Islamic Law of Inheritance* (Berkeley: University of California Press, 1986).

[12] and al-Nāṣir.[77] After this, it was preferred by Abū l-ʿAbbās, and Abū Ṭālib followed, and Abū Ṭālib even claimed that this view is the consensus (*ijmāʿ*) of the *ahl* [13] *al-bayt*. It is also elaborated upon by the scholar Ibn Miftāḥ in the *Sharḥ al-azhār* and [al-Faqīh Yūsuf] Ibn ʿUthmān in his book *al-Thamarāt*, which refers to the statement of God [Q 2:180]: [14]

> It is prescribed, when death approaches any of you, if he leave any goods, that he make a bequest [testament] to parents and next of kin, according to reasonable usage; this is due from the God-fearing.[78]
>
> This is also referred to in [the *fiqh* works] *Shifāʾ al-uwām*[79] and [15] also in *Bulūgh al-marām*.[80]

The decree lists major Zaydī scholars and authoritative works in classical Zaydism. Then it points even more specifically to the legal problem: The verse Q 2:180 is interpreted as a verse that proves that it is permissable to undertake testamentation to heirs. This verse, according to Sunnī consensus, was abrogated by the later revealed inheritance verses. However, it is difficult to argue that they also completely overruled any possibility of testamentation to heirs. To support this, the *ḥadīth* "no testamentation to an heir" was used and therefore the validity of this *ḥadīth* is an important part of the (Sunnī) argument, although usually a *ḥadīth* cannot overrule a Qurʾānic verse. The Zaydīs did not follow this argument; rather they made the jurisprudential explanation (given below) part of the decree. The problem is somewhat complicated and the clarification falls towards the end, in a somehow inverted structure:

> The essence of the question (*al-ḥāṣil*) is that concerning the sequence of revelation (*sabab al-nuzūl*) the *ʿulamāʾ* disagreed: Does this Qurʾānic verse [Q 2:180] still carry legal effect (*muḥkama*) or is it abrogated (*mansūkha*) [by the later revealed inheritance verses]? Indeed, most scholars inclined towards the view that [16] it was abrogated. This [theoretical position] is

77 Al-Murtaḍā and al-Nāṣir refer to the imamic titles of the two sons of al-Hādī, Muḥammad and Aḥmad, who were the successive imams after their father. See, for instance, the chronology of the early Hādawī imams: Gochenour, "The Penetration of Zaydi Islam," 64.

78 Trans. Abdullah Yusuf Ali, *The Holy Qur'an: Translation and Commentary* (Islamic Propagation Centre International, 1934), 71.

79 The *Shifāʾ al-uwām* is a commentary on al-Hādī's *Aḥkām* by Ibn Ḥusayn b. Badr al-Dīn al-Amīr, *Shifāʾ al-uwām fī aḥādīth al-aḥkām li-l-tamyīz bayna al-ḥalāl wa-l-ḥarām*. For a biography of al-Amīr (d. 1263 or 1264), see Ibn Miftāḥ, *Sharḥ al-azhār*, 1:48 and 1:59–60.

80 This may be a reference to the *Bulūgh al-marām* by Ibn Ḥajar al-ʿAsqalānī (d. 852/1449); it was later commented upon by Ibn al-Amīr in the work *Subul al-salām sharḥ bulūgh al-marām min adillat al-aḥkām*. However, it is a very common title and it could refer to other works.

built on the view that the testament (*waṣīya*) was originally obligatory (*wājib*). This view is attributed to the commander of the faithful, ʿĀʾisha, ʿUmar, and ʿIkrima [17] and this is the view that is held by the imams of the *ahl al-bayt*. The school of al-Hādī elaborated that it was only the obligatory aspect that was abrogated, not the [18] permissible aspect of the rule (*naskh al-wujūb dūna al-jawāz*) and further, that the statement "no testamentation to an heir" refers to the view that in the very beginning of Islam the testament to heirs was obligatory. [19] This was one of the two legal aspects of the rule, and the abrogation did not affect the second legal aspect, namely the permissibility of testamentation to an heir.

Despite this, in this noble decree there is a unification of views also in accordance with [20] the majority of the *uṣūl* scholars who validate the concept [that some verses] of the Book are abrogated and the concept of abrogation of a *mutawātir ḥadīth* by an *āḥād* [single transmission, weaker] *ḥadīth*. They took this claim to the point that this specific *ḥadīth*, even if it is recognized as originally *āḥād*, [21] was still given validity, as if it [had become] *mutawātir* because of the usefulness of this [*ḥadīth*].[81]

It is elaborated upon by al-Zamakhsharī that this restriction [to one-third] is only relevant in cases of intended damage (*muḍārra*)[82] from he who makes the testament (*al-mūṣī*) [22], according to the words of the exalted "no damage" [Q 4:12]. Al-Zamakhsharī states: "This refers to a testament of more than one-third, or one-third exactly. If less than one-third is given as testament, even if the testator's intention is to cause damage to his heirs, or anger between them, this is not God's concern."[83]

---

81 The actual wording is very unclear in the manuscript, but it could read *mutalqā bi-ʿumūd*. The argument, that the *ḥadīth* is given the status of *mutawātir* even if it clearly is *āḥād*, is stated by al-Zamakhsharī at Q 2:180. Abū l-Qāsim Maḥmūd b. ʿUmar al-Zamakhsharī, *Tafsīr al-kashshshāf ʿan ḥaqāʾiq al-tanzīl wa-ʿuyūn al-aqāwīl fī wujūh al-taʾwīl* (Beirut: Dār al-Maʾrifa, 2006), 111.

82 *Ghayra muḍārrin*. Here "damage" or "disadvantage" is perhaps a better term, as in "disadvantage for some of the heirs" as it refers to verse Q 4:12, which is one of the central inheritance verses. The latter half of the verse as translated by Yusuf Ali reads: "If a man or a woman whose inheritance is in question, has left neither ascendants nor descendants, but has left a brother or a sister, each of the two gets a sixth; but if more than two, they share in a third; after payment of legacies and debts; so that no loss is caused (to any one). Thus is it ordained by God, And God is All-knowing, Most Forbearing" "… *min baʿadi waṣīyatin yūṣā bihā aw daynin ghayra muḍārrin waṣīyatan mina Llāhi* …"4:12, 182. Ali (trans.), *The Holy Qur'an*. Yusuf Ali uses the term "legacy" for *waṣīya*. Often when this specific verse is referred to in similar debates, the first part of the verse "*waṣīyatan min Allāh*" is used as a reference as well.

83 al-Zamakhsharī, *Tafsīr al-kashshshāf*, 226.

The argument starts by referring to the mainstream Zaydī view, which explains why the *ḥadīth* "no testamentation to an heir" does not carry any legal prohibition. That is, in the early days of Islam the common understanding of Q 2:180 was that the testament was not only "allowed," but indeed "obligatory" (*wājib*). The crux of the argument is that only the testament's obligatory character (*al-wujūb*) was abrogated, not its permissibility (*al-jawāz*). Thus the testament to an heir changed from being obligatory to being permissible.[84] The Sunnīs and traditionists opposed to this somehow peculiar explanation responded by simply overlooking it. They refer to the strength of the *ḥadīth* and the principle that a strong, and preferably *mutawātir ḥadīth* indeed can abrogate the Qur'ān, or help in the argumentation of the abrogation. The author of the decree does not attack this directly, and he admits that the *ḥadīth* is considered important. However, he also points to the fact that the *ḥadīth* in question is not firmly defined as *mutawātir*, the reason the *ḥadīth* was given this strength, was its usefulness. Whether or not consensus can upgrade a *ḥadīth* from *āḥād* to *mutawātir* is not relevant here. Here the relevance is the way the author of the decree points to this human construction in an otherwise literalist, traditionist argument and uses it to implicitly undermine the argumentative power of the *ḥadīth*. The author uses al-Zamakhsharī as a source of authority[85] and points to al-Zamakhsharī's interpretation of Q 4:12, which states that inheritance shares can be distributed after payment of a loan or a non-damaging testament; less than one-third, if the testament does not produce damage or disadvantage.[86]

84 The discussion around the *waṣīya li-wārith* falls in the "chapter of *waṣāyā*," Ibn Miftāḥ, *Sharḥ al-azhār* (1980 ed.), 4:516, where it also, in brief terms, refers to the abrogation of the *wujūb* but not the *jawāz* and gives the example of the fasting of the day of *Ashūra*, which also became "permissible" and not "prohibited" after the "necessity" was abrogated, that is, it bolsters the argument that an abrogation can apply to one of the five categories of permissibility.

85 According to most informants, al-Zamakhshari's exegesis, *Tafsīr al-kashshāf*, is the most important Qur'ān exegesis (*tafsīr*) among Zaydīs today.

86 See *ghayr muḍārr*, n82 above. This topic is discussed by Powers, but he seems to understand from al-Zamakhsharī that he accepted the full abrogation of Q 2:180. In one way he did, but as the argument in the *Risāla al-mahdawiyya* explains, al-Zamakhsharī did not think that the abrogation also took away what was below the "free" third, which is an important specification. A testament of one-third does not cause "damage" and therefore is not abrogated by Q 4:12, an interpretation which necessitates the grammatical insight presented by al-Zamakhsharī. This latter statement is not treated under Q 2:180 in al-Zamakhsharī's *Tafsīr al-kashshāf* that Powers examines, but rather Q 4:12 (*ghayr mudārr: ḥāl … wa-dhālika an yūṣī bi-ziyāda 'alā l-thulth …*). Powers, however, does discuss other scholars who were against the abrogation, such as Fakhr al-Dīn al-Rāzī, however, he concludes that theirs became a minority position. Powers, "On the Abrogation," 280–285.

Later in the debate about this *ḥadīth*, al-Shawkānī states that according to the important scholar Muḥammad b. Ismāʿīl al-Amīr (d. 1182/1769), who was contemporary to this decree, testamentation to an heir is considered valid, while al-Shawkānī himself was opposed to this, and he elaborates upon this in his treatises on the topic in *al-Fatḥ al-rabbānī*.[87]

8.2 *The Question of* Waqf *for Some of the Heirs Without Others*

The second question the decree addresses is whether or not the exclusionary form of *waqf*, that is, a *waqf* made for some of the heirs that excludes others, is valid.

> [23] And among these [questions] is the question of *waqf* for some of the heirs without others. It is the law school of our imams, peace be upon them, [24] to allow this (*tajwīz dhālika*) and to argue for its validity (*al-qawl bi-ṣiḥḥatihi*). Such a valid exclusionary *waqf* rarely occurs, unless the founder's religion, piety, and knowledge about the law can be established, as al-Sayyid al-ʿAllāma ʿIzz al-Dīn b. al-Murtaḍā [25] b. al-Qāsim clarified, the view of Imam ʿIzz al-Dīn, who made the following response to a question from someone who made a *waqf* for his children (*awlādihi*) and excluded the *awlād al-banāt*.
>
> Imam ʿIzz al-Dīn upheld, as we can see from the [26] formulation of his answer, the exclusion of the *awlād al-banāt* and similar to what was mentioned, does not contradict a pious intention (*lā yunāfī qaṣd al-qurba*) and it is not prohibited for him to do (*lā yumnaʿ minhu*) if the founder made the exclusion with [good] intention [27] or if his intention can be known. However, Imam ʿIzz al-Dīn also stated,
>
> "But we do have a principle (*lakinna lanā ʿaqīda*) which is that the good intention of the founder only seldom appears absolute (*lā yukād yatamaḥḥaḍ qaṣd al-qurba illā nādiran*), such as in a person [28] whose religion, moral nature, piety, and knowledge about the rules of *waqf* can be established. These [persons] are few—even if they are not misusing this rule made by our forefathers—who made [29] *waqf* for the purpose which is outwardly claimed."[88] So, the role of doubt is emphasized by

---

Al-Zamakhsharī, *Tafsīr al-kashshāf*, 266. See also David S. Powers, "The Islamic Law of Inheritance Reconsidered: A New Reading of Q. 4:12b," *Studia Islamica* 55 (1982): 61–94.

87 al-Shawkānī, *al-Fatḥ al-rabbānī*, 10:4845. Ibn al-Amīr's works have not been consulted in this study.

88 This is a more or less direct quotation from the *fatwā* collection of al-Hādī ʿIzz al-Dīn, *Majmūʿ rasāʾil*, 2:466. These lines are otherwise fairly unclear and it is difficult to establish if they are based on the decree only.

> Imam ʿIzz al-Dīn, which means to avoid rushing to use this rule [30] that the imams made. Then he said in the end of the *fatwā*:
>
> "Let us not forget the element of doubt without mentioning those who did this among the imams and the pious forefathers; it is enough to mention as proof of that, the [31] *waqf* attributed to the most knowledgeable of imams and he who was himself an ocean of knowledge, [al-Hādī] Yaḥyā b. al-Ḥusayn, may peace be upon him, and similarly, more than one of the later imams, [32] among them our father Imam al-Hādī ʿAlī b. al-Muʾayyad.[89] Indeed, he excluded the *awlād al-banāt* and presented arguments for the validity of the *waqf* (*iḥtajja ʿalā iṣābatihi*) and produced proofs (*wa-ʿallala ʿilal*) and clarified and elaborated (*awḍaḥa wa-bayyana*) the pious intention he had by using weighty evidence (*adilla rājiḥa*)."[90]

The argument in this question is almost exclusively based on a *fatwā* by Imam ʿIzz al-Dīn. The author also refers to the practice of "several" imams and the very beginning of the argument refers to the fact that the *madhhab* indeed renders the exclusionary form of *waqf* valid. The crux of Imam ʿIzz al-Dīn's argument is that piety and pious intention is difficult to measure and that there could be piety even in an exclusionary *waqf*. The rule that pious intent is difficult to measure should not be used as an excuse hastily. This way of relating the validity of a *waqf* to piety and then saying that piety is difficult to establish, therefore the exclusionary *waqf* is valid, is a type of argument also found in al-Qāḍī ʿAbd al-Jabbār's *fatwā* below. The result is that a *waqf* excluding some heirs is valid if it is made by a knowledgeable person with good intentions.

9 al-Shawkānī's Views (d. 1250/1834)

Al-Shawkānī was opposed to the idea of allowing the exclusion of the *awlād al-banāt* in *waqf*. He did not accept the opinions of previous imams as valid simply because they were imams. Al-Shawkānī claimed that he was not bound by the Hādawī-Zaydī law school and that he could revert to the original sources of the *sharīʿa* and build the law from there.

89 Imam al-Hādī ʿAlī (d. 836/1432) was his grandfather.

90 See also al-Hādī ʿIzz al-Din, *Majmūʿ rasāʾil*, 2:466.

9.1 *The* Nayl al-awṭār

Already in 1795 when he was just thirty-five years old, al-Shawkānī had completed his *ḥadīth* commentary, *Nayl al-awṭār* [The achievement of the goal].[91] This work is a *ḥadīth* commentary in which important *ḥadīths* are collected according to legal topic; it includes a chapter on *waqf*. At the end of a section called "Section on the question that children of the children are included in the term children by circumstantial evidence, but not absolutely,"[92] he mentions: "Whoever makes a *waqf* for his children (*awlād*), [in this] the children of the children enter, whoever is born, and also the females, and in this [question] there is disagreement: What strengthens the argument of inclusion of the females is ..."[93] And then he mentions several *ḥadīths*, the relevance of which is sometimes hard to see for scholars not specialized in *ḥadīth*.[94] Then, very shortly after this, he excuses himself for not providing the full argument for the sake of shortening the discussion.

What we can understand from the above is that al-Shawkānī does not discuss the legality of excluding the females or the *awlād al-banāt* as such. He only discusses what the term "children" (*awlād*) means legally; whether or not the term includes the *awlād al-banāt* according to that specific *ḥadīth*. Thus in his statement there is no prohibition of exclusion per se. Nowhere in the *Nayl* does he address the issue of this type of family *waqf*. The *Nayl* is a typical example of scholarly, academic *fiqh* that is more oriented toward the *ḥadīths* as an academic science than towards legal debates in the field of codification. This is an example in which the question arises because there is material available in the form of *ḥadīths*, and not because the problem was encountered in "the real world." In this way, *fiqh* and certain knowledge is produced, but it is, arguably, poor material for law. Note that this work was done early in his career and we do see a development in his authorship over time, in that his later works are much more legally oriented.

9.2 *al-Shawkānī's* Fatwā *Collection,* al-Fatḥ al-rabbānī

There are at least two treatises in *al-Fatḥ al-rabbānī* that are highly relevant: Both these treatises also appear in very abbreviated form and slightly changed

---

91 Haykel, *Revival and Reform*, 19.

92 "Bāb anna al-waqf ʿalā l-awlād yadkhulu fīhi walad al-walad bi-l-qarīna lā bi-l-iṭlāq," al-Shawkānī, *Nayl al-awṭār*, 8:34.

93 Ibid., 8:36.

94 This is a peculiarity of al-Shawkānī: he continually stresses that the *sharīʿa* is so clear that the only thing needed is his specific, methodologically based deduction. However, many of the numerous *ḥadīths* he quotes are not easy to understand and their relevance and validity to rather different legal questions in diverse historical contexts is certainly not clear. Thus his references to validity are not as clear as he claims.

versions in his critique of Zaydī *fiqh, al-Sayl al-jarrār* [The raging flood]. The first *fatwā* is a compound of several related questions; below is a translation of the sub-question among those related to the form of family *waqf* that excludes the *awlād al-banāt*.[95] In this section of the *fatwā* he states that most *waqf* in those days were made with the purpose of excluding some of the heirs: "And when this situation reflects the general picture, then the a priori view of every *waqf* should be the lack of pious intention. The judges are not to render a *waqf* valid, except after the establishment of a strong probability (*ghalabat al-ẓann*) of the presence of pious intention."[96] His stand is clear and his argument opposes the exclusion of heirs in *waqf*, but what he means by "strong probability of pious intention" is not clear. Al-Shawkānī was a chief *qāḍī* and the question we must ask is, to what degree was such a *fatwā* meant as law, or was it a polemic against the Hādawī-Zaydīs who allowed for these "legal ruses." In order to answer that question we must find evidence that his view in these matters was enforced in court, and this is a topic that has, unfortunately, not been researched.

9.3 *al-Shawkānī's Views in the* Sayl al-Jarrār

Several of al-Shawkānī's *fatwā*s and treatises were abridged and compiled in the *Sayl al-jarrār*. Below is a *fatwā* including argumentation against the exclusion of heirs. It is written in clear language, but scattered with polemical metaphors, in an almost populist style. It is here that for the first time in this debate we see the explicit use of the term *waqf dhurrī*:

> And he [Ibn al-Murtaḍā, the author of the *Sharḥ al-azhār*] says: When it comes to defining the beneficiaries, a condition is good intention (*qurba*).

---

95 The *fatwā* is found in the treatise of Muḥammad b. ʿAlī l-Shawkānī, "Su'al hal yajūzu bayʿ al-mawqūf ʿalā l-dhurriya ʿinda masīs al-ḥāja," in *Dhakhā'ir ʿulamā' al-yaman*, ed. ʿAbd al-Karīm al-Jirāfī (Beirut: Mu'assasat Dār al-Kitāb al-Ḥadīth), 174–175. The *fatwā* treatise is also found in "Su'āl fī waqf al-dhurriyya" (Sanaa: Dār al-Makhṭūṭāt, MS vol. 1195, fols. 18–18). And in *al-Fatḥ al-rabbānī*, 8:4111–4128. In the two last sources the treatise has the name "Suʿāl fī l-waqf ʿalā l-dhurriyya." Al-Shawkānī's treatises and *fatwās* are very comprehensive and partly overlap in content. In the *Fatḥ al-rabbānī* there are two *fatwās* specifically about *waqf*, the second one is mentioned above "su'āl fī waqf al-dhurriyya," and the first one is entitled "Baḥth fī man waqqafa ʿalā awlādihi dūna zawjatihi," al-Shawkānī, *al-Fatḥ al-rabbānī*, 8:4019–4025. He also discusses family *waqf* as a legal ruse: "Ḍarūrat tayaqquẓ al-bāḥith li-ḥiyal al-fuqahā' fa-lā yuʿtabar fīhā," in the *Adab al-ṭalab*, 237–246. According to the editor of the *Adab al-ṭalab*, al-Shawkānī has several other treatises on the topic, mainly related to the issue of *waṣīya*, see *Adab al-ṭalab*, 242–243 n3.

96 al-Shawkānī, "Su'al hal yajūzu." And in the treatise "Suʿāl fī l-waqf al-dhurriyya," *al-Fatḥ al-rabbānī*, 8:4121.

> I say: This *waqf*, that the *sharīʿa* brought us, and that God's Prophet encouraged us make, and which his followers also practiced—this is indeed what brings one nearer to God, *ʿazza wa jallā*.[97] *Waqf* is a continuous charity in which the merit is not cut off from the actor (*al-fāʿil*) even after his death. Therefore, it is invalid (*lā yaṣiḥḥu*) if a beneficiary is not pious, because this is against the essence of a *sharʿī waqf*. Pious intention (*qurba*) is found in everything that the *sharʿ* defined as meritorious for the actor, whatever it may be.
>
> For example, he who makes a *waqf* for the feeding of a specific type of respectable animal; his *waqf* is valid, because it has been established in the true Sunna: "that in every liver there is some good"[98] and similarly, if someone makes a *waqf* for the sake of cleaning a mosque or something that eases the lives of [fellow] Muslims, that calls the Muslim to his path,[99] then verily, this *waqf* is valid because of the strong presence of evidence (*li-wurūd al-adilla al-dālla*) pointing to an outcome in the form of merit (*ajr*) for the actor of those actions. Note that these examples of *waqf* mentioned above are similar and result in merit for its actor, and belong to what is certain knowledge when it comes to the production of merit.

So far, al-Shawkānī has explained that *waqf* in general is indeed valid, at least for certain types of beneficiaries, and that these types of beneficiaries can be firmly established based on various *ḥadīth*s that state that a certain act produces merit. Then he changes his focus to the negative forms of *waqf*:

> As for the types of *waqf* that are made with the intention to prevent what God wanted to enhance, and to deviate from God's inheritance shares, then verily, these types are fundamentally invalid (*bāṭil min aṣlihi*) and such a *waqf* cannot ever have taken contractual effect in the first place. An example is he who makes a *waqf* for his male children without the females among them and similar to this. Verily, in this type of *waqf* there is no pious intention, rather there is an intention to circumvent God's rules and recalcitrance toward the *sharīʿa* He has made for his servants.[100]

---

97 Al-Shawkānī, like other Muslim scholars, uses a wide variety of these phrases following the mention of the name of God, the Prophet, and the Companions; such phrases have been left out hereafter.

98 "Anna fī kull kibd ruṭbatan ajran." The editor refers to where the *ḥadīth* can be found in the various *ḥadīth* collections.

99 "Aw yarfaʾu mā yuʾadhdhī l-muslimīn fī ṭuruqihim," also a *ḥadīth*.

100 "Mā sharraʿahu li-ʿubādihi."

> This person has thus made his un-godly *waqf* as an instrument for this diabolic purpose![101] Oh, how common is this type of *waqf* in our times! And the same [for] a *waqf* made by a person whose only intention is to keep the property within the male descent line (*al-dhurriyya*) and to prevent the property of leaving the descent line.[102] Such a person makes it into a family *waqf* (*waqf ʿalā l-dhurriyya*). Verily, this person only wants to deviate from God's rules which is the [intergenerational] transfer of property through inheritance (*intiqāl al-milk bi-l-mīrāth*), so that the heir is given his right and can do what he wants with his inheritance. Whether the heirs are rich or poor is not at all important in this question: *waqf* is for God.

His message is clear, at least in his moral condemnation. It is noteworthy that he explicitly states that God's rules are that the intergenerational transfer of property should follow the inheritance rules and not other concepts like *waqf* or *waṣīya*. Then he notes the exceptions:

> However, there may on rare occasions be found pious intention in family *waqf*s according to the needs of individuals. It is for the public administrator (*al-nāẓir*) to define the factors that are to be followed in this. Among these rare cases are *waqf*s for those among the descendants who maintain piety and good behavior, or those who engage in studies of *ʿilm*. This type of *waqf* may perhaps (*rubbamā*) contain a pure goal and an achievable pious intention (*qurba mutaḥaqqaqatan*).

The opening al-Shawkānī gives for the use of family *waqf*, is a family *waqf* that is explicitly tied to charitable purposes inside the family. This is also the position of the law today.[103] He does not specify how this should be legally specified for a judge in doubt. In the final paragraph he produces some polemical reflections in which he claims that although family *waqf* remains a moral question, the validity of family *waqf* in general is not a legal concept that man can simply validate himself, rather it is up to the *sharīʿa*. "All acts are judged according

101 "wa-jaʿala hādhā l-waqf al-ṭāghūtī dharīʿatan ilā dhālika al-maqṣad al-shayṭānī." Note that the word *ṭāghūt* is often referred to as tribal custom and practices not based on the *sharīʿa*, and the word is put next to the word *dharīʿatan*, which is very similar in sound to *dhurrī*, the term for family *waqf*. This sentence is just one of many that shows his virtuoso use of the language.

102 Here the term *dhurriyya* is used to refer to local perceptions that only include the male descent line, i.e., *awlād al-ṣulb*.

103 Wizārat al-Shuʾūn al-Qānūniyya, *Qānūn al-waqf al-sharʿī*, article 33.

to intention (*al-aʿmāl bi-l-niyyāt*), however, the validation of the exclusionary family *waqf* should be delegated to what God has ruled between his worshippers, and His approval is the better and right."[104]

9.4 *al-Shawkānī's Views in* al-Darārī

Among al-Shawkānī's later works is a *fiqh* work in a *matn-sharḥ* style called *al-Darārī l-muḍīya sharḥ al-Durrar al-bahīya*. It is very short, and the *matn* of the chapter on *waqf* is just a paragraph. Here, he has one rule, among other rules that seem to be included because of their basis in *ḥadīth*s rather than their direct usefulness, but this rule can be recognized from the previous debates: "Whoever makes a *waqf* that leads to disadvantage to an heir; this *waqf* is invalid (*wa-man waqqafa shay'an muḍārratan li-wārithihi fa-huwa bāṭil*)."[105] His explanation and commentary (*sharḥ*) on this is:

> This is so because it [*waqf*] is among the concepts that God the exalted did not authorize, except and only as continuous charity (*ṣadaqa jāriya*), which is of [continuous] benefit for the founder; not as an ongoing sin with a resulting eternal punishment. God the exalted prohibited harm (*ḍirār*) in His book, both generally and specifically (*ʿumūman wa-khuṣūṣan*), and the Prophet prohibited it in general in the *ḥadīth* "No harm in Islam" (*lā ḍarar wa-lā ḍirār fī l-Islām*). It was also mentioned previously, concerning specific rules related to harming [one's] neighbour (*ḍirār al-jār*) and [doing] harm by [one's] testament (*ḍirār al-waṣīya*) and similar to these two.[106]

His *sharḥ* adds arguments to underpin the rule. As a *sharḥ* compared to other *fiqh* debates, it is univocal. This aspect of univocality makes it very close to the genre of imamic decrees and codification and less a reconstruction of an academic *fiqh* discussion. By looking more closely at his arguments we see that they stop long before stating the exact relationship between "no disadvantage to an heir in *waqf*," and "no harm in Islam," and the relation between not "harming [one's] neighbour" and "[doing] harm by [one's] testament." He does not identify precisely how he takes validity from one rule and transfers it to the next. The principle of "no harm in Islam" is a general rule, while in the other two, which are considered more specific, a more specific underlying

104 al-Shawkānī, *al-Sayl al-jarrār*, 3:51–52.

105 al-Shawkānī, *al-Darārī l-muḍīya sharḥ al-Durrar al-bahīya* (Damascus and Beirut: Mu'assasat al-Kutub al-Thaqāfiyya, 1988), 303.

106 Ibid., 304.

cause (*ʿilla*), must be identified. This belongs to the technicalities of analogy (*qiyās*), but again, this *qiyās* is, as before in this debate, not explicitly invoked in this specific rule by al-Shawkānī. It is merely left for the reader to assume. By calling it a *qiyās*, it would probably not be up to the "standards" of argumentation that the *uṣūl* literature for a proper *qiyās* demands, thus the level of argumentation is deliberately kept vague, and the validity is invoked by numerous citations of *ḥadīth*s and citations from the Qurʾān. Reading his text, we almost forget that there are arguments against al-Shawkānī's views, which centre on the idea that it is not considered "harm" in the first place to favour some of one's children as long as it is within the limit, that is, the one-third, and that an individual is given a certain freedom concerning what he does with his wealth during his lifetime.

Al-Shawkānī has written extensively on his views on the *ḥadīth* "no testamentation to an heir," in a treatise called *Iqnāʿ al-bāḥith bi-dafʿ mā ẓannuhu dalīlan ʿalā jawāz al-waṣīya li-l-wārith* [The satisfaction of the researcher in correcting his assumption concerning the evidence of the validity of the testament to an heir].[107] And it suffices here to say that he takes a Sunnī stand, and opposes the argument as exemplified in the *Risāla al-mahdawiyya*. According to him, the treatise was made in response to a work by Ibn al-Amīr (d. 1183/1769), in which Ibn al-Amīr argued for the validity of testamentation to an heir. Ibn al-Amīr's treatise is called *Iqnāʿ al-bāḥith bi-iqāmat al-adilla bi-ṣiḥḥat al-waṣīya li-l-wārith* [The satisfaction of the researcher by presentation of the evidence of the validity of testamentation to an heir].[108]

In concluding the section on al-Shawkānī's views, we can say that in his later works he was firmly opposed to the exclusionary form of family *waqf*s. His moral condemnation is crystal clear, as is his legal prohibition, although there are some cases in which piety can be a valid foundation. We do not have the historical evidence necessary to determine to what extent the judges used this rule. Thus until the period of Imam Yaḥyā, the history of codification is only a history of the norm; the court practice can only be assumed from the normative text based in the assumed political power of the authorities. As Haykel reminds us, we should not forget that the act of producing and publishing *ikhtiyārāt* was also an act of demonstrating the ability to rule. Haykel mentions that the *ikhtiyārāt* thus had a "reflexive quality"; they made the ruler appear

107 Al-Shawkānī has several treatises on the matter of the *lā waṣīya li-wārith*. As with the questions related to *waqf*, these can be found in abbreviated form in the *Sayl al-jarrār*, in the *Fatḥ al-rabbānī* the treatise is referred to as "Iqnāʿ al-bāḥith bi-dafʿ mā ẓannuhu dalīlan ʿalā jawāz al-waṣīya li-l-wārith," 10:4839–4864 and "Jawwāb suʾāl wurida min Abī ʿArīsh ḥawla al-waṣīya bi-l-thulth," 10:4865–4880. al-Shawkānī, *al-Fatḥ al-rabbānī*.

108 Ibid., 10:4865.

learned.[109] Thus "codification" could also have a discursive aspect wider than the mere issuing of laws intended to be followed. This discursive element can be seen clearly in the quotation from *al-Sayl al-jarrār* above. Even if he was a chief *qāḍī* in a position to produce law, it is problematic to call his works "codification" until we have more historical evidence about actual court practice.

10 Imam Yaḥyā's Decrees

In 1911 when Imam Yaḥyā took over the political power and judiciary in the highlands from the Ottomans, he did not immediately issue any decrees on the matter of family *waqf*. The Ottomans used Ḥanafī judges in some cities, but we have little information about the extent to which they applied Ḥanafī law and hereunder *waqf* law.[110] With regard to legal rulings, we know that *waqf*s excluding *the awlād al-banāt* were legal, at least according to the most common views in the Ḥanafī law school, as is shown at the end of this chapter.

We do not know exactly when Imam Yaḥyā started to issue his decrees (*ikhtiyārāt*), only that he set up an appeal court in Sanaa even before he entered the city. The first decrees were not printed. One early handwritten example dates from 1934, and can be found in al-ʿAlīmī's *al-Taqlīdiyya*.[111] A printed version, and indeed a version that is versified and commented upon, *Ṣirāṭ al-ʿārifīn*, was made by al-Shamāḥī and published in 1937.[112] Both these versions contain codified legal rules related to the balance between the inheritance rules and the *waqf* rules.

10.1 *The Early Years of Imam Yaḥyā*

During the first years, that is from 1911 and into the 1920s, we do not know of any decrees directed to all the judges.[113] Some material that is relevant for this

---

109 Haykel, *Revival and Reform*, 202. In this case al-Shawkānī was not the imam, but rather representing his office and producing his own theories of how knowledge and power should be connected. Here Messick's work about the discursive power of *sharīʿa* texts is also highly relevant.

110 The Ottomans tried to reform and unify the courts, but it seems that this was achieved to an extent, and only in the larger cities. For details, see Kühn, "Shaping Ottoman Rule in Yemen"; Bostan, "Institutionalizing Justice in a Distant Province."

111 al-ʿAlīmī, *al-Taqlīdiyya*, 258–259.

112 al-Shamāḥī, *Ṣirāṭ al-ʿārifīn*.

113 An early *faṭwā* on the issue (from 1328/1910) by Imam Yaḥyā is given in Sālim, *Wathāʾiq Yamaniyya*, 202–204. Here Imam Yaḥyā answers a question from the judge in Kawkabān, al-Sayyid ʿAlī b. Aḥmad b. Muḥammad Sharaf al-Dīn. The *fatwā* states that all charitable dispositions are to be limited to the rules of the *waṣīya* and thus be limited to one-third and to take effect after death. Furthermore, "commoners" (*al-ʿāmmī*), despite their lack of

early period can be found in the first printed version of the *Sharḥ al-azhār* from 1913–14.[114] In the first pages there is a short collection of *fatwā*s and treatises (which were retained in the 1980 edition of the *Sharḥ al-azhār*) that centre on "practical" legal problems of the type a local judge would encounter: customary sharecropping, marriage, inheritance, and also *waqf*. It is unlikely that the *fatwā*s in the printed version of the *Sharḥ al-azhār* of these early years diverged significantly from the legal views of Imam Yaḥyā and they must at least represent some sort of consensus of the scholarly community around him at the time.

There are two *waqf* related *fatwā*s, both presumably issued by al-Qāḍī ʿAbd al-Jabbār al-Jabbūrī l-Ṣanʿānī (d. 1184/1771).[115] He was thus contemporary with Imam al-Mahdī l-ʿAbbās, but his text is included here because his *fatwā* was reused in the printed edition of the *Sharḥ al-azhār*. The first *fatwā* starts with a rule that is not directly relevant here, but the second rule is and the two rules are formulated together and conceptually linked: "A question [is related] about a man who made *waqf* of some of his property for his heirs (*al-waratha*), within the third (*qadr al-thulth*) as a charity (*ḥukm al-ṣadaqa*)." The usage of terms reveals that the one who asks, mixes several concepts. What should a judge or a *muftī* think when he hears the concepts *waqf, heirs, the third*, and *charity* together in one short sentence? The question demonstrates why this *fatwā* was included in the introduction of the *Sharḥ al-azhār*. The question continues: "Is (*hal*) the division (*al-qisma*) to be according to persons (*ʿalā l-ruʾūs*), where the males and the females are given the same, or is the division to be according to the inheritance shares (*al-farāʾiḍ*)? The *waqf* is for the *dhurriyya* and its division is not specified." Both options are legal in Zaydī *waqf fiqh*, and it is up to the founder to specify this. However, if it has not been specified, the former is to be assumed.

> And are (*hal*) the *awlād al-banāt* included after their inheritors have died, and are their children (*ʿayyāluhunna*) [of the *awlād al-banāt*] included in the aforementioned *waqf* or not?

---

knowledge about the *sharīʿa*, are to be allowed to undertake such dispositions. Ibid., 204. The *fatwā* does not address the issue of exclusion of the *awlād al-banāt*.

114 See the uncertainty concerning the date of the first version in chapter 4.

115 Ibn Miftāḥ, *Sharḥ al-azhār* (1980 ed.), 1:51. The *qāḍī* ʿAbd al-Jabbār al-Jabbūrī l-Ṣanʿānī (d. 1771) is the only man by the name of ʿAbd al-Jabbār in Zabāra's *Nashr al-ʿarf*. He was the judge of Sanaa under Imam al-Mahdī l-ʿAbbās, but withdrew because of a quarrel with chief *qāḍī* al-Saḥūlī. He studied under al-Amīr including the *ḥadīth* sciences. Zabāra, *Nashr al-ʿarf*, 2:30–31. Zabāra also quotes Aḥmad Qāṭin who quotes ʿAbd al-Jabbār about the *waqf* practices in Lower Yemen. *Nashr al-ʿarf*, 2:235. This is mentioned in the following chapter.

> Al-Qāḍī ʿAbd al-Jabbār answered: "The *waqf* is to be divided equally according to individuals (*ʿalā l-ruʾūs*) if the founder did not specify that the *waqf* is according to the *sharīʿa* fractions (*al-farāʾiḍ al-sharʿiyya*) [the shares of the inheritance rules] and as for family *waqf* (*al-dhurriyya*), the children of the females are included."[116]

Our focus is only on the last part of the *fatwā*: "As for the term descendants (*dhurriyya*), the children of the females are included." This is actually in harmony with most views, that is, that the term "descendants," *al-dhurriyya*, is a term or wording that includes the *awlād al-banāt*, while other terms can be used in the *waqf* initiation to exclude them. Thus this *fatwā* does not claim that the exclusionary *waqf* (which excludes the *awlād al-banāt*) is illegal, it simply claims that the term *dhurriyya* includes them. Before the following *waqf fatwā* no new author is introduced, thus presumably it is provided by the same author, al-Qāḍī ʿAbd al-Jabbār.

The answer to another question concerning whoever intends with a *waqf* to exclude heirs:

> The answer: He who intends with the *waqf* the exclusion of heirs, this *waqf* is invalid (*lā yaṣiḥḥu*) and no legal effects take place (*lā yunfadhu minhu shayʾ*). Pious intention is a condition in *waqf* and whoever expresses with his intent (*qaṣd*) to ignore what God has written [has committed] a great sin. However, and with no doubt, the plaintiff (*al-muddaʿī*) must produce evidence (*iqāmat burhān*) of his claim that the founder's intent was to exclude (*qaṣd al-ḥurmān*), because the intent is a matter of the heart (*amr qalbī*) that can only be established (*innamā yastadillu*) by what is expressed in words of legal meaning (*bi-mā ẓahara min al-aqwāl al-dālla*), thus he has to prove that the exclusion is intended (*maqṣūd*), such as is elaborated in the chapter of acknowledgements (*iqrār*) in the *fiqh* books.[117]

The first half of the *fatwā* follows the pattern of moral condemnation that we saw in al-Shawkānī's views. And similarly it turns around with a notable "however": An heir who feels excluded and who goes to the judge must be able to prove that the exclusion was "intended," and this can only be proven if the founder has used certain words. By this "however" the answer also changes from a philosophical and moral tone and into one of legal language: "plaintiff"

116 Ibn Miftāḥ, *Sharḥ al-azhār* (1980 ed.), 1:51.
117 Ibid.

(*muddaʿī*), "evidence" (*burhān*), "words of legal meaning" (*awqāl dālla*). The *fatwā* does not refer to which words would prove this intent, and thus invalidate the *waqf* or forcibly include the *awlād al-banāt*.[118] If this second part had not come after the "however," the *fatwā* would follow those who claim that the exclusion is illegal, and this is the first time we see more "procedural necessities" mentioned. Would not the mere exclusion of *awlād al-banāt*, as a fact in itself be enough? Does he mean that words like "*man yantasibu ilayya*" have to be found in the *waqf* document? Or does the *muftī* actually mean that there are no such words that can "prove" the intent? Does it mean that it is legal to exclude an heir from the *waqf* if this was not the primary intention of the founder, but merely a side effect? This *fatwā* would have been much more useful if the *muftī* provided the exact words necessary to clarify the intent to exclude. Perhaps they were left out in order to leave the *fatwā* open for further specification at a later point in a time, if the question was not settled. It is not necessary to try to establish the exact meaning of the *fatwā* here. What is important is to see this as part of the background and an example of the legal situation in the early years of Imam Yaḥyā's rule, when the *fatwā* was inserted into a section "useful for the judges" in the first printed version of the *Sharḥ al-azhār*. The legal problem of the status of the *awlād al-banāt* was clearly still there, and without a strong centralized court system, the question would in any case be left open to the discretion of the individual judges, thus producing a variety of legal practices. When Imam Yaḥyā started to issue his decrees, this was one of the most important legal matters in which *fiqh* had to be codified into clear, coherent, applicable law.

10.2 *The Decrees* (Ikhtiyārāt) *of Imam Yaḥyā*

In the 1930s, Imam Yaḥyā achieved stronger political control. In many rural areas women did not receive inheritance at all during al-Shawkānī's time, and this continued well into Imam Yaḥyā's reign. The tribal areas of Lower Ḥāshid were the last areas where this practice was allowed; it was put to an end in 1932.[119] Such an account is a very strong claim, but it is relevant as an example

---

118 As for which words carry which legal implication according to the *madhhab*, see the elaboration of the footnotes of Ibn Miftāḥ, *Sharḥ al-azhār* as treated below in the section dealing with *al-Tāj al-mudhhāb*.

119 Al-Shawkānī, *Adab al-ṭalab*, 243 n*. The editor of al-Shawkānī's *Adab al-ṭalab*, ʿAbdallāh al-Surayḥī, specifies that Lower Ḥāshid refers to ʿUdhar and al-ʿUṣaymāt. Dresch mentions punitive campaigns undertaken at this time by the imam against Ḥāshid, partly legitimated by the need to correct the tribal custom of denying inheritance to women. Dresch, *Tribes*, 227.

of how the imam's law was extended only gradually into the rural tribal areas and how the need for law was portrayed.

Imam Yaḥyā's decrees started as a list that was posted on the wall at the court of appeal. One example is the decree dated 23 Jumādā l-Ūlā 1352 [3 September 1934]:

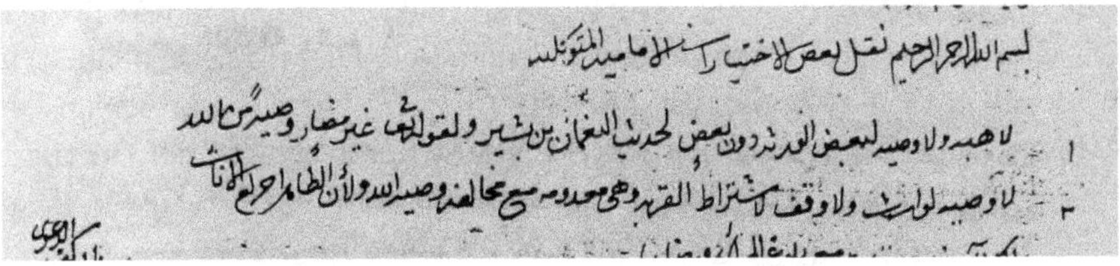

بسم الله الرحمن الرحيم نقل بعض الاختيارات الامامية المتوكلية

١ لا هبة ولا وصية لبعض الورثة دون بعض لحديث النعمان بن بشير ولقوله تعالى غير مضار وصية من الله

٢ لا وصية لوارث ولا وقف لاشتراط القربة وهي معدومة مع مخالفة وصية الله ولان الطامة حرمان الاناث

FIGURE 10 The two first *ikhtiyārāt* of Imam Yaḥyā's list (al-ʿAlīmī, *al-Taqlīdiyya*, 259).

The questions related to *waṣīya* and *waqf* are among the first rules of a list of twenty-eight.[120] These two rules read:

1. [There shall be] no gift and no testament for some of the heirs without others, according to the *ḥadīth* of Nuʿmān b. Bashīr[121] and according to His, the exalted's, statement: "No harm in testament from God" (*ghayr muḍārr waṣīya min Allāh*).[122]

---

120 Rule numbers 20, 21, and 22 also deal with aspects of family *waqf*, but parts of the sentences in the document are barely readable. However, in meaning, they are in full accordance with those found in the *Ṣirāṭ al-ʿārifīn* and *al-Tāj al-mudhhab* (in the latter they are given as footnotes), thus a tentative reading could be:

20: "*Waqf al-qirāʾa* for an heir is valid, not for consolation of the souls (*lā li-l-taysīr*) (*Waqf al-qirāʾa li-l-wārith bi-mā taḥṣil min al-ghilla fa-ṣaḥīḥ, lā bi-mā taysīr*). For the wording, see also *al-Tāj al-mudhhab*, 288 n1. Later, we know that this type of *waqf* was also used as a legal ruse—the salary for the recitation was often far higher than the actual work involved. See the court case and judgement from 1944 referred to in Mijallī, *al-Awqāf fī l-Yaman*, 37–38.

21: *Waqf* for the children, excluding the wives, is not allowed, unless the wife is the mother of the children.

22: All donative dispositions made by commoners (*ʿawwām*) are restricted like a *waṣīya*, unless the transaction is completed and takes effect during [one's] lifetime.

121 This is the *ḥadīth* "no testamentation to an heir." Powers notes that this *ḥadith* does not occur in the two authoritative *ḥadīth* collections of Muslim and al-Bukhārī. Powers, "On the Abrogation," 275. See also the discussion about this *ḥadīth* earlier in this chapter conserning *al-Risāla al-mahdawiyya*.

122 The *ghayr muḍārr* is the Qurʾānic reference (4:12) referred to in the *Risāla al-mahdawiyya*, above. The *Ṣirāṭ al-ʿārifīn* discusses how it should be read and al-Zamakhsharī's version is not mentioned at all. Al-Shamāḥī, *Ṣirāṭ al-ʿārifīn*, 40. It seems that the reading of the words *baʿda waṣīya yūṣā bihā aw dayn ghayr muḍārr waṣīya min Allāh* can produce several different meanings depending on how the word *waṣīya* relates to the context.

2. [There shall be] no testament to an heir and no *waqf*, because of the condition of good intention and this is absent if there is deviance from "God's testament" and because the clear [underlying intention] is to exclude the females.

Haykel argues that this list was developed over time as the cases came in to the appeal court.[123] If this is correct, then the fact that the *waqf* questions appear at the top of the list indicates their importance. Later, Imam Yaḥyā's decrees were extended, versified, and commented upon (elaborated and explained) in a work called *Ṣirāṭ al-ʿārifīn* by al-Shamāḥī (1937).[124] The decree is well noted in Messick's article "Textual Properties,"[125] thus I only give a brief summary. Further, Imam Yaḥyā's decrees are also found as footnotes in *al-Tāj al-mudhhab* of al-ʿAnsī (mainly on page 288).

The argumentation underpinning the rules, which are briefly indicated within each rule, are given in full in the *Ṣirāṭ al-ʿārifīn* and partly in *al-Tāj al-mudhhab*. The style of argumentation is similar to those that restrict the family *waqf* by focusing on diverse *ḥadīth*s and verses from the Qurʾān, without offering clear analogy (*qiyās*) or explicitly explaining the link. It is the mere sum or cumulative weight of arguments that seem be authoritative.

The legal result of the combination of arguments is the following: "No *waqf* to an heir." This is the indirect result of a lack of pious intent in exclusion and because of the "harm" that can be caused to heirs.[126] Both arguments have been seen before in different variants. However, there are exceptions: If the *waqf* does not favour some specific heirs, it can be made for the heirs. Wives, if they are mothers of the children who are beneficiaries, can be excluded. Needy and sick individuals can be preferred. The *waqf* is restricted to one-third, if it was established by a commoner. To put it positively: *waqf* for heirs is allowed if it follows the divisions of the inheritance rules, or needy individuals among the heirs can be preferred, and wives, if they are mothers of children who are beneficiaries, can be excluded if they are "sufficiently compensated."[127] This new law makes it easy for judges to invalidate the most blatant exclusions, but it also allows them to look quite specifically at each case and perhaps even treat each case differently. After all, the power constellations inside an

123 Haykel, *Revival and Reform*, 204.

124 al-Shamāḥī, *Ṣirāṭ al-ʿārifīn*. For a translation of the introduction to the *Ṣirāṭ al-ʿārifīn*, see Haykel, *Revival and Reform*, 205–206.

125 Messick, "Textual Properties."

126 al-ʿAnsī, *al-Tāj al-mudhhab*, 288 n1.

127 See the lengthy comment on "no testamentation to an heir," 33–44. On the *waqf*, see 44. On the *ʿawwām*, where it states that all dispositions are to follow the restriction of the *waṣīya* (non-charitable dispositions during one's lifetime are excluded from this), see al-Shamāḥī, *Ṣirāṭ al-ʿārifīn*, 44–45.

old family *waqf* belonging to a major, rich family is not something that a local judge can easily change; it is easier to prevent "commoners" from making new exclusionary family *waqf*s. In any case it would be difficult to establish a new family *waqf* excluding the *awlād al-banāt* without great care and the provision of compensation (e.g., to the mothers of the exogamously married daughters). The balance between the intergenerational transfer of wealth via *waqf* versus inheritance shifted in favour of greater respect for the inheritance rules.

10.3 al-Tāj al-Mudhhab: *Codification by Imam Yaḥyā or by the Zaydī* Madhhab?

During Imam Yaḥyā's lifetime he ordered the *Sharḥ al-azhār* to be re-written in a simpler style and include only the chosen views of the Zaydī *madhhab* and his own decrees. This was done to ease the training of and use by judges. The result was called *al-Tāj al-mudhhab* [The gilded crown] and was printed in stages between 1938 and 1947. In *al-Tāj al-mudhhab* there is no mention that a commoner cannot make a *waqf* of more than one-third, nor that the *awlād al-banāt* must be included, except on page 288 n. 1, where Imam Yaḥyā's *ikhtiyār* on this question is stated. *Al-Tāj al-mudhhab* is thus very "loyal" to the validated (*tadhhīb, taqrīr*) *Sharḥ al-azhār* and its footnotes, and is thus more a condensed version of the *Sharḥ al-azhār* than it is a work of scholarly *fiqh*.

As mentioned earlier in this chapter, the issue of the balance between the inheritance rules, the *waṣīya*, and the *waqf* is not discussed in the *matn*, nor in the *sharḥ* in the chapter on *waqf* of the *Kitāb al-Azhār* and the *Sharḥ al-azhār*. Discussions and validated rules are found in several glosses and footnotes dispersed in the chapter, but mostly under the rulings of definitions of "specified beneficiaries" (i.e., private or family *waqf*s). In *al-Tāj al-mudhhab* these footnotes are faithfully re-quoted in the main text, as "notes," or "topics" (*mas'ala, far'*). The references to the original sources of authority, which are important in the *fiqh* discourse, have been removed and these footnotes now appear as a part of a univocal text. These footnotes, which had been added gradually since Ibn Miftāḥ's time, existed parallel to the decrees and *fatwā*s discussed above. Once Imam Yaḥyā issued his *ikhtiyārāt*, most of these footnotes lost their legal power.

There are two notes in *al-Tāj al-mudhhab* that are directly relevant here and that are also given in the *Sharḥ al-azhār* (2003 edition, 8:297). The first one is very close in wording to the *fatwā* by 'Abd al-Jabbār quoted in the introduction of the *Sharḥ al-azhār* (1913–14 edition), as mentioned above:

> Topic (*far'*): *Waqf* for the children (*awlād*) and the children's children with a "then" (*fa*) or a "thereafter" (*thumma*) or with an "and" (*wa*) is a valid wording, or "generation after generation" (*baṭn ba'd baṭn*), or

> similarly. And the *awlād al-banāt* are included in that since they are children of the children, but not if the founder states "for the children of the male descent line" (*ʿalā awlād ṣulbihi*); if so [i.e., if he does that], the *awlād al-banāt* are not included since they are of someone else's male descent line (*min ṣulb ghayrihi*), and the custom speaks for their exclusion (*fa-iqtaḍā l-ʿurf khurūjuhum*).[128]

This note explains the position of the Hādawī-Zaydī *madhhab* quite concisely. There are various wordings that include the *awlād al-banāt* and various wordings that exclude them. And it is fully valid to exclude them. Furthermore, "custom" is a central conceptual source of validity both in claiming that there is precedence for exclusion, and as a way to establish the legal intention of a word as an act of speech. The second note admits that exclusion can constitute a loss for those involved in terms of inheritance, but that this is permissible if it is otherwise "compensated":

> Topic (*masʿala*): As for the rule (*al-ḥukm*) of excluding daughters and their children from the *waqf* (*al-banāt wa-awlāduhunna*): If they are given a compensation for the revenue in another way, such as [support] during visits [on] holidays (*ziyāra fī l-aʿyād*) and similarly for the married women (*muzawwajāt*) and otherwise sufficient support (*kifāya*) for the non-married [women] (*ghayr al-muzawwajāt*),[129] then this is valid, and this does not contradict pious intent (*qurba*).[130]

We can see that the project of simply "codifying" the strongest views found in the *Sharḥ al-azhār* keeps its stated goal; the main text of *al-Tāj al-mudhhab* is loyal to the *Sharḥ al-azhār*, not to Imam Yaḥyā's *ikhtiyārāt*. This is an attempt to separate the "Zaydī" codification from the codification of Imam Yaḥyā. One

128 al-ʿAnsī, *al-Tāj al-mudhhab*, 297. This note is inspired not only by ʿAbd al-Jabbār's *fatwā*; similar footnotes can also be found in the *Sharḥ al-azhār*. Here it is specified that there are disagreements over all the wordings, but that the validated consensus (*tadhhīb, taqrīr*) is that the wordings *nasl, dhurriyya, ʿaqb*, and *nasab* all exclude the *awlād al-banāt*, and one footnote adds that this is to be followed also by the term *awlād*, if the custom is so (*huwa mustaqīm idhā jarā bihi al-ʿurf*). Ibn Miftāḥ, *Sharḥ al-azhār*, 8:203.

129 Here it should be noted that in the learned families it is very common for unmarried women to have their own *waqf*s for their group, in order to confirm their right to remain in the paternal house or in a separate part of the house. Such a *waqf* does not have to be made for unmarried women only, it can also be established for others in the family. I have heard of several such individual *waqf*s.

130 al-ʿAnsī, *al-Tāj al-mudhhab*, 297.

single exception to this is found where *ḥurmān wārith*[131] is added as something that could invalidate the good intent, and thereby the *waqf*. Otherwise, the new decrees from Imam Yaḥyā are only given as footnotes under the text (in *al-Tāj al-mudhhab*, there are few other footnotes).

11 Imam Aḥmad's Decrees

Imam Aḥmad's decree does not mention family *waqf*, or the topic of exclusion of heirs or the *awlād al-banāt* explicitly, and he only mentions the "no testamentation to an heir," the issue of "equality between the children," and "no damage," but only in relation to the *waṣīya*, not explicitly in relation to the *waqf*.

As for the work *Taysīr al-marām*, it seems in general to be very close to Hādawī-Zaydī rulings and true to the *Sharḥ al-azhār* and not to the imamic decree. Article 695 states that the founder may exclude the *awlād al-banāt*.[132] Würth remarks that it is unclear to what extent the *Taysīr* was actually used.[133] The fact that exclusion of the *awlād al-banāt* was rendered valid supports the argument that the *Taysīr* was not intended to be used even if it has the form of codification.

12 Republican *Waqf* Laws on the Matter

12.1 *The Republican* Waqf *Decrees of 1971*

Under and immediately after the civil war, the judiciary remained unchanged and Zaydī *fiqh* in combination with the decrees of Imam Yaḥyā and Imam Aḥmad continued. Most of the judges in Lower Yemen had been educated under their regime, many of them in al-Madrasa al-ʿIlmiyya in Sanaa. As mentioned in chapter 3, some early decrees ordered that a ministry of *awqāf* be organised, but these did not address the legal institution of *waqf* as such, or any legal matters between private parties. It was in 1971 that the ministry of justice first issued a decree with sixty-eight rules that the judges of the country were obliged to follow. These remained in effect until the first *waqf* law was

131 Ibid., 289.
132 "… mā lam yaqil awlādī li-ṣulubī fa-lā yadkhulu awlad al-banāt," Qāsim b. Ibrāhīm and al-Sarḥī, *Taysīr al-marām*, 148, article 695.
133 Würth, *Ash-sharīʿa fī Bāb al-Yaman*, 43.

issued in 1976. The scholar and state *muftī* Muḥammad b. Ismāʿīl al-ʿAmrānī called them the *ikhtiyārāt* of the ministry of justice, as if to avoid any sense that there was a fundamental break with the imamic *sharʿī* past: the republican state simply took over the role the imam had. The list was published in the *Majallat al-buḥūth wa-l-aḥkām al-qaḍāʾiyya al-Yamaniyya* [Gazette of research and Yemeni legal rulings] number 1, 1980 and is also published in al-ʿAmrānī's *Nizām al-qaḍāʾ fī l-Islām*.[134] Rules 45–48 concern *waqf*. Note how the language, structure and style is changed into something between *fiqh* and modern law:

> 45. *Waqf* that contains exclusion, or that favours some of the heirs is invalid, because of incompatibility with the pious intent (*qurba*). The following cases are exceptions: (a) If the heirs approve, without any form of compulsion and with the full knowledge of their loss, and that this approval can later not be withdrawn. (b) If there is a personal reason, such as the beneficiary being blind or disabled or similarly, after that [the beneficiary's death] the *waqf* reverts to the heirs.[135] (c) If there has been a previous ruling [stating the validity of the *waqf*] by a competent judge, since a ruling can never be contradicted,[136] or, if one hundred years have passed and no one has protested.
>
> 46. Whoever makes a *waqf* for his children or heirs as a specified, personal *waqf* (*waqf al-ʿayn*), or a *waqf* of the *waqf al-jins* type,[137] the share of

134 For further comments on this see Haykel, *Revival and Reform*, 217. Haykel also points out that Sunnī-oriented Zaydīs like al-ʿAmrānī attribute many of the *ikhtiyārāt* of Imam Yaḥyā and Imam Aḥmad, and indeed also these first republican *ikhtiyārāt*, to the views of al-Shawkānī. Al-Shawkānī is portrayed by many in the republican generation as a source of authority.

135 Sic! One would expect, "the remaining beneficiaries," not "heirs." That the *waqf* reverts to the heirs of the founder is in accordance with validated Hādawī-Zaydī views. In the *fiqh*, the *waqf* does not revert to private property if the original purpose ceases to exist, but returns to the heirs as (family) *waqf*.

136 This is also found in Ibn Miftāḥ, *Sharḥ al-azhār*; it is an important principle from the time before the establishment of a hierarchical court system.

137 *Waqf al-ʿayn* is a *waqf* for specific persons: when they die, their shares are inherited and thus further split according to the inheritance rules. There are many complications of division and again we can see that *ʿurf* is invoked to clarify the legal meanings. See al-ʿAnsī, *al-Tāj al-mudhhab*, 293–294. The difference in the *ʿayn* and *jins* is often (but not always) related to rules used to determine whether or not the whole generation of children must become extinct before the next generation can have their shares. In this case the value of one share increases as there are fewer to share the *waqf* with in that one generation; when the last person of the generation dies, the *waqf* is shared among the following generation. This is more accurately treated under the *tartīb* issue, where the differences between the letters *wāw* and *fāʾ* matters, as "*awlādī, fa-awlādihim*" indicates that the entirety of the first generation must be extinct before the next can get their shares. See al-ʿAnsī, *al-Tāj*

whoever dies among them goes to his heirs, not to those of his generation until they are all extinct; in this there is [a form of] exclusion, and because the order of that description is not commonly[138] intended by many of the founders.

47. *Waqf* for the descendants (*ʿalā l-dhurriyya*) and for the children of one's relatives (*awlād al-aqārib*) and similarly (*wa-naḥwa dhālika*), is to be considered in light of the meaning the words have according to the customary usage in the area of the founder, unless he was a learned jurist (*faqīh ʿālim*), since it is not correct to assume another beneficiary [other] than the founder intended, even if the words in themselves are clear. In the most common custom, the term "child" (*walad*) is not used for other than males, the same is the case in the term "descendants" (*dhurriyya*), which means whoever belongs to the male descent line (*awlād al-ṣulb*). *Waqf*s containing these details can only be valid if there exists a permission from the ministry of *awqāf*,[139] or if there was previously issued a ruling of the validity of the *waqf*, or if the number of years, as mentioned in article 40(c) has passed.

48. If the beneficiary of a *waqf* ceases to exist (*idhā inqaṭaʿa maṣrif al-waqf*), the new beneficiary is to be of a similar purpose (*mā yumāthil al-mubarrira al-mawqūf ʿalayhā*), and it shall not return to the founder and his heirs, since the *waqf*[140] has exited from the realm of private property.[141]

This decree is an important link in the transition between the legal practices of the imamate and that of the republic. The *waqf* law further regulating private *waqf* practices did not come until 1976 and does not diverge much from the basic content of the decree.

The restriction to one-third is not mentioned in the 1971 decree in the rules related to *waqf*. However it is indeed treated under *waṣāyā* in the same decree, in article 64, under the inclusive concept "charitable dispositions" (*al-taṣarrufāt al-tabarruʿiyya*) which logically also includes *waqf* (that is, only

---

al-mudhhab, 296. This article in the decree seeks to clarify these rules and reduce the alternatives by prohibiting the issue of *tartīb* and leaving only one division model available.

138 Again, this is a reference to custom.

139 This was and still is the responsibility of the *nāẓir al-waṣāyā*. Thus, according to this principle, as long as no one takes the *waqf* to court, the *waqf* could be approved by the ministry.

140 Sic *bi-l-waqf*. Presumably, *al-waqf* is correct. If not, it would read "and it shall not return to the founder and his family as *waqf*, since it [the property] has exited from the realm of private propery." The basic meaning is the same.

141 al-ʿAmrānī, *Niẓām al-qaḍāʾ fī l-Islām*, 239–240.

those dispositions made by "commoners"). The reason this is not mentioned under the *waqf* section of the decree becomes more understandable if we see the period of the decree as one in which family *waqf*s were seldom established anymore, and the issues at stake were mainly related to older, already existing family *waqf*s. In this decree the *awlād al-banāt* can be excluded, but only from old existing *waqf*s. In new *waqf*s, such a practice is forbidden without ministry approval, the legal practice of which is little known. In 1971, when this decree was made, the "old" *waqf*s were mainly those that for various reasons were not privatized or confiscated by the state during the period of Imam Yaḥyā and Imam Aḥmad.[142]

12.2 *The 1976* Waqf *Law*

The 1976 *waqf* law[143] is the first republican, exclusive *waqf* law, that is, a single law code dealing only with *waqf*. The structure of the law follows the *Sharḥ al-azhār*[144] to a large extent. The matter of family *waqf* is in two sections near the section in the *Sharḥ al-azhār* structure that deals with the division of benefits between beneficiaries in the family of the founder,[145] but several articles relevant for this chapter can also be found in other places in the law:

> Article 14: A *waqf* is invalid if made with the intention to escape from a debt (*dayn*) or pre-emption (*shufʿa*) and legal ruse (*ḥīla*), such as circumventing the inheritance rules.

This article refers to a specific debate in the *Sharḥ al-azhār*[146] which is somehow peculiar; it concerns whether or not pious intention or absence of such can be legally established in acts such as in making a *waqf* in order to hide assets from a creditor, etc. The argument in favour claims that even though the act is outwardly reprehensible, the inner intent, as in the inner feeling of the founder, may still be one of piety. This debate in the *Sharḥ al-azhār* probably arose from the argument that if one cannot know the inner intent with certainty, then no *waqf*s can be legally invalidated because of lack of piety. This

142 For instance, Messick states that the 1940s to 1960s saw a wave of family *waqf* privatization in the city of Ibb. Messick, "Transactions in Ibb," 386.

143 The law was officially called "Decree by the *Majlis al-qiyāda* number 78 from the year 1976 regarding the issue of *waqf*." This law is published in Manṣūr, *al-Mawkib*, 313–323.

144 Several of the sections have the same headings as before, for instance, see the one called "Fī mā yajibu ʿalā l-mutawallī fiʿluhu wa-mā yajūzu lahu wa-mā lā yajūzu."

145 In Ibn Miftāḥ, *Sharḥ al-azhār* this is treated in the third section: "(Faṣl:) Fī bayān mā yaṣiḥḥu al-waqf ʿalayhi wa-aḥkām tattabiʿu dhālika."

146 It is the very latest rule in the *matn* of the *Kitāb al-Azhār*.

seems to have been the position of the *madhhab* (though with modifications)[147] and this article in the law takes a clear stand against this position by creating a fundament which is necessary for the other articles that restrict the family *waqf*. The article also mentions other "legal ruses" and "circumventing the inheritance rules." The article is included in the 1976 law in order to set aside any confusion of authority and validity and to set up a link and division of function between inheritance and *waqf* based on the concept of *qurba*. The article is a very complicated and *fiqh*-related way of stating that *waqf* is built on *qurba* and that *qurba* is the very fundament of validity in *waqf*, and that a *waqf* made with negative consequences cannot stand, even if the inner intention is good.

> Article 15: It is invalid for a person to make a *waqf* of more than one-third of his property if he has heirs at the time of the [establishment of the] *waqf*.

The restriction to one-third, even when making a public *waqf*, is commented upon further below, but here in article 15 it is spelled out explicitly. Article 30 continues in line with article 14:

> Article 30: All texts related to *waqf* (*nuṣūṣ al-waqf kullahā*) are to be followed, except those that contradict a pious purpose (*illā fī-mā yunāfī l-qurba*).

By "texts" the article probably refers to *waqf* documents or other administrative legal documents, but it could also include *fiqh* texts. The rule effectively relativizes all legal documents and laws and resets the new main criteria of validity to pious intention, as does article 14. Pious intention is a self-validating term and difficult to argue against. Yet its vagueness makes such an article little more than a doctrinal statement, the *waqf* law self-validating itself and creating a *sharʿī* image, rather than simply stating that "act X is illegal." It actually says that, if combined with article 15, *waqf* documents or other legal documents, even those valid under previous jurisdictions, are no longer automatically valid if they contradict the new law, as in matters of the exclusion of heirs. The main articles dealing with family *waqf* then follow:

> Article 31: *Waqf* for one's self, or for one or more heirs, or for the descendants (*al-dhurriyya*) or for the children, or the children's children is invalid (*bāṭil*), unless those mentioned are included as part of a general

147 Ibn Miftāḥ, *Sharḥ al-azhār*, 8:298–299.

> [public, charitable] definition specified by the founder, if so any of these have the same rights as others, or if the beneficiary is disabled (*ʿājiz*) such as blind or paralyzed (*ashall*) and does not have what he needs, and in this case, if the condition improves or the beneficiary dies, then the *waqf* is considered cut off from its beneficiaries[148] and will follow article 28[149] of this law.

The same is stated about the *waṣīya* from the personal status law: a *waṣīya* in favour of heirs is invalid, however, for a family member in dire need due to disability it is legal. This article effectively prohibits the new formation of family *waqf*s and the only opening remaining is various forms of charity within the family.

> Article 44: The old family *waqf*s whose stipulations are not in accordance with the stipulations in this law, if a judgement was issued in favour of their validity, or if the heirs agreed upon them, or if forty years passed, are to remain as they are, and are not to be invalidated unless the beneficiaries wish to, or the majority among them, according to their needs regarding sustenance. The request [for invalidation] is to be presented to the court …

Articles 45 and 46 regulate how a family *waqf* is to be divided between the heirs in case of privatization, dissolution or invalidation of the *waqf*. In practice, this means the *waqf*s that "survived" the period of Imam Yaḥyā and Imam Aḥmad.

A new *waqf* law was passed in 1992, however, with regard to the articles above, it is more or less the same as the 1976 law; the numbers of the articles changed (the numbers shifted up, i.e., no. 6 became no. 8). There is only one major legally oriented decree after this *waqf*, law called "The *waqf* of lease regulations" (*lāʾiḥat tanẓīm ijrāʾāt al-taʾjīr* …),[150] republican decree number 99 of 1996. It does not mention the issue of family *waqf* at all.

---

148 The phrase "cut off from its beneficiary" (*munqatiʿ al-maṣrif*) is often used in *fiqh* discussions on regulating a *waqf* that requires change when the income remains, but the beneficiary is gone.

149 Article 28 says that a *waqf* that is "cut off" from its beneficiaries should be spent in a similar purpose or type of beneficiary, or a better one. (This is the position of al-Muʾayyad and al-Shawkānī.) The change of beneficiary must be approved by a judge. Relatives of the original beneficiary and relatives of the founder are to be preferred if the intention of the *waqf* can be achieved.

150 These are treated in chapter 6.

12.3 *The Arguments Behind the Restriction of* Waqf *to One-Third*

Al-Waẓẓāf and al-Qirshī are university professors who have written student textbooks on *waqf* law and teach at the Faculty of *Sharīʿa* and Law at the University of Sanaa. Their views, commentaries, and arguments are being taught to students of law today. *Waqf* law is part of the curriculum for the bachelor's degree; once students graduate with this degree they are given the title of lawyer (*muḥāmī*). The following is an analysis of how "the restriction to one-third" in *waqf* is presented in these textbooks.

The restriction of making a *waqf* of only one-third of one's property is interesting as it represents one of the borders of validity of *waqf*, both related to family *waqf* and to public *waqf* and the restriction of a *waqf* to one-third of one's property follows closely the debate over exclusion of the *awlād al-banāt*. This restriction and the arguments behind it are especially relevant because they support the argument of this chapter, that the different models of intergenerational transfer of wealth are, in practice, strongly interrelated in codification and in everyday knowledge; this is particularly true in this patrilineal agricultural society. It relates to the perceived rights of the heirs in the property of their father, even before his death.

With regard to the family *waqf*, we have seen that in the Hādawī-Zaydī tradition, *waqf* is restricted to one-third because of its close relationship to the *waṣīya*. Interestingly, no one explicitly refers to the Hādawī tradition as a source for this restriction, even if we look at the debate from the time of Imam Yaḥyā until today. In addition, no one involved in the debate claims that it is a direct *qiyās* from the *waṣīya*. Imam Yaḥyā restricted it for the "commoners" only, since they "do not know the meanings of the legal terms";[151] he thus argued that commoners actually mean *waṣīya*[152] when they make *waqf*s, so he ruled that all charitable dispositions during one's lifetime should be regarded as *waṣīya* and that therefore they are restricted to one-third. This is also found in the decrees of 1971.[153] The *waqf* law of 1976, that is, article 17 of the 1992 law, does not provide any additional arguments in its favour, but simply states the norm straightforwardly:

> Article 17. It is invalid for a person to make a *waqf* of more than one-third of his property if he has heirs at the time of the *waqf*.[154]

---

151 "This is so because the commoners do not know the juristic implications of the terminology and often when they use terms like *hiba, nadhr* and similar [terms], they actually mean the *waṣīya*." See al-Shamāḥī, *Ṣirāṭ al-ʿārifīn*, 44–45.

152 Or "*waqf* that will take effect only after death."

153 Under the *waṣīya* section as mentioned, not explicitly in the *waqf* section.

154 Wizārat al-Shuʾūn al-Qānūniyya, *Qānūn al-waqf al-sharʿī*, 4.

Al-Qirshī's comment is that the only source for this restriction is the *qiyās* from the *waṣīya*:

> The clarification (*al-bayān*): Yes, and this is a *qiyās* of the *waṣīya*, as found in the *ḥadīth* by Sa'd b. Abī Waqqāṣ "a third and a third is much...."[155]

Al-Waẓẓāf[156] has a longer commentary than al-Qirshī. He starts by stating that "A majority (*aghlab*) of the jurists in Islam made the restriction to one-third in *waqf*."[157] He does not mention who and simply overlooks the whole Zaydī tradition we have followed in this chapter. Then, to make his argument, he includes more *ḥadīths* than al-Qirshī. He begins with a *ḥadīth* that focuses on *ṣadaqa* and in the footnotes he provides the many authoritative sources of the *ḥadīth*: "Verily God made for you, [to decide over] one-third of your property at your death, in order to make this an increase in your good deeds."[158] This is yet another *ḥadīth* that deals with the period shortly before death (*'inda wafatikum*), that is, it either looks like a *waṣīya* or as al-Waẓẓāf mentions, it relates to the so-called "death sickness," in which all dispositions are to be restricted like the *waṣīya*. But the *ḥadīth* alone does not "prove" that its restriction should also extend to the concept of *waqf*, or to other types of charity or dispositions during one's lifetime. Al-Waẓẓāf does not mention these counter arguments (i.e., that this *ḥadīth* only refers to issues related to "death sickness" or issues related to the *waṣīya*, and that these are not related to *waqf*s).

Calling this a *qiyās* is a way of using the term *qiyās* as if it, in itself, has some sort of validity. The term *qiyās* is often mentioned in textbooks as "one of the sources of Islamic law" and in *uṣūl* works there are discussions over different types of *qiyās* (strong, weak, etc.), and the criteria of what constitutes a valid *qiyās*. But in al-Waẓẓāf's modern law textbook it is used to prove that the rule in question "is valid," simply by invoking the term *qiyās*. This is done instead of encouraging the students to think critically and question the relationship between that *ḥadīth* and the rule. Instead of looking at the potential criticisms of article 17, al-Waẓẓāf instead focuses on the strength of that specific *ḥadīth* and

155 al-Qirshī, *al-Awqāf wa-l-waṣāyā*, 73.

156 Ismā'īl 'Abdallāh al-Waẓẓāf, *Aḥkām al-waqf fī l-fiqh al-Islāmī wa-qānūn al-yamanī* (Sanaa: N.p., 2006), 79–80.

157 Ibid., 79.

158 "Inna Allāh taṣaddaqa 'alaykum bi-thulth amālukum 'inda wafātukum ziyādatan fī ḥasanātikum li-yaj'alaḥā lakum ziyādatan fī a'mālikum." The *ḥadīth* can be understood in other ways as well. Here it is not important to clarify its potential meanings, but simply to point out that it is not readily understandable to everyone. The importance also lies in the way al-Waẓẓāf uses it and the claims he makes based on it.

in the footnotes he provides references to several *ḥadīth* collectors and *ḥadīth* collections, as if the *ḥadīth* collectors and collections themselves were fundaments of validity. My point is that the references to establish the validity of the rule do not extend back to a "clear text." Rather, we as analysts, anthropologists, and historians must see that the references quite often simply end early on in the chain, in certain concepts of authority and criteria of validity that frame the discourse. The sources and references are not as systematic as is claimed or assumed by the informants.[159]

Al-Shawkānī and others among the *ḥadīth*-oriented scholars referred to many of the same *ḥadīths* as al-Waẓẓāf does, and used similar methods of opaque inferences, but they never used or invoked the term *qiyās* in any of the rules analysed in this chapter. Authority and validity are "inferred" and the criteria of validity in inference shift according to context. Here, we can differentiate between a high-level *fiqh* debate (al-Shawkānī), a codification of Imam Yaḥyā, and a present-day student textbook commentary. When looking at these three different cases and the use of the word *qiyās*, we see that the first two share the criteria that the term *qiyās* should not be used, since the nature of the inference is not clear enough to be termed a *qiyās*. The modern-day university professors, who are educating today's lawyers, see this differently.

When a person has no potential heirs, he may give all his property as *waqf*. According to the 1976 *waqf* law, the restriction is only in the "presence of heirs." So again, the rationale in this article is related to the right of the heirs to the property of their living father. This is a clear legal right in the *waṣīya*, but it all comes down to the issues mentioned in the introduction, that a *waqf* produces just as many effects for the heirs in the future as a *waṣīya* does if the object is land and where the right to use the land is the rationale. And although the primary function of the *waqf* as a legal concept is as a carrier for charity, the borders becomes blurred when that charity is directed towards the heirs of the founder.

As for al-Waẓẓāf's comment on the invalidity of *waqf* in favour of heirs as found in articles 32 and 33 in the *waqf* law, his treatment is quite long and ventures even further into the *ḥadīth* sciences. This is in many ways indicative of many present-day law debates in Yemen. There is a shift to a more *ḥadīth*-based *sharīʿa* at the expense of the established *fiqh* from the "old" law schools. This new *ḥadīth*-oriented *sharīʿa* seems to be more populist and the demands for logic and coherence are not as strong as are those found in the established law schools. Al-Waẓẓāf, who seeks to validate the position of the Yemeni law

159 This point is also discussed in Dupret and Ferrie, "Constructing the Private/Public Distinction," 150.

in articles 32 and 33, interestingly also quotes opposing arguments, as if in a scholarly *fiqh* debate, in which the introduction and discussion of opposing arguments is a sign of quality. However, the opposing argument al-Waẓẓāf quotes also takes the form of a *ḥadīth*, one that states that *waqf* was made for heirs also during the time of the Prophet, one of them being that ʿUthmān made a *waqf* for his son Ibān. This *ḥadīth* has not been mentioned in the debate in this chapter. It is attributed to a certain *ḥadīth* collector al-Wāqiʿī. "However" al-Waẓẓāf says, "al-Wāqiʿī is not trustworthy," "Aḥmad states that he is a liar who alters *ḥadīths*" (*kadhdhāb yuqallibu al-aḥādith*) and "al-Bukhārī, Abū Ḥātim, and al-Nisāʾī state that he fakes the *ḥadīths*."[160] Al-Waẓẓāf wanted to show a dialogue, but did not choose a counter argument from the Zaydī tradition.

The whole shift in discourse is quite noticeable: it has shifted from a well-established and stable *fiqh* discourse over centuries, a discourse that takes into account legal problems in the real world, into a discourse about *ḥadīths* and *ḥadīth* collections, one that is rather detached from actual legal problems.

As for the exclusion of the *awlād al-banāt*, this issue becomes irrelevant in the debate hereafter since the modern *waqf* law (article 32 and 33) prohibit *waqf* for all heirs, not only *waqf* where exclusion is found.

Al-Shawkānī explicitly mentions the *awlād al-banāt*, but talks about the exclusion of heirs in general, and most of those who claim that the exclusion of the *awlād al-banāt* is invalid argue to include all heirs, not only the group of *awlād al-banāt*. The term *awlād al-banāt* is a technical legal term that belongs to a patrilineal agricultural society where the established legal practices are designed to circumvent the effects of the inheritance rules, while the term "heirs" is much more *sharʿī* in the sense that it is more easily found in the Qurʾān and the Sunna and neo-Sunnīs and Salafīs can more easily argue in favour of it. Claiming that the discourse is about "heirs" and "equality" and hence "no damage" (*lā ḍirār*), rather than "custom" and *awlād al-banāt* is a way of drawing upon more readily available arguments in the context of an increasingly modern and urbanized society.

A final remark on the restriction to one-third in *waqf* is that this restriction was also implemented (more or less the same way) in the Egyptian *waqf* law of 1946 (articles 23 and 24). This was upheld in law number 29 of 1960, even after the non-charitable *waqf* was abolished.[161] Thus it is possible that Egypt was the inspiration for the codification of this matter.

160 al-Waẓẓāf, *Aḥkām al-waqf*, 79–80.

161 Shalabī, *Aḥkām al-waṣāyā*, 385–387. Shalabī states that the old Ḥanafī law (*ẓāhir al-riwāya*) in these matters (practiced in Egypt until the 1946 law) gave the founder freedom to make all of his property into a *waqf*.

12.4 *The Gift* (Hiba) *in the Present Law*

A few notes on the gift (*hiba*) should also be made. If we return to the table in figure 9 "the relationship between *waqf* and *waṣīya* in a schematic form" at the beginning of this chapter, we might expect to find a loophole in the concept of the gift (*hiba*) during one's lifetime. Could the founder simply use a gift instead of *waqf* if he wanted to give his land to some, but not all of his children? There is no doubt that in classical Sunnī *fiqh*, one can give a gift during one's lifetime of all one's property and also to an heir, although favouring one child over others is considered morally wrong.[162] However, this does not seem to be as straightforward in Zaydī *fiqh*. According to the *Sharḥ al-azhār*, a gift to an heir is only valid for one-third of one's property. The *matn* of Ibn Miftāḥ declares it reprehensible (*makrūh*), but legally valid.[163]

The *muftī* of Zabid, Aḥmad b. Dāwūd b. Aḥmad b. Muḥammad al-Baṭṭāḥ al-Ahdal, gave the following *fatwā*, some time shortly before 1975:

> The question: Is it valid to give a gift to the son of one's son in the presence of heirs? The answer: "... The rules concerning a gift to an heir's heir follow the same rule as a gift to an heir; it is invalid, unless the rest of the heirs approve." Aḥmad Dāwūd Aḥmad al-Baṭṭāḥ al-Ahdal.[164]

Article 183 in the Yemeni Law of Personal Status (section on *hiba*) states that:

162 Y. Linant de Bellefonds, "Hiba," in *Encyclopaedia of Islam*, second edition, ed. P. J. Bearman, Th. Biancuis, C. E. Bosworth, E. van Donzel, and W. P. Heinrichs (Leiden: Brill, 1960–2004), 3:350.

163 Ibn Miftāḥ, *Sharḥ al-azhār*, Kitāb al-hiba 8:146–147. The *matn*: "Wa tukrahu mukhālafat al-tawrīth fīhimā" (the *hiba* and the *ṣadaqa*). The *sharḥ*: "If the favouring is done for good reasons, it is not reprehensible, as long as it is within the third." The discussions in the *Sharḥ al-azhār* on these pages are long and detailed. One footnote focuses on the father's right to give to his eldest son (*al-kabīr*, also known today as *al-bikr*) and the *tadhhīb* signs favour the possibility of this. It even claims that this is valid because the word *taraka* customarily means *waṣīya*. Some notes, among them some attributed to al-Saḥūlī, claim that it is not reprehensible to favour some of the heirs, if they are within the one-third. This statement provides a legal solution to a moral problem, and as such the limit between one-third and two-thirds is a practical one.

164 "... al-jawwāb: al-hiba li-wārith al-wārith ḥukmuhā ḥukm al-hiba li-l-wārith ghayr saḥīḥa illā an yujīzū baqīyat al-waratha ..." Aḥmad b. Dāwūd b. Aḥmad b. Muḥammad al-Baṭṭāḥ al-Ahdal, "Kitāb al-Tuḥfa al-qaddasiyya fī ikhtiṣār al-raḥḥabiyya fatāwā l-Shaykh al-ʿAllāma al-Sayyid Aḥmad b. Dāwūd b. Aḥmad b. Muḥammad al-Baṭṭāḥ al-Ahdal" (Electronic copy of handwritten manuscript edited by ʿArafāt ʿAbd al-Raḥmān ʿAbdallāh al-Ḥadramī, 1992), file DSC00033.

> Article 183. Equality (*musāwāt*) is compulsory in gifts and in similar dispositions, between the children and between the heirs according to the demands of the *sharīʿa*.
>
> Article 187. A gift for an heir or his heir during [one's] lifetime must follow the rules of the *waṣīya*, unless the receiver (*al-mawhūb lahu*) can consume the gift when the giver is alive, or following article 183.[165]

The reference to "consumption," would exclude land. Thus a gift is not unrestricted in the law. When informants today claim that a person can only dispose of one-third of his property, it is not only a "perception" of local *waqf* knowledge; it actually is the law.

12.5 *The* Nadhr *and the Recitation* Waqf

I came across several *waqf* documents in Rayma and Zabid in which the *waqf/waṣīya* was given by means of a conditional disposition, a so-called *nadhr*.[166] The *nadhr* is a separate concept and chapter in *fiqh* books, and in practice we would expect it to be a conditional *waqf*, as in, "I promise to make so-and-so a *waqf/waṣīya* if such-and-such happens." However, it seems to be a sort of transaction similar to a *waqf/waṣīya* since they overlap in practice, especially if the object at issue is land, as mentioned at the beginning of this chapter. When Imam Yaḥyā wanted to regulate all these intergenerational transfer practices, he did so in the rule that restricts dispositions during one's lifetime to heirs among the commoners (*ʿawwām*). In his decree he included a restriction of the *nadhr* in the very same rule as the restriction on the family *waqf*, as if they were part of the same legal phenomenon.[167] The informants who showed me the *nadhr* documents did not separate them conceptually from the concepts of *waqf* and *waṣīya*, and they explicitly pointed out that the purpose of all these concepts was to circumvent the inheritance rules and therefore they could only be valid within one-third of the property. Most non-scholarly informants

165 Wizārat al-Shu'ūn al-Qānūniyya, Qānūn al-aḥwāl al-shakhṣiyya: Qarār jumhūrī bi-qānūn raqm 20 li-sanat 1992 bi-sha'n al-aḥwāl al-shakhṣiyya wa-taʿdīlātuhu (Sanaa: Maṭbaʿat al-tawjīh, 2006), articles 183–187.

166 J. Pedersen, "Nadhr," *Encyclopaedia of Islam*, second edition, ed. P. J. Bearman, Th. Biancuis, C. E. Bosworth, E. van Donzel, and W. P. Heinrichs (Leiden: Brill, 1960–2004), 7:846.

167 Concerning the restriction to one-third in charitable dispositions: "This is so, because the commoners do not know the juristic implications of the terminology and often when they use terms like 'gift,' '*nadhr*,' and such, they actually mean the *waṣīya*." Al-Shamāḥī, *Ṣirāṭ al-ʿārifīn*, 44–45.

seemed to have the perception that a person is not free to do what he wants with his property, even during his lifetime.

Why use the *nadhr*? The answer is not entirely clear. Since Rayma is a Shāfiʿī area, one might expect the possibility of a full family *waqf*, even an exclusionary one, at least before the laws of Imam Yaḥyā. The explanation may lie in the fact that these areas were partly under Zaydī jurisdiction and one can only speculate over the influence of the Zaydī judiciary on the local Shāfiʿī practices of intergenerational transfer of property.[168] If *waqf* or *waṣīya* was invalid to heirs, perhaps the *nadhr* became a locally used legal ruse. The few *nadhr* documents I have seen state that the transaction is to take immediate effect, which means that it is more like a gift than a *waṣīya*. As pointed out by informants in Rayma,[169] such a transaction is only valid to an heir's heir, not a direct heir, which is also a normal Sunnī interpretation of the *waṣīya*.[170] In this book I do not address the *nadhr* further—I have included it here is to show how problems relating to the freedom of disposition are larger than the legal categories of *waqf* versus inheritance.[171]

Another type of *waqf* that also falls between categories is the recitation *waqf* (*waqf daris, qirāʾa, tilāwa, muqaddimāt*). This is a *waqf* in which the founder stipulates that the income of the *waqf* should go toward one who recites the Qurʾān for his own soul or someone else's, or for Qurʾān recitation only (*muṭlaq*). Usually, this work is done by the *mutawallī* himself. If the salary is

168 We do not know to what extent Zaydī rulers, such as the Qāsimīs or Imam Yaḥyā, enforced their law in the Shāfiʿī areas, and if so, in which exact areas of the law. Since the above mentioned rulers, as exemplified by the commentaries of their decrees, were Sunnī-oriented, it is possible that the differences between their law and local Shāfiʿī law was not very significant.

169 Such a *nadhr* document concerns one-third of a person's property, giving it as a *nadhr* to a grandson. Hovden, "Flowers in *Fiqh*," appendix 5.

170 The Law of Personal Status, Article 235 states that a *waṣīya* cannot be given for an heir or an heir's heir. Wizārat al-Shuʾūn al-Qānūniyya, *Qānūn al-aḥwāl*. Therefore one would expect the same restriction in the law of *nadhr*, see foonote below.

171 The *nadhr* also seem to be a "problem" in the *fiqh*. I have not pursued this matter in this study but it is indicated by the presence of a treatise mentioned in Zabāra, *Nuzhat al-naẓar, 363*: ʿAbd al-Rahman b. ʿAbdallāh al-Qadīmī l-Tihāmī (d. 1330/1912): *al-Tawḍīḥ wa-l-bayān fī tarjīḥ ibṭāl al-nadhr li-qaṣd al-ḥurmān* [The clarification and argumentation for preferring to invalidate the *nadhr* intending to exclude (heirs)].

The *Ḥawliyyāt* describes the *waqf* and *nadhr* as somewhat similar. Anon., *Ḥawliyāt yamaniyya*, 527.

The Yemeni law of *nadhr* is short and falls under the section of dispositions, under the Personal Status Law. Wizārat al-Shuʾūn al-Qānūniyya, *Qānūn al-aḥwāl*, 32–33. Article 212 states that a *nadhr* is restricted to one-third of one's property.

significantly higher than the effort of the recitation, he also in effect becomes a semi-beneficiary, and the *waqf* has an exclusionary potential.[172] This is also a reason one of the *ikhtiyārāt* of Imam Yaḥyā explicitly targets such a *waqf*. On the handwritten list of *ikhtiyārāt*, number 20 states: "*Waqf al-qirāʾa* for an heir is valid, not for consolation of the souls (*lā li-l-taysīr*)."[173] Interestingly, this type of *waqf* is not made invalid, the decree only specifies the correct religious form of recitation. However, we know that later, restrictions were added to this type of *waqf* limiting the "salary" to be proportionate with the actual effort involved.[174] Examples of such *waqf*s are elaborated by both Mundy and Messick.[175] Perhaps this type of *waqf* became more popular when the regular family *waqf* was increasingly restricted under Imam Yaḥyā.

12.6 *Summary of the Zaydī Trajectory*

Attempts to restrict some of the most liberal uses of *waqf*s can be seen when practices develop because "people on the ground" want to use the *sharīʿa* as a tool for their own agendas. The knowledge of *waqf* is highly specialized on the *fiqh* level; a comprehension of it requires years of education. This does not prevent "commoners" from using the institution for their purposes. On the *fiqh* level we can easily see that the knowledge needed to engage in this debate is situated in specific traditions, practices, in books, and texts. At the level of codification, which is not easily separated from that of the *fiqh*, if in fact it can be separated, we see that actors in academic *fiqh* (*fuqahāʾ*, *ʿulamāʾ*) seek to help the rulers to legitimize whatever rule they choose and that the rulers must support their laws with *fiqh* arguments. If we look at the historical trajectory, we can see that Sunnī *ḥadīth*s were increasingly used after the classical Zaydī period and with the onset of the Qāsimī dynasty. Imam Yaḥyā's decrees and restrictions on family *waqf* were not new in the history of codification, but many of the arguments were recycled from those of the commentary on the decrees of al-Mutawakkil Ismāʿīl. Those wishing to restrict the family *waqf* tend to use *ḥadīth*s to do this, but mainly after the classical Zaydī period. Those in favour of allowing an exclusionary family *waqf* refer primarily to the views and actions of previous imams.

---

172 See the case in Mijallī, *al-Awqāf fī l-Yaman*, 37–38.

173 "Waqf al-qirāʾa li-l-wārith bi-mā taḥṣīl min al-ghilla fa-ṣaḥīḥ, lā bi-mā taysīr." For the wording, see al-ʿAnsī, *al-Tāj al-mudhhab*, 288 n1.

174 See the court case and judgement from 1944 referred to by Mijallī, *al-Awqāf fī l-Yaman*, 37–38.

175 See Mundy, *Domestic Government*, 155, 158, 160, 231 n52, 232 n61. Messick, "Textual Properties." See also Hovden, "Flowers in *Fiqh*," appendix 6.

As we see from the debate, many of the arguments and clusters of arguments are reused over time. Following is a short summary of the history of codification in the matter of the exclusion of heirs from *waqfs*:

1. Around 900 CE, FOR the exclusion of heirs: al-Hādī introduced Zaydism and allowed the tribes to make *waqfs* for the male descent line only, however this was only allowable for one-third of the property. The remaining two-thirds, even if *waqf*, must follow the division of the inheritance rules.
2. Around 1200, AGAINST: al-Manṣūr disagreed with al-Hādī and said that the exclusion of *awlād al-banāt* is reason enough to say that there is no good intention and therefore he issued a *fatwā* that such a *waqfs* are invalid, at least formation of new ones. Old ones are allowed to remain.
3. Around 1410 and 1450 until today, FOR: Ibn al-Murtaḍā and Ibn Miftāḥ wrote the much used *Sharḥ al-azhār* and the community of Zaydī scholars later added validation signs over those views they agreed upon in the *fiqh*. Family *waqfs* follow the Hādawī *waqf* model. Good intentions are not easily measurable and only God can know if the founder is pious; thus, excluding heirs may be disliked and even reprehensible, but it is not contractually invalid.
4. Around 1475 FOR: Imam ʿIzz al-Dīn confirmed that this is the practice on the ground, and he accepted it even though he disliked it.
5. Around 1645, AGAINST: The powerful Imam al-Mutawakkil Ismāʿīl completely rejected any transaction that left some of the heirs with less inheritance, hereunder *waqf*. He based his views on several Sunnī *ḥadīths* in a supportive argument (*Sharḥ al-masāʾil al-murtaḍāt*). The decree was addressed to the judges of Yemen.
6. In 1774, FOR: al-Mahdī l-ʿAbbās took the position of Imam ʿIzz al-Dīn and the Hādawī-Zaydī *madhhab* in a decree form addressed to the judges of Yemen.
7. Around 1795, AGAINST: al-Shawkānī became chief *qāḍī* and remained so for forty years. He was critical of the exclusionary form of family *waqf* and stated that the intergenerational transfer of wealth should follow inheritance rules. He polemically attacked Zaydī authority and used Sunnī *ḥadīths*, but changes in court practice were not yet documented.
8. Around 1915 FOR: The *Sharḥ al-azhār* was printed and the burden of evidence was still on those who had been excluded from the *waqf*. Was it up to the local judges to interpret the details of wording? Imam Yaḥyā took over the judiciary from the Ottomans in 1911 and aimed to establish a court system for the country.

9. From 1920 to 1930, AGAINST: Imam Yaḥyā gradually issued his decrees: There is no good intention in excluding heirs or females. [There should be] no *waqf* to heirs, contrary to the Zaydī *madhhab*. A commoner (*ʿāmmī*) cannot make a *waqf* without the restriction of the *waṣīya* "because they do not know what they do." Recitation *waqfs* for heirs were still valid and many old family *waqfs* continued.
10. From 1940 to the 1950s: Attempts at Zaydī codification in the *al-Tāj al-mudhhab* and the *Taysīr al-marām* both take the stand of the *Sharḥ al-azhār* and allow the exclusion [of *awlād al-banāt*]. *Al-Tāj al-mudhhab* does, however, quote the views of Imam Yaḥyā in the footnotes.
11. Around 1950: Imam Aḥmad follows his father and limits the formation of new family *waqfs*, especially exclusionary ones, but old family *waqfs* are allowed to exist.
12. In the 1970s. New republican *waqf* laws allow for *waqfs* to heirs only if the *waqf* is pious and charitable. Old family *waqfs* remain in certain cases. In effect, these laws are very much a continuation of the laws formulated by Imam Yaḥyā. The restriction of one-third is extended to include charitable *waqfs*.

These views reflect only the level of codification, and regional variations and actual court practice could not be looked into here. As we can see from the summary, there is a tendency for the exclusionary form of family *waqf* to become more restricted over time, especially over the last hundred years. This could be related to a general "Sunnification" of Zaydism, at least state-sponsored Zaydism centred around Sanaa.

13 Exclusion of the *Awlād al-Banāt* in Other Law Schools

It is not my intention to make a systematic comparison with other law schools and legal orders, but a few remarks should be noted, since debates in the wider Islamicate world might have affected the Zaydī debate.

The important Palestinian Ḥanafī *muftī* Khayr al-Dīn al-Ramlī (d. 1671) discussed a question about the term "children and children's children" in the wording of a family *waqf*: Did it include the females? His answer was that Abū Ḥanīfa[176] said no, but that many later scholars said that the most correct view was that females were included. Al-Ramlī then stated that this specific question was famous and well-known, one in which the jurists were divided among themselves and that this question belonged to the questions of dispute

176 Abū Ḥanīfa's view is also mentioned in Ibn Miftāḥ, *Sharḥ al-azhār*.

(*ikhtilāf*) and *ijtihād* and therefore every judge must make his own decision in the matter; after that no one can oppose his verdict in this.[177]

Muḥammad Abū Zahra (d. 1974), a well-known Egyptian scholar, wrote *Muḥāḍarāt fī l-waqf* on the topic of comparative *waqf fiqh*; in it he addresses the status of the *awlād al-banāt*. He states that there is disagreement among the scholars on this issue, but that the majority of Ḥanafīs allowed for the exclusion of the *awlād al-banāt*. Further, he mentions that additional wording can be added in the establishment of a *waqf*, for example, "whomever belongs to the name of the family or the descent line" (*man yantasibu ilayhi*) as a possible exclusionary phrase, despite the fact that the term "children" originally includes the *awlād al-banāt*. He also refers to the argument that the meaning of any of these words is in any case dependent on local custom (*tadillu ʿurfan*).[178]

Wahba Muṣṭafā l-Zuḥaylī is a well-known Syrian *fiqh* scholar. In his authoritative, modern comparative *fiqh* work, *al-Fiqh al-Islāmī wa-adillatuhu*, he is very brief in his treatment of the topic. According to him there is disagreement over the term *awlād* (children), but not the terms *dhurriyya, nasl*, and *ʿaqab*, which are all, by consensus, terms that exclude the *awlād al-banāt*.[179] (This position is much in line with the footnotes of the *Sharḥ al-azhār*.) Although al-Zuḥaylī's project is modern, comparative *fiqh*, its concise character implies fewer details. The discussions that took place within the Ḥanafī and Shāfiʿī schools do not appear in his treatment of this specific rule.[180] If we look a bit deeper into the Ḥanafī debates, the Syrian Ḥanafī Ibn ʿĀbidīn (d. 1836) is a good starting point. In his commentary *Radd al-mukhtār* on the *Durr al-mukhtār* he is also very clear about the disagreement in the *fiqh* and states that both views (and many others in between) are found among Ḥanafī authorities:

> Section regarding the inclusion of the *awlād al-banāt*.
>
> ... Note that it is mentioned that the preferred view in the law school (*ẓāhir al-riwāya*), which is also stated in *fatwās* (*al-muftā bihi*), is that the *awlād al-banāt* are not included.... However, al-Khaṣṣāf stated that they are included ... al-Rāzī stated that if the founder used the word "male

177 Haim Gerber, "Rigidity versus Openness in Late Classical Islamic Law: The Case of the Seventeenth-Century Palestinian Muftī Khayr al-Dīn al-Ramlī," *Islamic Law and Society* 5, no. 2 (1998), 184–185.

178 Abū Zahra, *Muḥāḍarāt fī l-waqf*, 277.

179 "Yashmulu bi-l-ittifāq awlād al-dhukūr dūna awlād al-ināth, ayy, awlād al-banāt."

180 Wahba al-Zuḥaylī, *al-Fiqh al-Islamī wa-adillatuhu* (Damascus: Dār al-Fikr, 1997), 7663.

> child" (*walad*) in singular, instead of the plural (*awlād*), the wording is exclusionary ...[181]

He goes on to cite a long list of Ḥanafī authorities, *fiqh* works, and *fatwā* collections (including that of the above-mentioned Palestinian *muftī* Khayr al-Dīn al-Ramlī), and he cites views both for and against, including all the complicated positions in between. The crux of the arguments in favour of exclusion are similar to those used in the Zaydī debate, namely that a term has a certain usage, even "custom" (*ʿurf*) and therefore carries the meaning of exclusion, as intended by the founder of the *waqf.* This intention then is implicitly, on an aggregate level, admitted as a source of validity for the possibility of exclusion.

In Shāfiʿī *fiqh* as exemplified by al-Nawawī (d. 676/1277), the matter is crystal clear in the *matn* of the *Minhāj al-ṭālibīn*, the famous abridged textbook of Shāfiʿī legal theory:

> ... And, the *awlād al-banāt* are included in the *waqf* for the *dhurriyya*, the *nasl*, and the *ʿaqab*, and the children of the children, except if the founder states "whoever descends [in patrilineage] from me (*illā an yaqūla ʿalā man yantasibu ilayya minhum*) ...

Thus the term *nasab* and the verb *yantasibu* can be added to the wording of the establishment to achieve an exclusion of the *awlād al-banāt*. Al-Shirbīnī (d. 977/1570) adds in his *sharḥ* of al-Nawawī's *Minhāj* that this applies only to a *waqf* made by a man.[182] The comments in the *Tuḥfat al-muḥtāj* by Ibn Ḥajar (d. 974/1567) are very similar.[183] In sum, exclusion is considered valid.

As for the issue of "no testament to an heir" al-Zuḥaylī notes that the Egyptian testament law (*Qānūn al-waṣīya al-Maṣrī*) from 1946 allows for a testament in favour of an heir for one-third of the estate, contrary to most Sunnī *fiqh*, thus it actually takes a Shīʿī stand. As for the Syrian law, it has retained the Sunnī restriction, but a testament in favour of heirs is allowed if the all the heirs accept it.[184] As for practices in Mālikī *waqf,* Layish remarks that the exclusion of

181 Muḥammad Amīn Ibn ʿĀbidīn, *Radd al-mukhtār ʿalā l-Durr al-mukhtār* (Cairo: Sharikat Maktabat wa-Maktabat Muṣṭafā l-Bābā l-Ḥalabī wa-Awlādihi bi-Maṣr, 1966), 463–465.

182 al-Shirbīnī, *Mughnī l-muḥtāj*, 2:511.

183 al-Haytamī Shihāb al-Dīn Aḥmad Ibn Hajar, *Tuḥfat al-muḥtāj bi-sharḥ al-minhāj* (online from Islamweb.net). The section falls in the same place in the *matn* as it does in the *Mughnī l-muḥtāj.*

184 al-Zuḥaylī, *al-Fiqh al-Islamī*, 7478.

heirs in Mālikī *waqfs* was invalid according to leading jurists, while in practice it was usually allowed.[185]

As for the *waṣīya* in modern Yemeni law, this is regulated in the personal status law (*Qānūn al-aḥwāl al-shakhṣiyya*), where the law states that a *waṣīya* to an heir is invalid, as it also is for the heir of the heir.[186]

13.1 *Critique of the Liberal Family* Waqf *Outside the Zaydī Context*

David Powers argues that the contradiction between the *waṣīya*, the *waqf*, and the inheritance rules was a controversial issue from the very beginning of Islamic law. According to Powers, this is exemplified by the *ḥadīth*: no endowment in circumvention of God's shares (*lā ḥabs ʿan farāʾiḍ Allāh*).[187] Another very similar *ḥadīth* is quoted by al-Shawkānī in his *Sayl al-jarrār*: "No *waqf* after the revelation of the inheritance rules" or "… after the revelation of Sūrat al-Nisāʾ" (*lā ḥabs baʿda nuzūl sūrat al-nisāʾ*). This *ḥadīth* is an example of an argument against the *waqf*, but as al-Shawkānī explains, these are only odd examples.[188] *Waqf* in general is valid, without doubt, in all the major law schools. The general view among historians is that the institution of *waqf* as such was considered valid and was indeed frequently used throughout history, until restrictions were imposed in colonial and post-colonial times. The critique against the institution of *waqf* has arisen in modern times mainly in the colonial context, where the British especially focused on the balance between the *waqf* and the inheritance rules, and favoured the latter.

13.2 *Colonial Restrictions on Family* Waqf

There are two "problems" related to *waqfs* that have drawn the attention of modern jurists. The first is the negative effect of removing large amounts of assets from the local economy, since *waqfs* "cannot" be bought and sold. The

185 Aharon Layish, "The Mālikī Family 'Waqf' according to Wills and 'Waqfiyyāt,'" *Bulletin of the School of Oriental and African Studies* 46, no. 1 (1983), 8. This article is a useful basis for a comparison between Mālikī *waqf* and other law schools. See also Powers, "The Maliki Family Endowment."

186 Wizārat al-Shu'ūn al-Qānūniyya, *Qānūn al-aḥwāl*, article 235.

187 Powers, "Orientalism, Colonialism and Legal History: The Attack on Muslim Family Endowments in Algeria and India," *Comparative Studies in Society and History* 31, no. 3 (1989), 564.

188 al-Shawkānī, *al-Sayl al-jarrār*, 3:49. This *ḥadīth* is often mentioned in *fiqh* works, at the beginning of chapters of *waqf*, and is often used as one of the few arguments against the legality of *waqf*. The other well-known "argument" against *waqf*, also widely quoted, was made by Abū Ḥanīfa. For an example see al-Shawkānī, *al-Sayl al-jarrār*, 3:48. Otherwise none of the early jurists and companions opposed the institution of *waqf* as a whole. As for restrictions, this is another matter of course.

second problem is related only to family *waqfs* and focuses on the circumvention of the inheritance rules. The first problem has often been called the "dead man's hand" or "mortmain" and is of course also applicable to charitable or public *waqfs*, not only to family *waqfs*. This problem was mainly put forward by French orientalist scholars, colonial administrators, and their allies when French settlers and investors had problems obtaining full ownership rights over the land they wanted to acquire in their protectorates in the Middle East and North Africa. It was also seen as a problem for Muḥammad ʿAlī's taxation and agrarian reforms.[189]

The British, in contrast, did not raise the problem of the "dead man's hand" to the same degree, rather the second problem was more prominent for them and very controversial as it arose when judges in British colonial India began to enforce Islamic inheritance law in a systematic way. Muslims had their own family law under British colonial law, but it was sanctioned by British judges at a high level. The family *waqfs* created great problems of inconsistency as in practice they contradicted the inheritance rules. The focus was on the intention of the *waqfs*; if it was meant for the founder and his family it was conceived of as a way to circumvent the inheritance rules, and it was rendered invalid. In the latter half of the nineteenth century, British courts invalidated numerous family *waqfs* as the disinherited actors brought these *waqfs* to the courts. After protests from leading Muslim elites and Muslim scholars, the abolishment of the family *waqfs* made by the Privy Council in 1894 were withdrawn by an act in 1911 called the "Mussulman Wakf Validating Act."[190]

The debate investigated in this chapter has been remarkably free from references to similar debates in other law schools or societies and it can safely be termed "Zaydī" and even "Yemeni,"[191] although local legal debates and knowledge have of course always been a part of, and influenced by, the wider Islamic tradition of learning. It is possible that Imam Yaḥyā was inspired by the British colonial *waqf* law from India, East Africa, and Aden, and that Imam Yaḥyā's views were affected by the British solution. Actors in the debate in the period before Imam Yaḥyā clearly took their positions in the unique pre-colonial setting of Yemen.

While Powers claims that restrictions or even the abolishment of family *waqfs* by law is something that is only found in the colonial context, I have

189 Powers, "Orientalism, Colonialism and Legal History," 538.

190 Ibid., 554–563. See also Gregory C. Kozlowski, *Muslim Endowments and Society in British India* (Cambridge and New York: Cambridge University Press, 1985).

191 Zaydī *fiqh* is situated amidst, and constantly refers to, sources of validity in other law schools. As seen in this chapter, in the later period Sunnī *ḥadīths* are invoked a great deal. The debate on codification also affected those Shāfiʿī areas under Zaydī law.

shown in this chapter that this is not correct for Zaydī Yemen. Powers is correct in his argument that *waqfs* as an institution as such and then with an emphasis on the charitable aspect, did indeed enjoy an almost absolute consensus. The same applies to the general validity of family *waqfs*.[192] Some jurists did see the difference between the charitable *waqf* and the family *waqf*, even if the two concepts were not always clearly separated.[193] Powers states that despite some colonial administrators and judges who claimed that *waqfs* in general and family *waqfs* specifically were illegal, it is obvious that *waqfs* were considered valid by Muslim jurists: "To argue otherwise, as both British judges and French orientalists did, betrays either a profound misunderstanding of the historical development of Islamic law, or a willingness to manipulate the historical record for political reasons—or both."[194] Anderson states that there is no branch of Islamic law where "judicial infusion of alien ideas," "misinterpretation," "basic ignorance," and "rigidity of mind" by judges in British courts have frustrated Muslim people more than under British colonial jurisdiction.[195] Thus Powers and Anderson portray this as a matter in which Muslims were subjected to something completely new under colonial law when family *waqfs* were restricted. In this chapter however, we can see that the critique of, and restrictions on family *waqfs* also took place in non-colonial, Muslim settings.

•••

In this chapter we have seen a considerable interrelationship between the inheritance rules, the *waṣīya*, and the *waqf*. Over time, we see that the codification of the problem, in decrees and *fatwās*, alternated several times between those "for" and "against" the exclusion of the *awlād al-banāt*. The Hādawī-Zaydī debate sustained a model of an intergenerational transfer in which an individual could decide over one-third, as in the testament, this "free third" made its way into the Hādawī *waqf* model. In this "free third," pious intention (*qurba*) was not a condition, at least it did not restrict one from favouring some heirs over others. With the presence of this "free third" in the *fiqh* debates, the

192 Powers, "Orientalism, Colonialism and Legal History," 564.

193 Ibid., 564–565 n125. In his argument Powers even cites al-Shawkānī, *Nayl al-awṭār*, to prove the consensus of the legality of *waqf* in general. In the *Nayl al-awṭār*, which was one of al-Shawkānī's early works, al-Shawkānī does adhere to the overall consensus regarding the legality of *waqf in general*, however, in his mature phase al-Shawkānī took a negative position towards the concept of the family *waqf*, as shown in this chapter, though in contrast to Powers' use of him as an example.

194 Ibid., 564–565.

195 J. N. D. Anderson, "Waqfs in East Africa," *Journal of African Law* 3, no. 3 (1959), 152.

lines between the two otherwise different concepts of the *waqf* and the *waṣīya* became blurred. *Fiqh*, codification, legal cases, and local everyday knowledge mutually influence the formulation and counter-formulation of the arguments over validity.

This chapter has followed a chronologic trajectory of a set of rules centring on how to transfer property, in most cases land, from one generation to the next. Because of the local social and cultural context there is a "need" for a model of intergenerational transfer of wealth that is more flexible than the inheritance rules. And as we can see, both from the decrees, and from what we can infer from the legal discussions, family *waqfs* for the male descent line have been fairly well accepted, although as most admit, they require moral caution, invite criticism, and increasingly also became restricted legally through codification.

If we look away from the more theoretical, moral criticism we may ask who protested against the exclusionary family *waqfs* in daily life? Who took these *waqfs* to the judge or the court in order to challenge them? The exogamously married women's children, the *awlād al-banāt*, grew up in another family and if this family was of equal status, they would have their own *waqfs* from their father's side. By using the exclusionary family *waqf*, some of the lateral movement of land between families was replaced with a more vertical movement of wealth within the patrilineal group. Theoretically, seen from a distance, the system was fair if practiced equally by all landowning families. This could be part of the reason for the overall acceptance. What must also be noted here, and which has not been treated in this chapter in detail, is that there are different models for sharing a family *waqf* among the generations and among males and females. The most common is to share it by "heads" (*ʿalā l-ruʾūs*). This means that the females will get a full share equal to that of a male. Such a *waqf* does not discriminate against "females" in general; on the contrary, the females would then get more per person in *waqf* division than in inheritance division. Yet, what informants recount is that many conflicts arose over these issues and since many of the affluent families intermarry, the criss-crossing claims of inheritance and *waqf* shares can be very complex when accumulated over generations.

One other important distinction is to see the exclusionary form of family *waqf* in a class perspective. Among the poor and in the tribal areas, women have a weaker position in terms of their right of inheritance from their husbands or parents. Martha Mundy made one of the best ethnographic studies on this topic from the valley of Wādī Ḍahr near Sanaa.[196] In her material, her informants show how *waqfs* were actively used and contested. Yet she also states,

196 Mundy, *Domestic Government*; Mundy, "The Family, Inheritance and Islam: A Re-Examination of the Sociology of Farāʾiḍ Law," in *Islamic Law: Social and Historical*

that "farmers do not tie up their property in *waqf*."[197] It takes a certain amount of wealth and legal knowledge to use a *waqf* as a wealth management strategy. She also argues that on a more general level, in practice, women's rights to inheritance vary greatly from family to family and in the lower strata and in rural and tribal areas, women often do not receive their full share.[198] This leads us to look at the more affluent families. Clearly many of the large family *waqfs* still in existence are found among these "old rich" *sayyid* and *qāḍī* houses. For many, family *waqfs* were the economic glue that kept these families together and since the *waqfs* were usually controlled by the older, leading member of the family, it was also used as an instrument of power by the leading part of the family, over the more marginal members.[199] The status of women in these families, however, is fundamentally different from that of "tribal women" or women from poorer strata. The women from wealthier families were in general educated and could read and write. Through their close male relatives, they would have access to legal knowledge, that is, both the letter of the law and knowledge of how the court system functioned practically; thus this class of women knew their rights. We should also be careful about seeing this as a women's struggle against patriarchy. The opposition by men against the powerful core of their own extended family, who often controlled the *waqf*, is just as important. As for the category of *awlād al-banāt* specifically, these children included, of course, both males and females. From the perspective of the peripheral members of the extended family it must have been frustrating to be unable to sell one's part in the family *waqf*, that is, one might want to sell his share in the asset(s), instead of receiving a very limited yearly share. Once the family *waqf* system started to change under Imam Yaḥyā's decrees, these more peripheral members of the large families, or "houses," could take such *waqfs*

Contexts, ed. Aziz al-Azmah (New York and London: Routledge, 1988); Mundy, "Women's Inheritance of Land in Highland Yemen," *Arabian Studies* 5 (1979): 161–187.

197 Mundy, *Domestic Government*, 149.

198 This is also mentioned by Dresch. A standard scholarly and urban accusation of the tribal culture and "its un-Islamic ways of life" is that they deny women their inheritance. As for the sociological or ethnographic fact of this statement more research is needed and the answer will most probably be highly dependent on local context. Dresch states that the claim to inheritance from one's husband was often dropped (*isqāṭ*) and that this was even recorded in the marriage contract. Dresch, *Tribes, Government, and History in Yemen*, 186–187, 196 n35. Dresch also mentions that the typical landowning *sayyid* and *shaykh* families own significant amounts of land as family *waqf*. Dresch suggests that the term "collective holding" is just as descriptive as the term family *waqf*. *Tribes, Government, and History in Yemen*, 162, 211.

199 Vom Bruck also states that exclusion of the *awlād al-banāt* is found in such *waqfs*, according to her informants. Vom Bruck, *Islam, Memory, and Mortality*, 73–75.

to court and have them dissolved on the grounds that they were exclusionary. This way the assets could be sold, and for example, agricultural land in the vicinity of growing cities could reach high prices.

We can only speculate on what caused this change in policy and the ideas and motives behind it. What is certain is that once the new decrees went into effect, a domino effect started. The strategies of transferring wealth also differed from family to family; some families retained their family *waqf*s, others completely privatized them. We must not forget that the twentieth century saw fundamental changes, which make it difficult to compare the social context of today with that of earlier history. The mere growth in population and economy led to new forms of investment strategies. For instance, a family *waqf* that was not actively managed and economically reformed and re-invested, would be worth relatively less today than if it had been constantly reinvested in revenue producing assets. Further, a stable society with few fluctuations in land prices is very different from the situation in urban areas after the revolution. Owning land and "owning" a *waqf* share are not very different concepts as long as it concerns the yearly harvest and the right to a share of the income from the harvest. However, once the land itself becomes valuable as an asset, which can be sold, for example, for building plots for expanding cities, there arises a strong incentive to dissolve one's family *waqf*, especially, from the perspective of the marginal members of the family in need of cash. A few bags of grain a year cannot compare to the cash that could be obtained by selling the (now) urban land.

The houses and families that have retained their *waqf*s seem to be those that had a strong internal coherence. Messick suggests that changes in family ideology were important; more focus on the individual and the smaller nuclear family made the family *waqf* unnecessary and unwanted.[200] From this perspective we can imagine that once the validity of an exclusionary family *waqf* was disputed in a general cultural perspective, this also affected the laws. Once the laws and legal practices changed, the family *waqf* could not "return."

The presence of a national court system that could more or less systematically enforce its decisions is also central to this explanation. In periods of political chaos, the extended family is more important to individuals, and the court system is unlikely to be able to enforce laws contrary to the views of local shaykhs and elites, especially when the exclusionary family *waqf* is considered "valid" according to the *madhhab* as a whole, although morally doubtful. The level of codification that this chapter has focused on is ultimately dependent

200 Messick goes even farther and suggests that the emerging capitalist, individualistic ideologies made people want smaller families. Messick, "Transactions in Ibb," 437. See also the article "Textual Properties."

not only on a political force choosing and formulating the laws, but also on their enforcement. In periods during which this field of legal knowledge was not codified into coherent decrees that were enforced, legal subjects had to rely on local judges who serve their communities as notaries and who could consult directly the *fiqh* discourse making their own codification, circumventing the level of state codification.

When asking informants about the restrictions on the family *waqf* and how they came about under Imam Yaḥyā, few informants look back and give "sociological" explanations. Most claim that Imam Yaḥyā did so because of *sharʿī* reasons. The awareness that *waqf* was used as a tool to circumvent the inheritance rules is not found so much among the young. Among the older generation, and also in the countryside among landowning families, the concept of family *waqf* is a very well-known tool used in order to "not give inheritance to the women." Thus even without resorting to complicated *fiqh* arguments, "normal" landowning informants see the restrictions as an attempt to make a clearer and more just law with fewer legal ruses. The idea that a person is free to dispose of only one-third of one's wealth is widespread. Related to this is the concept of the *bikr* (the eldest son), who often has a closer relation to the family economy or politics than his younger brothers. It is often he who would wait to inherit a recitation *waqf*, or the position as the *waṣīy* (*mutawallī*) of a family *waqf* or a family controlled public *waqf* as treated in chapter 7. Legal conflicts between siblings are common, but many state that it is a great shame to summon one's father or brothers to court (*yusharriʿ*). It is also often mentioned that it can be extremely expensive and the judge may be corrupt.

A young *sayyid* from Sanaa told me that their family had retained their family *waqf*, and every year he received two large bags of coffee from the mountains of Ānis. They were more symbolic than economically important he said. Their relatives who were left in Ānis were so poor that they needed their own land and the same was the case of those sharecroppers who tilled the land with them. He had no wish to change anything about that.

One young informant in Sanaa, whose rather important and wealthy family came from al-ʿUdayn in Ibb, told me that they still had large amounts of land as family *waqf*. The *waqf* had been reformed to include all females,[201] and also consisted of a large, new community house in their village, with private flats for visitors from Sanaa. There were also some charitable works in their home village funded by the same *waqf*.

201 The issue of the *awlād al-banāt* was not clear, but his remark clearly meant "this *waqf* is not exclusionary anymore, and now follows the division of the inheritance law." Such a provision would perhaps make it easier to defend the *waqf* against court claims today.

Far more concrete cases and examples are needed to build a history or ethnography of practice of this topic, something that could not be followed further here. As discussed at the end of chapter 3, estimates of the percentage of *waqf* range from 5 per cent to 25 per cent to a much higher percentage in urban areas. The figures are uncertain and given the fear of government intervention, under-reporting is to be expected. The figure varies from area to area and the percentage of how much of this total is family *waqf* as opposed to charitable *waqf* is often not defined in such estimates. Even if defined, it is not well understood by informants for reasons clarified in this chapter. Asking questions about *waqf* when family *waqfs* are actually often termed *waṣāyā* will of course skew the result. It is fair to believe that the figure is generally fairly low today. Other forms of communal family-owned land or real estate ownership could be very similar to that of a family *waqf*. More research is needed about new forms of family estate ownership and joint family wealth management.

CHAPTER 6

The Tenant's Strong Hand

This chapter focuses on the relationship between two of the central actors in the institution of *waqf*, the administrator (*mutawallī*) and the tenant (*mustaʾjir, sharīk*). In this chapter I concentrate on one specific rule: the rule of the "three year maximum lease period." First and most importantly, I follow the historical trajectory of this rule chronologically, and examine how it was established in *fiqh*, what its validity is based on, and how it has been contested over time. Second, I follow this rule into other fields of knowledge: other fields of *fiqh* in the wider Islamic tradition, and into the field of Yemeni codification and applied law. Where I focused on the knowledge field of codification in the previous chapter, in this chapter I place a strong emphasis on the connection between *fiqh*, codification, the administrator's knowledge, and everyday *waqf* knowledge.

Waqf law is transactional law in which an object or a set of rights is transferred from one person to another.[1] The recipient is, at least in the ideal *waqf* model, the beneficiary (*al-maṣrif, al-mawqūf ʿalayhi*). If something is given to a person as a *waqf*, then this person cannot "own" the asset of the *waqf* as God is the legal owner of *waqf*; however, the person does possess the right to use the *waqf* and to have access to its benefit. The step of setting up a *waqf* is theoretically done only once, it is never repeated, and the effect is thereafter permanent and perpetual. However, the beneficiary may sell the right of use for a specific period if, for example, he does not want to till the land himself; through the *mutawallī* he can rent out the asset—this transaction is the lease.[2] The *waqf* asset is rented out, and the beneficiary can benefit from the rental income of the asset. Very often it is not the direct use of the asset that is useful for the beneficiary, but rather income in the form of harvest or money from rent/lease.

This second stage transaction involved in a *waqf* is not perpetual but temporary; it can be done several times and can involve different tenants. The lease contract can be terminated and contracted again with someone else. The so-called "three-year maximum lease period" breaks the ongoing, continuous rent into separate, successive three-year periods and prohibits leases longer than

1 To a natural or legal person. For a discussion of "legal personality" in *sharīʿa* generally and *waqf* specifically, see Behrens-Abouseif, "The *Waqf*."

2 In Zaydī *fiqh* a lease is the sale of the usufruct for a defined period.

 DOI:10.1163/9789004377844_007

three years, after which a new contract between the *waqf* (*mutawallī*) and the tenant must be made. If the lease contract were continuous, i.e., if the tenant had the right to rent the asset in perpetuity, the lease contract could become something close to a sale, which is invalid for a *waqf* according to the fundamental doctrine of *waqfs*. Before we proceed, it is necessary to step back and define what it means to "own" something.

1 Property and Lease Law

Property law or contractual or transactional law is an important part of Islamic law. A simple definition of property centres on the notion of ownership: "to own" a thing is, first and foremost, the right to use that thing, to have control over it, and to be able to give it away for a compensation (or not) if one so desires. Property is defined in diverse ways in western legal systems and in Islamic law, where the concept of property is somewhat vague. Delcambre writes about *milk*:

> D̲j̲urd̲j̲ānī defines the term *milk* thus: "It is a legal relationship (*ittiṣāl sharʿī*) between a person (*insān*) and a thing (*s̲h̲ayʾ*) which allows that person to dispose of it to the exclusion of everyone else." Yet for the classical Muslim jurists, the right of ownership became confused with the thing which is its object. For them, ownership is not a right (*ḥaḳḳ*) but a piece of property (*māl*) which has become ownership.[3]

In this book, I use a practical anthropological perspective that is not far from that of Jurjānī quoted above, thus I am not guided by the doctrinal meaning of *milk*, but focus instead on the right of access and use of the thing. In looking at leases we need to expand the definition to also include other actors, not only the relationship between the owner and the thing. Ownership in Islamic law can be transferred to other persons by means of inheritance, gift, lease (*ijāra*), sale (*bayʿ*) or *waqf*. A similarly practical definition of a lease is the sale of the right to use (usufruct), or access, for a specific period.

In a broader perspective, the right must somehow be recognized in a wider social and cultural system. There must be a more or less agreed upon system of rules that are defined and known to the main actors. When conflicts do arise, there must also be a more or less defined consensus on how to solve these

3 A. M. Delcambre, "Milk," *Encyclopaedia of Islam*, second edition, ed. P. J. Bearman, Th. Biancuis, C. E. Bosworth, E. van Donzel, and W. P. Heinrichs (Leiden: Brill, 1960–2004), 7:60.

conflicts in a manner that the majority respect and in a manner that can be enforced in the local community. Predictability and stability is important. Laws of ownership go to the very core of social and cultural life as also discussed in the introduction to chapter 5.

Messick quotes al-Shawkānī who uses the term *ʿismat al-amwāl* to mean something like "inviolability of property."[4] We could even translate the expression as "the sanctity of property." In *fiqh* there is a distinction between transactional law (*muʿāmalāt*) and religious obligations (*ʿibādāt*). For the *faqīh*, God is the origin of property law even if the property law regulates fairly mundane matters. Property, even if owned by a private individual, is religiously sanctioned, as seen from the perspective of *fiqh*. Arguably, we could also say that part of the importance of religion is its role in giving legitimacy and validity to the order of property and social power in society. To this day ownership documents start with the *basmala*: "in the name of God." Islam is conjured and invoked through the use and application of property law.

There are many terms for "property" and "rights" in *fiqh*, but by far the most significant are the terms *milk* or *māl*, both meaning ownership and the thing owned, and *manfaʿa* (usufruct). When referring to a "right" in a more abstract sense, the term *ḥaqq* is also fundamental. As mentioned in the basic *waqf* model in chapter 2, *manfaʿa* usually follows the asset (*al-raqaba*) and belongs to the owner (*al-mālik*), but in the very act of establishing a *waqf*, the *milk* and *manfaʿa* are split into two separate concepts, resulting in important theoretical and doctrinal implications in legal theory (*fiqh*).

As mentioned at the beginning of chapter 2, only some *waqf*s are types of "direct use *waqf*s," that is, the object made into the *waqf* is directly used by the beneficiaries; for example, a single book given as a *waqf*. Many *waqf* assets are intended to be rented out, at times even in favour of other, secondary *waqf*s. These primary *waqf*s are typically agricultural fields that are rented out to local farmers in order to produce income for a mosque or a cistern (secondary *waqf*s). In the cities, houses for dwelling and shops in the market areas are also typical *waqf* income-producing assets that are rented out. In such *waqf*s, or clusters of *waqf*s, the act of leasing is an important part of the management of the *waqf*. Leasing is the activity that the *mutawallī* undertakes that produces income and thereby secures the viability of the *waqf* and allows for its operation.

---

4 Brinkley Messick, "Property and the Private in a Sharia System," *Social Research* 70, no. 3 (2003): 711–734.

1.1 *Leases in* Waqf

One of the most significant and inherent problems of *waqf* legal theory and practices concerns issues of leasing, especially related to public *waqfs*. Ideally, the *waqf* should be rented out according to local fair rental rates, or the market price (*ajr al-mithl, ījār al-makān wa-l-zamān*). This doctrinal principle is generally agreed upon in most law schools and by most scholars, as we see in this chapter. Historical and contemporary practices, however, are far from this ideal, for several reasons. As I elaborate further below, often the rent is well below local market rents. This tension is reflected in the *fiqh* literature, which balances between formulating rules for the ideal *waqf* and at the same time formulating pragmatic but efficient rules for actual *waqf* practices. These diverging rules—the ideal ones and the pragmatic ones—co-exist in an intricate interplay in the *fiqh* texts.

Over time the tenant gains more extensive rights in the *waqf* asset than the ideal theory would allow. Often the tenant invests in the asset from his private funds. For example, a tenant might use his own time and capital to maintain and restore the asset (the agricultural terrace, house or shop) that he rents from the *mutawallī*. He might dig a new well to irrigate the agricultural field or install new shelves in the shop that he rents. If the value of this investment is not distinctly separate from the *waqf* asset, the *waqf* asset and the private asset of the tenant in practice become mixed (as discussed in chapter 7). When a tenant who rents an urban plot (*ʿaraṣa*) of *waqf* land is allowed (by the *mutawallī*) to build a house on that plot, the tenant cannot be expected to take his house and move after a year or two. His right to remain a tenant is complicated by the matter of how to distinguish what is *waqf* from what is the tenant's private property. As we see in this chapter, this right to remain a tenant tends to be inherited, bought and sold, although this is extremely problematic according to the legal theory of *waqf*. The last two *fatwās* in chapter 7 illustrate that these kinds of cases do occur in privately administrated *waqfs* (*waṣāyā*), as they do in the absolutely public *waqfs* (*al-waqf al-khāliṣ, muṭlaq*), where tenants often have rights not anticipated in the basic, ideal *waqf* model.

If one's family has been tenants of the same *waqf* asset (for example, land) for generations, then the right of the family to continue to till the *waqf* land becomes customary. This is possible and the rent of the lease contract remains somehow stable compared to the value of the asset because many leases are undertaken with the understanding that a fraction of the yearly harvest (sharecropping, *mushāraka*) will be part of the payment of the rent.[5] In a stable agricultural society this is an effective legal solution. For example, a certain family

5 For sharecropping in Zaydī law, see Donaldson, *Sharecropping in the Yemen*.

has the right to rent a *waqf* field as long as they pay an obligation of, for example, one-quarter of the harvest to the *waqf* administrator every year. One problem is that such customary leases are not time limited, but open-ended and continuous and thus cannot easily be terminated by the *mutawallī*.

The right to remain a tenant seems to be common in private leases, where this right is balanced against a "termination fee" (*ʿināʾ*), which the landlord would have to pay to the tenant if he terminates the contract.[6] Such a termination fee is also often connected to the investments the tenant has made in the asset. In leases of urban plots, this problem becomes more evident since the rent is often a fixed yearly sum. Inflation causes this sum to become relatively cheaper over time unless the rent is raised. A peculiar, but very common practice in contemporary urban *waqf* leases involves splitting the lease into an immediate and a deferred lease (*muʿajjal* and *muʾajjal*). This equals a one time "entrance fee" and a yearly lease, like the termination fee (*ʿināʾ*) in private leases. Such an "entrance fee" and a promise to remain a tenant gives the lease a sense of permanency, almost like a sale. This is very practical for the *mutawallī*, who then has access to cash in advance of the otherwise yearly leases. In Ḥanafī areas this phenomenon is termed *ḥikr, aḥkār* or *ijāratayn*, "dual lease."[7]

In Zaydī *fiqh* these issues have been debated for centuries; in this chapter I present the historical legal debate over a specific rule related to this issue, the so-called "three-year maximum lease rule," or simply the "three-year rule." The three-year rule can thus be seen as a "corpus" of knowledge, the trajectory of which can be followed through generations of legal experts. Further, I show how this rule is used in other legal fields such as codification and also in legal and administrative practices today. Over time, we see a complex interplay between the ideal doctrines on one hand and the need for a law that addresses the legal problems found in the "real" world, and legal solutions to these problems on the other hand.

The three-year rule is just one rule in the form of a sentence, among other rules in the *waqf* chapter.[8] Other rules and other chapters in the corpus of *fiqh* follow their own historical trajectories. Therefore, we cannot generalize the trajectory of the three-year rule to represent the trajectory of all *waqf* rules, or all rules in *fiqh*, however, the method of focusing on one rule only, and on its trajectory and its use in time and space, provides us with a systematic

6 Messick, "Transactions in Ibb," 153.

7 Gabriel Baer, "Ḥikr," *Encyclopaedia of Islam*, second edition, ed. P. J. Bearman, Th. Biancuis, C. E. Bosworth, E. van Donzel, and W. P. Heinrichs (Leiden: Brill, 1960–2004), 12:368.

8 There are more than eighty such "rules" in the *waqf* chapter of Ibn Miftāḥ, *Sharḥ al-azhār*, depending on how one defines a rule.

methodological perspective that allows us to see, understand, and describe the complex context of *fiqh*, law, and legal knowledge. In the last part of the chapter I focus on other issues and rules related to the problem of leases, those which do not directly relate to the three-year rule, but that are indirectly relevant. The chapter is thus divided into three main parts:

1. The genealogy and trajectory of the three-year rule;
2. The use of the three-year rule in the fields of codification and legal and administrative practices; and
3. Other important issues in *waqf* lease law and practices.

2 The Genealogy and Trajectory of the Three-Year Rule

The basis of the legal problem starts with the norm that a *waqf* should be rented out according to the market price. The reason for this is clear: if it is rented out for less than the market price, the rent will benefit the tenant and he will profit at the expense of the *waqf*. The lease is a contract between two parties, one in which the owner—in *waqf* issues, this means the representative of the owner, the *mutawallī*—sells the right of use for a specific period. In a normal (non-*waqf*) lease, it is not illegal to rent something at rates below market rents. In *waqf* leases, however, the case differs—the *waqf* must be managed as efficiently as possible to maximise its income and thereby respect the will of the founder and the need of the *waqf*. Ultimately, this is an issue of respecting God, who is doctrinally the private owner of the *waqf*.

In order to provide the *mutawallī* with the legal power to demand market rent (*ujrat al-mithl*) from the tenant, classical Zaydī *fiqh* suggests a relatively short lease time, usually three years, because this enables the *mutawallī* to say to the tenant: "the lease contract period has now terminated, you have two choices, accept the new lease contract, or leave the land and I will rent it out to someone who can pay more." Thus, a rule that *waqf*s cannot be leased for longer than a specific period is quite a useful instrument for the *mutawallī* and the *waqf*. However, neither the Qur'ān nor the Sunna states a rule specifically for this purpose. This means that according to the Shāfiʿīs, Zaydīs, and neo-Sunnīs or traditionists,[9] such a rule is necessarily a human construction that legal theorists must work with in the best way possible and so they base this on other types of arguments. How, if at all, such a human construction can be valid as Islamic law is indeed a point of criticism put forward by some jurists, as we see below.

9 Here, I mainly refer to al-Shawkānī.

As mentioned, in Yemen there is a strong custom of sharecropping leases; this is also true for *waqf*s. There are advantages to this for both parties. It creates less administrative work for the owner because he does not have to constantly inspect the work of the tenant and they can build a relationship of trust over time. The issue of asset maintenance is central; if this is delegated to the tenant, he naturally expects a lower rent. If this is normal in local non-*waqf* leases, then the fair rent, or the normal local land rent would be lower than in a lease in which the owner is responsible for maintenance. It seems that in *waqf* leases the job of maintaining the asset is usually assigned to the tenant, but subject to the inspection and approval of the *mutawallī*, who is ultimately responsible.

Instead of hiring external maintenance, the tenant can take care of the asset as it if it were his own agricultural field or shop. In actual, applied law and practice there are several different categories and types of lease and in some forms of lease, the tenant has the right to remain a tenant. This refers to the way people engaged in leases historically and how these leases were decided upon by judges, be they Islamic or customary. "Islamic law" has contradictory views on matters of sharecropping.[10] This is a good example that shows that a great number of diverging principles and rules are presented in *fiqh*, while applied law, by contrast, is fairly simple, applicable, and does not involve a direct extrapolation or deduction from doctrinal *fiqh* debates, but is much more practice oriented.

This right to remain a tenant can be very lucrative for the tenant if the rent is below market price, but not if the rent is near market rates. This right has many names: in Yemen it is often called *ḥaqq al-yad*, meaning "the right of the hand" or a slightly more formal concept referred to in *fiqh* as *ʿināʾ*. As noted at the end of chapter 7, this right can be bought and sold according to the Zaydī law school as presented in validated *fiqh* and *fatwā*s. Since *waqf* cannot be bought and sold, the use of the word "selling" (*bayʿ*), is controversial and the term "transfer" (*naql*) is often used instead. In an ideal *waqf*, it is unheard of for a *waqf* tenant to have such a right, but in practice it is common. This is something the jurists have had to face in recurring court cases and questions for *fatwā*s. They must try to regulate the issue as much as possible instead of just denying the existence of the problem. *Waqf* lease is thus different from other leases in that a component of piety and morality is added to normal lease law. This morality centres on the question of the very purpose and essence of *waqf* and bending those ideals subsequently involves bending the very concepts of community, morals, rule of law, and religion.

10 For a very good overview, see Donaldson, *Sharecropping in the Yemen*.

There is a wide span of possibilities between ideal *waqf* rules and more pragmatic legal rules. How can rules be formulated and discussed in the same text without undermining the legitimacy of each? Some scholars take the side of the *waqf*, saying that long lease terms are undesirable and therefore should be illegal; others are more pragmatic and examine the question of the degree of validity of the "right of the hand" in *waqf* leases.

2.1 *The Definition of a Rule*

The fact that the three-year rule is a legal "rule" (*ḥukm, aḥkām*) means that it seeks to regulate a hypothetical case or social act in its context. It is not only the core of the rule, as a sentence that states "act A is legal" or "act B is illegal"; it also refers to the context around the rule, other related rules, the legal discourse it is part of and actual practical issues on the ground. Typically, much of this context is clarified in the *sharḥ* (explanation, commentary), while the rule itself is given in short, almost symbolic form in the *matn*.

In leases of *waqf* property, the main issue is to identify what must be fulfilled in order to produce a valid lease contract. A lease is a contract, just as the creation of the *waqf* is a contract. Both regulate the transfer of a set of rights. The totality of necessary conditions is not limited by problems in the real world. Sometimes these problems are so interconnected that it is difficult to separate the rules from each other. In practice they tend to "cluster" and such clusters tend to be abbreviated in the *mukhtaṣar* genre into single separable sentences. In the *matn*, the rules follow each other on a linear string of fairly short sentences separated only by the particle "and" (*wa*). (Rules are often related to each other with criss-crossing intertextual ties and times subordinated to each other, but in the *matn* they come as pearls on a string in a linear manner that makes them easier to form into a corpus that has enough structure to be taught and learned, quoted, and claimed.) The connotations of the word "rule" in Arabic (*ḥukm*) lead the reader to think of something that has already been judged to be valid. The same root and even the same word can also be used for an individual court decision. In the hierarchy of the legal norms ranging from doctrines and principles, the rule is the lowest level, the most basic building block of *fiqh* which is often called "branch" (*farʿ*, pl. *furūʿ*), as if on a tree. Or, perhaps, according to Ibn al-Murtaḍā's title, a flower on the branch.

2.2 *The Three-Year Rule*

The three-year rule is a delimited, individual, legal rule (*ḥukm*) that is supposed to be applied to all lease contracts (*ijāra*) covering *waqf*. Still, there are other sub-rules, which are necessary in order to solve problems in real situations, and related rules. Because of the rather systematic arrangement of the *fiqh* works, it is easy to find the rule in question in other works. After the *Kitāb al-Azhār*, most Zaydī *fiqh* works follow the same structure.

The three-year maximum lease rule is designed to enable the *mutawallī* to terminate the lease; he has the power to threaten to change the tenant if he does not provide full market price rent. Furthermore, the rule not only helps the *mutawallī* in cases of need; it actually *demands* that the *mutawallī* always use this rule, in the interest of the *waqf*. The rule states that any lease contract not following the rule is invalid and thus not legally binding. Baber Johansen states:

> It is evident that, from a very early date, the jurists tried to protect certain types of properties against the disadvantages, which arose from the divergence of the contractually fixed rent (*musammā*) from the "fair rent" (*ajr al-mithl*). Already in the ninth century Khaṣṣāf discussed the problems that resulted from the fact that the contractually fixed rent (*musammā*) of *waqf* land fell below the rent level of comparable lands in a way that constituted a *laesio enormis* (*ghabn fāḥish*) to the interests of the *waqf*....
>
> Restricting the period of tenancy was another way of protecting the interests of the lessor against the dangers that result from the divergences between contractually fixed rent and the "fair rent." This possibility is already discussed during the eighth century. From the ninth century onwards, Hanafite jurists tried to restrict the period of tenancy with regard to *waqf* lands and big estates. Some of them formally interdicted periods of more than one year, others of more than three years. Still others wanted the *qāḍī* to examine regularly the difference between the contractually fixed rent and the "fair rent."[11]

The three-year rule is thus a legal instrument that enables the *mutawallī* to carry out the lease in the best possible way for the *waqf*. A tenant that stays for a long time may start to feel that the asset he is renting is "his," especially if he has undertaken repairs from his own pocket. In a stable agricultural society, there will not be much inflation, however, over the long term, prices tend to fluctuate and rise. When the *mutawallī* wants to raise the rent to market rent,[12]

---

11 Baber Johansen, *The Islamic Law on Land Tax and Rent: The Peasants' Loss of Property Rights as Interpreted in the Hanafite Legal Literature of the Mamluk and Ottoman Periods* (London: Croom Helm, 1988), 33–34.

12 In this book, "fair rent" (*ajr*, or *ujrat al-mithl*) is equated with the term "market price rent." This does not necessarily mean the highest possible rent, since issues of predictability and long-term aspects are important in any lease. As for the difference that relates to maintenance—whether different types of maintenance of the asset are included in the

as he is theoretically entitled to, the tenant will tend to refuse the increase and refer to the rent in the contract. It is the very lease contract that is the target of the three-year rule and it simply states that lease contracts can be legally valid for only three years.

The following outlines how the three-year rule is discussed in Zaydī *fiqh*.

3 The Three-Year Rule in Zaydī *Fiqh*: A Chronological Presentation

3.1 *The Three-Year Rule in the* Instiṣār *and* Nūr al-Abṣār

Perhaps the most important Zaydī *fiqh* work before the *Sharḥ al-azhār* is the *Intiṣār ʿalā ʿulamāʾ al-amṣār* by the famous Imam al-Muʾayyad bi-Llāh Yaḥyā b. Ḥamza (d. 749/1348 or 49). Since the chapter of *waqf* is considered lost, and thus not provided in the edited and printed version, here the *Nūr al-abṣār al-muntaziʿ min Kitāb al-Intiṣār*, a *mukhtaṣar* (abridgement), was consulted.[13] The lease rule is found in the *waqf* chapter of the *mukhtaṣar*:

> It is allowed to rent out the *waqf* (*ijārat al-waqf*) for a short period such as fifty years. It is reprehensible with a long [lease period] unless the *waqf* is of the *awqāf* that are well known and that do not become mixed (*allatī lā taltabisu*) over time, then there is no reprehensibility.[14]

Imam Yaḥyā b. Ḥamza does not provide the three-year rule, but rather a similar rule with another time estimate: fifty years. Imam Yaḥyā's text does not quote al-Hādī at all. After this work, almost one hundred years passed before the *fiqh* work, analysed below, appeared.

3.2 *The Three-Year Rule in* al-Baḥr al-Zakhkhār

Ibn al-Murtaḍā (d. 840/1437) wrote a short and concise passage concerning the three-year rule in *al-Baḥr al-zakhkhār*, presumably before he wrote the *Kitāb al-Azhār*:

---

rent or not—we cannot make generalizations, but must look at the specific lease or types of leases.

13 An electronic copy was provided with the gracious help of those at the Muʾassasat Imām Zayd b. ʿAlī l-Thaqāfiyya.

14 "Wa yajūzu ijārat al-waqf mudda qaṣīra naḥw khamsīn sana wa-tukrah fī l-ṭawīla illā an takūn min al-mawqūfāt al-mashhūra allatī lā taltabisu bi-ṭūl al-azmina fa-lā karāha." Yaḥyā b. Ḥamza, *Nūr al-abṣār*. The photo of the text discussed is very unclear and the page is unnumbered. The text is in black ink with occasional important words in red. The book has several stamps that say "waqf ʿalā Jāmiʿ Shihāra."

> Topic (*mas'ala*): It is valid (*yaṣiḥḥu*) to rent it out (*ta'jīruhu*), based on *ijmā'*,[15] since its usufruct is the property of the beneficiary (*tadhhīb*), less than three years only, similar to the period of demarcation (*taḥjīr*) (Y) [Imam Yaḥyā b. Ḥamza:] And it is valid [to rent it out] up to fifty years. A long [lease] period is reprehensible whenever [the long period] causes confusion (*iltibās*) [between *waqf* and] private property, such as in the period of pledge (*rahn*).[16]

The text is concise and clear. The usufruct (*manāfi'*) is the property (*milk*) of the beneficiary (*al-maṣrif*) "according to the *madhhab*." Most of the arguments and references found in the quotation are treated in detail further below. The way the three-year rule is treated in *al-Baḥr al-zakhkhār* is representative of the work as such and shows why *al-Baḥr al-zakhkhār* is a respected legal encyclopaedia even today—it is clear and concise and it gives the most significant rules with their most significant sources of validity.

3.3 *The Three-Year Rule in Ibn al-Murtaḍā's* Kitāb al-Azhār

The three-year rule falls under one of the nine sections (*faṣl, fuṣūl*) of the "chapter of *waqf*," in a section called the "Section on clarification of what the *mutawallī* is allowed to do and what he is not [allowed to do]."[17] The section is further structured into ten rules and the three-year rule is the sixth of these: "And to rent it out for less than three years."[18] The *matn* is given in bold; it is so condensed in the text that it hardly makes sense without contextual information.

3.4 *The Three-Year Rule in Ibn Miftāḥ's* Sharḥ al-Azhār[19]

As mentioned in chapter 4 concerning the texts used in this study, the *sharḥ* of Ibn Miftāḥ (d. 877/1472) appears on the margins of the *matn* of the *Kitāb al-Azhār*. If the *matn* had not been printed in bold in the 2003 edition or in brackets in the 1980 and earlier editions (i.e., in red ink in the manuscripts), the reader would not have been able to see two separate texts. This merging of the two texts is perhaps mainly a matter of style and eloquence. Ibn Miftāḥ

15 "Yaṣiḥḥu ta'jīruhu ijmā'an." This could also be interpreted as, "It is valid to rent all of it out, since ..." instead of "based on *ijmā'*," but to rent out only part of the asset in the first place sounds strange.

16 Ibn al-Murtaḍā, *al-Baḥr al-zakhkhār*, 159.

17 Faṣl. Fī bayān mā yajūzu li-l-mutawallī fi'luhu wa-mā lā yajūzu.

18 Wa ta'jīruhu dūna thalāth sinīn.

19 All the quotations are taken from Ibn Miftāḥ, *Sharḥ al-azhār* (2003 ed.), 8:271–272, unless otherwise noted.

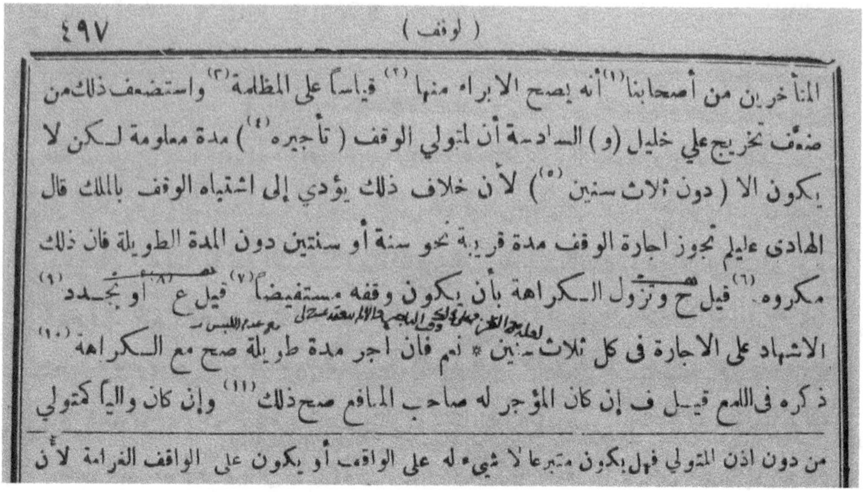
٤٩٧ (لوقف)

المتأخرين من أصحابنا(١) أنه يصح الابراء منها(٢) قياساً على المظلمة(٣) واستضعف ذلك من
ضعف تخريج علي خليل (و) السادسة أن لمتولي الوقف (تأجيره(٤)) مدة معلومة لكن لا
يكون الا (دون ثلاث سنين(٥)) لأن خلاف ذلك يؤدي إلى اشتباه الوقف بالملك قال
الهادي عليلم تجوز اجارة الوقف مدة قريبة نحو سنة أو سنتين دون المدة الطويلة فان ذلك
مكروه(٦) قيل ح وتزول الكراهة بأن يكون وقفه مستفيضاً(٧) قيل ع(٨) او بجدد(٩)
الاشهاد على الاجارة في كل ثلاث سنين * نعم فان اجر مدة طويلة صح مع الكراهة(١٠)
ذكره في اللمع قيل ف إن كان المؤجر له صاحب المنافع صح ذلك(١١) وإن كان والياً كمتولي
من دون اذن المتولي فهل يكون متبرعا لا شيء له على الواقف أو يكون على الواقف الغرامة لأن

FIGURE 11 The three-year rule in the *Sharḥ al-azhār* (1980 edition), 3:497.

treats the rule in two stages, as is common in the treatment of all the rules in his *sharḥ*: First he "decompresses" the text by adding some words of explanation, and then he discusses the sources of its validity. The two stages are given separately in the analysis below, thus first stage one:

> **And** the sixth [rule] is that the *mutawallī* of the *waqf* is entitled **to rent it out** [the *waqf* asset] for a defined period, however **for less than three years** only.

In this first stage, in the "decompressing" of the *matn*, the reader is given enough words to make meaning from the text, as the *matn* alone does not give enough meaning unless the reader knows the topic beforehand. The decompression explains, specifies, and expands the *matn*. However, both in the "explanation stage" and the "discussion stage" below, the author is rather economical with words. In general, his extra words make the text more readable and understandable.

The second stage, the "validation stage," or the "discussion stage," is a presentation of other scholars' views on the problem, further specification, potential alternatives in the form of rules, and the validity of each of those alternative rules and specifications. The author introduces this second stage by adding a short contextual explanation as to why this rule is needed in the first place:

> Because a deviation from this [rule] leads to confusion between what is *waqf* and what is private property (*milk*).[20]

It should be noted that the legal issue as such is presented as a problem that occurs because of social forces in the real, mundane world, whence the need of a rule; arguably, the rule does not originate in the texts of revelation, and certainly not in "clear text." Some informants point out (but not specifically related to this rule) that such rules are also "revealed," if not in the texts (*nuṣūṣ*) of the holy sources, then through human reason given by God. Quite a few Zaydī informants made an explicit point that the role of reason (*ʿaql*) is fundamental in the production of law, be it based on the holy texts or not.[21] This way a "secular" problem can be solved by a "secular" rule, yet still be part of a tradition of religiously validated law. Here the concepts of "secular" and "religious" seem to have limited value.

Then Ibn Miftāḥ starts an elaboration, discussion, and validation starting, as usual, with the "school founder" al-Hādī (d. 298/911):

> Al-Hādī stated: It is valid to rent out a *waqf* for a short period such as a year or two, but not for a long term because that is reprehensible (*makrūh*).[22]
>
> Al-Faqīh Yaḥyā l-Buḥaybaḥ said: The reprehensibility (*al-karāha*) is removed if the *waqf* is well known (*mustafīḍan*) [in the knowledge of the local community].[23]

This last argument has been validated with *tadhhīb*, as can be seen in the figure above. The fact that the *waqf* is well known in the local community means that there is no danger that the tenant and the *mutawallī* would be able to cheat the *waqf* through low rent. If the *waqf* assets are not well known among the local inhabitants, then the assets are more in need of protection through short lease

20 Li'anna khilāf dhālika yu'addī ilā ishtibāh al-waqf bi-l-milk. Another translation could be: Because a deviation from this [rule] leads to the resemblance of private property. The term *ishtibāh* means "semi" or "resembling" but in other places in the debate the terms *labs* and *iltibās* is used, and these terms are more related to "confusion."

21 This point is often used to highlight the "modern" and "intellectual" character of the Zaydī tradition in contrast to their "counterparts," the Salafīs and Wahhābīs.

22 Qāla al-Hādī, ʿalayhi al-salām, tajūzu ijārat al-waqf mudda qarība naḥw sana aw sanatayn dūna al-mudda al-ṭawīla, fa-inna dhālika makrūh.

23 Qāla al-faqīh Yaḥyā l-Buhaybaḥ wa-tazūlu al-karāha bi-an yakūnu waqfuhu mustafīḍan.

contracts only. Such local knowledge of *waqf* assets and their individual legal status is also called *shuhra*; we return to this below.

> Al-Faqīh ʿAlī said: Or, the witnessing of the lease is renewed (5) every three (6) years.[24]

This argument also carries the *tadhhīb* sign. Both of these are signs that were omitted from the *Sharḥ al-azhār* (1913–14 edition), but which reappear in al-Kuḥlānī's handwriting in the *Sharḥ al-azhār* (1980 edition), and also subsequently in the same places in the 2003 edition. This means that they override, at least in certain aspects, the main rule in the *matn*. It implies that the three-year rule is not absolute if the contextual conditions are right; if the *waqf* is well known in the local community it is not reprehensible to rent it out for a long period. We can see that the *sharḥ*, or more specifically, the validation signs combined[25] with the *sharḥ*, override the *matn* in several aspects, specifying it, and adding a new layer of validated meaning.

Then, Ibn Miftāḥ, the author of the *sharḥ*, returns to the active voice and explicitly agrees with what has been said so far and adds:

> Yes, so if [the *waqf* asset] is rented out for a long period, this is valid, though reprehensible, as he stated in the [*Kitāb*] *al-Lumaʿ*.[26]

Here Ibn Miftāḥ states a type of summary or conclusion, namely that a long-term lease *is* legally valid as a contract before a judge, but that it is morally reprehensible (*makrūh*) before God on the day of judgement. This division between law and morals is problematic, as exemplified immediately below. However, it shows that jurists did seek to separate legally valid, contractual law from the realm of morals and religious implications. In a sense, both are religious in their ultimate anchors of validity, but the admission that contractual law does not have to follow the same moral standards is an admission of some aspect of "secular" law. The same issue can be seen in al-Hādī's view above, but it is not entirely clear if he meant that a long-term lease is invalid because

24 Qāla al-faqīh ʿAlī: Aw yujaddadu al-ishhād ʿalā l-ijāra fī kulli thalāth sinnin.

25 The validation signs, at least in this systematized form, are probably younger than that *sharḥ*.

26 "The *Lumaʿ* was written by [al-Amīr] ʿAlī b. al-Ḥusayn and it has many *shurūḥ*." Ibn Miftāḥ, *Sharḥ al-azhār*, 1:87. Al-Amīr ʿAlī b. al-Ḥusayn died 656/1258. However the entry in the biographical dictionary does not explicitly use the title *faqīh*. Ibn Miftāḥ, *Sharḥ al-azhār*, 1:74. Qāla al-Faqīh ʿAlī: "Aw yujaddadu al-ishāda ʿalā l-ijāra fī kull thalāth sinīn. Naʿam, fa-in ujjira mudda ṭawīla ṣaḥḥa maʿa al-karāha, dhakarahu fī l-Lamʿ."

of its reprehensibility. There are five moral categories; the two negative types are *makrūh* (reprehensible) and *ḥarām* (forbidden). Making the determination that something is *ḥarām* is quite rare and the texts of revelation have to be clear about the matter. There is only one negative contractual, legal category: the invalid (*bāṭil, ghayr ṣaḥīḥ*).[27] The whole *waqf* chapter of the *Sharḥ al-azhār* follows the same pattern: it discusses contractual law regulating the transfer of rights from one actor to another actor. In some places in the *waqf* chapter and in some rules, the issue of morals does become entangled with contractual law.

The two previous arguments are validated later by *tadhhīb* signs and by the concluding sentence of Ibn Miftāḥ. If we look back at what Ibn al-Murtaḍā said in *al-Baḥr al-zakhkhār*, we see that he did not take a very firm stand on the three-year rule. And shortly after this was written, Ibn Miftāḥ was just as vague on its validity. Thus, the question is, why did he choose this rule specifically, and it alone, in the *matn*? Why quote it in the first place if he did not agree with it? We cannot answer this fully, except to say that he knew that his *matn* was a work that would be studied by beginners and used as a scaffolding and framework—it would never stand alone in the academic field of *fiqh*. It must always be read together with one or several explanations and commentaries (*shurūḥ*). The knowledge of exactly the correct rule can never be compressed into one sentence and still carry the same validity as *fiqh* knowledge.

Ibn al-Murtaḍā wrote his own *sharḥ, al-Ghayth al-midrār*,[28] but this work is seldom quoted. Ibn Miftāḥ ends the commentary on the three-year rule with a pragmatic argument in which he quotes his contemporary colleague from Thulā', al-Faqīh Yūsuf (d. 832/1429, who did not become especially well-known in later periods):

> Al-Faqīh Yūsuf said: If the tenant (*al-mu'ajjar lahu*) is the possessor of the usufruct (*ṣāḥib al-manāfi'*) then the longer lease contract is valid (9), and if he is in authority (*walī*) such as a *mutawallī* of mosque *waqf*s and the like, then the validity of the lease contract necessitates that there can be identified an interest for the mosque in the long lease and similarly, that this interest (10) cannot be achieved in a short lease, and if [an interest cannot be established for the mosque in a long lease], the lease is

27 It can be argued that there is a second negative category specific to Zaydī contractual law, see the main text below.

28 The *Ghayth* is mentioned in chapter 4 in the presentation of Zaydī *fiqh* texts.

> suspended (*fāsid*) (11) from the beginning, as stated in the [book called] *al-Zuhūr*.[29]

First, this quotation should be seen as two parts: The first deals with the case in which the beneficiary is the one renting the *waqf* asset; in such a case al-Faqīh Yūsuf states a long-term lease is valid. The question here is his use of the term "possessor of the usufruct" (*ṣāḥib al-manāfiʿ*). In a strict legal sense, this cannot be anyone other than the beneficiary (*al-maṣrif, al-mawqūf ʿalayhim*). This probably refers to the beneficiary of a family *waqf* or something similar to the *waṣīya-waqf* treated in chapter 7. If so, the descendants of the founder are also part beneficiaries, or, to state it in a legally correct manner, they are "holders of usufruct" (*ṣāḥib al-manāfiʿ*). In any case, it refers to a *waqf* in which the tenant and the beneficiary have a very close or overlapping role.

The second part of his argument, which supports the interpretation that the above relates to family *waqf*s or *waṣīya-waqf*s, switches to pure public *waqf*s. He uses the example of "mosques and similar [institutions]" and also uses the words: "And if he is a *walī*, such as a *mutawallī* for the mosque *waqf*s." The word *walī* here must refer to "a person with a general authority, acting for the interest of the society (or religion)." It can also be synonymous with the term *mutawallī*, but perhaps more in the sense of an imam-appointed *mutawallī* of the public *awqāf*. In any case, in this footnote he distinguishes between private *waqf*s and public *waqf*s and says that a long-term lease is allowed in private *waqf*s, while in public *waqf*s he adds a limitation, that a long-term lease can only be made if a preponderant interest can be identified that outweighs the disadvantage. And he adds, "if this interest cannot be identified, then the contract is suspended (*fāsid*)."

Hādawī-Zaydī contractual law is different from its Sunnī counterparts in that it distinguishes between three validities of a contract: valid (*ṣaḥīḥ*), invalid (*bāṭil*), and between the two there is a third with a conditional status (*fāsid*). A contract that is *fāsid* is temporarily invalid or suspended because one or more of its components or conditions is not fulfilled. If this component

29 Qāla al-Faqīh Yūsuf: In kāna al-muʾajjar lahu ṣāḥib al-manāfiʿ ṣaḥḥā dhālika, wa-in kāna walīyan ka-mutawallī awqāf al-masājid wa-naḥwa dhālika fa-sharṭ ṣiḥḥat al-ijāra an nafriḍa li-l-masjid wa-naḥwahu maṣlaḥa fī ṭūlihā tafūtu hādhihi al-maṣlaḥa maʿa qiṣr al-mudda, wa-illā fa-l-ijāra fāsida min aṣliha, dhakara dhālika fī l-zuhūr. The *Zuhūr* was written by al-Faqīh Yūsuf b. Aḥmad b. ʿUthmān al-Thulāʾī (d. 832/1429), who was a friend of Ibn al-Murtaḍā; Ibn al-Murtaḍā went to him when Ibn al-Murtaḍā was released from prison. He also wrote *Thamarāt al-yāniʿa wa-l-aḥkām al-wāḍiḥa al-qāṭiʿa* (a Qurʾān *tafsīr*) and the *Riyāḍ*. Ibn Miftāḥ, *Sharḥ al-azhār*, 1:109–110.

is fulfilled under the correct circumstances, then the whole contract takes legal effect once more.[30]

Al-Faqīh Yūsuf does not specify exactly how this "interest" should be defined or converted into a contractual condition. It is not at all controversial that "interest" supersedes the three-year rule, since interest or utility (*maṣlaḥa*) is central as a source of law if there is no "clear text" available in the revelation. This is also specifically pointed out by Ibn al-Murtaḍā at the end of the *waqf* chapter of *al-Baḥr al-zakhkhār*, where he states that most of *waqf fiqh* is indeed a matter of *maṣlaḥa* (we return to this matter in chapter 8).[31] Although not stated explicitly, it is probably the judge who is supposed to identify the *maṣlaḥa* that al-Faqīh Yūsuf calls for, since a *waqf* contract is valid unless it is taken to a judge to be contested.

This ends Ibn Miftāḥ's discussion of the three-year rule. In sum, four authorities are quoted, including al-Hādī, and two books are explicitly mentioned. The arguments overlap slightly and their views diverge. Of the three scholars quoted in addition to al-Hādī, al-Faqīh Yūsuf (d. 832/1429), was a contemporary of Ibn Miftāḥ (d. 877/1472). The two others, al-Faqīh al-Buḥaybaḥ and al-Faqīh ʿAlī[32] were earlier in time and are not referred to as often after the *sharḥ* was composed. There are several such figures[33] who are only referred to by advanced Zaydī scholars today; in other ways, they are "lost" from the debate.

In all editions of the *Sharḥ al-azhār*, except the new 2003 edition, most proper names are not given in full, rather they are indicated with one letter abbreviations. Where the *Sharḥ al-azhār* 2003 edition reads "al-Faqīh ʿAlī stated," all other editions remain in the passive "it has been stated [by] ʿ" (qīla ʿ), where the letter ʿayn stands for ʿAlī, the letter f for al-Faqīh Yūsuf, etc. (see figure 12 of the *Sharḥ al-azhār* 1980 edition above).

We do not see any references to scholars in other law schools at all. Ibn Miftāḥ's debate, specification, and discussion is purely local and Zaydī. This does not mean that other works do not contain such references to the origin of the three-year time period and to external authorities and sources. What we can assume is that Ibn Miftāḥ did not intend to do this in his *sharḥ*. It is not

30 Haykel mentions this, see Haykel, *Revival and Reform*, 224. See also the Qānūn al-madanī article 139 where there are indeed five categories, one of them "depending, suspended" (*mawqūf*). *Qānūn al-Madanī* [2002] (Sanaa: Wizārat al-Shuʾūn al-Qānūniyya, 2008), 24.

31 Ibn al-Murtaḍā, *al-Baḥr al-zakhkhār*, 166–167.

32 Al-Faqīh Yaḥyā b. Ḥasan al-Buḥaybaḥ (not dated but he "studied with a person … who was contemporary with Imam Yaḥyā" that is, shortly before 751/1350. Ibn Miftāḥ, *Sharḥ al-azhār*, 1:108. Al-Faqīh ʿAlī is not mentioned by that title in the biographic dictionary at the beginning of the *Sharḥ al-azhār*. Ibid.

33 Such as Abū Mudar. *Sharḥ al-azhār*, 1:59.

the ultimate, all-incorporating *sharḥ*, it was and is a practical *sharḥ* for *faqīh*s at the intermediary level. It is only later that this particular book, for a variety of reasons, became a reference work that continued to be added onto, in the margins, such as in the margins of the manuscript of al-Shawkānī and al-Suhayl that was chosen for the first printed edition. In that time span of around 350 years, from around 1450 until 1800, additional views were added as glosses. And, just as important, the validation signs were added. This is the third layer, which was undertaken by multiple authors; I treat this briefly below.

3.5 *The Three-Year Rule in the ʿIzz al-Dīn* Fatwā *Collection*

The three-year rule is mentioned once in a question in the *fatwā* collection of Imam al-Hādī ʿIzz al-Dīn b. al-Ḥasan (d. 900/1495). The question in the *fatwā* is long and complicated and deals with a family *waqf* in which one of the family members rented out his share (his right to use some agricultural fields) for 100 years and a "judge from the lands of Tihāma" judged that the lease was valid. Then, this family member died and his brothers wanted to make the lease invalid, presumably so they could end the lease contract and take on another tenant. The question leads to several sub-questions, for example, can the three-year rule be used to invalidate the lease contract? In the *fatwā* made by al-Hādī ʿIzz al-Dīn, he states that this is a family *waqf* and the beneficiary is the owner of the usufruct; therefore he can lease it in whatever way he wishes (quite in line with al-Faqīh Yūsuf above). This answer points to the problematic status of a family *waqf*: the property belongs to God, yet the right of use is transmitted from generation to generation (*yantaqilu ilā warathat al-wāqif bi-l-waqf*). If there was a common *mutawallī* for all of the *waqf* and all of the beneficiaries in question, and if the *mutawallī* did not rent out the *waqf*s according to the wishes of some beneficiaries and serve their interests, the judge should take his place and be the *mutawallī* (*tawallā l-naẓar al-ḥākim*).[34] Imam ʿIzz al-Dīn does not mention the three-year rule in his answer, probably because this was a family *waqf*. The "judges of Tihāma" would probably be Shāfiʿīs, who do not have the restriction of the three-year rule, as I elaborate on towards the end of this chapter. We can interpret the question above as an attempt by the beneficiaries to use the letter of the law selectively, and although the three-year rule was not absolute, nor very "powerful," they clearly believed that it could serve as the basis of a legal argument before a Zaydī judge. We do not know which geographical area this *waqf* was related to, that is, if it was located close to the Shāfiʿī lowlands. Al-Hādī ʿIzz al-Dīn mainly ruled in the northern areas of the highlands.

34 al-Hādī ʿIzz al-Dīn, *Majmūʿ rasāʾil*, 2:469–471.

In the *fatwā*, also related to *waqf*, immediately preceding the one above, the *Kitāb al-Azhār* is cited in both the question and the answer; this demonstrates that it was well-known at this time.[35] We shall now return to the glosses on the margins ("footnotes") that accumulated in the *Sharḥ al-azhār* over the following centuries.

3.6 *The Margins and Footnotes in the* Sharḥ al-Azhār

The *Sharḥ al-azhār* became the most used *fiqh* work in Zaydī Yemen; over time comments, specifications, and notes[36] were added in the margins. Many of these notes were made by anonymous authors, though quite a few were made by known scholars—this is often pointed out at the end of the note as an indication of validity. When the *Sharḥ al-azhār* was printed for the first time in 1913–14, the edition was based on a manuscript in which al-Shawkānī had copied out the *Kitāb al-Azhār*/*Sharḥ al-azhār* and his student ʿAlī b. ʿAbdallāh Suhayl (d. 1835) wrote the commentaries and notes. To a large extent, the content of these notes were well-known in the scholarly community and in other manuscripts of the *Sharḥ al-azhār*. These commentaries and notes form the

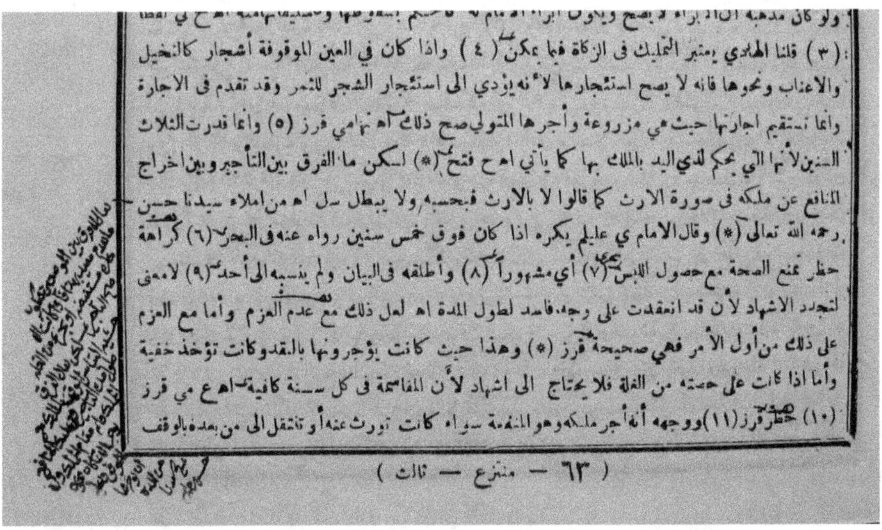
(٣) قلنا الهادي يعتبر التمليك في الزكاة فيما يمكن (٤) واذا كان في العين الموقوفة أشجار كالنخيل
والاعناب ونحوها فانه لا يصح استئجارها لأنه يؤدي الى استئجار الشجر للثمر وقد تقدم في الاجارة
وانما تستقيم اجارتها حيث هي مزروعة وأجرها المتولي صح ذلك اه تهامي قرز (٥) وانما قدرت الثلاث
السنين لأنها التي يحكم لذي اليد بالملك بها كما يأتي اه ح فتح (*) لكن ما الفرق بين التأجير وبين اخراج
النافع عن ملكه في صورة الارث كما قالوا لا بالارث فبحسبه ولا يبطل سل اه من املاء سيدنا حسن
رحمه الله تعالى (*) وقال الامام ي عليلم يكره اذا كان فوق خمس سنين رواه عنه في البحر (٦) كراهة
حظر تمنع الصحة مع حصول اللبس (٧) أي مشهوراً (٨) وأطلقه في البيان ولم ينسبه الى أحد (٩) لا معنى
لتجدد الاشهاد لأن قد انعقدت على وجه فاسد لطول المدة اه لعل ذلك مع عدم العزم وأما مع العزم
على ذلك من أول الأمر فهي صحيحة قرز (*) وهذا حيث كانت يؤجرونها بالعقد وكانت تؤخذ خفية
وأما اذا كانت على حصته من الغلة فلا يحتاج الى اشهاد لأن المقاسمة في كل سنة كافية اه ع مي قرز
(١٠) حظر قرز (١١) ووجهه أنه أجر ملكه وهو المنفعة سواء كانت تورث عنه أو تنتقل الى من بعده بالوقف
(٦٣ — منتزع — ثالث)

FIGURE 12 Photo of page 3:497 in the *Sharḥ al-azhār* (1980 edition)

35 This question was also directed to ʿIzz al-Dīn: how should a public *waqf* (*waṣāyā qadīma muṭlaqa*) be divided among three mosques entitled as beneficiaries. He states that if the mosques are equal in size and use, the *waṣāyā* (sic: *waqf*) is to be divided among them equally. The founder is termed "*al-muṣī*." Al-Hādī ʿIzz al-Dīn, *Majmūʿ rasāʾil*, 2:469.

36 One may use the term "glosses," but here the terms *sharḥ*, footnotes, and secondary footnotes have been used, following the structure of Ibn Miftāḥ, *Sharḥ al-azhār* (2003 ed.).

third layer of text and stem from the period that lasted from Ibn Miftāḥ to ʿAlī b. ʿAbdallāh Suhayl.

In order to better remember the sequence of these footnotes in the *Sharḥ al-azhār*, below I give the *sharḥ* one more time in its entirety. The *matn* is given in bold. All quotations are taken from the 2003 edition, in which the names of people are given in full.

> **And** the sixth [rule] is that the *mutawallī* of the *waqf* is entitled to **rent it out** (1) [the *waqf* asset] for a defined period, however for only **less than three years** only (2), because a deviation from this [rule] leads to confusion between what is *waqf* and what is private property (*milk*).
>
> Al-Hādī stated: It is valid to rent out a *waqf* for a short period such as a year or two, but not for a long term because that is reprehensible (*makrūh*). (3)
>
> Al-Faqīh Yaḥyā l-Buḥaybaḥ said: The reprehensibility (*al-karāha*) is removed if the *waqf* is well known (*mustafīḍan*) [in the knowledge of the local community]. (4)
>
> Al-Faqīh ʿAlī said: Or, the witnessing of the lease is renewed (5) every three (6) years.
>
> Yes, so if [the *waqf* asset] is rented out for a long period (7), then it is valid though reprehensible (8), as he stated in the [*Kitāb*] *al-Lumaʿ*.
>
> Al-Faqīh Yūsuf said: If the tenant (*al-muʾajjar lahu*) is the possessor of the usufruct (*ṣāḥib al-manāfiʿ*) then the longer lease contract is valid (9), and if he is in authority (*walī*) such as a *mutawallī* of mosque *waqfs* and the like, then the validity of the lease contract necessitates that there can be identified an interest for the mosque in the long lease and similarly, and that this interest (10) cannot be achieved in a short lease, and if not, the lease is suspended (*fāsid*) (11) from the beginning, as stated in the [book called] *al-Zuhūr*.

The system of footnotes comes from the first printed edition of the *Sharḥ al-azhār* (1913–14). Before that, numbers were at times used, but the notes were written in the margins of the *sharḥ*, not under it. There are some comments or notes that are notes on other notes, and sometimes there are several notes under one footnote reference. In the printed editions this is called a repeated footnote (*ḥāshiya mukarrara*), and is given as an asterisk *, or as an asterisk between parentheses (*) in order to separate them. Below they are given as 1a, 1b, and so forth. and the footnotes are renumbered so that they start at number one, while in the printed versions the numbers start at number one on each printed page.

Footnote (1) (footnote 4 in fig. 12 above)
The first note discusses whether or not fruit-bearing trees that happen to be situated on the land are included in the lease contract or not. I do not address this issue here, since it is not part of the paragraph of the *sharḥ* dealing with the three-year rule.

Footnote (2):
"The only reason for the estimate of three years is that it is the period that allows the possessor [of an asset such as land] to take full ownership, such as will be treated later. (*Sharḥ Fatḥ*)"

This note explains why the three-year rule has that exact time limit. The reason for the three years is not given in the *Kitāb al-Azhār* or the *Sharḥ al-azhār*, though Ibn al-Murtaḍā does mention it in *al-Baḥr al-zakhkhār*, where he states that the three-year estimate comes from the similar three-year estimate in issues of demarcation (*taḥjīr*).[37]

Taḥjīr is a legal concept regulated in detail in *fiqh*; it refers to the act of visibly demarcating borders by using stones (*ḥajar*, pl. *ḥajjara, taḥjīr*) or other border markers. According to the theory of Islamic and tribal law in Yemen, originally land is not "owned" unless it is actively claimed and used. Otherwise, according to Islamic law, it belongs to all Muslims, and in tribal law, to all members of the tribe. There are many types and degrees of such "un-owned" land and the issue cannot be explored in detail here. In theory, such land may be claimed by anyone who wants to revive and use it. The act of revival mainly refers to making a new agricultural field in common barren lands, with the permission of the local community. It is also regulated under the so-called "revival of barren lands" (*iḥyā' al-mawāt*), which is encouraged in Islamic law.[38]

In the *Sharḥ al-azhār*, there is a "Chapter of land revival and demarcation" (Bāb al-iḥyā' wa-l-taḥjīr).[39] It has its own section (*faṣl*), the "Section on *taḥjīr* and its rulings." The three-year rule in *taḥjīr* means that once border demarcation stones[40] have been placed to indicate that one has taken possession,

---

37 "Topic" (*mas'ala*): It is valid to rent it out, based on *ijmā'*, as its usufruct is the property of the beneficiary (chosen by the *madhhab*), less than three years only, such as the period of demarcation (*taḥjīr*) (Y) And it is allowed [to lease it] up to fifty years, and a long [lease] period is reprehensible because of [the long period] causing confusion (*iltibās*) [between *waqf* and] private property and as in the period of *rahn* [of the *waqf*]" Ibn al-Murtaḍā, *al-Baḥr al-zakhkhār*, 5:159.

38 Both the *iḥyā' l-mawāt* and the *taḥjīr* is found in the Civil Code, article 1242–1253 *Qānūn al-Madanī* [2002]. The three year estimate is mentioned in article 1243, sub-article 3.

39 It is located after Kitāb al-shuf'a (pre-emption) and Kitāb al-ijāra and Bāb al-muzāra'a (one of the forms of sharecropping), followed by the Kitāb al-sharika.

40 Typically a small pile of rocks at the corners of the plot.

that possession remains a right (*ḥaqq*) for the claimant until three years have passed and then the right becomes owned property (*milk*), as long as the land has been revived and used during that time. If anyone wants to protest, they must do so before the three years have passed. In the sentence dealing with the three-year estimate in *taḥjīr* in the *Sharḥ al-azhār*, immediately after the word "three" there is a footnote that refers directly to a *ḥadīth*:

> Concerning what was said about a man who made a *taḥjīr*, then another man came and revived that land and the two quarrelled and went to ʿUmar, may God be pleased with him. ʿUmar wanted to give them his judgement in favour of the one who revived [the land] when a man told him a story about the Prophet: "The right of the one who demarcates (*al-mutaḥajjir*) is valid until three years have passed," and ʿUmar said: If I had not heard this, then I would have judged otherwise ([Kitāb] al-bustān).[41]

The *ḥadīth* is never mentioned explicitly in the *waqf* rent issue, perhaps because the *ḥadīth* is considered weak, or more plausibly, the analogy between the two rules (the three-year rule in *taḥjīr* and three-year rule in a *waqf* lease) is too loose. The analogy is easy to understand in a broad sense, but the circumstances of the two cases are very different. While both deal with public property, *waqf* is a category of its own that can never be taken over by anyone simply by remaining on the land for three years. In *waqf*, even if hundred years pass, a testimony that this property is *waqf* is theoretically enough for it to revert to *waqf*. The concept of *qiyās* is not explicitly invoked here.

Footnote (1a)

Footnote (1a) is slightly complicated. It seems to be a question and an answer recorded during a study circle, as it ends with "explanation by Sayyidnā Ḥasan." The same person is quoted in footnote (9) below, which ends with: "by dictation of Sayyidnā Ḥasan." These two notes seem to belong together and relate to the topic raised by al-Faqīh Yūsuf; namely that which concerns the case of a tenant who is also the possessor of the usufruct (beneficiaries in a private, family *waqf*). Further, the question centres on what happens to a lease contract when a new generation of beneficiaries takes over the "possession." Another confusing aspect relates to the origin of the footnote: the second half of the footnote did not exist in the 1913–14 edition, rather it was added by al-Kuḥlānī as a handwritten marginal note, then printed in the photocopied 1980 edition (see the lower right corner of fig. 12. above). In the 2003 edition, this handwritten note was made into a proper footnote and inserted into (1a). This is a good

41 Ibn Miftāḥ, *Sharḥ al-azhār*, 7:353.

example of how a "lost marginal note" was "kept alive" outside the text and later reinserted.[42]

Footnote (2b)

> Imam Yaḥyā [b. Ḥamza[43]] (peace be upon him) said: it is reprehensible if it was more than five years. It has been stated in *al-Baḥr* [*al-zakhkhār*].[44]

When this is cross-checked with *al-Baḥr al-zakhkhār*,[45] (given above) we see that Imam Yaḥyā b. Ḥamza's view is indeed referred to, but there it is given as fifty years, not five. Can this mistake really have been made through all these editions of the *Sharḥ al-azhār*? Or is the mistake in the printed edition of *al-Baḥr al-zakhkhār*? As mentioned in chapter 4, the chapter on *waqf* from Imam Yaḥyā b. Ḥamza's (d. 749 or 50/1348–49) multivolume *fiqh* work, the *Intiṣār*, is lost. Only his *mukhtaṣar, Nūr al-abṣār* has the *waqf* chapter, which states: "fifty years" (*khamsīn sana*), not five.[46]

---

42 Footnote (1a): Lakinna mā l-farq bayna ikhrāj al-manāfiʿ ʿan milkihi fī ṣūrat al-irth, ka-mā qālū, lā bi-l-irth fa-bi-ḥasabihi wa-lā yabṭulu? Min imlāʾ Sayyidnā Ḥasan, raḥimahu Allāh taʿālā. Yuqālu: lā farq bayna al-mawḍiʿayn fa-yakūnu mā taqaddama muqayyidan bi-hādha, fa-idhā kānat al-ijāra mustafīḍatan aw bi-juzʾ min al-ghalla ṣaḥḥa al-taʾjīr. Lakinna yuqālu al-farq bayna khushiyat iltibās al-waqf bi-l-milk maʿa ṭūl muddat al-taʾjīr, wa-fī tamlīk al-manāfiʿ al-mumalllik qāʾim maqām al-mumallik wa-la yuʾajjaru illā bi-mā kāna yajūzu li-l-mawqūf ʿalayhi an yuʾajjirahā min al-mudda. (Sharḥ sayyidnā Ḥasan, raḥimahu Allāh.) Footnote (4): Wa-wajhuhu annahu ajjara milkahu wa-huwa al-manfaʿa, sawaʾan kānat tuwarrathu ʿanhu aw tunqalu ilā man baʿdahu bi-l-waqf, bi khilāf al-mutawallī fa-laysa bi-mālik li-l-manfaʿa. (Imlāʾ Sayyidnā Ḥasan, raḥimahu Allāh al-taʿālā.) The words "lā bi-l-irth fa-bi-ḥasabihi wa-lā yabṭulu" refers to the *matn* of the *Kitāb al-Azhār* (*Sharḥ al-azhār* (2003 ed.), 8:206–207) in the third section of the chapter on *waqf*. There is another similar note by Sayyidnā Hāsan there, Ibn Miftāḥ, *Sharḥ al-azhār* (2003 ed.), 8:207.

43 In Ibn Miftāḥ, *Sharḥ al-azhār* (1980 ed.), only "(Y)" is given, as in *al-Baḥr al-zakhkhār*. In the *Sharḥ al-azhār* (2003 ed.), this is given as "*Imām Yaḥyā*." Donaldson writes about the confusion of these abbreviations (he used *al-Baḥr al-zakhkhār* in his study); he has several theories on which of the potential imams (there were several Yaḥyās) the abbreviation could refer to. Donaldson, *Sharecropping in the Yemen*, 97. From this footnote in the *Sharḥ al-azhār* given above in the main text it is clear that the "Y" is Imam Yaḥyā b. Ḥamza.

44 Wa-qāla al-Imām Yaḥyā, ʿalayhi al-salām, yukrah idhā kānā fawqa khams sinīn, rawāhū ʿānhu fī (*al-Baḥr al-zakhkhār*). Perhaps "khamsin sana" became "khams sinīn" during the process of copying the manuscript.

45 (Y) wa-yaṣiḥḥu ilā khamsīn sana, wa-tukrah al-ziyāda allatī yaltabisu li-ajlihā bi-l-amlāk. Ibn al-Murtaḍā, *al-Baḥr al-zakhkhār*, 5:159.

46 The actual photograph of the page dealing with the three-year rule in the *Nūr al-abṣār* is slightly out of focus, but the difference between the words "five" and "fifty" would have been observable.

Footnote (3)

> Reprehensibility (*karāha*) is a hindrance (*ḥaẓr*), which prohibits legal validity if confusion (*labs*) occurs.[47]

"Confusion" is here translated from the word *labs*, or otherwise *iltibās*, and is frequently used in the discussion of the three-year rule. This refers to the state that occurs when the rights of the *waqf* become mixed with rights of other persons in a way that causes confusion about what exactly belongs to whom in the local community of owners.

First, the footnote says that if something is reprehensible, that is, morally wrong (*makrūh*), then it is automatically also invalid, contractually speaking. However, the second half of the sentence specifies this further and says that this is only the case if there is confusion. The footnote has not been validated by *tadhhīb*.

Footnote (4)

> That means: well known.[48]

This footnote is simply a lexical explanation for the word *mustafīḍ*.

Footnote (5)

> He stated it in the *Bayān* [*al-Shāfī*], but did not ascribe it to anyone.[49]

Footnote (5a)

> There is no point in renewal of the witnessing; the contract is contractually suspended (*fāsid*) because of the longevity of the lease term.
>
> Perhaps (*la'alla*) that is so if this is not emphasized (*'azm*) (*tadhhīb*), and if the renewal is emphasized from the very beginning, then the contract is valid (q-r-z).[50]

---

47 Karāha ḥaẓr tamna'u al-ṣiḥḥa ma'a ḥuṣūl al-labs.

48 Ayy: Mashhūran.

49 Wa aṭlaqahu fī-l(-*Bayān*) wa-lam yansabhu ilā aḥad. Note that the *Bayān al-shāfī* came after Ibn Miftāḥ's *Sharḥ al-azhār*, thus this footnote is an example of how the *Bayān* was later "imported" into the footnotes of the *Sharḥ al-azhār*.

50 Lā ma'nā li-tajdīd al-ishhād; li-anna qad in'aqadat 'alā wajh fāsid li-ṭūl al-mudda. La'alla dhālika ma'a 'adam al-'azm (tadhhīb), wa-ammā ma'a al-'azm 'alā dhālika min awwal al-amr fa-hiya ṣaḥīḥa (q-r-z).

The first half states that the long lease term only produces a "suspended" (*fāsid*) contract, not an invalid one. The second half is actually an independent note, again referring to the word in the *sharḥ* where it branches off, at "renewal." It states that if continuous renewal is "pointed out" or "emphasized" (*ʿazm*), presumably in the lease contract, then it can still be valid. This last part of the footnote is validated both by *tadhhīb* and *taqrīr*, and in effect it totally overrules the whole three-year rule.

In the 2003 edition, it looks as if this is one note and the two sentences are separated by a full stop. However, looking carefully at the 1980 edition (fig. 12), we can see that the first sentence ends with the abbreviation "ʾ-a-h" (*intahā*) meaning end of quote. The author of the second note is less strict in his view and he is the one whose note has been validated.

Footnote (5b)

> This is only so if it was rented out for money and the money was handed over covertly, however, if it was taken from a certain fraction of the harvest, then there is no need for witnessing because the yearly measuring of the harvest (*muqāsama*) is sufficient. Dictation by Shāmī (q-r-z).[51]

This is an important legal elaboration, and the note is clear. It refers to different forms of leases, which impose different challenges that do not need to be treated as strictly equal. The yearly crop estimation of the harvest, measuring the tenant's share according to the sharecropping fraction,[52] and the tenant handing over the rent in kind to the *waqf* administrator is an act, and as such does not need any further contractual confirmation or definition. It is an act that consists of contractual elements and aspects and is partly "public." The act of measuring and handing over the harvest confirms that there is a contract and it confirms the size of the rent as well as another public witnessing would. This is contrary to leases with fixed rents in cash; the payment of the rent *khufiyatan* (lit., "covertly") produces other challenges for the *waqf* lease situation, in terms of "publicness." It is this difference in contextual circumstances that is specified here and taken into consideration in this footnote.

---

51 Wa-hādha ḥaythu kānat yu'ajjirūnahā bi-l-naqd, wa-kānat tu'khadh khufiyyatan, wa-amma idhā kānat ʿalā ḥiṣṣatihi min al-ghalla, fa-lā yuḥtāj ila ishhād li-anna al-muqāsama fī kulli sana kāfiyatan (samāʿ Shāmī).

52 The fraction remains the same year after year, while the rent, in terms of absolute amount, depends on the size of the yearly harvest. In Yemen, rainfall varies greatly from year to year and is the most significant factor in the yearly variation in the size of the harvest.

The author of the note is presumably chief *qāḍī* Aḥmad b. ʿAbd al-Raḥmān al-Shāmī (1684–1759).[53]

Footnote (6)

> Perhaps so with the emphasis on that [that the contract can be renewed every three years] at the time of the lease, and if not, the contract is as if it was not made. (A comment by al-Saḥūlī.)[54]

This note is handwritten between the lines in the *Sharḥ al-azhār* (1980 edition), something that can be seen in figure 11 above. It is given as a full footnote in the *Sharḥ al-azhār* (2003 edition). It has no validation marks. This note specifies that such a renewal can perhaps (*laʿalla*) be valid, but only if it is pointed out in the lease contract or during the contractual situation (as a contract can also be oral) the first time it was made. Thus it is more restrictive than footnote 5b, which states a similar content. The absence of validation marks could stem from the edition of the *Sharḥ al-azhār*. The author of the note is the chief *qāḍī* al-Saḥūlī (d. 1209/1795), or he is the *qāḍī* of Sanaa, Yaḥyā b. Ibrāhīm al-Saḥūlī (d. 1060/1650). It could also mean that this was the law under al-Saḥūlī, but that the *madhhab* later favoured the less strict position.

Footnote (7)

> With the absence of confusion.[55]

This note is handwritten between the lines of the *Sharḥ al-azhār* (1980 edition). It means that if the *waqf* is rented out for a long period, and there is no confusion or ambiguity regarding the lease, then it is contractually valid though morally reprehensible.

Footnote (8)

> Hindrance (*ḥaẓr*). (q-r-z)

---

53 He was chief *qāḍī* under al-Mutawakkil al-Qāsim (r. 1718–27), under al-Manṣūr al-Ḥusayn (r. 1727–48) and into the reign of al-Mahdī l-ʿAbbās, before chief *qāḍī* al-Saḥūlī. al-Shawkānī, *al-Badr al-ṭāliʿ*, 105–106. See also Haykel, *Revival and Reform*, 112–113.

54 La'allahu maʿa ʿajzm ʿalā dhālika waqt al-ta'jīr, wa-illā lam yanʿaqid (ḥāshiyat al-Saḥūlī).

55 Maʿa ʿadam al-labs.

This means that "moral reprehensibility" (*karāha*) is a hindrance to the contractual validity of the lease contract. The note is with *taqrīr* (the letter q-r-z); this implies that if it is established to be reprehensible, then the contract is invalid. However, in the main text of the *Sharḥ al-azhār* al-Buḥaybaḥ is quoted, also with validation marks, stating that the reprehensibility is removed if the *waqf* is well known. This shows that the dialogue of scholars commenting on the main text and the footnotes, and even among the footnotes, is not systematic but continues to spiral on and produces consequences for all the other criteria.

Footnote (9)
The second note by Sayyidnā Ḥasan is given above in (1a), but here the end states that in contrast to a lease in which the *mutawallī* is a beneficiary and thus owns the usufruct, not all *mutawallī*s are in this situation (as in a public *waqf*, in which the *mutawallī*s do not own the usufruct and thus are not free to set up any lease. In short, it points to the distinction between family *waqf* and "public" *waqf*.

Footnote (9a)

> The *madhhab* does not validate (*tadhhīb*) a lease contract in which confusion [between *waqf* and private property] is taking place. There is no difference between the possessor of usufruct and others [regarding this matter]. Muftī. (q-r-z).[56]

This is a response to footnote 9 above, which states that there is a difference between private and public *waqf*s in this matter. Any lease contract in which the exact status and identity of the *waqf* asset is endangered is simply invalid. This footnote is also thoroughly validated by both *tadhhīb* and *taqrīr*. We do not know who the "muftī" was, it could have been Ismāʿīl b. Hādī l-Muftī (d. 1198/1783 or 84).[57]

56 Wa-l-madhhab lā yaṣiḥḥu (tadhhīb) illā ḥaythu lā yaḥṣulu al-labs, wa-lā farqa bayna ṣāḥib al-manfaʿa wa-ghayrihi (muftī) (q-r-z).

57 It could be al-Sayyid Ismāʿīl b. Hādī l-Muftī (d. 1783 or 1784), al-Shawkānī, *al-Badr al-ṭāliʿ*, 189. "Al-Muftī" is his *laqab*, not a reference to a position. If he was not the author of the footnote, it might have been one of his predecessors with the same *laqab*, as mentioned in Zabāra, *Nashr al-ʿarf*, 1:413–415.

Footnote (10)

> The concept of interest (*maṣlaḥa*) is valid when not countered by an equally strong disadvantage. This [the three-year rule] does not relate in any way with a specific number of years.
>
> (The author states:) This is when confusion is not feared or [something] similar. The same [applies] to every single rule (*ḥukm*) of the *sharīʿa*; if it is countered by a disadvantage, then this leads to the invalidation of the rule, if it indeed were so. (From the book *al-Wābil*)[58]

This note goes to the very foundation and origins of the rule and claims that the whole matter is simply one of *maṣlaḥa* and contextual circumstances, and further, that this even applies to all rules of the *sharīʿa*. This footnote has not been validated. The last, "from the book called *al-Wābil*"[59] was added by hand in the *Sharḥ al-azhār* (1980 edition).

Footnote (11)

> That means: invalid (*bāṭil*).[60]

This last footnote clarifies that if a lease contract becomes *fāsid* as a *consequence* of lack of interest or utility (*maṣlaḥa*) for the *waqf*, then this lease is not only *fāsid* (suspended), but also *bāṭil* (contractually invalid). This was stated earlier, but not as directly as it is here and not in relation to *maṣlaḥa*. There are no validation signs on the footnote.

Before summing up, we should note the complexity of the legal discussion. Obviously, the result of the discussion, i.e., what the *madhhab* agreed on, is something different from the strict form of the three-year rule. It is easy to see that such a deep and academic legal discussion is not a textbook for beginning students, nor is it a manual for judges. The conversion of this complicated discussion into more simplified genres, such as *al-Tāj al-mudhhab*, is discussed below.

---

58 Al-ʿibra bi-l-maṣlaḥa allatī lā tuʿariḍuhā mafsada musāwiya, wa-lā ʿibra bi-l-sinīn al-tabba (min al muʿallif) wa-dhālika ḥaythu lā yukhshā labs wa-naḥwa dhālika, wa-ka-dhālika kullu ḥukm min aḥkām al-sharīʿa idhā ʿāradahu mafsada fa-innahu yubṭal in kānat dhālika.

59 *al-Wābil al-maghzār al-maṭʿam li-athmār al-azhār fī fiqh al-aʾimma al-aṭhār* by Yaḥyā b. Muḥammad b. Ḥasan d. 1582 or 1583. It seems to be one of the many commentaries on the *Kitāb al-Azhār*. See chapter 4.

60 Ayy: bāṭil.

If we look at the explicit sources of validity for the footnotes above, we find five references to persons and five references to books. We also see concepts such as "confusion," "interest," "reprehensibility," "invalidity," and various ways of describing hypothetical situations and how these situations can be defined in relation to the real world. Many of the arguments refer to each other in a web of cross references, making it difficult to portray all of them in a systematic manner. Yet they are presented one by one in a textual sequence. Some of the views or comments seem confusing and do not contribute much and one may wonder why they were included at all. The answer is probably that they have accumulated over the centuries and no one has had the authority to remove them, since most of them have some sort of "original" content and contribution, if only in the sequence of arguments and scope of terms used.

The fact that something was said, and not removed, also produces more counter-arguments than if the most polemical or obscure notes were simply removed over time. Such removals might have made the text more readable as a book; indeed, this is what Ibn al-Murtaḍā did with his *al-Baḥr al-zakhkhār*, and al-ʿAnsī did in *al-Tāj al-mudhhab*. The *Kitāb al-Azhār* is not a good example of this simplification, as it goes too far in simplification and abbreviation; rather it belongs to another genre, one in which the didactic qualities of the text are central, while books like *al-Baḥr al-zakhkhār* and *al-Tāj al-mudhhab* had different purposes.[61] They both strike a balance between including and excluding arguments depending on their relevance. Each genre has its own criteria of validity and its own rationale for that validity. The *Sharḥ al-azhār* that appeared after Ibn Miftāḥ is at the opposite end of the continuum, where the discussion of all the minute footnotes must be seen as a cumulative "research" corpus; every statement is included and never erased. The *Sharḥ al-azhār* is a place where these minute details of legal knowledge are "stored" in a structured way, as they relate to the topic. This seems to be a purpose itself for the activity and practice of *fiqh*, in addition to an outcome in the form of new rules; it keeps alive a knowledge tradition and makes sense of it. But to a significant degree this becomes self-referential and one needs institutional frameworks and education to make sense of it fully.

As for the legal positions on the three-year rule, most footnotes allow for some degree of leniency under favourable circumstances. It is the definition of these circumstances that is the problem: What exactly is "fear of confusion" and when does it happen? The discussion is circular in the sense that the

61 They are of course different and made for different purposes. *Al-Tāj al-mudhhab* is univocal and *al-Baḥr al-zakhkhār* is more a work of comparative *fiqh* that contains references to validity beyond Zaydī scholars and imams.

three-year rule is an attempt to provide Muslims, not to mention the *waqf*, with a clear legal solution since the definition of "confusion" and "interest" is unclear. The three-year rule is an alternative to a rule that is too general and vague to be a rule. At the same time, the rule is perceived too rigidly, and many scholars seem sceptical toward it. This is what we get if we look at all the arguments in the debate. As I show below, the picture becomes clearer, and more useful in a legal sense if we isolate only those views "validated by the *madhhab*."

3.7 *The Three-Year Rule in the* Taftīḥ

The *Taftīḥ al-qulūb*[62] by Muḥammad b. Bahrān (d. 957/1550) is a commentary on a commentary (*al-Athmār*) related to the *Kitāb al-Azhār*. The *Taftīḥ al-qulūb* was not published in the twentieth century, though it was clearly important as a *fiqh* work, just as the *Sharḥ al-azhār* was at the time it was written. The catalogue of the *waqf* library of the Jāmiʿ al-Kabīr in Sanaa shows that there were many manuscripts of this work.[63]

The section dealing with the three-year rule in the *Taftīḥ* summarizes the whole discussion in the *Sharḥ al-azhār* much more concisely than the *Sharḥ al-azhār* does itself. Around this time, the mid tenth/sixteenth century, many of the footnotes of the *Sharḥ al-azhār* had not yet been written.

The author of the *Taftīḥ* starts with the final arguments made in the footnotes of the *Sharḥ al-azhār*, namely it begins with the issue of what is in the interest of the *waqf*. If it is feared that confusion of the tenants' rights might eventually lead to their ownership of the asset, even if the period is less than three years, then the interest of the *waqf* is threatened. But if this fear is not present, or if another disadvantage is present only to a small extent and balanced by a stronger interest, then the lease is valid. "This is what can be concluded in this question" (*hādha huwa taḥqīq al-masʾala*), the author says. Then he goes on to say that this is a re-alignment (*ʿadl*) of what Ibn al-Murtaḍā said in the *Kitāb al-Azhār*, that is, it is an adjustment of the three-year rule:

> … [W]hat is understood [from Ibn al-Murtaḍā's text] is that it is always invalid to rent out the *waqf* three years and more and that it is always valid to rent it out less, and this is not so.[64]

62 The Muʾassasat al-Imām Zayd b. ʿAlī l-Thaqāfiyya kindly provided me with a Word file of the chapter of *waqf* of a forthcoming printed edition of the *Taftīḥ*.

63 Al-Ruqayḥī, al-Ḥibshī, and al-Ānisī, *Fihrist makhṭūṭāt*, 2:993–998; thirteen manuscripts are listed.

64 Liʾanna mafhūmahu annahu lā yaṣiḥḥu taʾjīr al-waqf thalāth sinīn fa-ṣāʿidan muṭlaqan, wa-yaṣiḥḥu dunahu muṭlaqan wa laysa ka-dhālik.

He goes on to say that what is meant (*al-murād*) is rather what al-Hādī said in the *Muntakhab* (this is quoted in the *Sharḥ al-azhār*), that it is valid to rent it out for a short period, such as a year or two, but not a long period, as that is reprehensible.[65] Then he adds the two additional rules without referring to whom they are ascribed; that the reprehensibility is removed if the *waqf* is well known and that the lease could be re-witnessed every three years.

In terms of content, there is not a lot of new material. But the sequence of arguments is much more clear than the post-Ibn Miftāḥ *Sharḥ al-azhār*. The *Taftīḥ* is an example of works similar to the *Sharḥ al-azhār*—works that the *Sharḥ al-azhār* "overtook" in popularity. Another example of such a work is *al-Bayān al-shāfī*, from almost the same time as the *Sharḥ al-azhār*, not consulted here.

3.8 *The Three-Year Rule in al-Shawkānī's* al-Sayl al-Jarrār

Al-Shawkānī's view of the three-year rule is found in *al-Sayl al-jarrār*,[66] a rule-by-rule commentary or critique of the *Kitāb al-Azhār*. The *al-Sayl al-jarrār* is structured in a "He said—I say" style with one answer for each rule. When al-Shawkānī states "He is saying": he is referring to the author of the *Kitāb al-Azhār*, Ibn al-Murtaḍā, but also implicitly to the wider Hādawī-Zaydī tradition of *fiqh*. Although explicitly he structures his criticism only around the *matn* of Ibn al-Murtaḍā, there is also a large corpus of *sharḥ* and commentaries for each of the rules he deals with. When he criticizes "the fear of confusion between *waqf* and private property" (see below) he does not directly criticize the *matn* of al-Murtaḍā, but rather the *sharḥ* of Ibn Miftāḥ (*Sharḥ al-azhār*) since Ibn al-Murtaḍā (*Kitāb al-Azhār*) does not mention this at all. The nature of the text is very different from the *Sharḥ al-azhār*. It is univocal and he criticizes a text and a whole legal tradition at the same time. And he does this with confidence and style:

> I say: there is no reason for this estimate [of exactly three years] and if interest is found in the continuation of the lease and in prolonging the period of the lease, then this is what must be done, and if the circumstances make it necessary to shorten the lease period for [the sake of] a recurring interest for the *waqf*, then so be it.[67]

65 Ibn Miftāḥ, *Sharḥ al-azhār* also quotes al-Hādī's view before adding the more lenient arguments; this is a way to *claim* adherence to Hādawī doctrine as the core of classical Yemeni Zaydism or Hādawī-Zaydism.

66 al-Shawkānī, *al-Sayl al-jarrār*, 3:70–71.

67 Ibid.

This section simply refers to "circumstances" (*iqtiḍāʾ al-ḥāl*) and "interest" (*maṣlaḥa*) just as many others have done before him, but he does not refer to any of these scholars. He continues:

> And when it comes to validating this time estimate,[68] just because of fear that the tenant will claim that the *waqf* is his property, what is more obscure than such a validation (*fa-mā abʿada hādha al-tajwīz*)?[69]

The last rhetorical question refers to the validation (*tajwīz*) of using "fear of a crime" as the source of a specific rule in the *sharīʿa*. Al-Shawkānī vehemently claimed that only texts from the Qurʾān and the Sunna can be taken as sources of law and he was reluctant to use *maṣlaḥa* (and sources like it) as primary sources of law.[70] He continues:

> And indeed, the *awqāf* assets are in general well known in the local communities (*tashtahiru*) and stand out (*taẓharu*), therefore they do not become confused with private property over time.[71]

When using the word *awqāf* in plural, he means the many individual *waqf* lands and assets and not the concept of *waqf*. What is very important here, and indeed quite novel in the whole debate, is his simple denial of the existence of the problem of confusion (*iltibās*) of what is private and what belongs to *waqf*; this is the very problem that Ibn Miftāḥ explicitly gives as the basis for the need for the three-year rule.[72]

---

68 Wa amma taʿlīl al-taqdīr bi-hādhihi l-mudda.

69 al-Shawkānī, *al-Sayl al-jarrār*, 3:70–71.

70 His position on *maṣlaḥa* as a source of law is discussed in chapter 4 and also partly in chapter 5. In essence, he argues against Zaydism for being based on "human" views, while arguing that it is necessary to take out the human sources and revert to the textual evidence from the Qurʾān and Sunna.

71 Fa-inna al-awqāf tashtahiru wa-taẓharu ḥaythu lā taltabisu bi-l-amlāk baʿda mudda ṭawīla.

72 For example, his contemporary Ḥanafī scholar Ibn ʿĀbidīn states the opposite, namely that this is the very argument against long-term leases. See Miriam Hoexter, "Adaptation to Changing Circumstances: Perpetual Leases and Exchange Transactions in Waqf Property in Ottoman Algiers," *Islamic Law and Society* 4, no. 3 (1997), 326. Ibn ʿĀbidīn's comment is made in the *matn*, under the section on the three-year rule. He gives views for and against the three-year rule, but concludes that the judge can prolong the lease if it is in the interest of the *waqf*. Ibn ʿĀbidīn, *Radd al-Mukhtār*, 4:400–401.

> And if this validation (*tajwīz*) is what came out of it, then he who is the administrator [of the *waqf*] can simply be given the same powers; let him just do what follows the interest of the *waqf*.[73]

By "validation" (*tajwīz*) he refers to the ascribing of validity to the three-year rule as a *sharīʿa* rule and the related three-year estimate. Al-Shawkānī says that if they can say all this with no clear evidence and produce a *sharīʿa* rule out of it by means of *maṣlaḥa*, then why not just say that the *mutawallī* is allowed to act in the interest of the *waqf*, without having all these other rules and footnotes in the first place? Al-Shawkānī's style is polemical; he uses metaphors like "What is more obscure than ...?," much in line with his literary style in general. As for the topic of the rule as such, he does not seem to be very interested in it and does not mention the topic in other works.

4 The Three-Year Rule in Modern Yemeni Codification

As mentioned in chapters 2 and 4, the distinction between *fiqh* and codification is a fluid one. Because of the univocal voice and lack of discussion in *al-Tāj al-mudhhab*, I place it under the section of "codification." In support of this choice is the fact that *al-Tāj al-mudhhab* was written so that judges and students of law could more easily refer to the body of rules of Zaydī *fiqh*. But, it is a work that is based solely on the "chosen rulings" from the *madhhab*, and the imamic decrees of Imam Yaḥyā are only given as footnotes, although they are the ones that must be followed in court. The political factors behind the codification of the *Sharḥ al-azhār* are unclear and *al-Tāj al-mudhhab* presents itself as representing "the jurist's law" in *fiqh* language. In any case, *al-Tāj al-mudhhab* is a borderline case between *fiqh* and codification.

4.1 *The View in* al-Tāj al-Mudhhab

Al-Tāj al-mudhhab was an attempt to simplify the reading and use of the *Sharḥ al-azhār* and was ordered by Imam Yaḥyā.[74] It is based on the *matn* of the *Kitāb al-Azhār* as a traditional *matn* and *sharḥ* combination; however, the chapters are organised slightly differently with a separation between *ʿibādāt* (worship) and *muʿāmalāt* (transactions), the *waqf* chapter being placed in the *muʿāmalāt*. References to persons and books are removed and only validated

---

73 Fa-in kāna hādha al-tajwīz mimmā yaḥṣul mithluhu li-(la-?)man ilayhi al-wilāya faʿala mā yaqtaḍīhu al-maṣlaḥa.

74 See general information about *al-Tāj al-mudhhab* in Haykel, *Revival and Reform*, 215–216.

views are included. The treatment of the three-year rule is an excellent summary and repetition of the above discussion, in that it removes views that are either not validated by the *madhhab* or irrelevant according to the author:

> **And** the sixth [rule] is that the *mutawallī* is entitled to **rent it out** for a defined period of **less than three years** because more than this causes confusion between *waqf* and private property (*milk*). If the *mutawallī* rents it out for more than three years, then this is invalid (*kāna dhālika maḥẓūran*) and his guardianship is invalidated and the lease becomes invalid, be the tenant a possessor of the usufruct or the *mutawallī*.[75]

Here we see that the author of *al-Tāj al-mudhhab* repeats the three-year rule and its related phrases from the *Sharḥ al-azhār*, and mainly in the more restrictive and "ideal" form. However, then he introduces a chain of conditions functioning as exceptions to the above rule, starting with "unless":

> … unless the *waqf* is well known or not feared to be confused with private property, or if the *mutawallī* or his assistant takes the rent as a certain fraction measured out from the yearly revenue in the name of the *waqf*, then there is no significant objection (*lā ba's*) to renting out the *waqf* for three years or more. The same applies if a long term lease is in the interest of the *waqf* such as in a potential increase in the rent, or restoration of what has deteriorated in the asset or improvement in [its] maintenance, then a three-year lease period, or more, is valid if there is at the same time no fear of confusion [between *waqf* and] private property and if, in the contract, it is emphasized that [there is] the possibility of a renewal of the witnessing of the contract (*al-ʿaqd*) every three years, [in which case] the lease is valid. It is not valid if the witnessing is renewed without this having been emphasized in the contract, because it [the contract] has become inactive (*inṭawat*) by the suspended status (*fasād*) due to the long lease period.

Although the picture of exceptions is complicated, the rule is much easier to read than reading through all the footnotes of the *Sharḥ al-azhār* and taking into consideration all the validation marks. Actually, here we see that the author of *al-Tāj al-mudhhab* is loyal to the validated views of the *madhhab*, just as it claims. The element of discussion and dialogue is, however, absent and what remains is only a univocal, normative text without references to the origins of

75 al-ʿAnsī, *al-Tāj al-mudhhab*, 324.

the validity. A reader must either accept the text as authoritative in its entity or reject it.

4.2 *The View of the Three-Year Rule in the* Taysīr

The three-year rule is noted in the *Taysīr* in the same section of the chapter of *waqf* as in the other works based on the *Sharḥ al-azhār*. It is very short:

> Section on the clarification of what the *mutawallī* is allowed to do and what [he] is not allowed and what is obligatory....
>
> [Article] 720 ... It is allowed for him to rent out the *waqf* [for a period of] less than three years, not more than that, so that it [the *waqf* asset] does not become confused with other [assets].[76]

After stating the rule itself, this work lists the reason for *the three-year lease rule*: "so that it ..." just like Ibn Miftāḥ did. In addition, it has been given its own article; this makes it something closer to the typical modern codified law. The rule is presented in a much stricter form here than in *al-Tāj al-mudhhab*. None of the exceptions to the rule or references to *maṣlaḥa* are given—this is an argument that the *Taysīr* could not have been used as a law book on its own.

4.3 *The Three-Year Lease Rule in the Decree of 1968*

The next time the three-year rule is mentioned in codification is in the Republican decree no. 26 of 1968 concerning the organisation and responsibilities of the ministry of *awqāf* and the regulations of its application:

> Article 5: The *waqf* committee (*lajnat shuʾūn al-awqāf*) is only responsible for:
>
> First: Requests for exchange of assets (*ibdāl wa-istibdāl*) ... and renting out assets (*aʿyān*) longer than three years. All this [can be done] without consulting the court (*al-rujūʿ ilā l-maḥkama*).
>
> Second: The termination of long-term leases (*inhāʾ al-iḥtikār*).
>
> Third: Changing the beneficiaries of the public *waqf*s and their stipulations (*taghyīr maṣārif al-awqāf al-khayriyya wa-shurūṭ idāratihā*).
>
> Fourth: Other issues in which the minister finds it necessary to consult the committee ...[77]

---

76 Faṣl fī bayān mā yajūzu li-l-mutawallī fiʿluhu wa-mā lā yajūzu wa-mā yajibu ... wa-yajūzu lahu taʾjīruhu dūna thalāth sinīn lā akthar min dhālika li-an-lā yaltabisa bi-ghayrihi. Qāsim b. Ibrāhīm, al-Ānisī, and al-Sarḥī, *Taysīr al-marām*, 152.

77 Manṣūr, *al-Mawkib*, 279.

Immediately after the civil war and the fall of the imamate the new government assumed the same powers as that of a *sharīʿa* judge in *waqf* matters. It gave itself the right to enter into long-term leases and to end individual long-term leases that had already been made by buying out tenants and their rights, as is implied in the term "dual lease" or *iḥtikār*. It also gave itself the power to change beneficiaries and thus redistribute *waqf* funds, for example, from rich mosques to poorer ones. Here the way the three-year rule is mentioned indicates that the ministry or rather, its *waqf* committee, is allowed to disregard it even though they are very aware it exists.

4.4 *The Three-Year Rule in the* Waqf *Law of 1976 and 1992*

Interestingly, the three-year rule is found in the first *waqf* law of 1976 and in the same wording in the present *waqf* law from 1992, which is still valid today.[78] It is also located under a section with an almost identical name as that of the corresponding section in *Sharḥ al-azhār*:

> "The third section: In what the *mutawallī* must do and what is allowed for him and what is not allowed …"
>
> Article 72: The *mutawallī* is not allowed to rent out the *waqf* asset or its properties for longer than three years, be it for ploughing [agriculture] or building. This does not prohibit the renewal of the lease in accordance with what is stated in the following article.
>
> Article 73: The *mutawallī* is not allowed to rent out the *waqf* asset or its properties for less than the rent of the time and place [i.e., the local market rental rate].[79]

Here we see that the present *waqf* law takes the wording of Ibn al-Murtaḍā in the *Kitāb al-Azhār* and keeps the three-year rule. By doing this, the law invokes the validity of the *Sharḥ al-azhār* and the tradition of Zaydī *fiqh*. The first sentence states that the three-year rule is to be the norm, full stop. Then comes the exception that points to the possibility of renewing the lease and refers to the next article, which is also an article of its own. The second article states that the rent should be according to rates in the (free) market.

---

78 Wizārat al-Shu'ūn al-Qānūniyya, *Qānūn al-waqf al-sharʿī*, 10–11. Articles 72–73 in the law of 1992, but articles 68–69 in the law of 1976. See also Manṣūr, *al-Mawkib*, 321–322.

79 Māddat 72: lā yajūzu li-l-mutawallī ta'jīr ʿayn al-waqf aw amlākihi li-akthar min thalāth sanawāt sawā'an kāna li-l-ḥirth aw li-l-binā'. Wa-lā tamna'u dhālika min tajdīd al-ijāra maʿa murāʿat mā huwa manṣūṣ ʿalayhi fī l-mādda al-tāliya. Māddat 73: lā yajūzu li-l-mutawallī ta'jīr ʿayn al-waqf aw amlākihi bi-aqall min ujrat al-mithl zamānan wa-makānan.

There are two law textbooks/commentaries used in the present-day faculty of *sharīʿa* and law that focus on matters of *waqf*. Of these two[80] only the one by al-Qirshī comments upon the article:

> Article 72: ... The explanation: The fixation of the period of three years is an *ijtihād* for the benefit of the interest of the *waqf*, and if not so, there is no text [from the revelation] imposing it. Implementing it is far easier with regard to what is rented out for agriculture than for buildings. However, the article does allow for the renewal of the lease regardless [of whether it is] for ploughing [i.e., agriculture] or building.[81]

This is what the student of modern *waqf* law learns. If they want to know more, they have to use the works mentioned previously in this chapter. Many students come from scholarly Zaydī families, but few are comfortable investigating the *fiqh* debates on their own. Al-Qirshī calls the three-year estimate an *ijtihād*. He does not state exactly why he uses the term *ijtihād*; it is likely that he is simply pointing out that the three-year rule is not part of any of the texts of revelation and that it is humanly "constructed" and therefore does not have absolute validity, in his view. The ease with which he invokes *ijtihād* is also somehow similar to the ease with which he and al-Waẓẓāf invoke *qiyās*, as treated in chapter 5 in this book.

4.5 *The Three-Year Rule in the Civil Code of 1979 and 2002*

The Civil Code was established in 1979 and revised in 2002; below I analyse the 2002 version. Much of the transactional law in Yemen is in the Civil Code. Rules related to gifts, charity, and inheritance fall under the Law of Personal Status, while *waqf* law is a law of its own. In the Civil Code, most chapters are found in *fiqh*, and in general, the Civil Code looks *sharʿī* in its form and language, though there are modern implants in the Civil Code, like "legal persons" and the "association" (*jamaʿiyya*).

The three-year rule is found in both the section on leases (*ʿaqd al-ijār*) and in the chapter of the revival of barren lands (*iḥyāʾ al-mawāt, taḥjīr*). I do not address the latter here. The section of leases contains a section called "Lease of *waqf*."[82] First, the mere presence of *waqf* leases in the Civil Code (from 1979)

80 Mijāllī's book has a more historical and social science perspective. He does mention the three-year rule briefly in connection with a case he led as a lawyer for the *awqāf* of Taʿizz against actors usurping a *waqf*, Mijallī, *al-Awqāf fī l-Yaman*, 83.

81 al-Qirshī, *al-Awqāf wa-l-waṣāyā*, 92.

82 *Qānūn al-Madanī* [2002], 112–113.

is somehow strange when most issues of *waqf* leases are regulated in the *waqf* law (from 1976). The explanation for this could be that lease of *waqf* is also mentioned in the chapter of leases in Zaydī *fiqh* books; however, the three-year rule is not specifically mentioned there. Another contributing factor could be the vagueness of the republican *waqf* law, which says relatively little about leases. Thus when the Civil Code was written in 1979, three years after the *waqf* law, issues of *waqf* lease were included because of the need for additional operational *waqf* lease rules.

The first article, Article 773, states that leases of *waqf* are to follow the rules of leases of other property (private property), except what is mentioned in following articles:

> Article 774 states that "the *mutawallī* must follow the stipulations of the founder."
>
> Article 775 states that "the *mutawallī* is not allowed to rent out [the *waqf*] for less than local market rent (*ujrat al-mithl*), and if he does so,[83] the contract is invalid, unless the founder has stipulated otherwise."
>
> Article 776 states that "the *mutawallī* must renew the contract every three years, and each time use the free market rent."
>
> The last four articles (777–780) deal with leases in which the tenant is allowed to own his own building situated on *waqf* land and if the tenant wishes to transfer this ownership to someone else, the *waqf* committee (*lajnat al-waqf*) must agree to it and the new tenant must acknowledge the rights of the *waqf*. These articles regulating the lease were more detailed than those in the *waqf* law, until the appendix to the *waqf* law came in 1996.

4.6 *Republican Decree No. 99 of 1996*

This decree is called "Regulations concerning organising proceedings for leases and the use of *waqf* properties and real estate and their investment." The three-year rule is mentioned in no fewer than three individual articles: Article 4:5, Article 44:2:1 and Article 61. Article 4:5 states:

> Part 3. The general proceedings and conditions, section 1, article 4, sub. 5. In accordance with the general rules mentioned in the civil law there are conditions for the writing of the [lease] contracts (*in'iqād*) and the

83 Here the language seems similar to that of Ḥanafī *waqf* leases, as in the expression *ghabn fāḥish* (criminal fraud) as in al-Zuḥaylī, *al-Fiqh al-Islāmī*, 7689. See also the quotation of Baber Johansen at the beginning of this chapter.

> validity of the lease or usufruct contract, as follows: (sub-section) 5: That the period of lease or use (*intifāʿ*) is defined by what does not exceed three years before renewal, in accordance with the rules of these regulations.[84]

The other two articles do not add any content, perhaps they even provide more room for exceptions. They are all similar to their "mother" article in the *waqf* law mentioned above, in that a renewal must take place every three years. I do not analyse them further here, but we can note that article 61 explicitly adds an exception, namely that "long term investments" are to be valid as long as the rent is updated to the free market rent (*bi-ḥasab al-makān wa-l-zamān*) every three years. This is the last time we see the three-year rule in the chronological presentation of Zaydī *fiqh* and Yemeni codification.

5 The Three-Year Rule in Other Law Schools and Legal Traditions

In the Zaydī legal debate about the three-year rule discussed above there are remarkably few references to other (non-Zaydī) law schools. This may be exceptional or coincidental for this specific rule, since in other rules in the *waqf* chapter, authorities from other law schools are often invoked and quoted. The three-year rule debate and the knowledge of its authority and validity is inherently Zaydī. However, the three-year rule is also found in other non-Zaydī corpuses of legal theory. Before moving on to the three-year rule in present-day leases and ethnographically observed practices, I present a brief overview of the three-year rule outside Zaydism. This places the Zaydī debate in its "Islamic" setting and illustrates various levels of interconnections.

The very same three-year rule seems to be present in Ḥanafī *fiqh*, but not in Shāfiʿī *fiqh*. That does not mean that such a comparison is straightforward; the trajectory of the three-year rule in the Ḥanafī school might be very different than that of the Zaydī debate and a similarly in depth study would be needed to make a proper comparison. Likewise, the absence of the three-year rule in Shāfiʿī *fiqh* does not mean that the problem of long-term leases is not treated by Shāfiʿīs. It is beyond the scope of this chapter to investigate this in depth, however a few notes serve to illuminate our previous review of the Zaydī debate. The Syrian scholar al-Zuḥaylī (b. 1932) has written a well-known work of comparative *fiqh* called *al-Fiqh al-Islāmī wa-adillatuhu*. In this work there is a *waqf* chapter with a sub-chapter called "long-term leases."[85] This chapter is a

84 Wizārat al-Shu'ūn al-Qānūniyya, *Qānūn al-waqf al-sharʿī*, 18.

85 al-Zuḥaylī, *al-Fiqh al-Islāmī*, 7688–7692.

starting point from which we can briefly review the positions of the different Sunnī law schools.

5.1 *The Ḥanafī View According to al-Zuḥaylī*

Al-Zuḥaylī states that the Ḥanafīs uphold (*yuftā ʿindahum*) the rule that the maximum lease period for a *waqf* house is one year, and for agricultural *waqf* lands three years, as long as there is no interest for the *waqf* contrary to this time period, according to time and place. He uses terms as *maṣlaḥa, iḍṭirār, ḥāja, ḍarūra*; all of these have similar meanings, that the rule is not absolute, but open to leniency if interest or utility for the *waqf* can be identified. If there is no such interest that allows for the transgression of the rule, the rule is valid and must be followed. He quotes a *fatwā* collection called *al-Fatāwa al-Bazzāziyya*,[86] which quotes the one-year rule for leases of houses and the three-year rule for land and which includes a *fatwā* that further specifies that a lease contract can be worded to state that "I rent to you this house for one year for such an amount, and the year after for such an amount, and the next year such" etc., all in one cumulative contract that technically consists of several subsequently combined contracts. In such a contract, only the first contract would be valid in a strict sense; the subsequent contracts are valid by consensus (here, *riwāya*) of the Ḥanafī law school. Furthermore, the rent is defined as "property" and therefore can be taken in advance or promptly (*muʿajjalan*).[87]

The issue of dual *waqf* rent, immediate and deferred, also called *ijāratayn* or *ḥikr*, is an important part of Ḥanafī *waqf* lease law and practices;[88] a parallel can be seen in modern urban *waqf* leases in Yemen, as I show below. Al-Zuḥaylī continues by noting that if the free market rent or fair rent (*ujrat al-mithl*) increases over the rent stated in the contract, then the contract must be renewed. Here he quotes Ibn ʿĀbidīn, who states that if the tenant accepts the rise in the rent, no new contract is needed. If the *mutawallī* rents out the *waqf* for a rent below the free market rent, he himself is responsible for the difference.[89]

86 This probably refers to the work also called *al-Jāmiʿ al-wajīz* by Muḥammad b. Muḥammad al-Bazzāz (d. 827/1424).

87 al-Zuḥaylī, *al-Fiqh al-Islāmī*, 7689–7690. Van Leeuwen notes that al-Ramlī was against such subsequent contracts and similar devices to create long leases. Van Leeuwen, *Waqfs and Urban Structures*, 56.

88 Miriam Hoexter writes about perpetual leases (*ʿinā'* and *ḥikr*), but she does not mention the three-year rule. Hoexter, "Adaptation to Changing Circumstances." See also Baber Johansen, chapter 2: "The Contract of Tenancy (Ijāra): The Commodification of the Productive Use of Land," and the section in chapter 7: "The 'Contractually Fixed Rent' and the 'Fair Rent': The Special Status of *Waqf* and Big Estates" in Johansen, *The Islamic Law on Land Tax and Rent*, 33–34.

89 al-Zuḥaylī, *al-Fiqh al-Islāmī*, 7690.

5.2 *Egypt: Qadrī Pasha's* Waqf *Law*

Qadrī Pasha (d. 1888) of Egypt wrote the *waqf* law called *Kitāb Qānūn al-ʿadl wa-l-insāf li-l-qaḍā ʿalā mushkilāt al-awqāf*, which states:

> Section four: In clarification of what is allowed for the *nāẓir* of transactions and what is not allowed....
>
> Article 180 ... It is permissible for the agricultural lease period [to be] longer than three years if that is better and in the interest of the *waqf*.[90]

This is a very clear example of early *waqf* codification. The comparison to *al-Tāj al-mudhhab* and the *Taysīr* is apt; the *fiqh* has been reduced to coherent univocal statements, stripped of references of authority. Even though the rule is now an "article," vague traces from the *fiqh* remain in the title of the "Section" which can also be recognized as a section in the Zaydī *Sharḥ al-azhār waqf* chapter. We can say that the very mention of the three years is itself a reference to the *fiqh*, while the article itself simply identifies the "interest" of the *waqf* as the solution of the problem.

5.3 *Abū Zahra's Comment*

The well-known Egyptian legal scholar Muḥammad Abū Zahra (1898–1974) wrote a book called *Muḥāḍarāt fī l-waqf*. In this book he quotes, without references, Ibn ʿĀbidīn, who allows the tenant to invest in and build new structures on *waqf* land if it is in the interest of the *waqf*. After three years, the ownership of these things passes to the tenant (presumably according to the *taḥjīr* rule or some derivative of it).[91] Otherwise, he does not mention the topic of long-term leases. After all, the *ḥikr* or *ijāratayn* was a firmly established practice in Egypt.[92]

5.4 *The Three-Year Rule in Contemporary Egypt*

In a book called *Mawsūʿat al-awqāf: Tashrīʿāt qaḍāʾ—iftāʾ: Fatāwa al-awqāf mundhu 1890 ḥattā 1997*, we find a *fatwā* from 1 July 1981 that centres on the issue of authority in long-term leases. The *fatwā* reviews different legal authorities,

---

90 ... wa-lā baʾs min an takūna muddat al-muẓāraʿa akthar min thalāth sinīn in kāna dhālika anfaʿ wa-aṣlaḥ li-l-waqf. Qadrī Pasha, *Kitāb Qānūn al-ʿadl wa-l-inṣāf li-l-qaḍā ʿalā mushkilāt al-awqāf* (Maṭbaʿat al-Kubrā l-Amīriyya bi-Bulāq Miṣr al-Maḥmīya, 1906), 54–55.

91 Abū Zahra, *Muḥāḍarāt fī l-waqf*, 111.

92 Here one could also mention the work of Shalabī, *Aḥkām al-waṣāyā*, where the author does not mention these problems related to leases.

among them the Egyptian Civil Code. In the Egyptian Civil Code, the three-year rule is mentioned:

> Civil Code, article 633 section (1): It is not allowed for the *mutawallī*, without the permission of a judge, to rent out the *waqf* for a period longer than three years, even by subsequent contracts; if the lease is contracted for a period of more [than three years], then the contract is only binding for three years.[93]

The *fatwā* is an edited, anonymized *fatwā* in modern legal language. In addition to the above reference to the Civil Code it further claims that in these matters the authority of the judge has been transferred to the authority of the undersecretary (*wukalāʾ*) of the ministry of *awqāf*, and that this specific restriction does not apply if the ministry acts as the *mutawallī* (here, *nāẓir*). In this, the *muftī* refers to two laws specifying the authority of the ministry and its subsections.[94] Thus the *fatwā* invokes the three-year rule by referring to the Civil Code simply as a way of proving its own validity and relation to Egyptian law and *fiqh*. In fact, it states that the ministry is a *mutawallī* with the powers of a judge, thus free to base its actions on the "interest" of the *waqf* and thus it does not have to follow the three-year rule.

It is not a coincidence that in Egypt the three-year rule falls under the Civil Code and does not appear in the body of *waqf* laws. This probably has its origin in the structure of Ḥanafī *fiqh*. A quick look at the *Hidāya sharḥ bidāya al-mubtadī* by ʿAlī b. Abī Bakr al-Marghīnānī (the English translation by Charles Hamilton) reveals a short reference to the three-year rule in the "Book of Hire" concerning long-term *waqf* leases.[95]

93 Al-mādda 633 min al-taqnīn al-madanī, Fiqrat 1. "Lā yajūz li-l-nāẓir bi-ghayr idhn al-qāḍī an yuʾajjira al-waqf mudda tazīdu ʿan thalāth sanawāt wa-law kānat dhālika bi ʿuqūd mutarādifa, fa-idhā ʿuqidat al-ijāra li-mudda aṭwal inqaḍat al-mudda ilā thalāth sanawāt. Amīn Ḥasan Aḥmad and ʿAbd al-Hādī Fatḥī, *Mawsūʿat al-awqāf: Tashrīʿāt qaḍāʾ—iftāʾ: Fatāwa al-awqāf mundhu 1890 ḥatta 1997* (Alexandria: Manshāt al-Maʿārif, 2003), 353–356.

94 Ibid., 355.

95 The three-year rule is mentioned very early in the first section (chapter) of the Book of Hire. "It is to be observed that the expression of our author 'for whatever term' denotes that hire is valid, whether it be for a long or a short term, as the term is ascertained, and men, moreover, frequently require a long term. If, however, the Mootwalee [procurator] of a charitable appropriation let out the appropriated article, the hire of it for any long term is made unlawful, lest the lessee might be enabled to advance a claim of right to it. Hire for a long term signifies for any term beyond three years. This is approved." Charles Hamilton, *The Hedaya, or Guide: A Commentary on the Mussulman Laws* (Lahore: Premier Book House, 1963), 490.

5.5 *The Mālikī View According to al-Zuḥaylī*

In the Mālikī legal tradition, there is a maximum rule of "a year or two" in *waqfs* for specific persons and up to four years for public *waqfs* (i.e., for the poor and mosques, *'alā fuqarā' wa-l-masājid*). If there is a necessity (*ḍarūra*) and the *waqf* is in need of repair, the *waqf* can be rented out for forty or fifty years, but not more.[96]

All these Mālikī time periods are interesting for the Zaydī debate since most are mentioned in the Zaydī debate as well, although without reference to their origins. Al-Hādī used the "one or two year" period and Imam Yaḥyā b. Ḥamza used the fifty-year period. Much of al-Hādī's *fiqh* is taken from his grandfather al-Qāsim b. Ibrāhīm al-Rassī (d. 246/860), who grew up in, and lived near, Medina. He was a scholar there and in Cairo and also taught Medinan *ḥadīths*.[97] The link between the Zaydī and the Mālikī time periods could be better established by further studies. In this, the anthropological/praxiological study object ceases and the absolutely historical one takes over, as Zaydī texts commonly read by informants today do not direct readers to references farther back than al-Hādī and Yaḥyā b. Ḥamza, at least on this matter. The chains of references, and thereby the construction of validity and authority at the time of Ibn al-Murtaḍā and Ibn Miftāḥ do not extend beyond merely quoting these previous imams.

5.6 *Shāfiʿī* Waqf *Leases According to al-Zuḥaylī*

For the Shāfiʿīs, al-Zuḥaylī only quotes the *Mughnī l-muḥtāj*; however, the quotations are not direct, rather they are restatements in his own words and are self-contradictory. Al-Zuḥaylī's first statement is that it is absolutely (*qiṭʿan*) not valid to rent out a *waqf* asset for less than market price. The second view he notes seems to be quotation from al-Nawawī's *Minhāj al-ṭālibīn*, which states that the lease contract is not invalidated (i.e., it is valid) if the rise in market price happens after the contract is made or if a higher bid is made.[98] It is not strange for a theoretical legal debate to contradict itself, on the contrary, it is the nature of such "academic" dialogue. The problem for the commentator, in this case al-Zuḥaylī, arises when he wishes to concisely restate the Shāfiʿī view. The result is two sentences, one of which contradicts the other.

96 al-Zuḥaylī, *al-Fiqh al-Islāmī*, 7690–7691.
97 Madelung, "al-Rassī."
98 al-Zuḥaylī, *al-Fiqh al-Islāmī*, 7691.

5.7 *Shāfiʿī Leases as Mentioned in the* Mughnī l-Muḥtāj *and the* Tuḥfat al-Muḥtāj

This self-contradiction is elaborated upon in the *Mughnī l-muḥtāj*[99] and can be seen in almost the same language, structure, and references in the *Tuḥfat al-muḥtāj*.[100] These two commentaries are very similar in form, as compared to the *Sharḥ al-azhār*, but they quote other authorities. Shāfiʿī *fiqh* has not been an important part of this study, and only a few scholarly Shāfiʿī informants were consulted. Of the *fiqh* compilations, the most famous and the one most relied upon in Yemen is the *mukhtaṣar* called *Minhāj al-ṭālibīn* by al-Nawawī[101] (d. 676/1277). The *Minhāj* is organized differently than the *Kitāb al-Azhār*, but there are many similarities in the way it was used, as an introductory book in *fiqh* for *sharīʿa* students and also for different levels of study depending on the level of the *sharḥ* that is studied along with it. The *Minhāj* has a *waqf* chapter in which lease issues are mentioned in more than one place. In the *matn*, there is no reference to the three-year rule. To be more precise, there are several places in the *matn* where lease issues are mentioned, however the single most important place for us is at the end of the *waqf* chapter:

> If the administrator (*al-nāẓir*) rents out [the *waqf* asset] and the market price rises during the lease period, or if someone gives a higher bid, the most correct view (*al-aṣaḥḥ*) is that the lease contract is not invalidated.[102]

This is al-Nawawī's *matn*. In al-Shirbīnī's (d. 977/1570) *sharḥ*, *Mughnī l-muḥtāj*, al-Shirbīnī splits up the *matn*, adds more words, and starts a fairly long comment on this rule.[103] Al-Shirbīnī quotes a *fatwā* by a certain Ibn Ṣalāḥ who states that such a lease can be valid only if the market price remains stable. If it does not remain stable, the contract cannot be binding into the future since the future is unknown (and contracts cannot contain unknown elements).

A certain al-Adhriʿī states that "this is a highly complicated question" (*mushakkal jiddan*) and that if the intention of the original contract was the market price, then this must be followed. "The world is in constant change," he states, in regard to the problem of setting up the ideal lease for the *waqf*. And

99 al-Shirbīnī, *Mughnī l-muḥtāj*.

100 Ibn Ḥajar, *Tuḥfat al-muḥtāj*.

101 Muḥyī l-Dīn Abū Zakariyya Yaḥyā b. Sharaf al-Nawawī (d. 676/1277).

102 Wa idhā ajjara al-nāẓir fa-zādat al-ujra fī l-mudda aw ẓahara ṭālib bi-ziyāda lam yanfasikhu al-ʿaqd fī l-aṣaḥḥ. al-Shirbīnī, *Mughnī l-muḥtāj*, 2:507.

103 Ibid., 2:507–509.

as for the legal problem as such, he adds, "and in this [matter], the discussion is long."[104]

A very similar comment, quoting mostly the same sources, is made by Ibn Ḥajar in his *Tuḥfat al-muḥtāj*. The *Tuḥfa*[105] uses the same two quotations as the *Mughnī* does, but the author adds that even if a Shāfiʿī judge makes a ruling that such a lease contract is valid, that is, into the future, despite an increase in the free rent or despite the death of one of the parties, then such a ruling is invalid and no judge can say that such a contract would be valid into the future, since no judgement can be built on something that has not yet happened.[106] In other words, unless the founder wishes otherwise, the lease contract is invalidated if the rent is not kept up according to market rental rates. These Shāfiʿī references show that the legal debate is situated in its own context, and while it refers to different rules and authorities, at least compared to the Zaydī debate, there are also strong similarities between the various *fiqh* debates in structure, language, and content. How the lease issues have been codified or used in practice by judges in the Shāfiʿī areas of Yemen is another matter.

5.8 *Ḥanbalī* Waqf *Leases According to al-Zuḥaylī*

Al-Zuḥaylī's section on the Ḥanbalīs is brief and mainly states that the *mutawallī* is responsible for obtaining the full market rent.[107]

5.9 *The Trajectory of the Three-Year Rule in* Fiqh

A review of the trajectory of the three-year rule in this chapter demonstrates how the corpus of *fiqh* knowledge is represented by individual rules, strings of rules, necessary commentaries, texts, and debates that span centuries, which later actors must somehow relate to. As a legal problem, the three-year rule is only one aspect of many related problems of *waqf* leases. Questions related to leases of *waqf* are found in other parts of the chapters of *waqf* and also in other chapters of *fiqh* books, sometimes under the chapter of leases, the chapter of sharecropping, the chapter of agricultural revival and demarcation (*taḥjīr*), and so on. The configurations of the debate in the various law schools vary and the Zaydī debate is a distinct one.

In this historical presentation, the texts were chosen according to both the intertextual references and their relevance for informants today, as they

104 Ibid., 2:508. Ibn Ḥajar, *Tuḥfat al-muḥtāj*.
105 An unpaginated downloadable file was used, but the structure follows al-Nawawī's *mukhtaṣar*.
106 Ibn Ḥajar, *Tuḥfat al-muḥtāj*.
107 al-Zuḥaylī, *al-Fiqh al-Islāmī*, 6791–6792.

explained which books and sources are authoritative in Zaydī *fiqh* in general. Few informants today know the genealogy of this specific rule and in this aspect the focus of this chapter on one single rule may seem obscure. However, at the same time, the scholarly informants do relate to the scope and sequence of sources quoted in this chapter and for any rule they wish to discuss or study in depth, they must somehow apply a similar method, that is, they must trace the roots of legitimacy and validity back, to try to find the original sources in order to find the best possible evidence, according to their needs. And in most cases, the chains of references do not need to stretch back to reach an ultimate, absolutely clear source. On the contrary, in most debates they stop in the middle of certain frames or criteria of validity, which, it seems, the reader is expected to simply accept. Presumably, there is no need for a link that goes further back, as readers have confidence that the authorities have the correct view. The three-year rule is, as mentioned by many, an interesting tool that is useful for restricting the rights of the tenant. The problem is that as a rule, it has mainly been used in a way that is contrary to what it was explicitly intended for, namely to legitimize longer leases and continuous, perpetual renewals as in "yes, the three-year rule is the norm, which we of course adhere to as Muslims and Zaydīs, but…." In the following part of this chapter, I show how leases are undertaken in practice and how the law responds to actual situations.

6 *Waqf* Lease in Practice

The main focus of this chapter has been on the trajectory of the three-year rule in *fiqh* and codification, both "forward," as a historical and chronological genealogical trajectory, but also "backward," as a *faqīh* would conceptualize the roots of validity in older texts. The following part of this chapter does not deal specifically with the three-year rule, since it hardly exists outside the field of *fiqh* and codification. Rather, it focuses on some wider issues related to *waqf* leases at the level of the judge and administrator and in everyday *waqf* knowledge. In these fields of knowledge, we rarely see the three-year rule at all; rather we find different norms related to leases. The comparison between the validity of these norms at the local level and the validity of the three-year rule at the *fiqh* level is problematic because of the significant differences in context; however, as we see, the wording of the three-year rule can still be found in a few cases, and the problem it is supposed to address certainly also continued to arise.

Two important distinctions are "before" vs. "now," and "rural, agricultural leases" vs. "leases of urban plots and assets." These two distinctions overlap in part, since agricultural leases are still executed in the traditional way, while the lease of urban land is a somewhat new phenomenon that has emerged after the revolution. (Leases of urban buildings, such as shops in the market area, also existed before the revolution, but this type of lease is not treated below).[108] Another important way of categorizing leases is to separate leases undertaken by *waqfs* that for various reasons are kept out of reach of the public administration from those leases undertaken by the ministry of *awqāf*. The former tend to be called *waṣāyā*. This section focuses on public *waqfs*, but leases in private *waqfs* also deserve some mention.

In smaller family *waqfs* and in the *waṣāyā* type, leases are often not necessary, as the *mutawallī*, the tenants, and the beneficiaries are part of the same family. They have the right to the surplus of the *waqf* land and they till the *waqf* land. It is only when disagreements arise—over the flow of cash (or grain), or the transfer of shares from one generation to the next—that some family members may complain to the judge. Since family *waqfs* are difficult to defend under the present law (since Imam Yaḥyā), most *waqfs* of this type have been privatized. Many of these *waqfs* survived because of a public, charitable component, such as a small mosque or a cistern in addition to the family *waqf* (we return to this issue in chapter 7), and because many of these *waqfs* were not registered.

The larger family *waqfs*, some of which still exist, rent out their land according to methods and rules that follow local custom. Because there have been many changes in agricultural lease practices and sharecropping practices since the revolution, it is difficult to give a comprehensive description of this here. In brief, the *mutawallī* for the *waqf* is usually an important person in the clan or the extended family, and the power over the family assets and the salary he takes often re-affirm his position in the family. Many of the larger, *sayyid*, *qāḍī*, and shaykh families still have such family *waqfs*, and I have met several members of such families who receive cash or bags of agricultural produce from their lands in the countryside. These families often have family networks that cover large areas; their lands are typically in their main "home" areas, or in politically "docile," non-tribal areas in the Tihāma and western mountains where peasants farm their land. Almost nothing is known of the extent of this type of *waqf*. Even if these *waqfs* have been privatized, they still "need" an administrator. Here the definition of *waqf* is not crucial, rather it is the phenomenon of the family estate.[109] Messick also points out that the powerful families and

108 For leases of shops in the market area of Sanaa, see Dostal, *Der Markt von Ṣanʿāʾ*.

109 Dresch uses the term "collective holding." For instance, he refers to the large landholdings of the al-Aḥmar family. See Dresch, *Tribes, Government, and History in Yemen*, 211.

landowners are able to own lands far away, in contrast to smaller landowners who usually only own land near their villages.[110]

The *waqfs* administered by the public authorities are rented out through the administrative system of the *awqāf*. As mentioned in chapter 3, this system has changed somewhat, especially during the time of Imam Yaḥyā and today it is dominated by the ministry of *awqāf*. Other types of *waqf* are included under the heading of "public" *waqfs*, such as the *waqfs* for saint's tombs (*turab*), Islamic schools, and the many *waqfs* of the *waṣāyā* category that were entered into the government *awqāf* more or less by force in various regions and stages.[111] All these form "clusters" of *waqf* administration in which the Imam formerly, today the ministry of *awqāf*, is either the direct *mutawallī*, or in any case the inspector (*nāẓir*) with the power of a *sharīʿa* judge.

6.1 *Traditional Agricultural Leases*

A description of the traditional agricultural *waqf* leases is important since, in terms of the number of assets and physical areas rented out, this is still the most important lease activity for the ministry today. In general, these practices seem to have changed relatively little from the period before the revolution until today. The importance of *waqfs* varies greatly from area to area. The most fertile areas could, and still can, have several local *waqf* representatives, the so-called *ʿāmil al-waqf* (pl. *ʿāmilīn* or *ʿummāl*). In times of political order, these representatives answered, in turn, to a higher *nāẓir* either on the state or the regional level. Only in Ibb, Taʿizz, and Zabid do we know that Imam Aḥmad created local a *waqf* office (Maktabat al-awqāf). Until today, the ongoing reform has been to create a *mudīr waqf* in every district (*mudīriyya*), but this does not seem to have been fully implemented yet.[112]

There are two distinct ways of defining the rent, either according to a fixed yearly price, or according to a fraction of the yearly harvest. The first is less common and is often called *ḍamān*.[113] The latter is "sharecropping" and can have different names—a general term is *mushāraka*, or *al-sharika al-ʿurfiyya*. Both these types of leases are found in both private land leases and in *waqf* leases. At the level of the ideal *fiqh*, the *mushāraka* is illegal, since it is not

110 Messick, "Transactions in Ibb," 153–154.

111 See, for instance, the ordering of the state *waqf* administration during Imam Aḥmad in Hovden, "Flowers in *Fiqh*," appendix 2; and the registration of a public *waqf* in ibid., appendix 3.

112 For a fuller account, see chapter 3 and the references to Manṣūr, *al-Mawkib*, Messick, "Transactions in Ibb," and al-Farrān, *Athar al-waqf*.

113 For a reference to the use of this term, see Messick, "Transactions in Ibb," 150. He also points out that *ḍamān* was more common in leases of land in irrigation schemes.

only unlimited in time, but also contains an element of gambling, as the future yearly harvest cannot be known and thus the absolute rent itself is not known. Still, in Zaydī law schools the consensus is that most forms of *mushāraka* are legally valid.[114]

As for the fixed price leases (*ḍamān*), compared to the *mushāraka* these are more vulnerable to changes in the rate of market rents. This was also pointed out by the jurists in the footnotes of the *Sharḥ al-azhār* earlier in this chapter. In chapter 3 we saw that Aḥmad Qāṭin (d. 1199/1785) wrote about lease practices in Lower Yemen and quoted al-Qāḍī ʿAbd al-Jabbār (d. 1184/1771), who stated that the *waqf* income was called *ḍarāʾib* and that the rent was fixed independently of the harvest.[115] Even though the proper way of collecting the rent would be by *mushāraka*, in periods of weak centralized *waqf* administration the fixed rent would be easier to take. The practice of *mushāraka* is dependent on an assessment of the harvest; this is done by an individual hired by the *waqf*. The assessor must set the rent just before the harvest itself, otherwise, the tenant could manipulate the size of the rent if the *ʿāmil* is not present at the time of harvest.

We know that Imam Yaḥyā dispatched "assessors" to estimate the size of the harvest in two parallel systems, one for *waqf* income and one for *zakāt*.[116] The assessments around Sanaa were called *ṭuwwāf* or *ṭiyāfa*; the term *kharṣ* and *khurrāṣ* were also common. The *ʿāmil*s also had to send a yearly accountancy to Sanaa for approval. In Imam Aḥmad's time, this system seems to have disintegrated and *zakāt* was collected according to a fixed sum based on the amount of land. After the revolution, under al-Ḥamdī's presidency this was left to "trust" (*amāna*)—farmers were trusted to pay the correct amount voluntarily.[117] I was not able to establish to what extent, and in which areas the harvest assessment is still carried out. If assessors were not used to estimate *waqf* rent, then the previous years of accountancy could still be used to establish an average rent for a specific agricultural field and a minimum, basic *waqf* lease administration would keep record of the names of the individual agricultural fields and the average capacity of the field in terms of production of grains (these were usually measured in numbers of *qadaḥ*[118] of sorghum (*dhurra*)).

Until today, many *waqf* inventory registers (*miswaddāt al-aʿyān*) only state the name of the agricultural field and its average "capacity." Then, if the

114 For Zaydī debates over the legality of *mushāraka* in Yemen, see Donaldson, *Sharecropping in the Yemen*, 93–124.
115 Zabāra, *Nashr al-ʿarf*, 2:235–237.
116 This is also indicated in Messick, "Transactions in Ibb," 173–174.
117 See ibid., 172.
118 Approximately 41 litres. See Donaldson, *Sharecropping in the Yemen*, 141.

mushāraka could be used and the harvest assessed, other registers would keep track of each individual tenant and his payments for each year (*miswaddāt al-ajāʾir*).[119] This would be an administrative register for accounting, while the former, the inventory registers (*miswaddāt al-aʿyān*), were extremely valuable meta-ownership documents of the *awqāf* to be safeguarded in times of war or chaos so that they could be claimed when peace and order return. The primary importance was to keep records of the assets and in this way safeguard them, the secondary was to extract the highest possible income from them.[120]

The *mushāraka* type of lease is the most common form of private agricultural lease. Thus knowledge of a *mushāraka* is common among all individuals dealing with land in one way or another. Any local notary could write a *mushāraka* lease contract. The *waqf mushāraka* leases are unique, compared to private *mushāraka* leases, because the rent tends to be well below market rental rates, that is, the fraction given to the "landlord" is lower. In private leases, the rent, or fraction of the harvest, depends on access to irrigation water, the type of crop, whether or not the tenant or the landlord must pay the *zakāt*, who is responsible for maintenance, etc. *Mushāraka* fractions range from four-fifths of the harvest to less than one-tenth paid as rent to the landlord. These estimates, and the wide range they cover, are not important here. In a typical *mushāraka* lease on rain-fed sorghum land, where the tenant has a right to remain a tenant corresponding to a certain deposit or "entrance fee" (*ʿināʾ*), it is usually the tenant who pays the *zakāt* and takes care of the maintenance and his part of the harvest would commonly be one-half to three-quarters, that is, the rent paid to the landlord would be one-half or one-quarter.[121] In a field survey from the 1990s Donaldson found that the rent paid to *waqf* was often significantly lower than rent paid to private landowners. Informants told him "*waqf* trustees are more generous landlords than are private individuals."[122] One can imagine that if the tenant only has to pay one-sixth, and the local free rent is, say one-quarter (free rent, fair rent, *ujrat al-mithl, urjat al-makān wa-l-zamān*), then the difference between the two goes into the pocket of the tenant and thus represents a valuable yearly income. The right to remain a tenant can become lucrative, that is, if the leases are continuous and not terminated by a three-year rule and corrected to reflect the market price. The right to remain a

119 A *miswaddat ajāʾir ʿaraṣāt* in 1918 is mentioned in Serjeant and Lewcock, *Ṣanʿāʾ*, 429.

120 Personal communication with ʿAlī Muḥammad al-Farrān, a high ranking employee in the ministry of *awqāf* and author of *Athar al-waqf*.

121 Donaldson, *Sharecropping in the Yemen*, 142–144.

122 For a detailed study of the size of the sharecropping fraction, see ibid., 159. See also 59–61. He points out that the data is not built on a large survey, rather it is mainly from the highlands.

tenant is called *ḥaqq al-yad* or *al-ʿināʾ*[123] (for buildings, it is often called *ḥaqq al-miftāḥ*). Whether or not this right is something that can be bought and sold is a fairly theoretical legal problem, however, in practical terms and in practice-oriented *fiqh*, this is allowed and in any case circumvented by simply using other terms. Further, it was also explicitly allowed in *waqf* leases, as shown in the *fatwā* of al-Shijnī, which is analysed in chapter 7. In that *fatwā* the term "*naql al-yad*" is used for the sale of this right. Thus, in practice the tenancy could be "inherited," "bought," and "sold," but not with those words.

In the early 1950s, there was a great deal of chaos in the administration of the Zabid *waqfs*. *Waqfs* were rented out for indefinite periods with strong tenant rights attached to them. Imam Aḥmad ordered the *kawāʾin* type of *waqf* to be rented out for one-quarter of the harvest and further, to end the right of *ʿināʾ* altogether. Furthermore, he ordered that leases should be for a maximum of three years. The order was enforced and many farmers went to prison when they protested.[124] In 1957, Imam Aḥmad had to give up the implementation of this order after many complaints and problems, and he again allowed sale of the *ʿināʾ* and also returned to the custom of charging the tenants one-fifth of the harvest instead of one-quarter.[125]

It is important to ask, how valuable was this *ʿināʾ* right? If the *mutawallī* wanted to remove the tenant, how much would he have to pay the tenant? And if someone wanted to take over a tenancy, how much would he have to pay the landlord? This would depend on the difference between the agreed rent and the local free market rent. The size of the rent is balanced against the size of the *ʿināʾ*. A more exact answer is likely related to local geographical and historical context, but this is a matter that could not be followed more closely here. The distinction between private *waqfs* and "pure" public *waqfs* is extremely important here.

In a public *waqf* one would expect that the *ʿināʾ* would be minimal, but this does not seem to have been so simple. In al-Shijnī's *fatwā* cited in chapter 7, he

---

123 See, for instance, the treatise *Kitāb al-ʿInāʾ* mentioned in Anne Regourd, *Catalogue cumulé des manuscrits de bibliotèques de ʿAbd al-Rahman al-Hadrami*, fasc. 1: Zabid manuscript catalogue (Sanaa: Centre Français d'Archéologie et de Sciences Sociales (CEFAS)/SFD, 2006). This work is also listed in al-Ruqayḥī, al-Ḥibshī, and al-Ānisī, *Fihrist makhṭūṭāt*. "Bayʿ al-ʿināʾ" is a legal work mentioned in al-Ḥaḍramī, *Zabīd*, 252. It is probably the same work. The author was "an Egyptian scholar" Ibn Sirāj, who concluded that if the tenant invested in the improvement of the land, then this investment may constitute a sale (and thus private property of the tenant). Al-Ḥaḍramī adds that this became practise in Zabid, but the land could not be "sold," and the term "transfer" (*naql*) was used instead.

124 al-Ḥaḍramī, *Zabīd*, 255.

125 Ibid., 256–257.

explicitly claims that this right also exists in "pure" *waqf* (*al-waqf al-khāliṣ*).[126] The modern *waqf* law on the other hand is ambiguous in this question since article 73, as quoted above, states that leases must be according to free market rents, while in several other articles, it also allows for the *ʿināʾ* or *ḥaqq al-yad* wherever this "already exists." It also refers to something called "pure" *waqf* (*al-waqf al-ṣāfī*) whenever no *ʿināʾ* exists. The *waqf* law further states that the *ʿināʾ* can also be transferred to the following generations: Article 38 in the Regulation of Leases of 1996 states that "if a tenant dies, his heirs are not allowed to take over and share his "rented *awqāf*," unless "they need it," "by necessity of livelihood" (*maʿāyishatan*). This is the case as long as he obtains a permit by the local *mutawallī*[127] and other conditions are fulfilled, namely that no harm is done to the *waqf*, and it is "in accordance with the wishes of the founder," and the new tenants confirm that they will follow the same rules.[128] Article 38 thus opens the possibility of "inheriting" public *waqf* tenancy. The sentence "in accordance with the wish of the founder," clearly aims at the *waṣīya* type as discussed in chapter 7, yet the article as such also targets public *waqfs*.

In the sub-chapter concerning *waqf* in Serjeant's book on Sanaa, he reproduces a "rule" that is quite revealing. After Ḥusayn al-ʿAmrī's long quote that portrays a rather ideal *waqf* in Zaydī *fiqh*, Serjeant mentions in a brief paragraph a rule (of unknown origin) that explains some practices in *waqf*:

> When a *waqf* is sold half of the price of the land constituting the *waqf* (*qīmat ʿayn al-arḍ*) is paid to the Waqf, and the other half [is divided] between "the hand (*al-yad*), i.e. the owner(s) by inheritance (*wirāthah*) of the entitlement to the *waqf* (*aḥaqqiyyat al-waqf*) and the *shakhṣiyyah*, i.e., the cultivator or the *qabīlī* in return for the work which he has carried out (*muqābil al-ʿamal alladhī qāma bi-h*)."[129]

Several informants in the Sanaa area also pointed out a similar rule, and one who was a *mutawallī* for a prominent *sayyid* house in Sanaa also called the rule a *fatwā*. In the version of the rule quoted above there is also a piece of information added to the end that somehow explains the validity of an otherwise odd phenomenon; the reason is that the tenant may have invested his own resources in maintenance of the asset. If the *mutawallī* allows the tenant

126 For the sake of clarity, this *fatwā* is treated in its entity at the end of chapter 7.

127 Typically, the newer *waqf* laws do not refer to the old term *ʿāmil*, rather they use terms like the *mutawallī*, or they refer to the ministry with the abstract term *al-jihha al-mukhtāṣṣa* ("the relevant authority").

128 Wizārat al-Shu'ūn al-Qānūniyya, *Qānūn al-waqf al-sharʿī*, 29.

129 al-ʿAmrī and Serjeant, "Administrative Organisation," 152.

to invest in the asset, be it in maintenance or indeed in additional physical structures, then the ownership and value of this investment can belong to the tenant. In practice, it becomes difficult to separate the *waqf* component of the asset from the private component. The subsequent lower rent, as compared to the rent of an "absolute" *waqf*, is one result. If the *mutawallī* does not allow the tenant to invest in the asset, the tenant clearly does not have the right to keep his investment if the *mutawallī* terminates the lease. The problem arises in the grey areas in between. This rule above, as far as I have understood, refers to practices in the Sanaa area shortly after the revolution. The rule Serjeant quotes probably refers to normal, public *waqf*s in the Sanaa area and it is likely that this rule was originally made for judges or administrators in cases where it was important to get the old tenant off the agricultural land so that the land could be used for urban building plots (*ʿaraṣa* pl. *ʿaraṣāt*) instead. This implies that the public *waqf* (type A in the model in chapter 3) was not considered entirely "clean" (*ṣāfī*) or "absolute" (*muṭlaq*). There were rights attached to it that were not part of the ideal, basic *waqf* model.

With regard to agricultural leases the most common type of lease was a continuous sharecropping lease, and the rent was below free market rent. The difference between free market rent and reduced rent is important for understanding the value of the *ḥaqq al-yad* or the *ʿināʾ*. At the same time there could also exist fairly "pure" *waqf* leases in which the tenant paid close to full local rent. Thus the "confusion" referred to in the discussion of the three-year rule arises when tenants are allowed to invest in the asset and are then permitted to pay a lower rent. If someone remains a tenant for a long time, even normal maintenance, which is originally the duty of the *mutawallī*, gradually leads to the part "ownership" of the tenant in the asset and the confusion between *waqf* and private ownership becomes a reality. Thus, the three-year rule and the legality of *ʿināʾ* are conceptually related, however complex the relationship. It seems that *waqf* leases are affected by the practices and norms found in private agricultural leases where the *ʿināʾ* is a central concept. The jurists pointed out this problem hundreds of years ago, but the jurists' law does not seem to have been used, unless we are prepared to see that there are different levels in the jurists' law and that the text of the *matn* in the *mukhtaṣar* is not the only law that the jurists accepted as valid. The legally validated views are much closer to a codified law.

6.2 *Urban Leases*

There are two distinct new developments that the economic change after the revolution brought to the older rules: the concept of the *maʾdhūniyya* and the *taḥrīr*. These bear strong resemblances to the concepts of *ʿināʾ* and *ijāratayn*/

ḥikr. The dual rent was common in Ottoman-controlled areas and the concept of *ʿinā'*, which is similar, commonly appears in the *waqf* leases in Yemen discussed above. Yet, what we see in the debate about the three-year rule are strong notions of what a "pure" *waqf* should be, and that the tenant must not be given a position in which he can, over time, take over the asset in the name of maintenance or "interest." In the period after the civil war ended (around 1968), the solution of selling *waqf* land around the rapidly growing cities such as Sanaa seems to have tempted public *waqf* administrators. Perhaps this was related to the relatively low status of the "traditional" *waqf*, and the presence of *waqf* reforms and privatization programs elsewhere. Messick writes that the local *waqf* administration in Ibb at the time was controlled by a small number of individuals and families, who arguably benefitted much during this period.[130] We must also note that the 1970s saw massive changes in technology and economic growth. There was enormous need for urban building plots around the major cities, where much of the land was agricultural *waqf* land. Land prices skyrocketed. The new tenants did not want to till the land, but to build houses on it. The building of houses on the *waqf* land introduced permanent changes in the system and tenants could not be expected to move away at any time, and certainly not after three years.

6.3 Al-Maʾdhūniyya

The ministry settled for a dual lease option. Other options would have been to sell the land and focus on a strategy of *istibdāl*, which is to buy another *waqf* asset somewhere else, where the old investment strategy (agriculture) could continue. This would remove the *waqf* status from the urban agricultural lands. Another option would have been to demand full market rent for the plots, a right clearly stated in *waqf* law. A dual lease involves selling the right to use the plot, arguably for an indefinite period, and charging a substantial amount for allowing the tenant of the plot to build on it. This immediate rent (*muʿajjal*) appears in urban leases in Yemen after the revolution and is called the "allowance" *al-maʾdhūniyya*, as the tenant is allowed to build on the land. The yearly rent was set as a fixed rent per area[131] (*libna*) and was fairly low, especially after a few years of inflation.

From early on, there was criticism of this system, especially the problem of empowering the administrators of public *waqf* assets to raise rents. Several informants in the ministry of *awqāf* and indeed also the former minister of

130 Messick, "Transactions in Ibb," 261.

131 The city is divided into zones; the central commercial areas have higher rents than other areas.

awqāf, Aḥmad al-Shāmī,[132] states that from the time it was established the ministry had problems with its unorganized nature; and many of the employees accumulated more power than the leadership, particularly as they tended to protect practices that increased their own personal income. The salaries of most employees are still percentages of the transactions they administer, this includes percentages for issuing the *maʾdhūniyya*. Changing this policy thus meets resistance from both employees and tenants.

If the *maʾdhūniyya* is set too high, the rent must be equally low and the whole situation comes to resemble a sale. The law is not coherent in this issue because article 73 in the 1992 law and article 28 in the 1996 *waqf* lease regulations both state that the rent cannot be lower than free market rent (*ījār al-mithl al-ḥurr zamānan wa-makānan*).[133] The *maʾdhūniyya* could be restricted by applying the lease regulations of 1996, article 17, which states that the *maʾdhūniyya* cannot be higher than 25 per cent of the local price of land in the area.[134] The *maʾdhūniyya* is different from the *ʿinā* in that the tenant is not guaranteed that his money will be refunded if he wants of "step down" (*tanāzul*) from the lease; it was a one time fee related to the deferred rent. If the tenant sells the house to someone else, the new tenant must acknowledge the tenancy with the ministry. The second tenant would have to pay the first tenant privately and this way the first tenant gets most of his investment back. However, in old leases, the tenant may have acquired *ʿinā* rights, especially if the plot was originally rented through an old sharecropping agreement.

Today, article 22 in the regulations of *waqf* leases of 1996 states that if a tenant has an "obvious" right to *ʿinā* (*al-ʿinā al-ẓāhir*), and if the public *waqf* administrator (*al-mutawallī l-mukhtaṣṣ*) wants to terminate the lease, two expert witnesses should assess the value of the *ʿinā* "according to custom"; however, the *ʿinā* cannot be higher than 20 per cent of the market value of the land. Article 23 states that a court can rely on two expert witnesses in such a dissolution of a tenancy, in addition to the representative of the *waqf*, and further, that these proceedings can follow local custom (*ʿurf*) "as long as it does not contradict the law."[135]

132 Personal communication with former *waqf* minister, Aḥmad al-Shāmī, Jan. 2010.

133 Wizārat al-Shuʾūn al-Qānūniyya, *Qānūn al-waqf al-sharʿī*.

134 Ibid., 21–22.

135 Ibid., article 22, *Qānūn al-waqf al-sharʿī*, 23. The *ʿinā al-ẓāhir* only refers to old leases about which the *mutawallī* did not protest in the past; in new leases there is no *ʿinā*, since the *mutawallī* must first approve any repair or maintenance of the asset undertaken by the tenant. The value of this maintenance must be explicitly stated and recorded; the value then takes the form of a loan which can be paid as a reduction in the rent, but only for a limited time and the whole transaction and operation must be clearly defined and

These sharecropping leases are in effect perpetual as long as both sides respect the conditions. This is directly contrary to the three-year rule as it was originally put forward and it is certainly far from the ideal *waqf* model. Ironically, the three-year rule is stated in the *waqf* law as mentioned above, however, it is mentioned with exceptions that render it without effect; namely that leases can be renewed if they are below market rent. The wording of the three-year rule is also found on the standard lease contract that the ministry uses. The urban plots are rented out for three years at a time, whereupon they have to be "renewed." The renewal, however, remains a pro forma act. One example is a lease contract from 1986 in which 3.5 *libna* (altogether approximately 130 sq. metres) at Shuʿūb just outside the old city to the north was rented out for 168 *riyāl*s yearly (3.5 *libna* x 4 *riyāls* per *libna* per month). The immediate rent (later called *al-ma'dhūniyya*) was 12,250 *riyāl*s. Effectively, the immediate rent thus equals more than 70 years of yearly rent.[136] The ministry avoids the illegal selling of the land by adding the formulae of the three-year rule in the contract, in addition to a condition that states that the ministry is allowed to increase the yearly rent, which for various reasons mentioned above they only manage to do to a limited extent.

6.4 Taḥrīr

A concept that many "ordinary" informants have heard about, and one that is well known is that of *istibdāl, ibdāl, taʿwīḍ*: the act in which the *mutawallī* sells one *waqf* asset and buys another one. In *fiqh* this is portrayed as legally valid if it benefits the *waqf* as a whole. But as we saw in the letter from Ibn al-Amīr in chapter 3, large-scale *istibdāl* is seen as interfering with the notions of fixity and the sacred aspects of *waqf*. The ministry has also partly followed the policy of allowing *istibdāl*, but this is more commonly known by ordinary people as *taḥrīr* (privatization, lit. "making free"). *Waqf* tenants are given the choice to buy out of the *waqf* status by purchasing the land that they are renting from the *waqf*. In this case, the land becomes privatized, or "free" (*ḥurr*), to use the common term.

In the transition from agricultural leases to leases of urban land that took place after the revolution and still takes place, the value of the land according to local market price was simply split into two, as referred to in the rule

documented. In agricultural leases, such a loan cannot lower the rent more than 75 per cent (article 15).

136 For an English translation of this specific lease contract, see Hovden, "Flowers in *Fiqh*," appendix 7.

quoted by Serjeant above, when the tenant received their *ʿināʾ* or *ḥaqq al-yad*. But after this process was carried out once, the new tenants lost such rights and ideally would have to pay full market price if they want to buy the land from the ministry.

One informant mentioned he had recently privatized (lit., "*ḥarrar*ed" the land, or performed a *taḥrīr*) because he was afraid that his descendants would not respect the *waqf* status of the land and he wanted to keep his conscience and soul clean for the future. He told me the rent was fairly low; he rented 100 *libna* for around 20,000 *riyāl*s yearly while his own income from the land (partly *qāt* cultivation) was actually closer to 500,000 *riyāl*s yearly. Such stories can also be found relating to other types of assets: houses and shops are rented out well below market price and the tenants perceive themselves to have a strong right in the *waqf* asset. Most people prefer to remain *waqf* tenants, seemingly because of the low rents. The process of *taḥrīr* also involves many stages and operations, such as having the land measured by specialists (*massāḥīn*), demarcating it (*taḥjīr*), estimating a price (*tathmīn, muthamminīn*), calculating the portion of runoff rights (*rahaq, marāhiq*), engaging arbitrators (*muḥakkamīn*) and local neighbourhood representatives (*ʿāqil, ʿuqqāl*), and employing witnesses (*shuhūd*). Thus it is not necessarily an easy process and at each step the various actors must be paid and might seek to maximize their profit.

Ideally, *taḥrīr* is the better solution for the ministry and for the *waqf* in general as long as they obtain a good price. This way they can reform the bulk of assets into other investments, which produce a more normal rate of surplus and they can engage in investment strategies that are cheaper to administer. However, we see a strong cultural notion that the tenant is also a receiver and a sort of beneficiary. This notion is not easy to change. As one informant stated: "why shouldn't we get the flat cheaply, after all it is *waqf*; it is for the poor to enjoy and we are poor!" Such notions of what *waqf* "is" are also real, and produce real consequences, just as the ideal *fiqh* does. If the ministry was simply in charge of a large trust, disconnected from local knowledge about actual assets in the neighbourhood and how they are used, then this could also hurt its legitimacy and validity. When *waqf* assets are regrouped and shuffled around too much, they lose the connection to the original founder's intentions. If the ministry does not respect the intentions of those who make the *waqf*s in the first place, then few would make new *waqf*s for the future. People would start to choose other forms of local charity; in fact, this is what has happened. To a large extent, *waqf* and *awqāf* are now seen as synonymous with the bureaucracy of the ministry and its local *waqf* administration, and the "fact" that *waqf* is a prominent legal vehicle for organising public welfare is less known.

•••

When choosing a specific rule and tracing its trajectory, we see that its meaning and its validity varies across different fields of knowledge, as mentioned in chapter 2. In a narrow legal sense, the three-year rule is not much used and hardly relevant, yet it represents a sort of ideal of an absolute *waqf* and this ideal is invoked in the *waqf* law, in administrative practices,[137] in lease contracts,[138] and in *waqf* documents.[139] In all these documents and cases the rule is invoked to protect the rights of the *waqf*, or it is invoked to claim a connection to *fiqh*, *sharīʿa* and thus religious validity in a broad sense. This gap between the ideal norm and practical needs is discussed in minute details in works of *fiqh*, already many centuries ago, as we have seen. The jurists (*fuqahāʾ*) had a clear and strong consciousness about pragmatic lease problems in the real world. If we ask someone what is "Islamic law," the answer will not be shorter or any more coherent than what this chapter illustrates; it is a complicated and opaque discourse about both ideals and pragmatic rules.

When representing (Zaydī) Islamic law it is tempting to look at the main rule, which is clearly stated in textbooks: "the *mutawallī* of the *waqf* is entitled to rent it [the *waqf* asset] out for a defined period, however, for less than three years only." At first glance, it is a norm that *claims* to be valid, based on the text "itself," by having been written in an "authoritative" book. However, the *fiqh* and the *madhhab*-validated *fiqh* actually says that the three-year rule is not absolute, that it has exceptions, in fact quite a number of exceptions. Briefly, we can say that by looking at the *sharḥ* genre, and at the practice of the law, we emerge with a deeper insight than if we only look at a rule found in a *mukhtaṣar*. In a similar, but not entirely analogous way, this approach could also be used when representing Islamic law in more controversial rules, like *ḥudūd* or other topics. In representing the law, there is always a danger that the researcher has decided what to represent before researching the empirical material and the normative texts. The researcher risks reproducing a norm rather than a providing a description of how some views are codified and how that

137 Such as Imam Aḥmad's attempt to enforce the rule in Zabid as mentioned above.

138 For such a standard lease contract, see Hovden, "Flowers in *Fiqh*," appendix 7.

139 The three-year rule is not normally mentioned in the *waqf* documents I have analysed. The three-year rule is mentioned in the *waqf* document from 1552 for the Madrasa al-Naẓārī as edited by al-Akwaʿ, *al-Madāris*, 355. For the mention of the three-year rule in *waqf* documents in Iran, see chapter 11, "Ouqāf," 230–237. See also Ann Lambton, "Awqāf in Persia: 6th–8th/12th–14th Centuries," *Islamic Law and Society* 4, no. 3 (1997): 298–318. For *waqf* in Persia in general, see Lambton, *Landlord and Peasant in Persia* (London: Tauris, 1969), 234–235.

codification is used. This is why the inductive approach and praxiology can offer a corrective to the methods of the researcher. In the course of following the evolution of, and practice related to, the three-year rule we have been led, at times, down obscure paths, but as shown, the three-year rule is relevant to present-day legal practices, and by following one rule only, in a chronological and systematic way, we also establish a structure for seeing and representing the context of this "Islamic" rule.

CHAPTER 7

Private Rights in Public *Waqf*

This chapter focuses on a type of *waqf* that is very common in Yemen, namely *waqfs* that are partly private and partly public in terms of beneficiaries and in terms of administration and guardianship (*wilāya*). In these *waqfs* the benefits are not stipulated solely for one private or public beneficiary, rather these are *waqfs* in which the income or benefits (*manāfiʿ*) are divided for both types of beneficiaries. These *waqfs* pose specific legal problems in terms of regulating the balance between private and public, especially with regard to control of such *waqfs*.

Doctrinally, *waqfs* are portrayed as instruments to serve the public good. In reality, *waqfs* are pulled between different actors, many of whom seek worldly gain. This chapter focuses on the role of the descendants of the founder of public *waqfs* and on the role and the rights of the administrators or guardians, the so-called *mutawallīs*. Again, doctrinally speaking, the descendants of the founder have no rights in public *waqfs*, but in practice, and as acknowledged in practice-oriented[1] *fiqh*, they do have rights. These are important grey areas, or "border areas of validity" in the *fiqh* of Zaydī *waqfs*, investigations of which give us a unique insight into the range that extends between local practice and "Islamic law," as seen through the four fields of *waqf* legal knowledge defined in chapter 2.

I begin by presenting a detailed ethnographic case of a water *waqf* established in 2008, followed by the presentation of four *waqf* documents, which I have translated into English and commented upon. These four *waqfs*, established for urban *sabīls*[2] (public water stands) in Sanaa, are "cases" which we have access to only from the *waqf* documents. The next sections deal with theoretical and legal models by which private rights are inserted into public *waqfs*. These, in turn, illustrate ways in which Zaydī *fiqh* solves (or does not solve) the many grey areas and problems that arise in this legal field of human ingenuity and desire to remould *waqf* rules to fit local needs. Thus the chapter starts with local, everyday *waqf* knowledge, then looks at specific *waqf* documents

1 By practice-oriented *fiqh*, I mean the levels of *fiqh* meant for application and the level closest to codification as discussed in chapter 4.

2 As elaborated below, a *sabīl* is a water supply open to the public.

 | DOI:10.1163/9789004377844_008

and ends with the discussions of the *fuqahāʾ* and their attempts to clarify the confusion and the problems.

1 The *Waṣīya* of Three Cisterns: Bayt al-Laḥafa (2008): An Ethnographic Description

Early on in the fieldwork, through acquaintances, I got in touch with a young shaykh from a village[3] in the northwestern outskirts of Sanaa. His village was situated inside the checkpoints of Sanaa, thus travelling there was practical and simple. Throughout the fieldwork, I visited the village six to seven times and we also met in other settings. Our relationship developed after I mentioned my topic of study; the shaykh, ʿAlī l-Mujāhid, became interested and told me that he had recently found an old document which stated that he had inherited the right to the position as a *mutawallī* (administrator) for a water *waqf* and he was curious what this meant, what rights he had, and what he could legally do with the *waqf.* He had only taken over the position as a shaykh (*al-mashyakha*) four years ago, after his father's death. For reasons unknown to him, his father had not mentioned this *waqf.* Others in the village and his extended family now wanted to sell the *waqf* lands and thus privatize it, but Shaykh ʿAlī considered this wrong and wanted to revive the *waqf.*

The *waqf* consisted of twenty fertile, specifically named agricultural fields situated in the land around the village. The income from this *waqf* was dedicated to the upkeep of three, large public rainwater cisterns (*maʾjil, mājil*, pl. *mawājil*). These cisterns were located some distance from the village and in the past were mainly used for watering the livestock (*qurāsh, mawāshī*) that village members herded on the common lands (*kilāʾ, marʿā*). However, the same *waqf*, that is, the twenty agricultural fields, were also meant for the benefit of the descendants of the family of the "House of al-Mujāhid" (Bayt al-Mujāhid), (the shaykh's family or clan), one of six clans or extended families in the village. The division of income was to be one-quarter for the cisterns and the rest to the family (except for some details, elaborated below).

Shaykh ʿAlī came from the most important family in the village. His family had held the position as shaykhs. They owned the most land and also some real estate in Sanaa; this made them rather wealthy, at least in comparison to the other inhabitants of the village. Traditionally, they had owned much of the land around the village and rented this land out through sharecropping

3 Names of persons and places have been changed.

agreements to other villagers who tilled the land for them. Only one of the other families in the village was of a comparable status. The other four clans in the village owned a few pieces of land each and they were full "members" of the village, but they did not have the same wealth and economic power.

What did it mean that ʿAlī was a village shaykh? With the position of shaykh come certain responsibilities and also benefits, about which I was never fully informed. Most importantly, the shaykh was the spokesman of the village in inter-village matters. He also had a certain monopoly on the mediation of conflicts between the inhabitants of the village. He was not an important or renowned tribal mediator in the sense that the parties in a dispute made a deposit to him in order to effectuate the judgement. According to him, his word was enough to effectuate the judgement, but the ruling had to be grounded in the consensus of the village council. His responsibility was more to be the foreman of the village council, which was represented by the other five clans or extended families as well. He also had some extra funds for this job; I realized later that part of these funds came from another *waqf* in the village.[4]

The village was situated near Sanaa and in the last ten years many people from Sanaa came to buy land and build houses on the agricultural land and on the common lands of the village. These inhabitants were not considered members of the village nor were they under the authority of the shaykh and they were not represented in the village council. The village council was held by the shaykh in the shaykh's large reception room in the first floor of the house of his extended family. Here, weddings and various other important celebrations and gatherings in the village were held. When I visited the village, we often sat in this reception room, where I could overhear discussions of daily matters. The village also collected its own taxes (they used the term *zakāt*). Theoretically the collection of *zakāt* is overseen by the state, but this village collected the *zakāt* completely on its own. The funds were directed to a village "association" simply called "the association" (al-Jamʿiyya). This worked in tandem with the village council, but every member of the "original clans" (*bayt, buyūt*) held certain rights, mainly in the field of health services. A member in need could apply to al-Jamʿiyya for immediate cash in order to go to hospital, or to pay large hospital bills. Only individuals descending from families or clans from the original village were counted as full members of the village and "the association" today. Those who settled around the village as part of the ongoing urban expansion were considered outsiders. Some of these had their own networks and the whole area was also officially a sub-municipality

4 For *waqf*s funding the position of the local shaykh and his expenses in representation and hosting, see Weir, *Tribal Order*, 108.

of the governorate of the capital (*amāna al-ʿāṣima*). Thus the area had a state appointed sub-municipality leader (*ʿāqil*), though for the old village, this dual system of authority was not considered a problem. For them, it was the local rule, the village council and their association that was important and trusted.

1.1 *Domestic Water Supply*

Earlier, the village obtained its water from a small *qanāt*-like water conduit[5] that terminated in the centre of the village. For the last four decades domestic water supply has come from a couple of newly drilled private wells. As in much of the Sanaa area, the groundwater table has sunk a great deal during these last years and immediately after the shaykh took over, he initiated a public water supply project (*mashrūʿ*). A deep well (*biʾr*) was drilled to approximately 450 metres and water was found at around 250 metres. An electric pump was bought and lowered into the well and a generator house was built near the well; a generator (*muwallid, mātūr pl. mawātīr*) was purchased and installed in it.[6]

The pump was run approximately three hours daily in order to fill a large concrete water storage tank (*khizāna*) situated on a hill outside the village. From this storage tank, water reached some of the houses in the village through plastic pipes. These houses paid a fixed price per month per head for their water consumption. The three mosques in the village, of which two were fairly new, were connected to the water storage tank with pipes; they received water from the project free. Outside the mosques *sabīl*s (public water stands) were constructed so that the poor and those not connected to the water system could fetch water freely. These *sabīl*s were also frequently used by people not originally from the village, especially the poorer ones. Women and children could often be seen fetching water using the typical yellow plastic 20 litre containers called *dabba*. The shaykh called this a "good deed," and used the terms *maḥsana* and *ṣadaqa*. The shaykh's family, along with two other families, had contributed to the water project.

The ongoing cost of maintenance and diesel consumption was covered by a rather lucrative side business of the water project. Next to the water tank they had built a filling station for water trucks. Here, water trucks arrived from faraway and queued to tank up. These trucks were the sort of typical, small water

5 In Yemen this is usually called *ghayl* (pl. *ghuyūl*). This specific *ghayl* was rather small according to old informants in the village, and today it is completely buried and cannot be seen. At one time it began in a small valley about 250 metres away and in the rainy season it began to flow with enough force to provide water for irrigation. The old village mosque in the centre of the village had a large well attached to it and this well was the main supply of domestic water after the *ghayl* dried up and before the new water project was undertaken.

6 Such large water pumps require more electricity than the normal grid can supply.

trucks that people in Sanaa, especially the thousands of people in the suburbs who are not connected to the main water system, would buy household water from. There are hundreds of such private wells and filling stations in the Sanaa area, and this particular well was used profitably; since, after constructing and investing in a large and expensive well, operating it for a limited period of time would have been a waste of resources. I never understood all the details of the business side of the water project.

The shaykh was a religious person who was well aware of the religious dimension of various forms of giving and redistribution. The concept of *waqf*, however, was not fully clear to him, and during our discussions I understood that people's perception of *waqf* was mainly related to the ministry of *awqāf* and their lands and mosques, or, for the few learned people in the village, it was related to a chapter in the *fiqh* book, and mainly understood as distinct from various forms of local welfare and charity that were simply called "charity" (*ṣadaqa*). The local form of *waqf* was called *waṣāyā*, thus my insistence on focusing the conversations on *waqf* created quite some confusion in our first meetings. The fact that locals did not see *waqf* as relevant in their village was thus a matter of definitions. As discussed in chapter 2, this is an example of a type of everyday, local knowledge of what *waqf* is, and what is known about *waqf*. Methodologically, it is a problem because the same phenomenon is sometimes called something else. When the topic of the *waqf* (or rather, the *waṣīya*) of the three cisterns came up, it is important to note here that the water needs of the village were already taken care of. There was no real need to revive the *waqf* as a water *waqf*.

One of the first times we met, the shaykh took me to see the three cisterns in the fields around the village. These were what I had said were my main interest of study. They each had individual names and the largest one also served as a border marker; the land beyond it belonged to another village. In the mid-1980s, the inhabitants had stopped using the cisterns and they gradually fell into decay. The number of animals kept in the village declined and the need for the cisterns disappeared as many new wells were drilled. Agricultural activity also declined, especially since more and more land was sold for building plots for people from the city. The largest cistern was approximately fifteen metres across and five metres deep and had an inclined ramp inside, so that the livestock could descend to the lowest possible water level;[7] this eliminated

7 When such a cistern is full, the water can be reached easily, but when it is nearly empty, it must be hoisted up in buckets, or if there is a staircase, one must descend to the surface of the water.

the need for manual labour to lift the water out of the cistern and put it into small basins or troughs for the animals, as is common in other smaller cisterns. The two smaller cisterns in the same *waqf* did not have this feature. All three cisterns were located in the village's common grazing lands, although there were a few private agricultural fields nearby.

The common lands are available to the village inhabitants, who have the right to collect firewood (in the Sanaa area there is very little firewood) and graze their livestock (mainly in the rainy season). The one important right from the common land that is not available to everyone, a right that remains private, is the runoff rights. There are no surface streams in the area, but most of the area is divided into runoff zones where during heavy rains small shallow canals carry surface water to specific agricultural fields. Thus each agricultural field has a runoff area (*rahaq, marāhiq*) attached to it.[8] These runoff rights are well incorporated into local land and water law. Here it is important to note that the water source for these three cisterns was also this rainwater runoff from the adjacent land during heavy rain. This land belonged to the cisterns in a legal sense and the cisterns were common property for the village. Such common property is a type of *waqf* and Zaydī *fiqh* states that when such objects are given to the public, and the public is allowed to use them, it takes the effect of *waqf*, even if no document or contract exists.[9] This also applies, for example, to many of the traditional roadside *sabīl*s or shelters for travellers. Often certain families nearby benefit from *waqf*s on the condition that they take care of this infrastructure, and this specific *waqf* for these three cisterns is a typical example of this.

Today, these three cisterns are not very useful or important in terms of capacity to supply water. They do not collect much water, especially when compared to the amount of water that passes through the new village water system. What was important was the land that they occupied, directly, and even more importantly indirectly, through the runoff rights. The city of Sanaa is expanding

8 The canals are called *misqā* (pl. *masāqī*). The runoff water, or sometimes also the runoff area, is called *maṣabb*. See Helmut Eger's detailed study on the Qāʿ al-Bawn: Helmut Eger, "Runoff Agriculture: A Case Study about the Yemeni Highlands" (PhD thesis, Eberhard-Karls-Universität, 1986).

9 In Zaydī *waqf fiqh* there is a rule stating this. *Kitāb al-Azhār*: "Wa man faʿala fī shay mā ẓāhiruhu al-tasbīl khāraja ʿan milkihi," meaning that if someone does something with an object such that it is clear that he intends to make it accessible to the public (*tasbīl*), arguably through *waqf*, then that object automatically becomes *waqf*. *Tasbīl* is arguably one of the synonyms for *waqf*. Ibn Miftāḥ, *Kitāb al-Muntaziʿ*, 4:478. Ibn Miftāḥ, *Sharḥ al-azhār* (2003 ed.), 8:223–224.

rapidly and land prices are skyrocketing. To understand the value of the cisterns today we must first look to this urbanization process; when private agricultural fields are sold, it is an entirely private matter between the seller and the buyer.[10] In contrast, if the common lands are sold to outsiders, then the value should be split among the members of the village, through the village council. The one major exception to this is for parts of the common lands where private runoff-rights extend into the common lands. As mentioned, many agricultural fields have rights to specific parts of the common lands; these rights take the form of the potential rainwater runoff that flows, during heavy rain from the common lands, to the agricultural fields. If the common lands are divided and sold, the flow of water may be altered, and these agricultural fields may lose some of their water and thereby their value. Therefore a rule or a *fatwā* was followed, and it was said that this rule was slightly different from village to village. If a piece of the common land was sold, and that piece was also a private runoff area belonging to someone else, then half the price of the land would go to the village members collectively through the Jamʿiyya, and the other half would go to the private owner of the runoff rights, to compensate him for the loss of his runoff rights in the common land.[11] Thus if the runoff lands attached to the cistern were sold, the whole village would receive a part of it, and vice versa. The *waqf* of the cisterns therefore had rights in the form of cash if the nearby common land was sold and the runoff rights belonging to the cistern were cut off. Today the *waqf* status also made the whole case problematic: could the land be sold at all, and if so, who should enjoy the benefits? And should the funds be used to create a new *waqf* in order for the transaction to be religiously and morally valid? Furthermore, there was also confusion between the cisterns and the twenty fields that were *waqf* for the cisterns: were they the same legal unit as one *waqf*? Originally, the cisterns were not the same *waqf*, but a beneficiary (perhaps a secondary *waqf*) of the twenty fields.

---

10 Except in theoretical cases of pre-emption rights (*shufʿa*), and in this village, the village council simply kept watch over who the land was sold to and for what price. In addition, most agricultural lands do not have straight borders, as most fields are curved terraces. Here experts on land measurement (*qayyāsīn, massāḥīn*) are hired to ensure the accurate transition from organic-shaped plots to more rectangular or square plots suitable for building. In the process professional land price estimators (*muthāmminīn*) also become involved.

11 The issue on how to split the runoff rights is a large topic. Local political and geographical conditions lead to local solutions. In other cases agreements can be taken at the tribal level. See for instance the important *fatwā* from the Sa'da basin as explained by Gerhard Lichtenthäler, *Political Ecology and the Role of Water: Environment, Society and Economy in Northern Yemen* (Aldershot, UK: Ashgate, 2003), 53–55.

1.2 *The Document*

During my second visit, the shaykh showed me the document, not the original that he claimed he had, but a rather worn A4 photocopy of it. It must be noted here that whenever he referred to the document and the *waqf* case, he referred to it as a *waṣīya*, "our *waṣīya*" (*al-waṣīya ḥaqqanā*), or "the *waṣīya* of our grandfather" (*waṣīyat jaddinā*). We sat down and read the passages that were legible once together. I asked if I could photograph the document the next time I came and he agreed, and so I did not take many notes that day. It was also one of the first *waqf* documents I had seen, so I did not know exactly what to look for.

The *waqf* is around 200 years old and was made by an ancestor of Shaykh ʿAlī l-Mujāhid. The wording of the document was typical of a *waqf* document.[12] The document had been re-written (*naql*)[13] two times; each time the notaries who had done this added their name at the end of the previous document. Such re-writing was necessary because of the physical wear and tear over time, or because of the need to add new strong witnesses to the document, to make it fully public and valid again.

The founder had no sons, only two daughters. He thereby made one-third of his property a *waqf* for his male descent line (*ilā man yantasibūna ilayya*). The object of the *waqf* consisted of the twenty aforementioned agricultural fields located around the village. On the reverse side of the document the names of the fields were listed in a horizontal list[14] and under each entry, the average yearly production of grain (*al-qudra*) was given in numbers of *qadaḥ*. The document did not describe the borders and this bothered the shaykh quite a bit.[15] The income of the *waqf* was split between two separate, parallel beneficiaries: The first was designated for the upkeep (*iqāma, ṣiyāna*) of the three cisterns, and the beneficiaries were to receive one-quarter of the yearly harvest. The

12 "Ḥaḍara al-ḥājj ... wa-waqqafa wa-sabbala wa-abbada ..." Thus there is no doubt that the document was a *waqf* document and not only a *waṣīya* in the strict sense.

13 Often in such *naql* it is pointed out that not one letter has been changed and two new witnesses are added to testify to the validity of the new document and to certify that the new document has the same wording as the original.

14 This is typical of a *miswadda* with u-shaped lines dividing the entries in the horizontal list.

15 This seems to be common in many *waqf* registers as well: at the village level, at least in the past, the names of the fields were common local knowledge. The fields are also naturally bordered by the edges of the terraces. Even today the ministry of *awqāf* supervises many assets without knowing their size or borders; it only knows these assets by name and the yearly average harvest. This is not a problem in a stable, traditional, agricultural society, but it becomes a significant problem when *waqf* land is urbanized and the exact area of the land is needed in order set the rent.

rest was to be given to the descendants of the Bayt Mujāhid. This point also troubled the shaykh: was it to be divided according to "heads" (*ʿalā l-ruʾūs*) of households, or according to inheritance shares (*ʿalā l-farāʾiḍ*)? The handwriting was difficult for both of us to read and we struggled several times. He said that he had shown it to a learned man who had read it for him. Importantly, the founder stipulated that the *mutawallī* was to be the wisest (*al-arshad*) and best suited (*al-aṣlaḥ*) among the descendants. According to Shaykh ʿAlī l-Mujāhid, his inheritance of the position, along with many other responsibilities from his father, was not controversial.

There were three more interesting clauses that I cannot be certain were written since I did not study the document thoroughly; these may have been the perception of the shaykh. The first was the condition that if the family (Bayt Mujāhid) needed more than three-quarters of the income "in times of need" (*fī l-ḥāja, ḍarūra*), then this was to be preferred over the cisterns. This is an important "exception" to the public side of the *waqf* that is discussed later in this chapter. The second condition was that in any case, the descendants[16] of the founder were to be given the right to farm those twenty agricultural fields as sharecroppers (*shurakāʾ*). The third condition concerned the salary of the administrator, which according to the shaykh was 10 per cent (also called *ʿushr*). Bearing in mind that the shaykh was also central to the village *zakāt* committee, he also pointed out that 10 per cent of the yearly harvest was to be taken as *zakāt* tax (the *zakāt* in Yemen is often called a "tithe," or *ʿushr*). Prior to the revolution, this was paid to the state of Imam Yaḥyā and Imam Aḥmad. It is customary in many sharecropping agreements to specify whether it is the peasant or the tenant who must pay the *zakāt*.

1.3 *Transformation and Revival of the* Waqf

The shaykh was frustrated that some of his relatives had already started selling parts of the *waqf* land to outsiders. These, in turn, tended to move the borders and according to the shaykh, if he did not constantly protest, the land would have disappeared quickly. For a short time we decided to make a joint effort to try to find references to this specific *waqf* in public *waqf* registers. His explicit motivation was to see if the borders of the original assets were written somewhere. But we quickly gave up when we realized the many problems involved in accessing public *waqf* registers. Soon after, his openness with regard to the

16 *Man yantasibūna ilayya*, thus in legal terms, the male descent line. Some wordings have local meanings, as noted in chapter 5.

economic details of the *waqf* came to an end. Then, after four more meetings, he said that "it would better if we just forgot this document" and he said that he could not find it. Yet, before that point, during several semi-public discussions among villagers in the reception room of the shaykh, I gained some insight into the process of what could and should happen to the *waqf*.

I followed this case for one and a half years, during which time it seemed as if the shaykh had won over those of his relatives who wanted to sell the *waqf*. This was partly a result of his invocation of personal moral and religious principles—his brothers who had studied Zaydī religion and law had access to circles of religious scholars and notables and thus "religious capital." A written legal question (*istiftā'*) (which I saw) was sent to the highly revered Sanaa based Zaydī scholar al-Sayyid al-ʿAllāma Muḥammad al-Manṣūr.[17] This document asked the specific legal question: If we have a *waqf* for a specific purpose, in our case the provision of water, and if this service is no longer needed, may we then change the type of beneficiary? Can we make a school from it? The answer was given on the very same piece of paper, above the question: This is allowed, if no similar type of beneficiary (*maṣrif*) is needed and thus if the *waqf* is no longer useful. The answer, or *fatwā*, was given according to mainstream Zaydī *fiqh*, and is not controversial at all. From this point onwards, the contextual details of the *waqf*, which indeed had been converted from a water *waqf* to a school *waqf*, were not available to me, as my fieldwork ended. However, one last important change in the *waqf* had taken place by the end of the fieldwork. First, the school, allegedly a semi-religious evening school for women,[18] was built as a second storey over a public village building. But more importantly, the three cisterns and all the land and rights attached to them, and several of the agricultural fields, were sold for a very high price. New land (and again I have only the shaykh's version of this) was bought in a fertile part of the Tihāma, in the upper reaches of Wādī Sihām, a typical investment strategy for wealthy highlanders. The land in the Tihāma is considered a safe long-term investment, as it has flat areas with sufficient groundwater, it is situated in a politically stable part of Yemen, and at the same time it is rather close to Sanaa. As mentioned before, the cisterns themselves were not originally part of the

17 He is the *nāẓir al-waṣāyā* and mentioned in chapter 3.

18 In these tribal villages and specifically in this village, no one in the past had education. Some had a modern education, but the two brothers of the shaykh were the first to have a religious education. Women in the village tended to have no education at all; in this context "education" mainly refers reading and writing. The village was fairly conservative.

waqf of the twenty agricultural fields, yet they were included in the fate of the *waqf* from this point on. The *waqf* was, after all, though significantly changed, kept as a *waqf* and not converted to private property. It is unlikely that it was registered as a *waqf* in a public *waqf* register; it is more likely that the shaykh still holds the *waqf* as a private enterprise. However, it is no less a "real" *waqf* according to *fiqh*, law, or everyday knowledge. It is just kept at a distance from the state.

This is just one case—many more are needed in order to establish that this case is "normal." There are many strong indications that this form of complex *waqf*, in which public and private aspects are combined, indeed were very common in the past. I have seen a couple of similar *waqf* (*waṣāyā*) documents from the same area around Sanaa where local influential families had the responsibility of taking care of local cisterns.[19]

At the beginning of the fieldwork, I had doubts about the value of researching this case at all, especially because it seemed, in many ways, an odd example of *waqf*. At the end of the fieldwork I realized that, on the contrary, the case is typical in many aspects and perhaps just as common as the public mosque *waqf*s and as other forms of family *waqf*s, and therefore it is certainly in need of representation.

2 Four *Waqf* Documents of Public Sanaa *Sabīl-Waqf*s with Private Benefits

From the almost fifty *waqf* documents I obtained from the archives of the ministry of *awqāf*, I review and comment on four *waqf* documents below.[20] As mentioned in chapter 1, my initial focus was the study of water supply *waqf*s, and I asked the ministry for copies of *waqf* documents related to water supply. The documents below clearly fall into that category. The documents show the stability in the form of the *waqf* document (*waqfiyya*) itself, which span nearly 400 years from the first to the last. Because of the scant number of documents

---

19 An example, but one in which I did not see the document, is the *waṣīya* for the Bayt al-ʿArhab in Jirāf and al-Rawḍa. Some of these cisterns can still be seen. (I saw the cisterns and photographed them with the help and presence of the local *mudīr waqf* / *ʿāmil al-waqf* of al-Rawḍa, Muḥammad Baʿthār). I had personal communication with a member of Bayt al-ʿArhab.

20 This edition is given in Hovden, "Flowers in *Fiqh*," appendices.

analysed (just four),[21] the material lends itself to an explorative approach from which I raise questions, but do not fully answer them based on these four *waqf* documents alone. Some answers to these questions are, however, provided by the *fiqh* debates in the last part of this chapter. The *waqf* documents are important examples of *waqfs* that are not entirely public, but have distinct explicit or implicit private rights attached to them—rights that are not easily detected if compared to the ideal, basic *waqf* model.

The first document dates from 1621; it is a *waqf* comprising a shop for rent with a *sabīl* as beneficiary, both located in the market area of Sanaa, in the Madhhab Quarter. The second is the *waqf* of an estate in an affluent suburb named Bi'r al-ʿAzab; the *waqf* was founded in 1855 for a *sabīl* at al-Rawḍa just north of Sanaa. The third represents a *waqf* made in 1929 of a large tract of agricultural land outside Sanaa near Wādī Ḍahr for the benefit of one of the *sabīls* in the market area of Sanaa, the *sabīl* of Sūq Ḥārrat al-Madar. In this *waqf* the founder explicitly reserves the "surplus" of the *waqf* for himself along with the right to its administration (*wilāya*). Implicitly this also means that the surplus will go to his children after him, who will hold this position as *mutawallī*. The last *waqf* document is from 1982, it is a smaller *waqf* of two street side shops made for a small, modern *sabīl* with a water tap connected to the public water system. In this *waqf* there is also an explicit split in the rights to the *waqf*; the surplus is to go to an additional beneficiary. These last two *waqfs* are important examples of private rights inserted into seemingly public *waqfs*. The degree to which the two first *waqfs* also contain the same elements becomes clearer towards the end of the chapter.

2.1 *A Shop as* Waqf *for a Sanaa Market* Sabīl *from 1621*

This *waqf* was set up in 1621 and is one of the oldest *waqf* documents in this study. It was established during the reign of the second Qāsimī imam, al-Mu'ayyad Muḥammad (r. 1029–54/1620–44), the son of al-Qāsim himself. During this time, the Ottomans were still holding Sanaa.

---

21 Here, four *waqf* documents are presented in edited and translated form, though I read most of the approximately fifty documents obtained from the ministry. Some of the documents were also related to other forms of *waqf*. Often, I only received a copy of a single page, or a fraction of the document.

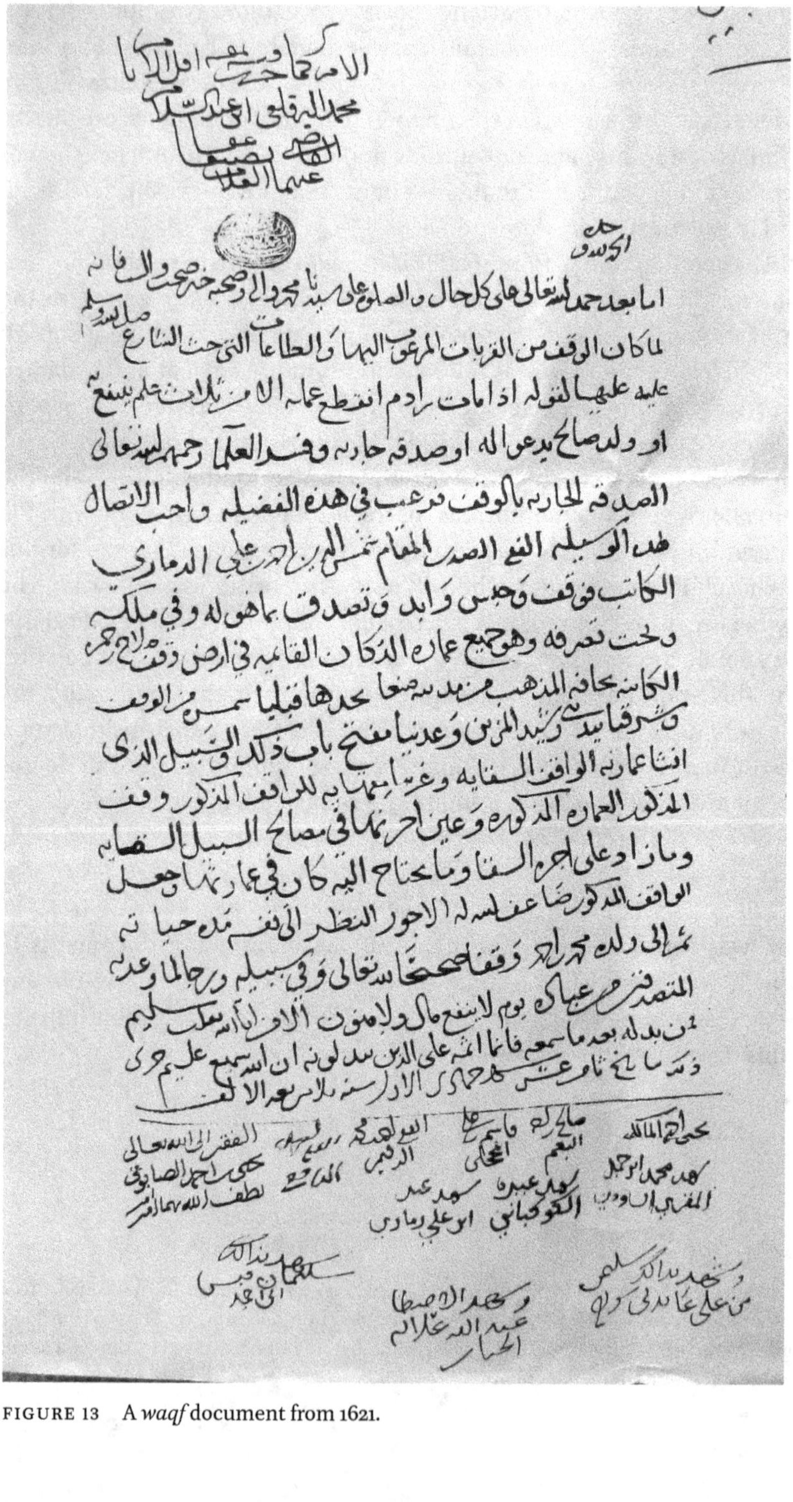

FIGURE 13 A *waqf* document from 1621.

Translation:

> The issue is to be followed xxx
> Muḥammad xxx
> Ibn ʿAbd al-Salām
> Judge of Sanaa
> (Stamp)
>
> Praise be to God
> alone
> After praising God the exalted for everything, and wishing peace upon Our Lord Muḥammad and his descendants and his companions, the best of companions and descendants. Then, indeed the [institution of] *waqf* is among the pious acts that are desired and requested and encouraged by the law-giver, peace and God's greetings upon him, as in his statement: "if a man dies, his [the rewards for his] good deeds are cut off except in three [things]: useful knowledge, a good son who prays for him, and continuous charity (*ṣadaqa jāriya*)." The scholars, may God the exalted be pleased with them, have established that continuous charity is the [concept of] *waqf*, and he [the founder of this *waqf*] wanted to perform this good act and wanted to use this instrument: Shams al-Dīn Aḥmad b. ʿAlī l-Dhamārī l-Kātib made *waqf* of what is his, and in his ownership, and under his right of disposal, being all of the erected shop (*dukkān*), standing on land of the *waqf* of Ṣalāḥ b. Ḥamza situated in al-Madhhab (city quarter) in the city of Ṣanʿāʾ. Its borders are, to the north the *samsara*[22] of the *waqf* and to the east the house under the hand of Rashīd al-Muzayyin, and to the south the door opening of that, and the *sabīl* that the founder initiated the building of,[23] and to the west, *miʿxxāya* for the aforementioned founder. The aforementioned [founder] made the aforementioned building a *waqf* and stipulated (*ʿayyana*) its income (*ujratahā*) for the interest of the *sabīl-siqāya*, and the surplus that is left after the expenditures for water supply (*saqā*), and what is needed [for the *sabīl*], is to be spent on its building (*ʿimāratihā*).[24] The aforementioned founder,

22 A *samsara* (pl. *samāsir*), is a large building where travellers and traders can rent or take free rooms for their animals and goods if they need to stay the night. The *waqf* used to own some such structures while others were private.

23 The word *siqāya* (water basin) is inserted and on the line below it is written *al-sabīl al-siqāya*.

24 It is not clear if the surpus should be spent on the building that houses the shop (*ʿimārat al-dukkān*) or the *sabīl* (and *siqāya*), but probably it is the shop, which is also the *waqf* asset.

> may God multiply the merits for him, made the guardianship (*al-naẓar*), to himself for the period of his life, then to his son Muḥammad b. Aḥmad, as a valid *waqf* for God the exalted, and in His way (*fī sabīlihi*), hoping for what the truthful ones among His servants have been promised [on] the day when property and funds are of no use, except for he who God provided with a good heart.[25] He who changes it [the wording of this *waqfiyya*] after having heard it, then the sin is only upon those who have changed it [the *waqfiyya*], verily God hears and knows everything. This took place on the 18th day of the month of Jumādā l-Awwāl, the year one thousand thirty [i.e., 10 April 1621].

Twelve witnesses are named at the end. The *waqf* document stipulates that the right to the guardianship, that is, the role of *mutawallī* shall remain in the family of the founder: it is first given to the founder himself, then to his son Muḥammad. Further, it states that the surplus of the *waqf* is to be spent on the maintenance of the *waqf* asset. If there is a surplus left after the maintenance of the asset, it is not stated where this shall be spent. This fact is discussed further below and compared to what *fiqh* texts say about such a surplus and the rights to it. It is not certain whether this is a Zaydī *waqf* or a Ḥanafī *waqf*, or if that would have meant any difference.

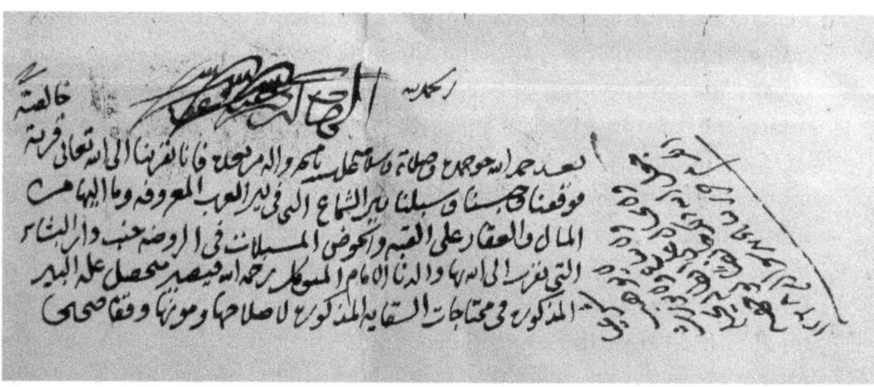

FIGURE 14 An entry from a *waqf* register concerning a *waqf* from 1852.

25 The last part of the sentence is unclear.

2.2 Waqf *of the Estate Bi'r al-Shammā'* (*1852*) *for a* Sabīl *at al-Rawḍa*

Translation:

Praise be to God
[Signature of the notary]

[1] After praising God, in gratitude, and the peace and greetings upon Our Lord Muḥammad and his descendants after him. Verily we sought proximity to God the exalted, an absolute piety (*qurba*); [2] We made *waqf* (*waqqafnā wa-ḥabbasnā wa-sabbalnā*) of the estate of Bīr al-Shammā' situated in Bi'r al-'Azab, the well known, and what belongs to it of [2] property (*māl*) and land (*'aqār*), for the dome (*al-qubba*) and water basin (*al-ḥawḍ*) made as *sabīls* (*al-musabbalāt*) in al-Rawḍa next to the palace of Dār al-Bashā'ir [3] that was founded in piety for God by our father, al-Imām al-Mutawakkil, may God grant him mercy. The income from the aforementioned estate [lit. *bīr*] [4] is to go to the necessities of the aforementioned water basin (*siqāya*), for its maintenance and its funding, [this being] a true *waqf* [being]

legally valid (*shar'īyan*),
not to be given away,
not to be sold, not to be inherited,
not to be circumvented by legal ruses,
made exclusively for God and His generous purpose.
Issued the date of the month Shawwāl in the year 1268 [1852][26]

This document[27] is very short and is probably a photocopy from a *waqf* register into which parts of the original *waqf* document were transcribed. It does not give the names of the founders, though the active voice in the *waqf* document indicates two or more individuals: "We make *waqf* ..." It could also be an imam who writes in plural. The *waqf* is made in favour of a *sabīl* that is not located in Sanaa, but in the nearby village of al-Rawḍa,[28] just to the north of Sanaa. In

26 The year is unclear, it may be 1238/1823. Sometimes the number 3 is written as it is shown in figure 14, with the number 2 curving upwards and the number 3 downwards.

27 As with many other documents provided by the keeper of *waqf* records (Ḥafiẓ al-miswaddāt), it was given without any further related information.

28 I visited another *sabīl* in al-Rawḍa. This *sabīl* complex, which was typical, also had a small dome and an old well and a larger open ground-level basin next to it. Now, the small doors of the *sabīl* are bricked up and a tap is attached to it. The well still works, but is now equipped with a small electrical pump (*daynamū*). I was told by the local *'āmil waqf* that

this case, what is made into a *waqf* is not an insignificant object, rather it is a complete estate in the suburb to the west of Sanaa where many wealthy people had garden palaces. The estate's name is Bi'r[29] (or Bīr) Shammāʿ. Unless this happens to be a very small estate, its income would be far more than what is needed for a *sabīl*.

This text not only leaves out the names of the founders, it also does not identify the *mutawallī*. This *waqf* was probably administered by a prominent family member together with many other *waqf*s "belonging" to the family. We do know that the "father" of the founder was "al-Imam al-Mutawakkil"; this could be the Imam al-Mutawakkil Aḥmad (r. 1809–1816), or Imam al-Mutawakkil Muḥammad (r. 1845–1849).[30]

The names of the founder(s) are missing; this information was probably lost during the process of entering the *waqf* document into the register. In any case, the missing information is undoubtedly covered legally by other contemporary documents and conventions such that this short form made sense.

Why make a *waqf* of an entire suburban estate for only one *sabīl*? One very obvious answer, but one that cannot be proven, is that this ensured that the estate would remain in the family, and that the *sabīl* was merely a cover of "charitability" to make the *waqf* valid.

2.3 Waqf *for* Sabīl *Sūq Ḥārrat al-Madar from 1929*

The *waqf* below is a *waqf* in favour of a *sabīl* consisting of agricultural land outside Sanaa, near Wādī Ḍahr. The *sabīl* itself deserves some mention.

2.4 *The* Sabīl *Itself*

The *sabīl* of Sūq Ḥārrat al-Madar, hereafter "the *sabīl*," is a typical example of the traditional *sabīl*s in the market areas of Sanaa.[31] In other parts of the city and especially in the residential quarters, the important *sabīl*s for household water supply were mainly attached to the local mosques, in the city quarter, and their wells.[32] In the main market area in the old city, the so called Sūq

---

the *sabīl* was still used and that a neighbouring family had taken on the responsibility of taking care of it. Thus the *sabīl* was a public *waqf*, but paid for by the family's *waṣīya*.

29 These estates are called "Bi'r" because they often have their own private well for irrigating the orchards and the land as one irrigation/land unit.

30 See the useful genealogical map made by Haykel (*Revival and Reform*).

31 For a list of the most important *sabīl*s in the market area, see Serjeant and Lewcock, *Ṣanʿāʾ*, 275. An earlier list was made by Dostal, *Der Markt von Ṣanʿāʾ*, 114.

32 These *sabīl*s outside the wall of a mosque were often called *muttakhadhāt* (places of fetching). Although not explicitly stated, one such can probably be seen in Serjeant and Lewcock, *Ṣanʿāʾ*, 205, photo 18.

al-Milḥ, there were several *sabīls* to serve the daily water needs of travellers and people coming to sell and buy products in the market. The market *sabīls* were not elaborate architectural structures like those in Cairo, where full-time employees served water in bowls to passers by. The elaborate examples of Cairene *sabīls* could comprise Qur'ānic schools on the second floor, where the chanting of students could produce a "religious soundscape" in the street surrounding the *sabīl* (*sabīl kuttāb*) and the first floor was often a lavishly decorated room containing a fountain or a small waterfall.[33] The Sanaa market *sabīls* were simpler and more practical; from the front they consist of a small wooden door behind which was a small basin. From this basin the person in need (also called *ibn al-sabīl*) could scoop out water with an attached cup or bowl. Some of the *sabīls* are separate, freestanding structures roofed with a small dome. For this reason, many *sabīls* are simply called *qubba* (pl. *qibāb*) (as in the previous *waqf* document). A few of them have a small well attached.[34] Most *sabīls* in the markets, and especially the smaller ones, did not have their own water sources and professional water carriers, who fetched the water from other public wells in water skins.[35] In al-Ḥajarī's book *Masājid Ṣanʿā'*, he mentions several of the *sabīls* at the time of Imam Yaḥyā (1940s); the *sabīl* discussed below is mentioned, the *sabīl* Ḥārrat Sūq al-Madar: "[N]ext to the Shāhidayn mosque there is a *sabīl* (*maḥsana li-l-shurb*) in the pottery market which was built by al-Ḥājj Muḥammad al-Maddār [the pottery trader] in recent times …"[36] According to older informants, many of the *sabīls* were torn down and rebuilt in the early years of Imam Yaḥyā's reign. This can also be seen from the dates found in the inscription above many of the *sabīls*—several date to that time period.

2.5 *The* Waqf *Document*

In addition to the general importance of this *waqf* document a more specific argument can be made. While all the *waqf* documents analysed here have

---

33 Saleh Lamei Mostafa, "The Cairene Sabil: Form and Meaning," *Muqarnas* 6 (1989): 33–42.

34 See drawing and plan of such a *sabīl* in Serjeant and Lewcock, *Ṣanʿā'*, 298 fig. 15.8, "Sabīl at Bāb al-Balaqa." Ronald Lewcock, "The Buildings of the Sūq/Market," in *Ṣanʿā'*, ed. Serjeant and Lewcock (London: World of Islamic Festival Trust, 1983), 298, fig. 15.8. For *sabīls* in the market area in general, see ibid., 293–296. For a picture of a *sabīl* drawn in the nineteenth centurys, see ibid., 111, fig 9.2.

35 For mention of water carriers taking water from the Ghayl al-Aswad, see Serjeant and al-Akwaʿ, "The Statute of Ṣanʿā'," 192 n224.

36 al-Ḥajarī, *Masājid Ṣanʿā*, 66; Serjeant says that "A *maddār* is a man who sells *fakhkhār* [that is, pottery], not a potter" that is, he is the merchant, not the craftsman. See Serjeant and Lewcock, *Ṣanʿā'*; on the law of the pottery market, see ibid., 228–230.

certain implicit aspects related to private rights, in this specific *waqf* document the private rights in the *waqf* have been set up in a detailed way. The *waqf* was made during the time that family *waqf*s were restricted (around 1930), as mentioned in chapter 5. This *waqf* document represents a *waqf* with a very large income to cover a rather limited expenditure and the difference represents a significant surplus. After making the *waqf*, the founder went to another notary/judge and asked him to add an explicit condition to the *waqf* document, namely that he could keep the surplus of the *waqf* after the needs of the *sabīl* were covered. Thus this *waqf* represents a creative move around the prohibition of the exclusionary form of family *waqf* treated in chapter 5.[37]

The text below is not a *waqf* document in a narrow sense, but rather an entry in a *waqf* register made to safeguard the original *waqf* document in a public place and to make the *waqf* publicly known. Such registers are called *miswaddāt al-taqyīd*, or registers where legal documents are "bound." Therefore, in addition to the active voice of the founder in the original *waqf* document and the active voice of the judge/notary who wrote the original *waqf* document, we also find the active voice of the *waqf* secretary who made the entry of the document (*naql*) into the *waqf* register.

Lines 10–24 seem to be the text of the original *waqf* document by the notary (/judge) al-Razzāqī, dated 14 Sept 1929. In the original *waqf* document most of the sentences are in the founder's active voice (lines 11–20), as is common in *waqf* documents. The rest of the *waqf* document, the beginning and the end, is in the active voice of the notary, that is al-Razzāqī.

On 18 October 1929, approximately one month after the original document was made, the founder went to another notary/judge, this one by the name of al-Ḥūthī, and added a clause to the *waqf* document; this clause stipulates that the surplus or what is in excess of the income (*al-fāʾiḍ*, lit. "the overflow") is to be taken by the founder himself after the *sabīl* and the *waqf* asset have been taken care of (lines 4–9).

Al-Ḥūthī was not just any scholar or notary: prior to 1929 he had been a member of the appeal court in Sanaa and shortly after this document was written he was appointed president of the same court, which was the highest court

37 Similar problems also arose in relation to the so-called recitation *waqf*s; in Imam Yaḥyā's new decrees and until today, these are legal, provided the salary is not greater than the burden of work the recitation represents. If the salary is higher, then that type of *waqf* is considered a legal ruse, *ḥīla*. These questions are almost impossible to codify in a more detailed manner; in each case local judges must estimate the income of the *waqf* and weigh it against the actual work performed by the "*waqf* holder" (who is not a beneficiary, but a *mutawallī*).

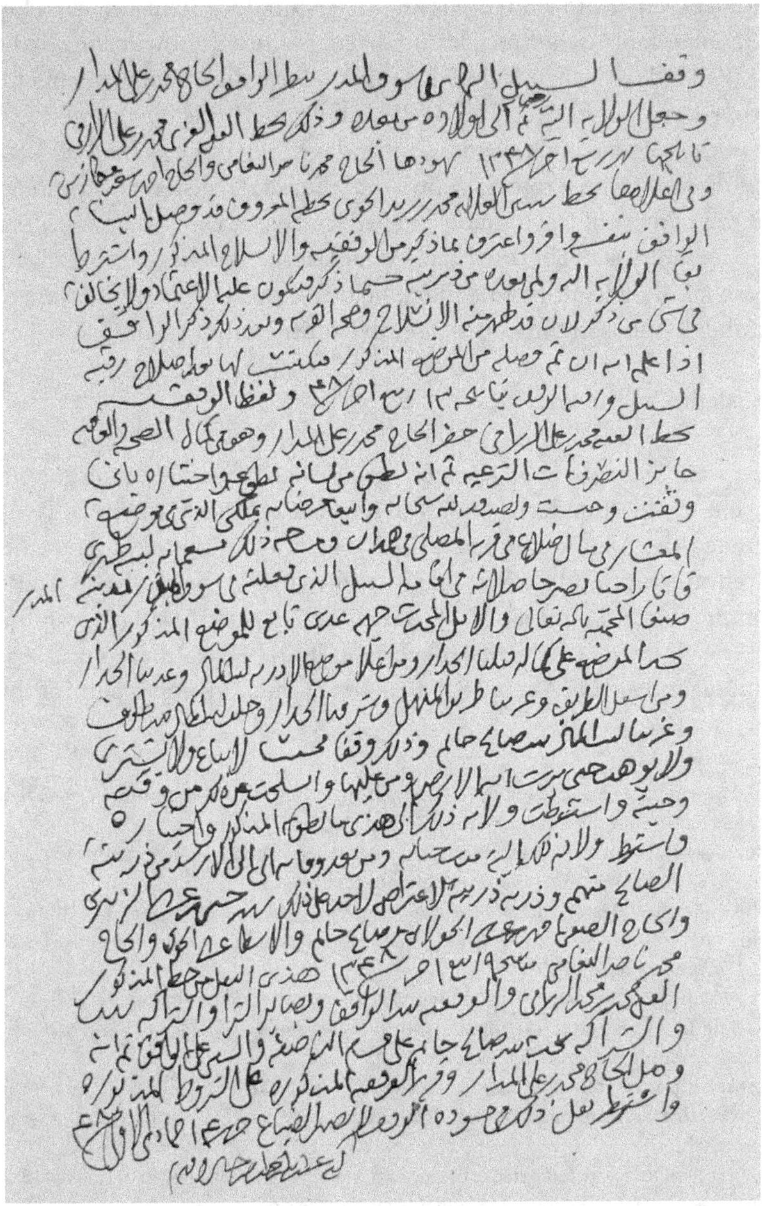

FIGURE 15 A *waqf* register entry for a *waqf* for a *sabīl* (1929).

under Imam Yaḥyā.[38] This document is written on top of the *waqf* document, on the very same paper above the main text. This practice is also common in

38 He was appointed a member of the appeal court of Sanaa (Maḥkamat al-Istiʾnāf al-Sharʿiyya) in 1330/1911 or 1912 by Imam Yaḥyā and was there for some time before he

ownership documents, and sometimes an ownership document can even become a *waqf* document[39] when an additional text is written above it such that a new owner is added to the ownership document above the original document.

The lines 1–4, 9–10, and 24–29 are "wrapped around" this new *waqf* document, that is, the original and the addition, and is in the voice of the *waqf* secretary (*kātib al-waqf*) who wrote this entry into the *waqf* register[40] (*miswaddat al-waqf*) at the request of the founder himself "so that it will not be lost." The name of the secretary is not entirely clear: it looks like ʿAbdallāh b. Aḥmad Abī l-Rijāl, whose family, according to Zabāra, held this position from the time of Imam al-Mahdī l-ʿAbbās in the mid-sixteenth century until 1938 or 1939.[41]

English translation of the text:

> [1] The *waqf*[42] for the *sabīl* situated in the pottery market under the supervision of the founder al-Ḥājj Muḥammad b. ʿAlī l-Maddār.[43] [2] He designated the role of administration[44] (*wilāya*) to himself, then to his children after him, and this was in the handwriting of the Faqīh[45] al-ʿIzzī[46] Muḥammad b. ʿAlī l-Razzāqī[47] [3] dated Rabīʿ al-Ākhir 1348 (September 1929). The witnesses [of the *waqf* document] are al-Ḥājj Muḥammad Nāṣir al-Naḥāmī and al-Ḥājj Aḥmad Saʿīd ʿAkāris [4] and the upper part [of the

---

returned to teaching Qurʾānic recitation. In 1349/1930 or 1931 he was appointed president of the same court, but died the year after. Zabāra, *Nuzhat al-naẓar*, 528.

39 I have copies of two such sales documents that were turned into *waqf* documents with the addition of some new sentences above the main text.

40 Thus he calls the register simply "the *waqf* register" (*miswaddat al-waqf*) as if there was only one, not *miswaddat al-taqyīd* (register for copying documents) or *miswaddat al-aʿyān* (inventory register).

41 Zabāra, *Nashr al-ʿarf*, 1:139–142. This reference is also mentioned by Haykel and Serjeant.

42 There could be a preceding text missing, but the genre of *waqf* registers often begin by directly mentioning the asset that is made *waqf*.

43 *Madar* means pottery, but a *maddār* is not the one who makes the pottery, but rather the trader of pottery. Serjeant and al-Akwaʿ, "The Statute of Ṣanʿāʾ," 228 n328.

44 Or guardianship.

45 *Faqīh* is a title of an educated person, usually a non-*sayyid*. Sometimes the term is used to refer to those with a legal education or in a legal profession.

46 Al-ʿIzzī is a honorary title for anyone named Muḥammad. In Sanaa many of the proper names used to have fixed honorary titles as a sign of respect. Similarly al-Ṣafīy is a title for Aḥmad, al-Fākhirī or al-Fikhrī for ʿAbdallāh, ʿAbd al-Raḥmān, or ʿAbd al-Salām; al-Wajīh. The origin is probably ʿIzz al-Islām, ʿIzz al-Dīn or something similar. A. Shivtiel, Wilfred Lockwood, and R. B. Serjeant, "The Jews of Ṣanʿāʾ," in *Ṣanʿāʾ*, ed. Serjeant and Lewcock (London: World of Islamic Festival Trust, 1983), 428 n262.

47 Or Razzāmī.

document] is in the handwriting of al-Sayyid al-ʿAllāma Muḥammad b. Zayd al-Ḥūthī, in his well-known handwriting.

The donor came to us [5] by himself, and affirmed (*aqarra*) and admitted what is mentioned in the *waqfiyya* and the aforementioned legal act (*insilākh*).[48] He put forward a new condition stipulating [6] that the guardianship (*wilāya*) should remain with himself and whoever comes after him among his descendants in accordance with what is mentioned, so this should be considered validated (*yakūnu ʿalayhi al-iʿtimād*)[49] and he is not deviating from anything by doing this [7] because both his withdrawal from his property (*insilākh*) and the purity of his good intent (*ṣiḥḥat al-qurba*) are obvious. After that, the founder mentioned [8] that knowing that if the separation[50] of the aforementioned property is complete [that is, that the *waqf* has taken place], then it is to be acquired for him (*fa-yuktasab lahu*[51]) after the asset of the *sabīl* (*raqabat al-sabīl*) [9] and the *waqf* asset (*raqabat al-waqf*) have been taken care of. Dated 13 Rabīʿ [al-Ākhir] 1348 [18 September 1929]. The wording of the *waqf* document (*al-waqfiyya*) [10] is in the handwriting of al-Faqīh Muḥammad b. ʿAlī l-Razzāqī. Present was [the founder] al-Ḥājj Muḥammad b ʿAlī l-Maddār and in complete health and well-being [11] and in a valid state for legal (*sharʿī*) dispositions. Thereafter he pronounced with his own tongue, with his free will and of his own choice: That I [12] made *waqf* (*waqqaftu wa-ḥabbastu wa-tasaddaqtu*) for God the exalted, for the purpose of His gratification, my property that is located in the place [13] of Maʿshār in the area of Ḍulāʿ in the village of al-Muṣallā[52] in Hamdān and the size of that is seven hundred *libna Ḍahrī*[53] (more than 2 hectars)

48 Here the term *insilākh* (withdrawal) refers to the act of making a *waqf*, as in withdrawing from the right to the usufruct of one's property. It means that the *waqf* took effect. See the use of the word in the contemporary case elaborated in Messick, "Textual Properties," 169 n9.

49 *Iʿtimād* means approval, validation. It can also mean "signature."

50 *Faṣl*, meaning "separating." The term is synonymous with the term *insilākh*.

51 If it reads *lahā*, referring to in the income (*al-ghālla*) the meaning would not be changed significantly.

52 This is a village to the northwest of Sanaa, half an hour drive outside the city.

53 A *libna* is a land measurement in the highlands that can have different sizes, depending on the locality. This one refers to the *libna* in Wadi Ḍahr. A *libna Ḍahrī*, as used in most of the area of Hamḍan, is smaller than a *libna Ṣanʿānī*. According to ʿAlī Muḥammad al-Farrān (forthcoming) the *libna Ḍahrī* is not given, but in Bānī Maṭar and in Bānī Ḥushaysh the *libna* is 49 m2. In this case, 700 *libna* would be just under 3.5 hectars (50 × 700), but a *libna* that some specify is equal to 30 m2 would give 2.1 hectars. Donaldson states that the *libna* varies much but that he uses an average estimate of 75 m2. Donaldson, *Sharecropping in the Yemen*, 141. *Libna* is usually pronounced *lubna*.

[14] of excellent[54] *qāt*, the income of which goes to the maintenance of the *sabīl*, that I made in the pottery market in the city of Sanaa, [15] protected by God the exalted.[55] The tamarix to the south is part of the aforementioned property, the borders of which [16] are in a complete [circle] from the north: the wall and from above the land of the public treasury (*bayt al-māl*) and to the south [is] the wall, [17] and from below [is] the road and from the west [is] the road of the water basin and from the east [is] the wall and behind it to the land of the treasury from the road [18] and to the west to the land of the public treasury, the house of Ṣāliḥ Ḥātim. All this is made *waqf*, not to be sold, not to be bought, [19] and not to be given away until God inherits the earth and those upon it. I withdrew from [all] this there [20] and then (*wa-nsalakhtu min dhālika min waqtihi wa-ḥīnihi*), and I stipulated the guardianship (*wilāya*) of this to myself, this is what he said about it, the aforementioned one, and what he chose. [21] And he stipulated the guardianship (*al-wilāya*) of that to himself, for the duration of his lifetime, and after his death to the wisest (*arshad*) of his descendants and [22] the best (*al-ṣāliḥ*) among them, and the descendants of his descendants, no one can protest this. This was witnessed by Ḥusayn ʿAbdallāh al-Zubayrī [23] and al-Ḥājj al-Ṣafiyy Aḥmad b. ʿAbdallāh al-Khawlānī and Ṣāliḥ Ḥātim and the master builder (*al-usṭā*) ʿAbdallāh al-Ḥūthī [or al-Jawfī] and al-Ḥājj [24] Muḥammad Nāṣir al-Nuʿāmī on the date of 9 Rabīʿ al-Ākhir 1348 [14 September 1929]. This is the copy (*naql*) of the aforementioned handwriting: [25] al-ʿAllāma Muḥammad b. Muḥammad al-Razzāqī, and the *waqfiyya* is under possession (*bi-yad*) of the founder, and the sales and sharecropping contracts are [also] in his hands[56] [26] and the [right of] sharecropping belongs to ʿAbdallāh Ṣāliḥ Ḥātim for half of the harvest (*ʿalā qisām al-nāṣifa*) and the irrigation (*al-saqiyy*) is [the responsibility] of the founder. Further, that [27] al-Ḥājj Muḥammad b. ʿAlī l-Maddār came and acknowledged (*qarrara*) the aforementioned *waqfiyya*, and the aforementioned conditions, [28] and he put as a condition the transfer (*naql*) of this into the *waqf* register (*miswaddat al-waqf*) for it not to be lost. Written 14 Jumāda al-Awwal 1348 [18 October 1929] [29] [Written by?] ʿAbdallāh b. Aḥmad Abī l-Rijāl(?), may God provide for him.[57]

---

54 The meaning of the word *qāt rājin, qātan rājiyan*, is not certain. It could be a type of *qāt*, or it could mean something like "good" or "re-occurring," or "walled."

55 This phrase is commonly mentioned after the name Sanaa: *al-maḥmīya bi-Llāh taʿālā*.

56 The last word of the line seems to just end in *bi-yad* ("in his hand"), presumably *bi-yadihi*.

57 The last line is unclear, perhaps *waffaqahu Allāh*.

2.6 *The* Sabīl *Today*

The *sabīl* in question is most probably the one that is today called *sabīl* Sūq al-Shāhidayn (see figure 16). The name of the *sabīl* has changed because the name of that part of the market has also changed. What used to be the pottery market is now located along the main passage from the Great Mosque to the Sūq al-Milḥ. The old pottery market is located at the northeastern periphery of

FIGURE 16 The *sabīl* Sūq Ḥārrat al-Madar today, known as *sabīl* Sūq al-Shāhidayn.

Sūq al-Milḥ and still specializes in "pottery," but now the "modern version" of it—plastic containers, metal pots, kitchen equipment, and so on. When asked, only a few of the older merchants knew that the market had been called the "pottery market" (Sūq al-Madar, Ḥārrat Sūq al-Madar). The market consists of one lane that follows the northwestern edge of the greater Sūq al-Milḥ market area. The market is dominated on the southeastern side by the old mosque called Masjid al-Shāhidayn. The present-day market took its name from this mosque, and is now called "Sūq al-Shāhidayn." The Shāhidayn mosque used to have its own *sabīl* and the remains of this can be seen a few metres to the east of the *sabīl* Ḥārrat Sūq al-Madar, though that one is no longer operating. As can be seen from the picture, the old *sabīl* Ḥārrat Sūq al-Madar, now called "Sabīl Sūq al-Shāhidayn" is still in operation. A typical stainless steel covered refrigerating/filtering device has been installed to deliver cool water and there is a stainless steel cup hanging on a chain for people to drink from. On the ground to the left, and barely visible in the photo is a tiny basin made in the concrete that provides drinking water for dogs and cats—this is a common feature related to *sabīls*. This little basin appears to be a new structure and the whole pavement where it is situated is new.

This *sabīl* is typical for the smaller market *sabīls*. One informant in the *waqf* ministry told me that most of these *sabīls* were *waṣāyā* and therefore were never under the direct authority of the *nāẓir al-waqf* or today's ministry. In contrast, the *sabīls* attached to the mosques were considered parts of the mosques and therefore were the responsibility of the "*awqāf*," that is, the ministry. The same informant told me that most market *sabīls* had been there from the late Ottoman period and that after this period they were "restored" by merchants, and new *waqfs* were attached to them. The actual *sabīl* is very similar to the other market *sabīls* in that it consists of a domed, one-room building inside of which is an old water basin called a *siqāya* (or *ḥawḍ*, both meaning basin). The term *siqāya* is often used synonymously with the term *sabīl*, the latter being a more formal term. This *sabīl* would have to have been filled by water carriers who filled goatskins with water from a public well. At night, the small wooden door at the front, leading to the *siqāya*, could be closed. We can only speculate about the cost of keeping the *sabīl* filled with water and well maintained. Once built, the structure could be relatively free of structural maintenance for decades. On a weekly basis or more frequently, the *siqāya* would need to be emptied completely, the last water scooped out, then the *siqāya* would be cleaned and refilled. Other *waqf* documents, such as those for the larger and more elaborate *sabīl*s in Cairo and other larger cities stipulated in detail what duties the *mutawallī* was responsible for.[58]

Today the structure of the *sabīl* is still considered *waqf*, but information about its legal representative and responsibility is not easy to obtain. Most of these types of *waqf*s were later privatized or changed drastically, although several of the *sabīls* are maintained by merchants in the market area who claim to take care of them "as charity" (*ṣadaqa*), but few are willing to admit any connections to a "*waqf*." One merchant in the Sūq al-Milḥ told me that his family had a *waqf* (*waṣīya*) that consisted of land outside Sanaa. They had closed the old *sabīl*, but made a new one nearby, converted from an old refrigerator.

Today most new *sabīl*s are quite small and consist of a plastic thermos-container[59] on a stall with a cup hanging from it, or a smaller steel tank with sackcloth wrapped around it that can be wetted to cool the water. Some house owners provide water taps outside the house for the poor, but these are often built in such a way that only a cup can fit under the water tap, not medium-sized water containers. According to the *Sharḥ al-azhār*, such *sabīl*s become *waqf*s by the act of providing the public with access to the services,[60] although this is a theoretical definition that few informants relate to. Most simply describe such new, urban *sabīl*s as "charity" (*ṣadaqa*).

2.7 *A* Waqf *Document of Two Shops for a Modern* Sabīl *(1982)*

This *waqf* document is the most recent of those provided by the ministry. Formation of new *waqf*s seems to have declined rapidly in recent decades, as charity and welfare have taken other forms. Yet this document is an example of a newer public *waqf*. Similar to those above, it also includes an undefined, but not insignificant, private component.

58 Mostafa, "Cairene Sabil," 41.

59 The domestic variant of this thermos container, present in a reception room (*mafraj*) when chewing *qāt* is also called a *thallāja*.

60 Ibn Miftāḥ, *Sharḥ al-azhār*, 8:223–224.

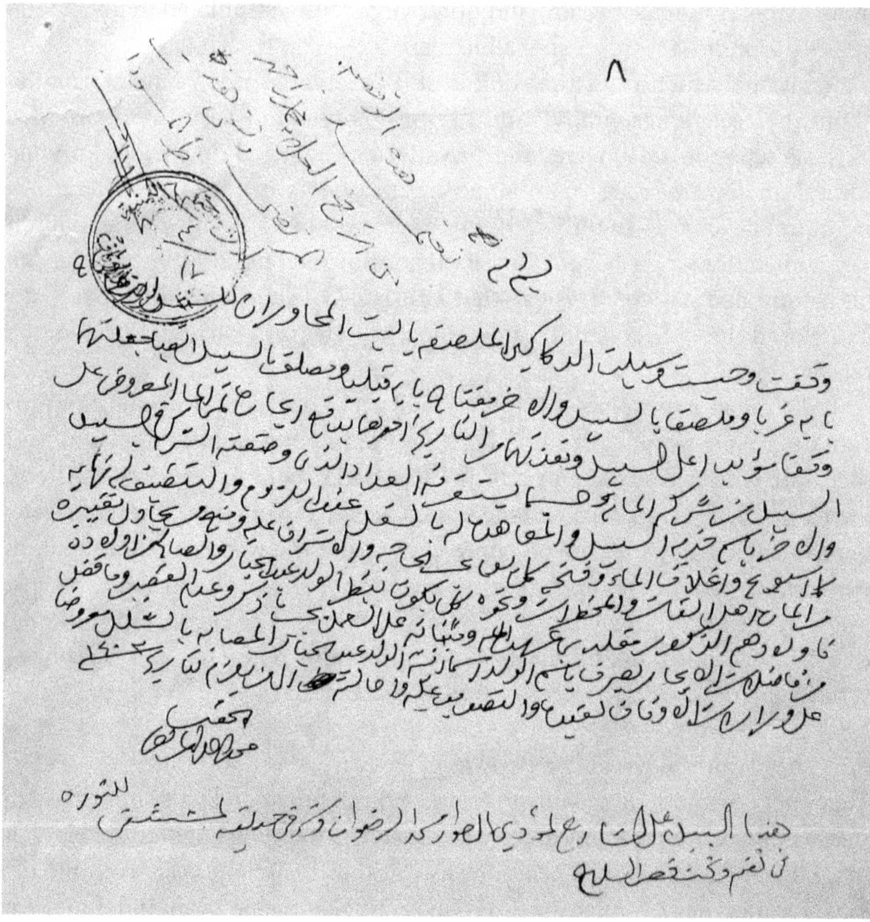

FIGURE 17 *Waqf* document from 1983.

Translation:

[Later added by the register secretary on top:] This *waqfiyya* is approved (*tuʿtamad hādhihi l-waqfiyya*).
by the brother, the learned Muḥammad Aḥmad
al-Murtaḍā xxx
entered into the *waqf* register (*miswadda*),
[signature and stamp:] (xxx)

In the name of God:

[1] I made [a] *waqf* (*waqqaftu, wa-ḥabbastu wa-sabbaltu*) [of] the two shops adjoining the house and next to the *sabīl* which is [2] facing

(lit. *al-muftāḥ*) the west and adjoining the *sabīl* and the other [shop] is facing north and next to the *sabīl* and adjoining the *sabīl* that I made, a [3] perpetual *waqf*, in favour of the *sabīl*. All this took legal effect (*nafadha*) from the date when the bill was paid [4] for water from the water company (*sharikat al-mā'*), which is used by the *sabīl*, according to its usage as indicated by the water metre that the water company installed in the *sabīl* [5] and the other [purpose of the *waqf*] is in the name of the service of the *sabīl* and its upkeep, such as washing it when necessary and cleaning it [6] every weekend and filling it with water, opening it every day according to need, and looking after it and preventing anyone from soiling the water [7] such as the passers-by of qat chewers (*ahl al-qāt*), vegetable sellers (*ahl al-mukhaḍḍarāt*),[61] and so on. All this is to be under the guardianship (*bi-naẓar*) of my son ʿAbd al-Jabbār and the righteous among his children, [8] after that, their children, the male ones among them who follow God and the work that is prescribed above. And, he is to set apart(?) and take [9] the surplus of the income and spend it in the name of the [my?] son for Asmā', the daughter of ʿAbd al-Jabbār who has suffered a handicap. [This document] has been shown [10] to the ministry of *awqāf* and for its registration (*qayd*) and its validation (*taṣdīq*) and to be available for whoever needs it. Dated the year 1402/1981–82.

The humble [before God],
Muḥammad Aḥmad al-Murtaḍā

[added by the registry]: This *sabīl* is located on the street that follows the wall of the Riḍwān Mosque, east of the garden of the Thawra Hospital.

2.8 *Comments on the* Waqfiyya

This *sabīl* is modern, in the sense that it is built in a new part of the city and gets its water from the "water company" (*sharikat al-mā'*) through the public water pipe network. However, by looking back at the other *waqfs*, we can see that the continuity of the tradition is very clear. The continuity is found in the formulations, the authorities invoked, the culture of legal documents, and the whole legal institution as such.

61 Many *qāt* chewers prefer to wash their *qāt* and when they are away from home, the public *sabīls* are very popular places to do this. Indeed it is very common to see written signs on the *sabīls* that discourage people from washing their *qāt* there, sometimes with strongly worded statements. The same applies to those who buy the leeks and salad on the way home for lunch and want to wash them at the *sabīl* along the way.

This *waqf* is a public *waqf*, however, it also has a private beneficiary, namely the disabled granddaughter. This is legal according to *waqf* law. What happens when she dies? Who is then to have the surplus, if there is any? Ideally, one could reason that the ministry of *awqāf* is ultimately responsible for such a public *waqf* and must supervise the *waqf* and demand yearly accounts etc., as is stipulated in *waqf* law. In that case, when the granddaughter dies, what happens if there is no one in the family who can be described as disabled such that they would qualify to have her share. According to the law, her share will go to a similar purpose, that is, someone else disabled outside the family. In reality, this *waqf* may not be considered a *waqf* but a *waqf-waṣīya*, and arguably should be supervised by the *nāẓir al-waṣāyā*.[62] It is even more likely that this is a semi-public type of *waqf*, that is, it is registered simply as other private property is registered in a public register and that neither the ministry of *awqāf*, nor the *nāẓir al-waṣāyā* were ever actively involved.[63] Probably it was also the custom of the time to allow such a *waqf* to exist simply on its own right without further involvement from the ministry, this would be based on the centuries-old rules found in *fiqh* books. The matter of the surplus in such *waqf*s is also characterized by a lack of strict rules, as I demonstrate later in this chapter, as long as the *waqf* is taken care of, the surplus is simply there for the *mutawallī* to decide over if the founder so wishes it. In effect, the surplus in the *waqf* above is not counted as part of the "charitable *waqf*" but belongs to the family of the founder; it either goes to the *mutawallī* himself or is divided among the family. In any case, it is a private matter.

Is such document a legal ruse? What if the son had two sisters and this *waqf* diminished their inheritance? Would such a *waqf* document be valid today? According to *waqf* law, this depends on the surplus: if it is larger than the amount of work needed to administer the *waqf*, then the *waqf* becomes, in part, a family *waqf*, which according to the law can be contested in court by heirs whose potential inheritance is threatened by it. The cost of taking such a case to court would argue against such a legal solution. We do not know how much the surplus in this actual *waqf* was.

Both issues in the *waqf* above, the surplus managed by the *mutawallī* and the girl who has a (temporary) right in the surplus, are aspects that could fall under the category of an "exception" to an otherwise ideal, public *waqf*. Such

62 In order to establish this, it would be necessary to study the registers of the *waṣāyā* administration; my request to do this was very politely refused.

63 Despite this, this very *waqf* is registered by the ministry. But what this mean in practice, is not clear.

exceptions are valid in Zaydī *fiqh*, but do not fall directly under today's republican *waqf* law.[64]

3 Theoretical Possibilities for Private Aspects of a Public *Waqf*

Looking at the last two *waqf* documents presented above, both were made at a time when it was not an option to use the family *waqf*, since, in its basic form, it is officially illegal. Thus the tendency was to insert private rights into a public *waqf*, in order to take the opportunity to create something similar to the exclusionary[65] family *waqf*. This motive was less clear in earlier periods when the exclusionary family *waqf* model could easily have been chosen instead. The need to keep family control over local charity and welfare infrastructure can also be seen as a way to ensure the continuity of charity in an uncertain society loosely governed by a weak state. Another intention could be to ensure that the continuity of the *waqf* remains in the hands of the founder's family, not in an outside governmental agency. If the *waqf* is kept local and only "semi-registered," it can be taken back by the descendants of the founder and reverted to private property more easily.[66] This is not very logical in "pure" or absolute public *waqf*s, for example, for mosques. Many think that it is better for a family to take back a *waqf* than to have the government mismanage it. In a society like Yemen, the state itself is also partly "private" and in our analysis, the private-public distinction must be used with caution.

---

64 Exceptions can be made in the income of the *waqf*, but not in the *waqf* asset itself. Further, this exception must be specified by a certain percentage of the income and not an absolute measure. Article 23 of the *waqf* law states: "If a *waqf* is made of a certain part—such as one-quarter or similarly—of the asset income, in a *waqf* for a specific purpose, then such a *waqf* is valid (*saḥḥa al-waqf*) and a joint ownership (*mushāʿ*) arises in the asset according to the percentage specified." In the *waqf* above the right to the surplus if the *waqf* is first considered public is also problematic. Wizārat al-Shuʾūn al-Qānūniyya, *Qānūn al-waqf al-sharʿī*, 4. The ministry, but again theoretically, has the right to the surplus such as in the article 38. Article 61 (and partly article 66) allows the *mutawallī* to expand the *waqf* with new assets from the surplus if a surplus occurs. The *fiqh* is clearer on this issue as I discuss below. First, it says that the whole issue of surplus is up to the founder to decide, and second, it says that if the founder does not specify this, which is the case in the *waqf* document above, then local custom is to be followed. In practice, this means that the surplus goes to the family of the founder. Here the law is "stricter" than the *fiqh*.

65 "Excluding" in a broad sense as discussed in chapter 5.

66 Mundy notes that small, informal *waqf*s ("among farmers") are often dissolved after a generation or two. Mundy, *Domestic Government*, 232 n61.

It is often stated that there are two types of *waqf*: public and private. Many scholars point out that both types of *waqf* have private and public aspects. For instance, Baer argues that public *waqfs* have clear benefits for certain families entitled to administer these public *waqfs* since the administration of the *waqfs* often entails many economic and social advantages.[67] Sometimes private rights can also be explicit parts of the *waqf*. Powers uses the term "semi-familial or mixed endowments."[68] Deguilhem calls them "shared" or "mixed *waqf*" (*waqf mushtarak*).[69]

The typical Ḥanafī family *waqf* is actually a charitable public *waqf* with a temporal exception added to it; this states that the family or descendants of the founder can enjoy the *waqf* as long as they live. Other law schools have other doctrinal foundations that relate to these questions, which again leads to other types of doctrinal dilemmas and possible legal ruses. Practice-oriented *fiqh* has developed differently according to the law schools and political contexts. This chapter deals almost exclusively with the Zaydī and Yemeni version of such a relationship between ideal doctrines and local *waqf* norms.

3.1 *Different Models of Mixed* Waqfs

In order to understand the questions discussed in the *fiqh* texts below it is necessary to clarify the different ways that private rights can be inserted into a public *waqf*. At least three types of mixed *waqfs* can be easily distinguished:

1) The split beneficiary *waqf*. This involves two parallel, separate beneficiaries: one public and one private.
2) The excepted income *waqf* (*waqf mustathnā l-ghalla*). This is a public *waqf* in which a part of the income (*al-ghalla*) or the usufruct (*al-manfaʿa*) is reserved, "excepted" (*mustathnā*) for a private purpose designated by the founder. The whole asset, theoretically, remains a *waqf*,[70] while parts of the income have a private character. Though the difference between the type above and this is arguably minimal, this legal construction is often used. It also makes the private part less explicit.
3) The *waqf* in which the *mutawallī* receives the surplus. This *waqf* is also fully public in theory, but the service it offers only requires a certain portion of the income; once that service has been taken care of by the *mutawallī*, he may take the rest of the income himself. This *waqf* is not

67 Gabriel Baer, "The Waqf as a Prop for the Social System (Sixteenth–Twentieth Centuries)," *Islamic Law and Society* 4, no. 3 (1997): 264–287.

68 Powers, "Orientalism, Colonialism and Legal History," 537.

69 Deguilhem, "Waqf in the City," 924.

70 In *fiqh*, this is the most common view; in modern *waqf* law (article 23 quoted above) there is a "joint ownership" in the asset. Thus the law takes a more practical stand.

fully legitimate on a doctrinal level and therefore it has no name. Yet, as this chapter shows, both in *waqf* documents and in *fiqh* (below) it does exist and arguably was/is common.

The first of these three types is not problematic and needs no further explanation. The last two types differ from each other in that the second theoretically leaves the surplus for the descendants of the founder, while the third leaves the whole surplus for the *mutawallī*. In practice they can overlap. In the following part of this chapter I analyse *fiqh* texts and *fatwās* that seek to regulate these "grey areas." These *fiqh* texts and *fatwās* are thus important indications of the presence of such forms of *waqf* and the perceived need for legal regulation in this field. Again, while doctrines state one thing, the more practice-oriented *fiqh* rules mainly refer to "custom." In any case, the legal solutions in these matters seldom refer to the texts of revelation; they are legal solutions that exist because they are needed.

The doctrines or ideal *fiqh* does not focus much on the role of the *mutawallī*, or presents him as one who is allowed to enjoy the benefits of the *waqf*. The obvious reason for this is that he is simply an employee; he administers the *waqf* for a certain fee. This fee is not explicitly mentioned in the *Sharḥ al-azhār*. It is given slightly more attention in al-Shawkānī's *matn/sharḥ* work, *al-Darārī*, in a rule based on a *ḥadīth*: "He [*the mutawallī*] can take from the *waqf* as salary what is considered custom (*lahu an ya'kula bi-l-maʿrūf*)."[71] As seen in chapter 3 and in the case of the "three cisterns" at the beginning of this chapter, according to local custom the *mutawallī* can take 10 per cent, be it for a private or a public *waqf*.[72] If we assume that in certain cases this fraction may be even higher, the legal right to be a *mutawallī* becomes important, as does having general control over the *waqf* and its assets. The role of the *mutawallī* is certainly much more important than what is foreseen in the ideal, basic *waqf* model. Thus the legal need for regulation in these matters is clear, and indeed the *fiqh* in these points is quite rich, as I demonstrate below.

3.2 *Regulating Public* Waqfs *with a Private Surplus*

In terms of *fiqh* doctrine, we can expect that if a surplus develops in an ideal *waqf*, this surplus would be spent on the *waqf* itself, in order to make it more useful, to expand its services, or to expand its assets and increase the *waqf*, or

---

71 al-Shawkānī, *al-Darārī l-muḍīya*, 304.

72 Vom Bruck mentions a large family *waqf* belonging to the Sharaf al-Dīn family in Kawkabān: It has two *mutawallīs* who share the job of administering the leases of the agricultural fields. The "trustees" are entitled to 10 per cent. Vom Bruck, *Islam, Memory, and Mortality*, 74.

make it "grow." If this cannot be done, the surplus should be diverted to other, similar *waqfs*. All this would enhance the merit of the founder, and thus the "spirit" of the *waqf* itself. It is ironic and quite revealing that the *fiqh* in the *Sharḥ al-azhār* barely mentions this ideal solution. Instead, it elaborates upon cases in which the founder specified that the surplus be diverted in other ways.

In Zaydī *waqf* doctrine, a public *waqf* can revert to the founder's family, in contrast to a Ḥanafī *waqf*, which requires a final, perpetual public charitable purpose. The *waqf*, "if its purpose/beneficiary ceases to exist" (*bi-zawāl maṣrifihi*) "is to revert to the descendants of the founder (as *waqf* not as private property)."[73] Once this doctrine is accepted, the strong position of the founder, his descendants, and the *mutawallī* is given preference over the "absolute," pure, or ideal *waqf*, though the ideal *waqf* is still valid and can be used. The founder may still, if he wishes, stipulate an alternative, ultimate public beneficiary, as is compulsory in Ḥanafī *waqf*. The break with the ideal *waqf* on this point is allowed in Zaydī *fiqh*, if the founder desires it. From this point, several discussions in Zaydī *fiqh* branch off, though they remain partly interwoven with each other.

The first debate, or elaboration, deals with the validity of making exceptions to the *waqf*. These exceptions are based on the theoretical bifurcation of the right to property and the right of use (as explained in the basic *waqf* model in chapter 2); some of the discussions try to correct some of the confusion and "innovations" that arise from this rather theoretical bifurcation. Below, I chose to focus on the more practically oriented rules and discussions, not the theoretical and doctrinal ones, although doctrinal elements are used as arguments and counter-arguments.

The first text I analyse is a discussion from Ibn al-Murtaḍā's *al-Baḥr al-zakhkhār*.

> Question: The statement of al-Mu'ayyad bi-Llāh:[74] If someone makes a *waqf* upon a right (*'an ḥaqqin*)[75] and then said: And my son is to be given from the income of the *waqf* what he needs, then this [*waqf*] is valid, as

73 Ibn Miftāḥ, *Sharḥ al-azhār*, 8:214. In this matter, only the dissent of al-Mu'ayyad is quoted in the *Sharḥ al-azhār*; he claims that the *waqf* should go the public treasury (*al-maṣāliḥ*). Al-Shawkānī also protests against this "pragmatism" in *al-Sayl al-jarrār*; he states that the *waqf* should rather be spent on a similar purpose, rather than reverting to the family.

74 Al-Mu'ayyad bi-Llāh (d. 411/1020), the Caspian Zaydī imam much quoted in the *Kitāb al-Azhār*/*Sharḥ al-azhār*.

75 *Ḥaqq* here probably refers to *waqfs* made for the sake of *zakāt*. This is indicated in the *Sharḥ al-azhār*: "fa-yaṣiḥḥu 'an yaqifa al-raqaba 'an ḥaqq min zakāt aw khums aw bayt māl wa-yastathnī l-ghalla." Ibn Miftāḥ, *Sharḥ al-azhār*, 8:218.

> he [the son] is like the exception (*al-mustathnā*). I [Ibn al-Murtaḍā] say: defining "needs" here refers back to custom.[76]

In Ibn al-Murtaḍā's time it was possible to make a *waqf* for a "right," such as *zakāt* for the public treasury. In several places such *zakāt waqfs* are mentioned in discussions over excepted income *waqfs*, but I do not look further into this peculiar aspect of *waqfs*.[77] Other footnotes clarify that any public *waqf* can also contain an "exception," therefore that specific detail should not divert our attention. In the citation above the significance is the validity of such an exception and second, the economic size of the exception is to be set by custom (*ʿurf*) if it is not specified by the founder.

A very similar statement is found in the *Sharḥ al-azhār*. One of the validated (*tadhhīb*) footnotes states:

> If the founder makes a *waqf* for a mosque, or [for a] similar [public purpose], and he excepts the income for himself (*yastathnī ghallatahu li-nafsihi*) then the income is his private property. But if he dies, does the excepted part revert to the mosque, or can it be inherited by his heirs? The closest view (*al-aqrab*), [validation by] *tadhhīb*, is that it can be inherited (*tuwarrath*), [validation by] *taqrīr*, unless he meant or stated that it [the exception] was only for his own lifetime.[78]

This footnote sparks further debate over whether or not the permanence of such an exception is in accordance with the doctrines. Being an "exception," in its nature it is temporary, but the line between ongoing temporality and perpetuity is theoretical. The validated views are the pragmatic ones, like the one above. The conclusion of the debate is that an excepted income *waqf* is doctrinally problematic, but legally absolutely valid.

---

76 Masʿala: (m) wa-law waqafa ʿan ḥaqq thumma qāl: wa-yuʿṭā ibnī min ghallat al-waqf ḥājatuhu, ṣaḥḥa, idh huwa ka-l-mustathnā. Qultu: wa-yurjaʿ fī tafsīr al-ḥāja ilā l-ʿurf." Ibn al-Murtaḍā, *al-Baḥr al-zakhkhār*, 5:154.

77 *Sharḥ al-azhār*, 8:219, clarifies that important imams were against *waqf* for "rights," such as *waqf* for *zakāt*. Imam Yaḥyā b. Ḥamza was one of these imams. Indeed, he produced a decree ordering the confiscation of all such *waqfs* since they were already made for a public purpose (a collection of Imam Yaḥyā b. Ḥamza's letters and treatises was shown to me at the Mu'assasat Zayd b. ʿAlī l-Thaqāfiyya). In the post-classical Zaydī period (after about 1600) such *waqfs* do not seem to be important anymore, though mention of them survives in the examples in the *fiqh* concerning excepted *waqfs*.

78 *Sharḥ al-azhār* 8:218, n2. The footnote is attributed to a certain work, *Bustān*. In any case, it is validated by both the *tadhhīb* and the *taqrīr* signs.

In effect, both of the last two types mentioned above, the excepted income *waqf* and the *waqf* in which the *mutawallī* receives the surplus are combined or mixed *waqfs* even though, initially, they were purely public *waqfs*. Formally, they have no private beneficiaries. The value taken out of the *waqf* by the relatives of the founder is not taken because they are beneficiaries. The rights are taken by someone who has been given the excepted part of the income, or through the "channel" of the *mutawallī*, through his salary. Whether or not the former are beneficiaries proper, as in any normal family *waqf*, is simply not clear, as is shown below.

The legality of such a *waqf* in the moment it is made is one question. Another discussion that is just as important is how these private rights are valid over the long-term and how these rights should be transferred from one generation to the next. Thus the rules of who should have the right to be the administrator or be the guardian (*mutawallī*) suddenly become highly important. The same applies to the rules of how to transfer the rights from one generation of recipients to the next. In the *waqf* in which the *mutawallī* receives the surplus this legal problem can be seen in the debates over the role of the *mutawallī*, an issue that I return to below. First we look deeper into the issue of how the *fiqh* justifies the concept that the *mutawallī* of a public *waqf* does not have to spend the surplus from the *waqf* assets on the original purpose or beneficiary of the *waqf*.

3.3 *What to do with a Surplus in the* Waqf?

Section eight of the nine sections in the "Kitāb al-waqf" (the chapter of *waqf*) in the *Sharḥ al-azhār* is called "Section clarifying what the *mutawallī* can validly do and not do." It has ten sub-sections or rules.[79] The last of these ten rules states that it is obligatory to spend the income of the *waqf* first on the maintenance of the *waqf* asset itself if it needs repair, and then, and only then, can the rest be spent on the beneficiary. Ibn al-Miftāḥ, the author of the *Sharḥ al-azhār* adds an exception:[80] "if the beneficiary is rich, i.e., his 'needs' are covered, then the *mutawallī* can buy another asset that can produce more income for the *waqf*."[81] It states explicitly that this is an option, not a duty. The duty is to maintain the asset. The encouragement to expand the *waqf* is no stronger in

79 The sixth of these deals with issues of lease; the maximum lease period rule is treated in detail in chapter 6.

80 Ibn Miftāḥ, *Sharḥ al-azhār*, 8:276–277.

81 "Fa amma law arāda al-mutawallī tawsīʿahā, aw taqwīyat binā'ihā [al-maṣrif] lam yaḥsan dhālika illā maʿa ghinā' al-maṣrif al-madhkūr, li-anna dhālika bi-manẓilat kasb mustaghill ākhar li-dhālika al-waqf." Ibn Miftāḥ, *Sharḥ al-azhār*, 8:277.

al-Tāj al-mudhhab[82] nor in the *Taysīr al-marām*.[83] Interestingly, the statement in the *Sharḥ al-azhār* has no validation signs and no footnotes.

There are some other elaborations on this topic in another part of the *waqf* chapter, namely the section dealing specifically with mosques. What is clear from the *Kitāb al-Azhār* and *Sharḥ al-azhār*[84] is that a *mutawallī* may validly (*yajūzu lahu*) take the surplus from the mosque *waqf*s and use it for whatever the founder wanted or for the general "revival" (*iḥyāʾ*) of the mosque. It does not explicitly say that the rule in question is relevant for other types of *waqf*s in addition to mosque *waqf*s. And, nothing seems to indicate that the rule is restricted to mosque *waqf*s only. Rather it is the nature of a mosque as a public beneficiary that must be understood. If the beneficiary is a specific person or persons (read: private, family *waqf*), he/they would make sure to take the whole income after the maintenance of the asset and the salary of the *mutawallī*. If the income from the asset increased more than expected in a certain year, the beneficiaries would simply take the surplus. However, if the beneficiary is a mosque or any other public structure, such as a water basin, the *mutawallī* might be left with a surplus after taking care of the needs[85] of the beneficiary. In general, these "needs" are, according to the *Sharḥ al-azhār*, decided by "local custom." If a certain set of services is expected from a certain mosque, such as water for ablution, carpets, the presence of a part-time imam, etc., then this must be upheld and respected by the *mutawallī*. However, if a water cistern is in good shape and not in need of further repair, and a surplus in the *waqf* emerges, is the *mutawallī* then obliged to expand the *waqf*?

The problem may sound theoretical and we could argue that there is no theoretical answer to it in practice-oriented *fiqh*. The reason for this is clear: the surplus has generally already been considered, either during the act of founding the *waqf*, or in later operational stages of the *waqf*, in the form of "custom." In order to look for legal ways to handle the problem of the surplus we must look at the division between publicly and privately managed *waqf*. This leads us back to the power of the founder in deciding who should be the *mutawallī*.

---

82 al-ʿAnsī, *al-Tāj al-mudhhab*, 4:326.

83 Qāsim b. Ibrāhīm, al-Ānisī, and al-Sarḥī, *Taysīr al-marām*, 152. Al-Shawkānī seems to hold the same opinion: *al-Sayl al-jarrār*, 2:71. However, in the comments on rules for mosques he says that it is "obvious" that if the *mutawallī* buys a new asset, then this becomes *waqf*. See al-Shawkānī, *al-Sayl al-jarrār*, 2:63.

84 Ibn Miftāḥ, *Sharḥ al-azhār*, 8:238–241.

85 The "needs" of a mosque are discussed in detail in that section of the "Kitāb al-waqf"; some of the needs are dependent on doctrinal stands, such as whether or not it is allowed to decorate the mosque, but most of the "needs" are defined by local custom (*ʿurf*), which varies depending on the size of the mosque.

If someone makes an agricultural field a *waqf* for a mosque (which is then a secondary *waqf*), and if the founder decides to administer the *waqf* himself, this constellation of the two *waqf*s is left with two *mutawallī*s (administrators, guardians), one for the agricultural field and another for the mosque. The founder of the *waqf* can "restrict" the *waqf* in the process of making it, that is, he can decide how his *waqf* should be used and thus influence whether or not the potential surplus is available for the mosque and its *mutawallī*. The texts from the *Sharḥ al-azhār* dealing with these questions are given below. In addition, there are many interesting footnotes, some of which I focus on below:

The *matn* (*Kitāb al-Azhār*) reads as follows; the footnote marked as (1) is important:

> **The *mutawallī* is allowed to acquire an investment object (*yajūzu kasb mustaghall*) from the surplus of the income, even if a minaret could be built from it.**[86] **And the new investment object does not become *waqf*. And the aforementioned object is to be spent on the mosque or its usage or its building in regard to what can increase its revival, such as education, except [in] cases in which the founder (1) restricted (*qaṣarahu*) the *waqf* for a specific purpose.**[87]

The *matn* (*Kitāb al-Azhār*) by Ibn al-Murtaḍā is given in bold. The *sharḥ* (*Sharḥ al-azhār*) of Ibn Miftāḥ (below) wraps around the *matn* that is given above, however, the *sharḥ* does not offer much "comment" other than rephrasing the same rule in different words, therefore I have not included it here. An exception might be the elaboration upon the very last sentences, where Ibn Miftāḥ adds:

> **... except in cases where the founder (1) restricted the *waqf* for a specific purpose.** This means: If the founder meant with the *waqf*; a specific usufruct (*manfaʿa makhṣūṣa*), [then] [the *mutawallī*] is not allowed to spend it otherwise, whether [the founder] pronounced this explicitly, or if this is known from his intention (*aw ʿurifa min qaṣdihi*).[88]

86 Al-Shawkānī comments on Ibn al-Murtaḍā's use of a minaret as an example; he finds this example theoretical, as it would rarely happen. Al-Shawkānī, *al-Sayl al-jarrār*, 63.

87 Ibn Miftāḥ, *Sharḥ al-azhār*, 8:238–239.

88 Ibid., 8:241.

An interesting footnote comes after the word "founder"; it states: "In words or custom (a comment made by al-Saḥūlī)."[89] Ibrāhīm b. Yaḥyā al-Saḥūlī (d. 1060/1650) was a judge in Sanaa who commented on the *Azhār*. The footnote has not been validated by *tadhhīb* or *iqrār* in the 2003 edition, but it is marked by *taqrīr* in the 1980 edition,[90] and it emerges in *al-Tāj al-mudhhab* as if it was so.[91] A second footnote follows immediately and this note *is* validated by *taqrīr*: "(*) And similarly: Such as in the giver of a *nadhr* [vow, conditional gift], the giver of a gift (*hiba*) and the giver of a testament (*al-mūṣī*). Validated (q-r-z)."[92]

The first footnote, which also later became a rule in *al-Tāj al-mudhhab*, implies several things: the interesting use of custom (*ʿurf*) as a source of law in a question that will be dealt in further detail below, and the founder's strong rights in deciding the setup of the *waqf*.

"Custom" contributes to validating a type of *waqf* that is valid just because it is custom. Invoking custom produces validity. For example, if a founder makes a *waqf* for a mosque (this is a form of *waqf* for another *waqf*), theoretically, the *mutawallī* of the mosque may take the surplus after taking care of the mosque and he can spend it to buy more income producing assets, or extra equipment, or additions to the mosque. This would be in the interest of the *waqf* and the founder. But if local custom says that founders generally do not give this freedom to the *mutawallī* of the mosque, then it is not necessary for the founder to say or write explicitly "I make a *waqf* for only a specific part or service related to the mosque, the surplus is not to go to the mosque," because custom supplies the intended restriction or exception. In this case, the *mutawallī* of the mosque cannot transfer the income or surplus from the *waqf* to other parts of the mosque, much less to other *waqf*s that he administers.[93] Further, we do not know exactly what al-Saḥūlī meant when he indicated that according to custom in some areas the founders restrict the *waqf*s they make; this is clarified

89 "Lafẓan aw ʿurfan." Ḥāshiyat al-Saḥūlī. Ibid., 8:241. See also Ibn Miftāḥ, *Kitāb al-Muntaziʿ*, 3:485.

90 This footnote is followed by an *iqrār* in Ibn Miftāḥ, *Kitāb al-Muntaziʿ* (1980 edition), 3:485.

91 al-ʿAnsī, *al-Tāj al-mudhhab*, 316.

92 "Wa naḥwahu; ka-l-nādhir wa-l-wāhib wa-l-mūṣī" (q-r-z). Ibn Miftāḥ, *Sharḥ al-azhār*, 8:241.

93 The following footnote states that the *mutawallī* of the mosque is indeed allowed to use the surplus on the building of the mosque itself, even if the founder did not intend this. This is attributed to the *Ghayth*, the *Wābil*, *al-Baḥr al-zakhkhār*, a certain *Sharḥ fatḥ*, and the fact that al-Shāmī confirmed ("*qarrara*") this view; however *al-Azhār* takes a position that is contrary to all these and this is what is given *tadhhīb*. Ibn Miftāḥ, *Sharḥ al-azhār*, 8:241, n2.

by other texts further below. The discussion sounds complicated unless we see this rule as part of what comes below; the custom of retaining the *wilāya* (guardianship) within the family of the founder and possibly also attaching additional benefits[94] to that role. Al-Saḥūlī's footnote above indicates the presence of such a custom and thus the need for a validated legal rule to explicitly implement it, and the second footnote extends the similar role of custom to the formation of other legal constructs such as a *nadhr* or a *waṣīya* (which are often synonyms for *waqf*s).

Many of the other footnotes deal with whether or not a minaret or other part of the mosque is "needed" and if this need is given priority over the income before the *mutawallī* can take the surplus, and if he buys something, whether or not these things automatically have a *waqf* status.[95] The opinions given vary, but the validation marks (*tadhhīb* and *taqrīr*) favour the view that newly acquired additions do not become new *waqf*s.[96] The "needs" of a mosque are defined in several rules related to local custom.

As noted, if a *waqf* is made for a public purpose such as a mosque, custom may say that the founder did not want the *mutawallī* to have full control of the *waqf*, or over the surplus of the *waqf*. In the case of such a *waqf*, the question of defining the authority or guardianship (*wilāya*) becomes a crucial issue. Al-Shawkānī often takes a stand that is contrary to the Zaydī tradition. The Zaydī tradition of *fiqh* in these questions is oriented towards practice and the *fiqh* has developed over the centuries alongside legal practices and legal needs. Al-Shawkānī attacks what he sees as "half-hearted *waqf*." His criticism is a doctrinal criticism of a pragmatic *fiqh*. The result is more academic and polemic than practical in terms of possibilities for legal implementation. For instance, he sees excepted income *waqf*s as doctrinally wrong. The same applies to the question of *waqf*s in which the beneficiary (which can be an institution or building) appointed by the founder has ceased to exist; he claims

94 As I argue below those benefits include control over the *waqf* as if it was a private *waqf*, and the possibility of extracting surplus income from the *waqf* in a way that is entirely legal.

95 Ibn al-Amīr touches on this last issue in the letter to al-Mahdī l-ʿAbbās, as translated in chapter 3. The present *waqf* law states in article 61 that new *waqf* assets bought from the surplus becomes the property of the *waqf* (*yuʿtabar al-mushtarā milkan li-l-waqf*). Wizārat al-Shuʾūn al-Qānūniyya, *Qānūn al-waqf al-sharʿī*, 9.

96 The *sharḥ* says that rugs and carpets are parts of the furniture inventory that the *mutawallī* should provide; one of the footnotes also adds water. One footnote, which is restated in *al-Tāj al-mudhhab*, says that the "*mutawallī* can pay for heating the mosque even if its white parts become blackened. And coal is better than wood for heating the mosque." Even details of which type of books deserve funding from the mosque is discussed. The details are many and interesting, particularly from a historian's perspective.

there are other worthy beneficiaries to receive the *waqf*: "The absence of the beneficiary does not remove the status of *waqf* [of the asset] since the status of *waqf* is absolute" (... zawāl al-maṣrif lā yarfaʿu hādha al-taḥbīs li-annahu taḥbīs muṭlaq ...).[97]

Thus far, we know that according to validated Zaydī *fiqh*, parts of a *waqf* can be reserved or restricted by the founder, even defined by custom, to be an a priori norm. Custom can also imply that the founder only makes a *waqf* for a specific service, for example, a service related to a specific mosque. The founder's right to keep the rest of the *waqf* income for himself once that service is taken care of is implicit in this, even though it is not stated explicitly, as long as it is local custom. We now return to the role of the administrator or guardian.

4 Questions Concerning the Right to Guardianship in Combined *Waqf*s[98]

In the ideal *waqf* model, once the *waqf* has been transferred from the founder's property and become God's property, one would not necessarily expect that the founder should have anything to do with the *waqf* anymore. However, many founders want to stay in control of the *waqf* even after it is made in favour of a public purpose. According to general agreement in Zaydī *fiqh*, the founder can declare that the role of the guardianship, the *mutawallī*, is to remain in his family.

If the founder does not stipulate that the *mutawallī* is to be from his family, the guardianship automatically goes to the beneficiary, according to the *Kitāb al-Azhār* and the *Sharḥ al-azhār*. If the beneficiary is another *waqf*, such as a mosque or a water basin, it is natural that the *waqf* made for that mosque falls under the authority of the *mutawallī* of that beneficiary. That is, the *mutawallī* of the mosque takes priority over the family of he who made the *waqf* for the mosque. One of the obvious reasons for this is the situation of management, it would become rather complicated if there were many such *waqf*s attached to one mosque and each one had its own *mutawallī*. The *waqf* clusters of the large urban mosque *waqf*s that today fall under the ministry may serve as an example: The original founders or their families do not have any claims to those *waqf*s at all (ideally, in practice they do in part). The *waqf*s that have existed for a long time, for which most of the origins are forgotten, are managed as one legal unit and administered by the public *waqf* administration. These are

97 al-Shawkānī, *al-Sayl al-jarrār*, 3:58.
98 al-ʿAnsī, *al-Tāj al-mudhhab*, 3:302; Ibn Miftāḥ, *Sharḥ al-azhār*, 8:249–250.

*waqf*s in which the founder has not stipulated the administration for himself, or in which, for various reasons, the administration has been taken over by the public *waqf* administration.

One can say that there is something suspicious about a *waqf* for a purely public purpose if it is explicitly pointed out that it is to be administered by the founder and his heirs, especially if the *waqf* that it is made for is large and consists of many assets and many different founders. The family of the founder has a dubious role in all this: Unless they receive benefits, why would the family be interested in the guardianship?[99] And what if the *waqf* is not *entirely* public? If the right of administration is given to the beneficiary and the family of the founder is also a beneficiary along with another public beneficiary, who should have the right to administer it?

The *fiqh* debates are initially correct in terms of doctrine: the guardianship goes first to the founder, then if he or his appointed *mutawallī* for some reason cannot hold the position, the position goes to the beneficiary. The *Kitāb al-Azhār* and the *Sharḥ al-azhār* do not mention the founder's descendants as having rights to the position as *mutawallī* at all. However, the question arises in the footnotes, which give us further information about what is perceived to be a common form of *waqf* in some areas. The text under scrutiny below is a footnote (*ḥāshiya*) in the *Sharḥ al-azhār*. It is found in the very beginning of the seventh of the nine sections in the *waqf* chapter:

> Section. Clarification of who has guardianship/authority (*wilāya*) of the *waqf*.
>
> **And** note that whoever made a *waqf*, **the guardianship** of that [*waqf*] **is to be for the founder** (6), and no one can oppose him in this, **then for his deputy by a testament or as an appointment … then** it is to be **for the beneficiary** if he is **a specific** person and of legal capacity, **then**, if there is no *wāqif* and no one appointed by him and no beneficiary that is defined and of legal capacity, the authority is to be **for the imam and the judge.**[100]

The sequence of authority is clear: (1) the founder, (2) whoever the founder has appointed, (3) the beneficiary if he/they are specific person(s), and if none of

99 According to Sālim BinSumayṭ, Shibām, Hadramawt, and all the public *waqf*s established by their family were administered by someone outside the family; this was done to ensure that a family member was not tempted to exploit the *waqf*. Personal communication, Shibām, Jan. 2009.

100 Ibn Miftāḥ, *Sharḥ al-azhār*, 8:249–252.

these are present, the *waqf* is to be controlled by the (4) imam or his judges. A judge under the imam's jurisdiction is technically called a *ḥākim*; the term *qāḍī* is much broader and can refer to any person working with issues of law and administration, and it is also the title of an educated person of a non-*sayyid*, tribal family.

The *matn* and the *sharḥ* move on to other topics, but again, what is of interest to us here is a footnote: Footnote (6) comes after the word "founder" in the *sharḥ* of Ibn Miftāḥ above:

> (6) A related topic, *tadhhīb*: If there exists a custom, such that a deceased [person] would not make a *waqf* unless he intends that the *waqf* will remain under the control of his children or similarly, and if this cannot be so he would not want [to make a *waqf*], as is common in some areas, [in those cases] he calls [that *waqf*] "the *waṣīya* of my grandfather" (*waṣīyat jaddī*) since the grandfather is the one who made the *waqf*. If so, the founder intends that [the *waqf*] does not leave the line of heirs and this [type of *waqf*] is as if he made a testament upon them: half of the income for the sake of upkeep of the other half [of the *waqf*]. And in that case, *tadhhīb*, he [the heir] is preferred over the beneficiary [in terms of guardianship] even if the beneficiary has requested to perform [the guardianship] for free (1). This is because the heir (*al-wārith*) has become an executor (*waṣīy*) for the founder (*al-wāqif*) [and a person who is] testamented to (*mūṣā lahu*) by the half [of the income] for the upkeep [of the *waqf* asset]. And thus there is no need for a *mutawallī* or guardianship (*wilāya*). God knows best. By dictation of Our Lord al-Manṣūr bi-Llāh (2) ʿAlī b. Muḥammad al-Sirājī, may God the exalted give him mercy (q-r-z).
>
> [Secondary footnotes:]
>
> (1) This means: He will till the land and submit all the income to them and they will give him half of the income only, as is found in the *Bayān*.[101]
>
> (2) Perhaps this footnote was dictated by al-Manṣūr, and if not, it is still found in *al-Baḥr*.[102]

101 Perhaps the famous *fiqh* work of *al-Bayān al-Shāfī*.

102 It is not found in the printed edition of *al-Baḥr al-zakhkhār* in the *waqf* chapter. We cannot establish who this al-Manṣūr is, since there are several imams with that title: al-Qāsim al-ʿIyānī, ʿAbdallāh b. Ḥamza, al-Qāsim b. Muḥammad. Ibn Miftāḥ, *Sharḥ al-azhār*, 8:249–251.

First we can say that the whole content of the footnote is thoroughly validated by two *tadhhībs* and one *taqrīr*.[103] It is also validated in the 1980 edition.[104] The validity of this footnote as a codified rule or possibly as law hinges on the existence, in time and space, of a certain "custom."

The footnote is placed in its specific context in the *Sharḥ al-azhār* in order to address the problem of who should have the guardianship or authority over the *waqf* (that is, take the role of the *mutawallī*). The purpose of analysing this footnote relates to the same topic as above, namely that of family-controlled public *waqfs*, in which the heirs of the founder automatically have the right to the guardianship, even if the *waqf* is made, at least partly, for a public purpose.

Here, if we return to the *waqf* case discussed at the beginning of this chapter, we find that the case of the *waqf* for the three cisterns fits very well into the legal picture of this footnote. It is as if this footnote was made to address such a case. If the *Sharḥ al-azhār* were to be followed,[105] the *waqf* of three cisterns would not only be a completely legal and normal *waqf*, there would also be no fear of government involvement or question about the power of the *mutawallī*.

Two other footnotes follow the footnote above, and belong to the same rule in the *Sharḥ al-azhār*; these further validate the content of the footnote above. These two footnotes are also validated by *tadhhīb*; they state that the rule is only valid if the *waqf* is made through a proper *waṣīya*[106] and that the founder's descendants have no legal rights to the guardianship doctrinally, their rights are only metaphorical.[107] Thus the authors of these footnotes seem reluctant to validate the "rule" that the founder automatically reserves the guardianship for his family.

In *al-Tāj al-mudhhab* the footnote has become a "question" (*masʿala*) or "topic" of its own. By using the term *waṣīya* as part of the solution to this question, in theory, jurists also encouraged the use of the *waṣīya-waqf* model even

---

103 For validation marks, see chapter 4.

104 Ibn Miftāḥ, *Kitāb al-Muntaziʿ*, 3:488.

105 It is the codification level that is validated. In a broad sense the *Sharḥ al-azhār* cannot be followed since it contains a multitude of views, but the validated views, in general, do not contradict each other.

106 It probably means that the *waqf* is restricted to one-third and made to take effect after death.

107 We cannot discuss these in detail here, as it would involve a lengthy discussion. However, it should be noted that both footnotes state that giving the guardianship to the heirs of the founder is legally valid, but only "metaphorically" (*majāzātan*). They also quote *fiqh* works or persons called (*Zuhūr, Bayān Maʿnā, Shāmī,* and *Hibal*). As for quoting the view of al-Faqīh Yūsuf (d. 832/1429), this helps us ascertain the age of the rule. Ibn Miftāḥ, *Sharḥ al-azhār*, 8:251.

more.[108] This adds to the explanations of the rationale behind insisting that the *waqf* controlled by one's family is a *waṣīya*, not a *waqf*: It legally secures the guardianship for the descendants of the founder. The notion of the executor of a testament is similar to that of a *mutawallī* of a *waqf*, however, an executor (*waṣīy*) is more private than a *mutawallī*, it is more a family matter and it does not invoke perpetuity as a *waqf* does.

The result and the implications of the above mentioned (footnote) rule that gives the rights for the administration of the *waqf* to the descendants of the founder is significant for our understanding of *waqf* in Yemen. The above rule was clearly made in response to the social reality of local *waqf* knowledge and practices that had been in place for centuries. The case it describes was a special form of *waqf*, we can say a *waqf* model, in which the beneficiary is in theory fully public, but for which only half, or any other specific estimate of the revenue, is made *waqf* for the public beneficiary. The other (second) half goes to the founder's heirs (or descendants). The founder's heirs retain their right to use (all of) the *waqf* land as tenants, but they have to pay half of the income, or any other specific amount, to the beneficiary, for example a local mosque or a water cistern in a sharecropping agreement (or as fixed rent). Or, they must take care of a certain service only, as mentioned above.

A third footnote after the words "then for the beneficiary"[109] is also attributed to al-Saḥūlī,[110] and also marked by *taqrīr* and *tadhhīb*. It has also become a *mas'ala* (question) in *al-Tāj al-mudhhab*. In *al-Tāj al-mudhhab*, such footnotes are anonymized, the result being that all that is said in *al-Tāj al-mudhhab* appears to be equally valid. Al-Saḥūlī's footnote says that if a *waqf* is made for a mosque (a *waqf* for a *waqf*) and the two *mutawallī*s disagree over the guardianship, the *mutawallī* of the first *waqf* (the *waqf* land for the mosque) is to be given priority unless the *mutawallī* of the mosque says he will do the job for significantly less that the other *mutawallī*.[111] This is slightly more restrictive than the footnote above that states "even if the other *mutawallī* will do it for free." It opens an element of competition between the two *mutawallī*s—who is willing to undertake the administration for the lowest price? Al-Saḥūlī's rule is logical, but not well-defined in practice, since it hinges upon the term "significantly." One can also wonder what is a "significantly" high salary for the *mutawallī*?

108 As noted in chapter 5, the other theory for the use of the term *waṣīya* in *waqf* centres on the combination of these two in the Hādawī *waqf* model.

109 That is, in relation to the sequence of priority of who should be in authority/guardianship.

110 *Samā'* al-Saḥūlī. Ibn Miftāḥ, *Sharḥ al-azhār*, 8:251.

111 al-'Ansī, *al-Tāj al-mudhhab*, 320.

As for family *waqf*s, in which the beneficiaries to a large extent overlap with the heirs of the founder, the "excepted *waqf*" or "*waqf* in which the *mutawallī* receives the surplus" is presumably not a frequently used model and indeed, there is no necessity or incentive for it, since the heirs (or descendants) of the founder and the beneficiaries would to a large extent overlap as a group.

The rule above takes the right to the surplus and the guardianship away from the beneficiary (the public *waqf*) and gives this right to the heirs of the founder, contrary to the *matn* of the *Kitāb al-Azhār*.

In the *waqf* model above it is the heirs, or the *awlād al-ṣulb* (the *nasab* line or the patrilineal descendants) who in any case tend to till the land (the actual asset) and maintain it. Thus the roles partly merge, as they also do in cases in which the *waqf* has a public beneficiary. One and the same person can be an "heir," *mutawallī*, a tenant, and a "semi-beneficiary" at the same time, provided he just pays a certain amount to the public beneficiary such as a local mosque or such, or takes care of a local cistern.[112] The *mutawallī* of this local mosque does not have authority over the primary *waqf*.

This model is very similar to an absolute charitable *waqf*, because the tenant of the land of a public *waqf* would in any case take his portion of the harvest as income for the work he has performed. The difference lies in the tenant's job security if he is also an heir of the founder. In the *waqf* model above, the tenant has the right to stay on the land as a tenant since what he receives from the *waqf* (the excepted part of the income) is not technically *waqf*, but his own property as it is given to him "as if over a testament (*waṣīya*)," as stated above. This stands in contrast to the case of a normal public *waqf*, in which the *mutawallī* might change his mind and lease the land to someone else.

This leads us back to the topic of the *waqf waṣīya* relationship. Twice in the translated footnote above the author invokes the concept of the *waṣīya*, while in the same two respective sentences he clearly refers to *waqf*. In this *waqf* model the "heir" is someone who has received a bequest or a testament (*mūṣā ʿalayhi*), and at the same time he has become the executor of the testament (*waṣīy*), that is, he helps the founder (*wāqif*) transfer his property to his heirs (as bequeathed to), and to the *waqf*'s beneficiary. This is indeed confusing. The model described in the footnote is indeed half *waqf* and half *waṣīya* and the confusion *is* complete. However, and most importantly in terms of its legal

112 For a more thorough description of the maintenance of communal village cisterns, see Eirik Hovden, "Birka and Baraka—Cistern and Blessing: Notes on Custom and Islamic Law Regarding Public Cisterns in Northern Yemen," in *Southwest Arabia across History: Essays to the Memory of Walter Dostal*, ed. Andre Gingrich and Siegfried Hass (Vienna: Verlag der Österreichischen Akademie der Wissenschaften, 2014).

validity, it also is based on custom. Further, since all the roles tend to overlap, the author of the footnote concludes with an answer that is both pragmatic and a theoretical solution to a Gordian knot of *fiqh*: in such a situation, there is no "need" for guardianship in the first place! (*lā yuḥtāj ilā wilāya. wa Allāh aʿlam*).

"Custom," in the wider Hādawī-Zaydī *madhhab*, is an authoritative source of law as long "as it does not contradict the undisputed, clear parts of the *sharīʿa*," as a well-known legal maxim.[113] The footnote starts by saying "if there is a custom," as if it is implicitly thought of as an a priori legitimate custom. But not only does this footnote or rule legitimate this type of *waqf* by the mere presence of a custom, it also refers to the topic in *waqf fiqh* in which custom is considered by many to be a clarifying necessity, namely that of the wording of the *waqf* initiation.[114] In *al-Tāj al-mudhhab* al-ʿAnsī also refers to custom where he says in a note that the wording "I bequeathed" (*awṣaytu*) is an indirect (*kiyānatan*) way of initiating a *waqf*, unless it is stated by a commoner (*ʿāmmī, ʿawwām*), then it is considered a clear and explicit wording producing a valid *waqf*, because "… a *waṣīya* is according to their custom a *waqf*."[115] When a commoner makes a *waṣīya*, he actually makes a *waqf*. If we understand this statement in an ethnographic sense, we have another strong indication for the presence of this special Yemeni type of *waqf*.

113 As in the legal maxim "al-ʿurf maʿmūl bihi fī l-ṣiḥḥa wa-l-fasād, wa-l-luzūm wa-l-suqūṭ, mā lam yuṣādif nāṣṣan." Ibn Miftāḥ, *Sharḥ al-azhār*, 1:17. For the role of custom in Islamic law in general, see especially Ayman Shabana, *Custom in Islamic Law and Legal Theory: The Development of the Concepts of ʿUrf and ʿĀdah in the Islamic Legal Tradition* (New York: Palgrave Macmillan, 2010).

114 The wording, or utterance of initiation (*al-ījāb*) refers to the utterance of the words that establish the *waqf*. The common words to use, such as "I hereby made *waqf*" (*waqqaftu*), are considered explicit and clear (*ṣarīḥ*), but there are other words that can be used which are not clear (*kināyatan*), but if used in combination still produce a valid *waqf*, such as "I hereby make to the poor, in perpetuity," etc. The *Kitāb al-Azhār*/*Sharḥ al-azhār* mainly follow the rules of the Shāfiʿīs in these questions, since these are fairly elaborate and practical. See also Messick's article about intent: Brinkley Messick, "Indexing the Self: Intent and Expression in Islamic Legal Acts," *Islamic Law and Society* 8, no. 2 (2001): 151–178.

115 "… **Aw kinānyatan** ka-taṣaddaqtu aw-jaʿaltu aw-awṣaytu(1). (1)illā fī ḥaqq al-ʿawwām, fa-ṣarīḥ, li-annahu fī ʿurfihim waqfan" (the *matn* of the *Kitāb al-Azhār* is given in bold), al-ʿAnsī, *al-Tāj al-mudhhab*, 3:377. The footnote in which he says that a commoner can make a *waqf* by saying "I bequeathed" is in accordance with Imam Yaḥyā's decree, in which he says that "commoners do not know what they do, and when they say "I made *waṣīya*," they actually mean "I made a bequest (*waqf*)." In chapter 5 we saw that as early as the time of Imam ʿAbdallāh b. Ḥamza most *waqf*s were made by using the initiation of a *waṣīya*.

4.1 *Al-Shijnī's* Fatwā *on the Regulation of Rights in a "Non-Absolute"* Waqf

Al-Shijnī's *fatwā* addresses the issue of how private rights in a public *waqf* can be transferred from one generation to the next and indeed also to others.

ʿAlī b. Aḥmad al-Shijnī lived from 1711 or 1712 until 1786 or 1787, which makes him contemporary with chief *qāḍī* al-Saḥūlī.[116] We know little of the authority of his *fatwā* or anything about its implications at the time he wrote it. What makes the *fatwā* treated below important for us is the fact that it is included in the small, but practically oriented *fatwā* collection in the beginning of the first printed version of the *Sharḥ al-azhār* in 1913–14.[117] This *fatwā* collection was very short, but was clearly intended to help judges in practical legal problems related to inheritance, customary sharecropping (*al-sharika al-ʿurfiyya*), divorce, and *waqf*. At this time, in the 1910s when Imam Yaḥyā took over from the Ottomans, there were few other printed *fiqh* works in the Zaydī tradition and this first edition of the *Sharḥ al-azhār* must have represented a significant step in the availability of *fiqh* texts that could be physically consulted, that is, they were not just in a library or memorised. Finding al-Shijnī's *fatwā* here thus means that it was as close to codified law as one could get before Imam Yaḥyā started issuing decrees a decade later. The *fatwā* collection is a very good example of how practical *fiqh* and the genres of *fatwā* and codification partly merge.[118] Later al-ʿAnsī reproduced this *fatwā* in *al-Tāj al-mudhhab*, where it appears almost identically as it was given in the *Sharḥ al-azhār*, this time less as a *fatwā* and *fiqh*, and more as a legal rule, since what *al-Tāj al-mudhhab* presents is a body of (fairly) coherent rules. The content of the *fatwā* is a good indication of the historical presence and continuity of the aforementioned *waqf* model, probably from the years of al-Shijnī himself (from 1750 to 1780), and at least in the years that this first printed edition was prepared (around 1900), including the 1930s and 1940s when *al-Tāj al-mudhhab* was printed. The *fatwā* refers to the area south of Sanaa, one of the most fertile and populated areas of Yemen. The version below is from *al-Tāj al-mudhhab*:[119]

116 Zabāra, *Nayl al-waṭar*, 2:154–155. Al-Qāḍī ʿAlī b. Aḥmad b. Nāṣir al-Shijnī l-Dhamārī studied under several of the famous *ʿulamāʾ* such as al-Ḥasan b. Aḥmad al-Shabībī and ʿAbdallāh b. al-Ḥusayn al-Dallāma. He was among the foremost in teaching the "*Sharḥ al-azhār, al-Baḥr al-zakhkhār*, and the *Bayān* [*al-Shāfī*]… and all the *shuyūkh* came to him concerning these works." One of his students later became the "*mutawallī* of the *awqāf* of the city of Damār"; that is, al-Sayyid ʿAlī b. Aḥmad b. ʿAlī l-Dhamārī. Zabāra, *Nashr al-ʿarf*, 2:170–171.

117 Ibn Miftāḥ, *Kitāb al-Muntazaʿ*, 1:52–53.

118 For this topic see Hallāq, "From Fatwās to Furūʿ."

119 al-ʿAnsī, *al-Tāj al-mudhhab*, 3:305–306.

Question: According to al-Qāḍī l-ʿAllāma ʿAlī b. Aḥmad b. Nāṣir al-Shijnī, may God grant him mercy. Concerning the custom of the transfer of possession of *waqf* (*fī jarīy ʿādat al-nās fī naql al-yad fī l-waqf*) in the areas of Ānis,[120] it is said that the custom (*alladhī jarā bihi al-ʿurf*) in the areas of Ānis and the adjoining districts is for the founder who makes the *waqf* for the mosques to make a *waqf* which remains under the control of the founder's heir (*bi-yad wārith al-wāqif*), and he [the founder] intends to present one-quarter of the harvest to the mosque if private land in the area is leased for half of the harvest.[121] This has become an established custom among them (*wa ṣāra hādhā ʿurfan lahum*). The founder only makes a *waqf* with [this] intention, according to this established custom, even though the founder does not utter this explicitly. And the heir (*wārith*) [sic] may transfer (*qad yunaqqil*) [this land] to someone else for compensation. The legal status of the land is taken over by the new possessor (*yad man ṣārat ilayhi*) and it remains under the same legal status as when the heir of the founder had it. This is an established custom that is widespread among them. So the surplus (*al-zāʾid*) that is excepted [after what is due to the beneficiary] goes to the heir, or to whomever the heir has transferred this *waqf* to (*li-man naqalahu al-wārith ilayhi*).

The following is mentioned in a gloss in [the book called] *al-Ifāda*: If a person makes a *waqf* out of fear that the land may be taken [illegally by force] by another person, then he can dispose of it himself [and make a *waqf*] and take from the revenue two *qafīz*es of grain (a measure of volume[122]) for the beneficiary, and it is legally valid for him to take from

120 Ānis is the fertile, mountainous area northwest of the city of Dhāmār.

121 This refers to the local "prize" for labour, the sharecropping fraction. This fraction varies slightly from area to area and from crop to crop. See Donaldson, *Sharecropping in the Yemen*. On rainfed land where sorghum is grown—this constitutes the majority of land in these areas—the fraction of one-half (paid to the landowner) is considered in the expensive range, but not uncommon. The most common would be to pay around one-third or one-quarter as rent. It seems that the author of the *fatwā* specifies that the *waqf* should receive half of whatever is the "free" market rent, but this exact systematic reduction in rent is not given anywhere else.

122 The *qafīz* is a measurement of grain, but we do not know the exact size intended here. In most of northern Yemen the *qadaḥ* (a bushel) is the common measure of grain, but a *qafīz* seems to be something different. As for the *qadaḥ*, Serjeant states that it was 36 litres (quoting Rossi), but there are obviously regional differences. His footnote also elaborates upon the fraction signs used in the accountancy. There were several attempts to standardize these measures of grain since the differences of each region's *qadaḥ* were a problem. See also Messick, where he states that the Ibb *qadaḥ* was previously larger than the Sanaani measurement, but that they now used the standard Sanaani *qadaḥ*. Serjeant and Lewcock, *Sanʿāʾ*, 188, n. 41. Messick, "Transactions in Ibb," 147–148.

the revenue what is left exceeding the two *qafīz*es. If this exception for himself is valid, then it is also valid to do so for someone else too, [end of quote].

This custom is not specific to the areas of Ānis only; indeed all the present *ḍarāʾib*-incomes[123] from *waqf* lands from Lower Yemen, that is southern Yemen, follow this rule: The founder dedicates a small amount of the income to the *waqf*, [a small amount as] compared to the whole harvest of that land and the founder makes the rest as an exception (*istithnāʾ*) [in the income of the *waqf*] in favour of the tenant, for the sake of the interest of the *waqf* land. This interest relates to the protection of the *waqf* land from degradation and this is compensated for by the excepted part of the *waqf* income. If such an exception is valid for this purpose, then other forms of exceptions are valid for other purposes as well, to the extent that the founder's pious intention can be known, according to his explicit utterances or according to established custom (*lafẓan aw ʿurfan*). In this, a sort of compensation is found (*muʿāwaḍa*), and [*waqf* land] continues to move from possessor to possessor (*min yad ilā yad*).

Al-ʿAllāma al-Shijnī states and confirms that this is in accordance with the *madhhab* (*qāla muqarriran li-l-madhhab*): "This is a *sharʿī* concept that must be followed and acted in accordance with (*hādhā wajh sharʿī yajibu al-maḍā ʿalayhi wa-l-ʿamal bi-muqtaḍāhi*) and it is only allowed to confiscate (*intizāʿ*) such *waqf* land from a possessor in case of fraud or mismanagement.

If the confiscation is valid due to of one of these two [aforementioned] reasons, the right of its possessor is not invalidated (*lam yabṭul*), rather the *mutawallī* of the land should lease it to someone who [will] take care of it so the beneficiary receives his defined share and the rest of the rent from the land [can] go to the one who has the right to that, that is, he who

123 *Ḍarāʾib* is a special type of *waqf* land rent, in which the *waqf* is rented out for a fixed annual sum, independent of the size of the harvest (this is the opposite of a sharecropping agreement, in which the tenant pays a fixed fraction of the yearly harvest, which may vary from year to year). This was explicitly stated by Qāḍī ʿAbd al-Jabbār around the same time as al-Shijnī, quoted by Qāṭin in Zabāra, *Nashr al-ʿarf*, 2:235–236. This *ḍarāʾib* form of payment seems to have been used at the time as a compromise between the public *waqf* administration and local tenants and one of the main purposes of this very *fatwā* could have been to legitimize this system, by claiming it is "custom" and something that was intended by the founders in these areas, and by explaining why tenants should not pay full market rent. Some of this is discussed at the end of chapter 6; the *ḍarāʾib* type of payment is also mentioned in chapter 3 about Qāṭin and his colleagues as public *waqf* administrators. See also Mijallī, *al-Awqāf fī l-Yaman*, 122–123.

the land was confiscated from. Further, the rule is the same if the one who possesses it[124] rents it out by his free choice.

This is not a transfer of possession in absolute *waqf* (*laysa hādha naql al-yad fī l-waqf al-khāliṣ*). In that there is no foundation in the law (*lā aṣl laha*) except, if that absolute *waqf* has been invested in [by the tenant] which necessitates a payment, then this is allowed, and if not, it is not allowed (*lam yaḥill*) to charge a compensation purely for the transfer of absolute *waqf* land to someone else for possession. God knows best.

The noble *madhhab* acknowledged and validated this [view] according to one of the recent shaykhs of the *madhhab*, al-Qāḍī l-ʿAllāma ʿAbd al-Qādir b. Ḥusayn al-Shuwayṭir, may God give him mercy.[125]

ʿAbd al-Qādir al-Shuwayṭir (d. 1198/1783 or 94)[126] was the student of ʿAlī b. Aḥmad al-Shijnī. Both of them came from the areas of Dhamār south of Sanaa and he also held an *ijāza* from al-Qāḍī Aḥmad Qāṭin, the famous *waqf* inspector of Yemen during his time, so he was certainly well informed about the various customs related to leases. Both were known and renowned scholars of the time. This longer *fatwā* raises several important points and indicates the presence of *waqf* practices that are arguably valid legally, but far from the ideal public *waqf*. The aspects that are related to the tenant and his rights to sell his investment to another holder (*ḥaqq al-yad, al-ʿinā*ʾ) were discussed in the previous chapter. The notion that a tenant is allowed to invest in the asset seems fairly uncontroversial, although the present *waqf* law requires that such an investment be specifically defined and documented, so that the reduction in rent does not become permanent. In this chapter the new aspect is that a *waqf* can (or could) be made for a public purpose while retaining part of the income already from the beginning of the *waqf*, thus producing a situation in which "reduced rent" is the starting point and not only something that develops over time.

---

124 Here Ibn Miftāḥ, *Sharḥ al-azhār* (1980 ed.) and *al-Tāj al-mudhhab* give two different words: *Sharḥ al-azhār* (1980 ed.): *al-ḥākim*, while *al-Tāj al-mudhhab* gives the word *al-ḥukm*. The translation above follows the latter.

125 The *Sharḥ al-azhār* version reads, at the end: "al-Qāḍī l-ʿAllāma ʿAbd al-Qādir b. Ḥusayn al-Shuwayṭir, may God give him mercy, said that this view is sound and strong according to the *madhhab* (*hādhā naẓar ṣaḥīḥ qawiyy ʿalā kalām ahl al-madhhab*). Ibn Miftāḥ, *Kitāb al-Muntaziʿ*, 3:53.

126 Born 1735 or 1736, died 1783 or 84. He was from Dhamār and studied under all the great scholars there, including al-Shabībī, Dallāma, and al-Shijnī and also under Aḥmad Qāṭin. Zabāra, *Nashr al-ʿarf*, 2:74.

We have already mentioned that there are forms of *waqf* which are not as "holy" as others.[127] One such example is in the letter from Ibn al-Amīr to Imam al-Mahdī l-ʿAbbās as translated in chapter 3.[128] And informants today still discuss the notion of the reduced *waqf* in the form of the *waṣīya*.[129]

Nothing can be fully owned twice and only God "owns" the *waqf*, and therefore, theoretically, it is prohibited to sell and buy and give away *waqf*. The terms used in the *fatwā* that relate to rights are terms that are not legally valid in the ideal *waqf*: the right to till *waqf* land can be "possessed," but not "owned," and this right can be "transferred for a compensation" but not "sold." The *fatwā* relates the right of the founder's descendants (the "heirs") with the role of the *mutawallī*. Like the previous *fatwā* above (or footnote or rule), the confusion of concepts is very much present here as well.

Al-Shijnī bases his claims of validity for this upon a certain present and ongoing (*jārin*) custom or legal practice that is allegedly found in a specific region. The practice is made into a *sharʿī* norm. The argument that the heir of the founder takes care of the land and therefore is entitled to reduced rent is rather baseless, since any *mutawallī* is required to take care of the asset in the ideal *waqf* model. It is simply the duty of any *mutawallī*. Perhaps the most interesting point is that this *waqf* remains split into a private and a public part and that because the part (of the income) that the heir is in possession of is not technically a *waqf*, but rather property (*milk*) "as given by means of a testament," the heir may freely sell his part of the income from the asset. The asset as such remains *waqf*, while the income is divided (between *waqf* and *milk* status). He mentions two ways of dividing the income, either by fraction or by absolute measures, such as a certain measurement of grain volume. Even "two

127 An old example from the *fiqh* is from *al-Baḥr al-zakhkhār*: Masʿala: (q) wa-mā lam yuʿayyan maṣrifuhu fa-li-l-fuqarāʾ (m) bal li-l-maṣāliḥ. Qulnā: al-ʿurf fī l-waqf al-muṭlaq mā dhakarnā. Ibn al-Murtaḍā, *al-Baḥr al-zakhkhār*, 154–155.

128 In chapter 3 we saw that Ibn al-Amīr, in his letter of protest, argued for a different status between a *waqf* and a *waṣāyā*. His main argument was that while the *waṣāyā* could be transferred, the *awqāf* could not, because of its more holy and absolute status. This leads us to the question of whether or not *waqf* land was registered differently because of this difference in status, but also to what extent there were regional differences in these practices. It is understandable that a family *waqf* could be classified as a *waṣīya*—the problem is if a *waqf* for a mosque could also be such a family-controlled *waṣīya*. It certainly produces a problem of definition in several ways.

129 Several people have told me that family *waqf*s are not the same as a "*waqf*." As one *mutawallī* of an important *sayyid* family *waqf* in Sanaa told me, "*waqf al-waṣāya tuḥarrar*," meaning, family *waqf* or privately managed *waqf*s may be terminated and sold. This is also the view of the present-day *waqf* law. The problem in this statement is that there are several so-called *waṣāya* that contain elements of public beneficiaries as well as being an ordinary family *waqf*, as in the case presented in the beginning of this chapter.

qafīzes" may be valid as the minimum given to the external beneficiary, if the circumstances necessitate it. This means that "if necessary," the *waqf* part of the *waqf* can remain almost symbolic and the "financial construction" of what appears to be a *waqf* becomes reality. This extreme is perhaps mentioned in the *fatwā* for the sake of argumentation, given that the *fatwā* does state that the custom in Ānis is to give half of the free market (thus one-quarter) as rent to the public *waqf* beneficiary.

Was there no criticism against this pragmatic *waqf*? Certainly there must have been but it was not given the same priority in the debate found in the *Sharḥ al-azhār*. According to the validation signs in the *Sharḥ al-azhār*, the criticism does not seem to be codified or carry the validity of law. One such criticism is found in footnote (4) in the *Sharḥ al-azhār* (2003 edition), 8:285:[130]

> (4) As for the sale of possession of *waqf* (*bayʿ al-yad*), this is *ḥarām* according to consensus. (the book of *Hidāya*) (1) And whoever claims that this is the custom among the people or that custom is a source of validity (*ṭarīq min ṭuruq al-sharʿ*), he is a liar. According to consensus, a sale is only valid if made by an owner (*mālik*), not if made by a possessor (*ṣāḥib al-yad al-shārik*). And custom [in these questions] is no different from custom in [topics like] interest on loans (*rabawiyyāt*), and this is also the case regarding the property of orphans, mosques, and the water supply (*manāhil*) where there exists (2) no such custom and where it is not accepted. (*hāmish* [a gloss from a book called the] *Hidāya*)[131]

There are two secondary footnotes in the *Sharḥ al-azhār* (2003 edition), as comments on this footnote:

> (1) There is a footnote (*ḥāshiya*): The transfer of the right of possession (*naql al-yad*) in *waṣāyā*, if there has been investment in repairs of a damage [to the asset] that the compensation is supposed to cover, then a sale is valid (*ṣaḥḥa al-bayʿ*), and not if not (*wa-illā fa-lā*).[132]
>
> (2) And the chosen view is the opposite (*wa-l-muqarrar khilāfuhu*) (q-r-z). In the presence of a custom, it is to go on as it is ongoing (*fī jary al-ʿurf, fa-yajrī ʿalayhi kamā yajrī lahu*).[133]

---

130 The text is also given in Ibn Miftāḥ, *Sharḥ al-azhār* (1980 ed.) 3:503, n7, see fig. 18.

131 Ibn Miftāḥ, *Sharḥ al-azhār*, 8:285.

132 In Ibn Miftāḥ, *Sharḥ al-azhār* (1980 ed.), as seen in the photo, this footnote is validated by *taqrīr*.

133 Ibn Miftāḥ, *Sharḥ al-azhār*, 8:285.

Interestingly, in the earlier versions (*Sharḥ al-azhār* 1980), the last of these two footnotes was only handwritten between the lines:

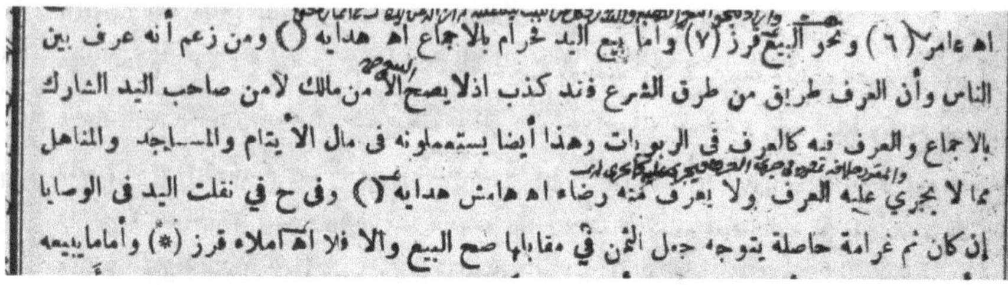
اه عامر (٦) ونحو البيع قرز (٧) وأما بيع اليد فحرام بالاجماع اهـ هداية () ومن زعم أنه عرف بين
الناس وأن العرف طريق من طرق الشرع فقد كذب اذ لا يصح الا من مالك لأمن صاحب اليد الشارك
بالاجماع والعرف فيه كالعرف في الربويات وهذا أيضا يستعملونه في مال الايتام والمساجد والمناهل
مما لا يجري عليه العرف ولا يعرف منه رضاه اه هامش هداية () وفي ح في نقلت اليد في الوصايا
إن كان ثم غرامة حاصلة يتوجه حمل الثمن في مقابلها صح البيع والا فلا اهـ املاء قرز (*) وأما بيعه

FIGURE 18 An inserted handwritten gloss: "Custom is to be followed" *Sharḥ al-azhār* (1980 edition), 3:503.

In any case, the footnote and the secondary footnotes clearly show that despite the criticism of "custom" being an absolute source of *sharīʿa*, the "*madhhab*" has validated the use of custom as a source for valid law regarding these issues in *waqf*.

The use of custom in the above *fatwā*s, rules, and footnotes, and also in al-Saḥūlī's footnote, all base their argument on the assumption that the intent of the founder can be known from the expressions he uses in the initiation of the *waqf* (or in the *waqf* document), but in certain cases, or rather, in certain geographical areas, there may be, or even *is*, with certainty, a custom of common underlying intent which is not expressed, because it is usually not necessary to be explicit. In this chapter, this concerns the idea that the guardianship is automatically kept in the founder's family, and to some extent *waqf*s are always of the excepted income type of *waqf*, and the tenants/heirs/descendants are automatically entitled to a reduced rent. The intent is important in that the will of the founder must be respected, therefore "custom" must be followed in order to follow the will of the founders.[134]

Thus have we found an admittance of an alternative "law" in the form of custom? Is this what Dupret means when he refers to "legal pluralism" as mentioned in chapter 2 of the present work?[135] Do my informants here point out that there are alternative bodies of law, "*sharīʿa*" and "custom"?[136] Is it a condition of "conflict" between two bodies of law, as posed by Woodman?[137] Or

134 For an analysis of "intent" in Zaydī *fiqh* in general and specifically in sales (*bayʿ*), see Messick, "Indexing the Self."

135 Dupret, "What is Plural in the Law?".

136 For Dupret legal pluralism is a term that is only relevant if the informants themselves point out that there are alternative bodies of law.

137 Woodman, "The Idea of Legal Pluralism."

is this what we can call an attempt to "unify" or "merge" two bodies of law? Perhaps all these ideas are right. When asking informants similar questions most answer with a standard answer, that there *is* only one valid law, the *sharīʿa*. The rest is simply a matter of specification and details, which the *ʿulamāʾ* know and commoners do not know. If asked directly, few would be comfortable in ranking *sharīʿa*, custom, and state law as equal. However, most informants also point out that there does not have to be a contradiction. Whether we see "unification" or "conflict" between *sharīʿa* and custom depends on the perspective and specific context and both views can be powerful concepts. Most would agree that custom can be an extension of the *sharīʿa* as long as it remains subordinated, while many would also have reservations in more specific matters, such as the footnote ascribed to the *Hidāya* above. Thus the question should not be researched on a doctrinal level only, it should also be "seen" at the level of context, at least from an ethnographic or historical point of view. And at the level of context, the level of correct doctrinal answers fades out of relevance and the legally valid ones—those validated by this or the other argument, scholar or institution—become important. Obviously, custom is vital to the very function of the more applicable *fiqh*, a point made specifically by Gerber in his study of *fatwā*s.[138]

Another related aspect of custom as a source of law, and one that is more abstract and probably closer to the legal maxim,[139] is the rationale of case law. If we imagine all those *waqf*s in Lower Yemen as operative and applicable to case law, then we would be saying that these must be followed, if not, all these *waqf*s must be taken to court and changed, or such new *waqf*s must be brought to the judge and invalidated. The fact that this has not been done, and that a legal innovation is used instead to circumvent the whole problem and simply redefine it, is an argument against the "classification" of *sharīʿa* as "the jurists' law" or

138 Gerber, *Islamic Law and Culture*, 9. See also the very useful review of this work made by Dupret, in which he summarizes: Though, Gerber argues, *ʿurf* "never quite attained the status of fifth basis of the law, it became a major practical fiction through which new material could be accommodated in practice, while preserving the sacred framework." (109–110) It could even contradict the main references of the schools of law, providing it did not run against one of the few clear injunctions of the Qurʾān. According to Gerber, "this is a practical secularization of the law without changing the formal framework of sanctity."(115) Baudouin Dupret, "Review of Gerber 'Islamic Law and Culture 1600–1840,'" *Journal of Law and Religion* 15, nos. 1–2 (2000–2001): 410.

139 The maxim that custom is to be followed. Ibn Miftāḥ, *Sharḥ al-azhār*, 1:17. Whether the validation of certain *fiqh* rules is built directly on the legal maxims, or the opposite, whether the legal maxims are induced from the *fiqh*, is a too theoretical question to answer. Validity is probably borrowed both ways.

other such types.[140] The "jurists" had to make concessions and compromises when facing social forces in the real world, and still do so in *sharʿī* language.

4.2 *The Rights of the* Mutawallī *in the Present* Waqf *Law*

Waqf law today allows for private guardianship. There were recent attempts to ban this and to force all forms of guardianship under the ministry, since all legal *waqfs* are now "public" *waqfs*, but this was met with great resistance and private guardianship was again made legally valid.[141] Similarly, the law demands that all *mutawallīs*, even private ones, present their accountancy to the ministry. Further, the law also gives the ministry right to take percentages (2.5 per cent)[142] of the income of the *waqf* in return for supervising it. These laws are highly theoretical and much further research is needed in order to establish to what extent many private *mutawallīs* actually follow these laws. This presents a major practical research problem: few would openly admit that they do not follow the laws and rules of the ministry. There are indications that there is a culture of mutual consensus and agreement not to press private *mutawallīs* too hard in these matters, as many of them, at least in certain areas, are much more respected locally than the representatives of the ministry and the representatives of the formal legal system. The *sharʿī* legitimacy of private guardianship is so clearly founded in *fiqh* works like the *Sharḥ al-azhār* that it is unlikely that the government will be able to construct laws that are considered more valid than the "law" of the Zaydī *madhhab* in these questions, at least in the near future.

•••

Reading the *fiqh* looking for the "ideal" *waqf* will simply produce a (normative) picture of the ideal *waqf*. However, reading with a methodological focus on problem areas, grey areas, and borders of validity produces a completely different picture and one that is more closely connected to historically established and ethnographically observed legal practices. The four *waqf* documents

140 See the overview of the debate in Vikør, *Between God and the Sultan*, 4–10.

141 Ministerial decree no. 18 of 2001 (*bi-sha'n ilghāʾ al-naẓarāt al-khāṣṣā*) caused so much resistance that a new decree was made, no. 51 of 2002, which abolished the former decree. al-Farrān, *Athr al-waqf*, 181.

142 This figure is stated in article 89 of the *waqf* law, but it is not entirely clear if this only refers to "confiscated *waqfs*" or any *waqf* registered by the ministry. We must also expect a divergence in practices. The 2.5 per cent perhaps refers to the *waṣāyā* administration, while in the mosque *waqfs* discussed in this chapter, the state-appointed administrator may take much more, as discussed at the end of chapter 3.

translated at the beginning of this chapter can be seen in a similar way: what they do not say may reveal important legal strategies used by the *waqf* founders that fit with local *waqf* law as explained in the last part of the chapter.

The four *waqf* documents referred to in this chapter have certain aspects in common: they are urban *waqf*s made in favour of *sabīl*s in Sanaa, thus in this respect, they do not relate fully to lease practices in Lower Yemen, which the *fatwā*s and footnotes in the last part of the chapter explicitly focus on. However, the four *waqf* documents do share several features relating to the "exceptions" of private rights.

In order to understand what happened historically with the institution of *waqf* in Yemen, it is necessary to understand how the institution was and still is situated in legal concepts and contexts that are sometimes quite far removed from the ideal *waqf* and ideal *waqf* administration. By shifting the analytical focus away from the ideal *waqf*, we can also better see how the four fields of knowledge are all necessary components in the explorative approach: *fiqh*, codification, cases of *waqf*, and everyday *waqf*-related knowledge. By looking at only one of these fields of knowledge, the argument of this chapter would be much weaker.

There is a strong pragmatic and practically oriented layer in *fiqh* that is strongly related to what goes on among judges and administrators and how they relate to real *waqf* cases. What ties these together is the field of codification. The codification is undertaken by jurists and written in the language of *fiqh*, something that slowly changed after the revolution when a more distinct modern legal language came to be used, something better seen in chapters 5 and 6. Many of the jurists mentioned by name in this chapter were close to the state, or the political establishment in one way or another and it was not always clear at what point *fiqh* stops and codification takes over. The exact border is not of interest as much as the claims, attempts, and results of the codification. The excessive rights of the *mutawallī* and the tenants, often as "heirs" or descendants of the founders, were given extensive legal validity, even if this diluted the ideal concept of *waqf*, despite critical voices. The sheer complexity of this field and the confusion between *waqf*, *waṣīya*, and related concepts makes it difficult for newcomers to the debate to state simple alternatives, unless the Zaydī *madhhab* is bypassed.

The institution of *waqf* cannot exist as an ideal only. The ideal state, court system, and administration apparatus needed to control, oversee, and administer ideal public *waqf*s did not and do not exist on the ground in Yemen. Validity of ideals is different than legal validity.

CHAPTER 8

Pure Law, *ʿUrf*, and *Maṣlaḥa*: Conclusions

In Yemen *waqf*s have been and are important legal institutions through which various forms of welfare, public services, and infrastructure have been and still are legally organised and financed. Power and political control over the *waqf*s is regulated by *waqf* law. In general, *waqf*s are non-state institutions established by private individuals who are allowed to retain control over their foundations. The state as an actor, and those elites to whom it has delegated power, try to occupy roles that control the power and economic resources that circulate in the *waqf* economy, especially with regard to aspects of "public services" related to religion, education, and mosques. In this, the *ʿulamāʾ* are central, but as a group they are not homogenous, they are partly "independent" and partly co-opted by the state, and sometimes they work directly for the state. This power struggle over who should control the resources involved in *waqf*s is reflected in the legal theory of *waqf*s and *waqf* law. In this chapter, I "zoom out" and focus on how the notion of Islamic law as "pure" is claimed and contested by legal scholars and ordinary Yemenis, and how notions of the public good, critical realism, and legal validity affect the potential to use *waqf*s as vehicles for welfare and finally, I engage in that ongoing debate.

1 Sources of Validity

Analysing constructions of validity in Zaydī *waqf* law is a more specific task than analysing constructions of validity in "Islamic law" in general. Furthermore, *waqf* chapters in Zaydī *fiqh* books have their own dynamic of sources underpinning them, for example, as compared to the chapter on inheritance rules (*farāʾiḍ*), which are more directly based on the Qurʾān. When explaining the sources of validity for any given legal topic, it is common to start with a review of how the issue is treated in the Qurʾān and thereafter in the Sunna. The Zaydī *waqf* chapter in the *Sharḥ al-azhār* also starts like that. However, according to Ibn Miftāḥ, *waqf* is not mentioned in the Qurʾān, as we see below:

 | DOI:10.1163/9789004377844_009

(كتاب الوقف)

قال في الشفاء: الوقف في اللغة هو الحبس. وفي الشرع: حبس مخصوص[(١)]، على وجه مخصوص[(٢)] بنية القربة[(٣)].

والأصل فيه السنة[(٤)] والإجماع. أما السنة: فما روي أنه ﷺ قال لعمر حين قال له: إني أصبت[(٥)] مائة سهم[(٦)]................

= مال العرصة، والحكم ما تقدم حيث بنى بنقض منه، وإن كان بناها بالنقض الذي منه جميعه، أو البعض بنية المالك، فالبناء لمالك العرصة، وعليه قيمة النقض الذي عمر به، وأجرة العمل، وإذا سكن الباني فعليه أجرة المثل للعرصة والبناء، ويتقاصان، أو يترادان، هذا تحصيل المسألة. (عامر ذماري) (قرز)

(١) ويزاد: من شخص مخصوص، في عين مخصوصة.

(*) ليخرج الرهن، والإجارة.

(٢) ليخرج الحجر. محذوف، وفي بعض النسخ: لأنه لا فائدة تحته.

(٣) ليخرج سائر التمليكات.

(٤) ومن الكتاب قوله تعالى: ﴿وَنَكۡتُبُ مَا قَدَّمُواْ وَءَاثَٰرَهُمۡۚ﴾[(١)] بهذا احتج الإمام الناصر الحسن بن علي، وذكر مثله الزمخشري، ورواه سيدنا (عامر) قال في (شرح الآيات): ﴿وَءَاثَٰرَهُمۡۚ﴾ قيل: ما بعدهم من وقف، أو تصنيف، أو بناء مسجد، أو قنطرة، وعليه قول الشاعر:

إن هذه آثارنا تدل علينا فانظروا بعدنا إلى الآثار

(٥) اشتراها، لا أنه غنمها، وفي رواية (أنه شراها من مالكها بمائة رأس) (شرح فتح) وذكر في (شرح الفتح) أنه غنمها وصدَّره.

(٦) أي: نصيبا، والمائة السهم هذه الذي حصلت له ممن تحت يده؛ إذ=

(١) والوقف ونحوه من الآثار.

FIGURE 19 The first page of the chapter of *waqf* in the *Sharḥ al-azhār* (2003 edition), 8:171.

> The chapter of *waqf* ("Kitāb al-waqf")
>
> He stated in *al-Shifāʾ*:[1] *Waqf* means linguistically, "restriction" (*ḥabs*) and legally (*fī l-sharʿ*), "a specific restriction for the sake of a specific purpose with the intention of piety (*qurba*)."

This first sentence of the chapter of *waqf* in Ibn Miftāḥ's *Sharḥ al-azhār* provides a definition of the term *waqf*. I do not treat the many footnotes here. What interests us is the following, second sentence:

> The origin (*al-aṣl*) [of the validity of the institution of *waqf*] is found in the Sunna and in the consensus (*al-ijmāʿ*). As for the Sunna: It is narrated that he [the Prophet] said to ʿUmar when [ʿUmar] asked him: "I have obtained one hundred shares [of productive land] in Khaybar and I want to undertake with these [shares of land] an act that makes me closer to God, the exalted (*ataqarraba bihā ilā Allāh*)." So he [the Prophet] said: **"Restrict the asset and give away its income"** (***ḥabbis al-aṣl wa-sabbil al-thamara***). It is also narrated that several of the foremost companions made *waqf*s (*waqqafū*).[2]

The bold text is the *matn* of Ibn al-Murtaḍā (*Kitāb al-Azhār*); these are the first words of the *matn* of the chapter of *waqf*. More *ḥadīth*s about various Companions and followers of the Prophet who made *waqf*s are cited in the *sharḥ*, and in the footnotes.[3] The footnote that follows the word "Sunna" is important: "And the Book [the Qurʾān] states: 'We prescribe [on the day of judgement] according to what they presented and what they left behind (*wa-naktubu mā qaddamū wa-āthārahum*) …'"[4] This verse is then explained by various authorities (in the same footnote). Imam al-Nāṣir al-Ḥasan b. ʿAlī and al-Zamakhsharī[5] are referred to, and then, the exegesis (*tafsīr*) of ʿĀmir in a book called *Sharḥ al-āyāt* is quoted. The words "what they left behind" (*āthārahum*) is said to mean, among other things, *waqf*s.

---

1 Most probably the *Shifāʾ al-uwām* by al-Ḥusayn b. Badr al-Dīn (d. 662/1263 or 64).

2 Ibn Miftāḥ, *Sharḥ al-azhār*, 8:171–172.

3 One such *ḥadīth* that is indicated as weak (by using the passive "it was said" (*qīla*) states that the Prophet "by his own blessed hand … made seven hundred wells and made them into *waqf*." This *ḥadīth* was narrated by a certain al-Qāsim al-Basatī l-Zaydī. It should be noted here that the Zaydīs have their own *ḥadīth* collection, the *Musnad* of Zayd b. ʿAlī, and although many of them are weak according to Sunnī standards, they represent an important source of legal validity in Zaydism.

4 Qurʾān, 36:12. See for instance the translation in ʿAbdullah Yusuf Ali, *The Holy Qur'an: Translation and Commentary*, 1171.

5 See al-Zamakhsharī, *Tafsīr al-kashshshāf*, 891.

> *Wa āthārahum*: It is stated (*qīla*) that "what comes after them" refers to *waqf*, or scholarly works (*taṣnīf*), or the building of a mosque, or a bridge (*qanṭara*) …[6]

This is how the Qur'ān indirectly mentions *waqf*. However, Ibn al-Miftāḥ, who wrote the *Sharḥ al-azhār*, did not mention that there are implicit references to *waqf* in the Qur'ān and explicit sources of validity that can be found there.

A much more useful treatment of the sources of validity in *waqf* law is given by Ibn al-Murtaḍā himself, at the end of the chapter on *waqf* in *al-Baḥr al-zakhkhār*. In some ways this is Ibn al-Murtaḍā's own "conclusion." Ibn al-Murtaḍā states that all *waqf* rules are based on the principle of *maṣlaḥa*:

> Most of what we have mentioned related to *waqf* is based on public interest (*maṣlaḥa*).[7] Most scholars[8] agree that to follow this is the *sharʿī way*,[9] except in the view of al-Dabūsī, who refuted it [the principle of *maṣlaḥa*], unless it is related to a clear, indisputable text (*naṣṣ*) [in the Qur'ān or the Sunna].[10]
>
> Sub-topic (*masʿala*) stated by Imam Yaḥyā b. Ḥamza (Y)
>
> The employment of *maṣlaḥa* can be found in the *sharīʿa* in the protection of life through [the establishment of] criminal legal punishment,[11] in the protection of religion by killing the apostate, in the protection of reason (*ʿaql*) by prohibiting drunkenness, even if [reason] may come back,[12] in the protection of property by the punishment of cutting the hand,[13] and in the protection [of the concept of family] descent (*nasab*) [identity] by the punishment for *zinā'*.[14] This means that the concept of public interest (*maṣāliḥ*) should be established by analogy even [in rules] without a specific textual source,[15] which most of them are anyway, such as the *waqf* for the poor, the public infrastructure (*al-maṣāliḥ*), the mosques,

6 Several of these purposes are also mentioned in the exegesis of al-Zamakhsharī referred to above.

7 Wa-akthar mā dhakarnā fī l-waqf riʿāyatan li-l-maṣlaḥa.

8 Actors are given in brackets in the printed edition so that "most scholars" are just given as "*al-akthar*."

9 Wa-murāʿātuhā ṭarīq sharʿī.

10 Fa-nafāhā illā bi-nāṣṣ.

11 Al-ḥifẓ li-l-dimā' bi-l-qisās.

12 *Wa-law binajan*. "Even if it can be saved?" The context indicates this, as does the fact that Yahyā b. Ḥamza does not mention the punishment. Or *banj*, the narcotic is meant.

13 Wa-l-māl bi-qaṭʿ al-yad.

14 Wa-l-nasab bi-ḥadd al-zinā'.

15 Fa-qayyis (qīsa?) ʿalayhā l-qawl bi-l-maṣāliḥ wa-in lam tastanid ilā aṣl muʿayyan.

> the *ʿulamāʾ*, and the orphans. So, in all of these cases, the concept of interest (*maṣlaḥa*) is to be followed....

"Public interest" is a slightly problematic translation here. The term "public" is a modern, western term that does not necessarily clarify the term *maṣlaḥa* accurately. Sometimes the term *ʿāmm* is added, and this makes it more appropriate to translate the term as "public interest." There is also a difference between *maṣlaḥa*, which tends to refer to the legal method or principle, and that of *maṣāliḥ*,[16] which rather invokes common infrastructure and welfare.

Maṣlaḥa as a principle can relate to the wider, general purposes of the law; these are commonly referred to as *maqāṣid al-sharīʿa*, as are more specific purposes of the law. The latter necessitates a critical epistemology of real (contextually situated) legal problems. An example is the problem of long term leases as treated in chapter 6. There we saw that the concept of *maṣlaḥa* "kicks in" as a way to create an efficient and thereby valid legal rule. Although the idea of *maṣlaḥa* as a tool can be seen as universal (or even as God's will), it becomes particular once it is employed to make a legal rule. In the discussion above, *maṣlaḥa* is understood as a tool in legal methodology in general, as well as a valid source of *waqf* law specifically.[17]

Ibn al-Murtaḍā and Imam Yaḥyā b. Ḥamza state that *waqf* law is to be constructed by using the concept of *maṣlaḥa*, and exceptions to this method or procedure should only be made if a "clear text" states otherwise. They invoke the general notion of *maṣlaḥa* as a principle in Islamic law and as a tool to establish the best possible *waqf* law that will serve the general public or society (*al-maṣāliḥ*). They also state that rules agreed upon by consensus are to be

16 In the Zaydī context *al-maṣāliḥ* in the plural with the definite article does not refer to the legal principle as found in *uṣūl* debates, but rather to the concept of the common, "public," infrastructure that is controlled by the imam or the state. In general, there is a clear distinction between the circulation of *zakāt* and the *bayt al-māl* (the treasury) on the one hand and the *waqf* economy on the other, since *waqf* is considered something separate from the state, even when the imam is the ultimate administrator. However, the term *al-maṣlāliḥ* is related, in part, to some types of *waqf*, for example, mosques and schools. According to the Caspian al-Mu'ayyad, *waqf*s revert to *al-maṣāliḥ* and not to the heirs of the founder, if the beneficiary or its category ceases to exist (*inqiṭāʿ al-maṣrif*). There are several other examples in the *waqf* chapter in the *Sharḥ al-azhār* that state that *waqf* can be made for *al-maṣāliḥ*, and this has the meaning of "general public infrastructure," but more research is needed to historicise the usage of this term.

17 For recent research and an overview over earlier research on the concept of *maṣlaḥa* in classical Islamic legal theory, see Felicitas Opwis, *Maṣlaḥa and the Purpose of the Law: Islamic Discourse on Legal Change from the 4th/10th to the 8th/14th Century* (Leiden: Brill, 2010).

considered legally valid and to be followed as long as there is an interest found in following the rule, even though there is no "clear text" directly underpinning the validity of the rule. Thus, *maṣlaḥa* is a concept that can be used to produce law, and already formulated law can afterwards be validated by *maṣlaḥa*. This perspective can also be seen in the use of a "meta-*qiyās*" to prove that the *sharīʿa* is there for a purpose and that it has a function, and that function is something that can be understood and reflected upon.[18] How should this work in practice? Ibn al-Murtaḍā continues in *al-Baḥr al-zakhkhār*:

> "Sub-section" (*masʾala*): al-Shāfiʿī (Sh) and al-Hādī (H) state that, concerning any rule that lacks a specific origin of validity (*aṣl muʿayyan*), the rule is also to be followed if *maṣlaḥa* can be found. (Y) [Yaḥyā b. Ḥamza adds]: Under the condition that it does not contradict a clear text,... it should not be used in cases where other equally significant interests work against it, such as, beating a person suspected for crime, for in doing so there is an interest in [protecting] property and by refraining from doing so, one refrains from injustice for a man, were he innocent ...[19]

Present-day liberals and reformists invoke the principle of *maṣlaḥa* as a source of law.[20] They often "excuse" the strong punishments prescribed in the *sharīʿa* which are pointed out above as "examples of *maṣlaḥa*" by referring to the strict demand for a number of witnesses, the offender's confession, etc., which would mean that these punishments would occur only rarely. And by eliminating this part of the *sharīʿa*, one is thus left with the idea that the *sharīʿa* is almost the

18 This is part of the rationalist, Muʿtazilī theology which maintains that humans have free will and are capable of distinguishing between "good" and "bad" by employing reason. The law then becomes a tool to help to correct the behaviour of man, who later faces the religious consequences in the hereafter. Other theological schools that allow for various degrees of predestination implicitly remove the "need" for a law, not to speak of those that completely reject the idea that man can understand what is "good" and "bad" outside the "clear" commandments in the revelation. If this is true, there is no "need" for law, it is simply there because God sent it. It is not the focus of this study to include such theological debates and arguably it is also not necessary in order to study *waqf* law in practice. It suffices here to simply point out that such advanced discourses can be found, though they are rarely relevant outside an "academic" and intellectual context.

19 Ibn al-Murtaḍā, *al-Baḥr al-zakhkhār*, 5:166, at the end of the chapter on *waqf*.

20 Here I refer to what I have heard from Yemeni intellectuals. For a more general treatment of the topic, see Felicitas Opwis, "New Trends in Islamic Legal Theory: Maqāsid al-Sharīʿa as a New Source of Law?" *Die Welt des Islams* 57 (2017), 7–32. Muhammad Qasim Zaman, "The ʿUlama of Contemporary Islam," in *Public Islam and the Common Good*, ed. Armando Salvatore and Dale F. Eickelman (Leiden: Brill, 2004). For a general overview of *maqāṣid*, see Vikør, *Between God and the Sultan*, 62, 68, 165.

same as *maṣlaḥa*. The concept of *waqf* is equally often seen as an instrument to fulfil the interests or the welfare of society, as a way of achieving social responsibilities (*takāful ijtimāʿī*), as several informants mentioned. An embarrassing example from the chapter on *waqf* is the rule regulating marriage with a slave girl who has been made into *waqf*. These "problematic" examples are treated in very different ways today. Some scholars simply ignore them and others use them in a "hypothetical" way. For example, in the commentary on the present Yemeni *waqf* law, certain university professors cannot completely avoid using theoretical, legal comparisons related to slavery, etc.[21]

As a principle and as a source of law, *maṣlaḥa* is open to change and to the possibility that the *sharīʿa* is suitable for a variety of times and places, similar to what happens when custom (*ʿurf*, *ʿāda*) can be acknowledged, as I show in chapter 7. Above, Ibn al-Murtaḍa and Imam Yaḥyā both render *maṣlaḥa* as part of *sharīʿa*. As we saw in chapter 7, *ʿurf* was incorporated into Islamic law, partly by rendering it neutral and even useful, as a legal precedent and as a social order. Of these two principles, *maṣlaḥa* is still the more abstract, theoretical principle and more integrated into Islamic legal methodology as an internal principle, while *ʿurf* is seen as something external to the *sharīʿa*, initially at least, while at the same time it is incorporated into it because *ʿurf* is subordinated to the overall validity of the *sharīʿa*.

Principles like *maṣlaḥa* and *ʿurf*, which both allow for flexibility, are necessarily threatening for those who claim a more literalist, traditionist stand. For them, this means that a *sharīʿa* that relies on *maṣlaḥa* and *ʿurf* cannot be a "holy" or "pure" entity, distilled and deduced from the texts of revelation, rather it is something that is gradually integrated into mundane, local, situational politics, discourses, and knowledge(s) where humans, rather than God, make the law. The literalists or the neo-traditionists, as exemplified by al-Shawkānī, prefer to rely on evidence and validity directly from the texts of revelation. Al-Shawkānī finds *maṣlaḥa* a dangerous, slippery slope like "unattested" *maṣlaḥa* (*maṣlaḥa mursala*), that is, *maṣlaḥa* with no textual basis at all.[22] By not admitting *maṣlaḥa* and *ʿurf* into the realm of what is "holy," he retains the fixed, pure quality of the *sharīʿa*, thus he is able to clearly separate between religious and mundane, human law. An example is the way al-Shawkānī critiques the three-year rule in his *al-Sayl al-jarrār* as seen in chapter 6. He opposes the view that the three-year rule carries *sharʿī* validity simply because it was in the

21 An example is al-Waẓẓāf, *Aḥkām al-waqf*, 79.

22 For his sceptical views on *maṣlaḥa* in the framework of *uṣūl* (*al-maṣlaḥa al-mursala*) and the related concept of *istiḥsān*, see al-Shawkānī, *Irshād al-fuḥūl*. For *istiḥsān*, see 786–789, for *maṣāliḥ mursala* 790–816. Al-Shawkānī, *Adab al-ṭalab*, 252–253.

interest of the *waqf* to follow this rule and because it was upheld by previous imams. He upholds that the three-year time limit cannot be made into a rule just by arguing based on *maṣlaḥa*. Yet, he also suggests an alternative rule, stating that the *mutawallī* should follow the interest of the *waqf* (a rule he does not include as an explicit "*sharīʿa* rule" in his *mukhtaṣar*).[23] Such an ideal view of the *sharīʿa* might be part of al-Shawkānī's polemical campaign to discredit the traditional or Hādawī-Zaydīs of his time. It is also a view that does not create problems for those who are mainly interested in the ritual laws (*ʿibādāt*) of the *sharīʿa*, such as many Salafīs. However, in the field of transactional law (*muʿāmalāt*), this leads to problems once newly occurring, real problems in daily life must be regulated and rules must be made, since "secular" knowledge about the world cannot be admitted as valid knowledge. The acknowledgement of the flexible elements in traditional Zaydī law, as given through *maṣlaḥa* and *ʿurf*, is important, as it allows for the future development and improvement of the law. It allows space to address problems on the ground.

2 Situating Legal Knowledge

The four levels of legal knowledge elaborated in chapter 2 enable us to see that there are theories and practices in all four fields of knowledge. The field of *fiqh* certainly has its actors, settings of transmission and use, its media and its corpus with conventions and frames of validity. The other fields of knowledge have not been as easy to define, but they are, arguably, still useful as analytical categories. In chapters 5, 6, and 7, we have seen that the field of *fiqh* is torn between an ideal, religiously-oriented, doctrinal debate on the one hand and debates that relate more to mundane law and the problems found in the "real" world on the other hand. These two are connected: when a certain act becomes religiously immoral it can also become invalid or illegal, but does not necessarily become so. Practice-oriented or legal-pragmatic *fiqh* also serves the "needs" of the local society, that is, the local community's need for commonly accepted, practical, transactional law. There is a need for a language in which to write contracts and legal documents, and there is a need for clear, applicable, and enforceable rules.

As I note in several places in this book, criticism of law and arguments of validity in law are often used by invoking arguments based on "essence," and "holiness," and "fixed" notions of divine will. Arguments built on "fixed" truths are employed and invoked, even in *waqf* law, which is scarcely mentioned in

23 al-Shawkānī, *Darārī l-mudīya*, 303.

the Qur'ān and the Sunna. However, the fact that these arguments are put forward and *claimed* does not mean that "Islamic law" *is* based on fixed and ideal truths, or that those arguments were actually effective or will continue to be effective in the future. This perspective aligns with that of Dupret, who argues for the necessity of methodological contextualization. The fact that someone claims Islamic validity does not mean that the actor will necessarily succeed over other counter-claims and the claim does not imply social reality or efficacy; nor does it imply that norms or claims must systematically relate to each other.[24] One can argue for or against *waqf* in a multitude of ways, *waqf* does not have to be "subordinated" to an all-encompassing "Islam" through a logical system of sources in one way only. The relevance of these claims to us as historians and social scientists are rather found in their social patterns and the frames in which they were thought of, taught, claimed, and used.

Instead of reverting to concepts like "religion" or "culture" or "Islam" or "*sharīʿa*" to describe the ideas and motivations underlying the texts and practices we observe, this book uses the concept of knowledge as formulated by Fredrik Barth. Barth's theory of knowledge allows us to theoretically connect norms, values, and claims to social context. His knowledge theory breaks down, in part, the division between values and acts and urges us to look at how knowledge is used and transmitted and under what circumstances. The criteria for what is proper, valid law and legal knowledge obviously vary greatly within Islamic law and even within Zaydism, and within various fields of knowledge of *waqf* law, as I focus on in this book.

What is valid *waqf* law? And for whom? In this book I show that the criteria of validity depends on which field of knowledge one looks at. This becomes clearer when we create four ideal analytical types of fields of knowledge: (1) *fiqh*, (2) codification, (3) individual legal cases, and (4) everyday knowledge. These fields of knowledge also all involve practices. This book prioritizes the *fiqh* and codification because of the relative availability of data and practical restrictions related to fieldwork.

In the four fields of knowledge, we see various levels of argumentation. For example, in *fiqh* we see arguments relating to the Qur'ān, *ḥadīths*, legal maxims, methodological arguments, references to public interest and custom, and the views of previous scholars, etc. We can see a hierarchy in the sources of arguments, where sometimes the "upper level" arguments are invoked and sometimes "lower level" arguments are invoked. We can imagine a system of

24 See the conclusion in Dupret and Ferrie, "Constructing the Private/Public Distinction." See also the "casuistic" perspective in the conclusion of Lynch, "Public Spheres Transnationalized."

hierarchy of arguments or sources of validity. The most famous textbook version is the four levels of Qurʾān, Sunna, *qiyās*, and *ijmāʿ*. This is, arguably, rather ideal and also Sunnī centred. One that would be more appropriate for Zaydī Yemen would be Qurʾān, parts of the Sunna, the views of previous imams and scholars, legal maxims, *maṣlaḥa*, and *ʿurf*. But do the lower-level arguments really necessitate an a priori "approval" by the higher-level arguments, and if so, when? Implicitly, certain upper-level arguments are, and must be, taken for granted in debates and must be accepted and "followed" in that sense. As exemplified in this book, most Zaydī scholars are of the view that *waqf* law is based on piety. When regulating legal practices that are not entirely pious, this principle is supposed to "kick in" and bring the law-making process back on track. In reality, we see that this is discussed, and often claimed, but not always followed in making the final rule chosen in codification. The same can be said about the principle of perpetuity or equality among the heirs. In chapter 5, such upper-level doctrinal arguments are often used, while in chapter 7, doctrinal arguments are seldom referred to, other than that custom is to be allowed if there is no clear text in the revelation contradicting the proposed rule. It is tempting to see this difference as resulting from the "need" for arguments (as discussed in chapter 5), where also the validity of the originally Sunnī *ḥadīth* "lā waṣīya li-wārith" becomes central, while in chapter 7, few seem to protest against the problems related to "non-absolute *waqf*." Some protests can be seen in chapter 6 and 7, but these protests are not taken into account in the codification. The hierarchy of norms and doctrines is arguably not systematic or coherent and it is therefore not possible to represent it as such. Each rule and its trajectory of debate need to be treated individually. While the systematic nature and coherence of the *sharīʿa* are often *claimed*, the truth of that claim must be investigated in the social and historical context. By following a *fiqh* debate historically, we can observe that some claims survive over time and others do not.

Indeed, several of the most controversial debates in Yemeni Zaydī *waqf* law are found in areas where there is a need for applicable, enforceable, codified law and where the arguments centre on local legal practices, interest, and custom. In this, the "Islamic" component is a language and frame for reasoning and not a definable essence. A book like the *Kitāb al-Azhār* can constitute a corpus, but not an essence. If we attach meaning to the corpus (text) and say that our informants would have to "believe," respect, and behave according to the *Kitāb al-Azhār*, then we as researchers are reproducing normative and religious concepts that were never used, especially when we see that the codification and the individual *waqf* cases followed quite different rules than those found in the *Kitāb al-Azhār*. We therefore also need to model and represent how hierarchies of norms are claimed and contested. In this book this has been done with the four fields of *waqf* knowledge as a model, but surely it is possible to use other such models, depending on the topic and what needs to be explained. In this book, we have deliberately not looked into *uṣūl* debates or theology, and some of the focus on everyday *waqf* knowledge also had to be taken out, partly for pragmatic reasons.

The continuity and stability of the tradition of Islamic law is striking, especially before the advent of "modernity."[25] We can see that by taking part in specific settings where *waqf* knowledge is used, actors must accept certain truths and criteria of validity in order to be accepted into the debate (and into the social institution—the *madrasa*, court, etc.). But even these criteria are not fixed; they can be challenged and the borders of validity can change under forces related to social and political power, communication technology, and under the influence of other novel knowledge traditions, such as the new, populist, fundamentalist, traditionist focus, or modern western law, popular culture, or science. Today, traditional Zaydī *fiqh* is only one among several settings where legal debates in Yemen take place. A study focusing more on contemporary legal debates in fields other than *waqf* might have to undertake a broader exploration than I have done in this study.

The inductive approach argued for in chapter 2 allows us to take a stand against previous, more essentialist academic perspectives, which build, in part, directly on emic and normative models and definitions. The ideal *waqf* model, as explained in the beginning of chapter 2, is not suitable as a model to use in the field in Yemen, when trying to see what *waqf* "is." It is even less useful to limit our investigation to "Islamic" phenomena only, just because *waqf* is "Islamic." However, the ideal *waqf* model is central in argumentation for—and constructions of—validity in *waqf* law. And it is also a good *starting point* for etic representations of *waqf* law, as long as it does not remain the central (hypo)thesis, and as long as one can investigate and represent contradictions of it. For historians of Islamic law who look farther back in time, the fact that sources become more normative is a problem. However, by acknowledging that there are pragmatic layers in *fiqh* that seek to solve problems in the "real" world, it is arguably possible to construct models of what we think could have been the practice(s) and the various tensions between ideals and pragmatic rules back then.

The historical and social data produce a picture that cannot be reduced to fit into an ideal Islamic *waqf* model. When discarding such a perspective and

25 Here, I use "modernity" in its widest sense, that is, as is evidenced by the advent of print and information technology, widespread literacy, etc. Arguably, in Yemen these changes came later than in the central areas of the Middle East.

employing an inductive one instead, new models, definitions, and theories can be made based on models that represent empirical findings from the field. Perhaps the best example of this is the terms *waqf* and *waṣāyā*: several forms of *waqf* in Yemen are called *waṣāyā*, despite the fact that *waqf* and *waṣāyā* belong to different chapters in the *fiqh* books (as explicitly pointed out by Imam al-Manṣūr ʿAbdallāh b. Ḥamza, as mentioned in chapter 5). Other examples relate to the fact that *waqf* law is tied to other forms of ownership law and that in reality *waqfs* are not only charitable and not only made with pious purposes. Central motives obviously relate to the control over resources, notably agricultural land, which in premodern Yemen was the central means of economic production and source of sustenance and position in society. This is a fact already well known to historians of *waqf*. This book goes further, to show that the legal theory (*fiqh*) and codified law is not the "ideal" found in the student textbooks of Islamic law, be it the modern western academic texts or the traditional Islamic texts like the *Hidāya*, the *Minhāj al-ṭālibīn*, and the *Kitāb al-Azhār*. When looking deeper into the legal literature, especially the *sharḥ* genre and footnote/commentary-debates of *waqf* law, one cannot avoid realizing that there are levels of jurisprudence and attempts at codification that are more pragmatic and oriented towards real life.

This book argues that at the level ("field of knowledge") of codification, the ideal *waqf* is linked with local, popular *waqf* practices and the need for law to regulate these. Such links extend through all four fields of knowledge. Concepts and arguments are borrowed and used interchangeably between these four levels. However, as this book also demonstrates, the dynamic of discourse within each of these four separate fields follows its own distinct "logic" and criteria of validity, again dependent on context. An argument in the field of *fiqh* may not necessarily be applicable and valid in court or in the reception room of a local *waqf* administrator and vice versa. The crux of these links is still the field of codification and the attempts to unify views and the ongoing debates centring on what is morally and legally valid law. This does not always have to be through the codification sanctioned by a centralized state that holds a monopoly of power, nor does it have to be a "modern" state, which is perhaps the ideal type of codification; at times we can imagine more local attempts arriving at law which can be respected and sanctioned by local elites.

In the field of *fiqh* we find in the *sharḥ* literature a culture of academic discussion. Deep academic discussions cannot exclude arguments and simultaneously claim to be "comprehensive" and "encyclopaedic." The same "freedom" and openness to opposing views can also be seen in legal disputes in court (a domain I have not focused on to the same degree in this book); in legal disputes, conflicting versions of truth are allowed into court. This does not threaten the validity of the court as such, on the contrary, the court needs to weigh the diverging views, it needs and depends on conflict. The validity of the judgement, on the other hand, is tied to the dynamic of witnesses and the power relations among the local elites, previous judgements, and "codification," all of which are connected. The judgement is not necessarily the ultimate word, the case may be appealed, and the case may live on in local knowledge. Both these fields, the *fiqh* and the court, can be seen as connected through the field of codification. Codification is a focus in Islamic legal studies with quite diverse views and we hope this book can contribute to the debate. Arguably, codification is an etic, analytic concept that is fruitful to consider even outside the context of a modern state. This way we can create an analytical distance from Islamic terms and concepts, while still allowing our analysis to be informed by them. Even if we choose to use another term, other than "codification," the same research questions regarding how *fiqh* relates to local legal cases must still be answered.

3 The Potential in *Waqf*

The potential of *waqf* can differ widely and can be seen from (at least) two perspectives: from modern, secular, western development discourse and from various local Yemeni perspectives. From a western perspective, to the extent that it is known at all, *waqf* is first and foremost problematic, since it is firmly situated in a discourse ("Islam") that is outside the control of the actors. Many are of the opinion that "Islam" is a totalizing discourse that, once accepted in its entirety, dictates certain lower-level outcomes and decisions. In general, although "local stakeholder involvement," "indigenous solutions," "capacity building," and "bottom up" is seen as good, religion and especially Islam is seen as something outside the development (or human rights) discourse altogether. "*Sharīʿa*" is a word with strongly negative connotations. I did not intend to analyse these issues in depth here. I believe that dialogue can be used and that one does not have to accept or reject "Islam" in its entirety. This study has shown that Zaydī *waqf fiqh* is much more nuanced, advanced, socially situated, and specific than what many assume from "an Islamic branch of law." This study allows us to see that we can enter into dialogue and conversations at different levels and from different entry points. It is also important not to overstate the Islamic component of *waqf*. *Waqf* is also situated in local Yemeni practices and cultures of law, administration, charity, and welfare. The nature of the "Islamic" component will always remain contested.

From a local Yemeni perspective, matters are, at least in part, quite different. Here, *waqf* is also problematic. Knowledge of *waqf* is very diverse and to a large extent unevenly distributed. Many feel alienated from discourses on *fiqh* and feel that they do not have the authority to question anyone's knowledge of *fiqh*. As the book demonstrates, *waqf fiqh* and law is complicated and the ideal *waqf* is conceptualized differently than *waqf* law that has been and is used in Yemen. Many see *waqf* as inseparable from the elites and actors who control it and as an especially traditional, opaque, and backward part of the government. Charity, organized welfare, and public infrastructure projects are therefore sought and conceptualized through other frames than *waqf*. Some modern liberals also see the traditional aspects of *waqf* and its context in religion as something incompatible with a civil state. However, most do not see any opposition, or "problem," in framing charity and welfare in Islamic terms and concepts.

Today, *waqf* is situated in distinct remnants of the past and is only one form of welfare management among various other forms of "state/civil" or "tribal" welfare. The "state" is not a very useful concept for our analysis of the Yemeni context, however, few clear alternatives exist. The state is a major actor in *waqf* law and management. If we look more broadly at the power relations between local rural communities and the political elites in the urban centres, we see a picture in which *waqf*s are managed by certain educated families who specialize in legal knowledge and administration. As in the judiciary, there is a tendency for *sharīʿa* education to be valued as important for social mobility; material wealth and clan identity are not the only decisive factors that determine who obtains administrative positions. At the same time, we can also see that many local and state *waqf* administrators were indeed members of the elite and passed their positions on to their children and close family members. The 1962 revolution did not produce significant changes in this pattern, and until today, the knowledge of *waqf* law and management is, to a large extent, still situated in the same elites, locally and nationally.

Under Imam Yaḥyā, the concept of *waqf* was revived and redefined as a political tool to finance public infrastructure (most notably his state *sharīʿa* education), much in line with his theocratic ideology. Under the republican government, little development has been seen and *waqf* is not important to the same degree for the state as such, except to the extent that the state attempts to exercise control over the mosques and what is preached there. The laws and decrees issued under the republican government have remained highly traditional, as have the forms of administration. The present-day *waqf* law remains partly "ideal," just as the *sharīʿa* books that inspired it, and sociological reality cannot be inferred uncritically from the law. As demonstrated in depth in chapter 6, in the discussion of the three-year rule, the rule is used to invoke an ideal, while the related rules in effect allow the opposite. Parts of the *waqf* law are not clear or coherent and much work is needed in order to create a better law and deeper knowledge of its potentials and functions.

Both western and Yemeni actors too quickly look to the ideal starting point ("Islam") when trying to understand the law and the institution of *waqf*. This is why we need a historical and ethnographically situated account of what *waqf* was in the past and what it is today. *Waqf* law still functions because of the strong presence of a semi-formal ownership law in Yemen, which although not always backed by the state, is still anchored in local communities and local elites who need a minimum of "order" to sanction their access to various forms of property, value, surplus, and wealth. *Waqf* is also respected in local communities as part of that law and is part of the vision of a moral order, both because of its moral-religious status and because it is deeply situated in the aforementioned ownership law. Despite all the problems in *waqf*, the moral aspect should not be underestimated, and this is something that is easy to do when analysing and taking apart a system. People believe in performing charity and setting up a welfare infrastructure, the "Islamic" essence of which is not always the best point of departure in trying to understand and interact with it.

In practice, much *waqf* has been privatized and nationalized and this makes it important to safeguard the old *waqf* documents and registers for future potential revival. Indescribably important values are at stake concerning the future of *waqf* in Yemen, related to both the economic dimensions and the human resources in the form of mobilisation, opportunity, and encouragement to perform good.

Bibliography

al-ʿAbbāsī l-ʿAlawī, ʿAlī b. Muḥammad b. ʿUbaydallāh. *Sīrat al-Hādī ilā l-Ḥaqq Yaḥyā b. al-Ḥusayn*. Edited by Suhayl Zakkār. Beirut: Dār al-Fikr li-l-Ṭibāʿa wa-l-Nashr wa-l-Tawzīʿ, 1401/1981.

ʿAbdallāh b. Ḥamza, al-Imām al-Manṣūr bi-Llāh. *al-Majmūʿ al-manṣūrī (al-qism al-thānī) Majmūʿ rasāʾil al-Imām al-Manṣūr bi-Llāh ʿAbdallāh b. Ḥamza*. Edited by ʿAbd al-Salām b. ʿAbbās al-Wajīh. 3 vols. Sanaa: Dār al-Imām Zayd b. ʿAlī l-Thaqāfiyya li-l-Nashr wa-l-Tawzīʿ, 2001.

ʿAbd al-ʿĀṭī, ʿAbd al-Ghanī Maḥmūd. *al-Ṣirāʿ al-fikrī fī l-Yaman bayn al-Zaydiyya wa-l-Muṭarrifiyya: Dirāsa wa-nuṣūṣ*. Cairo: ʿAyn li-l-Dirāsāt wa-l-Buḥūth al-Insāniyya wa-l-Ijtimāʿiyya, 2002.

al-Abdin, al-Tayib Zein. "The Role of Islam in the State, Yemen Arab Republic (1940–72)." PhD thesis, University of Cambridge, 1975.

ʿAbd al-Raḥmān ʿAbdallāh ʿIwaḍ Bakīr. *al-Waqf fī Ḥaḍramawt bayn al-salaf wa-l-khalaf*. al-Jamʿiyya al-Khayriyya li-Taʿlīm al-Qurʾān al-Karīm, farʿ Ḥaḍramawt, Mukallāʾ: Dār Ḥaḍramawt li-l-Dirāsāt wa-l-Nashr, 2002.

Abū Zahra, Muḥammad. *Muḥāḍarāt fī l-waqf*. Cairo: Dār al-Fikr al-ʿArabī, 1971 [?].

al-Ahdal, Aḥmad b. Dāwūd b. Aḥmad b. Muḥammad al-Baṭṭāḥ. "Kitāb al-Tuḥfa al-qaddasiyya fī ikhtiṣār al-raḥḥabiyya fatāwā l-Shaykh al-ʿAllāma al-Sayyid Aḥmad b. Dāwūd b. Aḥmad b. Muḥammad al-Baṭṭāḥ al-Ahdal." Electronic copy of manuscript edited by ʿArafāt ʿAbd al-Raḥmān ʿAbdallāh al-Ḥadramī, 1992.

Aḥmad, Amīn Ḥasan, and ʿAbd al-Hādī Fatḥī. *Mawsūʿat al-awqāf: Tashrīʿāt qaḍāʾ—iftāʾ: Fatāwa al-awqāf mundhu 1890 ḥatta 1997*. Alexandria: Manshāt al-Maʿārif, 2003.

al-Akwaʿ, Ismāʿīl b. ʿAlī. *al-Madāris al-islāmiyya fī-l-Yaman*. Sanaa and Beirut: al-Jīl al-Jadīd, Muʾassasat al-Risāla, 1986.

Ali, Abdullah Yusuf (trans.). *The Holy Qurʾan: Translation and Commentary*. Brentwood, MD: Amana Corporation, 1989.

al-ʿAlīmī, Rashād Muḥammad. *al-Taqlīdiyya wa-l-ḥadātha fī l-niẓam al-qanūnī l-Yamanī*. Cairo: Maṭābiʿ al-Shurūq, 1986.

al-Amīr, Ibn Ḥusayn b. Badr al-Dīn. *Shifāʾ al-awām fī aḥādīth al-aḥkām li-l-tamyīz bayna al-ḥalāl wa-l-ḥarām*.

al-ʿAmrānī, Muḥammad b. Ismāʿīl. *Niẓām al-qaḍāʾ fī l-Islām*. Sanaa: Maktabat Dār al-Jīl, 1984.

al-ʿAmrī, Ḥusayn ʿAbdallāh. "A Document Concerning the Sale of Ghayl al-Barmakī and al-Ghayl al-Awsad by al-Mahdī ʿAbbās, Imam of Yemen, 1131–89/1718–75." In *Arabian and Islamic Studies*, edited by R. L. Bidwell and G. R. Smith. London and New York: Longman, 1983.

al-ʿAmrī, Ḥusayn ʿAbdallāh. *Miʾat ʿām min tārīkh al-Yaman al-ḥadīth*. Damascus: Dār al-Fikr, 1988.

al-ʿAmrī, Ḥusayn ʿAbdallāh. *Yamaniyyāt fi l-tārīkh wa-l-thaqāfa wa-l-siyāsa II*. Damascus: Dār al-Fikr al-Muʿāṣir, 2000.

al-ʿAmrī, Ḥusayn ʿAbdallāh. *The Yemen in the 18th and 19th Centuries: A Political and Intellectual History*. London: Ithaca Press, 1985.

al-ʿAmrī, Ḥusayn ʿAbdallāh, and R. B. Serjeant. "Administrative Organisation." In *Ṣanʿāʾ: An Arabian Islamic City*, edited by R. B. Serjeant and R. Lewcock, 142–158. London: World of Islam Festival Trust, 1983.

Anderson, J. N. D. "Waqfs in East Africa." *Journal of African Law* 3, no. 3 (1959): 152–164.

Anonymous. *Ḥawliyāt yamaniyya: al-Yaman fī l-qarn al-tāsiʿ ʿashar al-mīlādī*. Edited by ʿAbdallāh b. Muḥammad al-Ḥibshī. Sanaa: Dār al-Ḥikma al-Yamaniyya, 1991.

al-ʿAnsī, Aḥmad b. Qāsim al-Yamānī l-Ṣanʿānī. *al-Tāj al-mudhhab li-aḥkām al-madhhab*. 4 vols. Sanaa: Maktabat al-Yaman al-Kubrā, n.d.

Asad, Talal. "The Idea of an Anthropology of Islam." In *Occasional Paper Series*. Washington, DC: Center for Contemporary Arab Studies, 1986.

ʿAslān, ʿAbd al-Wahhāb Muḥammad. *Ghuyūl Ṣanʿāʾ: Dirāsa tārīkhiyya āthāriyya wathāʾiqiyya*. Damascus and Beirut: Dār al-Fikr al-Muʿāṣir, 2000.

Aw-Hassan, Aden, Mohammed Alsanabani, and Abdul Rahman Bamatraf. "Impact of Land Tenure and other Socioeconomic Factors on Mountain Terrace Maintenance in Yemen." *CAPRi Working paper* 3 (2000): 1–40.

Baer, Gabriel. "Ḥikr." *Encyclopaedia of Islam*, second edition. Edited by P. J. Bearman, Th. Biancuis, C. E. Bosworth, E. van Donzel and W. P. Heinrichs, 12:368. Leiden: Brill, 1960–2004.

Baer, Gabriel. "The Waqf as a Prop for the Social System (Sixteenth-Twentieth Centuries)." *Islamic Law and Society* 4, no. 3 (1997): 264–287.

Bälz, Kilian. "Sharīʿa and Qānun in Egyptian Law: A Systems Theory Approach to Legal Pluralism." *Yearbook of Islamic and Middle Eastern Law* 2 (1995): 37–53.

Barth, Fredrik. "An Anthropology of Knowledge." *Current Anthropology* 43, no. 1 (2002): 1–18.

Bavenick, Maarten, and Gordon R. Woodman. "Can There be Maps of Law?" In *Spatializing Law: An Anthropological Geography of Law in Society*, edited by Frans von Benda-Beckmann, Keebet von Benda-Beckmann and Anne Griffiths. Burlington, VT: Ashgate, 2009.

Behrens-Abouseif, Doris. "The *Waqf*: A Legal Personality?" In *Islamische Stiftungen zwischen juristischer Norm on sozialer Praxis*, edited by Astrid Meier, Johannes Pahlitzsch, and Lucian Reinfandt, 55–61. Berlin: Akademie-Verlag, 2009.

Benthall, Jonathan, and Jerome Bellion-Jourdan. *The Charitable Crescent: Politics of Aid in the Muslim World*. London: I.B.Tauris, 2009.

Bonnefoy, Laurent. "Salafism in Yemen: A 'Saudisation'?" In *Kingdom Without Borders: Saudi Expansion in the World*, edited by Madawi al-Rasheed, 245–262. London: Hurst and Co., 2008.

Bonnefoy, Laurent. "Varieties of Islamism in Yemen: The Logic of Integration under Pressure." *Middle East Review of International Affairs* 13, no. 1 (2009). Also available online from the Rubin Center (rubincenter.org): http://www.rubincenter.org/2009/03/bonnefoy-2009-03-03/, accessed 12 November 2015.

Bostan, Hümeyra. "Institutionalizing Justice in a Distant Province: Ottoman Judicial Reform in Yemen (1872–1918)." PhD thesis, Istanbul Sehir University, 2013.

Bruinessen, Martiin van, and Stefano Allievi. *Producing Islamic Knowledge: Transmission and Dissemination in Western Europe*. London and New York: Routledge, 2011.

Buskens, Leon. "An Islamic Triangle: Changing Relationships between Sharīʿa, State Law and Local Customs." *ISIM Review* (2000), 8.

Cook, Michael. *Commanding Right and Forbidding Wrong in Islamic Thought*. Cambridge: Cambridge University Press, 2002.

Deguilhem, Randi. "The Waqf in the City." In *The City in the Islamic World*, edited by Salma K. Jayyusi, Renata Holod, Attilio Petruccioli, and André Raymond, 923–950. Leiden: Brill, 2008.

Delcambre, A. M. "Milk." *Encyclopaedia of Islam*, second edition. Edited by P. J. Bearman, Th. Biancuis, C. E. Bosworth, E. van Donzel and W. P. Heinrichs. Leiden: Brill, 1960–2004.

Donaldson, William J. *Sharecropping in the Yemen: A Study in Islamic Theory, Custom and Pragmatism*. Leiden: Brill, 2000.

van Donzel, E. "al-Manṣūr Bi'llāh ʿAbd Allāh b. Ḥamza b. Sulaymān b. Ḥamza." In *Encyclopaedia of Islam*, second edition. Edited by P. J. Bearman, Th. Biancuis, C. E. Bosworth, E. van Donzel and W. P. Heinrichs, 6:433–434. Leiden: Brill, 1960–2004.

Dostal, Walter. *Der Markt von Ṣanʿāʾ*. Vienna: Verlag der Österreichischen Akademie der Wissenschaften, 1979.

Dresch, Paul. "Legalism, Anthropology, and History: A View from Part of Anthropology." In *Legalism: Anthropology and History*, edited by Paul Dresch and Hanna Skoda. Oxford: Oxford University Press, 2012.

Dresch, Paul. *The Rules of Barat: Tribal Documents from Yemen*. Sanaa: Centre Français d'Archéologie et de Sciences Sociales (CEFAS) and Deutches Archäologisches Institut, 2006.

Dresch, Paul. *Tribes, Government, and History in Yemen*. Oxford: Clarendon Press, 1989.

Dupret, Baudouin. "Review of Gerber 'Islamic Law and Culture 1600–1840.'" *Journal of Law and Religion* 15, nos. 1–2 (2000–2001): 407–412.

Dupret, Baudouin. *Practices of Truth: An Ethnomethodological Inquiry into Arab Contexts*. Amsterdam and Philadelphia: John Benjamins Publishing Company, 2011.

Dupret, Baudouin. "What is Plural in the Law? A Praxiological Answer." Égypte/Monde arabe. Troisième série, 1 (2005). Available online: http://journals.openedition.org/ema/1869; doi: 10.4000/ema.1869, accessed 28 September 2018.

Dupret, Baudouin, and Jean-Noël Ferrie. "Constructing the Private/Public Distinction in Muslim Majority Societies: A Praxiological Approach." In *Religion, Social Practice, and Contested Hegemonies: Reconstructing the Public Sphere in Muslim Majority Societies*, edited by Armando Salvatore and Mark LeVine, 135–154. New York: Palgrave Macmillan, 2005.

Eagle, A. B. D. R. "Ghayat al-Amani and the Life and Times of al-Hadi Yahya b. al-Husayn: An Introduction, Newly Edited Text and Translation with Detailed Annotation." MA thesis. University of Durham, 1990.

Eger, Helmut. "Runoff Agriculture: A Case Study about the Yemeni Highlands." PhD thesis, Eberhard-Karls-Universität, 1986.

Fadel, Mohammed. "The Social Logic of *taqlīd* and the Rise of the *mukhtaṣar*." *Islamic Law and Society* 3, no. 2 (1996): 193–233.

Falzon, Mark-Anthony. *Multi-Sited Ethnography: Theory, Praxis and Locality in Contemporary Research*. Farnham, UK: Ashgate, 2009.

al-Farrān, ʿAlī b. Muḥammad. *Athar al-waqf wa-l-mubarrirāt fī l-takāful and ijtimāʿī*. Taʿizz: Muʾassasat al-Saʿīd li-l-ʿUlūm wa-l-Thaqāfa, 2009.

García Sanjuán, Alejandro. *Till God Inherits the Earth: Islamic Pious Endowments in al-Andalus (9–15th centuries)*. The Medieval and Early Modern Iberian World, vol. 31. Leiden: Brill, 2007.

Gelder, G. J. H. van. "Yaḥyā b. Ḥamza al-ʿAlawī." *Encyclopaedia of Islam*, second edition. Edited by P. Bearman, Th. Bianquis, C. E. Bosworth, E. van Donzel and W. P. Heinrichs, 11:246. Leiden: Brill, 1960–2004.

Gerber, Haim. *Islamic Law and Culture 1600–1840*. Studies in Islamic Law and Society, vol. 9. Leiden: Brill, 1999.

Gerber, Haim. "Rigidity versus Openness in Late Classical Islamic Law: The Case of the Seventeenth-Century Palestinian Muftī Khayr al-Dīn al-Ramlī." *Islamic Law and Society* 5, no. 2 (1998): 165–195.

Gerholm, Tomas. "Market, Mosque and Mafraj: Social Inequality in a Yemeni Town." PhD thesis, University of Stockholm, 1977.

Gilsenan, Michael. *Recognizing Islam: An Anthropologist's Introduction*. London: Croom Helm, 1983.

Gimaret, D. "Muʿtazila." *Encyclopaedia of Islam*, second edition. Edited by P. Bearman, Th. Bianquis, C. E. Bosworth, E. van Donzel and W. P. Heinrichs, 7:783. Leiden: Brill, 1960–2004.

Gingrich, Andre. "Tribes and Rulers in Northern Yemen." In *Studies in Oriental Culture and History*, edited by Andre Gingrich, Sylvia Haas, Gabriele Paleczek, and Thomas Filliz, 253–280. Vienna, Frankfurt, and New York: Peter Lang, 1993.

Gleave, Robert. *Inevitable Doubt: Two Theories of Shiʿi Jurisprudence*. Leiden: Brill, 2000.

Gochenour, David Thomas. "The Penetration of Zaydi Islam into Early Medieval Yemen." PhD thesis. Harvard University, 1984.

al-Hādī ʿIzz al-Din b. al-Ḥasan. *Majmūʿ rasāʾil wa-fatāwā l-Imām al-Hādī ʿIzz al-Dīn b. al-Ḥasan b. ʿAlī b. al-Muʾayyad: al-Mujallad al-thānī: Jumla min al-fatāwa al-mufīda ʿalā l-masāʾil al-fādiḥa al-farīda*. Edited by ʿAbd al-Raḥmān b. Ḥusayn Shāʾim al-Muʾayyadī. 2 vols. Sanaa: Muʾassasat al-Imām Zayd b. ʿAlī l-Thaqāfiyya, forthcoming.

al-Ḥaḍramī, ʿAbd al-Raḥmān ʿAbdallāh. *Zabīd: Masājiduhā wa-madārisuhā l-ʿilmiyya fī l-tārīkh*. Sanaa: al-Markaz al-Faransī li-Dirāsāt al-Yamaniyya bi-Ṣanʿāʾ, al-Maʿhad al-Faransī li-Dirāsāt al-ʿArabiyya bi-Dimashq, 2000.

Haider, Najam. *The Origins of the Shīʿa*. New York: Cambridge University Press, 2014.

al-Ḥajarī, Muḥammad b. Aḥmad. *Masājid Ṣanʿā: ʿĀmiruhā wa-muwafīhā*. Sanaa: Maktabat al-Irshād, 2007 [1942].

Hallāq, Wael B. "The Authenticity of Prophetic Ḥadīth: A Pseudo-Problem." *Studia Islamica* 89 (1999): 75–90.

Hallāq, Wael B. "From Fatwās to Furūʿ: Growth and Change in Substantive Islamic Law." *Islamic Law and Society* 1, no. 1 (1994): 29–65.

Hamilton, Charles. *The Hedaya, or Guide: A Commentary on the Mussulman Laws*. Lahore: Premier Book House, 1963.

Hārūn, ʿAbdū ʿAlī ʿAbdallāh. *al-Durr al-naḍīd fī taḥdīd maʿālim wa-āthār madīnat Zabīd*. Sanaa: Wizārat al-Thaqāfa wa-l-Siyāḥa, 2004.

Ḥawliyāt yamaniyya. See Anonymous.

Haykel, Bernard. "Order and Righteousness: Muḥammad ʿAlī al-Shawkānī and the Nature of the Islamic State in Yemen." PhD thesis. Oxford, 1997.

Haykel, Bernard. *Revival and Reform in Islam: The Legacy of Muhammad al-Shawkānī*. Cambridge Studies in Islamic Civilisation. Cambridge: Cambridge University Press, 2003.

Haykel, Bernard. "A Zaydi Revival?" *Yemen Update* 36 (1995): 20–21.

Haykel, Bernard and Aron Zysow. "What Makes a Madhhab a Madhhab: Zaydī Debates on the Structure of Legal Authority." *Arabica* 59, nos. 3–4 (2012): 332–371.

Heiss, Johann. "Tribale Selbstorganisation und Konfliktreglung Der Norden des Jemen zur Zeit des ersten Imams (10. Jahrhundert)." PhD Thesis. University of Vienna, 1998.

Heiss, Johann, and Eirik Hovden. "Competing Visions of Community in Mediaeval Zaydī Yemen." *Journal of the Economic and Social History of the Orient* 59, no. 53 (2016): 366–407.

Hoexter, Miriam. "Adaptation to Changing Circumstances: Perpetual Leases and Exchange Transactions in Waqf Property in Ottoman Algiers." *Islamic Law and Society* 4, no. 3 (1997): 319–333.

Hoexter, Miriam. *Endowments, Rulers, and Community: Waqf al-Haramayn in Ottoman Algiers*. Studies in Islamic Law and Society. Leiden: Brill, 1998.

Hovden, Eirik. "Birka and Baraka—Cistern and Blessing: Notes on Custom and Islamic Law Regarding Public Cisterns in Northern Yemen." In *Southwest Arabia across History: Essays to the Memory of Walter Dostal*, edited by Andre Gingrich and Siegfried Hass. Philosophisch-Historische Klasse, Denkschriften, 472. Band, 55–65. Vienna: Verlag der Österreichischen Akademie der Wissenschaften, 2014.

Hovden, Eirik. "Flowers in *Fiqh* and Constructions of Validity: Practices and Norms in Yemeni Foundations of Forever Flowing Charity." PhD thesis, University of Bergen, 2012.

Hovden, Eirik. "Rainwater Harvesting Cisterns and Local Water Management: A Qualitative Geographical / Socio-Anthropological Case Study and Ethnographic Description from the Districts of Hajja, Mabyan and Shiris." MA thesis, University of Bergen. Available online: bora.uib.no/handle/1956/2001, 2006.

Hovden, Eirik. "Shiʿa: Zaydi (Fiver)." In *Encyclopedia of Islam and the Muslim World*, second edition. Edited by Richard C. Martin. New York: Macmillan, 2016.

Hughes, Aaron W. *Situating Islam: The Past and Future of an Academic Discipline*. London and Oakville, CT: Equinox, 2008.

Ibn ʿAbd al-Majīd = ʿAbd al-Bāqī b. ʿAbd al-Majīd al-Yamānī. *Bahjat al-zaman fī tārīkh al-Yaman*. Edited by ʿAbdallāh Muḥammad al-Ḥibshī and Muḥammad Aḥmad al-Sanabānī. Sanaa: Dar al-Ḥikma al-Yamānīyya, 1988.

Ibn Abī l-Rijāl, Aḥmad b. Ṣāliḥ. *Maṭlaʿ al-budūr wa-majmaʿ al-buḥūr fī tarājim rijāl al-Zaydiyya*. Edited by ʿAbd al-Raqīb Muṭahhar Muḥammad Ḥajar. 4 vols. Sanaa: Markaz Ahl al-Bayt li-l-Dirāsāt al-Islāmiyya, 2004.

Ibn ʿĀbidīn, Muḥammad Amīn. *Radd al-Mukhtār ʿalā l-Durr al-mukhtār*. 7 vols. Cairo: Sharikat Maktabat wa-Maktabat Muṣṭafā l-Bābā l-Ḥalabī wa-Awlādihi bi-Maṣr, 1966.

Ibn Diʿtham, Abū Firās. *al-Sīra al-Manṣūriyya: Sīrat al-Imām ʿAbdallāh b. Ḥamza 593–614 H*. Edited by ʿAbd al-Ghanī Maḥmūd ʿAbd al-ʿĀṭī. 2 vols. Beirut: Dār al-Fikr al-Muʿāṣir, 1993.

Ibn Ḥajar, al-Haytamī Shihāb al-Dīn Aḥmad. *Tuḥfat al-muḥtāj bi-sharḥ al-minhāj*. Available online from Islamweb.net: http://library.islamweb.net/newlibrary/display_book.php?bk_no=20&ID=209&idfrom=5891&idto=5910&bookid=20&startno=6. Accessed 12 November 2015.

Ibn Miftāḥ, ʿAbdallāh Abū l-Ḥasan. *Kitāb al-Muntaziʿ al-mukhtār min al-ghayth al-midrār al-mufattiḥ li-kamāʾim al-azhār fī fiqh al-aʾimma al-aṭhār* (*Sharḥ al-azhār*). 4 vols. Sanaa: Wizārat al-ʿAdl / Dār Iḥyāʾ al-Turāth al-Islāmī, 1980.

Ibn Miftāḥ, ʿAbdallāh Abū l-Ḥasan. *Kitāb al-Muntaziʿ al-mukhtār min al-ghayth al-midrār al-mufattiḥ li-kamāʾim al-azhār fī fiqh al-aʾimma al-aṭhār* (*Sharḥ al-azhār*). 4 vols. Cairo: Maṭbaʿat Sharikat al-Tamaddun, 1913–14.

Ibn Miftāḥ, ʿAbdallāh Abū l-Ḥasan. *al-Muntaziʿ al-mukhtār min al-ghayth al-midrār al-maʿrūf bi-Sharḥ al-azhār*. 8 vols. Sanaa: Wizārat al-ʿAdl / Maktabat al-Turāth al-Islāmī, 2003.

Ibn al-Murtaḍā, al-Imām al-Mahdī li-Dīn Allāh Aḥmad b. Yaḥyā. *Kitāb al-Azhār fī fiqh al-aʾimma al-aṭhār*. Beirut: Dār Maktabat al-Ḥayat, 1973.

Ibn al-Murtaḍā, al-Imām al-Mahdī li-Dīn Allāh Aḥmad b. Yaḥyā. *Kitāb al-Baḥr al-zakhkhār*. 6 vols. Beirut: Muʾassasat al-Risāla, 1975.

Ibn al-Qāsim b. al-Muʾayyad bi-Llāh, Ibrāhīm. *Ṭabaqāt al-Zaydiyya al-kubrā: al-Qism al-thālith wa-yusammā: Bulūgh al-murād ilā maʿrifat al-isnād*. Edited by ʿAbd al-Salām b. ʿAbbās al-Wajīh. 3 vols. Sanaa: Muʾassasat al-Imām Zayd b. ʿAlī l-Thaqafiyya, 2001.

Jackson, Sherman A. "Taqlīd, Legal Scaffolding and the Scope of Legal Injunctions in Post-Formative Theory. Muṭlaq and ʿĀmm in the Jurisprudence of Shihāb al-Dīn al-Qarāfī." *Islamic Law and Society* 3, no. 2 (1996): 165–92.

Jāzim, Muhammad ʿAbd al-Raḥim. "Un nouveau corpus documentaire d'époque rasūlide: Les actes de waqf de Taʿizz." Chroníques du Manuscrít au Yémen 10 (2010). Available online at Chroníques du Manuscrít au Yémen (cmy.org): https://cmy.revues.org/1900. Accessed 12 November 2015.

Johansen, Baber. *The Islamic Law on Land Tax and Rent: The Peasants' Loss of Property Rights as Interpreted in the Hanafite Legal Literature of the Mamluk and Ottoman Periods*. London: Croom Helm, 1988.

King, James Robin. "Zaydī Revival in a Hostile Republic: Competing Identities, Loyalties and Visions of State in Republican Yemen." *Arabica* 59, nos. 3–4 (2012): 404–445.

Kogelmann, Franz. "Die Entwiklung des islamischen Stiftungswesens im postkolonialen Staat. Prozesse in Ägypten, Algerien und Marokko," in *Islamische Stiftungen zwischen juristischer Norm on sozialer Praxis*, ed. Astrid Meier, Johannes Pahlitzsch, and Lucian Reinfandt. Berlin: Akademie-Verlag, 2009.

Kozlowski, Gregory C. *Muslim Endowments and Society in British India*. Cambridge South Asian Studies. Cambridge and New York: Cambridge University Press, 1985.

Kreinath, Jens (ed.). *The Anthropology of Islam Reader*. London: Routledge, 2012.

Kuehn, Thomas. *Empire, Islam, and Politics of Difference: Ottoman Rule in Yemen, 1849–1919*. Leiden: Brill, 2011.

al-Kūfī, Muḥammad b. Sulaymān. *Kitāb al-Muntakhab*. Sanaa: Dār al-Ḥikma al-Yamaniyya, 1993.

Kühn, Thomas. "Shaping Ottoman Rule in Yemen, 1872–1919." PhD thesis, New York University, 2005.

Lambek, Michael. "Certain Knowledge, Contestable Authority: Power and Practice on the Islamic Periphery." *American Ethnologist* 17, no. 1 (1990): 23–40.

Lambton, Ann. "Awqāf in Persia: 6th–8th/12th–14th Centuries." *Islamic Law and Society* 4, no. 3 (1997): 298–318.

Lambton, Ann. *Landlord and Peasant in Persia*. London: Tauris, 1969.

Layish, Aharon. "The Mālikī Family 'Waqf' According to Wills and 'Waqfiyyāt.'" *Bulletin of the School of Oriental and African Studies* 46, no. 1 (1983): 1–32.

Layish, Aharon. "The Transformation of the Sharīʿa from Jurists' Law to Statutory Law in the Contemporary Muslim World." *Die Welt des Islams* 44, no. 1 (2004): 85–113.

Leeuwen, Richard van. *Waqfs and Urban Structures: The Case of Ottoman Damascus*. Studies in Islamic Law and Society. Leiden: Brill, 1999.

Lewcock, Ronald. "The Buildings of the Sūq/Market." In *Ṣanʿāʾ: An Arabian Islamic City*, edited by R. B. Serjeant and R. Lewcock, 276–303. London: World of Islam Festival Trust, 1983.

Lewcock, Ronald, Paolo Costa, R. B. Serjeant, and Robert Wilson. "The Urban Development of Ṣanʿāʾ." In *Ṣanʿāʾ: An Arabian Islamic City*, edited by R. B. Serjeant and R. Lewcock, 122–141. London: World of Islamic Festival Trust, 1983.

Lichtenthäler, Gerhard. *Political Ecology and the Role of Water: Environment, Society and Economy in Northern Yemen*. Aldershot, UK: Ashgate, 2003.

Linant de Bellefonds, Y. "Hiba." *Encyclopaedia of Islam*, second edition. Edited by P. J. Bearman, Th. Biancuis, C. E. Bosworth, E. van Donzel, and W. P. Heinrichs, 3:350. Leiden: Brill, 1960–2004.

Luṭf Allāh b. Aḥmad Jaḥḥāf. *Ḥawliyyāt al-muʾarrikh jaḥḥāf*. Min tārīkh al-yaman al-ḥadīth wa-l-muʿāṣir (silsilat al-ḥawliyyāt). Edited by Ḥusayn b. ʿAbdallāh al-ʿAmrī. Beirut: Dār al-Fikr al-Muʿāṣir, 1998.

Lynch, Cecelia. "Public Spheres Transnationalized: Comparisons Within and Beyond Muslim Majority Societies." In *Religion, Social Practice, and Contested Hegemonies: Reconstructing the Public Sphere in Muslim Majority Societies*, edited by Armando Salvatore and Mark LeVine, 232–249. New York: Palgrave Macmillan, 2005.

Macintosh-Smith, Tim. *City of Divine and Earthly Joys: The Description of San'a*. Yemen Translation Series. American Institute for Yemeni Studies (AIYS)/Middle East Studies Association of North America, 2001.

Macintosh-Smith, Tim. "The Secret Gardens of Sana'a." *Saudi Aramco World* 57, no. 1 (2006): 34–37.

Madelung, Wilferd. *Der Imam al-Qāsim ibn Ibrāhīm und die Glaubenslehre der Zaiditen*. Studien zur Sprache, Geschichte und Kultur des islamischen Orients. Neue Folge Band 1. Berlin: Walter de Gruyter & Co., 1965.

Madelung, Wilferd. "al-Rassī, al-Ḳāsim b. Ibrāhīm b. Ismāʿīl Ibrāhīm b. al-Ḥasan b. al-Ḥasan b. ʿAlī b. Abī Ṭālib." *Encyclopaedia of Islam*, second edition. Edited by

P. Bearman, Th. Bianquis, C. E. Bosworth, E. van Donzel, and W. P. Heinrichs, 8:453. Leiden: Brill, 1960–2004.

Madelung, Wilferd. *Religious and Ethnic Movements in Medieval Islam*. Aldershot, UK: Variorum, 1992.

Madelung, Wilferd. "Zaydiyya." *Encyclopaedia of Islam*, second edition. Edited by P. Bearman, Th. Bianquis, C. E. Bosworth, E. van Donzel and W. P. Heinrichs, 11:477. Leiden: Brill, 1960–2004.

Manṣūr, ʿAbd al-Mālik. *al-Awqāf wa-l-irshād fī mawkib al-thawra*. Sanaa: Wizārat al-Awqāf wa-l-Irshād, 1987.

al-Maqāliḥ, ʿAbd al-ʿAzīz. *Qirāʾa fī fikr al-zaydiyya wa-l-muʿtazila*. Beirut: Dār al-ʿAwda, 1982.

Marcus, Gerorge E. "Ethnography in/of the World System: The Emergence of Multi-Sited Ethnography." *Annual Review of Anthropology* 24 (1995): 95–117.

Marranci, Gabriele. *The Anthropology of Islam*. Oxford and New York: Berg, 2008.

Mermier, Franck. "Les Souks de Sanaa et la Societe Citadine." PhD Thesis, Ecole des Hautes Etudes en Sciences Sociales (EHESS), Paris, 1988.

Messick, Brinkley. *The Calligraphic State: Textual Domination and History in a Muslim Society*. Berkeley and Los Angeles: University of California Press, 1993.

Messick, Brinkley. "Cover Stories: A Genealogy of the Legal Public Sphere in Yemen." In *Religion, Social Practice, and Contested Hegemonies: Reconstructing the Public Sphere in Muslim Majority Societies*, edited by Armando Salvatore and Mark LeVine, 207–230. New York: Palgrave Macmillan, 2005.

Messick, Brinkley. "Indexing the Self: Intent and Expression in Islamic Legal Acts." *Islamic Law and Society* 8, no. 2 (2001): 151–178.

Messick, Brinkley. "Property and the Private in a Sharia System." *Social Research* 70, no. 3 (2003): 711–734.

Messick, Brinkley. "Provincial Judges: The *Sharīʿa* Judiciary of Mid-Twentieth-Century Yemen." In *Law, Custom and Statute in the Muslim World*, edited by Ron Shaham. 149–172. Studies in Islamic Law and Society, vol. 28. Leiden: Brill, 2006.

Messick, Brinkley. "Textual Properties: Writing and Wealth in a Shari'a Case." *Anthropological Quarterly* 68, no. 3 (1995): 157–170.

Messick, Brinkley. "Transactions in Ibb: Economy and Society in a Yemeni Highland Town." PhD thesis, Princeton University, 1978.

Mijallī, Ḥasan ʿAlī. *al-Awqāf fī l-Yaman: al-Itār al-sharʿī wa-l-qānūnī li-l-waqf wa-maqāṣidihi al-ʿāmma wa-tārīkh al-waqf wa-dawrihi al-iqtiṣādī wa-l-ijtimāʿī*. Sanaa: Maktabat Khālid b. al-Walīd, 2002.

Moore, Sally F. "Law and Social Change: The Semi-Autonomous Social Field as an Appropriate Subject of Study." *Law & Society Review* 7, no. 4 (1973): 719–746.

Mostafa, Saleh Lamei. "The Cairene Sabil: Form and Meaning." *Muqarnas* 6 (1989): 33–42.

Mundy, Martha. *Domestic Government: Kinship, Community and Polity in North Yemen*. Society and Culture in the Modern Middle East. London: Tauris, 1995.

Mundy, Martha. "The Family, Inheritance and Islam: A Re-Examination of the Sociology of Farā'iḍ Law." In *Islamic Law: Social and Historical Contexts*, edited by Aziz al-Azmeh, 1–123. New York and London: Routledge, 1988.

Mundy, Martha. "Women's Inheritance of Land in Highland Yemen." *Arabian Studies* 5 (1979): 161–187.

al-Mutawakkil, Ismāʿīl b. al-Qāsim b. Muḥammad. "al-Masā'il al-murtaḍāt fī mā yaʿtamiduhu al-quḍāt." ms 3013, fols. 104–106, Dar al-Makhṭūṭāt, Sanaa.

Opwis, Felicitas. *Maṣlaḥa and the Purpose of the Law: Islamic Discourse on Legal Change from the 4th/10th to the 8th/14th Century*. Leiden: Brill, 2010.

Opwis, Felicitas. "New Trends in Islamic Legal Theory: Maqāsid al-Sharīʿa as a New Source of Law?" Die Welt des Islams 57 (2017): 7–32.

Pedersen, J. "Nadhr." *Encyclopaedia of Islam*, second edition. Edited by P. J. Bearman, Th. Biancuis, C. E. Bosworth, E. van Donzel, and W. P. Heinrichs, 7:846. Leiden: Brill, 1960–2004.

Peters, Rudolph. *Crime and Punishment in Islamic Law: Theory and Practice from the Sixteenth to the Twenty-First Century*. Cambridge: Cambridge University Press, 2006.

Peters, Rudolph, D. S. Powers, Aharon Layish, Ann K. S. Lambton, Randi Deguilhem, R. D. McChesney, M. B. Hooker, and J. O. Hunwick. "Waḳf." *Encyclopaedia of Islam*, second edition. Edited by P. J. Bearman, Th. Biancuis, C. E. Bosworth, E. van Donzel, and W. P. Heinrichs, 11:59–99. Leiden: Brill, 1960–2004.

Powers, David S. "The Islamic Family Endowment." *Vanderbilt Journal of Transactional Law* 32 (1999): 1167–1190.

Powers, David S. "The Islamic Inheritance System: A Socio-Historical Approach." *Arab Law Quarterly* 8, no. 1 (1993): 13–29.

Powers, David S. "The Islamic Law of Inheritance Reconsidered: A New Reading of Q. 4:12b." *Studia Islamica* 55 (1982): 61–94.

Powers, David S. "The Maliki Family Endowment: Legal Norms and Social Practices." *International Journal of Middle East Studies* 25, no. 3 (1993): 379–406.

Powers, David S. "On the Abrogation of the Bequest Verses." *Arabica* 29, no. 3 (1982): 256–295.

Powers, David S. "Orientalism, Colonialism and Legal History: The Attack on Muslim Family Endowments in Algeria and India." *Comparative Studies in Society and History* 31, no. 3 (1989): 535–571.

Powers, David S. *Studies in Qur'an and Ḥadīth: The Formation of the Islamic Law of Inheritance*. Berkeley: University of California Press, 1986.

Qadri Pasha. *Kitāb Qānūn al-ʿadl wa-l-inṣāf li-l-qadā ʿalā mushkilāt al-awqāf*. Cairo: Maṭbaʿat al-Kubrā l-Amīriyya bi-Bulāq Maṣr al-Maḥmīya, 1906.

Qānūn al-Madanī [2002]. Sanaa: Wizārat al-Shu'ūn al-Qānūniyya, 2008.

al-Qāsim al-ʿIyānī, al-Manṣūr bi-Llāh. *Majmūʿ kutub wa-rasāʾil al-Imām al-Qāsim al-ʿIyānī*. Edited by ʿAbd al-Karīm Aḥmad Jadbān. Saʿda: Maktabat al-Turāth al-Islāmī, 2002.

Qāsim b. Ibrāhīm, ʿAlī b. ʿAbdallāh al-Ānisī and ʿAbdallāh b. Muḥammad al-Sarḥī. *Kitāb Taysīr al-marām fī masāʾil al-aḥkām li-l-bāḥithīn wa-l-ḥukkām*. Beirut and Sanaa: Manshūrāt al-Madīna, 1986.

al-Qirshī, Ghālib ʿAbd al-Kāfī. *al-Awqāf wa-l-waṣāyā bayna al-sharīʿa wa-l-qānūn al-Yamanī*. Sanaa: Iwān li-l-Khidmāt al-Iʿlāmiyya, 2008.

Redfield, Robert. "The Social Organisation of Tradition." *Far Eastern Quarterly* 15, no. 1 (1955): 13–21.

Regourd, Anne. *Catalogue cumulé des manuscrits de bibliotèques de ʿAbd al-Rahman al-Hadrami*, fasc. 1. Zabid manuscript catalogue. Sanaa: Centre français d'archéologie et de sciences sociales (CEFAS) and Social fund for Development (SFD), 2006.

Rosen, Lawrence. *The Justice of Islam: Comparative Perspectives on Islamic Law and Society*. Oxford: Oxford University Press, 2000.

al-Ruqayḥī, ʿAbdallāh, Muḥammad al-Ḥibshī, and ʿAlī Muḥmammad al-Ānisī (eds.). *Fihrist makhṭūṭāt Maktabat Jāmiʿ al-Kabīr Ṣanʿāʾ*. 4 vols. Sanaa: Wizārat al-Awqāf wa-l-Irshād, 1984.

al-Ṣaʿdī, Muḥammad b. Yaḥyā b. Aḥmad Bahrān. *Taftīḥ al-qulūb wa-l-abṣār li-l-ihtidāʾ ilā kayfiyyat iqtiṭāf athmār al-aẓhār (sharḥ kitāb al-athmār)*. Sanaa: Maktabat Zayd b. ʿAlī, forthcoming.

Ṣāliḥ b. Dāwud al-Ānisī. "Kitāb Taftīḥ abṣār al-quḍāt ilā azhār al-masāʾil al-murtaḍāt." "Fiqh/ʿilm kalām" MS 693 fols. 8–61, Dār al-Makhṭūṭāt, Sanaa.

Sālim, Sayyid Muṣṭafā. *Wathāʾiq Yamaniyya: Dirāsa wathāʾiqiyya tārīkhiyya*. N.p.: al-Maṭbaʿ al-Faniyya, 1985.

Salvatore, Armando, and Dale Eickelman (eds.). *Public Islam and the Common Good*. Leiden: Brill, 2006.

Salvatore, Armando, Dale Eickelman, and Mark LeVine (eds.). *Religion, Social Practice, and Contested Hegemonies: Reconstructing the Public Sphere in Muslim Majority Societies*. New York: Palgrave, 2005.

al-Samāwī, Muḥammad b. Ṣāliḥ b. Hādī. *al-Ghaṭamṭam al-zakhkhār al-muṭṭahhir li-riyāḍ al-azhār min āthār al-sayl al-jarrār*. Edited by Muḥammad b. Yaḥyā b. Sālim ʿAzzān. 6 vols. Amman: Maṭābiʿ Sharikat al-Mawārid al-Ṣināʿiyya al-Urduniyya, 1994.

Schacht, J. *An Introduction to Islamic Law*. Oxford: Oxford University Press, 1964.

Schwarb, Gregor. "Muʿtazilism in the Age of Averroes." In *In the Age of Averroes: Arabic Philosophy in the 6th/12th Century*, edited by Peter Adamson, 251–282. London: Warburg Institute, 2011.

Serjeant, R. B. "The Mosques of Ṣan'ā': The Yemeni Islamic Setting." In *Ṣan'ā': An Arabian Islamic City*, edited by R. B. Serjeant and R. Lewcock, 310–322. London: World of Islam Festival Trust, 1983.

Serjeant, R. B. "The Post Medieval and Modern History of Ṣan'ā' and the Yemen, ca. 622–1382/1515." In *Ṣan'ā': An Arabian Islamic City*, edited by R. B. Serjeant and R. Lewcock, 68–107. London: World of Islam Festival Trust, 1983.

Serjeant, R. B., and Ismā'īl al-Akwa'. "The Statute of Ṣan'ā' (*Qānūn Ṣan'ā'*)." In *Ṣan'ā': An Arabian Islamic City*, edited by R. B. Serjeant and R. Lewcock, 179–232. London: World of Islam Festival Trust, 1983.

Serjeant, R. B., Paolo Costa, and Ronald Lewcock. "The Ghayls of Ṣan'ā'." In *Ṣan'ā': An Arabian Islamic City*, edited by R. B. Serjeant and R. Lewcock, 19–32. London: World of Islam Festival Trust, 1983.

Serjeant, R. B., and Ronald Lewcock. *Ṣan'ā': An Arabian Islamic City*. London: World of Islam Festival Trust, 1983.

Shabana, Ayman. *Custom in Islamic Law and Legal Theory: The Development of the Concepts of 'Urf and 'Ādah in the Islamic Legal Tradition*. New York: Palgrave Macmillan, 2010.

Shalabī, Muḥammad Muṣṭafā. *Aḥkām al-waṣāyā wa-l-awqāf: al-Ma'mūl bihā fī l-jumhūriyya al-'arabiyya al-muttaḥida*. Alexandria: Maṭba'at Dār al-Ta'līf, 1964.

al-Shamahi, Abdulla. "Al-Imām al-Manṣūr 'Abdullāh b. Ḥamzah b. Sulaymān (d. 614/1217): A biography by his disciple Al-Faqīh Ḥumayd b. Ahmad al-Muḥallī (d. 652/1254), in his work *Al-Ḥadā'iq al-Wardiyyah fī Manāqib A'immah al-Zaydiyyah, v.2*." PhD dissertation, University of Glasgow, 2003.

al-Shamāḥī, 'Abdallāh b. 'Abd al-Wahhāb al-Mujāhid. *Ṣirāṭ al-'ārifīn ilā idrāk ikhtiyārāt amīr al-mu'minīn*. Sanaa: Maṭba'at al-Ma'ārif, 1937.

al-Shawkānī, Muḥammad b. 'Alī. *Adab al-ṭalab wa-muntahā l-arab*. Edited by 'Abdallāh b. Yaḥyā l-Surayḥī. Sanaa: Maktabat al-Irshād, Dār Ibn Ḥazm, 1998.

al-Shawkānī, Muḥammad b. 'Alī. *al-Badr al-ṭāli' bi-maḥāsin man ba'da al-qarn al-sābi'*. 2 vols. Damascus and Beirut: Dār Ibn Kathīr, 2006.

al-Shawkānī, Muḥammad b. 'Alī. *Darārī l-mudīya sharḥ al-durrar al-bahīya*. Beirut: Mu'assasat al-Kutub al-Thaqāfiyya, 1988.

al-Shawkānī, Muḥammad b. 'Alī. *al-Fatḥ al-rabbānī: Fatāwā l-Imām al-Shawkānī*. Edited by Muḥammad b. Ḥasan Ḥallāq. 12 vols. Sanaa: Maktabat al-Jīl al-Jadīd, 2002.

al-Shawkānī, Muḥammad b. 'Alī. *Irshād al-fuḥūl ilā taḥqīq al-ḥaqq min 'ilm al-uṣūl*. Edited by Muḥammad Ṣubhī b. Ḥasan Ḥallāq. Damascus and Beirut: Dār Ibn Kathīr, 2000.

al-Shawkānī, Muḥammad b. 'Alī. *Nayl al-awṭār: sharḥ muntaqā l-akhbār min aḥādīth sayyid al-akhyār*. 8 vols. Beirut: Dār Iḥyā' al-Turāth al-'Arabī, 2001.

al-Shawkānī, Muḥammad b. ʿAlī. *al-Sayl al-jarrār: al-mutadaffiq ʿalā ḥadāʾiq al-azhār*. Edited by Muḥammad b. Ḥasan Ḥallāq. 3 vols. Damascus and Beirut: Dār Ibn Kathīr, 2005.

al-Shawkānī, Muḥammad b. ʿAlī. "Suʾāl fī waqf al-dhurriyya." Sanaa: Dār al-Makhṭūṭāt. MS, vol. 1195, fols. 18–18.

al-Shawkānī, Muḥammad b. ʿAlī. "Suʾal hal yajūzu bayʿ al-mawqūf ʿalā l-dhurriya ʿinda masīs al-ḥāja." In *Dhakhāʾir ʿulamāʾ al-Yaman*, edited by ʿAbd al-Karīm al-Jirāfī. Beirut: Muʾassasat Dār al-Kitāb al-Ḥadīth, 1990.

al-Shihārī, Jamāl al-Dīn ʿAlī b. ʿAbdallāh b. al-Qāsim. *Waṣf Ṣanʿāʾ: Mustall min kitāb al-manshūrāt al-jalīya*. Edited by ʿAbdallāh b. Muḥammad al-Ḥibshī. Sanaa: al-Markaz al-Faransi li-l-Dirāsāt al-Yamaniyya (Centre Français d'Archéologie et de Sciences Sociales), 1993.

al-Shijarī, Yahyā b. al-Ḥusayn. *Sīrat al-Imām al-Muʾayyad bi-Llāh al-Hārūnī*. Edited by Ṣāliḥ ʿAbdallāh Aḥmad Qurbān. Sanaa: Muʾassasat al-Imām Zayd b. ʿAlī l-Thaqafiyya, 2003.

al-Shirbīnī, Shams al-Dīn Muḥammad b. Aḥmad al-Khaṭīb. *Mughnī l-muḥtāj ilā maʿrifat maʿānī alfāẓ al-minhāj*. Beirut: Dār al-Maʿrifa, 2007.

Shivtiel, A., Wilfred Lockwood, and R. B. Serjeant. "The Jews of Ṣanʿāʾ." In *Ṣanʿāʾ: An Arabian Islamic City*, edited by R. B. Serjeant and R. Lewcock, 391–431. London: World of Islam Festival Trust, 1983.

Singer, Amy. *Constructing Ottoman Beneficence: An Imperial Soup Kitchen in Jerusalem*. Albany: State University of New York Press, 2002.

Smith, G. Rex. "The Early and Medieval History of Ṣanʿāʾ ca. 622–1382/1515." In *Ṣanʿāʾ: An Arabian Islamic City*, edited by R. B. Serjeant and R. Lewcock, 49–67. London: World of Islam Festival Trust, 1983.

Strothmann, R. "Mahdī li-Dīn Allāh Aḥmad." *Encyclopaedia of Islam*, second edition. Edited by P. Bearman, Th. Bianquis, C. E. Bosworth, E. van Donzel, and W. P. Heinrichs, 5:1240–1242. Leiden: Brill, 1960–2004.

Tesco-Viziterv-Vituki. "Survey of the Agricultural Potential of the Wādī Zabīd." Budapest and Rome: United Nations Development Programme/Food and Agricultural Organization (UNDP/FAO), 1971.

Thiele, Jan. *Theologie in der jemenitischen Zaydiyya: die naturphilosophischen Überlegungen des al-Ḥasan ar-Raṣṣāṣ*. Leiden: Brill, 2013.

Thielmann, Jörn. "A Critical Survey of Western Law Studies on Arab-Muslim Countries." In *Legal Pluralism in the Arab World*, edited by Dupret Baudouin, Berger Maurits, and Laila al-Zwaini, 41–55. The Hague, London, and Boston: Kluwer Law International, 1999.

Varisco, D. M. *Islam Obscured: The Rhetoric of Anthropological Representation*. New York: Palgrave Macmillan, 2005.

Vikør, Knut. *Between God and the Sultan*. Oxford: Oxford University Press, 2005.

Vom Bruck, Gabriele. "Disputing Descent-Based Authority in the Idiom of Religion: The Case of the Republic of Yemen." *Social Anthropology* 4, no. 2 (1998): 150–191.

Vom Bruck, Gabriele. *Islam, Memory, and Mortality in Yemen: Ruling Families in Transition*. New York: Palgrave Macmillan, 2005.

Vom Bruck, Gabriele. "Regimes of Piety Revisited: Zaydī Political Moralities in Republican Yemen." *Die Welt des Islams* 50 (2010): 185–223.

al-Wāsiʿī, ʿAbd al-Wāsiʿ b. Yaḥyā. *Tārīkh al-Yaman al-musammā Farḥat al-humūm wa-l-ḥuzn fī ḥawādith tārīkh al-Yaman*. Sanaa: Maktabat al-Irshād, 2007.

al-Waẓẓāf, Ismāʿīl ʿAbdallāh. *Aḥkām al-waqf fī l-fiqh al-Islāmī wa-qānūn al-yamanī*. 2nd ed. Sanaa: N.p., 2006.

Wedeen, Lisa. *Peripheral Visions: Publics, Power and Performance in Yemen*. Chicago and London: University of Chicago Press, 2008.

Weir, Shelagh. "A Clash of Fundamentalisms." *Middle East Report* 204, no. 27 (1997). Available online at MERIP.org: http://www.merip.org/mer/mer204/clash-fundamentalisms, accessed 12 November 2015.

Weir, Shelagh. *A Tribal Order: Politics and Law in the Mountains of Yemen*. Austin: University of Texas Press, 2007.

Wizārat al-Shuʾūn al-Qānūniyya. *Qānūn al-aḥwāl al-shakhṣiyya: Qarār jumhūrī bi-qānūn raqm 20 li-sanat 1992 bi-shaʾn al-aḥwāl al-shakhṣiyya wa-taʿdīlātuhu*. Sanaa: Maṭbaʿat al-Tawjīh, 2006.

Wizārat al-Shuʾūn al-Qānūniyya. *Qānūn al-waqf al-sharʿī (qānūn raqm 23 1992) wa-lāʾiḥat tanẓīm ijrāʾāt al-taʾjīr wa-l-intifāʿ bi-amwāl wa-ʿaqārāt al-awqāf wa-istithmārihā (qarār jumhūrī raqm 99 1996)*. 2nd ed. Sanaa, Wizārat al-Shuʾūn al-Qānūniyya, 2007.

Woodman, Gordon R. "The Idea of Legal Pluralism." In *Legal Pluralism in the Arab World*, edited by Dupret Bauduion, Berger Maurits, and Laila al-Zwaini, 3–21. The Hague, London, and Boston: Kluwer Law International, 1999.

Würth, Anna. *Ash-sharīʿa fī Bāb al-Yaman; Recht, Richter und Rechtspraxis an der familienrechtlichen Kammer des Gerischts Süd-Sanaa (Republik Jemen) 1983–1995*. Soziologische Schriften Band 69. Berlin: Dunker & Humblot, 2000.

Würth, Anna. "A Sana'a Court: The Family and the Ability to Negotiate." *Islamic Law and Society* 2, no. 3 (1995): 320–340.

Yaḥyā b. Aḥmad al-Muẓaffar, ʿImād al-Dīn. *Kitāb al-Bayān al-shāfī l-muntaziʿ min al-burhān al-kāfī*. 4 vols. Sanaa: Maktabat Ghamḍān li-Iḥyāʾ al-Turāth al-Yamanī, 1984.

Yaḥyā b. Ḥamza, al-Imām al-Muʿayyad bi-Llāh. *al-Intiṣār ʿalā ʿulamāʾ al-amṣār*. Edited by ʿAbd al-Wahhāb b. ʿAlī l-Muʾayyad and ʿAlī b. Aḥmad Mufaḍḍal. 4 vols. Sanaa: Muʾassasat al-Imām Zayd b. ʿAlī l-Thaqāfiyya, 2002.

Yaḥyā b. Ḥamza, al-Imām al-Muʿayyad bi-Llāh. *Nūr al-abṣār al-muntaziʿ min kitāb al-intiṣār*. Electronically photographed manuscript 43 n. 4. Fihrist al-Makhṭūṭāt al-muṣawwara bi-muʾassasat Zayd b. ʿAlī.

Yaḥyā b. al-Ḥusayn, al-Hādī ilā l-Ḥaqq. *al-Majmūʿa al-fākhira: Majmūʿ kutub wa-rasāʾil al-Imām al-Hādī ilā l-Ḥaqq Yaḥyā b. al-Ḥusayn*. Sanaa: Dār al-Ḥikma al-Yamaniyya li-l-Tijāra wa-l-Tawkīlāt al-ʿĀmma, 2000.

Yaḥyā b. al-Ḥusayn b. al-Qāsim b. Muḥammad. *Ghāyat al-amānī*. Edited by Saʿīd ʿAbd al-Fattāḥ ʿĀshūr and Muḥammad Muṣṭafā Ziyāda. 2 vols. Cairo: Dār al-Kātib al-ʿArabī li-l-Ṭibāʿa wa-l-Nashr bi-l-Qāhira, 1968.

Yanagihashi, Hiroyuki. "The Doctrinal Development of 'Maraḍ al-Mawt' in the Formative Period of Islamic Law." *Islamic Law and Society* 5, no. 3 (1998): 326–358.

Yukleyen, Ahmet. "Production of Mystical Islam in Europe: Religious Authorization in the Süleymanlı Sufi Community." *Contemporary Islam* 4, no. 3 (2010): 269–288.

Zabāra, Muḥammad b. Muḥammad b. Yaḥyā. *Aʾimmat al-Yaman bi-l-qarn al-rābiʿ ashar li-l-hijra*. Cairo: al-Maṭbaʿa al-Salafiyya wa-Maktabatuhā, [1956].

Zabāra, Muḥammad b. Muḥammad b. Yaḥyā. *Nashr al-ʿarf li-nubalāʾ al-Yaman baʿda al-alf*. Vol. 1. Photo reprint.

Zabāra, Muḥammad b. Muḥammad b. Yaḥyā. *Nashr al-ʿarf li-nubalāʾ al-yaman baʿda al-alf*. Vols. 2–3. Beirut: Markaz al-Dirāsāt wa-l-Buḥūth al-Yamanī, Dār al-Ādāb, 1985.

Zabāra, Muḥammad b. Muḥammad b. Yaḥyā. *Nayl al-waṭar min tarājīm rijāl al-Yaman fī l-qarn al-thālith ʿashar min hijrat sayyid al-bashar ṣ*. Edited by ʿAdil ʿAḥmad ʿAbdallāh al-Mawjūd and ʿAlī Muḥammad Muʿawwiḍ. 2 vols. Beirut: Dar al-Kutub al-ʿIlmiyya, 1998.

Zabāra, Muḥammad b. Muḥammad b. Yaḥyā. *Nuzhat al-naẓar fī rijāl al-qarn al-rābiʿ ʿashar*. 2 vols. Sanaa: Markaz al-Dirāsāt wa-l-Abḥāth al-Yamaniyya, 1979.

al-Zamakhsharī, Abū l-Qāsim Maḥmūd b. ʿUmar. *Tafsīr al-kashshshāf ʿan ḥaqāʾiq al-tanzīl wa-ʿuyūn al-aqāwīl fī wujūh al-taʾwīl*. Beirut: Dār al-Maʿrifa, 2006.

Zaman, Muhammad Qasim. "The ʿUlama of Contemporary Islam and their Conceptions of the Common Good." In *Public Islam and the Common Good*, edited by Armando Salvatore and Dale F. Eickelman, 129–156. Leiden: Brill, 2004.

Zayd, ʿAlī Muḥammad. *Muʿtazilat al-Yaman: Dawlat al-Hādī wa-fikruhu*. Sanaa: Markaz al-Dirāsāt wa-l-Buḥūth al-Yamaniyya, 1985.

Zayd, ʿAlī Muḥammad. *Tayyārāt muʿtazilat al-Yaman fī l-qarn al-sādis al-hijrī*. Sanaa: al-Markaz al-Faransī li-l-Dirāsāt al-Yamaniyya, 1997.

el-Zein, Abdul Hamid. "Beyond Ideology and Theology: The Search for the Anthropology of Islam." *Annual Review of Anthropology* 6 (1977): 227–254.

al-Zuḥaylī, Wahba. *al-Fiqh al-Islāmī wa-adillatuhu*. 11 vols. Damascus: Dār al-Fikr, 2002.

Index of People and Places

Index of Terms and Subjects

www.ingramcontent.com/pod-product-compliance
Lightning Source LLC
LaVergne TN
LVHW010638300926
849161LV00005B/979